BEST IN SHOW

THE WORLD OF SHOW DOGS
AND DOG SHOWS

BO BENGTSON

Kennel Club Books®

40 Broad Street, Freehold, NJ 07728

PRAISE FOR *BEST IN SHOW*:

"At long last a factual and meticulously researched history of the purebred dog scene around the world. It's an everything-you-ever-wanted-to-know book about the fascinating world of show dogs. . . . And who better to have written it than Bo Bengtson, who has traveled the world successfully experiencing practically every facet of the dog world's vast array of opportunities and challenges."

—Richard G. Beauchamp, breeder, exhibitor, judge, and dog writer

"What incredible good fortune, for the dog world, to have someone with Bo Bengtson's enthusiasm, passion, intelligence—not to mention his research and writing skills—take on this monumental task. The result is a must-read for dog lovers, breeders, judges, and historians alike."

—Bill McFadden, handler and breeder

"To every endeavor under the sun, each generation is given a gift of greatness . . . and Bo Bengtson is the greatest living dog writer of our times. . . . Bengtson's work will be discussed, shared, and quoted for years to come. . . . This book deserves a quiet nook, a glass of wine, and a favorite dog curled by your feet. . . . Everyone who considers themselves a dog aficionado simply must have this book. . . . *Best in Show* is a gottahaveit."

—Kerrin Winter-Churchill, president of Alliance of Purebred Dog Writers

"Based in large part on the author's nearly 50 years' participation in the sport, *Best in Show* details the joys and the disappointments that invariably accompany success in this complex but ultimately rewarding hobby of breeding and keeping those beautiful dogs that ultimately end up in the show ring."

—Gretchen Bernardi, AKC judge and delegate, breeder, and author

"[This book] provides a definitive picture of how the modern purebred was shaped by kennel clubs and dog shows. Historical perspective . . . offers surprising revelations about the state of the game today. No one is better prepared to present this complex subject than Bo Bengtson. This book is a gift to the dog world precisely when it is needed most."

—Amy Fernandez, artist, author, breeder, and president of Dog Writers Association of America

"There has never been a dog book like this because only one man could have written it. . . . *Purist* is the word that always comes to mind when I think of Bo Bengtson and his perspective of the sport of purebred dogs. This book is a fascinating read."

—Betty-Anne Stenmark, multigroup judge and breeder

Karla Austin • *Director of Operations and Product Development*
Nick Clemente • *Special Consultant*
Barbara Kimmel • *Editor in Chief, BowTie Press*
Andrew DePrisco • *Consulting Editor*
Jessica Knott • *Production Supervisor*
Bill Jonas • *Design Concept*
Amy Stirnkorb • *Design and Layout*
Melody Englund • *Index*

Library of Congress Cataloging-in-Publication Data

Bengtson, Bo, 1944–
  Best in show : the world of show dogs and dog shows / by Bo Bengtson.
      p. cm.
  ISBN 978-1-931993-85-2 (hardcover) — ISBN 978-1-933958-17-0 (hardcover with slipcase)   1. Show dogs. 2. Dog shows. I. Title.

SF425.3.B46 2007
636.08'11—dc22

                              2007001200

Kennel Club Books®
A Division of BowTie, Inc.
40 Broad Street, Freehold, NJ 07728 USA

Printed and bound in Singapore

15 14 13 12 11 10 09 08 07   1 2 3 4 5 6 7 8 9 10

CONTENTS

The Pekingese Ch. Chik T'Sun of Caversham, born in England, Top Dog in Canada 1956, Top Dog in the United States 1957, 1958, and 1959. No dog has won this award three times since then.

PREFACE

In the torrent of new dog books published year after year, I have never seen a book that deals comprehensively with dog shows in general. Some deal with specific aspects of purebred dogs and the sport of dog shows: breeding, training, grooming, exhibiting, and judging. But how did dog shows begin and develop? Where are they heading? Which shows around the world are most important? Who are the human players and the canine stars?

Initially, I was surprised that nobody had written such a book. Dogs, after all, are a worldwide infatuation: hundreds of thousands of people around the globe participate, millions more watch on TV. It didn't take me long, however, to find the reason no such book existed: much of the basic information about this sport is surprisingly difficult to locate. Contrary to what many dog people in the United States believe, the American Kennel Club (AKC) does not have all the answers. Although excellent in so many ways, the AKC does not maintain records of who the all-time top winners, producers, or breeders are. Until recently, the AKC did not even keep any comparative records of the yearly achievements of the top show dogs. Naturally, getting information from other countries was often even more difficult. Despite the challenges involved in tracking down the necessary information for a comprehensive dog show book, I wanted to fill the void.

To compile these data, I consulted multiple sources: my own collection of old dog books; official show and stud records from AKC and other organizations; and scores of publications. Official Best in Show judging started in 1924, but results from the first few decades had never been compiled, so it was necessary to go through every issue of the *American Kennel Gazette* for these years at AKC's library in New York to establish just who won what. Year-end records of the top dogs were first published in *Popular Dogs* magazine from 1943–1969, then in *Kennel Review* into the early 1990s. In recent years, annual records have been published in most of the show dog publications as well as by the AKC itself. Having access to complete and accurate year-end results of the top dogs from 1925 through 2006 made it possible to reasonably estimate which dogs won the most.

In the end, however, the names and figures give only the bare bones, and very little color or substance. To paint a fuller picture, I leaned heavily on old magazines—the *American Kennel Gazette* (now the *AKC Gazette*) as well as other publications, such as the now nonexistent *Dog Fancier* and *Dogdom*, graciously lent to me by Kerrin Winter-Churchill. I also dipped frequently into my old stacks of *Popular Dogs*, going back as far as the 1920s. Most of all, a bound set of *Kennel Review* magazine was a great source of both information and inspiration. In 1992, when that venerable publication closed its doors forever, I was fortunate to be allowed to take over its photo and magazine archives going back almost 100 years. *Kennel Review* was founded in 1898; the oldest preserved copies are from 1918.

It goes without saying that many wonderful dogs and worthy breeders are not featured in this book. Best in Show wins are not necessarily the best measure of success in the dog world, but it's just about the only one that's available. Even using that yardstick, there are so many of these awards—about 1,500, every year, in the United States alone—that it's necessary to focus only on those dogs featured most consistently among the all-breed winners in the annual rankings.

Unfortunately, over the years, a tremendous amount of information about the wonderful dogs, great shows, and colorful people from the past has been lost. People die and relatives clear out "all that stuff," leaving the dog world poorer for it. I have always wanted to rescue as much as possible from oblivion and put it together within covers; this book is an attempt to do just that.

This book is not primarily about how to achieve success in show dogs. There are already excellent books on that subject: Patricia Trotter's *Born to Win* (1997) and Richard G. Beauchamp's *Solving the Mysteries of Breed Type* (2002) come immediately to mind. This is simply a book of facts and photographs about dog shows gathered from every possible source. If in some small measure it succeeds in showing the enjoyment this sport has provided me for half a century, I will consider myself amply rewarded.

ABOUT THE AUTHOR

I was born in Sweden, attended my first dog show there in 1954 when I was ten years old, and started going to shows regularly as soon as I could. In 1959, my sister and I got our first show dog, an Afghan Hound, whom we took turns showing to her championship. I spent the school holidays working at kennels in England and saved enough money to import a Whippet that I handled to Best in Show at the international Stockholm show in 1963. I was 18 years old, and there was nothing I wanted so much as to be involved in dogs and dog shows.

In 1967, after earning my degree at the University of Stockholm, I crossed the United States by Greyhound bus, visiting kennels and dog shows all along the way. A few years later, I became licensed to judge a few of my favorite breeds and over the years have officiated in many parts of the world, including at the FCI World Show, Crufts, and Westminster. In the 1980s, I was heavily involved in the Santa Barbara Kennel Club, which then held the biggest and probably best dog show in America. I have remained immersed in the sport of breeding, showing, and judging ever since, continuing to learn about and just plain admire all kinds of dogs. Although I have been involved in Greyhounds as well, Whippets remain my primary breed. My Bohem "kennel" has never consisted of more than four or five dogs but has produced many champions, including twenty-nine Best in Show winners at specialty or all-breed shows.

I wrote my first dog book at age twenty-two, had a regular dog column in the daily press, and was in charge of the Swedish Kennel Club's show coverage for several years. In the early 1970s, I started writing for

The author with a litter of homebred Whippet puppies, early 2000s.

Kennel Review in the United States and for *Dog World* in England, and in 1979 I left Sweden to take a position at *National Dog* magazine in Australia before accepting a partnership in Paul Lepiane's Show Dog Publications in the United States. In 1997, we started publishing *Dogs in Review* magazine, which was sold to BowTie, Inc., in 2003, although I remained as editor (now editor-at-large). I have lived in California since 1980.

NOTES ON THE TEXT

The title Champion has consistently been abbreviated as Ch. Unless otherwise specified, this refers to a title gained in the dog's country of residence. Many dogs have earned champion titles in more than one country, but a complete list of titles for all the dogs mentioned in this book would have made the manuscript twice as long and much more difficult to read. The only distinctions that have been made are between Sh. Ch. (Show Champion) for some dogs in the United Kingdom and Gr. Ch. (Grand Champion) in Australia and New Zealand.

The breed names used—and their spellings—generally follow the practice established by the American Kennel Club. In some cases, this may be frowned upon by purists. (What sort of tribute to Herr Dobermann is it that we in America accept the misspelling of his name in the breed he created, the Doberman Pinscher?) Sometimes the breed names can be confusing, especially in the case of the Cocker Spaniel: what we call a Cocker Spaniel in America is known as an American Cocker Spaniel in the rest of the world; and conversely, what is elsewhere named a Cocker Spaniel is called an English Cocker Spaniel here.

It is not possible to list owners of all the dogs mentioned in the book, partly for space reasons but also because ownership of a top show dog often changes during or after its show career.

The German Shepherd Dog Ch. Covy–Tucker Hill's Manhattan, America's Top Dog 1984 and 1985.

ACKNOWLEDGMENTS

I am very much indebted to Kerrin Winter-Churchill and Amy Fernandez for permission to use information from their articles in *Dogs in Review*, written during the 1990s and early 2000s, when I was editor of that magazine. Working with writers as good as these was a joy. Both have been of great assistance in helping me find historically significant illustrations. I am also indebted to Paul Lepiane and Amy Fernandez for helping me gather information from the *American Kennel Gazette* for the years from 1925 through 1942 and to Kate Romanski for providing missing later links.

I have also found useful information in the following books: *The American Kennel Club Blue Book of Dogs* (1938), Irene Khatoonian Schlintz's *Great Show Dogs of America* (a unique documentation of the top dogs from the mid-1950s through the mid-1960s), *Who's Who in American Dogdom* (1958), *The AKC's World of the Pure-Bred Dog* (1983), *The American Kennel Club 1884–1984: A Source Book* (1985), Frank Jackson's *Crufts: The Official History* (1990), *Who's Who in Handling* (1993), Anne Hier's very informative *Dog Shows Then and Now* (1999), and William Stifel's magnificent *The Dog Show: 125 Years of Westminster* (2001), one of the most beautiful books ever published about show dogs. I owe them all a debt of gratitude.

For records of foreign dog shows, I had access to complete records of all-breed championship show Best in Show winners in the United Kingdom for the past century, provided courtesy of Dr. Desiree Scott and Simon Parsons. Without them, it would have been impossible to compile records from Britain's early shows, and I am grateful also for Simon's help and response to my interminable questions. I kept referring to piles of magazines collected over the years, primarily to the wonderful English *Dog World* and *Our Dogs* annuals. I have saved each issue of the former since 1958; they now occupy two full bookshelves in my office and provide useful information.

I also received invaluable help from Paula Pascoe and Greg Soyster in the United States; Zena Thorn-Andrews and Glen Dymock in the United Kingdom; Wayne Burton, Barbara Killworth, and Sally Stasytis in Australia; Dawne Deeley in Canada; Joyce Crawford-Manton in Ireland; Espen Engh in Norway; Paula Heikkinen-Lehkonen in Finland; Renée Sporre-Willes and Elisabet Levén in Sweden; Karl Donvil in Belgium; Thomas Münch in Germany; Richard Hellman in Italy; Joan Whittingham in South Africa; Beth Warman in New Zealand; and Philip John and C.V. Sudarsan in India.

Additional thanks for assistance in various areas related to this book to:

The American Kennel Club's Dennis Sprung, James Crowley, David Roberts, Mari-Beth O'Neill, and AKC librarian Barbara Kolk and her staff;

Karolina Hedstrom at the Kennel Club library in London for helping me select suitable photos and letting me borrow them;

Yves de Clerq, general secretary of the Fédération Cynologique Internationale in Brussels, Belgium;

Wayne Ferguson of the Morris & Essex Kennel Club for providing a treasure trove of club memorabilia, mostly from the 1930s and 1940s, including photos, letters to and from Mrs. Dodge, press clippings, and much more;

David Frei of the Westminster Kennel Club for the use of general overview images from the show;

Dawne Deeley; Beth Marley, managing editor of *Dogs in Canada*; and Allan Reznik, editor-in-chief of *Dog World, Dog Fancy*, and *Dogs in Review* for help with photographs of top dogs in Canada;

Mrs. Fukie Yoshimoto and Mr. Hiroshi Kamisato for helping me get information from the Japan Kennel Club;

Valerie Reid of Williamstown, Ontario, for donating a collection of Westminster and Morris & Essex Kennel Club catalogs going back to the 1940s;

Bill McFadden for the loan of the wonderful out-of-print *The Fox Terrier Scrapbook,* by John T. Marvin, as well as *The American Fox Terrier Club's Centennial Year Book* (1987) and *Millennium Book* (2001);

Gail Sprock, former editor of the *German Shepherd Dog Review*, for the loan of photographs, two fascinating bound volumes of the *Shepherd Dog Review* (before German was in the title) from the mid-1920s, and Geraldine Dodge and Josephine Z. Rine's classic *The German Shepherd Dog in America* (1956);

David Landau, who has visited the German Shepherd Dog Sieger show in Germany most years since 1973, for information about that unique event;

Denise Humphries in Australia for reports from past dog shows down under and some historical information;

Nikki Riggsbee in the United States, Agnes Ganami Kerteis in Israel, Miguel Angel Martinez in Argentina, and Jaime Ganoza in Peru for assistance in compiling the list of FCI World Show winners.

Thanks also to my longtime partner in publishing and most other ventures, Paul Lepiane, for reading through the entire manuscript, for offering many excellent suggestions, and for unending patience during the long and often difficult production of this book.

Without cooperation from the photographers, a book such as this could not be published. My eternal gratitude goes to those wonderful dog photographers, both in the United States and abroad, who so generously provided even more photographs than could possibly fit on these pages. They are all credited elsewhere, but John Ashbey and Kim Booth rate special mention. Their records of top show dogs in America go back several decades, in Kim's case partly through the work of his father, Martin. In addition to the *Kennel Review* photo archives, I am also lucky to have access to our own *Dogs in Review* photo

Briards Ch. Deja Vu Four Leaf Clover (left) and her son Ch. Deja Vu In Like Flynn, a top Herding Group winner in the late 1990s.

The Poodle is one of the most successful show breeds ever. Pictured is the white Toy Ch. Smash JP Win A Victory, born in Japan and a leading contender for Top Dog in the United States in 2006 and 2007.

files. Since Paul Lepiane and I started that magazine in 1997, I have been almost literally swimming in a flood of wonderful dog photographs, arriving in an unending and colorful stream every month. In 2003, *Dogs in Review* was purchased by BowTie, Inc., but I remained as editor until late 2005, when I cut back my magazine activities, partly to write this book.

Finally, thanks to BowTie, Inc., for going ahead with such a demanding and unusual project as this one. My gratitude to Norman Ridker and Karla Austin for responding to the initial idea and helping bring it to fruition; to Andrew De Prisco and Seymour Weiss, who combined canine expertise with professional publishing skills; to Jessica Knott and Heather Powers, who had the overwhelming task of dealing with all the photographs; and above all to my patient and sensible editor, Barbara Kimmel, without whose calming influence this whole project could never have been completed.

Although I appreciate all the information provided by many helpful contributors, they cannot in any way be held responsible for mistakes or omissions, all of which must fall squarely on my shoulders.

The Australian Shepherd Ch. Caitland Isle Take A Chance, American owned, Canadian born, and winner of Britain's top award, Best in Show at Crufts in 2006.

INTRODUCTION

WHAT'S IT ABOUT?

From mostly humble beginnings in the rat pits of Queen Victoria's England, dog shows have evolved into a complex, highly sophisticated, billion-dollar industry. These shows compose a worldwide, ongoing circus involving people from all walks of life: from the modest housewife with two dogs in the kitchen and a dream of winning Westminster to the top professionals and high rollers who make the pursuit of success in this field a full-time, lifelong quest. In the United States alone, more than 1.5 million dog show entries were made at more than 3,700 licensed or member AKC conformation events during 2005. In Great Britain, across Europe, and in Australia, the major dog shows are even bigger than those in North America. Asia and Latin America are currently producing some of the world's best show dogs. The recent emergence of Russia and China as powers to be reckoned with in the future dog world will inevitably shift the balance. Millions now watch dog shows on TV.

To an outsider, a dog show can seem faintly ridiculous, but it's serious stuff for the participants: the level of intensity before the final decisions at an important show can be almost palpable. The joy of winning at dog shows is very basic and no doubt a key reason so many people keep returning. For that one moment, perhaps a whole day, you are the chosen one: you've won the lottery, the sun shines, and all is well with your world. Of course, what you've won is probably just a satin ribbon, and it was your dog that won it, not you. However, most people identify so strongly with their dogs that it's sometimes hard to tell where one begins and the other ends.

Beyond winning and the ephemeral glory of show ring success, the most immediate appeal is that this activity allows unlimited access to dogs in several hundred different forms. You needn't be partial to purebred dogs, of course, but one of the charms of the fancy is the variety of breeds to choose from. Whether you like big dogs or little dogs, hairy dogs or smooth-coated dogs, slow and dignified dogs or fast-as-quicksilver dogs, there will be a dog that's right for you. Much more than snob appeal, the predictability and variety that purebred dogs offer are their major selling points. When you know a dog's ancestors, what it was bred to do, and what characteristics it is known for, you have a much better chance of getting a puppy that's compatible with your lifestyle.

The variety of dogs is matched only by the panorama of human participants. The dog world welcomes everyone, regardless of age, sex, race, education, background, or occupation. In few other activities is there such a wide sampling of people doing their own thing side by side and, at least theoretically, all equal as they start out. Money helps, as it does almost everywhere else, but although you won't get rich from dog shows (money prizes, contrary to popular belief, are almost never offered), you don't need to make a major financial outlay to get involved. If you become known for breeding good dogs, you will still not get rich from your hobby, but you will almost invariably find people of means who are willing to help take your dogs to greater (and more expensive) glory.

One aspect of the competitive element is almost exclusive to dog shows: amateurs compete on equal terms with professionals. In how many other sports can a rank amateur—with a little luck and a lot of work, or vice versa—walk right in and have at least a chance of defeating the top pros? It doesn't happen often, but the fairy tale comes true frequently enough to keep the competitive flame alive. There are no novice or professional classes at dog shows: at your very first dog show, you and your dog may find yourselves in direct competition with one or more famous professional handlers.

The worldwide connections that showing dogs engenders are another important aspect of the fancy. It is not unusual for dog people to maintain regular contact with like-minded fanciers around the world. When traveling abroad, a dog fancier is almost never really "lost." In most countries, it is easy to find people who share your interests, who know (or at least know of) the same people, who speak a common dog language: a little English, a little local, and many gestures and facial contortions. If dog shows have some deeper meaning beyond the pure pleasure they give the participants, it may be that they encourage people to reach across borders and make friends in faraway lands they would probably not know much about otherwise.

The main reason so many people stay in dogs once they become involved is probably that however much one learns about dogs, no one will ever know everything about the sport. The greatest experts, with decades of experience, are the first to acknowledge this truth: after five years you think you know it all, after ten you begin to realize how much you still have to learn. Sometime after that, you might just become an expert in at least some area yourself. And you will never, ever have to be bored!

The Black and Tan Coonhound Ch. WyEast Why Not, one of the top-winning Hounds of 1988 and twice Best in Show at the national specialty.

The Skye Terrier Ch. Glamoor Good News, Best in Show winner at Westminster Kennel Club in 1969.

CHAPTER I

HISTORY
HOW DOG SHOWS BEGAN

It is usually agreed (although not necessarily true) that the first organized dog show was held in England in 1859. The dog classes at this event did not constitute a separate show but were simply an addition—possibly an afterthought—to an already well-established poultry show. The exhibition and conformation judging of many kinds of livestock had been an important part of English country life for many years. Only two classes for dogs were offered at this event, which was held at the New Corn Exchange in Newcastle on June 28 and 29: one for Pointers and one for Setters. Sixty dogs participated and were judged by two panels of three experts each. One of the Pointer judges won first prize with his Setter, and one of the Setter judges owned the winning Pointer, thereby setting a precedent of subjectivity that has haunted the sport ever since.

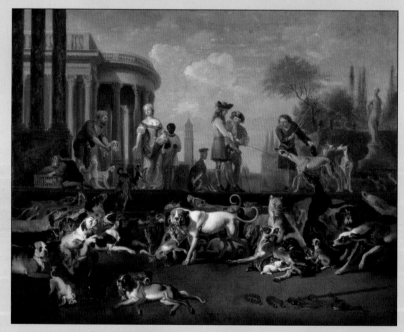

The Dog Market, a 1677 painting by Dutch artist Abraham Hondius, shows clearly that the concept of separate dog breeds that are distinguished by specific physical characteristics was recognized long before competitive dog shows had been introduced. Hondius was born in Holland but lived in London from 1665 on, and it is believed that the painting was completed there.

Perhaps surprisingly, in view of both the meager entry and the immediately controversial judging decisions, the attempt was deemed a success and reportedly attracted an almost unbelievable 15,000 spectators. Later that year, the same organizers held another dog show, this one in Birmingham under the august presidency of Viscount Curzon. This time, in addition to Setters and Pointers, classes for Retrievers and Clumber and Cocker Spaniels were scheduled, as well as separate puppy classes, and the event was an even bigger success than its predecessor. The Birmingham Dog Show Society was founded as a direct result of this venture, and the following year that organization held the first "national" dog show for all breeds, attracting an entry of 267 dogs. Still going strong almost a century and a half later, the Birmingham Dog Show Society reigns as the world's oldest active dog show club. Its annual all-breed championship show, now a four-day affair held at the Staffordshire County showground in May, regularly attracts well over 10,000 dogs.

The die had been cast, but it would take several decades before dog shows developed a set format and strict regulations. (No judge today can, for instance, participate as an exhibitor at a show where he or she is judging.) What those early Victorian sporting gentlemen would think of the vast, global, and very sophisticated institution their modest early endeavors spawned is impossible to guess. They would certainly be impressed by the size of the shows, no doubt surprised by the variety of people involved, and probably struck speechless by the sight of some of the dogs exhibited today.

THE EMOTIONAL BOND

Historically, dog shows are a comparatively recent phenomenon, a blip on the radar of dog's long association with man. The dog has faithfully followed us for at least 10,000 years (the figure varies depending on the point at which you consider the half-wild camp dogs to be domesticated). In the early days, dogs were permitted to share food scraps and relative safety close to the fires in exchange for sleeping with one eye open and guarding the camp and, later, for their increasingly useful assistance as hunters.

Gradually, an emotional bond between man and dog was formed. Exactly when the dog moved from its purely utilitarian role as hunter and guard to family member is impossible to say. We know that many early civilizations kept dogs for more than practical reasons. One of the more touching stories comes from Homer's *Odyssey*, the epic poem based on Greek mythology, and concerns "patient-hearted Argos," the dog raised by the hero, Odysseus.

When Odysseus returns home from the Trojan War and years of seafaring, no one, not even his wife, recognizes him—no one but old Argos, who licks his master's hand and then dies.

Here's a passage from the *Odyssey*:

> Now, as he [Argos] perceived that Odysseus had come close to him,
> he wagged his tail, and laid both ears back;
> only he now no longer had the strength to move any closer
> to his master, who, watching him from a distance, . . .
> secretly wiped a tear away, and said . . . :

Beautiful dogs of different breeds were highly valued far outside Europe. These illustrations are from the series *Ten Prized Dogs*, painted in the first half of the 1700s by Giuseppe Castiglione, an Italian missionary who became court painter to the Chinese emperor Qian-long and was later known as Lang Shih-ning.

"This is amazing, this dog. . . .
The shape of him is splendid, and yet I
cannot be certain
whether he had the running speed to go
with this beauty,
or is just one of the kind of table dogs
that gentlemen keep,
and it is only for show that their
masters care for them."

—Homer *Odyssey 17*, trans. The University of Toronto

This passage not only illustrates the affection between master and dog but also implies that as early as Homeric times, dogs were to some extent kept for status: "It is only for show that their masters care for them." This sounds a lot like some superficial dog show fanciers today, some 3,000 years later. Indeed, the ownership of particularly impressive dogs became a status symbol for the ruling classes very early. Sometimes, however, the dogs were too impressive for their own good. The fifth-century-BC Athenian statesman Alcibiades, known as much for his good looks and overweening pride as for his involvement in the disastrous Peloponnesian War, had a dog that was so handsome that Alcibiades reportedly had its tail cut off because the dog attracted more attention than its master did.

Over the centuries, the dog became an image of selfless love and undying faith, and the historian and art student will find innumerable representations through the Middle Ages and the Renaissance, often with religious overtones, of dogs that were obviously held in the highest esteem. Many of these dogs were used for hunting, but others were obviously kept as "luxury pets," judging by their diminutive sizes and extravagant coats. The admiration of beautiful dogs was not limited to Europe. The Jesuit priest Guiseppe Castiglione went from Italy to China as a missionary in 1715 and eventually became a court painter, famous under his Chinese name of Lang Shih-ning for exquisite portraits of flowers, birds, and horses. He also painted a series titled *Ten Prized Dogs*, which included several sighthounds, a Mastiff, and a dog of Great Dane type, all lovingly rendered in a landscape, and most wearing elegant, feather-adorned collars.

One of the most detailed early records of canine care is shown in *Le Livre de la*

Even in the 1300s, kennels could be elaborately planned. This one, pictured in Gaston Phoebus's *Le Livre de la Chasse*, has quarters for a kennel attendant, a fireplace, straw for the dogs to sleep on, good ventilation, and even sticks leading into gutters for the dogs to urinate on.

Distinct types or breeds of dogs were established early. Different hunting dogs are tenderly cared for by their keepers in the 1300s.

Chasse (ca. 1400) by Gaston Phoebus, count of Foix. Among the splendidly illuminated pages, most depicting the glories of the hunt, is one that shows the kennel staff ministering tenderly to their charges. Also from the fourteenth century, Geoffrey Chaucer's gentle prioress in *The Canterbury Tales* fed her pet spaniels bread and milk and cried bitterly "when one of them was dead."

THE DEVELOPMENT OF BREEDS

Initially, nobody cared what the dogs looked like. Over the centuries, however, different types of dogs developed different talents that were intrinsically linked to their appearance: the long-legged sighthounds, for instance, proved useful in open-field hunting of hares and deer; the heavier scenthounds used their noses and persistence in following their prey; the heavy-set, muscular mastiff types were efficient guard dogs; small but tough and usually rough-coated dogs were particularly well suited for rooting out rats and other vermin. Eventually, man started to help nature by selecting dogs with specific characteristics to reproduce.

In her book *Hunting, Hawking and Fishing* (1496), Dame Juliana Berners, abbess of Sopwell Priory near St. Albans, describes fourteen distinct kinds of dogs. Her word painting of the Greyhound ("headed like a Snake / And necked like a Drake / Footed like a Cat / Tailed like a Rat") is quoted by breed specialists to this day and may have been used as the basis for the first official breed standard. In the following century, William Shakespeare made more than 200 references to dogs in his plays and was the first to coin the word *watchdog*. It is obvious that there were many established dog "breeds" in his time:

> Ay, in the catalogue ye go for men;
> As hounds, and greyhounds, mongrels, spaniels, curs,
> Shoughs, water-rugs and demi-wolves, are clept
> All by the name of dogs: the valued file
> Distinguishes the swift, the slow, the subtle,
> The housekeeper, the hunter, every one
> According to the gift which bounteous nature
> Hath in him closed.

—*Macbeth*, act 3, scene 1

Shakespeare contemporary John Caius, chief physician to Queen Elizabeth I, made an attempt at a systematic classification of the existing breeds. His *De Canibus Britannicis*, published in Latin in 1570 (the first English translation, *Of Englishe Dogges*, came five years later), divided the various breeds into groups that surprisingly closely resemble some modern classifications—although more those of the FCI (Fédération Cynologique Internationale) than those of the English-speaking clubs. Caius listed "Sighthounds and Scenthounds, Water and Land Spaniels, Setters, Hunting and Guard Terriers, Mastiffs and Herding Dogs." The "Venatici or Dogges" were used for the purpose of hunting mammals and were divided as follows: "Leverarius, or Harriers; Terrarius, or Terrars; Sanguinarius, or Bloodhounds; Agaseus, or Gazehounds; Leporarius, or Grehounds; Lorarius, or Lyemmer; Vertigus, or Tumbler; and Canis Furax, or Stealer." The "Aucupatorii" were used for hunting fowl and comprised "the Index, or Setter; and the Aquaticus, or Spaniell." The third group of Caius's table of species was devoted entirely to the "Spaniell Gentle," or "Comforter," and the fourth section, for farm dogs, consisted of the "Canis Pastoralis, or the Shepherd's Dogge; the Mastive, or Bandogge, called Canis Villaticus or Carbenarius." The final section contained "the Admonitor, or Wapp; the Vernepator, or Turnespet; and the Saltator, or Dauncer."

Surprisingly, Caius did not specifically mention Toy dogs other than "Comforters." Dame Juliana had made a point of listing

A kennel plan from the 1600s.

"small ladyes' [pets] that bere aweye the flees"—indicating one reason small dogs were popular as pets. In fact, a small dog was not only thought to attract fleas that would otherwise move over to the dog's master but also considered a remedy for intestinal ills and various other ailments when lying on a person's stomach. The medical benefits of such a treatment may be discounted today, but the psychological comfort of a "bed-bug" pet can still be confirmed by almost anyone who has had a small dog as a companion.

It is worth noting that the first breed club, although hardly what we mean by that term today, was formed soon after William of Orange was crowned king of England in 1688. The new ruler brought with him Pugs from his native Holland, and so popular did these dogs become at court that an Order of the Pug was formed. It was apparently a lighthearted, aristocratic spoof of the Freemasons' order, but it is clear from existing records that Pugs not only were held in the highest esteem (each royal Pug carried an orange silk band as an indication of its elevated status) but also were considered a distinct, pure breed—a status that up to that time could not be taken for granted even for the most well-bred pets.

Both small "luxury" dogs and larger hunting dogs were immensely popular among the aristocracy everywhere. The French court of Louis XIV seems to have been swarming with toy

Louis XIV, King of France, 1643–1715; a great dog lover.

spaniels and the ancestors of today's Papillons, which were one of the king's most popular gifts to his female favorites. Louis was a great dog lover and had a separate room where he enjoyed feeding his own dogs, each from its own named bowl.

During the Age of Enlightenment, the naturalist Georges-Louis Leclerc, count of Buffon, compiled descriptions and illustrations of a large number of dog breeds for his enormous, multivolume *Histoire Naturelle*, published in France in 1755. This work included detailed information about almost every recorded mammal, bird, reptile, and insect known to the world at that time. Several of the twenty-seven full-page canine illustrations depict recognizable breeds. There is a Great Dane, a Greyhound, a Bloodhound, a Mastiff, a Pug, and even breeds that would be known today as Löwchen and Bichon Frisé. Buffon was the greatest naturalist of his time, as prominent in his sphere as Voltaire and Rousseau in theirs, and he influenced future generations of naturalists, Charles Darwin among them.

BLOOD-SPORT ROOTS

In spite of many individual exceptions to the contrary, it was not until the end of the 1700s that a more humane attitude toward animals in general began to pervade European society. Dog owners today may find it difficult to accept that some of the roots of the modern dog show lie in the so-called blood sports, which were wildly popular even in civilized, animal-loving England well into the 1800s. Bullbaiting and bearbaiting had been introduced by the Romans and for many centuries provided great entertainment for the masses. Even horses and donkeys were used on occasion

One of the most historically important of all dog paintings depicts a scene at Jemmy (or Jimmy) Shaw's pub in London, Queen's Head Tavern, in 1855. The link to earlier ratting matches (and Shaw's own pugilistic past) are evident in the wall illustrations, but conformation shows were already well on the way to becoming a reality. Among the breeds shown are Bulldogs, Bull Terriers, Black and Tan Terriers, and Toy Spaniels.

when bears were scarce. The animal, the more aggressive the better, was tethered to a pole and then set upon by mostly bulldog-type dogs. (The dogs, as is evident from contemporary illustrations, were closer in appearance to today's Staffordshire Bull Terriers than to modern Bulldogs.) Organized dog fighting was also considered great sport and still exists on the fringes of civilization in many countries, including the United States.

The first animal welfare laws were introduced in England in the early 1800s. The Royal Society for the Prevention of Cruelty to Animals was founded in 1824, and bullbaiting and bearbaiting were finally outlawed in 1838. The more extreme forms of blood sport gradually ceased to exist, but what were called matches remained popular at many more or less reputable pubs in London through much of the century, eventually changing shape and, in fact, providing one part of the foundation for what would become the dog shows of today. (The other part, of course, was supplied by the hunting and shooting fraternity.)

The match consisted of a number of rats tossed into a pit while spectators—a mixed group of roughnecks, regular working-class men, and sporting swells—bet on which of two or more dogs would kill the most rats within a given interval. There was a famous small English Terrier (somewhat similar to the modern Toy Manchester Terrier) named Tiny the Wonder, who weighed less than six pounds and was reputed to have killed 200 sewer rats in a record fifty-four minutes. Tiny, who wore a lady's bracelet as a collar, was a great favorite of the proprietor, the ubiquitous Jemmy (or Jimmy) Shaw. An earlier star of the pits was Champion Billy, a white terrier with a patch on his head, weighing in at twenty-seven pounds with a record of dispatching 500 rats in five and a half minutes.

For a firsthand report of a rat-killing match, Henry Mayhew's amazingly detailed account in *London Labour and the London Poor* (originally published in 1851) is unsurpassed. In parts, it reads as if it were written by a non-doggy intruder at a modern-day kennel club meeting:

> I arrived at about eight o'clock at the tavern where the performances were to take place. I was too early, but there was plenty to occupy my leisure in looking at the curious scene around me, and taking notes of the habits and conversation of the customers who were flocking in. The front of the long bar was crowded with men of every grade of society, all smoking, drinking, and talking about dogs. Many of them had brought with them their "fancy" animals, so that a kind of "canine exhibition" was going on; some carried under their arm small bull-dogs, whose flat pink noses rubbed against my arm as I passed; others had Skye-terriers, curled up like balls of hair, and sleeping like children, as they were nursed by their owners. The only animals that seemed awake, and under continual excitement, were the little brown English terriers, who, despite their neat black leathern collars by which they were held, struggled to get loose, as if they smelt the rats in the room above, and were impatient to begin the fray.

Mayhew was shown "an enormous white Bulldog," which he was assured was "a great beauty" and "was the admiration of all beholders." He describes the dog's front legs as bowed, "leaving a peculiar pear-shaped opening between them, which, I was informed, was one of its points of beauty." He was told of the breeding of some of the dogs and noticed "clusters of black leather collars, adorned with brass rings and clasps, and pre-eminent was a silver dog-collar, which, from the conversation of those about me, I learnt was to be the prize in a rat-match" coming up in a future event. According to Mayhew, "The dogs were standing on the different tables, or tied to the legs of the forms, or sleeping in their owners' arms, and were in turn minutely criticized—their limbs being stretched out . . . and their

As a precursor to organized dog shows, many of the London pubs staged rat matches for terriers in the early 1800s, attracting large numbers of spectators and participants. Many of the dogs became famous: this uncredited painting shows Billy, one of the wonders of his day, with a record of killing 500 rats in five and a half minutes at the Westminster Pit in March 1825.

BIG BUSINESS IN RATS

Rat-killing matches were big business in mid-nineteenth-century England. Contemporary author Mayhew estimated that there were at least seventy regular pits in London at that time, plus an unspecified number set up for temporary purposes. To get some idea of the scope of these activities, it must be understood that Jemmy Shaw, proprietor of the largest sporting public houses in London, celebrated for the rat matches that were held weekly at his establishment, alone purchased some 500 rats per week—an annual total of 26,000—for his rat pit. Shaw described himself as "the oldest canine fancier in London" and the one who started ratting as a sport in a big way. Women did not watch ratting matches—not officially. However, Shaw admitted to Mayhew "in a kind of whisper" that he had "noble gentlemen and titled ladies come here to see the sport—on the quiet, you know."

mouths looked into as if a dentist were examining their teeth." It is worth noting that "beauty points" were obviously a major concern even for the owners of these pure working dogs.

FORERUNNERS OF TODAY'S SHOWS

Almost imperceptibly, as the years passed and the rat-killing matches came to be regarded as offensive, various fancy aspects of the little rat dogs became more important as the pubs began offering a forerunner to "real" dog shows. As early as 1834, a Fancy Toy Dog Show was advertised at the Elephant and Castle pub in London; it was probably more an exhibition than a competition, but with the rat pits falling into disrepute, the time was ripe for a change.

A concern with specific conformation points long before modern breed standards had been established is evident from a report published in *Illustrated London News* in 1851 from a dog show held at a London pub, St. Giles, owned by one Charlie Aistrop:

> At this place a club is held, by one of the rules of which, each member is expected (in fact, we believe, compelled) to bring a dog for show or sale, as he thinks proper; thus ensuring a good show night, which is on a Tuesday evening; and here may be seen the most beautiful specimens of spaniel, Italian greyhound, and, of late years, of the Isle of Skye terriers. . . . The show dogs, or Fancy Pets, as they are termed, are solely valued for beauty of their respective sort.

By the mid-1800s, there was a great demand for fancy pet dogs in London. As there were no pet shops or organized shows, the dogs were supplied by itinerant dog sellers.

The King Charles, that has now for many years stood as prime pet with ladies, ranks in estimation as he more or less exhibits the following perfection:—Smallness of size, symmetry as to proportions, richness of colour, and length of ears. . . . Spaniels are often to be seen at spaniel shows for which £150 would not be taken, and those not the property of gentlemen or men of large means either. The author offers as his opinion that "The price these dogs are valued at is no doubt perfectly ridiculous," but adds that "anyone wishing to learn what merit and recommendation [these dogs] have, may see some of the choicest specimens at Aistrop's."

The illustration accompanying the article shows at least two dozen well-dressed gentlemen, some identified by name, assembled around long tables, on which are seated a number of toy spaniels. Other small dogs are held in the arms of the men, and several larger dogs can be seen in an enclosure on one side of the room; at least one of these shows distinct Greyhound type.

Although toy spaniels were by far the most expensive, other breeds could fetch high prices, sometimes at public dog auctions, which in those days carried none of the stigma associated with such a proceeding today. (This was the case as late as 1936, when after King George V's death his gundogs were auctioned off at Aldridge's.) In the 1880s, a well-known Pointer, Ightfield Dick, was auctioned off for £145, and the average for a lot of six Pointers was about £40 each.

(Remember that £1 in the mid- and late 1800s is the equivalent of about £70 today,

The first dog shows were held at taverns, and women were not present. A Fancy Dog Show of 1851 at the Eight Bells shows several recognizable early exhibitors and at least a dozen dogs, mostly Toy Spaniels but also a Greyhound and some other dogs in the back.

or about $140. Therefore, Ightfield Dick sold for what would have been about £10,000 or $20,000 today. Only the best modern show dogs change hands for more than that.)

A famous oil painting that now hangs at The Kennel Club in London illustrates the changing times better than any words can. Titled *A Jemmy Shaw Canine Meeting*, 1855, it shows a number of well-dressed, pipe-smoking gentlemen gathered at Shaw's pub, the Queen's Head Tavern, together with a dozen dogs, including several recognizable

FROM THE UNDERWORLD TO THE DOG FANCY

Charlie Aistrop, who held early "dog shows" at the St. Giles club, was a colorful character. According to Frank Jackson in his official history of Crufts, Aistrop, the son of a well-to-do family, turned his back on respectable society to indulge his passion for dogs among the denizens of London's underworld. He ran a notorious Westminster bear pit until his wife was killed while feeding one of the bears; he then opened a pub. Most of his colleagues were failed or former pugilists. It is unlikely but true that the rough environment of bare-knuckles boxing, organized dog fights, and rat killing helped spawn the popularity of something as inherently nonviolent, even genteel, as today's conformation dog shows.

breeds. These are obviously well-cared-for, well-groomed pets, some of them taking their places on the counter with every air of knowing they belong there. There is an English White Terrier (a now-extinct breed), a King Charles Spaniel, a dog that resembles a purebred Lhasa Apso (but most likely was a Cumberland Terrier), a couple of English Toy Terriers, a Bulldog, and a Bull Terrier. Shaw, shown in his shirtsleeves next to the fireplace, had earlier supported himself as a professional boxer, as a terrier breeder, and as the founder of one of the many toy dog clubs that were springing up. Breeding fancy dogs could be a lucrative business at this point; the former rat terrier breeders were eager to find a new clientele for their puppies, and society ladies were willing to pay exorbitant prices for the most exclusive, most beautiful little dogs. What had been rough-and-tumble dogs that earned their living by killing vermin were becoming pampered pets and exotic fashion accessories.

From a careful examination of the painting, it is obvious that a rougher past was not too distant, the well-dressed gentlemen notwithstanding: on the pub's walls are illustrations not only of boxing matches but also of pits with terriers and dead rats.

THE GROWING FANCY

That dogs were bred for specific breed points and intrinsic beauty in England many years before dog shows were held or The Kennel Club founded is an established fact. The indefatigable Henry Mayhew, in his seminal work about London life in the mid-1800s, quotes a House of Commons report of July 26, 1844, concerning the value of pet dogs: "From the evidence of various witnesses it appears, that in one case a spaniel was sold for 105*l*., and in another, under a sheriff's execution, for 95*l*. at the hammer; and 50*l*. or 60*l*. are not infrequently given for fancy dogs of first-rate breed and beauty." (The *l*. stands for a guinea, or a pound and a shilling, long a common denomination in pricing animals and goods and used up to the decimalization of British currency in 1971.) The spaniel alluded to was a "black and tan King Charles's spaniel," then by far the most fashionable and expensive of the small fancy dogs, worth more than $15,000 in modern U.S. currency. Evidence shows that other dogs of the same type had been sold for almost as much. A witness for the House of Commons report stated, "There are certain marks about the eyes and otherwise, which are considered 'properties'; and it depends entirely upon the property which a dog possesses as to its value."

Mayhew devotes several pages to the trade in breeding and selling different types of pet dogs to the aristocracy and burgeoning middle class. Without dog shows and kennel clubs to turn to, how could one find a fancy dog? There were at least twenty-five street sellers of dogs in London at this time—the closest things to a pet shop today, the main difference being that these vendors operated out of doors. Only the dogs for sale on that day were brought out into the street; most of the vendor's inventory remained on his private premises. Mayhew points out that a high level of hygiene was necessary for a successful establishment: "The scrupulous observance of cleanliness is necessary in the rearing or keeping of small fancy dogs, for without such observance the dog would

The support of the British royal family helped make purebred dogs and dog shows acceptable to polite society. The future Queen Alexandra is shown with her Chow Chow, Plumpy, and two of her Japanese Chins in 1897.

have a disagreeable odour about it, enough to repel any lady-buyer. It is a not uncommon declaration among dog-sellers that the animals are 'as sweet as nuts.'"

The dog seller would ply his wares in Regent Street, outside Whitehall, or in one of the London parks—wherever wealthy patrons might gather and be attracted by a few well-groomed toy spaniels or other dogs. As Mayhew observed:

Two dogs, carefully cleaned and combed, or brushed, are carried in a man's arms for street vending. A fine chain is generally attached to a neat collar, so that the dog can be relieved from the cramped feel he will experience if kept off his feet too long. In carrying these little animals for sale—for it is the smaller dogs which are carried—the men certainly display them to the best advantage. Their longer silken ears, their prominent dark eyes and black noses, and the delicacy of their fore-paws, are made as prominent as possible, and present what the masses very well call "quite a pictur[e]." I have alluded to the display of the Spaniels, as they constitute considerably more than half of the street trade in dogs, the "King Charleses" and the "Blenheims" being disposed of in nearly equal quantities. They are sold for lap-dogs, pets, carriage companions or companions in a walk, and are often intelligent and affectionate. Their colours are black, black and tan, white and liver-colour, black and white, and entirely white, with many shades of these hues, and interblendings of them, one with another, and with gray.

The other breeds that were available from these street sellers included small terriers, which were coming more into fashion at the time, "usually black, with tanned muzzles and feet, and with a keen look," and with either a smooth coat or "long and somewhat wiry hair." There were Skye Terriers, "little Scotch terriers," Pugs (no longer as popular as they used to be), French Poodles, Italian Greyhounds, and—interestingly—a breed that Mayhew describes as "an odd 'plum-pudding,' or coach dog (the white dog with dark spots which runs after carriages)"—obviously an early version of the Dalmatian.

Yorkshire Terriers are still judged on boxes in Great Britain. Details of this 1910 photograph are not known, but notice that all the lady exhibitors wield brushes (even the one sitting outside the ring). Notice also what appear to be forerunners of today's armbands on the ground in front of each box. At least seven Yorkshire Terriers can be seen in this photo.

Other breeds could be purchased elsewhere, but the distinction between the sellers of fancy dogs and those who dealt in what was called sporting dogs was very clear, and the two didn't mix. The fancy dogs sellers aspired to some gentility. As Mayhew points out, their customers were all of the wealthier class, which had its influence on the manners of the dog sellers, who were "in the majority of cases, quiet and deferential men, but without servility." The sporting dogs were not, as in modern America, the gundog breeds but instead those that had in earlier years been used for bearbaiting, dog fighting, and most recently rat matches—the rougher terriers, bulldogs,

and mastiff types. (Mayhew points out that, even in his time, "Bull-dogs cannot now be classed as sporting, but only as fancy dogs, for they are not good fighters, I was informed.") The sporting dog sellers were, perhaps naturally, a somewhat rougher group than the fancy dog sellers—there were, after all, still organized dog fights, even if the practice was increasingly frowned upon and, in fact, illegal.

The hunting and shooting breeds— Mayhew mentions "fox-hounds, harriers, pointers, setters, cockers, &c., &c." (in other words, what we now may call Sporting/ Gundogs and Hounds)—were never part of the street trade. If you hunted, you lived in the country, and a good hunting dog would be easy to find. Keeping one of those breeds in the city was almost unthinkable.

Eventually, the street dog sellers set up more or less permanent shops in the so-called dog markets at Club Row and Caledonian Market, which have remained popular flea markets and tourist traps well into modern days. From there, it was a short step to the regular pet shops, or dog bureaux, as they were called, which in the early days had none of the negative associations they later acquired. Among the best known was Mme. Lesmoir-Gordon's Entente Cordiale Dog Bureau on Regent Street, which, as Amy Fernandez put it in a *Dogs in Review* article, carried "a tempting inventory of toy Pomera-

nians, Pekingese, Yorkshire Terriers, French Bulldogs, and 'Sleeve' Griffons" and was in business until 1930. No less an august Victorian society personage than Mrs. Clarice Ashton Cross found it perfectly acceptable to run an exclusive and apparently highly lucrative pet shop in Mayfair. Her Pekingese kennel had been founded in the late 1800s on stock descending from dogs imported from China only a couple of decades earlier, and the Alderbourne Pekingese remained world famous—they were later bred by two of her daughters—into the 1960s. Mrs. Ashton Cross made headlines around the world in 1907 when she turned down a solid offer of £32,000 (over $4.6 million today) for her champion dog Ch'êrh of Alderbourne from

One of the most valuable show dogs of all time, the Pekingese Ch. Ch'êrh of Alderbourne. His owner, Mrs. Clarice Ashton Cross, turned down a multimillion-dollar offer for him from J. P. Morgan in the United States in 1907.

Alderbourne was one of the world's oldest and most prolific kennels, exporting champion Pekingese worldwide for several decades. Ch. Yu-Tong (top), Ch. Tong-Tuo (center), and Ch. Lin-Yu-Tang (bottom), all of Alderbourne, were photographed in 1953.

the American industrialist J. P. Morgan. Morgan then sent a blank check, which she promptly returned. The press had a field day, with headlines such as, "Only two things in England are not for sale: a London policeman and Mrs. Ashton Cross's Pekingese!"

THE FOUNDATIONS OF DOG SHOWS

It is apparent from the above that as early as by the mid-1800s, there were a number of different more or less pure breeds in England and even the beginning of what kennel clubs today would call distinct groups of breeds. The number of breeds increased sharply during the latter part of the 1800s, helped along by the popularity of dog shows and the public's demand for new, appealing, and "exotic" types of dogs. British dog fanciers traveled to the early dog shows in continental Europe and brought previously unknown, foreign breeds back home with them. The East India Company shipped tried-and-true British breeds to the empire's civil servants on duty in the most far-flung corners of the world, and the same ships often brought back exotic, more or less authentic breeds on the return trip. There was a lively trade in purebred (or purportedly purebred) dogs between London and New York, and by the end of the century the onetime British colonies had, in fact, produced their own first really popular native breed—the Round Head, now known as the Boston Terrier.

Today there is a vast, ever-increasing variety of breeds. There is no final or absolute verdict on what is a pure breed and what is not, although a certain level of predictability as far as physical and mental

One of the first show dogs to be heavily campaigned, the Pointer Wagg. Owned by Richard J. Lloyd of Wales, Wagg was exhibited at more than sixty shows in Great Britain and Germany in the 1870s, winning several cups for Best Pointer, Best Sporting Dog, and even "Best Dog in all Classes of the Show."

characteristics, and a certain number of generations of recorded breeding, are universally required.

The American Kennel Club fully recognizes more than 150 breeds, with more in the process of joining the fold each year. The Kennel Club in England registers approximately the same number, while the FCI's list of recognized breeds includes at least 350 and is growing steadily. (That's a conservative count, not including all the many color, coat, and size varieties of many breeds.) With many member countries around the world, the FCI sometimes seems to accept new breeds as much for diplomatic reasons as for anything else. Great national pride may hinge on minor details of color or conformation that differentiate almost identical breeds; sometimes the main difference appears to be on which side of a geographic border the dog was born. This is a matter of some ridicule among many people, at least until it concerns their own country or their own breed. Does the world really need both a Swedish Lapphund and a Finnish Lapphund? Neither breed exists in the United States, but if you pose that question to a Swede or a Finn, you may start a fight.

The creation of new breeds continues today and is likely to persist for as long as man's fascination with the varying forms of all things canine remains.

It is clear that the undeniably famous first show in Newcastle in 1859 was, in fact, not the first dog show at all, as exhibitions of fancy dogs of various kinds had been held well before that. There were the afore-mentioned various toy spaniel shows in the pubs of London as well as a forerunner of today's Peterborough Hound Show, known to have been held regularly in Kent since the 1770s. This exhibition, held in the countryside, was a forum for the huntsmen to show off their young stock during the summer off season. The agricultural societies, so important to rural life, might offer classes for sheepdogs as well as other livestock, often as a part of a sheep-shearing contest. Agricultural shows have continued to host dog classes into the present in both England and Australia.

THE FIRST COMPETITIONS

What was new at the historic show in Newcastle was real conformation compe-tition, with an official announcement of the winners, which puts this event in a category of its own. It should be noted, however, that the only two classes—one for Setters, another for Pointers—were limited to males; bitches were not included, and although there was an exhibition of puppies, they were apparently not graded competitively. The Setter judges were J. H. Walsh (of the famous Stonehenge pseudonym, then editor of *The Field*), Richard Brailsford (game-keeper to Lord Derby and Lord Chester-field), and Frances Foulger (gamekeeper to the Duke of Northumberland). Their winner was Joseph Jobling's dog—the exhibits did not carry names other than those of their owners. The Pointer judges were Joseph Jobling, Thomas Robson, and, again, J. H. Walsh; the winner was Mr. Brailsford's Pointer.

The "national" Birmingham Dog Show in 1860, which followed as a result of the Newcastle show, opened a new avenue of activity for dog fanciers. This show was organized by Richard Brailsford, judge and winner at the 1859 event. According to later accounts, Brailsford had tried for many years to arrange "public competition for dogs" before succeeding with his national show in Birmingham. To call it an all-breed show might be an overstatement. It was advertised simply as the First Exhibition of Sporting and Other Dogs but offered many different classes, in a first merger between the field dogs of the countryside and the ratters of the town, for Gundogs, Hounds, Terriers of different kinds, Toy Dogs (including, surprisingly, such breeds as Mastiffs, Newfoundlands, Dalmatians, and "Bull-dogs"), Foreign Non-Sporting Dogs (which did not have a single entry), and Sheepdogs. The official Kennel Club division of breeds into groups was several decades away, but Brailsford had set the stage.

The early shows lacked the amenities and smooth organization that we take for granted at most shows today. The dogs were judged not in a ring but "on the benches"—often without being taken out at all, similar

Dreams of glory, human and canine, from the Peterborough show in the first half of the 1900s.

Above: The National Dog Show at the Agricultural Hall, Islington. The early dog shows could be chaotic affairs. Note the straw on the benches and the lack of dividers between the dogs.

Right: Prize dogs in the National Dog Show at Islington.

to modern shows for poultry and other birds. These benches were, in fact, not raised but on floor level, which made viewing the dogs difficult. Nobody seems to have complained; the main concern was that the space between the rows of benching must be wide enough to allow for two well-dressed female spectators in voluminous crinolines to pass each other in the aisle without discomfort. As the *Illustrated London News* put it, "The dogs were polite to the last degree; and, though they occasionally had a battle royal among themselves, we only heard a rumour of one man having been bitten. . . . [I]t was a grand success, great was the disappointment that it did not continue open for another day or two." About 7,800 spectators attended, and

the show made a profit of nearly £500. Within five years the number of spectators had risen to more than 20,000 and the profit to £3,324. It must have been obvious that this was a new twist on the entertainment business that might have a future. (The sum of £3,324 in 1865 equals approximately $440,000 today.)

The judging, then as now, could be refreshingly unpredictable. From the same source, the *Illustrated London News*, just a few years after the first show: "Great things were predicted of Lord Bagot's Bloodhounds, but Mr. Jenning's winner . . . flung them completely in the shade, and sat up, a very king among dogs, lazily blinking over his victory."

The timing was perfect for the creation of a new sport. The Industrial Age had created a large middle class with sufficient money, energy, and time to devote to dogs as a hobby. The new railways connected formerly distant cities and allowed both people and dogs to travel. In 1873, The Kennel Club was founded. As it was the first such club in the world, no national designation was considered necessary, something that even today fanciers in the United States and Australia on occasion find confounding. (It is *never* the English Kennel Club, just *The* Kennel Club.) The first dog show under The Kennel Club rules, held at London's Crystal Palace June 16–20, 1873, was a huge success, with 975 dogs entered. The first Cruft's Dog Show was held in 1891. Over the following decades, purebred dogs and dog shows developed into almost a national craze in the United Kingdom, which still has the biggest (and some say the best) dog shows in the world. Crufts—the apostrophe disappeared in the 1980s—is now the world's biggest dog show with more than 20,000 dogs entered at the National Exhibition Centre in Birmingham during four days in March each year.

Just over a decade after the establishment of The Kennel Club, the United

Toward the end of the 1800s, kennel clubs were formed and dog shows held in many countries. This illustration from 1886 shows King Gustav V studying a few of the Pointers entered at the first dog show ever held in Sweden. The Swedish Kennel Club was founded three years later.

Scene from Scottish Terrier judging at Mineola Fairgrounds on Long Island, New York, in 1915.

States followed the British lead by founding the American Kennel Club (AKC), in 1884. Even before that, the Westminster Kennel Club had been in existence for several years. The first Westminster Kennel Club show, which is America's equivalent to Crufts, was held in 1877, attracting an entry of 1,201 dogs. (In the mostly friendly rivalry between the AKC and Westminster Kennel Club in recent years, it is a source of great satisfaction to the latter that the AKC was actually formed at the Westminster show— during the lunch break, to be precise.)

Kennel clubs in most European countries were formed soon thereafter. In 1911, several joined forces, forming the FCI, which regulates international competition at dog shows and serves as a counterbalance to the heavyweight British and American clubs. Over the past century, the FCI has spread far beyond Europe, incorporating kennel clubs in South America, Asia, and recently most nations of the former Soviet Union. Almost 100 years old, the FCI is now setting its sights on China, where it was illegal only a few years ago to even own a dog but where the opportunities for expansion now seem endless.

The present day continues to see exciting developments: the newly formed national kennel club of Turkey holds its first dog show, an Airedale Terrier from Russia wins at

Crufts, Pomeranians from Thailand top the breed competition at Westminster, and the Top Dog in India—a country from which little has been heard in dog circles since the days of the British Raj—is a Siberian Husky from Australia. The leading winners in both British and American Best in Show competitions come from countries that just a few years earlier would have been considered unlikely contenders in the Top Dog race. What started as a rarefied Victorian pursuit with a small following has truly become a worldwide passion for millions.

The Ladies Kennel Association is one of Britain's oldest and largest dog shows. This illustration shows Skye Terrier judging at one of the LKA shows in the early 1900s.

CHAPTER 2

THE BREED STANDARDS

What exactly are the judges looking for at dog shows? What makes one dog better than another? How can an Irish Wolfhound be compared with a Chihuahua? How can it be a beauty contest if the Bulldog beats the Irish Setter? Is it all just subjective, depending on whatever the judges' preferences are?

These are some of the questions a first-time dog show visitor may ask. It's not easy to respond in just a few words. At the center of every dog show stands not the judge but the breed standards, the official description of an imaginary, ideal specimen of each breed. Using the breed standard as the yardstick, the judge must determine which dog in each class comes closest to that ideal and place the dogs accordingly—an often difficult but not impossible task, provided the judge knows the breed standards thoroughly and is also well versed in each breed's history, function, and development.

The breed standard in most cases was heavily influenced by the dogs that were considered the greatest in the early days, when the standards were written. In the case of Afghan Hounds, the "father of the breed" was Ch. Sirdar of Ghazni, imported from Afghanistan to England in 1925. Considered close to the ideal, he is now the ancestor many times over of all modern Afghan Hounds.

Note: For details on show rules, judging systems, and so on, see Appendix A, p. 557.

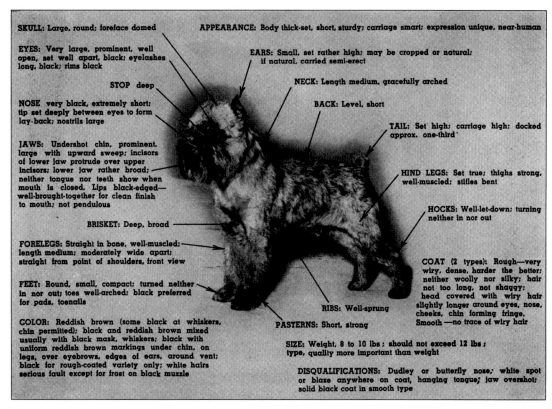

SKULL: Large, round; foreface domed

EYES: Very large, prominent, well open, set well apart, black; eyelashes long, black; rims black

STOP deep

NOSE very black, extremely short; tip set deeply between eyes to form lay-back; nostrils large

JAWS: Undershot chin, prominent, large with upward sweep; incisors of lower jaw protrude over upper incisors; lower jaw rather broad; neither tongue nor teeth show when mouth is closed. Lips black-edged—well-brought-together for clean finish to mouth; not pendulous

BRISKET: Deep, broad

FORELEGS: Straight in bone, well-muscled; length medium; moderately wide apart; straight from point of shoulders, front view

FEET: Round, small, compact; turned neither in nor out; toes well-arched; black preferred for pads, toenails

COLOR: Reddish brown (some black at whiskers, chin permitted); black and reddish brown mixed usually with black mask, whiskers; black with uniform reddish brown markings under chin, on legs, over eyebrows, edges of ears, around vent; black for rough-coated variety only; white hairs serious fault except for frost on black muzzle

APPEARANCE: Body thick-set, short, sturdy; carriage smart; expression unique, near-human

EARS: Small, set rather high; may be cropped or natural; if natural, carried semi-erect

NECK: Length medium, gracefully arched

BACK: Level, short

TAIL: Set high; carriage high; docked approx. one-third

HIND LEGS: Set true; thighs strong, well-muscled; stifles bent

HOCKS: Well-let-down; turning neither in nor out

COAT (2 types): Rough—very wiry, dense, harder the better; neither woolly nor silky; hair not too long, not shaggy; head covered with wiry hair slightly longer around eyes, nose, cheeks, chin forming fringe. Smooth —no trace of wiry hair

RIBS: Well-sprung

PASTERNS: Short, strong

SIZE: Weight, 8 to 10 lbs; should not exceed 12 lbs; type, quality more important than weight

DISQUALIFICATIONS: Dudley or butterfly nose; white spot or blaze anywhere on coat, hanging tongue; jaw overshot; solid black coat in smooth type

The American Kennel Club issued "visualizations" of its breed standards in the 1950s and 1960s. The Brussels Griffon standard was modeled by Ch. Barmere's Mighty Man, the top-winning Toy Dog of 1962 and 1963.

KNOWLEDGE OF THE STANDARDS

Clearly, this is no common beauty contest, at least not unless you are able to take the concept that beauty is in the eye of the beholder to extreme lengths. Many top show dogs are far from beautiful to the untrained eye, so it can be disconcerting for an outsider to listen to the cognoscenti rave about these dogs' great quality, soundness, and even star quality when all you see is a common, not-so-pretty garden-variety dog. That said, many of the best show dogs have such charisma and immediate appeal that you would have to be blind not to see that there's something special about them.

Without breed standards, dog shows could not exist. It would be impossible to conduct any meaningful comparison of dogs without universally accepted descriptions of each breed. The same applies to most other domestic animals. At their best, the standards are far more than a collection of anatomic phrases and measurements: they give a vivid, colorful word picture of the image each breed represents, in motion and standing, when alert and at rest.

Anyone who wants to be considered a true expert in a particular breed, however, needs to go far beyond rote memorization of the standards. To really know a breed, you must know why this breed should look the

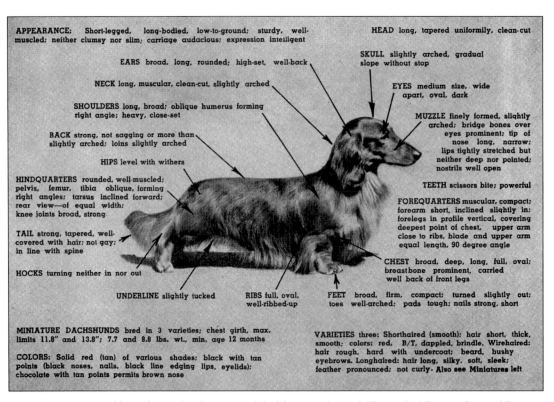

APPEARANCE: Short-legged, long-bodied, low-to-ground; sturdy, well-muscled; neither clumsy nor slim; carriage audacious; expression intelligent

HEAD long, tapered uniformily, clean-cut

EARS broad, long, rounded; high-set, well-back

SKULL slightly arched, gradual slope without stop

NECK long, muscular, clean-cut, slightly arched

EYES medium size, wide apart, oval, dark

SHOULDERS long, broad; oblique humerus forming right angle; heavy, close-set

MUZZLE finely formed, slightly arched; bridge bones over eyes prominent; tip of nose long, narrow; lips tightly stretched but neither deep nor pointed; nostrils well open

BACK strong, not sagging or more than slightly arched; loins slightly arched

HIPS level with withers

TEETH scissors bite; powerful

HINDQUARTERS rounded, well-muscled; pelvis, femur, tibia oblique, forming right angles; tarsus inclined forward; rear view—of equal width; knee joints broad, strong

FOREQUARTERS muscular, compact; forearm short, inclined slightly in; forelegs in profile vertical, covering deepest point of chest, upper arm close to ribs, blade and upper arm equal length, 90 degree angle

TAIL strong, tapered, well-covered with hair; not gay; in line with spine

CHEST broad, deep, long, full, oval; breastbone prominent, carried well back of front legs

HOCKS turning neither in nor out

UNDERLINE slightly tucked

RIBS full, oval, well-ribbed-up

FEET broad, firm, compact; turned slightly out; toes well-arched; pads tough; nails strong, short

MINIATURE DACHSHUNDS bred in 3 varieties; chest girth, max. limits 11.8" and 13.8"; 7.7 and 8.8 lbs. wt., min. age 12 months

COLORS: Solid red (tan) of various shades; black with tan points (black noses, nails, black line edging lips, eyelids); chocolate with tan points permits brown nose

VARIETIES three: Shorthaired (smooth); hair short, thick, smooth; colors: red, B/T, dappled, brindle. Wirehaired: hair rough, hard with undercoat; beard, bushy eyebrows. Longhaired: hair long, silky, soft, sleek; feather pronounced; not curly. Also see Miniatures left

The AKC Dachshund breed standard was modeled by Longhaired Ch. Roderick von der Nidda, one of the Top Dogs of all breeds in 1955.

way it does, how the breed standard was written and changed over the years, and in what ways it might differ from standards for the same breed in other countries, especially in the breed's native country. For international judges, it is imperative to know, in depth, the official standard for the breed in each country where they are judging.

Judging each breed against its own standard is one thing; comparing dogs of different breeds with each other is quite another. At the point in a show that the chosen best of each breed are competing against each other for Group and Best in Show awards, the judging technique obviously must shift slightly. Now each dog is compared with its imaginary ideal, and whichever comes closest to the ideal wins.

This explains how "ugly" breeds can defeat "beautiful" ones. The whole concept of what's beautiful assumes a different meaning for dog people.

FRAMING THE STANDARDS

Who wrote these breed standards, and why do they matter? The first ones were written centuries ago, long before anything resembling today's dog shows were imagined. Dame Berner, Caius, and Buffon have already been mentioned. The dowager Empress of China, Cixi (Tzu Hsi) wrote (or caused to be written) a detailed, supremely poetic description of the Pekingese even before the first specimens had been looted from the Summer Palace and brought to England in 1860. The empress decreed that the

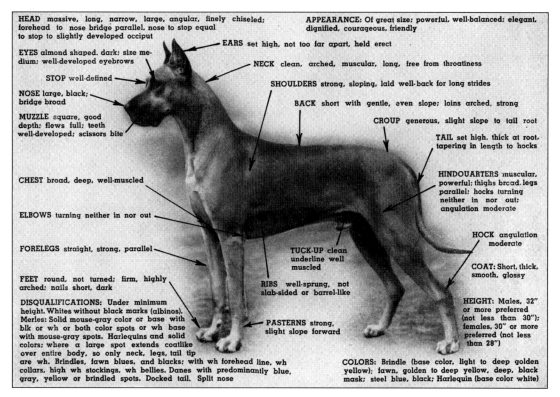

HEAD massive, long, narrow, large, angular, finely chiseled; forehead to nose bridge parallel, nose to stop equal to stop to slightly developed occiput

EYES almond shaped, dark; size medium; well-developed eyebrows

STOP well-defined

NOSE large, black; bridge broad

MUZZLE square, good depth; flews full; teeth well-developed; scissors bite

CHEST broad, deep, well-muscled

ELBOWS turning neither in nor out

FORELEGS straight, strong, parallel

FEET round, not turned; firm, highly arched; nails short, dark

DISQUALIFICATIONS: Under minimum height. Whites without black marks (albinos). Merles: Solid mouse-gray color or base with blk or wh or both color spots or wh base with mouse-gray spots. Harlequins and solid colors; where a large spot extends coatlike over entire body, so only neck, legs, tail tip are wh. Brindles, fawn blues, and blacks; with wh forehead line, wh collars, high wh stockings, wh bellies. Danes with predominantly blue, gray, yellow or brindled spots. Docked tail. Split nose

APPEARANCE: Of great size; powerful, well-balanced; elegant, dignified, courageous, friendly

EARS set high, not too far apart, held erect

NECK clean, arched, muscular, long, free from throatiness

SHOULDERS strong, sloping, laid well-back for long strides

BACK short with gentle, even slope; loins arched, strong

CROUP generous, slight slope to tail root

TAIL set high, thick at root, tapering in length to hocks

HINDQUARTERS muscular, powerful; thighs broad, legs parallel; hocks turning neither in nor out; angulation moderate

HOCK angulation moderate

COAT: Short, thick, smooth, glossy

HEIGHT: Males, 32" or more preferred (not less than 30"); females, 30" or more preferred (not less than 28")

TUCK-UP clean underline well muscled

RIBS well-sprung, not slab-sided or barrel-like

PASTERNS strong, slight slope forward

COLORS: Brindle (base color, light to deep golden yellow); fawn, golden to deep yellow, deep, black mask; steel blue, black; Harlequin (base color white)

The AKC Great Dane standard was illustrated by Ch. Honey Hollow Stormi Rudio, a multiple Best in Show winner in the late 1950s.

Pekingese should be small (so it is easy to carry) and that it should have an abundant coat around its chest and on the tail (described as a "swelling cape of dignity around its neck" and "the billowing standard of pomp above its back"). "Let its face be black; let its forefront be shaggy; let its forehead be straight and low"; the empress also specified that the eyes should be "large and luminous," its ears "set like the sails of a war junk," and its forelegs "bent so that it shall not desire to wander far, or leave the Imperial Precincts." Barring the poetry, this isn't far from the modern Pekingese standard, which was obviously based on descriptions of the early imperial imports, if not on the empress's own description. The empress, as if knowing what would come, also wanted the Pekingese to "immediately bite the foreign devils." That didn't make it to the modern breed standard, but it remains a typical breed trait that the Pekingese displays a certain arrogance toward strangers.

How Standards Evolved

Most breed standards, of course, are more recent and less fancifully worded, but almost all are based on a combination of tradition and function. They were written when most dogs were still used primarily for the activities for which they had been developed. Dogs that excelled in their particular activities were designated as the ideal, and their most outstanding characteristics were those that breeders sought to preserve for future generations. Often these characteristics are

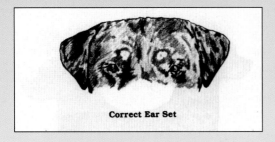

Correct Ear Set

Incorrect - Ears too High, "Terrier Set"

Incorrect - Ears too Large

Incorrect - "Rose" Ear

Incorrect - Ears Break at Outer Edge

Incorrect - Ears Set too Low

Ears
Pendant, proportionately small, triangular in shape; set well apart and placed on skull so as to make it appear broader when the dog is alert. Ear terminates at approximate mid-cheek level. Correctly held, the inner edge will lie tightly against cheek.

Commentary — Too long or too large ears give the Rottweiler a "houndy" look, as do ears set too low. Ears set too high give a terrier look. Many Rottweiler puppies, during the teething stage, will hold their ears incorrectly — either manifesting a "rose ear" or an incorrect crease in the ear. It is particularly true of puppies with smaller ears. Breeders and owners may tape a puppy's ears during teething to aid in correct carriage. Properly set and carried ears are essential to true Rottweiler expression and deviations should be penalized.

From the Rottweiler Club of America illustrated standard, 1986: ears.

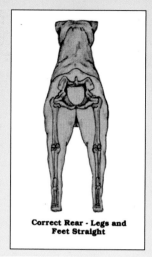

Correct Rear - Legs and Feet Straight

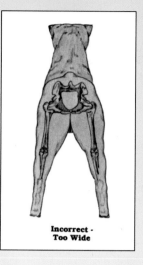

Incorrect - Too Wide

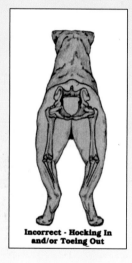

Incorrect - Hocking In and/or Toeing Out

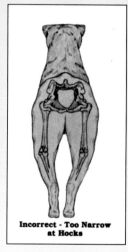

Incorrect - Too Narrow at Hocks

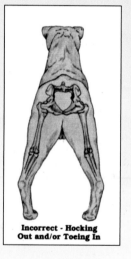

Incorrect - Hocking Out and/or Toeing In

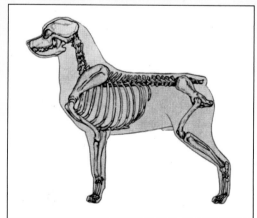

Hindquarters
Angulation of hindquarters balances that of forequarters.

Commentary — The degree of angulation of forequarters and hindquarters must be compatible to achieve balance and correct movement.

Upper Thigh
Fairly long, broad and well muscled.

Commentary — Prominent muscling of the inner and outer thighs should be visible when viewed from the rear.

From the Rottweiler Club of America illustrated standard, 1986: hindquarters.

vital to the dog's function: most good Greyhound judges today would agree, for instance, that legs, feet, and muscle development are far more important characteristics in this breed than color, eye shape, or ear carriage. A Bloodhound must follow a scent and so is not expected to carry its head high, while an Afghan Hound must do so because it hunts by sighting its prey from afar. A Dachshund and some terriers must be short legged to go underground; a toy dog needs simply to be pleasing to the eye and have an affectionate temperament. The Bulldog, to take an extreme historical example, needed to have a nose pushed up into its muzzle so it could breathe even while hanging on to a bull. It also needed to be heavier in front than in the rear for the same reason. There has been no bullbaiting with dogs for at least 150 years now, so the anatomical distinctions are more a cultural heritage than an actual necessity. Even seemingly insignificant details in the breed standards often prove to have a rational explanation if you dig back far enough into breed history.

Over the past century, old standards have been revised and modernized, often by decree of the various national kennel clubs in well-meant, but often self-defeating, attempts to clarify the original meaning. In the process, the reason that certain characteristics were included is forgotten, and the hallowed breed standard of old may slowly deteriorate, becoming just a description of what "this year's model" of a breed should resemble. Sometimes the changes describe a dog that looks very different from the original breed; sometimes it has even been necessary to call in veterinary expertise to determine if a standard's requirements are in fact not conducive to the breed's physical and mental health.

WHAT'S IN THE STANDARDS

Ideally, the standard begins with a short paragraph that places the breed in a historical context, alludes to the breed's original use, and includes a description of the "general impression" it should make. There should be a note about the breed's desired temperament: "calm and dignified," "lively and friendly," even "somewhat reserved with strangers." There should follow a detailed description of the dog's anatomy from the tip of the nose to the end of the tail:

DECIPHERING STANDARDS

The best breed standards have remained unchanged for the longest time—although possibly with some additional explanations for modern readers. How many dog people today know what a "cleverly made hunter, covering a lot of ground, yet with a short back" looks like, as described in the current Fox Terrier standard? How many people know what the original "hackney-like action" required of a Miniature Pinscher means? (A high lifting of the front feet accompanied by flexing of the wrist.) A century ago, most readers could be expected to know enough about horses for these terms not to need the explanations they might require today.

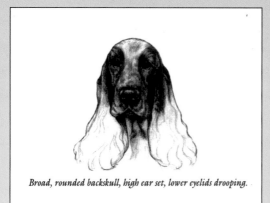

Broad, rounded backskull, high ear set, lower eyelids drooping.

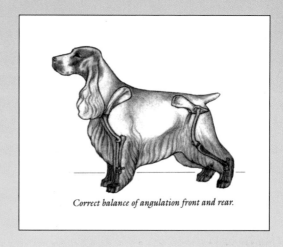

Correct balance of angulation front and rear.

A frequently seen fault in otherwise good dogs. A prominent frontal bone may be confused with stop. Note receding backskull.

Lack of balance between front and rear angulation, as in the above picture, will contribute to faulty gait, short steps and/or sidewinding

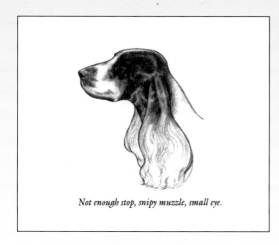

Not enough stop, snipy muzzle, small eye.

Correct side movement while keeping proud head carriage, firm topline and correct tail set

From the English Cocker Spaniel Club of America's illustrated standard, 1995: head (left), profile of body (upper right), gait (lower right).

One of the Top Dogs of all breeds in both 2003 and 2004, the German Shepherd Dog Ch. Kaleef's Genuine Risk.

muzzle, skull, ears, eyes, bite and teeth, neck, front legs and shoulders, body and topline, hind quarters, feet, and tail. Coat, color (or colors), and size for both dogs and bitches should be specified.

There should also be a description of the breed's gait and movement, how this breed looks in action: some breeds, such as the German Shepherd Dog, are expected to move with an extremely elastic, far-reaching stride, covering the maximum amount of ground with each step; others are expected to take shorter steps or may even have a stilted action. Some breeds may amble or pace; still others may have a lighter, airier

way of going. (Incidentally, show dogs are normally judged either standing or trotting; on rare occasions, walking; never at the gallop, however logical that may seem for the sighthound breeds.)

All males are required to have two normally descended testicles; monorchids (one testicle) or cryptorchids (no testicles) are barred from competition in most countries and should not be used for breeding even if they are able to sire puppies (as is sometimes possible with monorchids). Judges are required to check that all male dogs shown have normally developed testicles. In the United States, a dog without two "normally developed testicles" must be disqualified. In the United Kingdom, this is merely considered a fault, and it is up to the judge to determine how severely it should be penalized. Each breed standard ends with the note "Male animals should have two apparently normal testicles fully descended into the scrotum." In other words, if the judge thinks the dog is outstanding enough in other areas, one or both missing testicles may be considered the same as any other fault. On occasion, such a dog may even win; reportedly, at least one such dog has even become a champion.

FAULTS AND VIRTUES

With a clearly written breed standard, one would think it should not be difficult for a judge to determine the best of several dogs of the same breed. If the standard says that the front legs should be parallel, how could the judge possibly select a dog whose front looks almost like a rococo bureau?

The reason, of course, is that no dog is perfect; all have some characteristics that could be improved. If the dog that won has some easily visible imperfection, it doesn't necessarily mean the judge is incompetent. The winner probably has great qualities elsewhere that, at least in this judge's opinion, outweigh the fault. The others in the class probably lack those merits and perhaps have additional faults of their own, some of which may not be easily discernible from outside the ring. The ability to process and efficiently evaluate a huge amount of information and make clear-cut decisions in a very limited time frame is something every judge must possess.

The way in which two different people assess the faults and virtues of the same dog is, in fact, fundamental to both the attraction and the frustration of the dog show experience. The written word can describe only so much, and how you interpret the breed standard's words—filter them through your experience and match them to your mental image of what that particular breed should look like—virtually guarantees that no two people will ever see the same dog in exactly the same way. Consider also the fact that dogs change, mature, age, and are affected by a wide variety of external conditions, which means that the results can vary greatly from one show to another, from one judge to another.

No one ever suggested that all judges should agree on everything. In fact, there would not be much point to dog shows if they did. However, ideally we should expect that serious, experienced people within one breed are able to agree at least on which are the really good dogs—even if they may not agree on all the details.

ORIGINAL STANDARDS AND BEYOND

The FCI has saved the rest of the dog world from utter confusion by requesting that all its more than eighty member countries adhere to the same breed standards. The standards that the FCI uses are approved by each breed's country of origin, or in the case of breeds that hail from areas where no organized kennel club activity existed at the time the breed was established in the West (the Afghan Hound, the African Basenji, and the Japanese Chin, for instance), the standard is that used by that breed's country of development, usually England. This is a sound principle, at least in theory, but it does not always work. What if the country of origin is not

The American Cocker Spaniel Ch. Artru Hot Rod, a top all-breed winner in 1958 and Best in Show at the American Spaniel Club in 1959.

The Crufts Best in Show winner in 1938 and 1939 was Sh. Ch. Exquisite Model of Ware, illustrating the English Cocker Spaniel type then desired worldwide.

A UNIVERSAL STANDARD

Although in the best of all possible worlds there would be one universal standard for each breed, there are usually several. The reasons are historical, geographic, and political. In the dog sport's early days, breed standards drawn up by The Kennel Club in England were generally accepted in most other countries as well. Eventually, as breeds started developing along different paths in different countries—especially in America—fanciers called for changes in the breed standards. (It usually is not the standard that changes a breed so much as it is the breeders who change the standards to fit what appeals to them, with or without historical justification.) Over time, the specifics listed in the new standards for some breeds have come to clash quite strongly with those listed in earlier versions.

This is what happened with the Cocker Spaniel, where the type favored in America in the 1930s eventually led to the development of a separate breed; fanciers in many other breeds feel this is happening still. The other English-speaking countries, once a part of the British Empire, have generally shown more respect for the original standards, but in extreme cases the requirements for the same breed can differ not only from England to the United States but also among the standards used in Canada, South Africa, Australia, and New Zealand.

NOT SO UNIVERSAL STANDARDS

One extreme example of differing breed standards is presented by the Akita, a Japanese breed that has developed a strong, worldwide following. The type favored in the United States and the United Kingdom came to differ so strongly from what the FCI—and its Japanese members—felt was historically correct that the breed was eventually split into two separate breeds in FCI countries: one is called, simply, Akita; the other, which was officially approved in 2005, is the American Akita.

As another example, many German Shepherd Dogs that win at AKC shows are scorned in those parts of the world that adhere to the German standard approved by the FCI. Great Britain had its own distinct type for many years both before and after World War II and even gave the breed a new name, the Alsatian, in an effort to deemphasize its country of origin. In recent decades, the British have started to follow Germany's lead in this breed. A strong American segment also prefers to abide by the country of origin's standard but operates mostly outside the AKC framework.

A couple of other examples may illustrate how complicated the question of original breed standards may be. The original Afghan Hound standard was drawn up in the 1920s, based on the first imports from Afghanistan into England. For the most part, that standard was dutifully adopted by the fledgling Afghan Hound Club of America shortly afterward. Even as that was happening, a resourceful fancier in England succeeded in convincing The Kennel Club there to accept a new standard, different from the original but closer to this breeder's idea of how the breed should look. The American standard remains based on the first, older standard, but Britain is the country of development—so which standard is more correct?

The Brittany was developed in France and exported to the United States as well as to other countries. However, after the ravages of World War II, so few purebred Brittanys remained in France that these had to be crossed with other breeds. Although this guaranteed the breed's survival, it also introduced black, a color that had previously been a disqualifying fault. The FCI standard was altered to allow black, which is still not acceptable in the United States, where a translation of the "old" French standard is still used.

Afghan Hounds, imported from Afghanistan to England in the 1920s.

Fifty years later, in 1973, Ch. Khayam's Apollo won the Group at Westminster, handled by Eugene Blake under judge Joe Tacker.

SAME BREED OR NOT?

A top-winning English Springer Spaniel in the United Kingdom, Sh. Ch. Calvdale Call Off the Search, is shown by Nicole Calvert to Group 2nd at the Scottish Kennel Club show in 2006.

The American version of the English Springer Spaniel is illustrated by Ch. Salilyn's Condor, winning Best in Show at Wallkill Kennel Club in 1991, handled by Mark Threlfall under judge Dr. Anthony DiNardo. Condor was also Best in Show at Westminster in 1993.

One of the top-winning English Setters in the United Kingdom, Sh. Ch. Bournehouse Royal Colours, Reserve Best in Show at Crufts 2005, shown with Penny Williams.

The English Setter in America is portrayed by Ch. Set'r Ridge Wyndswept In Gold, top Sporting Dog in 2002, shown winning Best in Show at Greenwich Kennel Club in 2001, handled by Kellie Fitzgerald under Canadian judge James Reynolds.

The top Siberian Husky in England, Ch. Forstal Kaliznik, with Ali Koops handling after he won the Pedigree Chum all breed Veteran Stakes qualifying round at the Welsh Kennel Club Championship show in August 2004. The judge was Brenda Banbury; the presenter is Dave Williams, representing the sponsor, Pedigree Chum. "Cub" is the winner of a record thirty-nine Challenge Certificates.

Siberian Huskies win often in American all-breed competition. Ch. Kontoki's One Mo' Time was among the Top Dogs of all breeds in 1984. He is shown handled by his breeder, Tommy Oelschlager, to Best in Show at New Brunswick Kennel Club in 1986 under judge Judith Goodin. Trophy presenter was Marjorie Martorella.

The American Akita (formerly Great Japanese Dog) has been separated from the Japanese-type Akita at FCI shows since 1999. The latter breed differs from the American Akita in many ways, as exemplified by Ch. Akasta's Hedzi-wig, an FCI World Champion, shown with judge Dr. José Luis Payro, Mexico.

One of America's top Working Dogs in 1997 and 1998, the American Akita Ch. Crownroy-als Getoff My Cloud, shown winning Best in Show at Willamette Valley Kennel Club in 1998 under judge Carl Liepmann.

DOCKING AND CROPPING

Originally, the docking of dogs' tails and cropping of ears served some practical purpose. Fighting and guard dogs would have their ears and tails partly cut off to make them less vulnerable during fights and to make them look more ferocious. Many hunting breeds' tails were docked to prevent them from becoming injured in the field, and herding dogs had their long tails docked so they would not get caught in a gate behind the livestock.

Today, docking and cropping is performed almost entirely for aesthetic and historical reasons. A groundswell of feeling against these practices has resulted in regulations outlawing them in many countries; long-tailed Boxers and Rottweilers as well as flop-eared Great Danes and Dobermans, to mention just a few breeds affected by the cropping and docking bans, are now exhibited at shows throughout Europe.

In the United Kingdom, ear cropping was not an accepted practice even in the first days of dog shows, reportedly because of the royal family's disapproval. As early as the 1870s, Vero Shaw referred to cropping as a "barbarous and utterly useless practice." Dog shows, and most of the breeds that are cropped elsewhere, have flourished in Great Britain in spite of the long-established anticropping laws there. However, many fanciers predict that similar legislation would have a devastating effect on the sport if introduced in the United States.

Docking, a far less invasive measure that is performed shortly after birth with barely discernible discomfort for the puppy, is nevertheless often lumped with ear cropping and is currently illegal in an increasing number of European countries. Although laws against docking dogs were introduced in Great Britain in 2007, both North and South America have so far held out against cropping and docking bans.

Several AKC breed standards penalize undocked or uncropped dogs, but the American Kennel Club itself has no rules that require docking or cropping of show dogs of any breed.

The uncropped and undocked Bouvier des Flandres Ch. Sarol Tailfeather, a Group winner in Finland in 2006.

A black American Cocker Spaniel, Ch. Caci's Cute Carmen at Ld's, was Top Dog in Sweden in 2006, handled by breeder Carina Östman. Notice the dog's undocked tail.

capable of drawing up a sensible breed standard or keeps changing the standard for no apparent reason? What if the country of origin of some breeds is doubtful? The Poodle, for instance, is listed by the FCI as a French breed, but although France, Germany, Switzerland, and perhaps even Russia all had a hand in the creation of this breed, almost no one would deny that England must be considered the primary country of development, at least for the Miniature Poodle. Therefore, an international Poodle judge must be thoroughly familiar with several different breed standards.

The official FCI standards exist in four languages: French, German, Spanish, and English. In addition, each country will naturally translate the standard into its native tongue. This can create further problems, as very few capable translators are equally gifted in their knowledge of dog terms. Many of the subtle changes in priorities and emphases that develop in different countries may be the result of something as simple as a flawed translation of the original standard.

All in all, standards are not necessarily the stone tablets that they should be, but they are necessary and must be treated with much more respect than is often the case. For a breeder striving to attain perfection by breeding to a time-honored standard, it is upsetting to find that the goal, the ideal he or she has been striving toward for years, has suddenly been changed. It is a testament to the talent and adaptability of the best breeders that, despite the earth's shifting under their feet, they are able to continue producing great dogs, generation after generation.

CHAPTER 3

THE SHOWS

Among the thousands of dog shows held around the world every year, a few stand out. For different reasons, they have achieved a level of recognition that makes them classics in the annual calendar. They are the kind of event dog fanciers everywhere talk about and where a win is a lifetime achievement. Ambitious new fanciers dream of going to these shows someday, and many who make the pilgrimage return home inspired, with memories lasting for years. Your local show may be wonderful in its own way—everybody knows your name and you don't have to squeeze through crowds to see the dogs—but if you want to learn what the sport of purebred dogs is really about, you must visit some of the truly world-class events.

Overhead view of some of the breed rings at the Westminster Kennel Club dog show.

Indisputably, the two most famous and most historic dog events in the world are Crufts and Westminster. These shows must be discussed separately: one is in England, the other in the United States, and each is so bound by its own history and particular rules that the two could hardly be more different. What they have in common is the attention of millions of dog fanciers worldwide; most watch on TV, but thousands make the journey to one or both of these shows each year. Every true dog fancier should visit Crufts and Westminster at least once: anyone who is accustomed to one is bound to be intrigued by the other. Which one you prefer is a matter of taste, but both can provide memories for a lifetime if you are seriously interested in dogs.

BEST OF BRITAIN

Nowhere else will you see the purebred dog fancy blossom into such splendid flower as in the United Kingdom. Some have described it as a sort of noble folly, born during the years that these isles were the uncontested center of the world, both politically and culturally; perhaps one reason that dog shows are so popular in Great Britain is that they represent a tradition from a glorious past. Whatever the reason, dog shows are more popular in Great Britain than anywhere else, and as a consequence there are more large dog shows there than anywhere else on earth.

There are, in all, just over two dozen general British championship shows that are a regular fixture each year; the number has changed very little in the past few decades. Many of these shows are household names among dog fanciers far beyond the British Isles. The season starts in Manchester in January; there's Crufts in March and the first of the big outdoor shows, West of England Ladies' Kennel Society (WELKS), in April. By May, the show season is in full flower, with the world's oldest dog show, Birmingham, followed within a couple of weeks by the first Scottish Kennel Club show in Edinburgh and then Bath. June has Southern Counties close to London, Three Counties in Malvern, Border Union in Scotland, and Blackpool. July starts with the Windsor classic, followed by South Wales, Paignton, Peterborough, and Leeds. August has Bournemouth, the Welsh Kennel Club, and the second Scottish Kennel Club show. September is the last busy month for the all-breed shows, starting with the younger of the two Birmingham shows, followed by Richmond, Darlington, and the only Irish all-breed championship show under Kennel Club rules, Belfast. The year winds down with the Driffield and Midland counties shows in October and ends with a flourish at the huge Ladies Kennel Association (LKA) show, held in Birmingham in December.

First Prize card for Crufts in 1891.

There are also separate shows for each of the seven Groups into which The Kennel Club has divided the breeds. There are three shows for Gundogs, two for Hounds, three for Working and Pastoral Dogs, one for Terriers, one for Toys, and one for Utility breeds. In addition, there are breed club shows, a varying number for each breed, many with big entries but seldom carrying as much cachet as the best American specialty shows.

Which of these shows are the best is a difficult question. Size does not equal quality. Although Crufts is by far the biggest dog show in the world, usually with more than 20,000 dogs entered, it is not necessarily the "best" of the British shows. Many connoisseurs feel that some of the outdoors summer events better represent what British dog shows are all about. Windsor is a perennial favorite, especially with overseas visitors. It is held in the Home Park and used to have Windsor Castle as a suitably scenic backdrop, and even after its move a short distance away, it remains one the most beautiful dog shows anywhere. Always held in the beginning of July, Windsor is inextricably

Charles Cruft in the late 1800s, around the time he started his famous show.

linked to Wimbledon, to the Henley Regatta, to strawberries and cream, and to the sometimes fickle charms of the British summer.

Certainly, Crufts is the biggest ticket, however, not just in Britain but in most of the rest of the world. For Americans accustomed to the much smaller, more elitist, more formal, and tightly choreographed Westminster, Crufts can come as a shock: it is vast, sprawling, and surprisingly commercial, like a huge fair with vast numbers of dogs and even more people participating. Oddly enough, both Crufts and Westminster turn the national stereotypes on their ears: it is the American show that is smaller, more conservative, with much greater emphasis on protocol than is seen in its British counterpart. In earlier years, the two shows ran almost simultaneously over a few days in February, separated only by an ocean and a time difference, which had globe-trotting dog fanciers red-eyed with fatigue and overdosing on dogs. Since Crufts moved from London to Birmingham in March, they are held a month apart.

CHARLES CRUFT: ENTREPRENEUR AND MASTERMIND

Crufts dog show was named after its originator, Charles Cruft. Born in 1851, Cruft, without any particular interest in or experience with dogs, started out working first as office boy, then as a salesman for the Spratt's dog food company when he was in his midtwenties. In that capacity, he visited the World Exhibition in Paris in 1879. A dog show was planned as part of that event, and Cruft was asked to help organize it. The success of this

View of Crufts when it was held at Olympia in London, 1955.

endeavor was such that young Cruft realized he had found his niche. Cruft, who came back from Paris with his head full of enthusiasm from that experience, was not the first to feel that the world was ready for a truly great dog show event, but he would be the one to make it a reality. He promptly organized a show for terriers at the Royal Aquarium in London. Then—in 1891—came the first of what he advertised, with the remarkable absence of humility that would be his trademark, as "The Great Cruft's Dog Show" with "the largest and the finest collection of dogs ever brought together. Every breed represented. Dogs from all parts of the world." Never a shrinking violet, Cruft knew how to work the publicity machine, and the success of his show was in no small measure the result of his very modern use of advertising.

Charles Cruft, founder of Crufts Dog Show.

The British royal family's patronage of Crufts has continued through the decades. Queen Elizabeth is seen watching English Springer Spaniel judging in 1969.

As Frank Jackson put it, "Much of the incredible success of Crufts Dog Show was . . . the result of Charles Cruft's almost uncanny ability to attract publicity."

In a masterstroke of planning, Cruft secured sole rights to the only suitable showgrounds in London, the agricultural exhibition halls at Islington. Part of the con-

tract was that no other major dog show could be held there to compete with Cruft's show for several decades. There were 2,437 entries at that first show, an impressive figure even by today's standards, although, of course, the total number of dogs was smaller, with many dogs entered in more than one class. Cruft was also known to employ a somewhat imaginative manner of counting the entries, on occasion resorting to duplicates and omissions to reach his grand totals. No matter, the show was a huge success: "Surpasses any previous canine exhibition," said the *Standard*. "A dog show of unprecedented dimensions," announced the *Daily Telegraph*.

One feature that helped establish this as an event worthy of notice far outside the dog world was the patronage of the royal family. Queen Victoria exhibited a Collie and several Pomeranians. Her son the Prince of Wales showed his Samoyed and won every prize in the class for Rough Bassets, the early forerunner to today's Petit Basset Griffon Vendéen, which would not be reintroduced into England until many decades later. Dogs from the royal Sandringham kennels were shown at Crufts for several years, and even today some member of the royal family is likely to turn up at the show. (Queen Elizabeth's cousin Prince Michael of Kent has been president of Crufts for several years.) Until the introduction of quarantine restrictions in 1901, foreign dogs were encouraged to participate, and the fact that an occasional Indian maharaja or grand duke from Russia was listed among the exhibitors certainly boosted Cruft's publicity. The public found the "exotic" foreign breeds—even such now-established varieties as the Afghan Hound and the Chow Chow—quite irresistible and stood in line around the block to get in to see the dogs at Mr. Cruft's exhibition.

Even literary recognition came the great show's way. As early as 1926, Nobel Prize–winner John Galsworthy mentions Crufts in *The Forsyte Saga* as one of the reasons, together with the Beefeaters and the Derby, that an American visitor would want to visit England.

In 1936, Charles Cruft achieved a lifetime ambition of having more than 10,000 entries at his show. He succeeded in doing this at least partly by announcing this as the Golden Jubilee Show; the entries poured in until a final figure of 10,650 entries was reached. It was, in fact, only forty-five years since the first show, but Cruft was not one to be bothered by such details, and his time was running out. Charles Cruft died in 1938. The following year, his widow took over the management, but after one successful attempt and with the threat of war looming, Mrs. Cruft decided that she would not be able to continue the show. She accepted an offer from The Kennel Club to purchase the name and all rights to the show. The Kennel Club had, for many years, kept an envious eye on Cruft's show: its own annual championship show was forever running second to it, never quite emulating either its entry figures or public acclaim. Since the acquisition, Crufts has been the jewel in The Kennel Club's crown and the most valuable commodity in the dog show world.

THE POSTWAR CRUFTS

There were no major dog shows in England during World War II, but Crufts made its comeback in 1948. The halls in Islington had been destroyed by bombs, so the show moved to a new home at Olympia, then London's largest indoor arena. It still wasn't big enough: by 1950, participation had reached a new record of 5,700 dogs, which made more than 12,000 entries. (Multiple entries for the same dog are still common in

The first time a "foreign" dog won Best in Show at Crufts was in 1975, when Albert Langley handled the Wire Fox Terrier Ch. Brookewire Brandy of Layven to Best in Show. Brandy was born in Britain but owned by Italians Giuseppe Benelli and Paolo Dondina, shown being interviewed after the win by Stanley Dangerfield (far left).

England; at that time, the practice was more popular than it is today.) By the mid-1960s, it was necessary to introduce entry restrictions, at first by excluding young puppies, then by requiring that all dogs entered must have won an award at some prior show. Even the 1979 move to a more spacious venue at Earls Court did not ease the congestion. Getting from one breed ring to another could take hours, and once you got to the breed you wanted to watch you might encounter a five-row-deep wall of spectators. For the Crufts Centennial Show in 1991, The Kennel Club made the momentous decision to finally move the show out of London. The plan had many critics, but it made sense: it would be impossible to bring so many dogs and even more people together into any big city without major problems.

The Centennial Show, celebrated in the vast, modern National Exhibition Centre outside Birmingham, was a huge success. The NEC consists of twenty interconnected halls covering a total of forty-five acres; just five of the halls were enough to house the 22,921 dogs that were entered in 1991—the largest number ever recorded for a dog show anywhere. There were also several hundred commercial booths, selling every dog-related item you could possibly imagine, and quite a few other products as well. (One of the perennial criticisms of Crufts is that it is at least as much about shopping as it is about dogs.) There were also events separate from the regular dog show, such as the Discover Dogs information booths manned by breed fanciers with live dogs, not to mention obedience, agility, and other attractions. Some visitors missed the atmosphere of the old show and the big-city energy, but it was obvious that Crufts had moved north to stay. Birmingham, of course, was already home to the oldest dog show in the world—the Birmingham National dog show, held since 1860 and still going strong. With four of the world's biggest and most important dog shows held in or near the city, Birmingham must be considered the undisputed dog show capital of the world. London has not hosted a single major dog show since Crufts moved north.

The opening ceremony for the modern Crufts finale has become increasingly spectacular.

A new feature at Crufts is the Breeders' Team competition, consisting of four dogs bred by one person. In 2005, the finale was judged by Clare Coxall (center); the winners were a group of Weimaraners carrying the Ansona prefix.

Crufts is more than the world's biggest dog show; it is also a huge fair selling everything even remotely linked to dogs. This view shows a small part of one of the vast exhibition halls with trade stands.

Most of the Best in Show winners at Crufts have a champion title in front of their names. The only one who did not become a champion was the Pyrenean Mountain Dog (Great Pyrenees) Bergerie Knur, who was never shown after his 1970 win. He was sired by a de Fontenay dog.

The Keeshond Ch. Volkrijk of Vorden, Best in Show at Crufts in 1957.

CRUFTS AND THE CHANGING FACE OF QUARANTINE

One of the most exciting aspects of Crufts in recent years has been the participation of foreign dogs, following a gradual easing of the quarantine restrictions that for almost a century made it impossible for dogs from other countries to compete. Considerable red tape and paperwork are still required, more for dogs coming from certain countries than for others, but the result has been an invasion of foreign dogs that meet the requirements set up for overseas competitors to participate. The prestige of Crufts is such that even qualifying to compete is something to brag about, but many of the visiting dogs have done much better than that. Imported or foreign-owned dogs had won Best in Show at Crufts before (a Canadian-born Kerry Blue Terrier in 1979, a Wire Fox Terrier and an Airedale Terrier, both Italian-owned and the latter Italian-bred, in 1975 and 1986, respectively), but those dogs were all British residents shown by British handlers.

In 2002, a new era of international competition was officially launched when a white Standard Poodle, Ch. Topscore Contradiction, came over from his native Norway just for Crufts and went all the way through to Best in Show. Three years later, this win was repeated by American visitors. For the Norfolk Terrier Ch. Cracknor Cause Celebre, it was a case of returning to native soil for both dog and handler: "Coco" was born in England and handled by Welsh emigré Peter Green to win Crufts in 2005. The Australian Shepherd Ch. Caitland Isle Take A Chance, who won in 2006, came from California but was born in Canada and was shown by American handler Larry Fenner. In 2007, when Larry Cornelius handled the Tibetan Terrier Ch. Araki Fabulous Willy to the top spot, it was the third year in a row

American and British at Crufts: U.S. handler Linda Pitts shows Great Britain's Top Dog 2005, the American Cocker Spaniel Ch. Afterglow Douglas Fashion, in the Gundog Group at Crufts 2006. The judge was Freda Marshall. Douglas later continued his winning after being exported to the United States.

The Sporting Group at Westminster in 1970 was judged by Arthur Zane, who found his winner in the Pointer Ch. Counterpoint's Lord Ashley, handled by Corky Vroom. Lord Ashley had been the top Sporting dog and one of the top dogs of all breeds the previous year.

that a professional handler from America won Crufts, but Willy, like "Coco" before him, was born and bred in England.

WESTMINSTER

The Westminster Kennel Club show provides one of dogdom's longest unbroken links to the past: it has been held in New York City every year since 1877, fourteen years before the first Crufts. It is not only the oldest of all American dog shows—older than the American Kennel Club itself—but also the second oldest of all American sporting events, edged out of first place by the Kentucky Derby by a neck of only two years. It is not a particularly big show—the entry is limited to 2,500 dogs—but every dog entered must be an AKC champion of record. The combination of history, location, and the high percentage of top dogs present guarantees a spectacle that is virtually unri-

valed, not just in the United States but anywhere in the world. The Westminster Kennel Club's dog show is now a fixture held on the second Monday and Tuesday in February—the most important dates in the American dog show calendar.

The idea of gathering more than 2,000 dogs in the heart of Manhattan in the middle of winter is, by any reasonable standard, insane. That it works, year after year, is testament to the basic need for the dog sport in this vast country to have at least one great collective experience, one single show where the best meet the best. The expense and trouble involved in getting the dogs to the show weeds out almost anyone who is not a serious contender, and with the stakes so high, the TV cameras rolling, and the whole world watching, both dogs and people are on their very best behavior. How the dogs can understand that this show is serious business is a good question, but many of them certainly do.

"Westminster week" encompasses far more than the show itself: the days leading up to it are packed with social events, awards dinners, specialty shows, and other opportunities for America's dog show aristocracy (past, present, and wannabes) to rub shoulders in a frenzy that can be explained only by the fact that this is *the* dog event of the year for most of the fancy, unrivaled in importance by any other. With most of the serious competitors spread out over a vast continent for the rest of the year, this is often the only time that they are all in the same spot at the same time. The air is fairly crackling with energy, and one would have to be very blasé not to be impressed by seeing so many superb show dogs in such close proximity.

WESTMINSTER'S ORIGINS

It all started in the 1870s, when a group of gentlemen gathered to talk about dogs at the Westminster Hotel in New York. They formed a club and apparently named it after their gathering place. (Although other explanations for the club's name have been offered, none is conclusive; the idea of naming a dog club after a public hotel was unusual but seems most plausible.) The club members established their own kennel outside the city and imported both kennel managers and dogs, primarily Setters and Pointers, from England. Soon enough it seemed a natural development to organize a dog show where both the members' dogs and those belonging to other fanciers could participate. The first location was Gilmore's Garden, which by the early 1880s had been rebuilt and renamed Madison Square Garden. The Garden has changed location several times since then: the current Madison Square Garden Center in midtown Manhattan has been the home of Westminster since 1969.

The American Kennel Club had not yet been born, but even in the early days the Westminster club had enough prestige to carry it off on its own. The first show, in 1877, attracted an amazing entry for the time: 1,177 dogs.

GETTING A DOG INTO WESTMINSTER

The show became popular quickly: even in the 1920s, the number of dogs entered was as high as it is today. By the 1930s, the total exceeded 3,000 dogs, and since no indoor arena in New York City large enough to comfortably house all these dogs could be found, some measure to limit the numbers had to be introduced. At first the only requirement was that each dog entered must have won a first prize at some other AKC show, but the qualifications have been tightened several times in a largely vain attempt to stem the tidal wave of entries from fanciers who want to show at Westminster. By 1967, all dogs entered had to have won at least one point toward their championship; by 1969, they had to have won major points. In 1992, the champions-only rule was introduced, and since even that did not suffice to keep the figure within an acceptable total, the Westminster Kennel Club has had to resort to the extreme measure of accepting only the first 2,500 acceptable entries opened. It does not matter if you send in your entry early: a first date of entries acceptance is always given, and the window of opportunity reportedly closes in a matter of minutes.

Limiting entries invariably results in some hopeful winners being excluded, and ambitious handlers can be seen tearing their hair out in frustration at having missed the year's premier dog show event. Some top-winning dogs can be sure of getting in, however: Westminster now sends a special invitation to the five dogs in each breed that have defeated the most competitors in their own breed during the year prior to entries closing.

First Annual N. Y.

Bench Show.

CATALOGUE

1877.

NEW YORK:
ROGERS & SHERWOOD, PRINTERS, 51 BARCLAY STREET.
1877.

The first Westminster Kennel Club catalog.

General view of Westminster at the old Madison Square Garden in 1887.

A view of the judging rings at the 1943 Westminster show. The old Madison Square Garden looks almost identical to the Madison Square Garden Center, where the show has been held since 1969.

The Wire Fox Terrier Flornell Spicy Piece of Halleston won Best in Show at Westminster in 1937, fresh off the boat from England. This could not happen today, as an AKC champion title is required for entry. The handler (right) was Percy Roberts; the judge was George S. West.

Exactly how many entries are sent in to Westminster each year, and how many dogs would be at the show if all restrictions were lifted, is uncertain. As it is, a very high percentage of the dogs participating are the top winners in their own regions, all vying for a spot in the national limelight. It is a sight to behold a couple of dozen of the top dogs in a breed, all perfectly trained and in gleaming condition, being put through their paces by a Westminster judge. Space is at a premium and experience, performance, and stage presence can play almost as big a part in the outcome as breed type and conformation.

THE GLITTERING FACE OF WESTMINSTER

The action takes place in a surprisingly small arena. The floor at Madison Square Garden barely holds six or seven rather small judging rings, with spectators squeezed in five or six deep in the aisles. A few lucky spectators may get a pass to stand in the entrance aisle by the wall, but this space is usually reserved for handlers and their assistants awaiting their turns. Some spectators prefer to sit in the stands and look down on the judging through binoculars. As compared with Crufts, you don't have to walk miles to see the different breeds; however, because of the comparatively small breed entries, the judging you most want to watch could be over in a matter of minutes.

The Westminster judging arena has now become a very glamorous spectacle. It was not always so, but the face presented to spectators and TV cameras today is lush with purple and gold, elaborate flower arrangements, velvet ring dividers, and an immaculate green carpet that shows off almost any breed to great advantage. (The carpet is one of the amenities Crufts and Westminster share. Obviously both shows realize that getting as close as possible to what could resemble a lawn is appealing to the eye.)

Once you leave the judging arena, however, the scene changes dramatically. The backstage area where the dogs are benched is so chaotic and crowded that it is difficult to believe you are at the same show. That handlers manage to prepare their shining masterpieces of grooming under such circumstances is amazing, and that the dogs take it all with such remarkable sangfroid is admirable. A top American show dog simply cannot be a wilting flower, and backstage at the Garden is no place for a shy puppy.

The press coverage at Westminster can be overwhelming. Joyce Shellenbarger presents the 1974 Best in Show winner, the German Shorthaired Pointer Ch. Gretchenhof Columbia River, to the photographers.

Breed entries at Westminster are seldom as big as at other major shows, but the competitors are all champions. Borzoi contestants line up in the ring at the 2005 show.

The daytime breed judging is for the cognoscenti, the serious insiders who come for a close look at top dogs in each breed. However, it is the evening spectacular that is the real Westminster for most people, including the millions watching at home on TV. The arena is opened up into one giant ring, the famous green carpet is immaculate and makes the dogs really stand out, the silver bowls and rosettes on the trophy table glisten under the lights. The judges are in evening dress, and the thousands of spectators behave as if they were at a Broadway show or perhaps at the Super Bowl, hooting and applauding for their favorites. Sometimes, on rare occasions, there is booing, when the usually knowledgeable and always wildly partisan New York ringsiders don't agree with a judge's choice. Showing in the big ring at Westminster can be a daunting experience for an inexperienced dog or handler, but the performances are almost always flawless as the judges work their way through the breed winners in one Group after another. Even Westminster is

Some of the trophies at Westminster Kennel Club's show.

not immune to the media, however. Since the introduction of live TV coverage, all judging stops for a few minutes' commercial break at regular intervals.

Toward midnight on the second day, the seven finalists sweep under spotlights into the vast arena, one by one, lining up along one side of the ring for the Best in Show judge's inspection. It is the ultimate honor

The Ibizan Hound Ch. Gryphons Stellar Eminence takes to the air during Hound Group judging at Westminster in 2005.

The Westminster dog show is a big event for New Yorkers, often requiring that the Sold Out sign be posted on the Madison Square Garden marquee.

New York loves Westminster: the Empire State Building is lit up in the club's purple and gold colors for the duration of the show.

to judge Best in Show at Westminster, and the person elected to make the final selection will have spent a couple of days secreted away from all the dog show events in a lonely hotel room. During the examination of each dog and its individual turn around the ring, the audience support for the favorites can be deafening, but as the judge, duty done, takes a last look at the finalists and walks back to the table to mark the book, an almost eerie silence falls over the arena. Carrying the magnificent Best in Show rosette and accompanied by two officials carrying silver trophies, the judge walks out toward the dogs again, stops— and announces the winner. For the handler and owner, this is the moment a lifetime dream comes true. It's the sort of experience that changes people's lives and makes its

The English Springer Spaniel Ch. Felicity's Diamond Jim on his way to winning Westminster in 2007, handled by Kellie Fitzgerald.

own particular demands on both people and dogs: the round of public appearances, press, and TV interviews following a Westminster win require a degree of media savvy that cannot reasonably be expected of dog show winners but that most seem to possess as a matter of course.

No matter what, a Westminster Best in Show ensures fame forever on a list of winners that goes back to 1907. For the other finalists, having *nearly* won Westminster is more than most people ever accomplish, and for the rest of the fancy there's always next year. The dream of winning Westminster is very distant and almost unattainable for most—but the possibility, however remote, is there, and the drama of the elimination process provides one of the most fascinating spectacles in this sport.

Terrier Group judging at Westminster in 2006. The ultimate winner, the Colored Bull Terrier Ch. Rocky Top's Sundance Kid, who also went on to Best in Show, is seen on the monitor being examined by the judge, Peggy Beisel McIlwaine.

Labrador Retrievers at Westminster in 1974. Judge Graham Head from Australia is looking over a lineup of dogs handled by (left to right) Richard Whitehill, Roy Holloway, Stan Flowers, and Marna Pearson.

INTERNATIONAL COMPETITION

One aspect that is largely missing from Westminster is international competition. The panel of judges may include some carefully vetted overseas name, but other than an occasional expert from Canada, the list is much less cosmopolitan than at most other shows of this stature. In 2006, James Reynolds from Ontario became the first foreign judge to award Best in Show at Westminster since W. L. McCandlish from Scotland did so in 1930. The participation of visiting dogs is almost as rare: the Westminster Kennel Club has no means of checking foreign champion titles and limits entry to AKC champions exclusively, so the only way overseas enthusiasts can show their dogs is to send them to the United States first. Once they have won a champion title under AKC rules, they can—perhaps—get an opportunity to compete at Westminster.

Best in Show at Westminster 1982, the Pekingese Ch. St. Aubrey Dragonora of Elsdon, with handler William Trainor and judge Mrs. Robert V. Lindsay.

Canadian dogs participate as a matter of course, and several have won Best in Show, but all of the imported dogs that have won Westminster over the years were owned and shown by American owners and handlers.

The 1978 Westminster winner was Ch. Cede Higgens, a Yorkshire Terrier handled by his owners' daughter, Marlene Switzer (right), under judge Anne Rogers Clark (left). Mrs. Clark won Westminster three times as a handler in the 1950s; in 2002, she was one of the breeders of the Best in Show–winning Miniature Poodle there.

A slight imperfection does not necessarily stop the dog from going to the top. The Siberian Husky Ch. Innisfree's Sierra Cinnar had lost the tip of one ear in an accident but nevertheless had a stellar show career, which included winning Best in Show at Westminster in 1980. He was handled by his owner's daughter, Trish Kanzler.

The only dog ever to win Best in Show at both Westminster and the FCI World Show is the Papillon Ch. Loteki Supernatural Being. Born in 1990, "Kirby" was already a veteran when he won the World Show in 1998 and Westminster in 1999. He was still winning specialty Best in Show as a fourteen-year-old!

The Newfoundland Ch. Darbydale's All Rise PouchCove on the way to his Best in Show win at Westminster in 2004, handled by Michelle Ostermiller, who took the top spot there again in 2005, becoming the only handler ever to win Westminster for two successive years with different dogs.

Several foreign-owned dogs from South America have won their Groups at Westminster, but they were usually bred in the United States, and their handlers were either Americans or at least trained in the United States.

There have been many suggestions for changes that would allow more dogs to participate at Westminster. Moving to a larger arena outside of the big city worked for Crufts, but hardly anyone believes that taking Westminster out of Manhattan would be a good idea. Holding the show over more days would not be anything new: Westminster was held over three or even four days for several decades up into the 1940s. Moving the preliminaries somewhere less central and more spacious, with just the finals held at Madison Square Garden, is another suggestion. Whatever happens, the Westminster tradition is likely to continue as strong in future decades as in the past.

THE AKC NATIONAL CHAMPIONSHIP

In recent years, the American Kennel Club has made a strong bid to challenge Westminster's position as the top dog show in the United States by organizing a high-profile event of its own. Westminster predates even the birth of the AKC, and although it soon acknowledged the national club's supremacy, the annual Westminster show has been the shining star in the AKC calendar

The Bloodhound Ch. Heathers Knock On Wood and his handler, Ken Griffith, after their victory at the AKC National Championship show in 2005.

for over a century. Technically, it's just one of about 1,500 all-breed shows approved by the AKC each year, but it obviously occupies a singular position in the hierarchy. The relationship between the two clubs has not always been free of friction. In 2001, Westminster Kennel Club show chairman Ronald H. Menaker left that post; he was later elected chairman of the American Kennel Club, which soon announced plans to hold its own annual show. This was not quite unprecedented: the AKC hosted a show at the U.S. sesquicentennial in 1926 and celebrated its own centennial with a show in 1984, at which 8,075 dogs were entered—by far the biggest dog show ever held in America. An early attempt to hold an AKC Invitational show was made in 1992 but had only a few hundred dogs competing.

The new show was different, however, and destined to become an annual event. The first AKC National Championship show was held on December 12, 2001, in Tampa, Florida, exactly two months before Westminster. The event itself, the timing,

THE FIRST AKC NATIONAL WINNERS

The AKC National Championship continues to be held on either a December or a January date in Florida or California. That the Best in Show wins have gone to already famous competitors has not hurt the show's reputation. The first winner, in 2001, was the Bichon Frisé Ch. Special Times Just Right, who came out of retirement after his Westminster BIS earlier that year especially for the AKC National show. The following years' winners were the Kerry Blue Terrier Ch. Torum's Scarf Michael, the Norfolk Terrier Ch. Cracknor Cause Celebre, the Bloodhound Ch. Heather's Knock On Wood, the Alaskan Malamute Ch. Nanuke's Snoklassic No Boundries, and the English Springer Spaniel Ch. Felicity's Diamond Jim—all among the country's top dogs and some also Best in Show winners at Westminster.

The AKC National Championship event features a special award for the best Bred-by-Exhibitor in Show. In 2003, this was won by the Norwich Terrier Ch. Huntwood's First Knight, handled by co-breeder and co-owner Susan Kipp under judge Maxine Beam.

and the TV coverage seemed calculated to capitalize on the public's pre-Westminster interest in dogs, but the AKC show offered a few twists that generated genuine enthusiasm among many fanciers. For one thing, through the sponsorship of a dog food company, Eukanuba, the AKC was able to offer more prize money to the winners at its show than anyone in dogs had seen in decades. In the distant past, both Westminster and the Morris & Essex shows paid generous money prizes—the $20,000 those clubs offered at their shows in the late 1930s and 1940 would be worth even more in today's dollars than the $250,000 that the AKC show now distributes to the winners. (The owner of the Best in Show winner receives $50,000 and the breeder gets $15,000, with lower sums awarded for other wins.) The focus on the breeders was further enhanced by a ceremony held before Best in Show judging at the show, honoring a selected few of the past year's top breeders. The AKC show also offers substantial money prizes for the best Bred-by-Exhibitor competitors, and there are Meet the Breeds booths, allowing the public to see the various breeds close up, following the example of Crufts and manned by volunteers from different breeds' parent clubs. There is even an international component, with overseas judges and a number of foreign dogs invited to participate.

With all it has going for it, the AKC National Championship, held annually in either Florida or California, could become the great national showcase for breeders that the sport in the United States so sorely needs. However, the AKC has chosen to limit entries to dogs that have won Best in Show, gained their champion title entirely from the Bred-by-Exhibitor class, or are among the top twenty-five (initially the top twenty) dogs in breed competition during the year prior to entries closing. These restrictions, by eliminating nonchampions, puppies, and young dogs, add up to a much smaller entry than would otherwise be possible. Even if all those qualified to enter did so, the total would hardly exceed 4,000. So far, the highest number of dogs entered at the AKC Invitational show was 2,472 in January 2006, with slightly fewer than 2,000 dogs actually participating.

Especially when held in California in December, the AKC Invitational show has created its own image distinct from Westminster. If the AKC decides to open up its show to the entire fancy, the show might in time become a worthy American equivalent of Crufts. The AKC's published claim that this event is "The Planet's Greatest Dog Show," "unequaled in prestige and scope" with "the world's greatest dogs" on view, and so on, may be in keeping with such past centuries' larger-than-life promoters as Charles Cruft and P. T. Barnum, but it is as yet not strictly true.

MORRIS & ESSEX

Unlike Great Britain, America has a vast number of fairly small shows, with just a few that stand out from the crowd. None comes even close in size to the big shows in Great Britain and the rest of Europe; and only Westminster can rival them in prestige and reputation.

This was not always the case. At one time, several decades ago, another American dog show was bigger than Westminster, comparable to Crufts, and as famous as either. The Morris & Essex Kennel Club was

Morris & Essex Kennel Club held what many still feel was the greatest dog show ever in the United States. In the late 1930s, it was the biggest dog show in the world, attracting more than 4,000 dogs for several years. This shot shows most of the rings at the 1935 show.

virtually the private enterprise of the very wealthy Mrs. Geraldine R. Dodge and set a standard for dog shows that is unlikely ever to be matched. At its peak in the late 1930s and 1940s, Morris & Essex had well over 4,000 dogs entered for several years in a row, making it the biggest dog show in the world at that time.

Starting in 1927 and for the next three decades, Mrs. Dodge invited the dog world to an annual party at her magnificent estate, Giralda Farms, in Madison, New Jersey. Mrs. Dodge was the daughter of oil tycoon William Rockefeller; her husband, Marcellus H. Dodge, was president of the Remington Arms Company—together the Dodges were one of the wealthiest couples in Amer-

ica. The show grounds occupied only a small part of the vast estate, with the judging arena located near the manor house and the stately Giralda Kennels, which at its peak housed more than 100 of Mrs. Dodge's own dogs. On seemingly endless, perfectly manicured lawns, a staff of some 800 helpers erected long rows of tents and set up more than sixty large rings, of which the biggest remained unused for most of the day and was employed exclusively for Group and Best in Show judging.

There was parking for thousands of cars at a time when the automobile was still not every family's possession. Even more visitors came by train: it helped that one of the Dodges' main business interests was in the

Fox Terrier judging at Morris & Essex in the 1930s.

One of the great traditions at Morris & Essex was the lunch break. Notice the cars in the background; there was also a special train for spectators from New York.

THE FLAVOR OF MORRIS & ESSEX

Here is how Don Reynolds, author of *Champion of Champions*, saw Morris & Essex in his time:

"The sun kept its early promise of a beautiful day and by noon America's largest dog show had taken on the air of a huge and happy carnival on this last day of May in 1941. Refreshment stands were thronged and many picnic parties helped carry out the merrily informal spirit of the day. The sixty-five rope-enclosed rings in which the dogs were being judged stretched over an eighty-acre polo field whose emerald-green grass looked as though it had been carefully cropped by hand. In each ring was a judge's table, painted a dazzling red and surmounted by a large, orange-colored umbrella. Along the tops of the orange tents, which lined the two long sides of the rectangular field, hundreds of small American flags flapped lazily in the breeze. And flying here, there and everywhere were the bright orange and purple pennants of the Morris and Essex Kennel Club, vainly attempting to vie with the spring hues of the dresses, shirts and coats worn by the spectators who crowded the wide aisles between the rings. And all around were the dogs, each one a thing of beauty in itself.

"Exactly 3,840 dogs, representing ninety-one breeds, were here. They had started to arrive shortly after sunrise. All morning long, a steady, bumper-to-bumper procession of trucks, trailers, station wagons and passenger cars had wound through the narrow roads that criss-crossed this vast and lovely estate near the town of Madison, New Jersey. Now, with the sun high overhead, fully 16,000 vehicles were parked in the spacious meadows surrounding the judging area. All of the 2,400 exhibitors were on hand. Most of the spectators had arrived, but at one time or another during the day more than 35,000 persons would be attracted to this biggest and gayest of all dog shows."

Lackawanna Railroad, which offered visitors from the Metropolitan New York area quick and convenient access to the show. At lunchtime, all judging stopped, and not only judges and officials but also all exhibitors picnicked from box lunches, sometimes served by butlers on proper china with silverware and linen napkins, all courtesy of Mrs. Dodge. To win at Morris & Essex was an honor few would experience, but the visit was usually a memorable event regardless of what type of ribbon (if any) your dog carried home.

Technically, Morris & Essex was not an all-breed show, in spite of the large number of dogs competing. Mrs. Dodge herself determined which breeds classes would be offered for, and she definitely favored those whose fanciers might appreciate and support the exclusive, often foreign, specialist judges she invited. The result was big entries in the selected breeds, while the rest could only compete in the AKC Miscellaneous class. At its peak in 1939, Morris & Essex attracted a world record entry of 4,456 dogs of eighty-three breeds. Only one or two all-breed shows in the United States today have similar figures, in spite of the fact that nearly twice as many breeds are featured. The average breed entry at Morris & Essex then was more than fifty dogs, twice what a modern show of this size could hope for.

JUDGES FROM AROUND THE WORLD

All dogs were benched under the tents, and judging started at the civilized hour of ten o'clock, one hour earlier only for those breeds that had more than 200 entries. Captain Max von Stephanitz, the father of the German Shepherd Dog, had so many of his breed (271) entered the year Mrs. Dodge brought him over from Germany that he had to judge for two days. The inimitable H. S. Lloyd, from the famous of Ware kennels in England, judged a huge number of Cocker Spaniels. (There were more than 200 Cockers entered at Morris & Essex in 1936, the last year before the American and English types were divided—largely because of the influence of Mrs. Dodge, herself an active and successful English Cocker fancier. In the next few years, the total

rose to more than 300, with the vast majority being American.) Norwegian specialist John Aarflot attracted an entry of almost fifty Norwegian Elkhounds in 1955, more than one would have thought existed in America at the time. A young Australian, David Roche, judged a good-size entry of Kerry Blue Terriers at Morris & Essex before becoming even more famous as a Crufts Best in Show judge. Mrs. Dodge was very well aware of the advantages of using the right judge for the right breed, and she would bring them to her show from wherever in the world they were to be found. This factor, even more than the perfect lawns and the elegant lunch, was what set her show apart from the rest.

AN END AND A NEW BEGINNING

In 1954, the show was canceled after a dispute with the American Kennel Club over available dates, and the last three shows had to be held on a Thursday, preceding three other shows the same weekend. After the 1957 event, plans for the following year's show were suspended because of "conditions over which the members had no control," as the official news release put it. There was still a chance that a 1959 show might be held, but Mrs. Dodge decided that if she could not

The 1935 Best in Show winner at Morris & Essex, the Irish Setter Ch. Milson O'Boy, handled by Harry Hartnett. Club president Geraldine Hartley Dodge presents the trophy.

After the 1957 Morris & Essex show, the club and the show were inactive until 2000, when both were resurrected with a successful show held on the old Giralda Farm grounds, shown above.

maintain the standard for which Morris & Essex had been known, she did not wish to hold the show at all.

In her later years, Mrs. Dodge devoted most of her time and energy not to her own dogs but to the St. Hubert-Giralda shelter she had started in 1939. At her death in 1973, she left $85 million to the Geraldine R. Dodge Foundation, still located in Morristown, New Jersey. In 2005, the foundation awarded $4.7 million in grants to various environmental organizations.

The end of what was generally acknowledged as the best dog show ever in America was strongly felt throughout the fancy. Nothing like it was seen for a long time, but in 1997, as Morris & Essex was beginning to enter the area of myth, and the stories about the show had taken on a distinctly nostalgic glow, a second chapter of the show's history began. A team of enthusiasts, some of whom had firsthand memories

The Bedlington Terrier Ch. Rock Ridge Night Rocket, one of the few dogs ever to win both Morris & Essex (in 1947) and Westminster (in 1948). He was handled by Anthony Neary for the Rockefellers. The judge is probably Joseph Quirk, who awarded Rocket Best in Show at Morris & Essex when the dog was only fourteen months old.

of the original show, led by Wayne E. Ferguson, decided to resurrect the club in a spirit of sportsmanship and regard for history that Mrs. Dodge would have found gratifying. In its new incarnation, the Morris & Essex Kennel Club show was first held at the old Giralda Farms on Thursday, October 5, 2000, with an entry of 2,992 dogs. The success of this venture was such that, although an annual event could not be contemplated and a midweek date had to be accepted because of the crowded calendar, it was determined to hold the show every five years. The 2005 show attracted an entry well in excess of 3,000 dogs.

SANTA BARBARA

Other shows tried to fill the void left by Morris & Essex, usually with only moderate success. The best one, the Santa Barbara show, still remembered fondly by those who were present during its peak years of the late 1970s and 1980s, was held on the opposite side of the continent. California's Santa Barbara Kennel Club had existed since the early part of the twentieth century, its first records dating from 1919. The show had the natural advantage of being located in one of

In the 1970s, the Santa Barbara Kennel Club emerged as not just the top California show but also one of the biggest and best anywhere. The showground on the University of California campus had to be vacated when the university expanded in the late 1980s.

The Santa Barbara Kennel Club trophy table has long been one of the most impressive anywhere.

One of America's most popular judging couples for many years, Tom and Ann Stevenson, at home in Santa Barbara with friends.

the world's most beautiful resort towns, just a couple of hours' drive north from Los Angeles. The Hollywood connection also heightened the show's cachet: Santa Barbara has always had close ties to the entertainment industry, and spotting the occasional movie star or pop singer on the grounds was not unusual.

By the 1960s, the Santa Barbara show had already become one of the biggest in the country under the guidance of German Shepherd Dog enthusiast Sidney Heckert. It became a world-class international event when Tom and Ann Stevenson took over the reins in the 1970s. Former professional

Best in Show at Santa Barbara in 1985, the Pekingese Ch. St. Aubrey Bees Wing of Elsdon, handled by Luc Boileau. Judge Hans Lehtinen from Finland is on the far left; next to him with trophies are club officer Bo Bengtson, actress Bo Derek, and officers Barbara Stephenson and Tom Bradley.

handlers and Poodle breeders, the Stevensons had retired to Santa Barbara, and each year for the next couple of decades they spent virtually the entire year polishing the plans for their next show. It was as beautiful as Morris & Essex had been, with the added bonus of the dramatic backdrop of the Santa Ynez Mountains on one side and a fresh breeze from the Pacific on the other. The lawns were perfect, the tents were striped in bright yellow and white, the trophy tables groaned under antique silver and bronzes,

and the catalog was a work of art. The air was one of an elegant summer garden party, but as with Morris & Essex, what made the entry figures shoot up over 4,000 dogs was Santa Barbara Kennel Club's attention to its judging panel.

Just like Mrs. Dodge, the Stevensons realized what seems so obvious but few other clubs pay much attention to: if each breed is provided with a truly knowledgeable judge, exhibitors will come. Santa Barbara soon became known for introducing interesting new judges, many from overseas. The Stevensons were international judges themselves, and during their travels around the world, they kept their eyes open for new talent that could be successfully utilized at their show. It did not always work: bringing over foreign expertise can be risky, and there were some upsets from the established form. However, even the Santa Barbara failures did more to generate serious discussion about matters such as breed type and judges' priorities than most other shows' more predictable judging panels.

One asset the Santa Barbara Kennel Club did not have was its own show grounds. Hosting a major event in a tourist destination meant that the dog show on occasion had to be moved from one location to another. The most memorable shows were held at Hope Ranch, on the Polo Field, and on the University of California campus, but when the university needed to build, the dog show had to move. This coincided with the Stevensons' retirement from active involvement, and although the show remains a fixture in the California show calendar and retains many touches of its former glory—including one of the most impressive trophy tables anywhere—it is now less than half its peak size.

OTHER NOTEWORTHY EVENTS

Many other beautiful, well-organized, and ambitious shows are held all around the United States each year, but none has caught the fancy's attention to such a degree that it has become a national showcase for all the best that American breeders produce.

Some of the most beautiful dog shows in the United States were among the smallest. Del Monte Kennel Club in California, held for many years on the famous golf course by the Pacific in Monterey, was limited to 500 dogs.

That function has mostly been taken over by the various breed club specialty shows. A couple of dozen all-breed shows regularly draw up to 2,500–3,500 dogs; almost all are one-day unbenched events; and many are held as part of clusters of shows, with other clubs hosting all-breed or specialty events in the same building on the days before or after. This can sometimes make the weekend seem like one very long show, except with a new opportunity for each dog to compete every day. When one long weekend is followed by another one nearby, you are talking about circuits—typically American institutions that have been around since at least the 1930s but gain extra urgency during any oil crisis. Without cars, vans,

and motor homes, there would almost literally be no dog shows in America!

Usually the top spot in the annual show rankings, released by the American Kennel Club and based on number of dogs in competition, are the Kentucky spring shows hosted by the Louisville and Evansville Kennel Clubs. Out west in California, there is the beautiful New Year's show in Palm Springs, and farther north the Del Valle breeders' showcase in the fall, so called for the large number of specialty shows held on the same grounds that weekend. In the Midwest is the International Kennel Club of Chicago, and in the East are classic shows such as Bucks County and Harrisburg in Pennsylvania and Trenton in New Jersey.

The Del Valle Dog Club of Livermore has become one of California's premier showcases for breeders. The 1997 Best in Show winner was the Bichon Frisé Ch. Sterling Rumor Has It, that year's top Non-Sporting dog and one of the top winners of all breeds. He was handled by Paul Flores under judge Bettie Krause. At right is club officer Betty-Anne Stenmark.

PROFESSIONAL DOG SHOW MANAGEMENT

The large number of shows held in the United States created an opportunity for professional dog show organizers—firms that are hired by the kennel clubs to do everything from setting up the judging rings to providing the ribbons and printing the premium list and catalog.

The oldest existing dog show superintendent—still going strong—is Jack Bradshaw Dog Shows. The first of four generations of the same family in the business, Jack Bradshaw, Sr., came from England to California in the late 1800s. He exhibited, stewarded, and judged, reportedly superintending his first show in Los Angeles in 1898. More than 100 years later, the family still runs the company and superintends most of the top shows on the West Coast with superb efficiency.

America's biggest dog show superintendent, however, is MB-F, Inc., which is made up of three older organizations. George Foley started superintending dog shows in 1900; he was one of the first group of individuals to be licensed as a dog show superintendent by the AKC and was responsible for adapting many of the rules governing dog shows today. His company superintended many of the top shows in the East, including Morris & Essex Kennel Club as well as Westminster from the late 1930s to the early 1970s. After Mr. Foley's death, the Foley company merged with those of two other superintendents, one founded by A. Wilson Bow in the Midwest and the other by Edgar Moss in the South in the 1930s. Under the guidance of past professional handler Tom Crowe in the 1970s, MB-F grew to become a giant of the dog show industry, now superintending almost 800 shows per year, processing about 740,000 entries (almost half the total of all AKC entries), and distributing more than 3 million dog show premium lists.

Many of the approximately dozen dog show superintendents that the AKC licenses on an annual basis are small operations, and some clubs—especially smaller, single-breed clubs—choose to organize their own shows.

There are major all-breed shows in practically every urban area, most with at least a thousand dogs entered. The smallest AKC all-breed shows attract only a couple of hundred dogs in the more isolated parts of the mainland and in Alaska, Hawaii, and Puerto Rico.

In the 1960s and 1970s, *Kennel Review* magazine selected one show as the Best of the Year—the accolades usually went to Westminster or Santa Barbara. In the 2000s, the monthly *Dogs in Review* has done something similar with a Best Show category in its annual Show Dogs of the Year awards, which are announced during a ceremony in New York immediately prior to Westminster. The first three years' nominated shows included the Atlanta Kennel Club, the Bucks County Kennel Club, the Detroit Kennel Club, the Dog Fanciers Association of Oregon, the Middleburg Kennel Club, the Wichita Kennel Club in Kansas, and the Lima Kennel Club in Ohio; the wins went to the aforementioned Kennel Club of Palm Springs, the Del Valle Dog Club of Livermore, and the International Kennel Club of Chicago.

The Smooth Fox Terrier Ch. Mirolinda Superstar was the Sydney Royal show Best in Show winner in 1986. He is shown with judges Rainer Vuorinen (left) from Finland and Carl-Johan Adlercreutz (center) from Sweden.

THE ROYAL SHOWS OF AUSTRALIA

Beyond the top shows in England and America, a few other events in the English-speaking world must be mentioned. New Zealand has its annual National show, and South Africa has the Goldfields event, but it is the so-called Royal shows in Australia that attract the most dogs and the greatest interest from overseas visitors in the Southern Hemisphere.

These shows are unique in many ways, not only for their close links to the Royal Agricultural Society in each state but also for the fact that they often go on for a week or more, usually employing just three or four judges who work through at least a couple of hundred dogs per day for about a week. This means that all-rounders are the order of the day: employing a breed specialist, however knowledgeable in his or her particular area, would just not be practical at these shows. The judges are nearly always foreign; Australia is one of the few countries to almost invariably reserve its plum judging assignments for overseas visitors. In the past, judges usually came from the United Kingdom and, in recent years, from America or Canada as well, but an ever-increasing presence of South American, European, and Asian judges has been facilitated by the fact that many of these have at least formal FCI approval to judge all breeds—something that is much rarer for judges from Great Britain and the United States.

The "Royals" represent a link to the huge exhibitions of livestock and farm products for which Australia is famous, organized by the Royal Agricultural Society in each state. The annual Royal shows, held on the fairgrounds outside the biggest cities, can attract huge entries: up to 5,000 or 6,000 dogs in Melbourne, somewhat fewer in Sydney, which limits its entry. Each state and territory has at least one Royal show (some have several, in diminishing degrees of size and prestige); Adelaide and Brisbane hold important Royal shows as well, and Perth in the far west has a smaller equivalent, a couple of thousand miles away from the others.

The Royal shows have a simpler classification than most other Australian shows, with only Puppy, Junior, Intermediate, and Open classes offered. A Best of Breed and a Best Puppy are selected in each breed; the Best of Breed winners are placed First through Fourth in the Group, and there is a separate Best Puppy in Group competition, with only a First placement. Similarly, in the Best in Show competition, the top four Group winners are placed in order of merit, with the winner as Best in Show, whereas the Puppy Group winners compete for just the one placement of Best Puppy in Show.

THE FCI WORLD SHOW

The FCI World Dog Show provides one of the most colorful and interesting experiences in the dog world. Held annually in a different country and usually in early summer, the World Shows differ considerably from one year to the next, taking on the character of the host country. The arrangements range from utterly chaotic to superbly smooth; the entries vary from barely in the four figures to more than ten times that number. Invariably, however, the World Shows always provide a meeting ground for widely disparate views of how

When held in Europe, the FCI World Show often attracts huge entries. At the 2003 event in Dortmund, Germany, more than 18,000 dogs were entered. Best in Show was the U.S. born Australian Shepherd Ch. Propwash Syzygy, handled by American-born but Italian-based Richard Hellman.

The Komondor Ch. Jaszkoseri Kocos Csupor started out as a farm dog in Hungary but went all the way to Reserve Best in Show at the 2001 FCI World Show in Oporto, Portugal. Judge Tamas Jakkel from Hungary is second from left.

show dogs—and dog show people—should look and deport themselves, and a large number of breeds that are never seen at the big shows in the United States or Great Britain are always on display.

According to the records of the FCI, the first World Show was held in Paris in 1974. Other sources indicate that something approximating today's World Shows was held in conjunction with the FCI World Congresses as early as in the 1930s, although the international participation then was fairly limited. As traveling from one country to another, even from one continent to another, has become easier, the World Show has proved to be one of the great windows to the world of purebred dogs. The World Winner titles that are conferred on the best dog and best bitch in each breed, and the Junior World Winner titles to the best young dog and bitch, have

The Bracco Italiano has emerged as one of the leading show breeds in Europe, with two World Show Best in Show winners in the early 2000s. Ch. Axel del Monte Alago won the 2006 World Show in Poland, the biggest ever of its kind with some 21,000 dogs entered. Axel is handled by his owner, Bitte Ahrens, of the famous Sobers Kennel.

proved strong magnets for dog people from many countries. When held in Europe, the World Show can now attract

In many countries, the Europe Winner Show is second in importance only to the World Show. At the 2004 Europe Winner Show in Barcelona, Spain, Best in Show was the Newfoundland Ch. Three-pond Council Cup Bogart. Runner-up was the Yorkshire Terrier Ch. Quoccles Oliverlightsome, and third was the Afghan Hound Ch. Xenos Joselito.

more than 15,000 dogs from all over the world. The biggest so far were those in Helsinki in 1998; Dortmund in 2003; and Poznan, Poland, in 2006; the last mentioned show attracted some 21,000 entries, making it one of the biggest dog shows ever held anywhere. South and Central America have hosted four World Shows in the past decade, all much smaller than those in Europe. No World Show has been held in Asia since Tokyo hosted it in 1982.

SHOWS IN EUROPE AND ASIA

The annual French Championship exhibition was held at Longchamps outside Paris throughout the 1990s; it has since moved to different locations. It attracts strong competition (often 6,000–7,000 entries) partly

The 2003 Europe Winner Show, held in Bratislava in Slovakia, attracted 10,000 dogs from all across Europe and beyond and was won by an American Staffordshire Terrier from Croatia, Ch. Milwaukee de Ngorong-Ngorong. The judge (left, with flowers) was Renée Sporre-Willes from Sweden.

The German Shepherd Dog Ch. Triumphs Blaze was Best in Show at the Stockholm show in both 1986 and 1987, as well as Top Dog of all breeds in 1987. He is shown with his breeder, Bo Nyman, and judge Ulla Segerström.

because of its unique status in the rules for the French champion title: however much a dog wins elsewhere, it must have won at both the all-breed French Championship show and at the breed national specialty to become a French champion.

The Amsterdam Winner show in December invariably attracts big entries, as do the two most important German all-breed shows—the VDH Bundessieger and the VDH Europasieger shows, both held in Dortmund, the former in October with about 6,000 dogs, the latter in May with almost as many. The competition at these shows is fierce and very international, and because the breed clubs in Germany are much stronger than those in most other

One of the most important annual dog events in Latin America, the Exposición de la Américas y el Caribe, was held in Bogotá, Colombia, in 2006. Judge Rafael de Santiago awarded Best in Show to the Dogo Argentino Ch. Bombon de Don Ata, from Argentina.

countries, they invariably have much to say in the choice of judges. Obviously, at these shows at least, breed specialists are the order of the day. However, as one German exhibitor put it: "The emphasis at our shows here in Germany seems to be more on health and soundness than on glitz and glamour."

The Scandinavian countries are, on a per capita basis, probably more active in dogs than any others on earth. In spite of small populations, these countries regularly mount world-class shows that are among the biggest and best organized anywhere, particularly the spectacular year-end shows in Stockholm and Helsinki. Those events

sometimes attract as many as 7,000–8,000 dogs each, and the Stockholm extravaganza in particular has a solid reputation for glitz and glamour—sometimes to the extent that it has been called Hollywood Goes to Sweden. The Scandinavian shows are also among the most international dog events anywhere; the judges' panels feature a large number of names from all over the world. Usually these are two-day affairs, with about half the dogs judged the first day, and the other half on the second; but in late 2005, Helsinki topped all previous records by holding two back-to-back one-day shows with about 7,500 dogs at each. More than

The Boxer Ch. Jacquet's Urko was one of the first big American-bred winners in Japan, winning numerous Bests in Show there between 1982 and 1986. He was owned and shown in Japan by Dr. Hideaki Nakazawa but later returned to spend his retirement with his breeder, Richard Tomita, in the United States.

40,000 spectators watched the Wire Fox Terrier Ch. Ashgrove Highwaystar win Best in Show both days, defeating more than 15,000 entries. In one of those international exchange programs that have become increasingly popular in the new century, Highwaystar was born in Italy, lived in Sweden, and was scheduled to go to the United States to be shown later.

Russia, which has been a member of the FCI since 1995, is fast becoming cosmopolitan at least as far as dogs are concerned: foreign judges are extremely popular, and many European all-rounders are in great demand. Among the more than 1,000 shows held annually, the so-called Eurasia Show in Moscow in late February stands out as the biggest, with more than 4,000 dogs entered; followed in importance by the Russia show, also in Moscow but held in September; and by the White Nights event in St. Petersburg in June.

The top show in Asia is easily the annual FCI Asian Dog Show, held in Tokyo each spring during cherry blossom time since 1984, with only a couple of excursions to other cities. It usually has an international panel of judges, a strong American presence among the winners, and a total entry of about 3,000 dogs.

LATIN AMERICA

The FCI Section show in Latin America, the Las Américas y el Caribe show, rotates from one country to another each year and vies for the honor as the top dog event in Latin America with the so-called SICALAM show (Sociedad de Intercambio de la Canofilia de Latinoamericana). The southern part of the American continent has almost as many dog shows as the northern, with Brazil alone

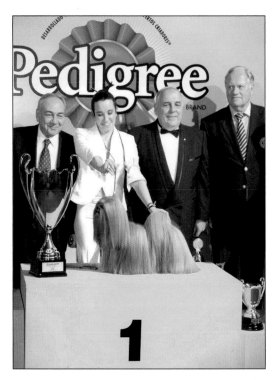

Although usually held in Europe, the FCI World Show has been held in Latin America several times. In 2005, it was hosted by Buenos Aires, Argentina, and won by the Lhasa Apso Ch. Homero del Alcazar. The judge was Miguel Angel Martinez; far right is the FCI President, Hans Müller, from Austria.

hosting about 800 dog shows per year. The entry figures are generally lower than those in the United States, but the dogs are often spectacularly good, as proved by the many that have traveled north to be campaigned to AKC titles.

In the late 1900s and early 2000s, Latin America hosted the FCI World Show with great frequency. The first World Show on the American continent was held in Acapulco in Mexico in 1984 and attracted only limited interest, but the next ones in Mexico City in 1999 and 2007 made big international news. The 1988 World Show in Lima, Peru, did not quite succeed in catching the world's attention either and had less than a thousand entries, but later World Shows in Argentina, Brazil, and Puerto Rico have all proved that this event belongs in Latin America as much as in Europe. The entries may not be quite as large, but the mixture of European tradition and Latin American culture, with a dash of U.S. professionalism, has created an event with unique flair and style.

The 2005 World Show in Buenos Aires was particularly well organized, and the host club could not be blamed for an incident that affected the entire show. Following a scuffle early in the week between a disappointed Dogo Argentino exhibitor and a judge, security guards had to be called to escort the judge from the show. The follow-ing day, after a similar incident in the same breed, an unknown person detonated two tear-gas bombs, one near the ring, one in a grooming area. Panic ensued, with thou-sands of people and dogs trying to get out of the building, smashing windows and breaking doors on the way. Nobody was killed, but fifteen people were taken to the hospital, and all judging had to be sus-pended for a few hours while fresh air was pumped into the judging pavilions. The show committee suspended all Dogos Argentinos from the show and all further judging. Best in Show was awarded at nearly 2:00 a.m. by senior Argentinean judge Miguel Angel Martinez to the native-born but American-sired Lhasa Apso Ch. Homero del Alcazar.

The Smooth Fox Terrier Ch. Torquay S Demetrio, a top winner in his native Brazil and the United States, where he won twenty Bests in Show in 2006 and remained a top winner in 2007.

CHAPTER 4

SPECIALTY SHOWS

U p to date the honors [for furthering the interests of a breed] are certainly due Mrs. G. R. Dodge for her wonderful hospitality bestowed on the remarkable gathering of shepherd dog fanciers at her beautiful Giralda Farms, Madison, N.J., when over 500 fanciers enjoyed the very interesting demonstration and lecture. Amid the most beautiful surroundings, with Dame Nature at her best, and the most lavish hospitality, the finest collection of famous champions ever brought together were put through a very educational test for soundness, of which moving pictures were made, and then paraded and posed before the crowd when the various points were thoroughly demonstrated by Messrs. Anton Rost and R. Cleveland. To assist one to follow the lecture, copies of the standard were issued which made it most instructive, and these were retained as pleasant souvenirs of a truly remarkable outing, for which sincere thanks were tendered Mrs. Dodge, who has certainly proved herself to be a 'guardian Angel' for the very sagacious shepherd dog."

—From *Dogdom* magazine, August 1924

Best of Breed at the English Cocker Spaniel Club of America in 1997, Ch. Stardust Cimarron. The judge (left) was James Reynolds from Canada; the trophy presenter was David Flanagan.

Some national specialties feature a Top 20 competition for the previous year's top winners, with a panel of judges officiating. In 1995, the Afghan Hound Club of America hosted a World Congress in California, and Top 20 was an international event, judged by Frank Sabella from the United States, Pauline Hewitt of Australia, Bo Bengtson (originally from Sweden), and Andrew Brace from Great Britain. The winner, Ch. Applause Majic Show, is flanked by owner-handler Cindy Chandler and Irish co-owner James Dalton.

The epigraph sums up the basic philosophy behind specialty shows. A number of fanciers—preferably a large number—gather in one place with an even larger collection of dogs of a single breed with the object of immersing themselves in breed lore, learning what that breed is about, and studying the finer points of breed type, all the while aided by experts with a deep background in that particular breed. All that was missing from the Giralda experiment was the competitive factor.

Specialty shows are in many ways closer to the original idea of what dog shows were meant to be than are most of the more popular all-breed shows today. All the first exhibitions of dogs in the mid-1800s were limited to either a single breed or to a few related breeds: Setters and Pointers, Toy Spaniels, Terriers, and Bulldogs, for example. Many of the annual single-breed specialty shows still held today were started in the first part of the twentieth century.

The all-breed shows came later but caught on with the public to such a degree that the specialty events were soon outnumbered. Then in the latter part of the twentieth century, after being overshadowed for many years, specialty events started to come into their own again, especially in the United States. By 1970, there were actually *more* specialties than all-breed shows in America, and this has remained so: in 2005, more than 2,000 specialty shows were held, as opposed to fewer than 1,500 all-breed shows. The average specialty entry in the United States is now about seventy-five dogs of a single breed, easily ten times higher than the average breed entry at most average all-breed shows.

Prior to full recognition by the AKC, breed clubs must prove themselves by holding specialty matches—often prestigious without having official status. The Bichon Frisé was officially recognized in April 1973, the day after a historical match show, judged by Tom Stevenson, where Mike Dougherty showed one of the breed's early greats, Cali-Col's Scaliwag (later a champion), to Best in Match. The trophy presenter is actress Betty White, a great Bichon fancier. Dougherty later became a multigroup judge; Scaliwag became one of the breed's first champions and Best in Show winners.

Specialty shows can be family affairs: Lydia Coleman Hutchinson is handling Flair's Flirt of Wolfpit (center); her father shows Easter Bonnet of Wolfpit (right); while her mother handles the sire, Ch. Cairnwood Quince, winner of the Stud Dog class at the Cairn Terrier Club of America specialty in Chicago in 1972. The judge was Ann Stevenson.

THE PURPOSE OF SPECIALTY SHOWS

The single-breed specialty shows have, in fact, become one of the greatest glories of the American dog show world. There is an obvious reason for this. Most American dog fanciers are so widely scattered across a vast continent that the national specialty show may provide their only opportunity to meet a large number of like-minded fanciers and see an even larger number of their favorite breed. The big specialties provide an unparalleled opportunity for breeders to look for a potential stud dog, and they offer an invaluable gauge for how the homebred

The Vizsla Club of America's national specialty in 1999 was judged by Anne Rogers Clark and won by Ch. Sandyacre's Russet Majesty, JH. "Maggie" was handled by Bobby Schoenfeld.

The Scottish Deerhound Ch. Jaraluv's Sindar Star Image, shown by Ray Brinlee, is having fun during the photo session after a win during the Sighthound weekend in California in 1999. The judge is Carol Reisman.

dogs stack up against the best from other areas. Westminster, after all, attracts only a dozen or two top campaigners in most breeds; the biggest specialties may have several hundred participants of that same breed. The competition at a national specialty show can be such that even placing in a class with perhaps forty or fifty entries carries more prestige than winning at most other shows. Sometimes the breed fanciers take over an entire hotel for several days, and the regular conformation judging, at the core of the event and held in the hotel's ballroom, may be accompanied by social

and educational side events of many kinds: seminars, health clinics, informal competitions, and field activities, which provide an all-around education within almost every aspect of that particular breed.

THE EVOLUTION OF SPECIALTY CLUBS

The oldest surviving breed clubs in the United States date back well over 100 years; some of them attract a strong following still. The American Spaniel Club was founded in 1881, three years before the American Kennel Club. The American Fox Terrier Club was established in 1885 and held its first show the following year. Both clubs still host annual shows: the American Spaniel Club celebrated its 125th anniversary in January 2006, with a show that had more than 700 dogs participating in the official classes. Most clubs for today's established breeds were founded in the 1930s and 1940s, but new national clubs are formed on a regular basis as additional breeds are approved and gain in popularity to such a degree that an annual national gathering is warranted.

The biggest and best of the American specialty shows are well-organized week-long affairs that dwarf anything else of their kind in the world. They cater to just a single breed, with the rare exception of the American Spaniel Club, which has classes for all the flushing spaniel breeds, and a couple of others. The American Fox Terrier Club is open to both Smooths and Wires, which are now separate breeds but were once classified as varieties of the same breed; the Norwich & Norfolk Terrier Club was founded when the Norfolk was still considered a "drop-eared Norwich" before following the British lead and achieving separate breed status.

THE PRESTIGE FACTOR

The National Specialty Best in Show award is almost invariably the highest possible accolade for a dog at the breed level, and the

The Boxer bitch Ch. Bayview Some Like It Hot, one of the top winners of all breeds in 2006, is shown winning the American Boxer Club's Top 20 competition that year, handled by Michael Shepherd. The judges were James Reynolds, Kimberly Pastella Calvacca, and Ida Baum. The presenter (right) is ABC President John Connolly. "Monroe" won more Bests in Show than any other Boxer bitch ever.

The Chinese Shar-Pei Club of America's national specialty was won by Ch. Royals Simon Says in 1997. The judge was J. D. Russell.

sight of perhaps 100 champions of one breed literally overflowing the ring, as sometimes happens at the biggest specialties, is something enthusiasts willingly travel long distances to witness. Many big national specialty shows attract scores of overseas visitors, and on occasion they have served as hosts for a World Congress, at which breed concerns can be discussed with international participants in a congenial setting.

The American Kennel Club recognizes only one national club for each breed, and that parent club can apply for permission

to hold its own show or shows. Some parent clubs hold one show per year, others several—in which case one of the shows is usually designated as the national, the rest as parent club regional specialties. The national clubs for Chinese Shar-Pei, Bulldogs, and Gordon Setters lead the way, each with a dozen or more parent club specialties per year. A few clubs have both a summer national and a winter national, perhaps even a roving national in addition to one that may stay in the same location from year to year. The AKC, somewhat surprisingly, does not regulate the use of the term *national specialty* and does not indicate that specialty shows are nationals in its official *AKC Awards* publication. In some cases, it can even be unclear which of the parent club shows really is the national specialty.

As a breed becomes more popular, new clubs are formed to cater to local fanciers—with or without the explicit blessing of the national club. These clubs may eventually reach official status and hold their own specialty shows. Some breeds are intensely specialty driven, meaning that the fanciers focus on specialty shows to the almost complete exclusion of all-breed competition. The most obvious example is German Shepherd Dogs, which in addition to having one single parent club show every year offers fanciers the opportunity to participate at more than 100 other regional specialty shows around the country.

SPECIALTY SHOWS AND BREED POPULARITY

The top fifty specialty shows held under AKC rules since 1985 have all had at least 600 dogs present and competing in the official breed classes (see "Largest AKC Breed Club Specialty Shows"). The entry figures released by many breed clubs are always considerably higher than those recorded by the AKC. Neither total is necessarily incorrect: breed clubs routinely include sweepstakes entries, futurities, obedience trials, and other performance events in their totals, while the AKC records only the number of dogs actually competing in the official classes. Unsurprisingly, the most popular breeds often had the largest entries: Golden and Labrador Retrievers are almost always at the top of the

list. It is interesting to consider the number of show entries in relation to registration figures. In the early 2000s, Labrador Retrievers were almost twice as popular as Goldens according to American Kennel Club registrations, but in spite of this their specialty show entries were similar. German Shepherd Dogs, Beagles, and Yorkshire Terriers followed closely on the Golden Retriever's heels on the popularity charts, yet none of them had a single show among the largest specialties. That is not necessarily a reflection on the clubs or the active fanciers in those breeds, simply an indication that there is a large pet segment of owners who prefer not to participate in conformation events for their breed.

A Labrador Enigma

Almost without exception, the shows with the highest entries are hosted by each breed's parent club. There is only one major exception: the largest Labrador Retriever specialty shows have been held for many years by the Labrador Retriever Club of the Potomac, a regional club founded in 1973 serving the Virginia and Maryland areas. With more than 700 participating Labradors at many of the club's annual shows over the past decade, this is now one of the biggest single-breed events in the world. The parent club, The Labrador Retriever Club, Inc., consistently has lower entries; its seventy-fifth specialty show in 2006 had 266 dogs competing. The two largest specialty shows ever in America were both held in 2005, by the Golden Retriever Club of America and the Labrador Retriever Club of the Potomac, respectively: each had exactly 849 dogs competing in the official classes and total entry figures well into the thousands.

LARGEST AKC BREED CLUB SPECIALTY SHOWS

Following is a listing based on number of dogs in competition at the largest single-breed specialty shows according to official AKC records of 1985–2005. The figure includes only dogs present and competing in the official classes.

849	Labrador Retriever Club of the Potomac	2005
849	Golden Retriever Club of America	2005
813	Collie Club of America	2001
818	Labrador Retriever Club of the Potomac	2006
791	Collie Club of America	1996
790	Golden Retriever Club of America	2003
770	Golden Retriever Club of America	1999
753	Golden Retriever Club of America	1997
737	Labrador Retriever Club of the Potomac	2002
729	Collie Club of America	1994
726	Labrador Retriever Club of the Potomac	2003
724	American Shetland Sheepdog Association	2003
724	American Shetland Sheepdog Association	1993
712	Collie Club of America	2005
708	Labrador Retriever Club of the Potomac	1999
700	Labrador Retriever Club of the Potomac	2000
700	Golden Retriever Club of America	1996
699	Golden Retriever Club of America	1990

Many of the biggest specialty shows attract several hundred dogs of the same breed. The Golden Retriever Club of America national specialty in 1999 was one of the biggest ever, with 770 dogs in competition. Judge Beth G. Speich selected Ch. Briarwoods My Hi Flying Legend as Best of Breed.

The American Spaniel Club, founded in 1881, is one of the oldest dog clubs in the United States—three years older than the American Kennel Club. It attracts several hundred spaniels at its annual January show. In 2005, Best in Show was judged by Marilyn Spacht, who chose the particolor Cocker Spaniel Ch. San Jo's Born To Win as her winner. He was handled by Michael Pitt.

698	Poodle Club of America	1993
687	Collie Club of America	1998
685	Collie Club of America	1990
677	Labrador Retriever Club of the Potomac	2001
672	American Shetland Sheepdog Association	2005
667	Labrador Retriever Club of the Potomac	1998
662	Collie Club of America	2004
651	Labrador Retriever Club of the Potomac	1996
646	Labrador Retriever Club of the Potomac	1997
645	Siberian Husky Club of America	1986
642	Collie Club of America	2000
642	Golden Retriever Club of America	2006
641	Poodle Club of America	1990
640	American Whippet Club	2004
637	Golden Retriever Club of America	2000
637	Poodle Club of America	1992
637	Poodle Club of America	1991
635	Siberian Husky Club of America	2000
635	American Whippet Club	1999
635	Poodle Club of America	1998
634	Poodle Club of America	1997
631	Poodle Club of America	1995
631	Poodle Club of America	2006
629	Labrador Retriever Club of the Potomac	2004
627	Poodle Club of America	2000
625	Dachshund Club of America	1995
625	American Shetland Sheepdog Association	2006
624	American Shetland Sheepdog Association	1990
623	Labrador Retriever Club of the Potomac	1995
622	Poodle Club of America	2002
622	American Shetland Sheepdog Association	1999
617	Collie Club of America	2003

Specialty shows can afford fanciers the opportunity to bring in judges from foreign countries. The National Shiba Club of America's specialty in 2001 was judged by Mr. Y. Mori from Japan, the breed's native country. His Best of Breed winner was Ch. Sho Go Gold Typhoon.

Winning at a breed's national specialty show is one of the highest honors a dog person can hope for. Best of Breed at the National Beagle Club of America's specialty in 1987 was the 13-inch bitch Ch. Teloca Lacoste Judith Anne. The judge, as is usually the case at these shows, was an established breed specialist, Anthony Musladin, of the famous The Whim's Beagles.

The Wildweir Yorkshire Terriers had a great run at both specialty and all-breed shows for many years, owner-handled by sisters Joan Gordon and Jane Bennett. Judge Maxwell Riddle awarded Ch. Wildweir Fair N' Square Best of Breed at the Yorkshire Terrier Club of America show in 1967.

The Poodle Extravaganza

One of the classics of the dog show world, the Poodle Club of America's annual event in June has long attracted visitors from around the world. The Poodle Club has held specialty shows since 1932, and until the mid-1970s, they were located only on the East Coast. In 1974, the PCA regional specialties were introduced and are held in different parts of the country in most years. The show in Maryland, held in April starting in 2008, remains the largest and most prestigious. At first, only Standard Poodles were classified; Miniatures were added in 1933, and Toys in 1947. The first show, described by Poodle specialist Del Dahl as "an elegant little garden party," had a total of twenty-three dogs entered; today, PCA is unquestionably the world's premier Poodle event and usually gets close to a thousand dogs entered in the conformation classes alone, even more if obedience, agility, and hunt tests are included.

No individual Poodle has won the Poodle Club of America national more than twice, and no modern Poodle kennel has surpassed the old Blakeen establishment of Mrs. Hayes Blake Hoyt, who won PCA six times with five different Standards in the show's first eleven years. The still-active Dassin kennels of Joseph Vergnetti and the late "Bud" Dickey come close, with five wins over the past few decades.

The three Variety winners at the 1999 Poodle Club of America specialty: the Standard Ch. Aleph Blue Skies Outrageous (also Best of Breed), shown by Tim Brazier; the Miniature Ch. Reignon Dassin Alexandra, handled by Joseph Vergnetti; and the Toy Ch. Appli Age of North Well Chako, imported from Japan and shown by Kaz Hosaka.

One of America's biggest and best organized specialty shows is hosted each year by the Poodle Club of America, often with close to 1,000 dogs entered. The 1984 show was won by the white Miniature Ch. Wavir Hit Parade, handled by Harold Langseth. Judge Frank Fretwell holds the ribbon; trophy presenters (left to right) are Frank Sabella (kneeling); Dr. Sterg O'Dell; Anne Rogers Clark; Doris Cozart; Norma Strait; "Happy's" breeder, Virginia Milroy; and Dr. Samuel Peacock. "Happy" is the only Poodle to win four PCA specialty shows.

Many specialty shows have additional judging as well as the official classes. Sweepstakes classes, open only to puppies, young dogs, or veterans, are especially popular. At the Poodle Club of America in 1992, the winner of Best in Veteran Sweepstakes under judge Richard G. Beauchamp was the Standard Ch. Rimskittle Romp, handled by Del Dahl. Left is Gene Cozart; right, Dr. Jacklyn Hungerland.

Exceptional Entries

It is worth noting that some breeds have exceptionally high show entries entirely out of proportion to their popularity. The Collie Club of America and American Shetland Sheepdog Association specialties are among the largest of all, in spite of the fact that neither breed is close to Goldens, Labradors, or Poodles in registration statistics. Other breeds that do not score high on the popularity charts manage to attract exceptional entries at their specialty shows. Whippets are the most obvious example. They hover around the middle of the annual registration statistics for all breeds yet have had more than 600 competitors at their national specialty—more than most of the more popular breeds—on at least a couple of occasions. Even more exceptional figures have been noted for a relatively rare breed: the Saluki usually stands among the least

numerous of the breeds listed on AKC's registration rankings, yet 300–400 Salukis may participate at the Saluki Club of America's annual outdoor show in Lexington, Kentucky. This is, in fact, one of the few breeds in which the number of dogs shown at the national specialty may *exceed* the total registered with AKC annually. To have comparable participation from Labrador Retrievers, for example, there would have to be more than 100,000 dogs at a single show!

Dogs that win at specialty shows do not always do as well in all-breed competition. In an ideal world, breed specialists and all-rounder judges would agree on which dogs are best, but in reality, the emphasis is often placed on different points at a specialty show. To simplify a little, at all-breed shows, general soundness, showmanship, glamour, and charisma may be taken more into account than specific breed points, whereas the opposite can be true at a specialty show judged by a breeder.

The top winners at specialty shows are not always the same dogs that win in all-breed competition. The 2003 Basset Hound Club of America, however, was won by Ch. Topsfield Bumper Cars, who went on, with handler Bryan Martin, to win numerous all-breed Bests in Show. The judge was Augusto Rizzi from Argentina, shown (left) with owners Claudia Orlandi and Claire Steidel.

Leading Specialty Winners

No official records are kept regarding the top winners at specialty competitions. It is obviously impossible to compare the records for one breed with those for another because the size and the number of the specialty shows vary so much. In spite of their popularity, Labrador Retrievers, for instance, have relatively few specialty shows, which makes each specialty a big event: winning even one or two of these puts a dog into a very select category. In other breeds, most notably German Shepherd Dogs and Poodles, there are so many specialty shows to choose from that entries drop, and the prestige of being a multiple specialty winner is not high enough for anyone to keep records.

The highest number of wins at independently held specialty shows (as far as was known during most of the research for this book) is shared by two dogs: the Afghan Hound Ch. Pahlavi Puttin' On The Ritz ("Taco") in the 1980s and early 1990s, and the Saint Bernard Ch. Aksala's Arie from 2002 to 2006. Both won all-breed Bests in Show as well, but their careers were obviously focused primarily on specialty shows: each is credited with winning Specialty Best in Show fifty-one times. Taco succeeded in winning the Afghan Hound Club of America specialty three times and became a top sire, with champion get in many countries around the world. He was shown to all his specialty wins by his breeder and owner, Karen Wagner. Arie won the Saint Bernard Club of America's regional specialty in 2003, and when he won the national in 2004, he also won the Stud Dog class at the same show, handled by Melody Kirkbride. In addition to his show career, Arie earned his Canine Good Citizen and Therapy Dog International certificates. He has also earned the Rally Novice title and two legs on his Companion Dog obedience title. Arie is owned by Ed and Linda Baker.

Amazing as the records of those two dogs are, further investigation turned up one who had won even more: the Rough Collie bitch Ch. Shoreham Triumph Timeless won an almost unbelievable—but well documented—ninety-one Specialty Best in Show wins in the late 1990s and early 2000s. "Mocha" won some Groups in all-breed competition, but it was specialty shows that were her métier and, true to her name, she got better with age: thirty-five of her specialty wins came from the veteran class, and in 2004, when she turned ten years old, she won a total of sixteen Specialty Bests. She was also a fixture at the Collie Club of America's annual national specialty, one of the biggest of all breeds: she won it in 2000, was Best of Opposite Sex in 1998, and received Awards of Merit in 1999, 2002, and 2004. One of her owners,

The Miniature Schnauzer Club of America holds its specialty show at the Montgomery County Terrier event each year. Ch. Regency's Twist of Fate won the specialty three years in a row, in 2004, 2005, and 2006.

One of the all-time top winners at breed specialty shows, the Afghan Hound Ch. Pahlavi Puttin' On The Ritz. He was a Best in Show winner at all-breed shows and is seen during Hound Group judging at Westminster, but "Taco" took most of his wins at Afghan Hound shows: he won fifty-one Specialty Bests in Show, almost invariably handled by his owner, Karen Wagner.

Elaine Goto-Tamae, tells how Mocha survived a bout with cancer and lived until nearly twelve years of age.

Not all the biggest or best single-breed events take place in the United States. It makes sense, however, that UK specialty shows—or breed club championship shows, as they are called in the United Kingdom—don't have quite the status there that they have in America. Distances are shorter and entries at the all-breed shows so big that most active people in a breed compete on a regular basis at the same shows throughout the year; getting together for a breed show makes a pleasant break in the calendar but is not quite the unique experience it usually is in the United States.

The Rough Collie bitch Ch. Shoreham Triumph Timeless secured a record with her ninety-one specialty Best in Show wins.

The Great Dane Club of America celebrated its centennial with a specialty show in 1989. Best of Breed was Ch. Rojon's Rumor Has It, handled by breeder Ray Cataldi, Jr., under judge Hazel Gregory.

THE GERMAN SHEPHERD DOG SIEGER SHOW

Other countries are catching on to the idea of single-breed celebrations, and many of them hold specialty shows with big entries. The biggest single-breed dog event in the world does not take place in America, but in Germany. David Landau, vice president of the German Shepherd Dog Club of America's Working Dog Association, Inc., and authorized as a judge by the German parent club, has been attending Sieger shows in Germany since 1973. He reports that the annual Sieger show hosted by the Schäfer

Verein (SV, officially Verein für Deutsche Schäferhunde) is usually held in August or early in September. It is a huge event, akin to a three-ring circus with more than 40,000 visitors and about 2,000 German Shepherd Dogs entered. An entire football stadium is needed for the judging of the Working dog classes, plus several adjacent large fields for four additional 120-by-120-foot rings, and two large fields for the protection work. Additional space is needed for about 100 vendors, office space, and a large tent for picking up the bibs with identifying numbers that are worn by the handlers instead

In homage to the German Sieger title, the best dog and best bitch at the German Shepherd Dog Club of America national specialty are called Grand Victor and Grand Victrix, respectively. The 2000 Grand Victor—and also Best of Breed—was Ch. Hickory Hills Bull Durham, handled by Bart Bartley under breed specialist judge Joseph Bihari.

of regular armbands. There are multiple beer and food stands, several large campgrounds, and parking for 5,000 cars and buses.

Only three conformation classes are offered, each separated by sex: Youth class (twelve to eighteen months), Young class (eighteen to twenty-four months), and Working class (over twenty-four months). There are prerequisites for entering the Working class, including a sufficiently good show rating at local or regional shows and a working (Schutzhund) title. Dogs from outside Germany may qualify with a recognized foreign working title. The winners of the Working dog classes, which can have 300 or 400 entries each, are the Sieger (VA-1 male) and Siegerin (VA-1 female). There is no Best of Breed award. VA stands for Vorzüglich Auslese, which translates as "Excellent Select." The VA ratings, typically from first to tenth, can be awarded only in the Working dog and bitch classes. The VA animals must have complete, correct dentition; certified hips and elbows; and at least a Schutzhund 2 title; the parents must have been breed surveyed (approved by the parent club), and the grandparents must also have Schutzhund titles. The dogs must pass a protection work test at the show as well, and there is a very extended period of gaiting to test endurance and drive.

The Schutzhund protection work trials (which are open to all Working breeds, not just to German Shepherd Dogs) have always been controversial, both in the United States and in Europe. In 2004, in response to political pressure within Germany, the SV and the VDH (Verband für das Deutsche Hundewesen, or German Kennel Club) made substantial changes in the requirements, and although SV still uses the term *Schutzhund*, the German clubs, at least on paper, gave up control of the sport to the FCI.

Following the Sieger show, there is a meeting of the World Union of German Shepherd Dog clubs. The World Union consists of seventy-four organizations in sixty-three countries, incorporating almost a half million breed fanciers.

Germany's biggest contribution to the dog world is no doubt the German Shepherd Dog. Ch. Zamp vom Thermodos won not only the Sieger title at the Schäfer Verein in 2006 but also Best in Show at the German Kennel Club's centennial show in Dortmund the same year. The judge was Uwe Fischer (left); right is club president Christofer Habig.

THE GROWTH OF GROUP SHOWS

A separate category of specialty shows is formed by the so-called Group shows, which occupy a level somewhere between all-breed shows and the single-breed specialty events. These shows are limited to one of the groups of breeds into which all national kennel clubs divide the breeds: it could be a show open only to toy dogs, or terriers, or hounds, or any of the other groups.

GROUP SHOWS IN GREAT BRITAIN

Group shows have been popular in Great Britain for many years without any perceptible change in recent times. The current National Terrier Show, for instance, had a forerunner that was started in 1886 at the instigation of the Duchess of Newcastle, herself a formidable Fox Terrier breeder; Charles Cruft was one of its early secretaries. All seven groups have their own championship shows in Great Britain today, and some have two or three. There is even a separate show for the Scottish breeds, regardless of which official group they belong to. Most British Group shows are big, in the tradition of British shows in general, attracting between 2,000 and 3,000 dogs each.

TERRIER CLASSIC IN PENNSYLVANIA

In the United States, there were hardly any Group shows for many years, Montgomery County Kennel Club being the outstanding exception. Technically, this is an all-breed organization, but all activities have been focused exclusively on terriers for so long that it is commonly thought of as a terrier club. The Best in Show records go back to 1929 and consist entirely of terriers. (In the

United States, the Miniature Schnauzer is classified as a Terrier and has won Montgomery three times in the past, all before 1970.) Fewer than 200 terriers competed at the 1929 show, but that figure doubled after World War II and was already into the four figures by the early 1970s. Since the mid-1980s, well over 2,000 terriers have been entered each year at Montgomery, making this the biggest terrier show in the world, surpassing even the parent club in England.

Held in October in Pennsylvania each year, Montgomery sometimes suffers from the elements, but by the seemingly simple expedient of cooperating with the breed clubs and inviting world-class specialist judges, Montgomery regularly attracts bigger entries in most of the terrier breeds than can be seen anywhere else in the world. At least twenty national breed clubs choose to hold their specialty classes as part of the Montgomery event, and the Best in Show competition is usually judged by a high-profile terrier name—as often from a foreign country as from the United States. Montgomery is, in fact, a very cosmopolitan show; terrier lovers travel from all over the world to watch, and large numbers of judges and fanciers from other breeds congregate there for the pure pleasure of seeing

Many of the older breed clubs were founded in the late 1800s. The Whippet Club in England celebrated its centennial with a well-attended championship show in 1999. Best in Show (second from left) was Ch. Nevedith Veefa Vanity at Roguesmoor. The dog CC went to Dumbriton Dream Lover (far left). Best Puppy was Moonlake Making A Splash and Best Veteran was Summersway Spring Board.

The Terrier show hosted by Montgomery County Kennel Club in October each year is the biggest in the world: well over 2,000 Terriers are usually entered. The 2005 finale was judged by Ferelith Somerfield from England (with the big ribbon) and won by the eight-year-old Smooth Fox Terrier Ch. Pennfox Trackway's Wicked Brew, handled by Elizabeth Tobin. Trophy presenters are the show committee: from left, Walter Goodman, Daniel Shoemaker, Dr. Josephine Deubler, James McTernan, and Carol Carlson.

large entries of good dogs judged by breed experts. Most of the popular terrier breeds may have at least 100 dogs entered; some will have far more.

No dog has won Best in Show at Montgomery three times, but several have won it twice—most recently the Kerry Blue Ch. Torum's Scarf Michael, in 2001 and 2002, and the Norwich Ch. Chidley Willum The Conqueror, in 1992 and 1993.

In spite of the undisputed success of the Montgomery County terrier show, the AKC was long reluctant to approve Group clubs. In the 1990s, there was a change, the result of strong pressure from exhibitors, and a number of Group clubs were offi-

cially recognized. They are now a popular fixture in the show calendar, especially for Toy breeds, Hounds, and Terriers. Some attract big entries and do full justice to the unique opportunity for comparison of related breeds that a Group show provides, but none comes close to approaching Montgomery County in size or prestige. The second-biggest Group show in America in the first years of the twenty-first century has been the Connecticut River Working Group Association, which gets more entries than any of the other official Group shows, although it still has only half as many dogs on show as the Montgomery terrier classic does.

Ch. Kazor's Johnny Come Greatly won the Basenji Club of America National under breed specialist judge Sandra Bridges in 1997; there were 351 Basenjis competing. The following year, he was one of the Top Ten dogs of all breeds. He was handled by Erin Roberts.

The first Smooth Collie to win Best of Breed at the Collie Club National Specialty, and one of the few Smooths to win big in all-breed competition, was Ch. Black Hawk of Kasan, seen with handler Leslie Canavan winning Best in Show under judge William Kendrick in 1970.

Best of Breed judging can on rare occasions include as many as 100 champions or more. At the American Whippet Club's 2006 national specialty, 101 dogs were in the ring at the same time, as the final day's judging began.

SIGHTHOUNDS IN CALIFORNIA

The American Kennel Club does not allow multibreed clubs to hold official shows unless the breeds they cater to conform exactly to the official Group division. Thus, one of the country's most beautiful and educationally significant dog events, hosted by the Western Sighthound Combined Specialties in California in late July each year since 1980, is technically a loose confederation of single-breed clubs—for Greyhounds, Whippets, Salukis, Borzois, and various other sighthounds that hold their specialties on the same grounds. It may look as if they are all one show, but the AKC does not permit any competition between different breeds at such an event, so there is no Best in Show or other interbreed judging.

In 2004, the Swedish Sighthound Club show was won by the Afghan Hound from France, Ch. Khafka's Exotic Spice, under judge Keke Kahn from the US (third from right). The judging panel consisted of Pauline Oliver (UK), Torbjörn Skaar (Sweden), Bernard Barjot and Jean-Louis Grünheid (France), Pat Latimer (UK), Janet Buchanan (Canada), and Sue Gillespie and Molly McConkey (UK).

Breed clubs make every effort to see that their shows live up to the specialty name. The Monterey Bay Afghan Hound Club even sports a genuine imported Bedouin tent for its show.

One of the great specialty dog show events in America, the Western Sighthound Combined Specialties, is held in California each summer. One of the features is the Parade of Winners, which incorporates many of the participating breeds. This photo is from the mid-1980s. Pictured from left are an Afghan Hound, two Ibizan Hounds, a Scottish Deerhound, three Whippets, an Italian Greyhound, a Pharaoh Hound, another Scottish Deerhound, a Saluki, and a Borzoi.

The Western Sighthound event has a counterpart in Europe that in some years is even bigger than the California event. It is still often called simply the Skokloster show, so named after the baroque castle overseeing the grounds where the Swedish Sighthound Club held the first shows in the 1970s and 1980s. Although the location has changed, in a good year the show still attracts nearly a thousand sighthounds, with almost twice the number of entries if the single-breed specialties held the same weekend are included. Exhibitors from all over Europe bring their dogs, the judges come from even farther away, and to win Best in Show is among the greatest honors imaginable for any sighthound fancier.

CHAPTER 5

THE JUDGES

Being a dog show judge can seem like a glamorous occupation. You fly around the world, sometimes to exotic locations in faraway lands. You stand in the spotlight; get wined, dined, and photographed—and you are treated like a celebrity, at least for a while. The top judges are booked years in advance, rather like opera divas; according to widely circulated stories, certain judges behave a little like that, too. In reality, being a judge is hard work for little (or no) pay, and judges need an abundance of cheerful flexibility to adjust to different circumstances in order to enjoy the vagaries of travel from one dog show to the next. Judges also need a thick skin: few people are exposed to as much criticism as dog show judges, and if you aspire to become a really good judge, you need a very specific combination of essential personality traits.

Judge Sandra Goose Allen examines the Sealyham Terrier Ch. Stonebroke Right On The Money during Breed judging at Westminster 2004. Handler Gabriel Rangel showed the dog to a spot among the top dogs of all breeds in both 2005 and 2006.

THE RESPONSIBILITY OF JUDGING

The responsibility of the dog show judge is a heavy one. Without good judges, there wouldn't be any point in holding dog shows—one might as well award the ribbons by lottery, which is in one form or another what disappointed exhibitors say when they are unhappy about a judge's decisions. No other subject causes as intense feelings among dog people as who is a good judge and who is not or what characteristics a judge must possess to qualify as someone you really respect. The judge may be all-powerful in the ring, but as soon as the assignment is over, every minute action he or she made will be scrutinized, analyzed, and interpreted in detail—often with wildly disparate conclusions, depending on how well your dog did.

There is one term dog people use that applies here: *kennel blindness*. It means that you look at your own dogs through rose-colored glasses with much less brutal clarity than you scrutinize the competition. That is a problem every single dog show judge must deal with. In the end, usually it is only the winners who are happy, and by the nature of the sport, there are always many more losers than there are winners.

The problem, but also much of the appeal inherent in conformation judging, is that it is, by its very nature, subjective. One person's opinion is what matters—his or her interpretation of how closely each dog compares with the ideal for its breed. It is not a question simply of who can run the fastest or jump the highest, as in many other competitive activities; dog shows are more similar to such Olympic sports as diving, figure skating, and dressage riding, except that in those sports there is always a panel of judges who share the responsibility. In dogs, there is almost invariably a single judge who determines the placements.

The use of a multiple-judge system was fairly common in the past, but the only shows in recent times that I am aware of that used a panel of judges to determine class placements are a few big specialty shows in France. I participated in a couple of those, and frankly it seemed that whoever put forward the most forceful point of view usually got to determine the winner. If the greater expense and time required for a multijudge panel aren't reason enough to stick to just one judge, there is also the fact that the dogs tend to get rather irritated if they have to be pawed over by several people at the same time—and most of the exhibitors, truth be told, actually prefer to have just one judge in charge.

It is surprising in some ways that so many people want to subject themselves to the difficult job of becoming judges. You work hard without getting rich (most judges get only their expenses paid; only a few earn a reasonable living), the power trip is short lived, and whatever you do is likely to be misinterpreted, and often misrepresented, in any of a dozen possible ways. The winners will always tell you what a brilliant job you did. What really warms the heart are those rare times when you hear an appreciative word from someone who did not do so well.

WHAT MAKES A GOOD JUDGE

The fact that there are judges whose opinions are almost universally respected within the sport is, in view of the above, remarkable. Those are the individuals who possess all the characteristics necessary to become a top-class dog show judge.

IN-DEPTH KNOWLEDGE OF THE BREED

The first requirement, of course, is that you need to know a lot about dogs, knowledge acquired not just from reading books but also by experience, through a long and close association with dogs—living with, studying, and learning from a large number of dogs over many years' time. That provides the foundation, an ease and comfort in dealing with dogs that's necessary if you are going to regularly get up close and personal with thousands of dogs on an ongoing basis. Most dogs sense immediately if a person is unfamiliar with animals, and it is necessary that the dogs trust and like the judge. Even if the judge is completely comfortable with most dogs, an occasional animal may be skittish, insecure, or even aggressive, and the judge needs to know how to deal with that. It is the judge's responsibility to excuse a dog that "menaces, threatens, or exhibits any sign that it may not be examined in the normal manner"—and a dog that attacks any person in the ring must, needless to say, be disqualified. It is not the judge's job to try to examine a dog that acts in a threatening manner.

The judge must also possess a thorough knowledge of basic canine anatomy. He or she must obviously have a deep, intimate knowledge of each particular breed he or she is approved to judge. That does not mean just knowing the official breed standard practically by heart; that's compulsory. To apply this standard while examining the dogs, the judge must also know the breed's function and development, as well as all the many details that go into the makeup of a really top-class specimen. A sense of history is a plus: if the judge knows under what circumstances a breed was developed, it's easier to prioritize the characteristics unique and essential for each separate breed.

EYE FOR A DOG

Even if you know all there is to know about dogs (which, of course, nobody does even after years of study), it is by no means certain that this alone will make you a good judge. You also need that elusive eye for a dog, a somewhat mysterious quality that is difficult to explain but is similar to an artist's eye: an appreciation for balance and proportions that immediately allows you to recognize a quality animal. Good horse people often make good dog judges, and anyone who is capable of judging dogs well can often apply that knowledge rather easily to other animals. Without an eye for the whole picture, it doesn't matter how much you know about the details.

In addition, the judge must have a sort of computer brain, capable of processing hundreds of impressions from many different dogs simultaneously and then making decisive, logical placements based on those impressions. What you need is "a cool brain and warm hands."

AUTHORITY, ENTHUSIASM, CLARITY, AND DIPLOMACY

You must also possess a degree of natural authority that makes it clear that you know what you are doing: if it doesn't at least *look* as if you know your business, the exhibitors and spectators are not going to take you seriously. You need the strength of character that discourages exhibitors from taking advantage of you or playing games in the ring, such as crowding or running into a competitor, resorting to more or less subtle body language asking for a win. The judge

Some judges prefer to specialize in just one breed. One such was Mme. Harper Trois-Fontaines, a towering presence in Great Pyrenees in England, seen here with three of her de Fontenay dogs in 1970.

A TOUCH OF STAGE PRESENCE

Some judges have such stage presence and such a sense of drama that watching them can feel a little like attending the theater. Big gestures and artificially prolonged suspense isn't what judging dogs is about, of course, but as long as the dramatic flair is paired with solid dog knowledge, it can make for a fascinating spectacle. I will never forget the majestic Mme. Harper Trois-Fontaines judging Great Pyrenees at Crufts a long time ago. She was probably past eighty years old at the time, and she simply sat on a chair—a throne, really—in the middle of the ring. Each dog was brought up to her for examination, more or less as if at a royal *audience*. She indicated her winners with a subtle yet imperious gesture, and nobody argued. Not everyone would get away with this procedure; the American Kennel Club demands that the judge be able to walk and stand unaided and have the full use of at least one arm and hand. Some clubs have even introduced age limits for judges, which is both inhumane and self-defeating: some people are better judges at eighty-five than others are at forty.

must be in total control of the ring and by his or her appearance make it clear that nothing improper will be acceptable. The behavior of dog handlers can sometimes resemble that of schoolchildren, testing their teacher to see how far they can go.

At the same time, the judge must remember that this is a hobby: most people are showing dogs for fun, and it should be an enjoyable experience for both handler and animal. Some exhibitors may be newcomers and many are nervous, so it helps if the judge exudes confident enthusiasm and positive energy. Some judges focus so intensely on the difficult task of finding the best dogs that they forget that this is supposed to be a pleasant endeavor; others can appear so bored and listless that you wonder why they chose to become judges in the first place.

It helps considerably if the judge also makes the judging process understandable for spectators. Following the same procedure when examining dog after dog, class after class, makes it easy for the ringside to know what to expect. If the judge is really clever, an observant spectator should soon be able to sort out that judge's priorities. It's not as easy (or rude) as the judge pointing to a sagging topline or cow hocks, but there is a certain subtle body language that an experienced spectator should be able to decipher.

A little diplomacy goes a long way. Most judges can see at a glance when a dog doesn't have a shadow of a chance of placing in a big class and then won't give it a second look. That may be necessary due to time restrictions, but everybody pays the same entry fee, and many a newcomer with a dog of indifferent quality has been turned off dog shows for the future by feeling they were not getting even a look at their first show. A second glance and a kind word have the power to work wonders.

STAMINA

Physically, a dog show judge's job may not seem particularly demanding, but it is much harder than it appears. Judges are expected to be on their feet for days on end, sometimes in cold and rain, sometimes in extreme heat; they must appear calm and composed, exude authority, put their hands on hundreds of dogs, and make quick and forceful decisions. Many judges are no longer in the first spring of youth—that comes with the territory since gaining the necessary experience takes time—yet they are supposed to bend over, check bites and testicles, and if possible kneel all the way down to the ground to make sure that those tightly knuckled feet are not just the result of a clever trimmer's handiwork.

FIXING THE WINS

One of the few cases in which an exhibitor has been known to resort to (and succeed in) bribing judges occurred during the infamous McKay affair in the 1980s. William McKay was a newcomer who wanted to make it big in dogs, and he had enough money to buy good dogs. As if that wasn't enough, he hired a few unscrupulous judges to tout his dogs to their colleagues. When the AKC got wind of these activities, McKay was suspended for life and some judges were disciplined, but the most serious fallout was for some dog people who had innocently become involved with McKay. Since the AKC ruled that any dog owned or co-owned by McKay could neither be shown nor participate in any other AKC activities, McKay's best dog, an all-time great Wire Fox Terrier, was in limbo during years of litigation and could not be used at stud until he was almost too old to be fertile—a major blow to serious breeders who wanted to use the dog.

The last show judged by Anna Katherine Nicholas was Bryn Mawr Kennel Club in 1999. Her Best in Show winner was the Bearded Collie Ch. Classic Image Of A Legend, handled by Jason Hoke. Legend had been Top Dog of all breeds in Canada in 1997.

Small breeds are always examined on a table, which spares the judge's back. Medium-size breeds can be judged on a ramp for closer inspection, but this doesn't happen as often as it should. As a result, many judges tend to neglect canine body parts not within easy reach. After a few hundred deep knee bends to inspect feet, it is easy to understand why.

HIGH ETHICAL STANDARDS

It is not possible to discuss judges without talking about ethics. If exhibitors cannot trust that the judge's opinions are his or her own, the whole point of judging is lost. It takes strength of character to remain completely unaffected by outside factors that

should not enter into the judge's decisions. Even when a judge knows that Dog A has a formidable record, that Dog B is owned by the judge's best friend, and that Dog C is shown by a famous professional handler, the judge must still have enough strength of character to place Dog D first if he sincerely feels that it more closely adheres to the breed ideal than the others do.

Actually, much of what many people consider dishonest judging is really ignorant judging: if you are sure that Dog A is better than Dog B, it is really difficult to put Dog B first just because you know that's the politically correct move. However, when judges are really not that certain about the breed, it is all too easy for some of them to just go with the flow and convince themselves that the most famous dog is the best one.

At the same time, a judge must be mature enough not to penalize a good friend's dog just because it belongs to a friend (in the circumstances, it probably should not have been shown in the first place). Neither should a judge succumb to the temptation to create a stir by selecting a completely unknown nonchampion over all the big stars unless it really deserves it. One basic premise is that judging is "on the day"—the dogs are assessed as they are at that moment, in the ring, without any consideration to what they may have looked like in the past or what they could be in the future. Most judges are not anxious to go out on a limb; if they do, history may or may not prove them right.

Exactly how close a relationship a breeder-exhibitor can have with a judge and still show dogs under him or her is impossible to define. Most clubs have rules prohibiting club officials, family members, and certain others from showing under a judge. The American Kennel Club, in a memorable phrase in its *Guidelines for Conformation Dog Show Judges*, puts it like this:

> Judges are often singled out for critical observation by the fancy. Therefore, always keep in mind that a perfectly innocent action or discussion can be misconstrued. . . . There will always be those "gray areas" that perplex judges. When faced with such a dilemma, ask yourself whether the situation, however innocent, maintains an outward appearance of propriety. A

good rule of thumb is: If you have concerns about whether something is inappropriate, you probably should avoid the situation.

No action taken by any judge is so innocent that it cannot be misconstrued by at least some exhibitors. Fortunately for the judges, most don't have to listen to what the exhibitors say back at the benches or grooming areas when the day's judging is over. It is probably natural that a competitor whose great new star has just suffered a painful defeat won't be singing that judge's praises, and because a lot of work and high hopes go into every ring appearance, many handlers simply need to let off steam at times. When exhibitors calm down, most of them may even acknowledge that perhaps the judge did what he or she felt was right after all, that there is room for many interpretations of the ideal, and in any case there's always another show next week.

In real life, there are very few judges who deliberately and knowingly put up the wrong dog. This may sound naive, but it's not that judges are morally superior to other people; rather, as a judge one is in a very visible position, and since there are always knowledgeable people watching what the judges are doing, one would have to be very foolish to not even try to put up the best dogs. It's more a question of judges who are not quite confident in their own minds and therefore tend to follow the leader.

THE ROAD TO BECOMING A JUDGE

How long does it take to become a judge? As a rule, don't even start to think about it until you have been actively involved in dogs for

The famous English judge Judy de Casembroot, herself a Cocker Spaniel breeder, awards Best of Breed to Ch. Ascot's Donny of Squirrel Run, handled by Anne Rogers Clark, at the English Cocker Spaniel Club of America's specialty in 1966. The trophy presenter is the club president, Louis Kleinhard.

at least five years. At that point, if you have done your homework and experienced some success as an exhibitor and breeder, you could be asked to judge some unofficial match show or sweepstakes classes—which may immediately tell you (and perhaps the spectators) if you have the right temperament to become a judge. After another five years of learning, you may be ready to apply to become an official judge. Some people, however, don't enjoy being in that position. It is regrettable but understandable when an experienced dog person does not want to jump through the hoops required by the authorities to become a fully approved judge.

BECOMING A JUDGE IN THE UNITED KINGDOM

The requirements vary from country to country, but judges in the United Kingdom in the past had less formal training than did those in most other countries. More recently, since around the turn of the twenty-first century, the requirements have changed dramatically, and now no person can be approved to judge at championship level without having attended breed seminars and taking breed club examinations and assessments. A judge is also required to undergo various other Kennel Club tests, including hands-on examinations,

Mrs. Geraldine Rockefeller Dodge awards Best in Show to the Irish Setter Ch. Conifer's Lance, one of the top Sporting dogs of 1961, handled by Dick Cooper. The trophy presenter is Mrs. Groverman Ellis of the Killybracken Irish Wolfhounds.

and to attend conformation and movement seminars.

A new judge begins gaining experience at small Limited or Open shows, where no championship awards are available. Before being approved to award Challenge Certificates, the prospective judge must be on at least one breed club's list of desired judges. These judging lists are at different levels, with stringent requirements and at least seven years of judging the breed at lower level shows required to get on the A-list. The prospective judge then has to wait for an invitation to judge a championship show. The Kennel Club always asks the breed clubs for their opinions concerning a first-time championship appointment, and an approval to award Challenge Certificates is for one particular show only. The judge, no matter how experienced, is always evaluated on the first appointment for each new breed, and a written form is submitted to The Kennel Club.

There is also a judges' development scheme, in which those who have already awarded CCs in some breeds can attend postgraduate seminars and be subjected to practical tests. It usually takes at least a couple of decades before one is able to award Challenge Certificates in enough breeds to judge a group (although a judge does not, in fact, have to be approved for all the breeds in that group). Before a person can be approved to judge Best in Show at a general championship show, he or she must already have judged a minimum of two groups and some breeds within other groups.

BECOMING A JUDGE IN THE UNITED STATES

In the United States, a judge has to fulfill certain specified criteria before he or she can apply to become a provisional judge for a first few select breeds. The requirements have been changed frequently in recent years; currently those criteria involve having been involved in dogs for a minimum of twelve years and bred at least five litters that resulted in at least four champions. There are some alternatives, but basically each applicant is required to have been actively involved (which means being officially listed as an owner or exhibitor or breeder) in each first-time breed they apply for. Once the applicant has successfully judged all these breeds on five separate occasions, he or she may be regularly approved and can then apply for a few more breeds—never more than the number one already has. (If at first a judge is approved for one breed, one more may then be added; once a judge has two breeds, he or she can apply for two more.) The maximum number of breeds anyone can request in a first-time application is fourteen, but most applicants would have a difficult time filling the requirements for more than one or two breeds.

Very few of the more than 3,000 judges approved by the American Kennel Club are content to judge just a couple of breeds. If they do, they would not be in high demand by most clubs, who want each judge to be able to tackle 150–175 dogs per day to cover expenses. Since the average breed entry at most shows consists of only 5 or 6 dogs, the judge may have to adjudicate as many as twenty-five or thirty breeds in a single day. Whether it helps the sport or not that most judges try graduating to multibreed, Group, and Best in Show status as quickly as possible is debatable. Judges with in-depth knowledge of a single (or a few) breeds often have different priorities than has someone who is only superficially familiar with a large number of breeds. The result of the all-rounder predominance in the United States is that the finer points of breed type may suffer at the expense of more easily assessed characteristics such as showmanship, glamour, soundness, and general balance. Much of the difference that has appeared between the English type and the American type in some breeds can be traced directly back to the difference in the judges' backgrounds, with the huge entries at British shows allowing more opportunities for breed specialists to exert their influence.

One cannot start judging Group competition at AKC shows until one has been approved for *all* the breeds in this group—but once approved to judge even a single group, one may become eligible to judge Best in Show. This is one of the little-known facts that few people talk about in American dogdom—the anomalous situation that allows AKC's top show award to be determined on a regular basis by judges who are not officially licensed to judge many (or most!) of the breeds competing for it. The reason is simply that there are too many shows and too few judges who are so experienced, ambitious, and knowledgeable that they become approved to judge all breeds. At present, less than 1 percent of the approximately 3,000 AKC judges are true all-rounders, approved to judge all breeds. Obviously, this situation requires a remedy, and it can be argued from both sides whether it is better to compromise on the requirements for Group judges, as is done in the United Kingdom, or to allow almost every judge approved for a single group to also award Best in Show, as in the United States.

Becoming an FCI Judge

Most of the FCI countries have formal tests and examinations for aspiring judges, but the requirements vary from one national kennel club to the next. Judges from some FCI member countries progress with astonishing speed from their first breed to the position of being at least nominally licensed to adjudicate over all the several hundred breeds the FCI classifies at its shows. Unsurprisingly, this fosters some resentment among the FCI judges' British and American colleagues, who may be bypassed for shows at which the convenient all-rounder status is appreciated. However, most of the really important dog shows around the world tend to assign judges on the merit of their particular expertise, not on the number of breeds for which they have passed tests. It is not that difficult to learn the difference between a good and a bad specimen of most breeds, but it's a different matter to become the kind of judge who can, with some claims to authority, determine which of several good dogs is the best and why.

There is also some risk of tunnel blindness if a judge stays involved in just one or two breeds for many years. Hitting the right balance between focusing too hard on a narrow goal and becoming the type of judge who knows a little about everything but not much about anything is not always easy. One learns more about dogs in general and acquires a new perspective on one's own breed when judging others.

For anyone judging in a foreign country, there is a whole new set of rules to deal with. English is, so to speak, the lingua franca among dog people, but the priorities change with the geography and judging systems, as does how dogs are shown. Even what is considered a good dog may differ more than one would think possible. Aspiring judges go against local custom at their peril, so before setting off on an overseas assignment, one must learn both how shows are run in that country and what the standards are like for the breeds to be judged. If a person is not willing to adjust to the local rules, he or she should probably stay home: such judges will do more harm than good trying to tell people that "this is how *we* do things"—unless asked, of course. Word spreads remarkably fast in the international dog community.

AMERICAN JUDGES

Who are the best judges? That always depends a great deal on whom you ask. There is no grade for judges, and the fact that someone officiates on a regular basis all over the country does not necessarily guarantee that he or she is a better judge than one who specializes in just a few breeds and only judges a few shows occasionally. One could even make a case for the advantage of being a specialist judge, since whenever one is invited, it is usually to a major event. For obvious reasons, the small shows with low breed entries rarely cater to breed specialists.

THE ALL-ROUNDERS

Having said that, judges approved by the American Kennel Club to judge all breeds form a unique group of their own, having demonstrated the experience, knowledge, and determination required to fulfill all AKC criteria. The backgrounds of these judges vary considerably. Some were professional handlers; others, successful breeders and exhibitors. There are two husband-and-wife all-rounder couples; several other all-rounders have spouses who also judge one or more groups. Another half dozen judges are in the midst of being added to this elite list, as they are now approved to judge six of the seven AKC groups.

THE GROUP JUDGES

Of the approximately 750 people who judge at least one full AKC group, about half are approved for one or more additional groups as well, and of those who judge "only" one group, the vast majority are also approved to judge Best in Show. The remainder are either gaining the requisite experience before they can become Best in

AKC JUDGES APPROVED FOR ALL BREEDS (Based on AKC Judges Directory 1978–2007)

Mrs. Barbara Dempsey Alderman*
Mr. Roy L. Ayers, Sr.
Mr. Maurice L. Baker
Dr. Robert J. Berndt*
Ms. Michele L. Billings*
Dr. Frank R. Booth
Mr. Edward W. Bracy
Mr. Robert Braithwaite
Mr. Len Carey
Mrs. James Edward Clark
Mr. Thomas E. Conway
Mr. Herman G. Cox
Mr. Melbourne T. L. Downing
Mr. J. J. Duncan
Mr. Joseph Faigel
Mr. Glenn T. Fancy
Mrs. Jean Fancy
Mr. Robert S. Forsyth*
Mrs. Robert S. Forsyth*
Mrs. Marcia A. Foy*
Mr. Thomas M. Gately
Mr. Rutledge Gilliland
Mr. Kenneth W. Given
Mr. Joseph E. Gregory*
Mr. Denis J. Grivas
Mrs. Virginia S. Hampton*
Mr. Clinton M. Harris*
Mrs. Paula Hartinger *
Mr. Roger M. Hartinger*
Mr. Heywood R. Hartley
Mrs. Winifred R. Heckman
Mr. Charles P. Herendeen
Mr. Stephen J. Hubbell*
Mrs. Dorothy O. Hutchinson*
Mrs. Helen Lee James*
Mrs. John Marshall Jones (Van Court)

Mrs. Keke Kahn*
Mrs. Jane G. Kay*
Mr. William L. Kendrick
Mr. Emil R. Klinckhardt
Mr. A. Peter Knoop
Ms. Denny Kodner*
Mr. Phil Marsh
Mr. Robert J. Moore*
Mr. Louis Murr
Ms. Dorothy D. Nickles*
Mr. Gordon M. Parham
Mr. Vincent G. Perry
Mr. Gerhardt Plaga
Mr. Derek G. Rayne
Dr. Lee Anthony Reasin*
Mr. Maxwell Riddle
Mrs. Augustus Riggs IV
Mr. Isidore Schoenberg
Mr. R. Stephen Shaw
Mr. Langdon L. Skarda
Dr. Harry Smith*
Dr. Robert D. Smith*
Mr. Glen M. Sommers
Mr. Robert Stein*
Mr. Henry H. Stoecker
Mr. Joe Tacker*
Mr. Peter B. Thomson
Mr. E. W. Tipton, Jr.
Mr. James W. Trullinger
Mr. Howard H. Tyler
Mr. Robert Waters
Mr. Robert G. Wills
Mr. Theodore Wurmser
Mr. Arthur K.Y. Zane

Indicates active judge in 2007

Show judges or simply do not want to judge that competition. There are even a couple of rare bird multigroup judges who do not judge Best in Show either, more likely because of their own disinclination to do so than because of any resistance from

Judge Michele Billings awarded Best in Show at Westminster in 1988 to the Pomeranian Ch. Great Elm's Prince Charming II. The handler was Skip Piazza.

the AKC. If you are interested only in terriers or hounds, it may seem unnatural that you should make important decisions that concern other breeds. However, that feeling is obviously not shared by most judges.

The most active Best in Show judges at AKC shows in the first years of the twenty-first century were Keke Kahn, Dr. Harry Smith, and Michele Billings, all of whom officiated in that capacity more than seventy times between 2001 and 2005. The two most active married couples were Dr. Robert and Polly Smith and Roger and Paula Hartinger. The two most active foreign judges came, not surprisingly, from Canada, James

Reynolds and Virginia Lyne; the only judge from outside North America to have more than an occasional Best in Show assignment was Enrique Filippini from Buenos Aires, Argentina.

THE LEADING WESTMINSTER JUDGES

Judging the most prestigious shows is what really counts, of course, and no dog show in America carries more prestige than the Westminster Kennel Club. Following is a list of contemporary judges who have officiated at least ten times at Westminster through the year 2006:

- Melbourne T. L. Downing, twenty-two times 1949–2000, including Best in Show in 1992
- Edd Embry Bivin, seventeen times 1970–2005, including Best in Show in 1999
- Michele L. Billings, thirteen times 1978–2006, including Best in Show in 1988
- Dr. Bernard E. McGivern, Jr., thirteen times 1976–2007
- Frank T. Sabella, thirteen times 1970–2007, including Best in Show in 1990
- Anna Wanner (Mrs. George J. Wanner), twelve times 1975–2000, including Best in Show in 1986
- Dorothy Welsh, twelve times 1981–2004, including Best in Show in 1991
- Louis Auslander, eleven times 1979–2000, including Best in Show in 1987
- Walter F. Goodman, ten times 1982–2005, including Best in Show in 1994
- Patricia W. Laurans, ten times 1990–2006
- Kenneth M. McDermott, ten times 1982–2005

The Legendary Mrs. Clark

Few people would deny that Anne Rogers Clark's contributions to the sport of dogs are unique. Mrs. Clark, who was born into a doggy family (her mother was a successful breeder of Poodles and English Cocker Spaniels), often said that she did not blossom as a junior handler: even as a youngster she set her sights directly on the adult competition. In this she was singularly successful, winning her first Best in Show with her mother's English Cocker Spaniel Ch. Comanche of Ranch Aero in 1950. A high-profile career as a professional handler resulted in, among many other achievements, three Best in Show wins with Poodles at Westminster in 1956, 1959, and 1961. Her many judging assignments at this and other shows were crowned with the Best in Show appointment in 1978; her winner on that occasion was the Yorkshire Terrier Ch. Cede Higgens. In 2002, when the black Miniature Poodle Ch. Surrey Spice Girl took

The Rhodesian Ridgeback Ch. Kwetu Oakhurst Bronco, one of the top Hounds of 1986, is shown winning at Contra Costa Kennel Club that year with handler Leroy Stage and judge Robert Ward.

In the past, active professional handlers were eligible to judge occasional specialty shows. Anne Rogers Clark is shown in the mid-1950s, at the height of her professional career, judging a Poodle specialty in California. The dog is the Standard puppy Bel Tor Hugues Capet; the handler, Tom Stevenson.

Best in Show at Westminster, Mrs. Clark became the only person ever to have been involved in the finale at America's top show as a handler, as a judge, and as a breeder.

In spite of her success as a handler and breeder, there is no question that Mrs. Clark's most important contribution was as a judge of undoubted authority. Her talent was obvious from the start. In the 1950s, professional handlers could accept occasional judging assignments, and when Mrs. Clark, then Miss Rogers, did so at a Poodle specialty show in California in 1955, her colleague Tom Stevenson paid her the ultimate tribute to a judge in writing: "Miss Rogers' manner was so courteous and her placings so right that, under her, it was even a pleasure to be left out of the ribbons." Profiled in both the *New Yorker* and *Wall Street Journal,* Mrs. Clark was one of American dogdom's few bona fide stars and shared generously her long, deep experience both in her book, *Annie on Dogs,* and in monthly articles in the *AKC Gazette* and in *Dogs in Review* magazine.

Anne Rogers Clark judged her last assignment, a huge entry of Smooth Fox Terriers, at the great Montgomery County terrier extravaganza in October 2006. She died a little over two months later.

Mrs. Clark is not the only one to have both won and judged Best in Show at Amer-

Anne Clark won Best in Show as a handler three times at Westminster. Her 1959 winner was the black Miniature Ch. Fontclair Festoon, who also became an influential brood bitch.

ica's top show. Frank Sabella, for instance, took the top spot in 1973 with the Standard Poodle Ch. Acadia Command Performance, shortly before retiring as a professional handler, and came back as a Best in Show judge in 1990. Walter Goodman is one of the relatively small number of owner-handlers to ever have won Westminster; he did so in 1969 with his homebred Skye Terrier Ch. Glamoor Good News, then judged Best in Show there in 1994.

Anna H. Whitney, Trailblazer

Anna H. Whitney's background is interesting for several reasons. She was vice president of a splinter group of fanciers who were dissatisfied with the American Kennel Club and formed what was called the National Kennel Club of America. The new organization did not last long, but it is worth noting that the first time Miss Whitney judged at Westminster was in 1888—the same year that the new club was formed. Anne M. Hier suggests, in her *Dog Shows Then and Now* (1999), that Westminster, in an effort to placate Miss Whitney for convincing the National Kennel Club to amalgamate with the AKC, offered her what in effect was a carte blanche to judge at Westminster. Of course, even in those days Westminster and the AKC were not necessarily one and the same, but for whatever reason,

Anna H. Whitney at Westminster in 1897. A breeder of St. Bernards and Pugs, she was one of the leading lights of the National Kennel Club of America, a short-lived AKC rival. In 1888, Miss Whitney was the first woman to judge at Westminster and officiated there sixteen times through 1913.

Miss Whitney continued to judge at Westminster almost every year well into the next century. She was, by all accounts, extremely good at it: at her first assignment, she had an entry of 118 St. Bernards, and according to Hier, she consistently received "rave reviews in the press for her fairness, honesty, and judicial abilities."

Miss Whitney was the first female judge in the United States; in England, a Miss Holdsworth and a Mrs. Jenkins had judged toy dogs at a small show two years earlier. Women gained equal footing with men as judges on both sides of the Atlantic within a few decades, but full representation in national canine affairs took longer. The first female delegates to the AKC were elected in 1974 (they were Carol Duffy, a multigroup judge; Gertrude Freeman, of the Bulldog Club of New England; and Julia Gasow, of the Salilyn Springer Spaniels); the first woman on the AKC Board of Directors, Dr. Jacklyn E. Hungerland, was seated in 1985.

WESTMINSTER BEST IN SHOW JUDGES

No living person has judged Best in Show at Westminster more than once, but in the history of the show a number of judges had that honor several times. Dr. Henry Jarrett judged Best in Show four times at Westminster between 1912 and 1934, and C. Frederick Neilson judged four times between 1926 and 1936. At their first three assignments, however, both acted as a part of a panel, usually consisting of three to five judges, who determined Best in Show at most of the Westminster shows together until the late 1920s. The last two individuals to judge the Westminster finale more than once were Len

The Maltese Ch. Joanne Chen's Maya Dancer, top Toy Dog of both 1971 and 1972, was also Runner-up to Top Dog of all breeds in 1972. Dancer is shown with handler Peggy Hogg winning the International Kennel Club of Chicago that year under judge Len Carey.

The Pekingese Ch. Dan Lee Dragonseed was campaigned in California by John Brown and was among the Top Dogs of all breeds in both 1968 and 1969. He is shown winning Best in Show under judge Beatrice Godsol, with trophy presenters Vicki Draves (far left) and Ramona Van Court. Mrs. Godsol and Mrs. Van Court were among the top judges in America for many years.

Carey, in 1964 and 1974, and William Brainard, Jr., who judged Best in Show three times, in 1958, 1972, and 1976.

Carey owned the Doberman Pinscher Ch. Rancho Dobe's Storm, who won Westminster twice, in 1952 and 1953, making him the only person to have both won and judged the Westminster finale twice. Brainard's Downsbragh kennel was best known for Smooth Fox Terriers and Greyhounds. Another judge who was involved in three Westminster finales was Thomas Carruthers III, who judged Best in Show twice, in 1949 and 1959, after having taken home top honors in 1946 for a Wire Fox Terrier bitch, Ch. Hetherington Model Rhythm, which he owned with his wife.

The first woman to officiate as a Westminster Best in Show judge was Mrs. R. F.

The Westminster Best in Show finale in 2006: judge James Reynolds watches the eventual winner, the Colored Bull Terrier Ch. Rocky Top's Sundance Kid, with the other finalists lined up in the background.

Mayhew, part of the 1928 panel. Five years later, the redoubtable Mrs. Dodge became the first woman to award the top honor as a single judge; only a year earlier one of her Pointers had won Best in Show there, and she would win again six years later with a Doberman Pinscher.

It took nearly a quarter century before another woman was asked to judge Best in Show: Beatrice Godsol did so in 1957 in a memorable performance that launched the career of the great Afghan Hound Ch. Shirkhan of Grandeur. Mrs. Godsol's husband, Major B. Godsol, judged Best in Show at Westminster in 1968, making the Godsols the first husband-and-wife team to have done so. The second and third such couples are Chester F. and Dorothy Collier (2000 and 1997, respectively) and Edd E. and Irene Bivin (1999 and 2003, respectively). The imbalance between the sexes began to level off in the 1970s, and since the late 1980s the otherwise all-male Westminster Kennel

Brace classes were popular at Westminster for many years. They have been discontinued there but are still held at other shows. James Edward Clark is shown winning Best Brace in Show at Westminster in 1968 with the Whippets Ch. Rimskittle Seashell and Ch. Stoney Meadows Sealark. The judge was Major B. Godsol.

Club has had at least as many women as men judges occupy the top spot.

Foreign judges are not often invited to Westminster, and then almost always only at the breed level: the exception was the British all-rounder W. L. McCandlish, who took part in the Best in Show panel in 1926 and then judged the finale alone in 1930. It took seventy-six more years until a judge from outside the United States was given the honor of making Westminster's final decision: the 2006 Best in Show judge was James G. Reynolds from Ontario, Canada. Even at the breed level, it is difficult to find more than very sporadic visits from overseas guest judges.

Over the more than eighty years that Group judges have been recorded at Westminster, only a small number have judged a Group final more than once. Mrs. Clark leads the way, having judged a Group there eight times, followed by Melbourne Down-ing with five. Four judges from the past—Virgil Johnson, Peter Knoop, Theodore Offerman, and Henry Stoecker—judged four Groups. Mrs. Clark is also the only judge to have officiated for all seven AKC groups at Westminster.

JUDGING THE AKC NATIONAL CHAMPIONSHIP

The only current U.S. show that can possibly compete with Westminster in terms of prestige is the much younger American Kennel Club's National Championship event, held in either Florida or California two or three months before Westminster. Two of the Best in Show judges at the AKC show have also judged the finale at Westminster—Frank Sabella and Michele Billings. The first AKC National Championship finale in 2001 was judged in superb style by Dorothy M. Nickles, one of America's most active and popular

The Shih Tzu Ch. Hallmark Jolei Raggedy Andy was Runner-up to Top Dog of all breeds in 2002. He is shown with handler Luke Ehricht and judge Dorothy Nickles, winning Best in Show at Beaumont Kennel Club in 2001.

judges for many decades. At the second AKC show, Best in Show was determined by Constance M. Barton, and in 2006 Robert and Jane Forsyth were honored by determining the outcome of the two most important awards: Mrs. Forsyth judged Best in Show, her husband the Best Bred-by-Exhibitor award. As it turned out, the same dog won both competitions—the Alaskan Malamute Ch. Nanuke's Snoklassic No Boundries. Mr. Forsyth followed his wife as Best-in-Show judge at the next AKC National show, placing the English Springer Spaniel Ch. Felicity's Diamond Jim in the top spot.

From handler to judge: Frank Sabella is one of the few to have both won Best in Show as a handler at Westminster and judged the finale there. He is shown judging the Standard Poodle Ch. Longleat G. Willikers, handled by Michael Pawasarat, in the Non-Sporting Group in 1986.

Few American shows have a greater tradition of inviting overseas judges than the Santa Barbara Kennel Club. In 1995, the Best in Show judge was England's top all-rounder, Terry Thorn, who awarded Best in Show to the Australian Shepherd Ch. Summertime Showdown of Old West. Also in the picture are club officers John Reeve-Newson from Canada, Carmen Visser, and Derek and Gerda Rayne.

BRITISH JUDGES

In the United Kingdom, The Kennel Club does not license judges: it approves each judge for every specific assignment on a one-time-only basis. Even if an individual has awarded Challenge Certificates in a breed in the past, it is not necessarily certain that he or she will be approved if invited to judge that breed a second time. (In practice, once someone has been approved for a breed, he or she is seldom turned down for this breed after that, but it's not automatic.) At intervals, a list is compiled of judges who have been approved to award CCs in a large number of breeds. Although less official than the AKC's annual directory, this list is occasionally published in the dog press, attracting considerable attention.

AWARDING CHALLENGE CERTIFICATES

For many years, no judge was approved to award CCs in all the eligible breeds in the United Kingdom. Throughout the 1980s, the two who judged the most were Joe Braddon and Catherine Sutton, both among the most colorful and brilliant judges of all time. A big personality in a big body, Braddon at his best was an education to watch, and if he ever had an off day, his background and solid experience were such that it was never, ever boring. Like most British all-rounders, Braddon was originally a breeder and exhibitor; his "of Ide" kennel included numerous top Pointers, Spaniels, and later Pugs. Mrs. Sutton was as active as a breeder under the Rossut prefix (famous mostly for

Joe Braddon (right) awarding Best in Show to George Down with his Smooth Chihuahua Ch. Weycombe Antonio, at Hammersmith open show in 1963. Between them is show secretary Harry Jordan. Hammersmith is not a championship event, but all three individuals pictured went on to judge Best in Show at Crufts.

Beagles) and club official as she was as a judge; she died in the mid-1980s at the peak of her career. By the end of the decade, a younger judge, Robert M. James, had been approved to award CCs in more breeds than anyone else. Like Mrs. Sutton, James was primarily a hound man and had a particularly solid background in Whippets, although he had a deep appreciation for all breeds; his premature death was a great loss. These three judges were among the first rank of international experts. Catherine Sutton and Robert James judged on a regular basis in the United States; Joe Braddon did not.

Approximately 150 breeds are now eligible to compete for CCs in the United Kingdom, and the number is rising slowly but steadily each year. Currently, the only judge The Kennel Club has approved to

award CCs in all breeds eligible for them is Terry Thorn. He was well established as a breeder and exhibitor with his Tahawi Salukis and an occasional Greyhound champion in the 1960s and 1970s before rising to the top as chairman of Crufts and as the United Kingdom's premier all-rounder judge. Thorn is also one of the world's most traveled international judges, as familiar with shows overseas as in the UK. His wife, Zena Thorn-Andrews, has been approved to award CCs in almost as many breeds as her husband. She also started with hounds: her Drakesleat Irish Wolfhound and Miniature Wirehaired Dachshund kennel has produced more champions in the UK than any other since records began in 1873 and has had a great impact overseas as well. The only two other judges to have been approved for more than 100 breeds are Ferelith Somerfield, who has a lifetime's experience of show dogs through her family's Oudenarde kennels of mainly Cairn Terriers, and Brenda Banbury, whose primary background has been in Pugs and Schipperkes. Based on the number of breeds they have been approved for, they are followed by Ellis Hulme, Liz Cartledge, Andrew Brace, Michael Quinney, Jean Lanning, and Frank Kane, all of whom have solid backgrounds and great international experience.

AWARDING BEST IN SHOW

To judge Best in Show at one of the general championship shows in Great Britain is an honor reserved for very few people. There are, after all, only a couple of dozen such shows each year, and even the top judges usually award Best in Show barely once a year. Interestingly, one of the most active Best in Show judges, Geoff Corish, is also one of the most successful exhibitors and professional handlers. This could not occur in America, where the division of labor is more strictly defined, but it seems to present no problem at British shows.

There are far more American judges officiating at the top level in Great Britain than the reverse, and more international judges in general. An analysis of the Best in Show finales indicates that nearly 20 percent of these competitions at the biggest shows in the early 2000s were determined by non-British judges. American judges who recently have awarded Best in Show at a top British championship show are Michele Billings, Dr. Jacklyn Hungerland, Dr. Harry Smith, and Dorothy Welsh. Peter Green must also be included in this group. Best known in America as a top handler, Green retired after Westminster 2006 to pursue a judging career. Born in Wales, he has lived in the United States since the 1950s and has been asked back to Great Britain to judge several times. Also among the most popular foreign judges are Hans Lehtinen, Rainer Vuorinen, and Kari Järvinen (Finland), who regularly officiate at the top shows; Ole Staunskjaer (Denmark);

Ch. Blossom Hill Full Circle set new records for both Smooth and Rough Collies, placing among the top Herding dogs in both 2001 and 2002. She is shown handled by her owner and breeder, Mary Wells, at Westminster in 2000 under judge Dorothy Welsh.

In 2005, the Pug Ch. Kendoric's Riversong Mulroney was Runner-up to the Top Dog award for all breeds. He is shown with his handler, Barry Clothier, winning Best in Show at Baltimore County Kennel Club under Pug specialist and all-rounder judge Dr. Harry Smith.

Rodi Hübenthal (Norway); Moa Persson (Sweden); Paolo Dondina (Italy); Luis Pinto-Teixeira and Carla Molinari (Portugal); and Hans van der Berg (Holland), all of whom judged Best in Show at major all-breed championship events. More than forty years after his 1969 Crufts assignment, David Roche came back from Australia to judge Best in Show in Britain, as did another Australian, Peter Luyten. Most of these judges are known around the world and regularly officiate at American shows as well.

It is not possible to analyze the British Crufts judges of the past as carefully as those at Westminster simply because Crufts is so much bigger and has different judges

for almost every breed. In Best in Show judging, however, the development was very similar to Westminster's in the early decades, with a small group of names cropping up every year. There was no real Best in Show award until 1928, but there was judging for Best Champion most years from 1906. Just as at Westminster, the final award was long determined by a panel of judges— three or more individuals sharing the responsibility each year until after World War II. (On at least one occasion it seems that the panel consisted of nine people.) As far as is known, the panel judges never disagreed; in such a case a referee would have to be called, as sometimes still happens when there are separate judges for dogs and bitches and the two cannot agree which one is better. Usually that referee will be the person chosen to judge the Group competition.

The three dominant names into the 1930s were Theo Marples (founder of the still active weekly *Our Dogs*), Harding Cox, and A. Croxton Smith. Two of them, sometimes all three together, participated in almost every Crufts Best in Show (or Best Champion) finale for several decades. Mr. Marples judged Best in Show twelve times in the years from 1906 to 1931. Mr. Cox was on the panel a record twenty-one times between 1912 and 1937, and Mr. Croxton Smith participated as one of the Best in Show judges at Crufts every year from 1930 to 1939, when shows were disbanded for the war. He came back to Best in Show judging for the first four Crufts that were held when dog showing resumed in 1948.

In more recent years, Air Commodore Cecil-Wright, Sir Richard Glyn, and the Earl of Northesk judged Best in Show three times each, and in 1970 Stanley Dangerfield—well known to American exhibitors at the time—was the first to be allowed to determine a Crufts Best in Show finale alone. The one-judge rule became the standard practice from then on.

Crufts also mirrors Westminster in the part women played as early

judges. Mrs. Harry Cowell was a part of the Best Champion panel as early as in 1927, and the great Lorna, Countess Howe, who had won Crufts the previous two years with a Labrador Retriever and would do so once again a few years later, judged Best in Show in 1934. (Countess Howe was announced as Westminster's Best in Show judge in 1938, which would have made her the only judge ever to judge the finale at the world's two greatest dog shows, but for unknown reasons she did not fulfill the assignment.)

In the early years after World War II, two women—Winnie Barber and May Pacey (of the famous Wolvey West Highland White and Sealyham terriers)—dominated the final

Lorna, Countess Howe, one of the most successful dog people ever in England, raised the Labrador Retriever to heights it has not experienced in later years. Countess Howe's Banchory kennels were later successful in Pugs as well, and she is shown here with her Petit Brabançon Binkie in 1936.

The Wolvey kennels of May Pacey were a major force in establishing the West Highland White Terrier as a contender for top awards. They won several Best in Shows, both in England in the 1920s and 1930s and at Westminster in 1942. Mrs. Pacey was one of the leading judges of her day.

FCI JUDGES

It is not possible to compile reliable statistics regarding FCI authorized judges. Currently, there are nearly 8,000 FCI judges, more than 5,000 in Europe (several hundred each in Germany and France), and more than 1,000 in Russia. Japan, surprisingly, in view of its very active dog show community, has fewer than 100 FCI judges. Argentina has only 18 judges, and the following members just 1: Cyprus, Hong Kong, Malta, Monaco, Panama, and the Philippines. Many of these judges travel from one international FCI show to another in different parts of the world for most of the year, and a few have also made a name for themselves in the United Kingdom and America. The invitations to judge Best in Show at FCI's World Show ought to be a good barometer of how highly esteemed a judge is held internation-

awards, co-judging Best in Show together and with others several times.

As Crufts became increasingly international in the late 1990s, the number of foreign judges increased in direct proportion to the participation of foreign competitors. Just as at Westminster in America, overseas judges are almost never invited to judge Groups, although two Australians, David Roche and Harold Spira, have judged Best in Show there. The only two judges to have judged a Group at both Crufts and Westminster, at least in recent decades, are the prominent American sportswoman Mrs. Augustus Riggs IV in the 1970s and, more recently, the Canadian toy dog specialist R. William Taylor. It is still safe to say that no other judging assignment in the United Kingdom is as coveted as a Crufts appointment, although some breed specialists may feel that judging breed club shows is at least as important.

One of the most active foreign judges in both the United States and Canada, Enrique Filippini from Argentina, is pictured awarding Best in Show to the Shih Tzu (Mr. Filippini's own original breed) Ch. Wenrick's Hollywood Hit at the Ottawa Kennel Club in 1999. The handler is Jody Paquette, whose parents, Wendy and Richard Paquette, bred "Woody."

RECENT CRUFTS BEST IN SHOW JUDGES

The list of Best in Show judges at Crufts in recent decades reads like a who's who of the British dog world. Three individuals were in the unique position of having won Best in Show at Crufts prior to being asked to judge the same competition there: Judy de Casembroot (Treetops Greyhounds and Cockers), Bill Parkinson (Blenmar and Daviam Pointers), and Clare Coxall (Tiopepi Poodles). Those who have won Best in Show at other major championship shows before being selected for the ultimate honor of judging the Crufts finale include Thelma Gray (Rozavel Welsh Corgis, German Shepherd

The Afghan Hound Ch. Dzum Pollyanna, a multiple Best in Show winner at Adelaide Royal show in Australia. She is pictured with owner-handler David Roche and judges Ulla Magnus from Sweden (left) and Pamela Cross-Stern from Great Britain. Both Mr. Roche and Mrs. Cross-Stern judged Best in Show at Crufts.

Dogs, and Chihuahuas), Joe Braddon ("of Ide" Pointers and Pugs), Group Capt. "Beefy" and Mrs. Catherine Sutton (Rossut Beagles), Gwen Broadley (Sandylands Labrador Retrievers), L. C. James (Wendover Irish Setters), Robert M. James (Samarkand Whippets), Bill Pinches (Turlshill Smooth Dachshunds), Ann Argyle (Harque Whippets), Ellis Hulme (Tongemoor Papillons), Albert Wight (Sharval Shetland Sheepdogs), and Zena Thorn-Andrews (Drakesleat Irish Wolfhounds and Miniature Wirehaired Dachshunds).

Pamela Cross-Stern is in the unique position of being a second-generation Crufts Best in Show judge: her father, the great terrier man Fred Cross, did so twice in the 1960s. Mrs. Cross-Stern has been involved in several different breeds and won Best in Show with two: her Japanese Chin Ch. Sternroc Dikki was Top Dog of all breeds in 1981, and the Lhasa Apso Ch. Cheska Alexander of Sternroc became the first of his breed to win Best in Show in the United Kingdom in 1973 and also won a Group at Crufts.

ally, but the top award at these shows is invariably determined by a judge from the host country—usually a longtime native judge and club official. This does not mean that the World Show judges are not as well qualified as others, but it is obvious that the top spot on the judges' panel is considered more a reward for services rendered to the sport in general than necessarily an appointment to the best-qualified all-rounder judge.

CHAPTER 6

THE HANDLERS

T aking a dog into the ring at a show—surely that can't be difficult? If you ask the question, it's pretty certain that you have never tried to do so yourself, have never been one of the first-timers who fumble and drop the leash and step on their own toes. Everyone at ringside is laughing at you (or at least it feels that way), you get progressively redder in the face, and the dog tries very hard to get away from you. What happened? That dog looked so good at home!

Two of the greatest handlers of all time, Anne Hone Rogers (later Rogers Clark) and Jane Kamp (now Forsyth), in the early days of their show careers, winning with two English Setters under judge Geraldine Rockefeller Dodge in 1957.

The Lakeland Terrier Ch. Cozy's Mischief Maker lives up to her name in the Group ring at Westminster. Handler Eddie Boyes keeps his cool.

THE CRAFT OF SHOWING DOGS

Actually, showing dogs is a craft. It can be a profession, and it can almost be an art when done really well, so well that it looks as if dog and handler are in perfect unison and the dog enjoys doing exactly what he is supposed to do. This can be a beautiful sight, but it is usually the result of years of work and training.

A dog show is not the most natural place for a spoiled household pet to be, and if you expect your normally well-behaved dog to just walk into a show and act like the champion you always knew it was, you are probably in for a disappointment. Dog shows are chaotic, noisy, and stressful, and even a confident, extroverted dog must

learn to enjoy them. A shy or nervous dog probably will never consider showing to be fun and is better left at home. Dog shows, in fact, constitute a sort of temperament test in themselves; it is very difficult for even a talented handler to make a winner out of a dog that doesn't have a good time.

You also have to realize that the judge only has a couple of minutes to spend on each dog. There is a strict timetable, and however much the judges wish otherwise, they cannot give extra time to a dog that won't stand for examination or that plants all four feet on the ground and won't move. Especially in the United States, the atmosphere is fairly unforgiving. You are supposed to have done your homework before you come to the show, although

Ted Young, the top Cocker Spaniel handler of the 1960s and 1970s, moves the Top Dog of 1972, Ch. Sagamore Toccoa, for the judge.

TEACHING A DOG TO SHOW

To be a show dog, your dog does not have to know anything unusual—it must simply walk happily on a loose leash, not get in the way of the other dogs in the ring, learn to stand for examination, and let the judge get intimate (checking both bite and testicles, if applicable) without protest. The dog must look generally alert and attractive, preferably standing still in the lineup with the other dogs, arching its neck, and looking attentively for a little piece of cooked liver you have hidden in your hand or pocket. There is nothing very complicated about this, but it is amazing how difficult it can be to make the dog's ring performance look smooth and natural. So how do you teach your dog to become a show dog, and how do you learn to become a good handler?

You start with your puppy when it's just a few weeks old—it is practically never

today, as informal match shows are becoming more of a rarity, it is not easy to find a place to train. Many kennel clubs organize handling classes for beginners, and some retired professional handlers travel around the country giving seminars, but the conditions of a "real" dog show are difficult to emulate.

In most other countries, especially those governed by the FCI, the ring procedure tends to be more informal. There are almost no professional handlers, many of the other exhibitors are as new to this as you are, and the judges usually have a more flexible schedule.

The Irish Setter Ch. Meadowlark's Anticipation, a Westminster Group winner, is shown winning Best in Show at Middlesex County Kennel Club in 1981, handled by Elliott Weiss under judge Council Parker.

The Cairn Terrier Ch. Rose Croft Best Foot Forward, one of the top Terrier winners of 1999, is pictured handled by Peter Atkinson winning Best in Show at the Eastern Dog Club that year under judge Dorothy Collier.

too early. At first, all you do is get the puppy used to you (and eventually to other people, including strangers), posing it on the ground or on a table, petting it while holding a hand under its chin. Expect it to stand still for just a couple of seconds before you reward it with a little treat and much praise. The time gets longer; the leash is put on. Some trainers recommend that the puppy should be allowed to lead the way and you just follow wherever the dog goes, in the conviction that this is the way to get a show dog with "go!" Certainly the less dragging and force used the better. Absolutely the worst thing you can do is overtrain or discipline a puppy so much that it starts hating the training sessions. A young dog that does not like showing will never grow up to become a big winner.

The Basset Hound Ch. Slippery Hill Hudson, top-winning Hound of 1975, is shown with handler Bobby Barlow and judge Mrs. Nicholas Demidoff winning Best in Show at Central Ohio Kennel Club in 1974.

Grooming is part of show training: if your breed is normally judged on a table, let the puppy stand on one while it gets used to being groomed and having every part of its body inspected (and make sure it doesn't jump down). Eventually, move your training outside, to the driveway in front of your house, a quiet street or park, or even a shopping center where the puppy can get used to lots of people. Car training is crucial: a dog that has been sick the whole way to the show will be a sad sight in the ring and not likely to win any awards. Always, always encourage the puppy with lots of praise and little treats; it is far better if the puppy is overly exuberant and jumps around a bit than the opposite. As a wise handler put it, "You can always take it out of the puppy later if you need to, but you can't put it back in once you've taken it out." It's an odd paradox: you need a well-behaved, obedient dog that at the same time looks ebullient, as if it's almost jumping with joy.

A last-minute touch-up on the examination table can make all the difference in a coated breed. Sue Vroom puts away the brush, as the Lhasa Apso Ch. Rufkins Bonnie Reight is ready for the judge.

How-to books, training classes, and seminars will teach you and your dog to become a winning team, but the best thing you can do if you are interested in learning is to simply go to dog shows and watch—really watch. Study the top handlers, and follow their every step in the ring.

GOING TO REAL SHOWS

As soon as your dog is trained enough so that at least it won't get in the way of anyone else in the ring, start going to shows. Don't expect to win, just try to have a good time, and make sure your puppy has fun, too. There is so much to look at, for you and your puppy, that you should both be able to enjoy yourselves quite apart from the competitive aspects.

After the first show, the puppy will need plenty of sleep. Don't make the mistake of dragging a young dog to too many shows early in its show career, especially if

One of the top professional handlers for many years, Russell Zimmermann, stands in front of what was the latest mode in dog travel in 1939. According to his advertisement, "This modern equipment will be a familiar sight throughout America, being seen at all the major shows." Zimmermann lived in Van Nuys, California.

Most professional handlers in the United States today work out of motor homes specially outfitted to house dogs. The trend took flight in the 1960s; Jack Dexter's setup includes both the obligatory grooming tables and exercise pens.

the shows are indoors, crowded, and noisy. Once you and the puppy have both learned to enjoy the whole process, you will find that your dog can't wait to get going when you get out the show paraphernalia. In fact, when a show dog's career is over, it can be rather sad to see it wanting to jump into the car with the younger dogs. Some people bring along senior citizens even after they have been retired so they can get a whiff of show business once again.

SHOWING OTHER PEOPLE'S DOGS

At one time, when showing dogs was primarily a rich man's sport, wealthy owners maintained large kennels with a large, full-time staff. It made sense that the kennel managers were often those who handled the dogs at the show; they usually knew the dogs better than anyone else did, and most owners were happy to sit at ringside, bask in the reflected glory of their dogs, and

The West Highland White Terrier Ch. Balinbrae Stonewash Genes, the top-winning West Highland White Terrier 2003 and 2004, shown by Sally George.

accept a silver trophy or two. As the sport became more sophisticated, kennel managers with a flair for displaying their charges might leave the at-home kennel duties to others and focus entirely on showing their employers' dogs—in the process becoming what were, in effect, the first private professional handlers.

As time passed, dog shows became accessible to an increasing number of regular middle-class fanciers. Most of the large kennels dwindled, and as the managers and private handlers saw their jobs disappear, they had to adjust to current realities and start showing other people's dogs—anyone's dog, in fact, as long as handler

The first Norfolk Terrier to win top Terrier in America, Ch. The Duke of Copperplate, was also one of the top dogs of all breeds in 1999. He is shown with handler Larry Cornelius winning Best in Show at Carolina Kennel Club in 2000 under judge Barbara Heller.

The only English Foxhound to win a Group at Westminster, Ch. Mr Stewart's Cheshire Winslow, did so in 1984. He had been the country's top-winning Hound the previous year. The Westminster judge was Thelma Brown, and the handler was George Alston.

The Wire Fox Terrier Ch. Zeloy Mooremaide's Magic, one of the eleven Wire Fox Terriers that have won Best in Show at Westminster. Magic's win came in 1965; like her handler, Jimmy Butler, she was originally from England.

and customer could agree on a price. Many of the great British professional handlers became world famous, especially those in terriers, such as Bobby Barlow, Albert Langley, Ernest Sharpe, Joe Cartledge, Les Atkinson, and Vincent Mitchell. Some of the best, from Percy Roberts in the 1920s to Peter Green a few decades later, moved to the United States and became hugely successful professional handlers, and later judges, at American dog shows.

Today there is barely a handful of professional handlers left in Great Britain. Most people in the United Kingdom now show their own dogs, and many of these owner-handlers are extremely talented. In the United States, the development has gone in the opposite direction: there are no reliable

figures for how many people make their livelihood from showing dogs, but there are several hundred. The Professional Handlers' Association has well over 100 registered members and represents only a portion of the total. If you include all those people whose income is at least partly derived from their handling activities, the number certainly rises into four figures.

TURNING PROFESSIONAL

When they have become established as talented handlers with their own dogs, many people start helping others who are either unwilling or unable to show their dogs—sometimes just for the fun of it, sometimes in return for payment or other services. Some of the most enthusiastic hobby exhibitors manage to pay their own dog show expenses by helping others handle their dogs in the ring on a fairly regular basis. Once you reach that level, you are on your way to semiprofessional status: one day a friend can't get to the show and asks if you would be able to bring his dog, and the money the owner saves by staying home can go into your pocket. In America, where long distances, the price of gasoline, and the large number of shows are major factors, the semiprofessional handler has become a permanent fixture—someone who does not make a living from showing dogs but sometimes accept payment for doing so.

The step from occasionally showing your own or your friends' dogs for fun to becoming a full-fledged professional handler is a big one. It might seem like a very appealing profession for a dog-crazy kid—play with dogs all day and get paid for it, too!—but being a professional handler means getting involved in what must be one of the world's most highly specialized professions, one that on occasion also requires its practitioners to be a jack of many other trades: veterinarian, psychologist, business- and salesperson, chauffeur, auto mechanic, accountant, and artist in residence. You must have an iron physique, capable of functioning on very little sleep; you must be a good traveler, able to adjust to uncomfortable, often cramped, living conditions; and you must have an even temper to be able to deal with recalcitrant dogs, grumpy owners, mean-spirited competitors, and demanding judges. Above all, you must love dogs deeply, not just so they will love you back and want to do whatever you ask of them in the ring, but so much that you want to live with a large number of dogs, twenty-four hours a day, seven days a week for most of the year. Handlers spend much of their lives on the road,

on the way from one show circuit to another, and the brief time they are at home is usually taken up with plans for the next long trip.

An understanding, dog-loving spouse or partner willing to keep the home fires burning while you are away is a vital prerequisite. Alternatively, your partner may also be a handler and come along to the shows, which increases the importance of finding reliable staff to look after the kennel and the dogs left behind. In either case, most handlers must hire assistants, usually star-struck kids who want to be handlers themselves one day. They graduate from picking up after the dogs to grooming and eventually showing the odd dog when the handler has a conflict, such as when two of his charges are being judged in different rings at the same time. Some of the assistants work part time, perhaps just for a limited number of show week-

Most professional handlers start young: Corky Vroom is shown with the Doberman Pinscher Ch. Ziegmers Bali Hi in 1957. Vroom would go on to have the country's top show dog three times in later decades.

TWO DAYS, TWO WINS

Most of the Best in Show wins naturally go to established champions with top professional handlers. An owner-handler with a good dog will often do well, but winning two Best in Shows in two days with a homebred youngster that's not yet even a champion is a rare occurrence. That's what happened to Shelley Kruger and her Whippet Fanfare's Tequila Rose: they won Best in Show from the Bred-by-Exhibitor class at Packerland Kennel Club on April 30, 2005, and then repeated the win at the same club's other show the next day. The judges were Keke Kahn (top) and Lesley Hiltz (bottom). "Cheers" soon became a champion and took more Groups and Best in Show wins.

ends; others live for years with the same handler, learn the trade from the bottom up, and become a part of the family before either branching out as professional handlers on their own or getting back to what may be termed a normal job.

One of the most important tools of the handler's trade is the vehicle he or she drives. Most professional handlers own motor homes, some of a size that incorporates living quarters for several people (in varying degrees of comfort) as well as kennel facilities and crates for a couple of dozen dogs, sometimes more. (To see a flock of these forty-foot-long giants slowly pull onto the grounds for a big show weekend, looking a little like a herd of prehistoric monsters, is to realize what big business dog shows can be.) The expense of buying a motor home is often one of the largest obstacles to establishing oneself as a handler. A

new one can cost more than a small house, not including the retrofitting necessary to make it safe and convenient to travel with a large number of dogs and all the gear that's necessary for their maintenance and show preparation.

At the show, a handler's work starts hours before the judging begins. Dogs must be exercised and sometimes fed (sometimes not, depending on condition and individual habits). Conditioning, grooming, and trimming will have started months before the show for most breeds, but every dog requires a final once-over in the morning before going into the ring with every hair in place. The detailed judging program, which specifies to the minute when the judging of a breed is expected to start, is gone over with a felt-tip marker, so both handler and assistants know exactly when each dog must be ready to go in the ring. A small

One of the most colorful and talented handlers for several decades, Lina Basquette, specialized in Great Danes and is shown on her way to a Group placement at Westminster in 1977 with Ch. Heather of Braeside. Before settling on dogs as her second career, Basquette had danced in the Ziegfield Follies, acted in Cecil B. DeMille and Frank Capra movies, and been married to Sam Warner.

army of handlers and assistants can be seen criss-crossing the show grounds all day, usually with a dog in tow or under each arm, often with a walkie-talkie or cell phone in hand, trying to get to each ring as smoothly and efficiently as possible. That the dogs almost invariably arrive on time is impressive; that they usually look happy and show well is a testament to how well they are treated. Most of the handlers succeed in looking businesslike and well dressed—always jacket and tie for the men, usually skirts for women, never shorts or jeans for anyone.

The fact that most handlers, in spite of tremendous pressure, stress, and a physically demanding job, manage to be upbeat, polite, and even cheerful is something of a miracle. Anyone who has studied a professional handler in full flight at a big show, handling a dozen dogs or so in perhaps as many different rings during the day, will agree that these men and women truly earn their money.

COMPENSATION

Can you get rich showing dogs? It might seem so to an owner who is paying a hefty handling bill, and there is certainly a lot of money floating around at dog shows. Depending on the breed, and not including extra grooming expenses (which are considerable in the long-coated and trimmed breeds), you can expect to pay anything between $50 and $100 for a handler just to take your dog in the ring. That's a lot of money, considering that each dog may

The Whippet Ch. Starline's Sweet Sensation is moved on a loose lead by her handler, Lori Wilson. "Jeep" was one of the top Hounds in 2003 and won fifteen Bests in Show.

The English Setter Ch. Goodtime's Silk Teddy, handler Bruce Schultz, and judge Michele Billings meet the press after a Group win at the Santa Barbara Kennel Club (above). Teddy was one of the top dogs of all breeds in both 1989 and 1990. Below are the backs of photographers Vicky Fox Cook, Missy Yuhl, Joan Ludwig, Rich Bergman, and Jim Callea as they vie for a shot of the winner.

PROFESSIONAL HANDLERS IN BRITAIN

Most top winners in the United Kingdom are handled by their owners, sometimes by their breeders; often the owner and the breeder are the same person. Only a few full-time professionals provide the extra edge that has made American dog shows as much a competition in presentation and showmanship as anything else. However, the long tradition of professional handlers that began in England, primarily in terriers, is still alive. The two best-known contemporary professionals in England, partners since 1985, are Geoff Corish and Michael Coad. It is no coincidence that both are accomplished breeders as well as talented handlers, guaranteeing a degree of involvement in breed specifics not always apparent in their American counterparts.

Michael Coad with the Standard Poodle Ch. Pamplona Something Special, Top Dog of all breeds in the United Kingdom in 1994.

Corish started in West Highland White Terriers in the 1970s, won Crufts for the first time in 1976 with Ch. Dianthus Buttons, and repeated that achievement in 1984 with the Lhasa Apso Ch. Saxonsprings Hackensack. His Sealaw prefix has also graced many Lhasa Apso champions: Ch. Saxonsprings Fresno was owned by Corish for the latter part of her career, retired to the whelping box after winning forty-seven CCs, and produced at least a half-dozen champions.

Michael Coad started in dogs in Ireland and purchased his first great winner from Clare Coxall, the Bichon Frisé Ch. Tiopepi Mad Louie at Pamplona, who won Best in Show at the Scottish Kennel Club championship show in 1986, handled by Corish. Another Bichon, Ch. Si'Bon Fatal Attraction at Pamplona, was Top Dog in 1990, and the homebred black Standard Poodle bitch Ch. Pamplona Something Special took the same title in 1994. The winner of eleven Bests at the major all-breed shows, Something Special ranks among the top all-time winners in the United Kingdom. Her sire, Ch. Härbovis Heaven Can Wait for Vanitonia, was born in Sweden and, among many other champions, also sired the successful show and stud force in America Ch. Maneetas Del Zarzoso Fuego Fatuo—indicating how intensely cosmopolitan the breeding of the top Standard Poodles has become. Coad also won Crufts in 2000 with the great Kerry Blue Terrier Ch. Torum's Scarf Michael, before "Mick" came to the United States.

The 1984 Crufts finale was won by the Lhasa Apso Ch. Saxonsprings Hackensack, handled by Geoff Corish, with Runner-up going to the Pomeranian Ch. Lirevas Shooting Star, owner-handled by Averil Cawthorne Purdy. Center left is Jean Blyth of the Saxonspring Lhasas, next to Kennel Club chairman John MacDougall and judge Molly Garrish of the Fleeting Whippets and Italian Greyhounds.

In 2004, the partners were to the fore again, with Coad showing the imported American Bichon Ch. PaRay's I Told You So to a half-dozen Best in Show wins, making him Top Dog of all breeds. "Buster" had by then already been a top winner in his native country for three years. They also experienced a great deal of success with the Smooth Fox Terrier Ch. Sunrise Rascal Fair. He had flown with his owner, Claire Hoffman of California, to compete at Crufts in 2005, took a Group Second there, and stayed on to become a Best in Show winner, handled by Coad.

spend only a few minutes with the handler, and it includes just the in-ring presentation, not the owner's share in the show and traveling expenses. Many handlers do not accept what are termed ringside pickups in any case, feeling that they need to know a dog better than is possible if they first meet each other just a few minutes before going into the ring together. Certain shows and certain breeds involve greater expense than do others, and there is also a bonus system that means the more the dog wins, the more expensive it gets.

Certainly, the sums brought in by busy, successful handlers over a long show weekend look impressive at first sight. There are always stories floating around of fabulous rewards, sports cars, and luxury cruises paid as bonuses by grateful rich owners after a great win. On one occasion, the owner of a new dog reputedly agreed that the handler, as an incentive, should get a bonus of a dollar for each competitor his dog managed to defeat, and since the dog went on to become a top Best in Show winner, that handler collected a windfall. However, the unvarnished truth is that when expenses are deducted, it must be clear that no one ever became a professional dog handler to get rich.

FROM HANDLER TO JUDGE

The greatest handlers of the past often became the most influential judges of the next generation. Most of the twenty people inducted into dogdom's own Hall of Fame since it was inaugurated in 1986 earned their early stripes as professional handlers, and most became equally influential as judges. Robert and Jane Forsyth, the only married couple to both win Best in Show at

The competition between the top handlers is intense—but hardly as lethal as this photo might imply. Bill McFadden, Kellie Fitzgerald, and Larry Cornelius have fun after the judging is over.

Westminster (he with a Whippet in 1964 and she with a Boxer in 1970), became one of America's most respected judging couples. Their contemporary, Anne Rogers Clark, won Best in Show at Westminster three times and was as commanding a figure in the ring when she was a handler as she later was as a judge. William Trainor, Michele Billings, Ric Chashoudian, Maxine Beam, and Peter Green were all professional handlers turned judges. Dick Cooper, a wizard with the sporting breeds, and George Ward, another of the great terrier handlers, were unusual in that they remained professional handlers all their lives. Jimmy Moses, the youngest of the Hall of Fame inductees, is of a different generation and remains active as a German Shepherd Dog handler after more than two decades of unparalleled wins. The only owner-handler in the Hall of Fame is Pat Trotter of Vin-Melca Elkhound fame.

THE OWNER-HANDLER

As noted above, in most parts of the world the normal state of affairs is for an owner to show his or her own dog. America is different, and the owner-handler faces overwhelming odds. There are good reasons that the professionals reap what may sometimes seem, at least to the defeated owner-handler, like more than a fair share of the wins. To begin with, it is logical to expect that people whose livelihood depends on an ability to present dogs in a manner that impresses judges should be good at their profession; if not they would be forced to find other work. They must also possess an advanced knowledge of grooming and conditioning that can be difficult for nonprofessionals to match.

In some ways, the handlers' success is self-perpetuating: winning handlers are likely to be offered their choice of the best young dogs to show. Since their professional future depends on how well they assess a dog's potential, they cannot afford to look at future show prospects through rose-tinted glasses, the way a loving owner

The Dalmatian Ch. Four-in-Hand Mischief set new standards for his breed by becoming one of the top Best in Show winners of any breed in the late 1930s. He was bred and owned by Leo Meeker in California but shown by Harry Sangster.

Left: The Welsh Terrier Ch. Anasazi Annie Oakley, top Terrier in 1985 and one of the top dogs of all breeds, was shown by Clay Coady and is pictured winning the Group at Westminster the following year. The judge was Kenneth McDermott.

Below: Best in Show at Westminster in 1979 was the Irish Water Spaniel Ch. Oak Tree's Irishtocrat. He is pictured handled by William Trainor to one of two Group wins at Westminster, this one under judge Elsworth Howell.

might if the dog sleeps on his couch. Professional handlers get many opportunities to practice, bringing dogs into the ring hundreds, even thousands, of times each year, gaining much more experience than most amateurs can ever hope to get. As a fringe benefit, an observant professional handler will also, after many years and hundreds of shows, have some inside knowledge of the different judges' likes and dislikes in the various breeds, which makes it easier to pick the right dog for each judge. *Of course* professional handlers usually win more than the amateurs do—that's why they are professionals!

Nevertheless, owner-handlers have a few advantages, too. Foremost among them is the fact that as an owner-handler you can focus on a single dog: you don't have to worry about several dozen clients whose dogs you are showing. You don't have to deal with their hopes and wishes and their individual quirks or priorities, and you are not dependent on them for your livelihood. Because your dog has your undivided attention, you can train it better and condition and feed it on a more individual basis than most kennels can. If you do everything right, the dog will respond by showing with more sparkle and enthusiasm than any other. The bond between handler and dog is never as strong as when the handler is also the dog's closest friend. That bond may be invisible to a nondoggy outsider, but it is easily apparent to anyone who knows dogs. At its best, it can result in the kind of charismatic ring performance that will make it difficult for anyone—least of all the judge—to take his eyes off your dog.

As an owner-handler, you will also be able to tailor your dog's show career exactly

Akita breeder-owner-handler B. J. Andrews takes Best in Show with Ch. The Widow-Maker O'BJ under judge Dorothy Nickles. A ten-time Best in Show winner, Widow-Maker sired sixty-five champions.

The Miniature Pinscher Ch. Rebel Roc's Casanova von Kurt remained one of the top Toy dog winners for a record five years, winning seventy-four Bests in Show between 1959 and 1963. Handled by his owner and breeder, E. W. Tipton, Jr., "Little Daddy" was Runner-up to Top Dog of all breeds at his peak in 1961. He also sired scores of champion sons and daughters.

The Komondor Ch. Lajosmegyi Dahu Diga, handled by owner and breeder Patricia Turner to a Group win at Westminster in 1993 under judge Irene Bivin.

George Bell, a top owner-breeder-handler of Salukis in the 1970s and 1980s, moves one of his top winners, Ch. Bel S'mbran Aba Fantasia.

as best suits you and the dog, without concern for where anyone else wants you to go. Your dog will be of a breed that you are obviously interested in, so you have the opportunity to learn more about that breed than most professional handlers will ever know. You can also learn more about the judges in that breed, about your competition, about where to find the best shows for your specific purpose than most handlers can—all of which will help level the playing field.

Even in the best of circumstances, it won't be easy to make your mark as an owner-handler, but when you win, the satisfaction of having done it all on your own is difficult to match. The best professional handlers and the best owner-handlers all learn from each other. The mutual respect that often develops in spite of the intense competition in the ring can be one of the most rewarding aspects of your dog's show career.

Early Successes

In spite of the obvious handicaps and an increasing reliance on professional talents in recent years, owner-handlers have scored some memorable wins in the toughest American competition.

The outstanding example was for many years provided by Patricia Craige Trotter, who burst on the scene in the 1960s with her Norwegian Elkhounds. One of the very few owner-handlers to win the award for Top Dog of all breeds, Mrs. Trotter showed a contender for the top honors most years for the quarter century she remained active at this level. She has shown dogs she herself bred and owned (sometimes in partnership with other fanciers) to ten Group wins at Westminster—more than any other owner-handler and much more than most full-time professionals. Mrs. Trotter must without question be considered America's most successful owner-handler.

One particularly impressive aspect of Mrs. Trotter's success in dogs is that she worked as a schoolteacher during her most active career. Some owner-handlers enjoy the luxury of being able to spend most of their lives going to dog shows, without the encumbrance of having to maintain a full-time (or even part-time) job. Not so Mrs. Trotter: regardless of her dog show activities during weekends, she was back in front of her students on Monday morning. In a 2004 interview with the author, Mrs. Trotter pointed out that maintaining a full-time job and achieving dog show success at the highest level was not easy in the past and may no longer even be possible because campaigning a top show dog today has virtually become a full-time occupation in itself.

As an example, Mrs. Trotter mentioned two of her own dogs. When she won Top Dog with Ch. Vin-Melca's Vagabond in 1970, he went to about 75 shows, won fifteen Bests in Show and forty-one Hound Groups, earning a little over 31,000 points for defeated competitors. That was an impressive record, but twenty years later, Ch. Vin-Melca's Calista had to go to almost twice as many shows, win forty-five Bests in Show and

The Norwegian Elkhound started to gain national attention in the late 1960s, and in 1970, Ch. Vin-Melca's Vagabond was Top Dog of all breeds, handled by his owner and breeder, Patricia Craige Trotter. They are shown winning Best in Show at the Santa Barbara Kennel Club under judge Derek Rayne in 1970.

Owner-handler Amanda West's French Bulldogs had a long streak of success in the 1950s and 1960s. West's most successful dog was the homebred Ch. Ralanda Ami Francine, who won at least fifty-five Bests in Show and was among the top dogs of all breeds for three years in the early 1960s.

almost one hundred Groups, and defeat more than 80,000 competitors to get as far as the Number Two of all breeds. That pace has not slackened in recent years; some of the top dogs go to as many as 200 shows in a year.

Mrs. Trotter's Vagabond is not the only owner-handled dog to take home the Top Dog spot of all breeds, however. In the 1950s, one of Mrs. Trotter's inspirations was the English Setter Ch. Rock Falls Colonel, winner of 100 Bests in Show and Top Dog in both 1952 and 1953, who was handled to all his wins by his owner, William T. Holt. The Afghan Hound Ch. Kabik's The Challenger was Top Dog in 1982 and won Westminster the following year, handled by his owner and breeder, Chris Terrell. In 1989, the Bulldog Ch. Hetherbull Bounty's Frigate was owner-handled by Jean Hetherington to the Top Dog spot at a very young age—he had not yet turned two at the end of his winning year!

Very few people have been consistently successful showing their own dogs over many years.

Terriers have traditionally been more heavily dominated by professionals than most, but Walter Goodman created a stir in the early 1960s with his two Skye Terrier bitches, Ch. Evening Star de Luchar and Ch. Jacinthe de Ricelaine, both imported from France and both among the Top Ten dogs of all breeds. A few years later, he did even better with his homebred dogs, including Ch. Glamoor Good News, who won Westminster in 1969. In the Non-Sporting Group, Amanda West and her French Bulldogs were a force to be reckoned with for at least a decade around that same time: her Ch. Ralanda Ami Francine placed among the Top Ten dogs for three years in a row. The success of the Flakkee Keeshonden shown by past professional handler Porter

Skye Terriers came to the forefront in the early 1960s, largely through Walter Goodman's French imports and their offspring, carrying the Glamoor prefix. Ch. Jacinthe de Ricelaine was owner-handled by Goodman to thirty-five Bests in Show and placed among the top Terriers for five years.

The Keeshond Ch. Flakkee Sweepstakes, the top Non-Sporting Dog of 1967 and 1968 and Runner-up to Top Dog of all breeds in 1968, owner-handled by Porter Washington.

Washington for his wife, Dickie Doheny Washington, in the 1960s and 1970s was even more impressive. Their biggest stars were Ch. Flakkee Sweepstakes (Number Two of all breeds in 1968) and a Pomeranian, Ch. Rider's Sparklin' Gold Nugget, the only dog shown by the Washingtons that was not a Keeshond. This celebrated Pom was one of the country's Top Ten dogs of all breeds for three years in a row.

LATER SUCCESSES

In later years, the small group of consistently successful owner-handlers at the top level—meaning exhibitors whose dogs placed among the Top Ten of all breeds more than once—has included Debbie Butt,

The Pomeranian Ch. Rider's Sparklin' Gold Nugget had the distinction of being the only non-Keeshond shown by Mr. and Mrs. Porter Washington's Flakkee kennels. Porter Washington showed Gold Nugget to a spot among the Top Ten dogs of all breeds for three years in the late 1950s.

who took over the career of the family's great Whippet Ch. Sporting Fields Clansman when his regular handler, Bob Forsyth, retired to become a judge in 1980. She also showed Clansman's great-grandson Ch. Sporting Fields Kinsman to a spot among the top dogs in 1992. Thomas Oelschlager ("Tommy O") and his Siberian Huskies Ch. Kontoki's One Mo' Time (1987) and Ch. Kontoki's E-I-E-I-O (1995), Sandra D'Andrea and the Alaskan Malamute Ch. Nanuke's Take No Prisoners (1997), and Karen Black with her Saluki Ch. Sundown Alabaster Treasure (1999) are other owner-handlers who have placed among the Top Ten dogs of all breeds.

The most consistently successful owner-handler in the late 1900s and early 2000s, however, has been Jere Marder and her Lambluv Old English Sheepdogs. Starting with Bahlambs stock in the 1970s, Mrs. Marder has shown her dogs to a spot among the top Herding dogs for many

years, hitting the all-breed Top Ten in 1997 with Ch. Lambluv's Desert Dancer and winning the Herding Group at Westminster with two different dogs, Desert Dancer in 1998 and Ch. Lambluv Moptop Show Stopper in 1991.

Some later Top Dog winners can also boast of having been at least in some sense owner-handled. For instance, the Standard Schnauzer Ch. Parsifal di Casa Netzer, Top Dog 1996 and Westminster Best in 1997, was co-owned by Rita Holloway, whose handler husband, Doug, also showed "Pa." In this case, however, it was more a question of a professional handler who also was one of the winning dog's "family members." In fact, in recent years the owner-handler definition has become increasingly vague. Some full-time handlers are lucky enough to get paid, by a co-owner or sponsor, to show the dog they also own. If you don't need to work beyond dog shows, or if your hobby does not incur any expenses, it does not

Jere Marder has experienced great success as an owner-handler of Old English Sheepdogs, including two Group wins at Westminster. In 1998, she won with Ch. Lambluv Desert Dancer under judge J. Donald Jones.

The Great Pyrenees Club of America specialty in 1985 was judged by James Bennett and won by Ch. Karolaska Bristol Bay, owner-handled by Carol Kentopp. Bristol Bay was a multiple Best in Show winner and sired more than thirty champions.

OWNER-HANDLERS AT WESTMINSTER

Westminster, a show that is frequently, but not quite fairly, considered a playground for the top professionals, has seen some major success for owner-handlers from different parts of the country in recent years. At the 2006 show, for instance, Keith Carter from Georgia showed his Rottweiler Ch. Carter's Noble Shaka Zulu to become the first of his breed to win the Group at this show. The Sporting Group that same year was won by the Golden Retriever Ch. Chuckanut Party Favour O Novel, shown by co-owner Ken Matthews from Bellingham, Washington, and the Herding Group was won by the Old English Sheepdog from Colorado Ch. Bugaboos Big Resolution, shown by his breeders' and co-owners' son, Colton Johnson (who is admittedly a professional handler as well.)

One of the most successful owner-handlers in the early 2000s, Keith Carter, with his Rottweiler Ch. Carter's Noble Shaka Zulu. They won the Working Group at Westminster in 2006.

make the wins any less impressive, but it is obviously more difficult for the person who has a full-time job outside the dog show world to compete.

SHOW DOG OF THE YEAR AWARD

One way of assessing a handler's success is to add up the number of times he or she has shown dogs that won what used to be called the Quaker Oats award, now named the Show Dog of the Year award and presented in February each year since 1954 to the dogs that won the most Group Firsts in each of the AKC-recognized variety Groups during the preceding year. Based on these criteria, and including both professional and ama-

teur handlers, Jimmy Moses has been by far the most successful, winning sixteen times, all with German Shepherd Dogs, between 1984 and 2005. Peter Green won nine times with terriers and is followed by Richard Cooper (eight wins, mostly with the Salilyn English Springer Spaniels) and Dennis McCoy (seven wins, most of them with Standard Poodles). Dennis's partner, Randy Garren, is included in six of the wins; both have since retired as handlers and have turned to judging.

Patricia Craige Trotter won seven times as an owner-handler with her Norwegian Elkhounds; Porter Washington won six with the Flakkee Keeshonden (and one Pomeranian); Michael Kemp won six times with breeds as diverse as a Wire Fox Terrier and a Bichon Frisé; George Ward won five times with terriers. Two contemporary toy dog handlers have won five times each: Luke Ehricht with Shih Tzu and David Fitz-patrick with Pekingese. An old-time handler who was active long before the awards existed, Harry Sangster, won five times toward the end of his career in the 1950s. The early Toy Poodle exhibitor Robert Levy won an impressive six times with his own dogs, Ch. Blakeen King Doodles and Ch. Loramar's I'm A Dandee.

Going one step higher, it is possible to limit the analysis to a select group of people who have handled more than a single Top Dog of all breeds since the early 1950s.

The bond between handler and dog can be strong. Jimmy Moses and the top Herding dog in 2005, German Shepherd Dog Ch. Kenlyn's Tenacity of Kaleef, have a pep talk.

Among those are the two great terrier specialists Peter Green and Ric Chashoudian. Green has shown four different terriers to five such wins (a Sealyham, a Wire that won twice, and two Norwich Terriers); he was also heavily involved in a sixth winner, the Norfolk Terrier shown by his partner, Beth Sweigart. Chashoudian showed three different terriers that won in the 1960s and 1970s before he turned to judging: a Wire Fox, a Kerry Blue, and a Lakeland. Jimmy Moses handled three different German Shepherd Dogs to Top Dog, of which two won not once but twice. The great Poodle handler Frank Sabella took two Miniatures and one Standard to Top Dog of all breeds in the short span of a few years in the 1960s, and Corky Vroom handled three dogs of three different breeds—a Doberman, a Grey-hound, and a Bouvier des Flandres—to Top Dog between 1973 and 1990. Most remark-ably, these three latter dogs all had the same owners, Mr. and Mrs. Nathan Reese.

In addition, Clara Alford showed the great Pekingese Ch. Chik T'Sun of Caver-sham to Top Dog for three consecutive years in the 1950s. Robert and Jane Forsyth both won Top Dog in the 1960s, he with the Whippet Ch. Courtenay Fleetfoot of Penny-worth and she with the Boxer Ch. Arriba's Prima Donna. Michael Kemp showed one dog, the Wire Fox Terrier Ch. Registry's Lonesome Dove, to the top spot two years in a row in the early 1990s, and so did Den-nis McCoy with the Standard Poodle Ch. Lake Cove That's My Boy later in the same decade.

Early in the twenty-first century, the Show Dog of the Year awards, announced in New York before Westminster, introduced two separate categories for Best Handler in

In 2005, the Pekingese Ch. Yakee If Only was Top Dog of all breeds, handled by David Fitzpatrick, after having been runner-up to the top spot the previous year. They are pictured winning Best in Show at the International Kennel Club of Chicago in 2005 under specialist judge R. William Taylor from Canada. At left is Louis Auslander, the man behind the International's success.

their annual polls, one for professionals, the other for owner- (or owner-breeder-) handlers. The first couple of years saw Bill McFadden and Michelle Ostermiller win the professional categories. The former won Westminster in 2003 after having taken the great Kerry Blue Terrier Ch. Torum's Scarf Michael to Top Dog the previous year; the latter became the first handler ever to win consecutive Bests at Westminster with two different dogs, a feat she achieved in 2004 and 2005 with the Newfoundland Ch. Dar-

bydale's All Rise PouchCove and the German Shorthaired Pointer Ch. Kan-Point's VJK Autumn Roses. Wendell Sammet of the Alekai Standard Poodles was best owner-breeder-handler in 2004, and Jere Marder of the Lambluv Old English Sheepdogs won the owner-handler category the following year. In 2006 David Fitzpatrick, of Pekingese fame, won the professional handler award, while Sandra D'Andrea of the Nanuke Alaskan Malamutes won among the owner-handlers.

One of the greatest show dogs of all time, the Kerry Blue Terrier Ch. Torum's Scarf Michael, on the move in California.

JUNIOR HANDLERS

There are no age restrictions for dog handlers: the only requirement is that the handler must be able to get around the ring at the appropriate speed (which varies from breed to breed) and capable of controlling the dog in the ring. In fact, in few other occupations are people of such diverse age groups involved in the same activity, competing on equal terms.

However, young and less experienced exhibitors are often at a disadvantage, and it was for this reason—and to ensure the education of future generations of dog show handlers—that what is now termed Junior Showmanship was established. Children would compete with other children and be evaluated on their handling abilities. In other words, the handlers, not the dogs, are judged.

The founding father of Junior Showmanship in the United States was Leonard Brumby, Sr. A successful professional handler, Brumby convinced his local club, Westbury Kennel Club in Long Island, New York, to organize the first Children's Handling class at its 1932 show. The maximum age was initially fourteen years; no minimum age was stated. The idea caught on quickly, other shows followed suit, and by the following year the competition was divided into one class for children under ten years, another for children over ten and under fifteen years of age. This was later amended to the current requirements: a Junior class for boys and girls at least nine but under twelve years old on the day of the show; an Intermediate class for those at least twelve but under fifteen years old; and a Senior class for teenagers at least fifteen but under eighteen years old. The dog shown must be owned by the junior handler or by a member of the junior's household or extended family.

In 1933, Westminster Kennel Club was one of the first clubs to sponsor Children's Handling classes. Even in the first year, participation at Westminster was limited to juniors who had won at least one first place at another show during the preceding year. As in the regular competition, the urge to compete at Westminster has led to further restriction. Participants must now have placed first in ten or more Junior Showman-

The Junior Showmanship finalists at Westminster in 2000: the winner was Nicholas Urbanek (with Pointer), followed by Lindsay Balder (with English Springer Spaniel), Carley Simpson (with Golden Retriever), and Ryan Wolfe (with Cocker Spaniel). The judge (left) was Frank Sabella.

The International Junior Handler competition at Crufts in 2007 had finalists from thirty-seven countries participating. The winner was Adell Brancevich (center) from Latvia, showing a Pointer; second was the United Kingdom's representative, Emma McLaughlin (right), with a Papillon; and third was Juan Miranda (left) from Mexico, also showing a Pointer. The judge was Bo Bengtson, USA; at right is Stephen Rendu, representing the sponsor, Pedigree.

ship Open classes, with competition present, during the year preceding entry. Still, more than 100 junior handlers usually compete at Westminster.

In addition to age, Junior Showmanship classes are divided by experience. The Novice class is open to all competitors who have not won three first-place awards with competition present in this class; the Open class is for those who have won their way out of the Novice class. If at least two class winners are present, the club may offer a Best Junior Handler award.

The early Children's Handling classes were often judged by a local celebrity with no particular knowledge of dogs or handling. The awards naturally would often be based more on perceived cuteness of dog and child than on handling talent. This resulted in an involvement by the Professional Handlers Association, which had been formed in 1926, with Brumby as its first president. For many years, it was primarily professional handlers who judged the Junior Showmanship classes (as the Children's Handling was renamed in 1951). The the AKC did not grant official recognition to Junior Showmanship until 1971, and when AKC stopped licensing professional handlers in 1977, only AKC-approved judges could officiate—some approved for many breeds and groups as well as Juniors, others specializing in Junior Showmanship judging only.

In the United Kingdom, the early support for Junior Handling classes in the 1960s came from one of the top judges, Judy de Casem-broot, and the great handler Joe Cartledge. There has been an annual competition for Junior Handler of the Year in the United Kingdom since 1970. In 1984, under the expert guidance of Joe Cartledge's widow, Liz Cartledge, this developed into the international handling competition at Crufts, which rivals that of Westminster for prestige and excitement. The finale, now incorporating young finalists from more than thirty different countries, has become a big draw with the general public. There is also the Young Kennel Club, which offers separate awards for conformation handling as well as for other activities (for example, obedience and agility). Junior Handling classes soon became popular at dog shows in other countries as well, with the competition at some of the World Shows having become every bit as intense as that at Westminster and Crufts.

As noted earlier, some of the greatest handlers did not shine as juniors. Anne Rogers Clark famously told how she did not excel in this type of competition and went on to concentrate on the adult competition instead, with spectacular results. Other of the early Westminster-winning juniors, however, had brilliant careers as professional handlers in mature years—notably George Alston, the 1954 winner. In later years, Teresa Nail and Valerie Nunes both won the Westminster Junior Showmanship competition before going on to successful adult handling careers. Clint Livingston, who won the International Junior Handling finale at Crufts in 1988, and Simon Briggs, who did the same one year later, are now among, respectively, America's and Australia's most successful handlers.

The top junior handlers can compete internationally: Juan Miranda qualified for and participated in the Junior Handling finales at both Crufts in England and Westminster in the United States, and he won the finale at the World Show in his native Mexico in 1999 under British judge Liz Cartledge. Now a judge, Juan judged the Junior Handling competition at the 2007 World Show. He is shown with the Afghan Hound Ch. Karamoor Llacue's Edelweiss at Westminster.

CHAPTER 7

THE BREEDERS

A dog breeder, according to the most basic definition, is any person who owns or leases a bitch and raises a litter out of her. No great talent is necessary for this, just a modicum of familiarity with animal husbandry and a lot of hard work.

However, when dog people talk about breeders, they mean much more than that. A real breeder is an idealist who works for decades, often for a lifetime, to produce a family of home-bred dogs of such consistent soundness and beauty, with excellence of breed type and temperament to match, that their quality is apparent to all within the fancy. A talented breeder will produce dogs with a particular look recognizable as coming from this particular kennel.

To achieve this goal, the breeder must have a clear view of what he or she is trying to accomplish and great perseverance against overwhelming odds.

German Shepherd Dog breeders Gloria Birch (left) and Cappy Pottle, of Covy-Tucker Hill's fame, in the 1980s.

WHAT IT TAKES TO BE A BREEDER

In many ways, a true breeder is like an artist, but instead of marble or oil, the medium is living flesh. At the least, it takes months—more often years—before you can evaluate your efforts, but the work can never be put away, mistakes cannot easily be wiped out, and the raw material one is working with needs constant attention and care. What a person achieves as a breeder is never permanent and keeps changing, sometimes for the better and sometimes not, sometimes thanks to one's efforts and sometimes in spite of them. As soon as the breeder succeeds in improving one feature, a different one begins to slip, and getting all the pieces of the puzzle right in even a single dog—let alone an entire family—is *almost* impossible.

While having lofty goals and a high degree of idealism, the breeder must also be able to function on the most basic, down-and-dirty practical level. Breeding dogs is not for the squeamish. It often involves an uncomfortably close acquaintance with blood, bodily fluids, and other organic materials, both from the reproductive and the digestive systems. It is possible to hire help for some of the dirty work, but to get the most out of the dogs a breeder needs to know every single one of them intimately, almost literally inside and out. There is nothing like sitting up at night with a bitch that is having puppies to show you the wonder of birth and realize what a perilously close line there is between life and death, the beginning and the end. No breeder with a few years under his belt will be spared tragedies, which are always close to the daily experience of anyone involved

Hundreds of champions in many countries descend from the Dreamridge kennels, primarily American Cockers but also English Toy Spaniels. Breeder Tom O'Neal is shown circa 1980 with a group of hopeful young Cockers.

in dogs. Being able to rebound from them is an important ingredient in success.

A breeder has to be ready to act as veterinarian and midwife, surrogate mother if anything goes wrong, nutritionist and trainer, geneticist, psychologist—and even psychic. Being able to predict the future for a prospective show puppy is an invaluable but somewhat elusive talent. Each year, thousands of promising show prospects turn out less well, conformation-wise, than had been hoped, while some that were deemed less likely to succeed and sold as pets grow up so handsome that they could become champions if given the opportunity.

Arlene Butterklee and two Gingery Chinese Cresteds (a Powderpuff and a Hairless). Since the breed first started competing at AKC shows in 1991, more than 150 Gingery Cresteds have won the AKC champion title.

The Chelsea breeding program has produced well over 100 Whippet champions in the show ring since the mid-1980s and more than 20 field champions as well. Breeder Deann Christianson is pictured with Ch. Chelsea Gold Rush of Keynote, the breed's top sire for several years in the early 2000s, and his half sister Ballad.

Rick Tomita and two Jacquet Boxer puppies. There have been more than 200 AKC champions from the Jacquet kennels, and there have been many more champions abroad as well.

THE INVISIBLE PLAYER

The breeder is the foundation of the dog fancy. Without breeders, there would be no dogs, and without dogs, there would be no kennel clubs, no dog shows, no judges, no handlers, no dog food companies, no dog publications—in short, no dog sport at all.

In spite of their vital importance, breeders are easily the least visible segment in the sport, often the most admired, sometimes the most criticized, and always the most misunderstood. When all goes well, the whole world will flock to the successful breeder's door, but even the best ones have their critics. Since breeding activities, for obvious reasons, are conducted in the privacy of the home, away from prying eyes, it is easy for rumor and legend to take wing. There is no set pattern to reach the top, and

exactly why one breeder succeeds while another fails is the subject of much speculation within the dog fancy. Very few breeding kennels employ an open-book policy, happily sharing their methods with anyone; most prefer to keep their secrets to themselves. A few talented individuals seem to deliberately nurture an image as brilliant hermits, lonely souls isolated from the rest of the world and dedicated to the pursuit of excellence in dogs to the exclusion of almost everything else.

Although some breeders like to show their own dogs, especially in the early stages of their careers, the shows are not the primary interest for most: they usually have dogs at home, puppies growing up or an expectant mother who can't be left alone. Because they are rarely interested in breeds

John Buddie with six champion Tartanside Rough Collie bitches, all tracing back to the kennel's foundation sire, Ch. Tartanside the Gladiatior, a Best in Show and three-time national specialty winner in the 1970s.

Karen Staudt Cartabona in the 1970s with a few of the 350 champions that have come from her Majenkir Borzoi kennel.

Jeffrey Pepper, with the Petit Basset Griffon Vendéen Ch. Pepperhill's O'Henri. There have been more than 100 Pepperhill Golden Retriever and PBGV champions.

other than their own, breeders are more likely to congregate at specialty shows than anywhere else. When they appear at all-breed events, even the greatest breeders are seldom immediately recognized by the rest of the fancy, in spite of the fact that they may have achieved worldwide fame through the dogs they produce. A true breeder is perfectly happy if his kennel name is better known than his own, and most breeders prefer to leave it to others to reap the glory of their work at the shows: handlers who present the dogs they have bred and owners with the means to campaign these dogs as they deserve. The breeder is busy at home, raising the next generation and planning the one after that, trying to figure out how the stars of the future can shine even brighter than those of today.

THE TRUE INCENTIVE

Because breeding dogs is hard, dirty, and often lonely work, often fraught with disappointment and sometimes tragedy, why do people breed dogs at all? It certainly is not for the money. Nobody ever got rich from breeding top-quality dogs, although many outsiders think it's possible. It may seem to be a good economic investment to breed from your bitch and watch the dollars roll in; after all, a single puppy can bring anywhere from $1,000 to $2,000, sometimes more, depending on breed (and breeder). However, once you realize just how much time, expense, and labor is involved in raising a litter, the financial incentive will weaken. There is a stud fee to be paid, the cost of transporting the bitch to the most suitable dog (which may live a great distance away), and all the expensive health testing that conscientious breeders subject their dogs to on a regular basis. Add to this the possibility that the bitch may not have any puppies at all or that there may be problems requiring veterinary intervention during the whelping or the following eight or ten weeks until the puppies can leave the nest. The cost of showing and bringing one's breeding stock to such prominence that the public—serious fanciers and pet buyers alike—becomes interested in buying the puppies must be considered. Anyone who raises a litter should be satisfied if the puppies are all in good homes by two months of age and if the income from puppy sales covers basic expenses. The endless work is unpaid, literally a labor of love.

Lou Ann King with a group of her Loteki Papillons in the 1990s.

The appeal of breeding dogs comes from something less tangible but every bit as important as money: the satisfaction of having, in effect, created a living being. By selecting this particular bitch to be bred to that specific dog, you are having an impact on the future of the breed with which you are involved. The puppies are the result of your decisions, and if you repeat the process many times over a period of years, you can have a profound effect on that breed. This is a huge responsibility: you are helping produce sentient beings, each of which will probably live for ten to fifteen years and must be able to function first as a healthy, happy family companion. In the best of cases, it should also become a successful show dog, and perhaps later a producer of future generations. The most inveterate ribbon-chaser will agree that soundness of mind and body is paramount. Even a heavily campaigned dog spends only a small part of its life at shows, and basic humane aspects aside, it is clear that dogs need to be both healthy and happy to do well in the show ring.

THE CONSCIENTIOUS BREEDER

The basic fact of life that in each litter there will almost always be more puppies than the breeder is willing to keep, that they live for many years and demand far more from life than commercial livestock, is an undeniable obstacle for an ambitious breeder who wants to get to the top as quickly as possible. The more you breed, the greater the chances are that you will hit the jackpot and produce a superstar, but every single dog you produce has as much right to a good life as any other.

How breeders deal with this reality varies widely. Some feel that once the sale is final, their responsibility is over, but for a conscientious breeder finding a good, permanent home for every puppy is one of the greatest and most difficult responsibilities. Few breeds offer an unlimited supply of such homes waiting for each puppy; in some breeds the prospective buyers are as scarce as hen's teeth. Even in the popular breeds in which there is a steady demand for pets, no reputable breeder would hand over a puppy to anyone willing to pay the price without subjecting the prospective buyer to a close interrogation about past dog experience, home conditions, and plans and long-term goals for the puppy. Access to a fenced yard and someone who stays home most of the day can determine whether there will be a sale. In fact, if you are considering buying a puppy and the breeder does *not* ask a number of questions, it's a pretty sure sign that this is not a conscientious breeder. In many ways, the puppies are part of the breeder's family, and ideally, sending a puppy to a new home does not end the relationship. All good breeders will offer the new owner help and advice after the sale and provide help in an emergency later in life as well.

BECOMING A BREEDER

How do you become a breeder? It usually starts with a bitch. You love your girl and feel the world would be better off with a few more like her. If she is healthy, happy, and handsome, you may be right—but don't trust your own opinion. Purebred dogs are among the most closely scrutinized of all animals for health problems, and it is wise to check with your breed's parent club to find out what medical screenings are advisable. Needless to say, the prospective

Myrtle Klensch produced a long line of top-winning Manchester Terriers of both sizes over many years. Her top winner was Ch. Salutaire Surely You Jest, top Toy Dog and among the Top Ten of all breeds in 1986. They are shown winning a Group at the Ventura County Dog Fanciers Association in 1985 under judge Tom Stevenson.

sire should have passed all the required health tests as well.

As for happy and handsome, you know better than anyone else how well adjusted and easy to live with your future brood bitch is, but if you really want her to contribute to the breed, you should talk to someone with considerable experience in your breed—preferably a judge or another experienced authority. Unless your bitch has a show or performance record to fall back on, it may be difficult to justify breeding from her. In some cases, a long, hard look at your bitch may result in the decision that, as much as you love her, perhaps it's just as well not to try for a litter from her—and seek a better one from a top breeder instead. If you want to be successful, being able to separate your brain from your heart is of paramount importance. Many breeders waste years by starting out with a less-than-outstanding foundation bitch.

In the 1950s and 1960s, the English Seagift kennels of Dorothy Whitwell produced more Whippet and Greyhound champions in both England and America than did any other kennel. This group of Whippet champions was photographed in 1955; several of them were later exported to the United States.

CONTROLLING NUMBERS

After you have successfully raised your first litter, found that you enjoyed the process, and decided that you want to get seriously involved in breeding dogs, that's the time to decide if you want a kennel. Many of the best breeders don't have any real kennel facilities; for most, it is simply a matter of keeping a couple of bitches in the kitchen, perhaps fixing up a guest room for the puppies and part of the garage for the adults. The temptation to keep too many dogs is always a factor. You should keep at least one daughter of your first bitch from which to breed on. You may acquire an additional brood bitch; you may want to run on some youngsters to see how they develop; and you may even plan to get your own stud dog. At this stage, keeping a male is usually neither a smart idea nor a necessity. You need bitches if you want to breed, but excellent-quality males are usually available at public stud. With your own stud dog, it's too easy to use him simply because it's convenient, even when he may not be the ideal choice for your bitch. You must also cope with the hassles of raging hormones whenever any of your bitches are in season.

A few years after your first litter, you often realize that you have too many dogs and too little space and that some changes need to be made. The neighbors may complain; perhaps a city or county ordinance limits the number of dogs you are allowed to keep. Your choice is either cutting down the number of dogs or moving out into a real kennel in the country. In the former instance, co-ownerships are an increasingly popular method to stay involved with a minimum number of dogs at home. Even a cursory look at any show catalog, especially in America, will indicate that a very high percentage of the dogs are listed as having two, three, or even four owners and breeders. It can be a convenient, practical way of sharing the joys as well as the disappointments and the expenses of the dog world with other people.

Many of these partnerships develop into close, lasting friendships, but exactly what everyone wants to get out of the joint responsibilities must be clearly spelled out from the start. Some breeders use intricate, multipage legal contracts to guard themselves against disagreements, but there is no way to predict all eventualities, and differences of opinion are all too common. If you care so strongly about a puppy that it would be a tragedy if you lost it in a conflict with a co-owner, it makes good sense to simply keep it—even if you are short of space.

ESTABLISHING A KENNEL

It is on such occasions that having your own kennel facilities may be the solution. Starting a real kennel is a major step, involving considerable planning, expense, and added responsibility, but it can be a very rewarding lifestyle if you are able to live in the country and have the resources to provide a number of dogs with good facilities. Big kennels were a feature of the past more than they are in the present. Wealthy owners maintained vast establishments, sometimes with more than 100 dogs on the premises, complete with a kennel manager and a uniformed staff of kennel help. It has become customary to regret the demise of the grand kennels of the past, but there is no question that the dogs in many of those kennels were often treated more like cattle than like the pets they have become today. Some of those kennels relied for their success on what was euphemistically called culling (which meant that any puppy or dog not up to the kennel's standard was put down). Many of today's kitchen-variety kennels provide a much better environment for the dogs and foster a deeper personal relationship between people and canines than most large establishments can ever hope to do.

A hundred champions is an impressive record for any kennel. In Great Britain, where champion titles are more difficult to achieve than elsewhere, the first kennel ever to reach this milestone was Drakesleat, owned by Zena Thorn-Andrews. This occurred in 2005; most of the champions were Irish Wolfhounds or, in recent years, Miniature Wire Dachshunds.

A kennel can consist of anything from a few dogs in the kitchen to a professionally planned building just for the dogs. Few private kennels were as carefully designed as the Grandeur kennels, owned by Roger Rechler during the last three decades of the 1900s.

In a best-case scenario, however, life in a kennel can be very good for the dogs. They have the company of their own kind, their own space indoors and out, and usually lots of activity to keep them interested. Two modern kennels that stand out in different respects can serve as examples.

The Grandeur Afghan Hounds were inherited by Roger Rechler after the death of the original owner, Sunny Shay, in 1978. Rechler, a real estate investor, built a show kennel in Dix Hills, Long Island, which in every respect was worthy of its top-winning residents, a long line of champions coming down from the 1957 Westminster winner Ch. Shirkhan of Grandeur. Finished in 1984 at a reported cost of over a million dollars, the two-story structure of concrete and glass block was located on over five acres, with steeply angled paddocks for isometric exercise. A staff of four looked after the twenty-odd canine residents. The kennel included a separate puppy room, office, and bathing and grooming area, with closed-circuit cameras throughout and special dog-drying cabinets that could bring an Afghan Hound in full show coat from wet to completely dry in twenty-five minutes. There were indoor-outdoor practice rings, complete with bleachers, to train the youngsters in show ring procedure. Michael Canalizo was hired as full-time kennel manager and for nearly two decades showed the Grandeurs to more than 300 Best in Shows, climaxing with the great Ch. Tryst of Grandeur, America's top hound for four years during the late 1990s. The kennel was closed down just a few years later, although both Rechler and Canalizo maintain an active interest in dog shows.

Whereas Grandeur was a small, private show kennel, Skansen Kennel in California

Sylvia Hammarström is most likely the world's most successful breeder, based on the number of champions produced. At her Skansen Kennel in California, she has bred well over 1,000 champions, mostly Giant Schnauzers. Sylvia is shown with the Giant youngsters Skansen's Charles de Gaulle and Skansen's American President and the Swedish-born Great Dane Diplomatic's Nora Jones.

is very different altogether. One of the few big breeding establishments of note in America, it was started by Sylvia Hammarström in her native Sweden and established in Sebastopol, outside San Francisco, in 1964. It now consists of a 100-acre ranch where, on most days, a visitor can see, in addition to other animals, as many as 100 Schnauzers, mostly Giants, including puppies and young stock. The dogs live in big, open half-acre fields, two or three dogs together, and there is constant activity, with many visitors coming and going, eight kennel girls working nonstop, and enough

Shows in Europe often feature classes for Breeders Teams, as represented by this winning quartet of Badavie Salukis from Sweden at the 2006 FCI World Show in Poznan, Poland. Runners-up that day were the famous Finnsky Skye Terriers from Finland (left); third were the Rhodesian Ridgebacks from the Tina Trading kennel in Russia.

At the same show, another Swedish kennel topped the Breeders Team competition during the last day's competition: the Almanza Flat-Coated Retrievers. The judge was Tamas Jakkel.

experiences and challenges to keep any dog on its toes.

For those who are used to thinking of kennels in terms of a dozen dogs and two or three litters per year, the Skansen experience may come as a shock: about fifty annual litters have been produced on a regular basis for many years. For anyone expecting the usual long, narrow concrete runs and the unmitigated boredom of many large boarding kennels, Skansen feels like a breath of fresh air. Dealing with so many puppy buyers and providing backup services and help is pretty much a full-time job. Skansen is extremely professionally run, with a strict daily regimen that keeps every dog occupied. There is a clear price list: $800 for a pet puppy, $1,300 for a good-quality pet, and $2,300 for a pick-of-litter show puppy, guaranteed to become a champion. The price includes an eighty-page Schnauzer manual, three ninety-minute audiocassettes about routine care and training, a one-hour videocassette showing how to tape ears, a kennel information booklet, and newsletters with nutritional information for both dogs and humans. The kennel is never expected to make a profit. Skansen has bred more champions than any other kennel in the world, more than 1,000 in all, among them the all-time top Giant Schnauzer winners in America and numerous Best in Show winners around the world.

Most kennels are neither as luxurious as Grandeur nor as expansive as Skansen. You can succeed extremely well with more modest facilities and fewer dogs, as proven year after year by top dogs that have been born and bred in a talented and dedicated small breeder's kitchen or bedroom.

Marjorie Butcher's Pembroke Welsh Corgi kennel produced more than 100 champions. One of her top winners was Ch. Cote de Neige Pennysaver, shown winning Best in Show at the Kennel Club of Philadelphia in 1967, owner-handled by Mrs. Butcher under judge Albert Van Court. The trophy presenter is William Kendrick.

EVALUATING BREEDERS

Although there are many ways to rank the top show dogs, there is no way to reliably assess the relative merits of the breeders. There are too many variables: is it more impressive to have a small kennel that produces a consistent stream of nice dogs, including an occasional superstar, or one that is larger in scope and able to seriously affect the whole breed in a positive way? There is no way to compare the two, and in any case, at least in America, the data necessary for studying each kennel's activities are not available to anyone except the breeder and the AKC. There are also many other questions that are difficult to answer. Does the breeder keep the dogs in a healthy environment? Does he or she deal ethically with puppy buyers? What about health testing? Did the dogs achieve their big show ring successes handled by their owners or with the help of a professional handler? In what sort of competition were the kennel's wins achieved? Just having produced a large number of champions does not necessarily prove much.

AMERICA'S MOST SUCCESSFUL BREEDERS

Despite the difficulty of comparison, few would disagree that the two most successful breeders of the twentieth century in America—in the sense that they raised their respective breed to a new level of competitiveness—were the Salilyn English Springer Spaniels and the Vin-Melca Norwegian Elkhounds. There had been top-winning English Springers before Julia Gasow established her breeding program in the 1930s, but no other kennel has produced such a consistent stream of contenders for the Top Dog spot for as many years as Salilyn Kennels of Troy, Michigan. The total adds up to more than 400 Best in Show wins, starting with the first one, Ch. Sir Lancelot of Salilyn, in 1945. Those who placed among the Top Ten dogs of all breeds are: Lancelot's grandson Ch. King Peter of Salilyn (Number Two of all breeds 1953), Ch. Salilyn's Macduff (Number Two of all breeds 1959), Ch. Salilyn's Aristocrat (Number One of all breeds 1967), Ch. Salilyn's Classic (1974–1975), Ch. Salilyn's Hallmark (1978–1979), Ch. Salilyn's Continental (1979), Ch. Salilyn's Private Stock (1982), Ch. Salilyn's Condor (Number Two of all breeds 1992, BIS Westminster 1993), and Condor's daughter Ch. Salilyn 'N Erin's Shameless (BIS Westminster 2000). Condor's pedigree shows judicious linebreeding to Aristocrat through his grandson Classic, with the use of top stud dogs from other kennels, prima-

Julia Gasow of the Salilyn English Springer Spaniels had one of the longest and most successful careers of any breeder, producing Best in Show winners for more than sixty years, including two Westminster Best in Show winners.

rily Ch. Telltale Author (by Aristocrat) and Ch. Filicia's Bequest (by Classic).

The Vin-Melca situation was very different. For the most part, Patricia Trotter's kennel was kept quite small—if not of the kitchen variety, then nearly so. For another, although the Salilyn dogs, at least in later years, were always presented by professional handlers, the Vin-Melcas were almost invariably owner-handled. There had been an occasional top-winning Elkhound before the 1960s, but Mrs. Trotter took what had essentially been an overlooked, nonglamorous breed and succeeded in making it a real contender in all-breed competition.

What was even more impressive was that she stayed close enough to the original type in Norway to satisfy a succession of Scandinavian breed experts who came over to judge the national specialty and awarded both praise and high honors to Vin-Melca-bred dogs. (This is one area in which Salilyn and Vin-Melca differ: the Springer Spaniels in America have long differed greatly in type from their British ancestors.)

The first to make the ratings was Ch. Vin-Melca's Howdy Rowdy in 1968, but the big breakthrough came with his half brother Ch. Vin-Melca's Vagabond (Number One of all breeds 1970), followed by several others who placed among the Top Ten of all breeds: Ch. Vin-Melca's Valley Forge (1975), Ch. Vin-Melca's Nimbus (Number Two of all breeds 1978), Ch. Vin-Melca's Calista

America's top owner-breeder-handler, Patricia Craige Trotter, with the dog that first brought her to the top, Ch. Vin-Melca's Vagabond, Top Dog of all breeds in 1970. Vin-Melca Norwegian Elkhounds have been among the year's top Hounds twenty-nine times in all!

(Number Two of all breeds 1990), and Ch. Vin-Melca's Bombadier (1992). There is also an unprecedented line of ten Westminster Group wins and many more recent champions, although Mrs. Trotter no longer campaigns her own dogs since she began judging in the early 1990s. An analysis of the annual statistics indicate that Vin-Melca champions placed among the top ten hounds twenty-nine times between 1968 and 2003.

Not surprisingly, the only two breeders ever to be inducted into dogdom's own Hall of Fame—an honor usually reserved for judges, handlers, and club officials—were Julia Gasow in 1986 and Patricia Trotter in 1990.

ACCREDITED BRITISH BREEDERS

The United Kingdom does not currently have any awards or contests to distinguish Britain's top breeders. However, The Kennel Club introduced a new program in 2004 that, although it will not tell which breeders produce the most winners at the shows, should prove useful for prospective puppy buyers who want to purchase healthy, sound pets. To participate in the so-called Accredited Breeder Scheme, a breeder has to agree to the following basic requirements:

- Compliance with Kennel Club registration requirements
- Permanent identification of breeding stock
- The use of relevant official breed-specific health checks on breeding stock
- The provision of advice to new owners on issues such as feeding and worming, exercise, puppy socialization and training, and immunization measures
- The use of a sales contract

TOP STUD DOGS

The record for the most champions sired by any dog has been held since the 1970s by the English Springer Spaniel Ch. Salilyn's Aristocrat. He is credited with 188 AKC champion sons and daughters.

The second-highest number of champions sired comes from Aristocrat's contemporary, the Norwegian Elkhound Ch. Vin-Melca's Howdy Rowdy, with 166 AKC champions to his credit.

It is difficult to compile records of the top show dogs, but it's almost impossible to compile a list of the top stud dogs and brood bitches. No official statistics are kept, and although various organizations and publications on occasion attempt to rate the top producers, the work involved is almost overwhelming, especially in the United States, where the number of dogs involved is so large.

The usual way of assessing a stud dog's success is by the number of champion get he has sired. With more than 20,000 new champion titles awarded each year at AKC events, the figures change all the time; but it is generally acknowledged that, on the basis of these criteria, the top stud dog ever in AKC competition was the English Springer Spaniel Ch. Salilyn's Aristocrat, who sired 188 champion sons and daughters. His closest rival was the Norwegian Elkhound Ch. Vin-Melca's Howdy Rowdy, who is credited with 166 AKC champions.

Both these great stud dogs were born in the 1960s. It is impressive that their records have not been surpassed several decades later, particularly in view of the much greater number of champion titles awarded in recent years and the increasing use of artificial insemination with stored, frozen semen, which makes it possible for a stud dog to continue siring puppies indefinitely, even after his own death.

Among those dogs that have sired around 150 AKC champions are the Shetland Sheepdog Ch. Halstor's Peter Pumpkin, the Rough Collie Ch. Fantasy's Bronze Talisman, the Standard Poodle Ch. King's Champagne Taste, and the Doberman Pinscher Ch. Cambria's Cactus Cash, of which at least the latter three, born in the late 1980s or 1990s, might possibly surpass the all-time record. Several dozen other stud dogs have more than 100 AKC champion offspring to their credit, not counting additional titleholders in obedience or other activities or champions in Canada and other countries.

Since the champion title is several times more difficult to achieve, statistically speaking, in the United Kingdom than in the United States, the number of champions in the United Kingdom is much smaller and therefore more easily processed. According to current statistics, the stud dog with the highest number of Kennel Club champions to his credit is the Labrador Retriever Sh. Ch. Sandylands Mark, born in 1965, who sired twenty-nine titleholders in the United Kingdom alone. The closest contenders are the Golden Retriever Ch. Camrose Cabus Christopher and the Beagle father-and-son duo Ch. Dialynne Gamble and Ch. Soloman of Dialynne, each with twenty-six champions. Others with more than twenty UK champions to their credit are the English Springer Spaniel Sh. Ch. Hawkhill Connaught; the Irish Setters Sh. Ch. Kerryfair Night Fever and Sh. Ch. Caspians Intrepid, another sire-and-son combination; the English Setter Sh. Ch. Latest Dance of Bournehouse; the Airedale Terrier Ch. Jokyl Gallipants; the Scottish Terrier Ch. Kennelgarth Viking; the Bull Terrier Ch.

The top stud dog in the United Kingdom, sire of a record twenty-seven champions according to Kennel Club records, was the Labrador Retriever Sh. Ch. Sandylands Mark.

Souperlative Jackadandy of Ormandy; the Afghan Hound Ch. Amudarya Shalar; and the Smooth Dachshund Ch. Silvae Sailor's Quest. All these are from the second half of the twentieth century; easily the top sire of the first fifty years of recorded British dog show history was the Wire Fox Terrier Ch. Talavera Simon, sire of twenty-one champions in the United Kingdom as well as a large number overseas, including America.

For obvious reasons, it is much more difficult for a bitch to exert as much influence over a breed as a popular stud dog: the latter may sire more than a hundred litters, depending on breed, whereas few bitches owned by responsible breeders produce more than three or four.

There are, of course, many other ways of assessing the top producers' influence than simply by their number of champion offspring. Getting a clear picture of a dog's producing ability requires knowledge of the less-than-outstanding winners and of how high the percentage of top winners is, and of course a keen awareness of all-important and less easily measured characteristics such as the temperament and health of the dog's offspring.

One of the United Kingdom's most successful breeders of Deerhounds, Nora Hartley (right), shown in 1950 with eight of her Rotherwood hounds at home at Fletton Tower, Peterborough.

- Agreement to act as a point of contact for their new puppy owners in case problems arise once the puppy has gone to its new home

None of these points is different from what would be considered desirable for a good breeder in the United States; the difference is that The Kennel Club is publicizing a formal list of positive practices. Obviously, an important aspect of the scheme is a policing system that can check for breeder compliance. The program is still in its infancy, but approximately 1,200 breeders have already joined and agreed to comply with the requirements.

Some other countries have different types of competitions, ratings, and awards. Sweden, for instance, has both a contest for top breeder each year and a separate award,

England's top breeder of Samoyeds in the pre–World War II era, Miss M. Keyte Perry of the Arctic kennels.

the Hamilton plaquette (named after the Swedish Kennel Club's founder, Count A. P. Hamilton), which has gone to a handful of deserving breeders each year since the early 1900s, somewhat along the lines of the much newer AKC award.

Carol Harris has bred well over 300 champion Italian Greyhounds and Whippets, including many Best in Show winners. She is also a top breeder of Quarter Horses at her Bo-Bett Farm in Florida.

BREEDER OF THE YEAR

In the early 2000s, the American Kennel Club started an initiative to honor a Breeder of the Year at its annual Invitational show. The criteria state only that "[t]his award is bestowed on individuals who have dedicated their lives to improving the health, temperament and longevity of their breed," but surely success in conformation judging is also a major concern. The nominees must have a dog entered in the Bred-by-Exhibitor competition at the show where the award is made. The first five winners of this prestigious award are David and Peggy Helming of PouchCove Newfoundlands (the only kennel to be nominated twice so far), Cathy Nelson of Pennywise Dandie Dinmont Terriers, Mary Rodgers of Marienburg Doberman Pinschers, Wendell Sammet of the Ale Kai Standard Poodles, and Douglas and Michaelanne Johnson of the Bugaboo Old English Sheepdogs.

One of the most interesting attempts to encourage breeders was made through *Kennel Review* magazine's Tournament of Champions, which included a special class for teams of homebred dogs. In 1991, the last year of the competition, the Breeder of the Year award went to the Black Watch Lakeland Terriers of Jean Heath and William H. Cosby. The judge at far left is Max Magder from Canada, at center is Dr. David Doane, and at right is Darryl Martin.

Left: Cathy Nelson handles her home-bred Dandie Dinmont Terrier. Right: In the early 2000s, the American Kennel Club started an award for Breeder of the Year. The 2005 winner was Cathy Nelson of the Penny-wise Dandie Dinmont Terriers, here showing Ch. Pennywise Matilda of Ride-out to Best of Breed at Westminster in 2001 under judge Elliott Weiss.

Breeder-owner-handlers don't often go to the top at Westminster. Chihuahua breeder Linda George won the Toy Group in 1991, under judge Sari Tietjen, with her homebred Smooth dog Ch. Ouachitah For Your Eyes Only.

(Breeder of the Year cont.)

The Alaskan Malamute Ch. Nanuke's Take No Prisoners was the top Working dog in 1997 and Runner-up to Top Dog of all breeds. He is shown with his breeder and owner, Sandra D'Andrea, winning Best in Show under judge Vernelle Kendrick at Bucks County Kennel Club.

The list of nominees for the AKC's Breeder of the Year award for the first five years includes Douglas Johnson (Clussexx Clumber Spaniels), Karen Staudt-Cartabona (Majenkir Borzoi), William and Rebecca Poole (Rocky Top Bull Terriers), Margery Shriver (Sheffield Pugs), Roberta Lombardi (Rufkins Lhasa Apsos), Michele Ritter (Britannia Bearded Collies), Sandra Bell (San-Jo Cocker Spaniels), Gayle Bontecou (Gaylewards Scottish Deerhounds), Patricia Turner and Anna Quigley (Lajosmegyi Komondorok), Dale Adams (Chindale Japanese Chins), Cody T. Sickle (Cherokee Bulldogs), Tom and Nioma Coen (Macdega Shetland Sheepdogs), Helen Szostak (Grousemoor Flat-Coated Retrievers), Patricia Trotter (Vin-Melca Norwegian Elkhounds), Capt. Jean Heath and William H. Cosby, Jr. (Black Watch Lakeland Terriers), Tom O'Neal (Dreamridge English Toy Spaniels), Joseph Vergnetti (Dassin Poodles), Jere Marder (Lambluv

Old English Sheepdogs), Melissa Newman (Setter Ridge English Setters), Damara Bolté (Reveille Basenjis), Barbara Miller (Max-Well's Norfolk Terriers), Linda George (Ouachitah Chihuahuas), Janina Laurin (Chateau Blanc Belgian Tervurens), Judy Colan (Colsidex Weimaraners), Susan LaCroix Hamil (Quiet Creek Bloodhounds), Sandra D'Andrea (Nanuke Alaskan Malamutes), Beverly J. Verna (Regency Miniature Schnauzers), Jose Cabrera and Fabián Arienti (Starfire Pomeranians), and Kathy and George Beliew (Imagine Chow Chows).

In 2005, *Dogs in Review* magazine began honoring outstanding breeders, with a nominating committee selecting five annual nominees based on an intricate list of requirements and the dog fancy voting for the final selection. The winners of the first award were the PouchCove Newfoundlands of Peggy and David Helming, of Flemington, New Jersey, who started breeding in 1968 and since then have bred or owned some 275 champions, including many top winners abroad and the 2004 Westminster winner, Ch. Darbydale's All Rise PouchCove. The other nominees were Judith M. Russell (Karnovanda Siberian Huskies), Jon Woodring and Wade S. Burns (Lanbur Beagles), Paula Pascoe (Lehigh Scottish Deerhounds), and Anne H. Bowes (Heronsway Pembroke Welsh Corgis). The 2006 winner was Joseph Vergnetti of the Dassin Poodles, mentioned above; his fellow nominees were Cindy Butsic (Northwind Lhasa Apsos), Sandra D'Andrea (Nanuke Alaskan Malamutes), Doug Hoffman (Broughcastl Pugs), and Doug and Michelanne Johnson (Bugaboo Old English Sheepdogs and Rocheause Bouviers des Flandres).

One of many top-winning Norfolk Terriers from Barbara Miller's Max-Well's kennel, Ch. Max-Well's Weatherman was among the top Terrier winners in both 1996 and 1997. He is pictured with his handler, Susan Kipp.

Best in Show at Westminster in 1996, the Clumber Spaniel Ch. Clussexx Country Sunrise, shown with handler Jane Alston-Myers, judge D. Roy Holloway, and trophy presenters Ron Menaker and Chester F. Collier.

THE KENNEL NAME

Choosing a kennel name is usually one of the lighter decisions, although not one without significance, since it will follow the breeder through the years and ideally serve to identify his or her dogs. Anything easily recognizable, distinctive, and preferably short will do. Most kennel clubs worldwide limit the number of letters used in a registered dog's name, so a long kennel name allows less space for each dog's individual name. It is easy to guess that Salilyn is derived from the name of an early beloved dog (Sally Lynne). Vin-Melca comes from a combination of the breeder's maiden name (Vincent) and the names of two of her first dogs, Melody and Candy, and Skansen is a popular tourist destination in Sylvia Hammarström's native Sweden.

In most countries, a kennel name must be approved and registered by the national kennel club and then cannot be used by anyone else. Exactly how many kennel names the FCI maintains in its register is not known, but the total is well into six figures. In the United States, the situation is slightly different: only a small number of prefixes are registered (and therefore protected) by the AKC, so any other name or names can be used in a dog's name without any kennel registration requirement. This explains how the same kennel name can be spelled differently in different dogs' names and how on occasion more than one kennel name can be part of a dog's name—sometimes it can, in fact, be difficult to tell which part of the name is a kennel name. It can become confusing when two well-known breeders unbeknown to each other are using the same kennel name—although this is not likely to occur in the same breed.

In the United States, once a dog has been registered by the AKC, its name cannot be changed. However, in the United Kingdom it is possible to change a registered dog's name to include a new owner's kennel name, provided the dog is still young and has not yet won any major awards. The breeder's kennel name is used as a prefix, the new owner's as a suffix. (As an example, the Whippet Ch. Hardknott Maestro of Bohem was bred by Hardknott Kennels in the United Kingdom, and the author's Bohem suffix was added after the puppy was transferred to new ownership.)

DISHONESTY AND ITS CONSEQUENCES

The paperwork for maintaining a breeding kennel is considerable but important: the AKC basically relies on the honesty and good faith of each individual breeder when it comes to vital matters such as birth dates, parentage, and the number of puppies born in a litter. There is little reason for most breeders to cheat, and with DNA testing a practical reality, the risk of discovery would in any case be great.

In a couple of instances, the AKC has taken action against breeders who demonstrably falsified pedigrees. One such case bordered on the ludicrous. A Whippet breeder, the late Walter Wheeler of the Windsprite prefix in Sherborne, Massachusetts, announced in the 1970s that he had discovered the long-lost gene for long coat in Whippets and had managed to produce purebred longhaired dogs of this breed. The Whippet has traditionally been smooth-coated for many decades, and investigation proved that Mr. Wheeler's longhaired dogs were the result of surreptitious crossing with other breeds (reportedly primarily small Borzoi and Shetland Sheepdogs). The dogs with falsified pedigrees were deleted from the AKC registry, and Mr. Wheeler was expelled from membership in the American Whippet Club.

More serious was the case of the Banchory Shetland Sheepdog kennels of Clare and Donna Harden. Banchory was a prolific and successful breeding operation in the 1970s and early 1980s, with numerous top producers and national specialty winners to its credit. The influence of its stud dogs was great, but rumors of unethical breeding practices and questionable pedigrees dogged the kennel for years. Most of the controversy centered on an outstanding male, Ch. Banchory Formal Notice, and on a few brood bitches that had been placed in a co-ownership by Donna Harden. The co-ownership turned acrimonious, and as AKC requires that all co-owners of the bitch must sign the litter application, the Hardens could not register litters from these bitches. Apparently, to get around this, they reregistered the bitches under different names and continued to breed them. In 1983, after an in-depth investigation, the AKC charged the Hardens with falsely registering dogs and suspended them permanently from organized AKC activities. Registrations for a number of Banchory dogs were canceled, and the AKC was forced to publish a number of corrections in its stud book. Because some of these Banchory dogs had been used for breeding outside the home kennel, other breeders suffered as well, and to make matters worse, Formal Notice was stripped of his national specialty win when it turned out that his ownership had been incorrectly registered. The Hardens, no longer able to remain active in

The win that wasn't. The Shetland Sheepdog Ch. Banchory Formal Notice is pictured after winning the American Shetland Sheepdog Association's national specialty in 1977. The win was later disallowed for technical reasons.

show dogs, were last known to have taken up breeding show cats.

Since there is little financial incentive, it is difficult to imagine anyone becoming involved in owning, breeding, and keeping show dogs without a strong and abiding affection for animals. Most dogs that live with hobby breeders are lucky in that they get expert care and attention; they probably live more active and interesting lives than many bored, lonely suburban pets; and they usually have the advantage of proper facilities that make their lives comfortable. Anyone who is in charge of animals must be aware that they are, in effect, an extension of their owners. Usually that's an advantage, and it is every breeder's and kennel owner's responsibility to make sure that is always the case.

CHAPTER 8

THE BEST OF BRITAIN

T he names of the clubs that hosted dog shows in Great Britain in the late 1800s make it clear that these events were originally planned as part of general livestock exhibitions: the North Yorkshire Horse and Dog Show Society; the Shropshire and West Midland Agricultural Society; the Liverpool Dog, Poultry, Pigeon, and Cat Show; and many others with similar names. Most of these early shows are long forgotten, but others are still held on a regular basis. Of the shows that featured only dogs, the oldest, of course, is the Birmingham Dog Show Society, which is still going strong. The Manchester Dog Show Society is only a couple of years younger (founded in 1861) and received championship status soon after the formation of The Kennel Club in 1873. The Scottish Kennel Club, the Ladies Kennel Association, and the Sountern Counties Canine Association all had their beginnings in the late 1800s, and all still hold annual major championship shows over a century later.

Probably the most successful British dog show exhibitor ever, H. S. Lloyd, won Best in Show at Crufts six times with his Cocker Spaniels between 1930 and 1950, in spite of a hiatus in show activity during World War II. Lloyd is shown with his 1948 winner, Sh. Ch. Tracey Witch of Ware, and Mrs. Cruft.

THE KENNEL CLUB AND EARLY SHOWS

Officially recorded dog show history began when The Kennel Club gave permission for its rules to be used at fifty-one dog shows in 1897. At this time, The Kennel Club also made a distinction between the elite events—championship shows—and the rest of the British shows. This was an important decision, and since it is at championship shows that the most important action takes place, all the following refers to all-breed championship events only unless otherwise specified. The seventeen all-breed championship shows held that first year were: Derby, Liverpool, Leicester, Manchester, Dublin, Royal Aquarium (Pet Dog Show), Armagh, Limerick, Strabane, Darlington, Nottingham, Birkenhead, Edinburgh (Scottish Kennel Club), Crystal Palace (Kennel Club), Belfast, Birmingham, and Crufts. The Dublin and Limerick shows were, of course, held in what is now the Republic of Ireland, which had not yet achieved independence from Great Britain.

The results of breed judging at those early shows were recorded in the annual Kennel Club Stud Book, but competition between dogs of different breeds was still in its infancy. In the late 1800s, a cup for the best-conditioned dog at the show was awarded at Crufts and won for three years running by an Irish Setter owned by the show's president, Sir Humphrey de Trafford. At that time, club officers could still exhibit at their own shows, which would not be considered acceptable today. A Best Dog in the Show was awarded at some shows from the start, but just what it meant was not quite clear for many years. Some clubs did not offer any such competition at all; others did but did not necessarily broadcast the results—and in any case, it took several decades before Best in Show developed into a logical elimination of previously undefeated class winners through breed and Group competition until only one winner was left standing. Dogs that had been defeated in their class during the breed judging could compete for Best in Show later the same day; others might participate in spite of having bypassed the breed competition entirely. Obviously Best in Show did not necessarily mean then what it does today.

That such dogs could be considered eligible for, and sometimes even win, the Best in Show award did not make sense to most exhibitors, but the rules were not changed until after the "considerable controversy" (to quote Theo Marples) that occurred at Crufts in 1935. At this show, a Pointer, Pennine Prima Donna, was declared Best in Show without ever having competed for Best of Breed; another Pointer had, in fact, won some of the challenge trophies offered to Best Sporting Dog. The owner of the dog that was awarded Reserve Best in Show, the Chow Chow Ch. Choonam Hung Kwong, not unreasonably lodged a protest. Although the results from that show stood as awarded, new rules were introduced to ensure that only dogs that had competed and remained undefeated in their breed classes would be allowed to participate in further competition. In view of the above, many of the early Best in Show awards—which really often just denote a winner of a trophy offered to the Best Champion in the Show or something similar—have to be taken with a grain of salt.

UNITED KINGDOM: ALL-TIME TOP BEST IN SHOW WINNERS

Minimum five times Best in Show at general championship shows as recorded 1901–2006 (an asterisk indicates additional wins in 2007):

Afghan Hound Ch. Horningsea Khanabad Suvaraj, six BIS (1961–1963)
Airedale Terrier Ch. Ginger Xmas Carol (imp. Italy), six BIS (1985–1986)
Airedale Terrier Ch. Jokyl Gallipants, seven BIS (1983)
Airedale Terrier Ch. Riverina Tweedsbairn, seven BIS (1960–1962)
Akita Ch. Redwitch Dancin In The Dark, six BIS (1996–1999)
American Cocker Spaniel Sh. Ch. Misticolas Over the Moon with Afterglow, five BIS (1994–1995)
Basset Hound Ch. Bassbar O'Sullivan, six BIS (1993–1995)
Bearded Collie Ch. Potterdale Classic at Moonhill, five BIS (1986–1989)
Bichon Frisé Ch. PaRay's I Told You So (imp. U.S.), seven BIS (2004–2006)
Bouvier des Flandres Ch. Kanix Zulu, seven BIS (1998–2001)
Chow Chow Ch. Choonam Hung Kwong, six BIS (1934–1936)
Chow Chow Ch. Ukwong Adventurer, five BIS (1977)
Chow Chow Ch. Ukwong King Solomon, six BIS (1970–1971)
Cocker Spaniel Ch. Colinwood Silver Lariot, ten BIS (1956–1961)
Cocker Spaniel Sh. Ch. Exquisite Model of Ware, six BIS (1938–1939)
Cocker Spaniel Sh. Ch. Lucky Star of Ware, ten BIS (1929–1931)
Cocker Spaniel Sh. Ch. Tracey Witch of Ware, thirteen BIS (1947–1951)
Dachshund (Standard Wirehaired) Ch. Gisbourne Inca, five BIS (1964–1965)
Dalmatian Ch. Buffrey Arrabelle at Daedalus, five BIS (1999–2000)
Doberman Pinscher Ch. Iceberg of Tavey, six BIS (1965–1967)
English Setter Sh. Ch. Silbury Soames of Madavale, five BIS (1961–1964)
English Springer Spaniel Sh. Ch. Hawkhill Connaught, seven BIS (1972–1977)
Flat-Coated Retriever Ch. Shargleam Black Cap, six BIS (1980–1986)
Fox Terrier (Wire) Ch. Gosmore Kirkmoor Craftsman, five BIS (1969–1970)
German Shepherd Dog Ch. Asoka Cherusker, five BIS (1959–1962)
Giant Schnauzer Ch. Jafrak Philippe Olivier, twelve BIS (2003–2005)
Greyhound Ch. Solstrand Double Diamond, five BIS (1978–1979)
Hungarian Vizsla Ch. Hungargunn Bear Itn Mind (imp. Australia), nine BIS (2005–2006)*
Irish Setter Sh. Ch. Caspians Intrepid, seven BIS (1997–1999)
Irish Wolfhound Ch. Cloghran of Ouborough, six BIS (1931–1934)
Kerry Blue Terrier Ch. Another Prince of the Chevin, five BIS (1933–1934)
Kerry Blue Terrier Ch. Torum's Scarf Michael, six BIS (1999–2000)
Labrador Retriever, Dual Ch. Bramshaw Bob, twelve BIS (1932–1935)
Lhasa Apso Ch. Saxonsprings Fresno, eight BIS (1981–1984)
Lhasa Apso Ch. Saxonsprings Tradition, seven BIS (1997–2000)

Old English Sheepdog Ch. LamedaZottel Flamboyant, ten BIS (1991–1992)
Pekingese Ch. Caversham Ku Ku of Yam, seven BIS (1954–1957)
Pekingese Ch. Yakee A Dangerous Liaison, nine BIS (2000–2003)
Poodle (Miniature) Ch. Mickey Finn of Montfleuri, five BIS (1971–1973)
Poodle (Miniature) Ch. Minarets Secret Assignment, five BIS (2004–2005)*
Poodle (Standard) Ch. Frenches Honeysuckle, five BIS (1958)
Poodle (Standard) Ch. Midshipman at Kertellas Supernova, five BIS (1979–1980)
Poodle (Standard) Ch. Montravia Tommy-Gun, ten BIS (1984–1985)
Poodle (Standard) Ch. Pamplona Something Special, eleven BIS (1993–1996)
Poodle (Toy) Ch. Grayco Hazelnut, eight BIS (1980–1984)
Rottweiler Ch. Rolex Rumour Has It by Fantasa (imp. New Zealand), seven BIS
    (2004–2005)
Schnauzer (Standard) Ch. Khinjan American Express, five BIS (1995)
Scottish Terrier Ch. Gosmore Eilburn Admaration, six BIS (1967)
Scottish Terrier Ch. Gosmore Eilburn Miss Hopeful, five BIS (1968)
Scottish Terrier Ch. Heather Realisation, sixteen BIS (1934–1937)
Scottish Terrier Ch. Wildermist Clara, five BIS (1990–1992)
West Highland White Terrier Ch. Olac Moon Pilot, seven BIS (1988–1990)
Whippet Ch. Nutshell of Nevedith, seven BIS (1989–1990)
Yorkshire Terrier Ch. Blairsville Royal Seal, twelve BIS (1976–1978)

The Basset Hound Ch. Bassbar O'Sullivan, Top Dog in the United Kingdom in 1993, also runner-up to this title in both 1994 and 1995.

The first time The Kennel Club offered a Best in Show competition at its annual championship show was in 1904: the winner was the Pointer bitch Ch. Coronation.

THE FIRST BESTS IN SHOW

The first time the results of a best in show competition at a Kennel Club championship show were recorded was at the Cambridge Canine Society in 1900, a two-day event held on October 31 and November 1. There was no single winner of that show, however: one award was offered for the best dog (male) and another for the best bitch in the show, and that's where the competition ended. The winners were the Foxhound male Southboro'

The Curly-Coated Retriever Ch. Belle Vue Surprise was Best Sporting Dog in Show at both The Kennel Club show and the Birmingham Dog Show Society in 1903.

Ideal and the fawn Whippet bitch Ch. Rosette of Radnage. Many British dog shows well into the 1950s were, in fact, content to stop judging after a best dog and a best bitch had been designated, or perhaps a Best Sporting Dog and a Best Non-Sporting Dog. (The *Sporting Dogs* term used in the early years did not imply exclusively gundogs, as it does in America today. A Sporting Dog was any gundog, hound, or terrier breed, as opposed to Non-Sporting, which included all kinds of Working breeds as well as the pure companion and toy breeds.)

The first dog to be declared as winner of Best in Show among all breeds at a British championship show was a Schipperke, registered simply as Katawampus, owned by a Miss L. Whiting and winner of this momentous award at the Mallow & District Agricultural Society on October 17, 1901. (The word *katawampus* does not appear in modern dictionaries but was commonly used in 1890s nurseries to describe crabby little children.) Since Mallow, like Dublin and Limerick, was located in the present-day Republic of Ireland, the win qualifies as British only on historical grounds. Unfortunately, this win did not launch a glorious career for Katawampus. He did not become a champion; in fact, he never won a single Challenge Certificate—not even at the show where he won Best in Show, since although he defeated CC winners in other breeds, no CCs were offered for Schipperkes that day. The Mallow & District show also disappeared from the records after a second show the following year, at which an Irish Terrier, Ch. Straight Tip, won Best in Show.

In 1902, the Cambridge Canine Society offered a Best in Show award at its two-day November show. The winner was Curly-Coated Retriever bitch Ch. Belle Vue Nina. Although this is an uncommon breed to be seen on the Best in Show podium today, things were different then: Nina's owner, Mr. C. Flowitt, also scored some big wins

Coronation's equally admired contemporary, Ch. Lunesdale Wagg, won Best in Show at the Irish Kennel Club in 1907.

with a kennel mate, Ch. Belle Vue Surprise. He was chosen as the Best Sporting Dog in Show at both The Kennel Club show and Birmingham in 1903, thereby becoming one of the first multiple winners in recorded all-breed competition. Curlies were not the only retriever breed to produce top winners at the time. Although Labradors and Goldens were not yet represented at this level, a Flat-Coated Retriever, Ch. High Legh Blarney, was a consistent winner. It would take many decades before either of these retriever breeds would do as well again: not until the 1980s would another Curly- and Flat-Coated Retriever appear among the top winners, but those two— Ch. Darelyn Rifleman and Ch. Shargleam Blackcap, respectively—won many times over, Blackcap even at Crufts.

In 1904, The Kennel Club's own show announced its first official Best in Show competition, with the Spratt's pet food company offering a Coronation Gold Cup for dogs of all breeds born in the 1901 coronation year of Edward VII. It seems almost suspiciously apropos that the winner of this magnificent trophy should be a bitch named Ch. Coronation. Be that as it may, Coronation was a Pointer, one of the relatively few breeds whose success in all-breed competition has remained constant over the years. At least as much admired by his contemporaries was another Pointer, Ch. Lunesdale Wagg (namesake and possibly descendant of the top-winning Wagg of the 1870s), described by Harding Cox as a "brilliant exception" to most other, and apparently less handsome, Pointers of his day. English Setters did even better than Pointers during the same period, represented by a score of winners, the majority of which came from two of the most important early foundation kennels for the breed, Rumney and Mallwyd. Both exported top winners to the United States. The lemon belton Ch. Mallwyd Ned was one of the most consistent winners, while the blue belton Ch. Rumney Regal took the breed's first outright Best in Show. Many of the Mallwyd winners had a Rumney sire or dam, and vice versa, indicating a degree of cooperation between two intensely competitive and very successful breeders that has been evident only intermittently in later years.

Among other notable winners of the day were not one but two Field Spaniels. Ch. Matford Queen came from the same kennel as a Westminster-winning Wire Fox Terrier, and Ch. Clareholm Dora won the Best Champion trophy at Crufts in 1909. This represented greater success than the breed would reap at future British shows for the next century.

OUTSTANDING EARLY COLLIES

Among the earliest all-breed winners were several Rough Collies whose names still ring a bell among breed fanciers with a bent for historical research. Two were sable and whites, Ch. Parbold Pagoda and Ch. Squire of Tytton, and one was the tricolor Ch. Wishaw Leader. The latter won Best in Show at the Scottish Kennel Club and also

Field Spaniels were more successful in the early 1900s than they have been since: Ch. Clareholm Dora was Best Sporting Dog at the Irish Kennel Club in 1908 and the following year won the Best Champion in the Show award at Crufts. This painting by F. T. Daws was made into a postcard.

One of the early Collie winners, Ch. Squire of Tytton, Best Non-Sporting Dog in Show at Birmingham in 1907.

took home the first challenge bowl for Best Champion in the Show offered at Crufts in 1906—a precursor to the official Best in Show competition that materialized there two decades later. Leader was described as "a beautiful dog, with an enormous coat and beautiful flowing white mane." Even more sensational, but much less lasting, was the success of a sable-and-white bitch named Killucan Dreadnought, who in 1910 achieved the surprising feat of winning Best in Show at two separate Championship shows in two consecutive days: first at Weston-super-Mare & District Kennel Club on July 6, then at the Taunton and District Dog Association on July 7. (Obviously, the modern American trend of holding more than one show in a single weekend is noth-

ing new.) Like Katawampus before her and a large number of other once-only winners at the time, Dreadnought did not become a champion. In fact, she never won another Challenge Certificate after this one successful weekend.

THE FOX TERRIER POWERHOUSE

Fox Terriers were winning in all-breed competitions from the start and have remained among the dominant show breeds ever since. Smooths were more successful than Wires during this period, and names such as Ch. The Sylph, Ch. South Cave Siren, and Ch. Watteau Surprise are still familiar to breed fanciers with a passion for history. Surprise came from a kennel that would go on to greater glory in future decades; three

One of the most influential personalities of the British dog show world, the Duchess of Newcastle. Her of Notts champions are in the back of almost all Fox Terrier pedigrees. The Duchess won the challenge bowl presented for Best Champion in the Show at Crufts in both 1911 and 1916. She was also heavily involved in Borzoi and influential in several other breeds.

generations of the same family and a whole century later, Watteau is still a byword for quality Smooth Fox Terriers. The most successful show dog of all in the pre–World War I era was a Smooth Fox Terrier, Ch. Levenside Luke. According to published records, Luke was just a puppy when he won his first Best in Show at Birmingham in 1913; in spite of his age, he also won Best in Show at the Scottish and English Kennel Club shows and Best Sporting Dog at the Irish Kennel Club. Apparently, the idea of top all-breed show campaigns is a lot older than many of today's exhibitors would have imagined.

In 1907, Ch. Southboro' Salex became the first of a seemingly endless line of Wire Fox Terrier Best in Show winners. His owner, J. J. Holgate, was one of the era's leading exhibitors of many different breeds and later an all-rounder judge. An even more influential Fox Terrier personality was the Duchess of Newcastle, whose kennel produced two Wires, Ch. Collarbone of Notts and Ch. Chequebook of Notts, both of whom won the Best Champion cup at Crufts, in 1911 and 1916, respectively. The duchess was also interested in other breeds, notably Borzoi. She never won a "real" Best in Show at Crufts but remained involved in club affairs, helped launch the Ladies' Branch of The Kennel Club, and was active as a judge well into the 1950s.

Several of the top Wire Fox Terriers of the early twentieth century were exported to the United States, starting a trend that has continued to this day. One of them, Ch. Matford Vic, winner of the Best Sporting Dog award at Birmingham in 1914, would go on to greater glory on the western side of the Atlantic, winning Westminster in both 1915

The Smooth Fox Terrier Ch. Levenside Luke is credited with Best in Show wins at Birmingham as well as at both The Kennel Club show in London and the Scottish Kennel Club show in 1913. He was also Best Sporting Dog at the Irish Kennel Club show the same year and could be described as Great Britain's top winner in all-breed competition prior to World War I. On the back of this cigarette card, Luke is credited with winning "several championships and numerous firsts and special prizes."

and 1916. His contemporary, Ch. Wireboy of Paignton, was a Best in Show winner in his native country and won Reserve Best in Show to Vic at Westminster in 1915. (Those were the days when two dogs of the same breed could win both top awards at an all-breed show.)

BULLDOGS, POODLES, AND "COMPANION BREEDS"

The Bulldog, one of the first established of all show breeds, took home a number of early top honors, with Ch. Nuthurst Doctor, Ch. Woodend Thaddius, and Ch. Phul-nana among the best-known names. Poodles were still developing and would not become a really successful show breed for another half century, but the influential foundation breeder Mrs. L. W. Crouch saw

The Newfoundland Ch. Shelton Viking won the Best Champion in the Show trophy at Crufts in 1908.

her efforts rewarded with several impressive wins. The black Ch. Orchard Admiral and the white Ch. Orchard Challenger were the breed's first Best in Show winners; both were owned by Mrs. Crouch but descended from continental European stock. Although listed as Standard Poodles, they can be found far back in the pedigrees behind almost all modern Poodles in the United Kingdom. (British Toy Poodles were bred down entirely from Miniatures and Standards, as opposed to American Toy Poodles, whose background is more mixed.)

Newfoundlands had their first Best in Show winner, Ch. Milk Boy, at the Royal Ulster Agricultural show in 1906. The St. Bernard Ch. Destiny of Duffryn won Best in Show at Birmingham in 1913, but another

Several Bulldogs went to the top at the early British championship shows: Ch. Woodend Thaddius won Best in Show at Taunton in 1911.

Saint, Ch. The Pride of Sussex, had already won the Crufts Best Champion award the year before.

The Pomeranian Ch. Morceau d'Or, a top winner in 1920, including Best in Show at Bristol.

The Pomeranian Ch. The Sable Mite, a consistent top winner in the early 1900s and winner
of the Best Champion in the Show trophy at
Crufts in 1907.

POMERANIANS TOP TOYS

Among the toy breeds, Pomeranians were
enormously popular from the start, partly
through Queen Victoria's patronage. The
biggest show stars were Ch. Shelton Sable
Atom and his half brother Ch. The Sable
Mite, who reportedly weighed in at only
four and a half pounds. This was considered
tiny in those days, when Pomeranians were
quite a bit heftier than they are today; the
current Kennel Club standard lists four to
four and a half pounds as ideal weight for a
show-quality male. Mite won the Crufts
Best Champion cup in 1907.

ALL-TIME TOP DEERHOUND

The only dog other than Luke, the Smooth
Fox Terrier, to win Best in Show three times
during the pre–World War I era was,
remarkably, a Scottish Deerhound. Like
some of the other early top breeds, Deerhounds have not often been among the big
winners in later years. However, Ch. St
Ronan's Rhyme, born in 1902 and described
as a steel brindle, won Best in Show at three
major all-breed shows, including The Kennel

Club shows in both 1906 and 1907—the only
dog of any breed to do so twice. According
to a 1916 article in the magazine *Country Life
in America*: "In England the St Ronan strain
has long been famous, and there probably
never was a finer specimen of the breed
than St Ronan's Rhyme, who was champion
of champions at the Crystal Palace, London,
in 1906 and best dog in the Edinburgh show
the same year. The blood of these and other
good British dogs is to be found in our best
American specimens." No other Deerhound
has won as much as Rhyme in Great Britain
since her days.

BETWEEN THE WARS

Some dog shows, even all-breed championship events, were still held in Great
Britain during the first half of World War I.
After a last major event in December 1916,
there were only small shows for a couple of
years; the regular championship shows did
not resume until 1920. Many of the shows
still did not feature all-breed competition,
and of those that did, most only indicated a

Best Sporting and a Best Non-Sporting dog, or a Best Dog and a Best Bitch—not a Best in Show. Toward the end of the decade, that was beginning to change, and by the mid-1930s, most shows closed with a competition for an outright Best in Show award.

The Kennel Club show and Crufts still competed for the public's attention, with Crufts winning on almost every count. That Crufts let so many years go by without offering any real Best in Show competition—until 1928—seems like a surprising lapse, considering what an enterprising and forward-looking showman Charles Cruft was. The Kennel Club show was actually ahead of Crufts in that respect for a while but reverted to separate Best awards for each sex for a few years in the 1920s. (The first Crufts Best in Show winner, the Greyhound Primley Sceptre, died very young of jaundice and so never got the chance to become a champion.)

NOTEWORTHY DOGS AND EXHIBITORS

The two finalists at the first postwar Kennel Club show, held in November 1920, were among the top names in all-breed competition for several years. Best Dog in Show that year was a Bloodhound, Ch. Dark of Brighton, bred in a kennel that remained successful throughout the twentieth century and into the present. Brighton Bloodhounds are currently owned by Lily Ickeringill, whose great-grandfather started the kennel in 1908. Dark repeated his big win at The Kennel Club show for an unprecedented three years in a row. Best Bitch in Show in 1920 was a blue merle Smooth Collie, Ch. Laund Lynne, whose owner, W. W. Stans-

The only dog ever to win Best in Show at The Kennel Club show twice was the Scottish Deerhound bitch Ch. St Ronan's Rhyme, who did so in both 1906 and 1907, with a third win at Ulster for good measure. No other Scottish Deerhound has won as much in all-breed competition since Rhyme in the United Kingdom.

One of the oldest kennels in the world is that of the Brighton Bloodhounds, started by H. Hylden, the present owner's great-grandfather, in 1908 and still active a century later. Ch. Dark of Brighton was Best Dog in Show (there was no outright Best in Show award) three times at The Kennel Club show in the 1920s.

field, also scored big with another Smooth, Ch. Laund Luetta, a Best in Show winner in the 1920s. The Laund kennel exported a large number of Collie cham- pions to the United States, mostly Roughs, including a promising puppy named Laund

Loyalty of Bellhaven—famous for winning Best in Show at Westminster from the Puppy class and then never being shown again. Various reasons have been given for this; one of the more lurid versions suggested that Loyalty's owner, Florene Ilch, received death threats toward the dog from a disgruntled competitor. Mr. Stansfield's daughter, Ada Bishop, has continued the family interest in Collies into the twenty-first century.

THE TERRIERS

The 1920s saw a number of great British kennels make serious inroads in all-breed competition. In terriers, F. Calvert Butler continued the success of the prewar Watteaus with a string of Best in Show winners—Smooth and Wire Fox Terriers, Kerry Blues—that has seldom been equaled. May Pacey bred top-quality Sealyhams before focusing on her groundbreaking Wolvey West Highland Whites.

Crackley and Talavera

In the late 1920s, J. R. ("Bobby") Barlow started to win big with the Crackley Wire Fox Terriers and would

Smooth Collies had considerable success in England after World War I: Ch. Laund Lynne was Best Bitch in Show several times in the early 1920s, including at The Kennel Club show in both 1920 and 1922, and Best in Show at the Scottish Kennel Club show in 1923. The Laund kennels exported scores of Rough Collie champions to the United States, including the Westminster Best in Show winner of 1929, Laund Loyalty of Bellhaven.

The Wire Fox Terrier Ch. Crackley Startler won Best in Show at The Kennel Club show in 1931, and his son Ch. Crackley Surething did the same two years later. Bob Barlow's Crackley dogs remained a force to be reckoned with for several decades.

continue to do so for several decades. The first top winner bred by Barlow, Ch. Kemphurst Superb, who was Best in Show at the Royal Veterinary College Dog Show in 1927, was not registered with his kennel name. Four years later, Ch. Crackley Startler won Best in Show at The Kennel Club show, and his son Ch. Crackley Surething did the same in 1933. Most of the Wire Fox Terriers of the time, including the Crackleys, came down from Col. Phipps's Talavera stock—sometimes in a roundabout way via American-born Wildoaks descendants of the great stud dog Ch. Talavera Simon.

Terrier handlers made regular trips across the Atlantic, bringing with them scores of British exports to their American clients. Many of the handlers stayed to show their charges for a while; Bobby Barlow even won Best in Show at Westminster. In the early 1960s, he won Crufts, too, the only handler ever to win both these great shows until Peter Green did so in 2005. Some handlers liked America so much that they remained

Photo by] [Thurse
Ch CRACKWYN COCKSPUR, winner of eight CCs, best in show all breeds, Cardiff Ch Show, also at Brewood, Sutton Coldfield, Redditch, Halifax, Malvern and Thame, reserve best at Bakewell.

Photo by] [Thurse
Ch CRACKWYN ARDOCK ARTISTIC, winner of four CCs and best of breed at Crufts and Richmond.

Photo by] [Thurse
Ch CRACKWYN CAPRICE, winner of seven CCs and best all breeds Scottish Kennel Club show and several times best of breed.

CRACKWYN and CRACKLEY KENNELS
Owners: Messrs H L GILL and J R BARLOW, 409 Chester Road, Aldridge, Staffs. *Phone: Streetly 7295*

Photo by] [Thurse
Ch CRACKWYN CORRECTOR, winner of three CCs, best of breed Leeds, LKA. Now proving himself the greatest sire of modern times.

Photo by] [Thurse
Ch CRACKWYN CORRECT, winner of three CCs and the dam of some wonderful stock.

SOME OF THE STAR CRACKWYN CHAMPIONS

These seven champions are but a few of the many famous winners housed in this kennel and a visit is advised to any interested in the breed. The past year may have been a record but I venture to state that the coming one will be even more successful as there are many high class youngsters which are bound to make history.

Exports have been many, and one may obtain youngsters to make a start with. Mr J R Barlow, the expert, will be only too pleased to help the beginner up the ladder to fame. Stud cards willingly sent on request to the above address.

Vernon Hirst

Photo by] [Thurse
Ch CRACKWYN CAPTIVATOR (litter brother to Ch C Caprice, several times best all breeds in show. Already sire of ch show winners including Crackwyn Charmer, best puppy Richmond Ch Show.

Photo by] [Thurse
Ch WINDLEHURST SUSAN, winner of three CCs, dam of Ch C Cockspur and other good winners.

By the 1960s, the Crackley Wire Fox Terriers had joined forces with the Crackwyn kennels. Bob Barlow still showed all the dogs, and in 1962 he won Best in Show at Crufts with Ch. Crackwyn Cockspur. This ad appeared in *Dog World Annual* in 1961.

there permanently. Others returned home, and a few such as Barlow even brought some dogs back from the United States to England. The American handlers, of course, traveled to England frequently as well. The editor of England's *Dog World*, Phyllis Robson, wrote in the American *Popular Dogs* in 1952: "We have just said goodbye to George Thomas and Harry Sangster who sailed back to the States on the Queen Mary. Both have made a host of friends; incidentally it was Mr. Thomas's 78th crossing of the Atlantic, and Mr. Sangster took back with him ten dogs of various breeds."

Talavera Simon's influence as a sire was unrivaled by any other dog at the time, but the Kerry Blue Terrier Ch. Black Prince of the Chevin came close. Prince himself was a Best in Show winner, and both his son Ch. Another Prince of the Chevin and daughter Ch. Muircroft Thora were among the top winners of all breeds for some years in the early 1930s, each with a handful of Bests in Show. Black Prince was owned during his British career by F. Calvert Butler, of the famous Watteau kennels, but later moved to the United States and was a Best in Show winner there also.

Heather Scottish Terriers

The most successful terrier kennel of all, however, belonged to two brothers from Scotland, Robert and James Chapman. Their Heather Scottish Terrier breeding program was started by their father in 1896 and was a large operation, sometimes with as many as 100 dogs in the kennel, not all of them Scotties. (The family even bred Clydesdale horses.) The first major all-breed success came with Ch. Heather Necessity, originally registered as Snooker's Double. He had a

number of different owners until registered under the name he made famous. Necessity won Best in Show at Crufts in 1929, only the second time such an award had been presented at this show. He repeated his Best in Show win at a couple of lesser shows, as did several of his offspring from his home kennel and from other breeders. The biggest star came a few years later, when an eight-month-old brindle dog, Heather Realisation, won his way through to Best in Show at the Scottish Kennel Club in September 1934. This was the first in a series of wins that would set records. Although not a son of the Crufts winner, Realisation was cleverly line-bred in the classical tradition—his sire was a son of Necessity, his dam a Necessity granddaughter.

As a young adult in 1935, Realisation won three more Bests in Show—at Belfast, at the Scottish Kennel Club (again), and at The Kennel Club show. This was more than most British show dogs can hope to achieve in a lifetime, but it was just the start for this one: in 1936 Realisation won five Bests, and in 1937 he won seven more, for an amazing total of sixteen Bests in Show at all-breed championship shows—more than any other British show dog has ever won before or since. Who knows how much more Realisation could have won if he had not died prematurely soon after his last Best in Show. Realisation had won the Scottish Kennel Club show for four years in a row; after his death, exhibitors at the 1938 edition of the show must have heaved a sigh of relief—only to find that Best in Show went to Realisation's son, Heather Benefactor, that year. The new dog did not become a champion, however, and the Heather success story was basically over by the mid-1940s.

A fanciful rendition of the Heather Scottish Terriers at home in Glenboig, Scotland: obviously the dogs were added to the design afterward.

One of the top kennels ever in the United Kingdom, the Heather Scottish Terriers in Scotland, was started in the late 1800s but came to the fore when Ch. Heather Necessity won Best in Show at Crufts in 1929. This photograph is interesting especially because it is obviously not retouched—a very unusual occurrence in Terriers at the time.

Ch. Heather Realisation, whose record of sixteen Best in Show wins at general championship shows in Great Britain has never been exceeded.

BANCHORY LABRADOR RETRIEVERS

Alongside Heather, two other top kennels, Banchory Labrador Retrievers and the of Ware Cocker Spaniels, took home a very high percentage of the top awards in the 1920s and 1930s. These three top kennels had a virtual lock on the Crufts Best in Show trophy in the 1930s, winning that most prestigious of all shows eight times between 1929 and 1939. The Banchory Labradors, owned by Mrs. Quintin Dick, first surfaced with a couple of top winners in the 1920s, including the great stud dog Ch. Banchory Bolo, the first Dual Champion of any breed. A few years later, Mrs. Dick became Lorna, Countess Howe, and hit her stride with the biggest winner this breed has ever seen. Dual Ch. Bramshaw Bob won Best in Show at his first Crufts attempt in 1932, repeated that win the next year, and won a dozen all-breed Bests, making him one of the biggest winners in British all-breed competition, and certainly the top winning Dual Champion ever. In 1937, Countess Howe won Best in Show at Crufts for the third time, now with Bob's younger half brother Ch. Cheverells Ben of Banchory. No other Labrador kennel before or since, either in England or in the United States, has enjoyed as much all-breed success as

Labrador Retrievers have never received more recognition on the all-breed scene in England than they did through the Banchory dogs in the 1920s and 1930s. Some of them won in the field as well as in the show ring: left to right in Reuben Ward Binks's 1923 painting are Ch. Barrie of Faircote, Ch. Grateley Ben, Dual Ch. Banchory Bolo, Ch. Banchory Bruco, Ch. Banchory Lucky, Ch. Banchory Sunspeck, and Ch. Banchory Betsy.

When he first won Crufts in 1932, the Labrador Retriever Bramshaw Bob was not even a champion. He repeated the win in 1933, became a Dual Champion, and won Best in Show at a dozen all-breed championship shows, making him one of the top winners ever at British all-breed shows.

Bob's younger half brother Ch. Cheverells Ben of Banchory won Best in Show at Crufts in 1937. Both dogs were owned by Lorna, Countess Howe.

Banchory. Countess Howe remained actively involved in dogs into the 1960s; in later years, she turned her attention mainly to Pugs, again with great success. Her black bitch Ch. Banchory Lace was the first Pug to win Best in Show in the United Kingdom.

THE OF WARE COCKER SPANIELS

The great achievements of Heather and Banchory notwithstanding, the most successful show kennel in Great Britain at that time, possibly ever, was of Ware. A long line of Cocker winners, owned and impeccably shown by H. S. Lloyd, dominated British shows for many years both before and after World War II. Much of the Cocker Spaniel's worldwide popularity in the ensuing years was, in fact, attributed to Lloyd's tireless promotion of the breed and to the numerous exports from his kennel that circled the globe.

One of the early great Cocker Spaniel winners that helped make the breed—and the of Ware kennel—world famous: Show Ch. Lucky Star of Ware, Best in Show at Crufts in both 1930 and 1931.

The first big winners carrying the of Ware suffix appeared in the 1920s. By 1930, the kennel was going full steam, winning its first Best in Show at Crufts with the blue roan male Sh. Ch. Lucky Star of Ware. He repeated that win the following year. In 1934, Sh. Ch. Whoopee of Ware took Reserve Best in Show at Crufts, and Silver Templa of Ware (later exported to Australia, and a champion there) did the same in 1936. Whoopee was a great sire: his son Sh. Ch.

Manxman of Ware, owned by the maharaja of Patiala, was a Best in Show winner at the Ladies Kennel Association in 1935, and another Whoopee offspring, the tricolor bitch Sh. Ch. Exquisite Model of Ware, was an even bigger winner. Model won Crufts in 1938 and 1939, the last Crufts held until dog shows were resumed after the war, in 1947, and could quite possibly have continued her long string of successes if dog shows had not been canceled in September 1939.

It is worth noting that none of these outstanding winners carried a champion title in their own time: no matter how much a gundog won in the show ring, it did not become a champion until it had also qualified in the field. The Show Champion (Sh. Ch.) title was introduced in the late 1950s but is frequently bestowed retroactively as an honorific on dogs in the Gundog group that had qualified in the show ring earlier.

As if unaffected by the enforced eight-year wartime break of dog show activities, Lloyd hit his stride as shows resumed in 1947, launching his last and greatest star. The blue roan bitch Sh. Ch. Tracey Witch of Ware followed in the family tradition by winning, among other honors, back-to-back Bests in Show at Crufts—the first two shows held after the war. All told, Lloyd won Best

The last great star from Lloyd's famous kennel was Sh. Ch. Tracey Witch of Ware, who won back-to-back Bests in Show at Crufts in both 1948 and 1950 (there was no Crufts in 1949). Tracey Witch won Best in Show at championship shows thirteen times, making her one of the top winners of all time in the United Kingdom.

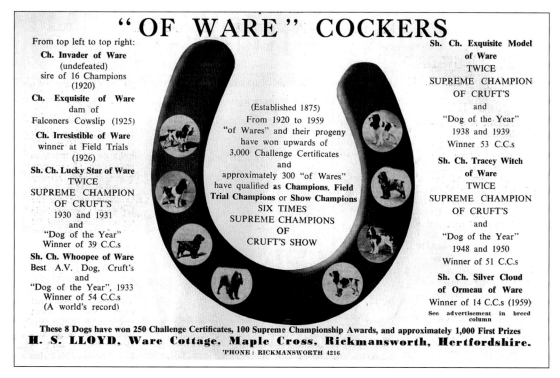

As late as the 1960s, the of Ware kennel was standing nine dogs at stud. This advertisement is from the 1959 Christmas issue of *Our Dogs*.

at all-breed championship shows thirty-six times: his greatest winners were Lucky Star (nine wins), Whoopee (five wins), Exquisite Model (seven wins), and Tracey Witch (thirteen wins). Six Bests came at Crufts; neither this achievement nor the total number of wins has been equaled in Great Britain by any other kennel before or since. The worldwide importance of the of Ware Cockers can hardly be overestimated, but by the end of the 1950s, H. S. Lloyd was mainly resting on his laurels. His daughter Jennifer Lloyd Carey and granddaughter Paula Carey have continued the family's Cocker Spaniel tradition but keep a much lower profile than Lloyd did.

Wendover Irish Setters

One kennel with homebred winners and tremendous influence for many decades was Wendover, owned by Mr. and Mrs. L. C. James. Their first Irish Setter winners appeared in the 1930s, but Wendover dogs enjoyed even more success after the war

One of the most outstanding examples of the great Wendover Irish Setter kennels: Sh. Ch. Wendover Gentleman, Best in Show at Southern Counties championship show in 1969 and a very influential sire.

and sired all-breed winners into the 1990s. In Great Britain and many other countries, it is almost impossible to find an Irish Setter pedigree without a large number of Wendover names in the earlier generations. Since the original owners' deaths, Wendover has been carried on by their son Peter James, a past chairman of The Kennel Club.

Ouborough Great Danes and Irish Wolfhounds

Another breeder who worked on the grand scale and almost always produced his own top winners was James V. Rank, whose Ouborough Kennels set records for both Great Danes and Irish Wolfhounds. A business tycoon from a prominent Yorkshire family and the brother of J. Arthur Rank, the movie mogul, James Rank founded his kennel in the 1920s and later expanded the establishment to 170 rolling acres in Surrey, incorporating a mansion, kennels, stables for thoroughbred horses, and a barn for his Guernsey cattle. According to an *Our Dogs* reporter at the time, "The Ouborough kennel is fortunate in its position. Away from the main road, it is possible to exercise in the numerous lanes, and I saw about thirty youngsters go out for their afternoon exercise with but one person in charge, and he on a bicycle; wonderful training, by the way."

The article also stated that "[o]ne of the greatest desires of Rank is to have nothing but home-breds in the establishment." It seems he got his wish. Rank's first big winner was his homebred Irish Wolfhound male Ch. Cloghran of Ouborough, who won a half dozen Bests in the late 1920s and early 1930s—more than any other Wolfhound in Great Britain before or since. His son Ch. Farnoge of Ouborough was also an all-breed

ANALYZING THE RECORDS

Wire Fox Terriers from the Travella kennels hit the top spots in both England and America in the 1950s but reached a new high a half century later through Ch. Travella Show Stopper. She was one of the top dogs in England in 2006 and won Reserve Best in Show at Crufts 2007. Show Stopper's pedigree is solid Travella breeding for several generations; both her parents were also Best in Show winners.

In spite of the vast number of dog shows held in later decades, the records set by the greatest stars before or just after World War II—Heather Realisation, Bramshaw Bob, and Tracey Witch of Ware—have not been exceeded by those of later generations. The relatively small number of British championship events has remained remarkably stable: there were twenty-three or twenty-four annual British all-breed championship shows in the mid-1930s; twenty-five each year in the early 2000s. However, since the shows have grown so much bigger over the years, it is obviously much more difficult for any one dog to dominate as heavily as the three above did in their day. This development is very different from that in America, where the vastly increased number of shows has created opportunities for heavily campaigned dogs to achieve records that are unimaginable in England. More dogs have won 100 Bests in Show in America than have won 10 in England, but the number of dogs defeated in the process may not differ very much, as the average all-breed championship show in Britain is about ten times bigger than that in the United States.

It may come as something of a surprise to realize that many of the successful kennels mentioned elsewhere did not breed the winners that took home their biggest trophies. (None of the top of Ware Cockers were, for instance, bred by Lloyd.) Then, even more than today, it was the custom and prerogative of an influential kennel to pick stud fee puppies from litters sired by their dogs out of other breeders' bitches. If these puppies turned out well, they were run on, and the new owner could reregister the dog with a completely new name, which could lead to much confusion. After the war, the rules were changed: a new kennel suffix could be added, but the rest of the dog's name stayed the same. With a little luck, the dog could then go on to add luster to its home kennel, while the breeder was relegated to just a name in the catalog.

The Ouborough kennels of James V. Rank were established on a grand scale in the 1920s and produced a string of homebred top winners in Great Danes and Irish Wolfhounds. The apex was reached with Best in Show at Crufts in 1953, shortly after Rank's death. Patsy Rank is shown in the 1930s with some favorites on the steps of the estate in Godstone, Surrey.

The Irish Wolfhound Ch. Cloghran of Ouborough won Best in Show at all-breed championship shows six times during the late 1920s and early 1930s.

winner, and the Great Dane results were similarly impressive. The homebred Ch. Ruffian of Ouborough and two of his sons, Chs. Ruler and Raider of Ouborough (as well as a daughter from another kennel, Ch. Billie of Lavrock), were all Best in Show winners. There were others, but the kennel's biggest win came after World War II, when the Great Dane Ch. Elch Edler of Ouborough swept all before him at Crufts in 1953. Rank did not live to see this final great victory for his breeding program; Elch Edler was owned and, like all Rank's other dogs before him, shown by W. G. (Bill) Siggers, who was Ouborough's kennel manager and later a widely traveled international judge.

OTHER PREWAR ACHIEVEMENTS

The achievements of some other pre–World War II enthusiasts must be mentioned. The Warlands Airedale Terriers, owned by a coal magnate in Durham, J. P. Hall, first sailed to the top in the early 1920s but came even further to the fore a decade later with Ch. Warland Prefect and his half brother Ch. Warland Protector. The latter was sold to an American fancier, S. M. Stewart, who brought both the dog and his handler, Bobby Barlow, to the United States. They promptly won Best in Show at Westminster—now with Mr. Stewart's suffix of Shelterock added to Protector's name—and helped establish a successful kennel in Montclair, New Jersey. A Protector son, Ch. Shelterock Merry Sovereign, then went in the opposite direction of his sire, following his American show career with an even more impressive

The Airedale Terrier Ch. Warland Protector was a Best in Show winner in England prior to being exported to the United States. With the suffix of Shelterock added, he also won Westminster in 1933. His handler was Bobby Barlow; the judge was Mrs. Geraldine Rockefeller Dodge. Right is John G. Bates, Westminster's show chairman and president of the American Kennel Club.

Ch. Shelterock Merry Sovereign, Protector's son, was the first American-born dog to win big in Great Britain. In 1937, he won Best in Show at The Kennel Club show—second in prestige only to Crufts.

record in England. Sovereign was, as far as is known, the first American, possibly the first foreign-born, dog to win Best in Show at a major show in Great Britain. He gained that title first at The Kennel Club show in 1937—second in prestige only to Crufts—and repeated the win twice more the following year.

The Chow Chow Ch. Choonam Hung Kwong, already mentioned in connection with the controversial 1935 Best in Show award at Crufts, was the best known of many top winners from Violet Mannooch's famous kennel. Hung Kwong's Crufts record was unequaled by any other dog at least up to the 1960s: he won Best in Show

there in 1936 and was Reserve in both 1935 and 1939. He did not move to the United States, but several others from the same kennel did. Hung Kwong's great-grandsire Ch. Choonam Brilliantine, reportedly sold for what would today equal a half-million dollars to an American fancier, Dorothy Mae Hoover, of the Hoover vacuum cleaner empire. Whether Brilliantine was worth the price is uncertain, but he had won a lot in England. With an added kennel suffix, "of Manchoover," Brilliantine won a number of Bests in Show in America as well.

The Pointer that defeated Hung Kwong at Crufts in 1935, Sh. Ch. Pennine Prima Donna, was a consistent winner, but it was another Pointer who very nearly succeeded in doing what no dog had thus far done: winning both Crufts and Westminster. Ch. Nancolleth Markable won Reserve Best at Crufts in 1931, then sailed to America, where he won top honors at Westminster the following year. Markable went on to a long string of wins as part of the stunningly successful team of show Pointers exhibited across America under Mrs. Dodge's illustrious Giralda banner. Markable, as well as many other imports to America in both Pointers and English Setters, went back to the hugely successful Crombie gundog kennels of L. Turton Price. One of his top English Setters, Sh. Ch. Pilot of Crombie, won Best in Show at the Scottish Kennel Club show in 1931, then went across the Atlantic and won a large number of all-breed Bests for the Happy Valley kennels.

It would take until the late 1960s before any dog succeeded in winning both Crufts and Westminster, and not until 2003 did a second dog repeat this achievement. Both were terriers. The first dual winner was the

The Chow Chow Ch. Choonam Hung Kwong had an impressive record at Crufts: Best in Show in 1936 and Reserve Best in both 1935 and 1939.

Lakeland Ch. Stingray of Derryabah; the second was the Kerry Blue Ch. Torum's Scarf Michael.

With war clouds gathering over Europe, the 1939 show season was curtailed. Some dog shows were canceled; others carried on. The last major prewar dog show in England was held by the Harrogate Kennel Association on September 2, 1939, one day after Germany invaded Poland and the day before Great Britain and France declared war on Germany. About 1.5 million people, mostly children, were evacuated from the cities to the countryside to avoid the expected air raids in the fall of that year. A strict blackout was imposed, and nearly all forms of popular entertainment—including dog shows—were abruptly curtailed. Many kennels closed down, and those that could sent their best dogs to safety in America. Dog activities did not stop completely, however. In spite of blackouts, food rationing, and fuel shortages, small radius shows continued to be held. However, there would be no major dog show events in Great Britain for nearly eight years.

AFTER WORLD WAR II

After the war, in spite of deprivations, a bleak economy, and a shortage of most consumer goods, dog activities resumed, enthusiastically supported by a British public eager to get back to peaceful pursuits. The first all-breed championship show was sponsored by the East of England Ladies Kennel Society on May 29–30, 1947. The winner was of a new breed—a Golden Retriever, Ch. Torrdale Happy Lad. It was the first time one of this breed had won Best in Show at championship level. Happy Lad was described by no less an expert than Joan Tudor, then starting her Camrose kennels, as "a very glamorous, heavily built, extrovert cream dog." A number of Golden Retrievers, several descending from Camrose, most famously the great stud dog Ch. Camrose Cabus Christopher, would win Best in Show at British championship shows over the following decades, but although the breed later became one of the most popular and breed entries skyrocketed, it has mostly been a case of single, individual successes. No Golden Retriever has ever been Top Dog of all breeds in England or Best in Show at Crufts.

PREEMINENT GUNDOG STARS

It did not take long for some prewar kennels to reestablish themselves at the top. Only a week into the first postwar show season, as an echo from an earlier era, H. S. Lloyd's last winner, Sh. Ch. Tracey Witch of Ware, took the first win in what would be a long and illustrious career that did not end until five years later. By then, she had amassed a record fifty-two Challenge Certificates and thirteen major Best in Show wins, including two at Crufts. She was not the only of Ware Cocker to reach the pinnacle of success after the war, but although other prewar kennels, such as Ouborough, also continued to win through the early 1950s, there was a natural and very definite sense of a new generation taking over.

This trend was very evident in Cockers, now safely established as the most prominent show breed. These were all English Cocker Spaniels, of course: the breed had been split into two before the war, but the American Cocker did not arrive in the United Kingdom in any numbers for another couple of decades and did not start winning Bests in Show until the 1970s. The competition was strong, the entries huge: at Crufts in 1950, 432 Cocker Spaniels made over a thousand entries, and a large number of ambitious new fanciers vied for the top spots. Ch. Colinwood Cowboy won a first Best in Show for A.W. Collins's successful kennel in 1949, and his greatest star, Ch. Colinwood Silver Lariot, made his first appearance just a few years later. His career was as long and almost as glorious as that of Tracey Witch; Silver Lariot was still winning as a veteran in the early 1960s, at which point he had also sired at least two other Best in Show winners for Colinwood. However, it is his own record of ten Best in Show wins at all-breed championship shows that made him one of Britain's all-time top winners of any breed.

Occupying a special niche among the gundog specialists who came to dominate their breeds in the future was Gwen Broadley, with her Sandylands Labrador Retrievers. No kennel has had greater international impact at the breed level. In spite of a couple of important Bests in Show at all-breed championship shows, Sandylands can serve as perhaps the most outstanding example of a breeder whose astounding

The Best in Show winner at Crufts in 1993, the Irish Setter Sh. Ch. Danaway Debonair, sired the 1999 winner, Show Ch. Caspians Intrepid. Both were owned and handled by Jackie Lorrimer, shown with Intrepid at Crufts.

The English Setter Sh. Ch. Silbury Soames of Madavale was one of England's top Gundog winners in the early 1960s: he was Reserve Best at Crufts twice before taking Best in Show there in 1964.

TOP ALL-ROUNDER JUDGES

The Greyhound Ch. Treetops Golden Falcon.

Two of Britain's most influential judges, Judy de Casembroot and Joe Braddon, were also successful in Cocker Spaniels. Mrs. de Casembroot had won Best in Show before the war with a red bitch, Treetops Turtle Dove, the first solid-colored Cocker to go that far; Mr. Braddon had a past in Irish Setters but took his first postwar win in 1948 with the Cocker Ch. Blue Flash of Ide. Both Treetops and Ide went on to do well in other breeds—Mr. Braddon primarily with gundogs and later Pugs, Mrs. de Casembroot with Greyhounds. The brindle Ch. Treetops Hawk won, among much else, the top award at an experimental all-British-breeds show in 1952 (which, in spite of a grand entry of 2,755, does not seem to have been repeated). Almost every show Greyhound in the world today descends from Hawk. His particolor son Ch. Treetops Golden Falcon won Crufts in 1956 and was later exported to Prince Husain in Pakistan, where, reportedly, he was a house pet until his death at age fourteen. Most important, however, both Mr. Braddon and Mrs. de Casembroot were among Britain's new generation of judges, able to circle the globe and officiate at dog shows worldwide as traveling by air became a practical reality for many people.

Best in Show at the Centennial Crufts Dog Show in 1991 was the Clumber Spaniel Sh. Ch. Raycroft Socialite, shown with his owner-handler and The Kennel Club chairman, Leonard Pagliero.

The Pointer Ch. Chiming Bells won Best in Show at Crufts in 1958. Her sire was the imported American dog Ch. Herewithem Royal Flush; her daughter Ch. Blenmar Bianca was also a Best in Show winner.

penetration of breeding programs around the world is derived primarily from its pre-potent stud dogs and brood bitches, rather than from all-breed campaigns. Mrs. Broadley owned and bred the top stud dog of any breed ever in the United Kingdom,

Irish Setters won Best in Show at Crufts three times in the 1990s. In 1995, the winner was Sh. Ch. Starchelle Chicago Bear.

Ch. Sandylands Mark, and she was one of the most respected all-rounder judges. Since her death, the Sandylands kennel has been continued by Erica Jayes together with Mrs. Broadley's longtime partners from Hawaii, Mr. and Mrs. Garner Anthony.

In the Best in Show rings, the spectacular English Setter Sh. Ch. Silbury Soames of Madavale was the most consistent gundog winner for several years in the 1960s. His record at Crufts was particularly impressive: he won Reserve Best there twice before occupying the top spot in 1964. English Springer Spaniels peaked in the 1970s with Sh. Ch. Hawkhill Connaught, a great sire and scion of a successful family that included several Best in Show winners. Connaught was Top Dog the first time the weekly *Dog World* announced such an award more or less in the present form.

Many Pointers did well at the top level. Ch. Chiming Bells won Crufts in 1958 and also made history because her sire was an American import, Ch. Herewithem Royal Flush—the first time that the top winner at this great show was of "foreign" breeding. Some later Blenmar and Daviam winners also had similar American breeding many times over in their pedigrees, including Ch. Daviam Titus Lartius, who won several Bests and was Runner-up at Crufts. Retrievers in general won less at the top level in the latter part of the 1900s than their huge popularity would indicate. Their biggest winner was neither a Golden nor a Labrador but a Flat-Coat, Ch. Shargleam Blackcap, who scored half a dozen Bests in Show, including Crufts in 1980. Irish Setters had a great run of success at Crufts with three wins in the 1990s: Sh. Ch. Danaway Debonair in 1993, Sh. Ch. Starchelle Chicago Bear in 1995, and Sh. Ch. Caspian's Intrepid in 1999. Intrepid was Debonair's son, and both were owned by Jackie Lorrimer, who had the unique distinction of owning two Crufts Best in Show winners in a small kennel consisting of just a handful of male Irish Setters. Intrepid won seven all-breed championship Bests in Show and was a great stud dog.

Other gundog kennels that made huge contributions to their chosen breeds over the next few decades and also did well in Best in Show competition were the previously mentioned Camrose Golden Retrievers, as well as Lochranza Cocker Spaniels, Raycroft Clumber Spaniels, Crookrise Pointers, and Bournehouse English Setters. Lochranza had a deep influence on Miniature Poodles as well as Cockers around the world, and Raycroft bred the Best in Show winner at the Centennial Crufts show in 1991, Sh. Ch. Ray-croft Socialite. Crookrise has had a great influence especially in America and an active branch in Australia, and Bournehouse won several Bests in Show with the great Cocker bitch Ch. Bournehouse Starshine, as well as with its English Setters. One of the latter, Sh. Ch. Bournehouse Dancing Master, won Best in Show at Crufts in 1977, and his descendant several times over, Sh. Ch. Bournehouse Royal Colours, was Reserve Best there in 2005.

CHOW CHOW GLORY

Chow Chows were well to the forefront at the big shows before and after the war. The Choonam blood was still in evidence, but there was also a strong influence from imported European breeding, although even this, to a large extent, went back to old English blood. Mme. La Comtesse Mary de Changy

Ch. Ukwong King Solomon, England's Top Dog of all breeds in both 1971 and 1972.

The Ukwong Chow Chow kennel was established on the famous Chang-Shi lines from Belgium in the 1950s. Owners Eric and Joan Egerton are shown in 1956 with four of their early champions.

bred the Chang-Shi Chows in Belgium, but this did not stop her dogs from having a tremendous influence in England and, through those exports, across the rest of the world. Canadian breed expert Paul Odenkirchen put it this way in a 1992 article in *Dogs in Canada*: "There simply is not a single successful Chow in the world whose pedigree does not trace back to the Chang-Shi lines." At least three of the dogs the comtesse sent to England won Best in Show at major all-breed events, and one of them, Ch. Chang-Shi U Kwong (himself a great-grandson of the old Crufts winner, Hung Kwong), is behind most of the top winners and producers in later years. His grandson Ch. Astom was also brought in from Belgium and leased for a

short but successful show and stud career by Eric and Joan Egerton, who used the Belgian blood to establish what would become one of Britain's foremost kennels up through the late 1970s.

Eric Egerton was a past professional boxer turned successful businessman, and his Ukwong kennel was planned on the grand scale, with top-quality imports and a string of homebred champions. The Egertons did not own Chang-Shi U Kwong, but he obviously served as an inspiration, and they named their kennel in his honor. (To make a distinction between the two, the Belgian dog's name consisted of two words, whereas the English kennel was usually written as one, sometimes with a hyphen.)

An English-born son of Chang-Shi U Kwong, Ch. Emperor of Jungwaw, was a great winner for the Ukwong kennel and was leased to the comtesse in exchange for the loan of Astom. Emperor sired his share of winners, but a litter brother, Ch. Minhow Edward of Jungwaw, was even more influential in that department. The Ukwong dogs were presented either by Mr. Egerton himself or by the kennel manager, Percy Whitaker, who later went on to an international career as an all-rounder judge.

After a series of top dogs in the 1950s and 1960s, the best winners for the Egertons were their last two. Ch. Ukwong King Solomon, seven generations down from Chang-Shi, was Top Dog of all breeds in both 1971 and 1972, amassing the amazing total seventy-eight CCs along the way—more than any other dog before him and an all-breed record until the 1990s. The Egertons' last big winner was Ch. Ukwong Adventurer, who in a brilliant but tragically brief

career sailed right up to the top and won five big British all-breed shows within just six weeks in 1977. At one of the last shows of the year, however, Adventurer and two other Ukwong dogs were poisoned. Adventurer died; the two others barely survived. This apparently calculated attempt to bring the Ukwong dynasty to an end caused an outrage in England, but the perpetrator was never caught. The Egertons soon afterward dispersed the kennel and retired to Spain. Since the Egertons left the breed, Chows have had some good winners but no stars of the caliber of the top Ukwong dogs.

POODLE POPULARITY

By the 1950s, Poodles were already on their way to becoming the supremely successful show dogs and popular pets they have remained ever since; whether popularity generated show ring prominence or vice versa is unclear. Two British Poodle establishments were particularly successful at top-level competition right from the start. One was Montfleuri, which specialized in glamorous black Miniatures, expertly owner-handled by Philippe Howard Price and later by his wife, Nadia, who reached an apex in the mid-1970s with the multiple Best in Show winner Ch. Mickey Finn of Montfleuri. The other was Rita Price-Jones's Frenches kennel, which housed mostly Standards. Her first champion, also the first Poodle champion after World War II, came from the already established Vulcan line, a

Poodle coats in the 1960s and 1970s were grown to huge proportions. England's leading Miniature Poodle in the early 1970s was Ch. Mickey Finn of Montfleuri, a multiple Best in Show winner at championship shows.

mainstay in Standards but seldom active at the all-breed level. Mrs. Price-Jones's bitch Ch. Frenches Honeysuckle (registered as an apricot) was Top Dog of all breeds in 1958 after sweeping a half dozen of the top shows that year. She was later reportedly exported to the United States, but her fate there is unclear; she did not become an American champion. Mrs. Price-Jones experienced similar success with her black male Ch. Frenches Rockaven in the mid-1960s, but the type of Standards winning in Britain changed drastically soon after that, with the influx of new-look North American lines. The Frenches Standards are primarily associated with old English blood, but Mrs. Price-Jones adjusted quickly to the new custom of importing dogs from abroad and had some of her last big wins with an American-born white Miniature, Ch. Round Table Brandy Sniff at Frenches, in the 1970s. She stopped breeding Poodles in 1974.

Miniature Poodles continued to increase their inroads in all-breed competition in the 1960s with even greater force than before. Montfleuri was going strong; Tophill and

In the 1950s, Poodles started on their way to becoming the most popular and successful show dogs anywhere. English Miniatures scored worldwide for the next couple of decades, largely through the efforts of individuals such as these: Philippe Howard Price of the Montfleuri Poodles is shown in the early 1950s awarding CCs to Mrs. A. D. Jenkins and her great stud dog Ch. Rudolph of Piperscroft and to Phyllis Austin-Smith and her homebred Ch. Braeval Betta. Rudolph had numerous champion offspring worldwide, including the Westminster Best in Show winner Ch. Fontclair Festoon, bred by Mrs. Jenkins.

The Canadian-born Standard Poodle Ch. Bibelot's Tall Dark and Handsome caused a stir when he became Top Dog of all breeds in Great Britain in 1966. After going Reserve Best at Crufts 1967, he returned to Canada but left a long legacy of top winners. He was shown in England by Marilyn Willis.

The top Best in Show winner of 1958, the Standard Poodle bitch Ch. Frenches Honeysuckle, was registered as a cream but often listed as an apricot. She won Best in Show at five regular all-breed championship shows that year.

Montmartre scored multiple all-breed wins; and newer names such as Beritas, Leander, and Tiopepi took their first big wins. A flood of glamorous exports from these and many other kennels streamed across the world, most noticeably to America, where British Miniature Poodles were pure gold for many years. The big sensation occurred in Standards, however, and represented a reverse of the usual transatlantic traffic: in 1966 a black import from Canada hit the British rings with a force that changed perceptions of what Standard Poodles should look like. By today's standards, Ch. Bibelot's Tall Dark and Handsome ("Tramp") did not look particularly extreme, but at that time he was a revelation to many Poodle fanciers, exhibiting a degree of style, elegance, and

showmanship that British Standard breeders had not seen before. He immediately split the fancy into two camps, for and against, but as he ended the year with enough wins to make him Britain's Top Dog of all breeds that year, he paved the way for future imports and a major change of direction for the breed.

Tramp ended his British career by going Reserve Best in Show at Crufts in 1967; the winner was the Lakeland Terrier Ch. Stingray of Derryabah, who went on to win Westminster a year later. On his way home to Canada, Tramp stopped over at Westminster but did not win, having to settle for Best of Opposite Sex to the great white Ch. Alekai Marlaine. However, he and his relatives left behind a rich legacy in England, in the high-profile Springett kennels of his handler Marilyn Willis and with other breeders. Since the 1960s, almost every Standard Poodle winner in England, and via them most Standards in other parts of the world, has carried a substantial infusion of Canadian and American blood.

Poodles would go on to further dog show glory later in the century. Some of the most successful and influential British breeders took them under their wings, but this would wait for another few years.

LEGENDARY PEKINGESE

The Pekingese had been an established show breed from the early years and attracted a large number of dedicated long-term breeders. Several of the best early dogs descended from Mrs. Clarice Ashton-Cross's Alderbourne kennel, which was continued by her daughters with much success and worldwide recognition into the 1960s. There were many other important kennels, but none could match the success of the Caversham string of champions in the 1950s. Started by Mary de Pledge in the 1920s, later in partnership with Herminie Lunham, the Caversham stud force exerted

The great Pekingese Ch. Caversham Ku Ku of Yam won six Best in Shows and forty Challenge Certificates in the mid-1950s. He is still held up as a model for the breed.

unprecedented influence and is still to be found far back in most Pekingese pedigrees. Their first great winner was Ch. Ku-Chi of Caversham, a Best in Show winner in 1950. The second was Ch. Caversham Ko Ko of Shanruss, who won more than any other dog in British all-breed competition in 1953, before being sent to the United States, where he only had time for a few early wins before his tragically premature death in a kennel fire.

The peak—at least as far as the show ring in England was concerned—came with the magnificent Ku-Chi son Ch. Caversham Ku Ku of Yam, who won a half dozen all-breed Bests and forty Challenge Certificates in the mid-1950s. The Pekingese is an intensely head-oriented breed (which means that the head properties are considered extremely important), and Ku Ku's head—as well as the rest of him—is still considered a model by many experts. He was also an important sire, and his son Ch. Ku-Jin of Caversham, a third-generation Best in Show winner in tail male line, was at least as influential for the future.

The Caversham exports were legion, with a particularly large number of top winners in North America. The most famous of these, of course, was the double Ku-Chi descendant Ch. Chik T'Sun of Caversham, winner of more than 100 Bests in Show and Top Dog of all breeds in both the United States and Canada. Miss de Pledge died in 1967; her past partner, now Mrs. Frank Warner Hill, then embarked on a successful international judging career with her husband, a successful gundog exhibitor before the war.

There have been many other important Pekingese kennels—Kyratown, Micklee,

It took nearly fifty years for the record set by the great Ku Ku in the 1950s to be broken. The new top Pekingese, Ch. Yakee A Dangerous Liaison, won Best in Show nine times at general championship shows. "Danny" and Bert Easdon are pictured after winning Crufts in 2003.

The Pekingese Ch. Micklee Roc's Ru-Ago, a Best in Show winner of the mid-1980s and Reserve Best at Crufts in 1985.

and Pekehuis, to mention just some of those that took home multiple Bests in Show in the next few decades—but none, at least until the turn of the next century, that could match Caversham's achievements. The one that comes closest and may eventually equal, if not eclipse, the old records is the Scottish kennel owned by Bert Easdon and Philip Martin. Their Yakee prefix has been successful in many breeds and started in Boston Terriers in the 1960s. (Easdon originally wanted to use Yankee as a kennel name, but The Kennel Club would not accept it until the one-letter change had been made.) The first big Pekingese winner was Ch. Yakee For Your Eyes Only, Reserve Best in Show at Crufts in 1989. A string of champions followed and was crowned by the great Ch. Yakee A Dangerous Liaison,

Top Dog of all breeds in 2001 and Best in Show at Crufts in 2003. "Danny's" total of nine all-breed Bests in Show is more than even Ku Ku won in the 1950s and secured him a place among Britain's all-time great show winners of any breed.

In America, two different Yakee exports dominated the toy groups for several years in the early 2000s, with Liaison's son Ch. Yakee If Only becoming Top Dog of all breeds in 2005. It was the first time ever that a sire and son of any breed succeeded in reaching the Number One spots in the United Kingdom and the United States.

GREAT POMS AND YORKIES

Of equal worldwide importance to any of the top Pekingese kennels were the Hadleigh Pomeranians. The breeding program established over several decades by Gladys Dyke bore fruit in a seemingly endless procession of champions. By the 1960s, Mrs. Dyke had won Best in Show with several different dogs, and Ch. Pixietown Serenade of Hadleigh was Reserve Best at Crufts before being sold to Bermuda, continuing his show career in America. Although the Hadleigh Poms enjoyed great success in many parts of the world, they were particularly influential in Asia, where Pomeranians are often among the most popular of all breeds at dog shows. Toward the end of her life, Mrs. Dyke transferred her kennel name to her most trusted acolyte in Japan, Kazumasa Igarashi, who has continued to keep the Hadleigh name to the forefront at the FCI shows there in the twenty-first century.

Great Britain's greatest winning toy dog of all did not appear until the late 1970s, however. The Yorkshire Terrier had been a popular pet and show dog since Hudders-

Gladys Dyke with three of her famous Hadleigh Pomeranian champions in 1948.

field Ben, 100 years earlier, and by the final quarter of the 1900s the breed had reached a peak of perfection that resulted in a series of outstanding winners. One of these was Ch. Blairsville Most Royale, who will remain in the history books not so much for her own wins (which included Reserve Best at Crufts in 1974), as for being the dam of the great Ch. Blairsville Royal Seal. This amazing little show dog first made the fancy sit up and take notice by going to the top at the West of England Ladies Kennel Society in the spring of 1976; he then dominated the British show scene for the next two years as no other dog had done for decades. Royal Seal won either Best or Reserve Best at over half of the biggest shows during this time, always handled by his owner and breeder, Brian Lister.

It is doubtful whether any dog before or since Royal Seal has won as consistently as he did, and the judges sang his praises almost unanimously. One of the few shows that Royal Seal didn't win was Crufts: the best he managed was a repeat of his dam's Reserve award. Another year at the same show, Royal Seal was actually defeated by another Yorkshire Terrier male. It caused big headlines, and according to some reports, the judge had to be spirited out of the show by a back door to avoid the wrath of Royal Seal's many loyal fans. When the smoke cleared, Royal Seal's total number of Bests in Show stood at an even dozen, making him the most successful British show dog in the quarter century that had passed since the great Cocker Tracey Witch of Ware.

Although Mr. and Mrs. Lister left the show scene in the 1980s, the Yorkshire Terrier did not. Another breeder who had already offered spirited competition for the Blairsvilles at the breed level took the place front and center. Osman Sameja's Ozmilion dogs were the result of an extensive and carefully planned breeding program, and the reward was success that makes this kennel one of Great Britain's top show and breeding establishments ever. What seems like an endless assembly line of homebred

The Yorkshire Terrier Ch. Blairsville Royal Seal with breeder and owner Brian Lister after winning Best in Show at East of England in 1977. Royal Seal was Top Dog of all breeds in both 1976 and 1977.

Best in Show at Crufts in 1997, Ch. Ozmilion Mystification, with owner and breeder Osman Sameja, judge Terry Thorn, and club official Sybil Churchill (far right). Mystification was Top Dog of all breeds the previous year.

champions and winning exports reaches across most of the world. A half dozen homebred Ozmilion dogs have won the top award at some of Britain's biggest all-breed shows since the mid-1980s, with an amazing new top winner produced every couple of years. The two greatest names were Ch. Ozmilion Dedication, Top Dog of all breeds in 1987, and his great-grandson Ch. Ozmil-ion Mystification, who repeated the Top Dog award in 1996 and also won Crufts the following February. "Justin" descends from several generations of pure Ozmilion dogs, incorporating all the homebred Best in Show winners that came before him. His pedigree reads like a textbook on expert linebreeding, with his dam being a full sis-ter to his sire's sire.

The Smooth Chihuahua Ch. Belmuriz Brevier was a multiple Best in Show winner and Reserve Best at Crufts in 1979. He is shown winning the Toy Group under judge Pamela Cross-Stern.

OTHER TOP TOYS

Smooth Chihuahuas forged ahead in the late 1970s and 1980s, thanks largely to two half brothers: Ch. Belmuriz Brevier, who won several Bests as well as Runner-up to the top spot at Crufts, and Ch. Apocodeodar Aristocrat, one of many British winners from a successful kennel that later, like Rozavel earlier, emigrated to Australia. More recently, Ch. Dachida's Master Angel has been a multiple Best in Show winner. The Griffons Bruxellois (Brussels Griffons in America) from Skibbereen and later Starbeck won well in their home country and have been influential around the world, and

Maltese have been represented first primarily by Vicbrita and more recently Snowgoose dogs. Young Sarah Jackson won her first Best in Show with a Snowgoose and then continued to do even better with her American import Ch. Hi-Lite Risque Gold Fever and his son Ch. Benatone Gold Ring.

TOP TERRIERS

There was no truly outstanding terrier winner in the United Kingdom for several years after the war. Terriers took their share of the top awards, but the honors were spread among many dogs. There were the Airedales Ch. Murose Replica and Ch. Weycroft Wyldboy, who won multiple Bests during the period and were both sired by Ch. Holmbury Bandit. The Scottish Terrier Ch. Walsing Winning Trick was a Best in Show winner in 1947 but earned his greatest fame in the United States with a new suffix, of Edgerstoune, added. His owner, Mrs. J. G. Winant, bought Winning Trick while living in England as the wife of the U.S. ambassador, then brought him back with her to the States, where he was Best in Show at Westminster in 1950. It was Mrs. Winant's second win there: the first had been with another British-born terrier, the West Highland White Terrier bitch Ch. Wolvey Pattern of Edgerstoune, who had won Westminster in 1942.

At the end of the 1950s, a Sealyham named Ch. St. Margaret Steve—from Cora Charters's famous kennel, which had already produced a Westminster Best in Show winner before the war—was Top Dog of all breeds. This was the beginning of an exciting decade for terriers. An Airedale, Ch. Riverina Tweedsbairn, who is still remembered fondly by old-timers, took his first big win in 1960 at Windsor (then a fairly new show and still called the Windsor Gundog Society, although obviously open to other breeds as well). Tweedsbairn ended the year on a high note as Top Dog of all breeds with consecutive wins at the Ladies Kennel Association and Birmingham, then won Crufts 1961—three of Britain's most prestigious all-breed shows. He continued to score well for the next couple of years and ranks

The Airedale Terrier Ch. Riverina Tweedsbairn, Best in Show at Crufts in 1961 and Top Dog of all breeds in both 1960 and 1961.

The Scottish Terrier Ch. Gosmore Eilburn Admaration was Top Dog in 1967. His owner, Audrey Dallison, had the top-winning dog of all breeds in the United Kingdom for three years in a row in the 1960s.

high among the all-time top winners—in terriers, one would have to go all the way back to Heather Realisation to find a dog that won more. Tweedsbairn's handler was the popular Joe Cartledge, whose widow, Liz, has continued the family business of shipping dogs worldwide and is one of the most respected judges at the top shows in Great Britain and overseas.

In Wire Fox Terriers, the Travella prefix, which would scale new heights in the early 2000s (including Reserve Best in Show at Crufts 2007), was already established with Best in Show winners in both England and America a half century earlier. Bridging the

gap between the generations was the seemingly evergreen Bobby Barlow. His last big star, Ch. Crackwyn Cockspur, was neither bred nor owned by "the maestro" himself, but handled by him and sired by a Crackley dog. Cockspur won Crufts in 1962 and, still handled by Barlow, topped international shows in Scandinavia and on the Continent after being exported to Mme. Lejeune of Belgium.

Cockspur was one of several winning Wires that hit the top spots in the early 1960s. The future great sire Ch. Zeloy Emperor won an all-breed Best in Wales and saw his daughter Ch. Gosmore Empress Sue do the same in Scotland just a few weeks later. Sue was only one of many champions sired by Emperor, but she was the first Best in Show winner owned by the redoubtable Audrey Dallison, whose Gosmore Kennels would introduce a new level of winning in the next few years. At least eight different Gosmore dogs won all-breed Bests at major shows in the following decade, all immaculately presented by Mrs. Dallison's handler, Vincent Mitchell. The Top Dog award for all breeds had become firmly established in England by this time, and Gosmore won it for three years in a row with three different dogs in the 1960s: the Scotties Ch. Gosmore Eilburn Admaration (who won six Bests in 1967) and his half sister Ch. Gosmore Eilburn Miss Hopeful in 1968; and the Wire Fox Terrier Ch. Gosmore Kirkmoor Craftsman in 1969. Admaration and Miss Hopeful had the same dam, Bardene Betwixt (possibly the only bitch ever to produce two Top

Dogs of all breeds by two different sires); Admaration's sire was the great stud dog Ch. Kennelgarth Viking, while Miss Hopeful was by Viking's son Ch. Inverdruie Scorchin. A large number of Gosmore terriers, including Admaration, found their way to the United States and took their share of the wins here as well.

Scottish Terriers had a great run during the 1960s. In addition to the Gosmore dogs, there was Ch. Bardene Bingo, a winner at Blackpool in 1963 and later exported to America, where he won Westminster in 1967 and, with a couple of other exported Bardene stud dogs, dominated the breed for many years. Later on, Scotties were represented as a family by the Gaywyns and their descendant Mayson winners, and individually especially by the top-winning Ch. Wildermist Clara, who won Best in Show five times at championship shows around 1990. There were also the Brio dogs, which

AUDREY DALLISON AND THE ROUGH-AND-READY TERRIERS

Not since the days of H. S. Lloyd and the of Ware Cockers had anyone won so much with so many dogs as the Gosmore kennels did. Mrs. Dallison was involved in other breeds—Miniature Schnauzers, Poodles, Maltese, and Whippets, and she won with them all. It was always more a show kennel than a breeding establishment (none of the biggest winners were homebred), but Gosmore stock has nevertheless had a strong influence in both Scotties and Wire Fox Terriers. Mrs. Dallison herself was a combative personality, frequently involved in some hotly contested issue, often as a result of her outspoken articles in the dog press. Her most controversial topic concerned whether the more rough-and-ready terrier breeds—Border, Norfolk, and Norwich Terriers—really deserved to win in Group competition with their more highly stylized cousins. At that time, few of those breeds had succeeded at this level, but the suggestion created a furor nevertheless. In later years, of course, Norfolks and Norwiches would routinely defeat other terriers and take Best of all breeds at some of the top shows, effectively ending any such discussion.

The White Bull Terrier Ch. Ormandy Souperlative Chunky had a unique record. Shown only three times, he won three Challenge Certificates, all with Best of Breed; two Group wins; and Best in Show at Leeds in 1960.

proved that owner-breeder-handlers can win big: Jane Miller's homebred Ch. Brio Wishbone (also sired by the great Ch. Kennelgarth Viking) and Wishbone's son Ch. Brio Checkmate both won Best in Show during the 1960s. In the early 2000s, Miss Miller was back at the top with the Swedish import Ch. Raglan Rose Maiden at Brio, Reserve Best in Show at Crufts in 2004.

Some dogs did not have to rack up a long list of wins to create a sensation. The white Bull Terrier Ch. Ormandy Souperlative Chunky had the shortest show career any champion could possibly have, attend-

ing only three shows in his life, winning the necessary three Challenge Certificates for his title. He did so with spectacular all-breed success, however, including a Best in Show at Leeds as the jewel in his crown. What such a dog could have achieved if shown consistently is anyone's guess, but this was a case of a man abiding by his principles. Raymond Oppenheimer—whose Ormandy kennels are still legendary long after his death—was nothing if not principled. His stated belief was that once a dog had become a champion it should not be shown. He also felt that comparisons between different breeds involved too many compromises to be meaningful. Hence, once they had gained their titles, the scores of Ormandy champions (as well as the Souperlative dogs shown by his partner and kennel manager, Eva Weatherill) could be viewed only at the so-called Trophy Shows for Bull Terriers or by invitation in their home surroundings at White Waltham, Mr. Oppenheimer's spectacular estate in Berkshire. Mr. Oppenheimer's two Bull Terrier books (*McGuffin & Co.* and *After Bar Sinister*, both privately published) are among the best dog books ever written, containing wit and wisdom that can be savored by anyone, regardless of breed affiliation.

The big terrier successes in the 1970s came, again, primarily through a celebrated Wire Fox family. Two half brothers, Ch. Sunnybrook Spot On and Ch. Cripsey Townville T'Other 'Un (both sired by Ch. Townville Tally 'O), vied with each other for attention in the big ring. The former went on to a brilliant career in America, and in 1975, at the same time as Spot On was winning Bests in Show in America, his daughter Ch. Brookewire Brandy of Layven won Best

The Airedale Terrier Ch. Ginger Xmas Carol, born in Italy but of British parentage, won Best in Show at Crufts in 1986. The previous year, she was Top Dog of all breeds.

in Show at Crufts. She was bred in England, handled by Albert Langley, and owned by Beppe Benelli and Paolo Dondina of Italy. In 1976, yet another half brother to Spot On and T'Other 'Un, Ch. Harrowhill Huntsman, shown by Evelyn Howles, became one of the few owner-breeder-handled terriers ever to go to the top at Crufts.

In the same decade, Airedale Terriers started a roll that would include three individual Top Dogs of all breeds in just a few years: Ch. Perrancourt Playful in 1979, Ch. Jokyl Gallipants in 1983, and Ch. Ginger Xmas Carol in 1985. Gallipants won seven all-breed Bests, as many as Tweedsbairn had in his day, and was the crowning glory of one of England's greatest terrier kennels. George and Olive Jackson had been successful with both Airedales and Welsh Terriers since the 1950s and exported scores of top-winning

Jokyl terriers all over the world. Xmas Carol, or "Emma" as she was called, was a different story. Although she was of entirely British breeding and handled in England by Mary Swash, manager and subsequently partner in the Jokyl kennel, Emma had been bred in Italy by Alessandra Livraghi, making this the first time ever that an imported dog won both Top Dog and Best in Show at Crufts.

A few years later, a daughter of Gallipants and granddaughter of Emma, Ch. Jokyl This Is My Song, was shown by Mary Swash to a record forty-five CCs and also won Reserve Best in Show at Crufts in 1996.

One kennel deserves more credit for the big Airedale wins than may be apparent at first glance. This is Siccawei, owned by Clare Halford, who was the breeder of Tweedsbairn as well as of Gallipants's sire and also responsible for many of the dogs in Xmas Carol's pedigree.

Many other terriers, in addition to those already mentioned, continued to score in the Best in Show rings during the latter part of the twentieth century. Bedlington Terriers produced their greatest all-breed winner in Ch. Stanolly Scooby Doo, who won several Bests in Show in the early 1970s. One of the most outstanding terriers was the West Highland White Ch. Olac Moon Pilot, Top Dog of all breeds in 1988 and Best in Show at Crufts in 1990. The Purston kennel, which had been best known for Westies and exported some of the all-time top winners of

The West Highland White Terrier Ch. Olac Moon Pilot, Top Dog of all breeds in 1988 and Best in Show at Crufts in 1990.

this breed in America, was behind the Crufts 1994 winning Welsh Ch. Purston Hit and Miss from Brocolitia, whose younger sister Ch. Purston Leading Lady at Wigmore won Reserve Best in Show at Crufts the following year. Michael Collings, the man behind the Purston prefix, had previously also won the Top Dog title in 1978 with the Welsh Terrier Ch. Groveview Jubilee.

The outstanding Norwich Terrier kennel, Ragus, bred and shown by Leslie Crawley and before her by her mother, Marjorie Bunting, took a sensational Best in Show with the young Ch. Ragus Gypsy Love at Windsor in 1979, in the days when this breed was not considered a serious contender for all-breed honors. Ragus has bred more champions than almost any other kennel in England, primarily in Norwich and Norfolk Terriers. It took some years before another Norwich would win Best in Show, but when that occurred it happened at the same show, and the winner, Ch. Elve the Sorcerer, was owned and bred by Michael Crawley, Leslie's husband. In the 1990s, their Ch. Ragus Devil's Own was a three-time Best in Show winner.

One of the top current terrier fanciers in the United Kingdom, Judy Averis, is following a family tradition as the daughter of professional handler Les Atkinson. He had won Best in Show at Crufts with the Lakeland Ch. Rogerholm Recruit in 1963, and his daughter, together with partner David Scawthorne, is responsible for a large number of top terriers carrying their Saredon prefix. The Welsh Ch. Saredon Forever Young was a multiple Best in Show winner in the late 1990s and won Best in Show at Crufts in 1998.

POODLE GREATS

Together, three of England's best-known kennels helped ensure that the Poodle remained among the most high-profile of all show breeds during the last quarter of the twentieth century. They all first made their marks with Poodles in the 1960s. All three—Leander, Tiopepi, and Montravia—went on to win Best in Show at Crufts, all had success in other breeds beyond Poodles, and all influenced breeding programs around the world through long lines of successful exports. The rivalry and cooperation, both among the three and with other kennels, helped raise the level of competition within the entire fancy.

The Leander prefix, owned by Wendy Streatfield, first scored big with Toy Poodles in the 1960s and then with Standards in the 1970s, primarily through the multiple Best in Show–winning American import Ch. Acadia Detonator of Leander. However, when Leander won Crufts in 1979, it was not with a Poodle but with a Canadian-born Kerry Blue Terrier, Ch. Callaghan of Leander. Mrs. Streatfield later emigrated to South Africa, and a black Standard Poodle she bred there, Ch. Leander Stockbroker of Montravia, was sent to England and did some important winning during the late 1980s.

The Tiopepi prefix is owned by Clare Coxall, who has had the unique distinction of owning one Crufts Best in Show winner and breeding another, neither of whom carried her kennel name. The first Crufts victory came in the shape of an owner-handled apricot Toy Poodle bitch Ch. Oakington Puckshill Amber Sunblush, who won in 1966 when Mrs. Coxall—then Clare Perry—had been involved in show dogs for only a few years. The second Crufts winner was a black Standard Poodle puppy who left Tiopepi before he had been registered with his breeder's prefix. This puppy grew up to become the great Ch. Montravia Tommy-Gun, whose sparkling career in the mid-1980s included, among much else, Best in Show at Crufts. There were numerous Tiopepi champions of all three Poodle varieties, with a particularly strong international influence on Miniature Poodles. Mrs. Coxall also bred the first Bichon Frisé to win Best in Show in England, Ch. Tiopepi Mad Louie at Pamplona. She and her husband, Dennis, are among Great Britain's most active Best in Show judges. Mrs. Coxall is the 2008 Best in Show judge at Crufts, making her one of the few people ever, possibly the only one, to have participated in this award in three different capacities, as an owner, a breeder, and a judge.

The third of the kennel trio, Montravia, must be considered one of the top British show kennels of this and any other period. Other breeding programs may have had an even deeper impact on Poodle pedigrees worldwide; certainly no other kennel has won as much as Montravia did in this breed. This was very much a family affair. Peter Gibbs did the backroom work and driving; his wife, Pauline, owned most of the dogs; and daughter Marita was the handler, starting at an early age in the late 1970s. Montravia was involved in many different breeds, but the first big star was the homebred black Standard Poodle Ch. Montravia Gay Gunner. His son Tommy-Gun did even better as Top Dog of all breeds in 1984, the winner of fifty-three CCs and ten all-breed Bests, making him one of the top all-time show dogs in Great Britain. Marita scored an amazing double by winning Best in Show at Crufts twice in three years while she was not yet thirty years old: first in 1983 with the Afghan Hound Ch. Montravia Kaskarak Hitari, then again two years later with Tommy-Gun. All in all, Montravia won Best in Show at all-breed championship shows at least twenty-four times with eight different Standard Poodles prior to Mrs. Gibbs's death in 2005. Her daughter, now Marita Rodgers, has continued to show different breeds with great success. She did not own but handled the Top Dog of all breeds in 1999, the Bichon Frisé Ch. Roxara He Drives You Wild (British born but sired by an Australian import, Ch. Charnel Born To Be Wild About Roxara).

Standard Poodles have continued to win much more than their smaller cousins in all-breed competition. In addition to those mentioned elsewhere, the greatest individual winner has been Ch. Midshipman at Kertellas Supernova, winner of five Bests in Show in the late 1970s and early 1980s. Miniatures took occasional wins but had no all-conquering stars in the Best in Show ring for many years after the last great Montfleuri winner, Mickey Finn, in the 1970s. In the late 1980s, Ch. Navarre's Executive won three Bests in Show, and in the early 2000s, Ch. Minarets Secret Assignment has won a fistful of Bests and become one of England's top winners of any breed. Interestingly, all these and practically all the other top winners in both Miniatures and Standards have been black, with no development of a parallel to the all-conquering American white Poodle winners.

Toy Poodles did not get championship status until 1958 in the United Kingdom, although they had been established in America since the beginning of the twentieth

Marita Gibbs Rodgers won Best in Show at Crufts twice in three years: first in 1983 with the Afghan Hound Ch. Montravia Kaskarak Hitari, and again in 1985 with the Standard Poodle Ch. Montravia Tommy-Gun. "Tommy" had been Top Dog of all breeds in 1984.

The Bichon Frisé Ch. Roxara He Drives You Wild, Top Dog 1999, again handled by Marita Rodgers, shown at Crufts with judge George Down and trophy presenter Dorothy Dearn.

The Toy Poodle Ch. Grayco Hazelnut was one of the most popular winners in England during the 1980s. She was Top Dog of all breeds in 1980 and won Best in Show at Crufts two years later.

century. The first British Best in Show winner took another five years to appear—Ch. Leander Tia Maria, who won at Windsor in 1963. Toy Poodles did have the benefit of a bona fide superstar for several years in the shape of the ebullient brown showgirl Ch. Grayco Hazelnut. She burst on the scene in 1980, ended that year as Top Dog of all breeds, and remained one of the most appealing and popular winners in all-breed competition for several years. Her wins included Best in Show at Crufts in 1982. Hazelnut had not even retired from the scene before a second multiple Best in Show Toy bitch appeared, the black Ch. Velveteen Boogy-licious, but since then most of the Poodle wins have been left to the two larger varieties.

The Standard Poodle Ch. Midshipman at Kertellas Supernova, five times Best in Show at general championship shows in 1979 and 1980.

WORKING AND PASTORAL BREEDS

Most dog people consider themselves lucky if they succeed in one breed. Few have a serious impact in two. One of Great Britain's most successful kennels in several breeds after World War II, with a vast influence both at home and abroad, was Rozavel. Thelma Gray pioneered the Pembroke Welsh Corgi before World War II and in 1950 was the first to win Best in Show in this breed with her Ch. Rozavel Rainbow. Mrs. Gray also did extremely well in such diverse breeds as German Shepherd Dogs and Chihuahuas, winning Best in Show with both and Reserve Best at Crufts with the Long Coat Chihuahua Ch. Rozavel Tarina Song in 1971. The kennel also had a big impact on Cardigan Welsh Corgis and Beagles. To the general public, Mrs. Gray probably remains best known as the breeder of Queen Elizabeth's first Corgis; Rozavel, in fact, owned a CC winner bred by the queen, appropriately registered as Windsor Loyal Subject. Later in life, Mrs. Gray immigrated to Australia, having scaled down her breeding activities considerably by that point.

Both Welsh Corgis and German Shepherd Dogs were a part of the Working Group until 1999, when the breeds used for herding were separated into what is now known as the Pastoral Group (a near-equivalent to the AKC's Herding Group).

Thelma Gray's Rozavel kennel was influential in several breeds, bred H. M. Queen Elizabeth's Welsh Corgis, and produced numerous Chihuahua champions, including Ch. Rozavel Hasta La Vista, a top winner in the 1960s.

German Shepherd Dogs, or Alsatians, as they were known for many years (the term is still included in parentheses after the current name in The Kennel Club's list of breeds), had a short period of great success in the Best in Show rings of the 1960s and 1970s. The first big all-breed winner was Ch. Asoka Cherusker in the early 1960s; a few years later his son Ch. Fenton of Kentwood won Crufts. That win was repeated twice more within six years, first by Ch. Hendrawen's Nibelung of Charavigne in 1969 and then by Ch. Ramacon Swashbuckler in 1971. Shortly before the show, Swashbuckler had been purchased by Prince Ahmed Husain (the same one who

had bought the Crufts-winning Greyhound from 1956), making Swashbuckler the first foreign-owned Crufts winner. Swashbuckler's son Ch. Spartacist of Hendrawen, a multiple Best in Show winner in the mid-1970s, is listed as having been bred by the prince. The type difference between the British dogs and the German dogs was quite pronounced at this time; there were even rumblings of making the British Alsatian a separate breed. However, by the 1980s a new group of fanciers took over; German Shepherd Dogs in the United Kingdom are now greatly influenced by the top German lines, although there are still English-type

The West of England Ladies Kennel Society is one of the big events in the British show calendar each spring. At the 1986 show, Best in Show was the Bearded Collie Ch. Potterdale Classic of Moonhill (also Best in Show at Crufts in 1989), with the Whippet Ch. Samarkand's Beau Ranger as Runner-up. From left to right: club official Sybil Churchill, owner-handler Brenda White, Ian Hampton, Mrs. E. Howard-Jones, judge Catherine Sutton, handler Anne Knight of the Dondelayo Whippets, and Mrs. Hampton.

These two German Shepherd Dogs, Ch. Hendrawen's Nibelung of Charavigne (left) and Ch. Fenton of Kentwood, both won Best in Show at Crufts, in 1969 and 1965, respectively.

Shepherds that win under judges who prefer that type. In spite of the fact that most people would no doubt agree that the change has been for the better, no German Shepherd Dog has emerged as a major player in British all-breed competition since the 1970s.

The leading pastoral breed during the latter part of the twentieth century, however, has been not the German Shepherd Dog but the Pembroke Welsh Corgi. Most of them won only once or twice—the only exception was Ch. Belroyd Lovebird, a four-

time Best in Show winner in the 1980s. Toward the end of the century, the Bearded Collie has moved further into the spotlight, largely thanks to the achievements of one kennel. Mike and Janet Lewis, owners of the Potterdale prefix, first shot to fame as breeders of the multiple Best in Show and Crufts winner in 1989, Ch. Potterdale Classic of Moonhill. She was followed by several other all-breed winners, notably Ch. Potterdale Privilege, the winner of forty-three Challenge Certificates, and Ch. Potterdale

Prophet, Top Dog of all breeds in 2000 and winner of forty-two CCs.

Another important kennel in the Pastoral Group is the Zamoyski Samoyeds of Mrs. C. A. Hamilton, who had tremendous success as the owner of the record-breaking Ch. Hurkur Jingles and then as a breeder of Best in Show winners on her own. That Samoyeds compete among the Pastoral (or Herding) breeds would come as a surprise to American dog show exhibitors; the AKC classifies the Samoyed as a Working breed.

Old English Sheepdogs were primarily represented by the Beckington dogs of Mrs. K. Gibson, who won several Bests in Show in the 1950s, and a couple of decades later by Ch. Aberfells Georgey Porgey, who in spite of being owner-handled by what was essentially a novice exhibitor, won several Bests in Show in the 1970s. The biggest wins for Old English Sheepdogs would come later in the century, however.

Among the breeds in the Working Group, two kennels that made a strong impact in the 1950s and 1960s were the Wardrobes Boxers and the Tavey Dobermans. The former, owned and handled by Constance Wiley, came to the forefront with the famous red and white Ch. Wardrobes Miss Mink, the first multiple Best in Show Boxer in England and one of the top dogs of any breed in the mid-1950s. A long line of other Wardrobes winners followed, including two more all-breed Best in Show winners in the 1960s. The kennel closed in 1973 with a total of thirty-one British champions.

The Tavey Dobermans were owned by Fred and Julia Curnow, who

The Doberman Pinscher Ch. Iceberg of Tavey, Top Dog of all breeds in 1965. Great Britain introduced laws against ear cropping early in the 1900s.

had already done well with Borzoi under the kennel name Woodcourt. They hit the jackpot by importing an American Doberman bitch in whelp to the great Westminster winner Ch. Rancho Dobe's Storm. From the resulting litter, born in quarantine, came Ch. Tavey's Stormy Achievement, who started the Curnows' impressive line of all-breed Best in Show winners in 1960. A granddaughter, Ch. Tavey's Stormy Wrath, continued the tradition, but it was Stormy Wrath's half brother Ch. Iceberg of Tavey who won the most, going on to become Top Dog of all breeds in 1965. The Curnows were heavily involved in the weekly newspaper *Dog World*; both also became popular international judges.

The Working Group has of late produced some of the strongest Best in Show contenders at the big shows. In the early 2000s, two dogs from this Group achieved records that stand among the most impressive ever. One was the Giant Schnauzer Ch. Jafrak Philippe Olivier, the British-bred result of a clever blend of continental European and American bloodlines. After three years at the top, Philippe retired in early 2006 with a total of twelve wins at all-breed championship shows—more than any other dog in the United Kingdom since Royal Seal, the Yorkshire Terrier, nearly thirty years earlier. Philippe was Top Dog of all breeds in 2003, Number Three in 2004, and Number Two in 2005.

Philippe's biggest rival for the limelight was the only slightly younger Rottweiler Ch. Rolex Rumour Has It by Fantasa. The first import from New Zealand to hit the high spots in Great Britain, "Ronan" won seven all-breed Bests in 2004 and 2005. His co-owner, Liz Dunhill, is responsible for the

The Afghan Hound Ch. Horningsea Khanabad Suvaraj, Top Dog of all breeds in 1962.

"Fantasa" part of Ronan's official name and deserves a separate mention as one of the most successful British exhibitors ever. She had previously won with two homebred Rottweilers and, using her other affix, Vormund, has had the only two Best in Show–winning Shiba Inus in the United Kingdom, as well as champion Akitas and Soft Coated Wheaten Terriers.

HOUND HEADLINERS

Dachshunds and Afghan Hounds, each at a far end of the Hound spectrum, were among the most successful breeds in the show ring after World War II. In Dachshunds, Mrs. Grosvenor Workman's Silvae Smooths included a pair of Best in Show winners that were full siblings, Ch. Silvae Lustre and Ch. Silvae Post Horn; the kennel is carried on with Wires today by daughter Jill Johnstone. The Turlshill Smooth Dachshunds of Bill Pinches were equally successful, while the Frankanwen Longhaireds had

FLORENCE NAGLE: MAKING A DIFFERENCE FOR WOMEN

In 1960, the Crufts Best in Show winner was a young Irish Wolfhound, Ch. Sulhamstead Merman. He was owned, bred, and handled by one of British dogdom's strongest and most colorful characters, Florence Nagle. The Sulhamstead dogs had already been successful for many years; even as early as the 1930s, some of the Ouborough hounds were of part Sulhamstead breeding.

Mrs. Nagle not only bred world-class Wolfhounds and outstanding field trial Irish Setters, she also bred, raced, and trained thoroughbred horses. This was at a time when the Jockey Club did not allow women to hold trainers' licenses, and The Kennel Club did not allow women to become full members—women were relegated to a separate ladies' branch with no voice in general matters. Having tried to reason, unsuccessfully, with both organizations for a change, Mrs. Nagle took both the Jockey Club and The Kennel Club to court for discrimination, and her success in these legal battles, after years of litigation, was instrumental in giving women equality in both the racing and the dog show worlds. Mrs. Nagle was also a forthright and much respected judge of her own breed (she judged the Irish Wolfhound Club of America national specialty twice) and a very active member of the Ladies Kennel Association. The 1960 victory at Crufts was simply the most visible manifestation of Mrs. Nagle's extremely productive life in dogs; the legacy she left for women's rights in sports was even greater than the one she left in Wolfhounds.

One of the strongest and most influential characters in the sport of dogs, Florence Nagle fought for women's rights with both The Kennel Club and the Jockey Club—and won. Mrs. Nagle's Sulhamstead Irish Wolfhounds were world famous. She is seen with two of her last champions and her Bentley in 1983.

some of their biggest successes in the 1990s. The foremost individual Dachshund winner was the Wire Ch. Gisbourne Inca, Top Dog of all breeds in 1964, the only time a Dachshund ever has taken this award in the United Kingdom.

The Afghan Hound Ch. Horningsea Khanabad Suvaraj was also Top Dog in the early 1960s. He was an immensely coated black-masked gold dog of all-English breeding and appeared on the scene just before the population explosion and influx of foreign blood would give this breed one of the highest profiles in Britain. However, none of Suvaraj's many glamorous successors won quite as much as he did. In fact, most of the Afghans that took the top spots in England through the rest of the century were of predominantly British breeding. This included the two Crufts Best in Show winners: the brindle Ch. Montravia Kaskarak Hitari in 1983, and the black-masked gold Ch. Viscount Grant in 1987.

One of Britain's greatest judges of the next couple of decades, Robert M. James, was involved in several hound breeds but made his name in Whippets. His fawn Best in Show winner Ch. Samarkand's Greenbrae Tarragon created a dynasty as the central figure in a tight in- and linebreeding program that resulted in numerous high-flying winners for Anne Knight's Dondelayo kennels in the 1960s and 1970s. Her first big star, Ch. Dondelayo Roulette, was the result of breeding a Tarragon son to a Tarragon daughter; her next was a Roulette-Tarragon daughter, Ch. Dondelayo Duette, Reserve Best at Crufts in 1972 and as streamlined and solid fawn as both her parents. Both Bobby James and Anne Knight died prematurely in the late 1980s, but in

The Whippet Ch. Pencloe Dutch Gold was still young when he won Best in Show at Crufts in 1992, but he was retired after this win and became a top sire instead. He was handled by his Scottish owner and breeder, Morag Bolton Lockhart.

The Crufts Best in Show winner in 2004, the Whippet Ch. Cobyco Call The Tune, is a great-granddaughter of the two earlier top Whippets, Nutshell and Dutch Gold. She was owner-handled by her breeder, Lynne Yacoby-Wright.

the limited time allotted to them they achieved more than most, one as a widely respected international judge and the other by providing a foundation for future Whippet fanciers in many parts of the world. Tarragon appears several times in the pedigrees of the top-winning Whippets in later years, including the 1990 Crufts Reserve

The Whippet Ch. Nutshell of Nevedith, Top Dog of all breeds in 1989 and Reserve Best at Crufts the following year.

Best in Show winner Ch. Nutshell of Nevedith, the 1992 Crufts winner Ch. Pencloe Dutch Gold (himself a top sire), and the 2004 Crufts winner Ch. Cobyco Call The Tune. Nutshell won seven all-breed Bests, more than any other hound before her, and was Top Dog of all breeds in 1989. A breeding of Nutshell to her cousin, Dutch Gold, produced champions that are behind a long line of current winners.

Equally successful, and even more influential on some levels, were the Rossut Kennels, owned by Group Captain "Beefy" and Catherine Sutton. Although the Suttons owned many breeds, Beagles were the most prominent. The first important Rossut wins came in the mid-1960s with the homebred half siblings Chs. Rossut Triumphant and Gaiety, but the biggest success came later, with the importation from the United States of Ch. Gradtrees Hot Pursuit of Rossut, one of the top all-breed winners of the early 1980s. The Suttons were extremely active in club work—primarily associated with Windsor, Richmond, and Crufts—and both judged widely at home and abroad. After her parents' death, daughter Patricia Sutton, already the owner of many of the top Rossut dogs, has continued the kennel on a limited scale.

Hot Pursuit was sired by the top American stud dog Ch. Starbuck's Hang 'Em High and proved to be an influential sire himself in Great Britain. His most famous daughter was Ch. Too Darn Hot for Tragband, Number Two of all breeds in 1984—

the same position her sire had held the year before. One of "Ada's" co-breeders was Ken Sinclair, who would go on to win many Bests in Show with the Araki Tibetan Terriers, including the breed record-holder Ch. Araki Fabulous Willy (a Best in Show winner in both the United States and England, including Crufts in 2007). "Ada" was the constant companion of her owner, Andrew H. Brace, whose later involvement in this breed coincided with that of another great British Beagle kennel, Dialynne: Ch. Dialynne Tolliver of Tragband was one of the most successful all-breed winners of the late 1990s. Following success in an eclectic

The multiple Best in Show winner Beagle Ch. Too Darn Hot for Tragband, Runner-up to Top Dog of all breeds in 1984.

A first for Tibetan Terriers, Ch. Araki Fabulous Willy won Best in Show at Crufts 2007, handled by Larry Cornelius from the United States and pictured with owners John Shaw of Hong Kong and Neil Smith, breeder Ken Sinclair, and judge Zena Thorn-Andrews.

mix of breeds—including, in addition to Beagles, Afghan Hounds, Boxers, and Pekingese—Brace has become one of the world's most active and widely traveled international judges. He is also a prolific and witty writer in dog publications both at home and abroad.

A young Irish Wolfhound breeder who had been inspired by Mrs. Nagle, Zena Thorn-Andrews, established the Drakesleat Kennel in 1967. Her biggest success in the Best in Show arena came with the great Ch. Drakesleat Kyak in the early 1980s. He won forty-one CCs, still a breed record; his wins under Mrs. Nagle were particularly treas-

ured. One of the kennel's last Wolfhound winners was Ch. Drakesleat Odyt, who was a multiple Best in Show winner and retired after winning Reserve Best in Show at Crufts in 1993. Drakesleat then shifted focus to its Miniature Wirehaired Dachshunds; the first of their many champions, Drakesleat Hussy, had won her title in 1971. By 2005, Drakesleat had produced a total of 100 British champions, a figure no other breeder had ever achieved. Together with her kennel partner, Jeff Horswell, and husband, Terry Thorn, who himself has a solid hound background through his Tahawi Salukis, Zena Thorn-Andrews is one of the most active judges both in the United Kingdom and around the world.

The top hound winner of the 1990s was the Basset Ch. Bassbar O'Sullivan with nine Bests in Show, Top Dog in 1993, and Number Two in both 1994 and 1995. Since then, the only hound to rack up more than an occasional Best in Show win has been the Saluki Ch. Mabrooka Jayid with four Bests in the early 2000s. That the Basset Hound's dam was a Dutch van Hollandheim import and the latter's sire came from the Australian-American Baghdad kennel was indicative of the increasing influence of imported blood around the turn of the century.

STARS FROM THE UTILITY GROUP

Of the breeds in the Utility Group, other than Poodles, the Bulldog has produced a consistent line of Best in Show winners. The influence of an American-imported son of the great Ch. Vardona Frosty Snowman resulted in the much admired Best in Show bitch Ch. Portfield So Small in the 1970s. Later on, Ch. Beechlyn Golden Nugget of Denbrough and Ch. Tyegarth Jacob of Kelloe became multiple all-breed winners, and in 2001 Ch. Rowendale Rum Truffle at Bollglade, the first champion for his owner-handler, won four all-breed Bests in Show.

Dalmatians did not have the same pre-war success as did Bulldogs. Both breeds won Best in Show at Crufts, however—the Bulldog Ch. Noways Chuckles in 1952 and

The Irish Wolfhound Ch. Drakesleat Kyak, winner of a record number of Challenge Certificates as well as three general championship Bests in Show in the 1980s.

The Bichon Frisé Ch. PaRay's I Told You So was a big winner in the United States for three years before going to England, where he was Top Dog of all breeds in 2004. He is shown with his handler in the United Kingdom, Michael Coad.

the Dalmatian Ch. Fanhilla Faune in 1968. In parallel to Rum Truffle, the top-winning Dalmatian at all-breed level, Ch. Buffrey Arrabelle at Daedalus, was also the first champion for her owner-handler. By 2000, she had won five Bests in Show at championship events.

The Utility Group—which most closely mirrors the AKC Non-Sporting Group but includes several breeds that are classified in the AKC Working Group—produced an increasing number of top winners in the late 1900s and early 2000s. The Akitas (of American type) from the Redwitch establishment of Dave and Jenny Killilea have enjoyed huge success since the breed was first established in the United Kingdom in the 1980s. Three different champion males imported from the Goshen kennels of Lewis and Julie Holm in the United States were all Crufts Best of Breed winners. Ch. Goshen Dark 'N Debonaire at Redwitch was one of the breed's first Best in Show winners in Great Britain but left the biggest winning to his son Ch. Redwitch Dancin' In The Dark. After being sent to Norway as a puppy and enjoying a successful career there, "Rave" went through the six-month quarantine to return to his native country and soon set breed records, winning six Bests in Show at the close of the twentieth century and Reserve Best in Show at Crufts in 1999. Redwitch dogs are winning all over the world in the early 2000s–even in Japan! In the United States, Ch. Redwitch Reason to Believe was one of the top dogs of all breeds in 2006 and became the first bitch of her breed to win the Group at Westminster in 2007.

The Schnauzer (as the British refer to the Standard Schnauzer) had an outstanding representative in Ch. Khinjan American

The Akita Ch. Redwitch Dancin' In The Dark was one of the top all-breed winners in the United Kingdom in the late 1990s and Reserve Best in Show at Crufts in 1999. The Redwitch kennel was founded on American imports but has later sent homebred winners all over the world, including to the United States, Scandinavia, Australia, and even Japan.

Express, winner of five Bests in Show in 1995. Miniature Schnauzers were consistently successful. Pam Radford and Dorrie Clarke of the Iccabod Kennel have been connected with three Best in Show winners, as owners of two very influential Travelmor imports from America and breeders of a third, Ch. Iccabod Olympic Gold. Peter Newman's Risepark kennel has been associated primarily with Miniature Schnauzers

GLOWING SUCCESS STORY

Perhaps England's most successful show kennel around the turn of the century has been the Afterglow establishment, owned by Michael Gadsby. He was not the first to experience great success with American Cocker Spaniels. Andrew Caine won that breed's first Best in Show at Birmingham City in 1971 with the imported particolor dog Sh. Ch. Dreamridge Delegate, and Michael Bottomley did even better with another American particolor import, Sh. Ch. Homestead's Tiffany with Boduf, in the early 1990s. The first big Afterglow success came around that time with a buff dog Gadsby co-owned with one of the breed's pioneers in England, Yvonne Knapper: Sh. Ch. Sundust Kream Kopper with Afterglow. He was the first of a half dozen Best in Show–winning Afterglow American Cockers, including four who either won Top Dog or were close to doing so: Sh. Ch. Mistico-las Over the Moon with Afterglow (1994), Sh. Ch. Boduf Pistols at Dawn with After-glow (Top Dog 1997), Sh. Ch. Afterglow Arrabella (2002), and Sh. Ch. Afterglow Douglas Fashion (Top Dog 2005). There have also been major successes with Afghan Hounds, Poodles, Petits Bassets Griffons Vendéens, and many other breeds. Gadsby has bred champions in many differ-ent breeds, with Afterglow exports doing particularly well in the United States.

Probably Great Britain's most successful breeder and exhibitor around the turn of this century was Michael Gadsby, whose Afterglow kennels have produced top winners in many breeds. Two of his American Cocker Spaniels have won Top Dog of all breeds, and one of them, Show Ch. Boduf Pistols at Dawn with Afterglow, pictured, was Reserve Best in Show at Crufts in 1997.

but has long been a successful exhibitor with a variety of breeds.

It is difficult to compare achievements of different times and different breeds, but certainly the Saxonsprings Lhasa Apso establishment has been one of the most monumentally successful of all British ken-nels. The owner, Jean Blyth, had bred cham-pions before she made what turned out to be a milestone decision to import Ch. Orlane's Intrepid from the United States in the late 1970s. Bred to two different bitches, he fathered the all-time greats Ch. Saxonsprings Fresno (Top Dog 1982) and Ch. Saxonsprings Hackensack (Best in Show at Crufts in 1984). In a classic combination of great dog and excellent handler, they were shown to a dozen Bests in Show by professional handler Geoff Corish. For several years, there were Saxonspring champions galore in many parts of the world and several more Best in Show winners in England. One of them, a Hackensack son, sired what turned out to be the last great winner to carry this kennel name. Mrs. Blyth was already ill when Ch. Saxonsprings Tradition won his way toward the Top Dog of all breeds title 1998, and with her premature death a glorious era of Lhasa Apso domination in the British show ring was over.

THE INTERNATIONAL INVASION

By the 1970s, it must have been obvious to any alert British exhibitor that importing a top-class dog from abroad could have great benefits. Clever breeders had done so for years, but the idea certainly got a boost by the success of such dogs as the Tall Dark and Handsome Poodle descendants and by Ch. Orlane's Intrepid's great impact at stud. Foreign exhibitors had brought their best dogs to England for many years in the hope of recognition where it mattered most. Many were disappointed, but it was in the most British of all breeds, the terriers, that foreign dogs harvested their first big wins in England. The Airedale Ch. Shelterock Merry Sovereign in the 1930s was an isolated example,

Ch. Balboa Belmondo, one of the Kerry Blue Terriers from an Italian kennel that has won big in England, was a multiple Best in Show winner and won England's National Terrier show in 1997.

One of the top-winning Hounds in all-breed competition in England, the Greyhound Ch. Solstrand Double Diamond, combined British, Swedish, and American breeding. He won Best in Show five times at general championship shows in the late 1970s.

but in the mid-1980s, two foreign-born dogs were Top Dog of all breeds in England: the previously mentioned Airedale Ch. Ginger Xmas Carol in 1985 and the Kerry Blue Terrier Ch. Balboa King Regal in 1986. Both were born and bred in Italy but descended directly from stock exported from the British Isles. The Balboa Kennels of Roberto Tasselli made more British headlines in 1997, when his home-bred Ch. Balboa Belmondo won Best in Show at the Birmingham National, the Welsh Kennel Club, and (perhaps most prestigiously) the National Terrier show. Both the Balboa dogs were shown by Don Munro, who had also handled Callaghan to his Crufts win years earlier.

The Kerry Blue Terrier has long been a very international breed, with a lively interchange of dogs going on between many different countries. The first—and long the only—Australian-born dog to win a major Best in Show in England was a Kerry Blue, Ch. Fermoy Knight O Terra, who won both Richmond and Manchester in 1990. Sired by an American Bluefire dog, Knight O Terra was owned, bred, and handled by David Roche of South Australia, who in earlier years had imported many top Kerry Blues and dogs of other breeds from England. Even the top British Kerry Blue breeders of later years, Ron and Carol Ramsay of the Torum prefix, have a dash of older American breeding in their pedigrees. The Ramsays' most brilliant star was Ch. Torum's Scarf Michael, who after an unbroken row of five big all-breed Bests in Show in late 1999 and early 2000 (including Crufts) flew to the United States and had an equally exciting career there. After his departure, the Ramsays made up for the loss by winning Bests in Show with Mick's younger brother Ch. Torum's Tunde Bayou, Reserve Best at Crufts in 2003.

The leading import in the early 2000s is of a different breed, however: the Vizsla Ch. Hungargunn Bear Itn Mind, born in Australia, was Top Dog of all breeds in the United Kingdom in 2006 and won nine Bests in Show in all, making him one of the all-time top winners of any breed there.

It was not just the dogs that came from abroad. An influx of foreign dog people characterized much of the last quarter of the twentieth century in Great Britain. Usually, they brought their dogs with them, succeeded in combining their "foreign" stock with British lines, and experienced a great deal of success. Among the most visible was Dagmar Kenis-Pordham, born in Sweden but living in California for several years before she brought her Solstrand Hounds to England. She was successful in both Greyhounds and Irish Wolfhounds (the latter based on the great Eaglescrag line), and her greatest winner was Ch. Solstrand Double Diamond, a five-time Best in Show–winning Greyhound of combined English, American, and Scandinavian ancestry in the late 1970s. Greyhounds had done well before—both the Shalfleet kennels of Barbara Wilton-Clark and the RP breeding program of Ralph Parsons had produced multiple Best in Show winners—but none won as much in Best in Show competition as the internationally bred "Johnny."

From Sweden also came Liz Cartledge, whose main influence has been through her kennel club activities and international judging career, and Elisabeth Matell, whose Cracknor Norfolk Terriers achieved dizzying success first in England with Ch. Cracknor Call My Bluff and then in America with the exported Ch. Cracknor Cause Celebre, who returned from America to win Best in Show at Crufts in 2005. Gerd and Geir Flyckt-Pedersen had been winning with several breeds in Scandinavia, but it was with the Louline Wire Fox Terriers that they won the most in England. Knut-Sigurd and Kari Wilberg both came from Norway, took their first big win in the United Kingdom

Elisabeth Matell of the Cracknor Norfolk Terriers was part of the successful "Scandinavian invasion" of England during the 1980s and 1990s. Her Ch. Cracknor Call My Bluff (pictured) was Runner-up to Top Dog in 1996, and Ch. Cracknor Cause Celebre returned from being Top Dog in America to win Best in Show at Crufts in 2005.

Above: The Old English Sheepdog Ch. Lameda-Zottel Flamboyant, Top Dog of all breeds in the United Kingdom in both 1991 and 1992.

Left: The Kanix kennels started in Norway but have achieved great success since moving to England, primarily with Bouviers des Flandres. Ch. Kanix Zulu, handled by owner-breeder Kari Wilberg, is shown winning Best in Show in Wales under Welsh-born but American-domiciled judge Peter Green.

with a Giant Schnauzer from Finland, Ch. Rosapik Othello of Kanix, in 1985, and did even better with Bouviers des Flandres in the late 1990s. The homebred Ch. Kanix Zulu's record included seven championship show Bests.

One of the most successful "immigrant" kennels represented a fusion of British and

The Giant Schnauzer Ch. Jafrak Philippe Olivier, the United Kingdom's Top Dog of all breeds in 2003 and winner of a round dozen Best in Shows at championship level—more than any other dog since the 1970s. He and owner-handler Kevin Cullen are shown winning Best in Show at the Scottish Kennel Club with, from left, club secretary Myra Orr, convener Anne McDonald, judge Ken Sinclair, and president J. A. Johnston.

continental blood. Christina Bailey's Zottel Old English Sheepdogs started in Germany in the mid-1970s, and when their owner moved to England in the 1980s she brought with her seven dogs, including a bitch puppy who would grow up to become Ch. Zottel's Miss Marple of Lameda. Descending from two of the top continental kennels (Elbe-Urstromstal and Reeuwijk's), Miss Marple was a great show winner and produced an amazing record of twenty-five

champions in several different countries. Miss Marple's son Ch. LamedaZottel's Flamboyant became one of the all-time top winners of any breed in the United Kingdom, co-bred by John Smith and owner-handled by Christina Bailey to fifty-seven CCs, ten all-breed Bests, and Top Dog in both 1991 and 1992. His son Ch. Zottel's You Don't Fool Me won nearly as many CCs and repeated his sire's win as Top Dog in 2002, making Bailey the only exhibitor to have

The Scottish Terrier Ch. Raglan Rose Maiden at Brio, shown handled by her Swedish breeder Dan Ericsson winning Best in Show at Windsor with, from left, president Leonard Pagliero OBE, judge Ole Staunskjaer from Denmark, vice president Terry Thorn, and owner Jane Miller. Rose was also Reserve Best at Crufts in 2004.

The Pointer Ch. Chesterhope Lets Be Serious with owner and breeder Dianne O'Neill in New Zealand in 2005. Bred from partly American lines and with the Kanix suffix added, Serious continued to win after being exported to England.

won this award three times since it was introduced in the 1950s.

A BRITISH MELTING POT

In the breed ring and in Best in Show competition, British dog shows in the early twenty-first century have become a melting pot of both people and dogs from all over the world, more cosmopolitan than the founders of dog shows over a century ago could ever have imagined. What would the old school English judges have thought if they knew that an American Bichon Frisé would be Top Dog of all breeds in the United Kingdom early in the twenty-first

ALL-TIME FAVORITES

In the 2007 *Dog World Annual*, a number of the top British all-rounder judges were asked to list the dream lineup they would most want to see if they were judging Best in Show at Crufts—a role that most of these people had, in fact, already performed. Several of the judges mentioned great dogs they had seen in America or elsewhere in the world, but the most frequently mentioned favorite was the great Lhasa Apso Ch. Saxonsprings Fresno, the Top Dog in the United Kingdom in 1982, who won almost everything in her brilliant show career except the top spot at Crufts. The second most mentioned dog, Pekingese Ch. Yakee A Dangerous Liaison, in fact won Crufts in 2003. The others who were mentioned repeatedly were the Smooth Chihuahua Ch. Belmuriz Brevier, the

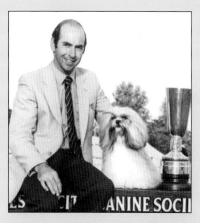

The Lhasa Apso Ch. Saxonsprings Fresno, all-time favorite, with her handler, Geoff Corish.

British-born but later American-owned Kerry Blue Terrier Ch. Torum's Scarf Michael, the Irish Setter Ch. Caspians Intrepid, and the Wire Dachshund from the 1960s Ch. Gisbourne Inca.

The Rottweiler Ch. Rolex Rumour Has It By Fantasa was bred in New Zealand and set new records for his breed after arriving in England, winning Best in Show seven times at general championship shows in 2004 and 2005. The handler is co-owner Liz Dunhill.

century? That a Vizsla from Australia and a Rottweiler from New Zealand would be contenders for some of the top spots? That an undocked Airedale Terrier from Russia would win Best of Breed and be shortlisted in the Group at Crufts, as happened in 2006? They would no doubt have taken comfort in the fact that British dog shows are bigger than ever and that, regardless of how many imports are brought in from far-flung places, the British dogs sent abroad continue to uphold the traditions of the past. For three years in the early 2000s, the winner in the Top Dog competition in the United States had been imported from either England or Scotland. Surely, the fact that the traffic continues both ways at the present time is to everyone's advantage.

CHAPTER 9

THE TOPS IN AMERICA

Most sources agree that the first organized dog shows in the United States were held in 1874, one in Hempstead on Long Island and one in Chicago. The exact date of the Hempstead show is not known, but the Chicago event took place on June 2 and was hosted by the Illinois State Sportsmen Association. According to a published report, "Dogs were judged informally, but without the awarding of prizes." A more formal dog show, perhaps more recognizable as such by modern standards, was held in Mineola, New York, on October 7, 1874; the American Kennel Club had not yet been founded, so the rules of The Kennel Club in England were observed. Only classes for Irish Setters, Gordon Setters, and Pointers were offered. Just a day later, a show for Sporting breeds was held in Tennessee, and early in 1875 the first real all-breed dog shows in America were held in Detroit, Michigan, on January 14 and in Springfield, Massachusetts, in April.

One of the most famous American show dogs of all time, the Boxer Ch. Bang Away of Sirrah Crest, with his owner-handler, Dr. R. C. Harris, after winning Best in Show at Westminster in 1951.

The first dog known to win Best in Show in the United States was a white Bull Terrier named Count, who won that award at the Western Connecticut Poultry, Pigeon, and Pet Stock Association show in 1885. Of course, a Best in Show award at that time did not mean what it does now, and the judging procedure was much different from that seen at dog shows today. Often, there was no judging beyond Best of Breed; sometimes there was not even any competition between the class winners, and the number of classes for each breed could vary from show to show, the way it still does in the United Kingdom. There might be a single class for all dogs and bitches of a breed at a show, or none at all, or a large variety of classes to choose from. There was no consistent division of breeds into variety groups either, and although a special trophy for the Best Dog in Show was sometimes offered, that prize might go to a dog that had been defeated in its breed class earlier in the day.

THE FIRST WESTMINSTER BESTS

In any case, most of the winners' names from the early years are lost in the mists of time. Even after the American Kennel Club was founded in 1884, results from interbreed competition were unofficial and often not reported in the press. The best records that

Smooth Fox Terrier Ch. Warren Remedy, the first Westminster Kennel Club Best in Show winner and the only one to win three times.

Winthrop Rutherfurd, New York socialite, winner of the first three Bests in Show at Westminster, and "father of the Fox Terrier" in America.

have been preserved are primarily those of the Westminster Kennel Club, whose annual New York event had emerged as America's premier dog show by the turn of the century. Westminster held its first annual Best in Show competition in 1907, and the early winners are still known to fanciers today, published in each year's catalog. Some of those dogs set records that remain difficult for any modern dog to break.

Among them is the first Westminster winner, who did what no other dog has done in the 100 years since: won Best in Show there three years in a row. The Smooth Fox Terrier bitch Ch. Warren Remedy was described as "perfect of her kind" and obviously must have had charisma to burn to achieve what she did. When she tried for a fourth win in 1910, however, she was defeated in her class. Another of her breed, Ch. Sabine Rarebit, took over the Best in Show title. In those days, when the Smooth was king and the Wire Fox Terrier had yet to earn its sea legs, the Warren and Sabine kennels competed heavily.

The backgrounds of the first two Westminster winners could hardly have been more different. Remedy came from New York; she was owned, bred, and handled by the patriarch of the Fox Terrier breed in America, Winthrop Rutherfurd. He belonged to a prominent New York family and was known to every reader of the tabloids as the "other man" in one of the era's greatest society dramas. Rutherfurd had become engaged to railway heiress Consuelo Vanderbilt, who was forced to renounce him, very much against her will, to exchange the family fortune for the title of Duchess of Marlborough in the 1895 "wedding of the century."

Ch. Sabine Rarebit (left) and Ch. Sabine Fernie. Rarebit defeated Ch. Warren Remedy at Westminster in 1910 and went on to win Best in Show, making it four wins in a row for Smooth Fox Terriers.

The Sabine Fox Terriers, by contrast, came all the way from the Wild West to compete in New York. It is sometimes felt even today that the eastern establishment has a lock on the top Westminster wins, but that obviously did not apply to F. H. Farwell, the colorful character and cattle rancher who owned the vast Sabine Kennels in Orange, Texas. He often traveled to shows with a corral of as many as sixty dogs and two handlers—one to groom and one to show the dogs. As different as these two leading Fox Terrier breeders may have been, they still managed to cooperate: Rutherfurd's great star, Remedy, was sired by a dog from Farwell's kennel, Ch. Sabine Resist.

The first two Westminster winners were both born in the United States, but after that the floodgates opened to imports. Only a handful of Westminster winners in the first few decades of the twentieth century were born and bred in America. Imported dogs dominated so heavily at the time, in fact, that a separate competition for Best American-Bred Dog in Show was introduced in 1917 and not abolished until 1961 (by decree of the American Kennel Club).

No Smooth Fox Terrier has won Westminster since those early victories. Wires have done so repeatedly—some of them more than once. The famous English bitch Ch. Matford Vic took home Best in Show in both 1915 and 1916, in the process escalating in value; from her initial English sale price of £2, she was sold first for $1,000, then for $2,500, and finally for $5,000 after her second Westminster win—huge sums at the time. Vic's last owner was Mrs. Roy A. Rainey, who obviously spared no expense in establishing her Conejo kennels in Huntington, New York. Having spent a small fortune on Vic, she paid a reputed $6,000 for another dog, added her kennel prefix to his name, and then won Westminster with Ch. Conejo Wycollar Boy in both 1917 and 1920. Wire Fox Terriers would go on to win Westminster nine more times in the following decades, more than any other breed.

Ch. Tickle 'Em Jock, a Scottish Terrier originally purchased for the equivalent of $15 from a butcher in London, won in 1911 and was followed to the top spot by a half dozen other Scotties at Westminster in later years. In 1918 Ch. Haymarket Faultless, a white Bull Terrier from Canada, won in one of Westminster's most hotly contested decisions: the two Best in Show judges could not agree on a winner, and a referee had to be called to break the deadlock. Faultless was not the last Bull Terrier to win Westminster, but it took almost ninety years until the charismatic Colored Bull Terrier Ch. Rocky Top's Sundance Kid did so in 2005. Three different Airedales won between 1912 and 1922, but none has won since then.

Terriers ruled almost every Westminster in the early years. The only exceptions until 1929 were the Bulldog Ch. Strathay Prince Albert in 1913, the Old English Sheepdog Ch. Slumber in 1914, the Cocker Spaniel Ch. Midkiff Seductive in 1921, and the Pointer Ch. Governor Moscow in 1925.

It also says something about Best in Show judging in those days that when Vic won in 1915, another Wire was awarded Reserve Best in Show—something that would be impossible today. Although there is no Reserve Best in Show award at American dog shows today, Westminster Kennel Club recognized a runner-up to the top spot for a few years up through the mid-1920s. Not only did both the Warren and Sabine kennels feature in these awards—although with dogs other than Remedy and Rarebit—but so did both the Old English Sheepdog Slumber and the Bull Terrier Faultless, who therefore have the distinction of being the only dogs ever to win both Best and Runner-up at America's top show.

Two dogs that are not featured in the list of Westminster Best in Show winners placed as runner-up to the top spot there not once but twice. The Pekingese Ch. Phantom of Ashcroft did so in 1917 and 1921 and was roundly booed by the rabble at ringside on both occasions. (Westminster spectators have become more polite over the years, but on at least some occasions as late as in the 1970s the spectators made their dissatisfaction with the judge's verdict known.) The Greyhound bitch Ch. Lansdowne Sunflower was Reserve Best in both 1920 and 1922 and reportedly won the Best in Show award at other shows forty-nine times, a record that is impossible to verify because AKC did not publish details of such wins at the time.

The only two generations of the same family to win Best in Show at Westminster are Margaret Newcombe, whose Whippet Ch. Courtenay Fleetfoot of Pennyworth won Westminster in 1964, and her mother, Claire Knapp Penney, whose Sealyham Terrier Ch. St Margaret Magnificent of Clairedale had also done so 1936. Mrs. Knapp is shown with one of her West Highland White Terriers, a breed she was also successful in. Mrs. Newcombe died in 2007 at eighty years of age.

THE STAGE IS SET FOR THE MODERN SHOW

In 1923, there was no Best in Show winner at Westminster—the only time in more than 100 years that a top award was not announced at this show. The American Kennel Club barred interbreed competition that year while investigating the irregularities that routinely occurred at this level of judging: for example, defeated dogs could win over dogs that had placed ahead of them in earlier classes at the same show, and even dogs that had not competed for Best of Breed might turn up to compete—and win—in the Best in Show judging.

The following year, the AKC announced new rules, which have basically remained in place ever since. At all-breed shows, a dog could now compete only at the Group level after winning its breed, and only the Group winners were eligible to compete for Best in Show, as they are today. At the time, there were only five groups, however. The Sporting Group incorporated both hounds and gundog breeds until the late 1920s, when the present Hound Group was created, and the herding breeds were part of the Working Group until it was split in 1983.

The new rules set the stage for modern dog show competition, and a look at the first few years' official Best in Show competitions makes it clear that the concentration on show campaigns and racking up big records is nothing new. A surprising number of dogs—even at a time when there were far fewer cars, no motels, no interstate freeways, and almost no airplanes—were obviously quite heavily campaigned. A few built up Best in Show records that are impressive even by today's standards.

Bearing in mind that there were not nearly so many shows then as there are now, these early records are particularly admirable. In the late 1800s, there were only a dozen or so AKC all-breed shows per year, and although the number grew steadily in the new century, it was not until 1923 that as many as 100 shows were held. The total didn't rise far above 200 shows per year

The Smooth Dachshund Ch. Herman Rinkton, one of the top Best in Show winners of the late 1930s.

until well after World War II. This number increased to 500 shows in the 1960s, to 1,000 in the mid-1980s, and currently hovers around 1,500. Obviously, with more shows it was easier to compete—and win—frequently and therefore possible to create bigger records.

The dog shows of the past were not necessarily much smaller than they are today. Many had only a couple of hundred entries, some even fewer, but by the 1930s several of the top shows attracted more than 1,000 dogs. With approximately 2,500 entries, Westminster was the same size then as it is today—in fact, it reached a peak of 3,146 dogs as early as 1937; there were no restrictions on entries at the time. The amazing Morris & Essex Kennel Club at its height in the late 1930s and early 1940s could draw entries of more than 4,000 dogs, more than almost any AKC show today. The size of an average AKC all-breed show reached a peak of almost 1,300 dogs in the late 1970s; by the early 2000s, that figure had dropped to well under 1,000, not because of any loss of interest in the fancy but because the number of shows has increased even faster than the number of dogs competing.

The quality of the dogs that won then and win now is, of course, a separate matter. Beauty is in the eye of the beholder, and that goes for show dogs as well as for anything else. Fashions change, and although some of the old winners still look wonderful, others probably could not get out of a class today. In some cases, there is no doubt that talented breeders have improved the quality of certain breeds; in others, perhaps it's more a matter of refining a look that's fashionable at the time. Before we dismiss a strange-looking famous old dog as a peculiar, inferior specimen that couldn't win a ribbon today, it might help to remember that the reverse might also be true: some of the top dogs today probably could not have won in the past either.

At Westminster in 1924, the first year that modern Breed, Group, and Best in Show judging was formally implemented, the top award went to an American-bred Sealyham Terrier, Ch. Barberryhill Bootlegger. He no doubt got his name from the Prohibition era, which began in 1920, the year Bootlegger was born. He was the first of a cavalcade of Sealyhams that would grace the top spots at AKC shows for the next few years. His owner and breeder, Bayard Warren, would later make a big impact on a breed that was as yet almost unknown in the Western world, the Afghan Hound.

The AKC did not consistently publish the results for the first year of official all-breed competition. Writer and historian Amy Fernandez, who helped the author gather early results at the AKC library in New York, reports, "Best in Show was not included in the listings of show results, and some clubs did not have a Best in Show award. [A] couple of show reports . . . actually said something like, 'Everyone agreed that Best in Show was a great choice' yet failed to mention which dog it was!" This means that there may have been impressive all-breed records at an earlier time, but there is no way to find out. As we have seen, a Best in Show prior to 1924 was not necessarily what we might expect it to be. Announcements of show records earlier than that should be taken with a grain of salt; hype is not a modern invention, as anyone who has read early twentieth-century kennel ads can testify.

Irene Phillips Khatoonian Schlintz, originator of the Phillips ratings system, which was introduced in *Popular Dogs* in the 1950s and upon which all the major current annual ratings systems are based.

THE RATINGS ARE BORN

In 1925, the American Kennel Club began publishing the results of Best in Show competitions in their monthly magazine, the *American Kennel Gazette*. Since no one had conceived of tallying the wins, there were no rating systems in existence and no Top Dog awards. No year-end summaries of the top dogs were published until the late 1930s, when *Popular Dogs* magazine established a new tradition by printing the names of all the Best in Show winners of the past show season, starting with those that had won the most at the top of the list. From there it was only a short step to a Dog of the Year award, but the real ratings craze did not start until the 1950s, when Irene Phillips Khatoonian Schlintz, herself a judge and past exhibitor, hit upon the idea of adding up not number of wins but total number of defeated competitors during a year. This is the idea behind most ratings systems to this day, although they can be (and have been) twisted in several different directions and for various purposes.

It is clear, however, that the large number of shows held in the United States—initially ten times more than in Great Britain, now sixty times more—requires a reliance on points, statistics, and summary records that just are not necessary when each show is an event in itself. The argument continues about whether it is better to defeat the most competitors or to take the highest number of wins.

That "average" people managed to show as extensively as they obviously did before World War II is surprising. Some big kennels had full-time handlers who were on the road with a string of dogs for much of the year, but it seems that many regular exhibitors also succeeded in attending many shows, even though just a single trip in those days must have been much more of an adventure than it would be today.

Obviously, most of the dog show activity was at first centered along the East Coast, but the number of shows—and top winners—in other parts of the country grew year by year. There was a perceptible shift toward California during the latter part of the 1930s, with a large number of top eastern dogs going West to new fanciers on the coast. The following appeared in the AKC's *Blue Book of Dogs*, published in 1938:

During 1937 the practice of competing in distant circuits was so wide-spread throughout the United States that for the first time since 1874, when the country's first bench show was held near Hempstead, L.I., N.Y., the leading dogs of the various sections of the country could be compared. The East, so long considered as having dogs of far better quality than other parts of the country, found many of its major awards going to dogs from other parts of the country. Dogs from the East that competed in the South and the Southwest for the first time met serious competition.

Another little-known fact is that there were indeed show circuits much earlier than is commonly believed. They were not necessarily as carefully planned or well established as they are today, but it is obvious, both from advertisements for upcoming shows and from the reports, that dog show organizers even then put some thought into picking a convenient date and location for exhibitors attending other nearby shows.

There were far fewer breeds in the past than there are now: in 1900, the American Kennel Club recognized only 43 breeds and by 1950 just over 100, compared with 156 in the early twenty-first century. A few breeds took a disproportionately large chunk of the wins. English Setters, Boston Terriers, Pointers, Doberman Pinschers, and especially Wire Fox Terriers were among the most popular Best in Show breeds at the time. Some breeds won much more then than they do now. For instance, at least 100 English Setters won about 300 all-breed Best in

The Best in Show finale at Morris & Essex in 1935, judged by G. V. Glebe. Louis Murr leads the way with his Borzoi Ch. Vigow of Romanoff, followed by Percy Roberts with the Standard Poodle Ch. Edelweiss du Labory of Salmagundi. William Shafer shows the Doberman Pinscher Ch. Muck v. Brunia, Mac Silver handles the Wire Fox Terrier Ch. Leading Lady of Wildoaks, and Harry Hartnett pulls up the rear with the Irish Setter Ch. Milson O'Boy. The Toy Group winner, the Pomeranian Ch. Little Sahib, is not shown.

Show awards between 1925 and 1941. English Setters again reached a peak in all-breed competition in the early 1950s; during the second half of the twentieth century, they remained competitive but were not nearly as dominant. Boston Terriers and Sealyham Terriers also appear far more frequently on the top lists in the early years than they have done since. Doberman Pinschers and Wire Fox Terriers have never lost their

appeal as Best in Show choices, and yet other breeds that were not serious contenders in the past have come to the forefront in more recent decades. Poodles, Afghan Hounds, and Bichons Frisés are some examples.

Some of the Best in Show totals listed for certain dogs in this chapter are lower than what has been published in some breed books. This does not mean that either source is incorrect. Today, pretty much everyone agrees that when a dog in the United States is credited with a given number of Bests in Shows, this applies to AKC all-breed wins. That was not necessarily so in the past, and in much published material about dogs of bygone years the records include wins before an imported dog came to the United States, wins in Canada, or wins at specialty shows. All figures in this chapter, unless otherwise specified, refer only to AKC all-breed shows.

THE FIRST "OFFICIAL" TOP DOGS

There were, of course, no ratings systems or official Top Dog awards in existence until much later, but the AKC's decision to offer a straightforward Best in Show competition as early as 1924 makes it possible to bestow that honor retroactively on those dogs that won more than any others in all-breed competition in the early years. Not all the results were published that first year, but from 1925 onward, it is possible to reconstruct the complete records and determine who the top dogs were, year by year.

THE GREAT GERMAN SHEPHERDS

Individually, the top winners in all-breed competition for the first few years on record were two German Shepherd Dogs. Ch. Teuthilde vom Hagenschiess won far more Best in Show awards than any other dog of the period—fourteen all-breed Bests in 1925 and 1926—and could perhaps be said to be the first ever Top Dog All Breeds winner in the United States, although that award did not yet exist. She and her litter brother Ch. Theodolf had been imported from Germany by Geraldine Rockefeller Dodge. For a dog

The German Shepherd Dog Ch. Cito von der Marktfeste, imported from Germany, owned by the Giralda kennel and the leading Best in Show winner of 1927 and 1928.

that made show history, Teuthilde remains somewhat elusive; there is no photo of her even in Mrs. Dodge's own book on German Shepherd Dogs. One reason could be her sex. Mrs. Dodge preferred to focus attention on her stud dogs, and although he won far less, brother Theodolf's photograph frequently graced the Giralda advertisements in the dog press of the period.

Fortunately, Mrs. Dodge's next top winner was a male, Ch. Cito von der Marktfeste, who won even more than Teuthilde did in 1927 and 1928. His photograph was often featured in the *Shepherd Dog Review* magazine in the 1920s. One admirer wrote simply: "With a dog like Cito, judging is made a good deal easier. . . . All a judge needs to do is single him out, place him in front and match the balance of the class up to him." Competition in the breed at that time was intense; there were 205 German Shepherd Dogs at Westminster in 1926. Cito's vital statistics, by the way, may be of interest to modern breed fanciers. He

UNITED STATES: ALL-TIME TOP BEST IN SHOW WINNERS

Minimum 100 AKC all-breed Bests in Show 1924–2006. Years denote first and last appearance in Top Ten all-breed rankings. Total number of Best in Show wins differ slightly depending on source; the figures published are the ones most commonly recognized.

Afghan Hound Ch. Tryst of Grandeur, 161 BIS (1994–1999)
Bichon Frisé Ch. Special Times Just Right, 101 BIS (2000)
Bouvier des Flandres Ch. Galbraith's Ironeyes, 100 BIS (1989–1991)
Boxer Ch. Bang Away of Sirrah Crest, 121 BIS (1950–1955)
Cocker Spaniel (Black) Ch. La-Shay's Bart Simpson, 106 BIS (1994–1995)
Doberman Pinscher Ch. Brunswig's Cryptonite, 123 BIS (1990–1991)
English Setter Ch. Rock Fall's Colonel, 100 BIS (1950–1955)
English Springer Spaniel Ch. Salilyn's Condor, 101 Bests in Show (1991–1992)
Fox Terrier (Wire) Ch. Galsul Excellence (imp. Ireland), 103 BIS (1986–1987)
Fox Terrier (Wire) Ch. Registry's Lonesome Dove, 216 BIS (1991–1993)
German Shepherd Dog Ch. Altana's Mystique (imp. Canada), 275 BIS (1992–1994)
German Shepherd Dog Ch. Covy-Tucker Hill's Manhattan, 200 BIS (1984–1986)
German Shepherd Dog Ch. Kaleef's Genuine Risk, 100 BIS (2003–2004)
German Shepherd Dog Ch. Kismet's Sight For Sore Eyes, 103 BIS (2001–2002)
Kerry Blue Terrier Ch. Torum's Scarf Michael (imp. UK), 109 BIS (2001–2002)
Lakeland Terrier Ch. Revelry's Awesome Blossom, 100 BIS (1995–1996)
Maltese Ch. Ta-Jon's Tickle Me Silly, 103 BIS (1997–1998)
Pekingese Ch. Chik T'Sun of Caversham (imp. UK), 126 BIS (1957–1960)
Pekingese Ch. Yakee If Only (imp. UK), 127 BIS (2004–2006)
Pekingese Ch. Yakee Leaving Me Breathless at Franshaw (imp. UK), 113 BIS (2002–2003)
Poodle (Standard) Ch. Lake Cove That's My Boy, 169 BIS (1997–1999)
Poodle (Standard) Ch. Lou-Gin's Kiss Me Kate, 140 BIS (1979–1980)
Poodle (Standard) Ch. Whisperwind's On A Carousel, 105 BIS (1989–1990)
Scottish Terrier Ch. Braeburn's Close Encounter, 200 BIS (1981–1985)
Welsh Terrier Ch. Anasazi Billy The Kid, 100 BIS (1995–1997)

weighed eighty-five pounds, was twenty-five and one-half inches (sixty-five centimeters) at the withers, and is described as twenty-eight inches (seventy-one and one-half centimeters) "long" (presumably from breastbone to buttock). Cito also traveled back to his native Germany at least once to compete at the great Sieger show. He placed third in the Adult Male class of some eighty competitors, which was pretty good, but not good enough for the perhaps slightly biased ringside commentator, who wrote that the winner had "absolutely no business" getting ahead of Cito.

It would be safe to say that no individual before or since has been as influential on as many different levels in dogs as Mrs. Dodge. She owned more top dogs of more breeds than anyone else either before or since; she was also a philanthropist, a writer, a judge, and—perhaps most important for the dog fancy—a dog show organizer. The annual Morris & Essex Kennel Club dog show, which she hosted each year on her magnificent estate in Madison, New Jersey, would become the biggest and best dog show in the United States.

Mrs. Dodge was not the only American to import top dogs from Germany at this point. In German Shepherd Dogs, the other big winners were Ch. Hamilton Aribert vom Saarland, Ch. Arko v. Sadowaberg of Jessford, and Ch. Dolf v. Düsternbrook, who in his younger years had been Champion of Germany in 1919 and was Reserve Best in Show at Westminster in 1924. Among other imports were two Doberman Pinschers, Ch. Freya vom Siegelberg and Ch. Claus von Signalsburg, and the Schnauzer (presumably a Standard, although size is not mentioned) Ch. Clause von Fürstenwald. The most significant wins for imports from continental Europe were still to come, however.

The American
KENNEL GAZETTE

Vol. 43, No. 10
Per Year $4

October 31, 1926
Per Copy 50 Cents

FREDERIC C. BROWN'S CH. PINEGRADE PERFECTION
Best in Show at the American Kennel Club Sesqui Exhibition

PUBLISHED OFFICIALLY by the AMERICAN KENNEL CLUB

The Sealyham Terrier Ch. Pinegrade Perfection graced the cover of the *American Kennel Gazette* after winning Best in Show at the AKC Sesquicentennial show in 1926. She repeated the win at Westminster the following year.

SPECTACULAR SEALYHAMS

The most important dog event of 1926 was AKC's Sesquicentennial show, in celebration of America's 150th birthday. (The AKC was only thirty-two years old at the time; it would one day celebrate its own centennial anniversary with a big show, but not until 1984.) It was the first time that the AKC hosted its own show. Held in Philadelphia as a part of the national celebrations, the dog show was a huge success, attracting 2,899 entries from 1,767 dogs. It was won by a Sealyham Terrier, Ch. Pinegrade Perfection, handled by Percy Roberts; Perfection went on to win Westminster the following February as well. She won "only" six all-breed Bests but obviously had a knack for doing well where it mattered, as she ended her career by winning at the three-day Eastern Dog Club show in 1928 with more than 1,000 dogs entered. Another dog from the same kennel, Ch. Delf Discriminate of Pinegrade, shared top all-breeds honors with German Shepherd Cito in 1928 and also won Morris & Essex that year—a show in which Mrs. Dodge's Cito did not, for obvious reasons, compete.

Sealyham Terriers were more successful in the 1920s and 1930s than before or since. The breed had been recognized by the AKC

The Sealyham Terrier Ch. St Margaret Magnificent of Clairedale, Best in Show at Westminster 1936.

only in 1911 but became popular very quickly, both among terrier people, the sporting set, and Hollywood's glamour crowd. (Movie star Gary Cooper was an active dog show competitor and won Best in Show at the Santa Barbara Kennel Club show in 1936 with Ch. Hollybourne Delia.)

After the Pinegrades came the Clairedales. In the mid-1930s, the country's top dog show exhibitor was undoubtedly Claire Penney, whose kennel had already achieved great success with the Clairedale Chow Chows. Turning her attention to Sealyhams, she quickly won scores of all-breed Bests with her two English imports Ch. Wolvey Noel of Clairedale and Ch. St Margaret Magnificent of Clairedale. In 1936,

Magnificent won Best in Show at Westminster, an achievement that would be matched nearly thirty years later by a dog owned by Mrs. Penney's daughter, Margaret Newcombe. That dog was a Whippet, Ch. Courtenay Fleetfoot of Pennyworth, also imported from England. Even more remarkably, at the 2006 Westminster show, seventy years after Magnificent's wins, Mrs. Newcombe and her daughter Claire co-owned the Hound Group–winning Scottish Deerhound Ch. Thistleglen Margot, which may be the only of case of three generations of the same family owning Westminster finalists.

There were many other top-winning Sealyhams during the 1930s, but at the end of the period, the breed's run of success petered out. It did not return until many years later, in 1977, with Peter Green and a Welsh-bred bitch named Ch. Dersade Bobby's Girl, and then again in the first decade of the twenty-first century with Ch. Stonebroke Right On The Money, one of the top show dogs of all breeds in both 2005 and 2006.

THE AGE OF THE WIRE FOX TERRIER

Even at their peak, Sealyhams, for all their spectacular wins, were neither quite as successful nor as numerous as Wire Fox Terriers. Most years up through the 1930s, Wires won at least twice as much as any other breed. In fact, their success was such that it was at first difficult for any single Wire to dominate breed competition on a regular basis. With wealthy owners, new imports regularly arriving from England, and hard-edged professional handlers in the ring, the competition was intense. It was not unusual for a couple of hundred Wires to compete at the top shows, and the atmosphere bristled with energy among the human players almost as much as between their feisty dogs.

The first Wire to win big on a consistent basis was a bitch who stayed at the top for several years. Ch. Talavera Margaret was owned by Reginald Lewis of Warily kennels in Ridgefield, Connecticut. She, like almost all the other great Fox Terrier stars, was imported from England, and among her many other all-breed wins took Best in Show at Westminster in 1928. The following year, a dog named Ch. Newmarket Brandy Snap of Welwire won even more than Margaret did and became the first dog to win ten Bests in Show in a year. That is an impressive record even today, and in those days, with the small number of shows held, it must have seemed an almost impossible achievement. Brandy Snap was owned by Dr. and Mrs. Homer Gage, whose Welwire kennel in Shrewsbury, Massachusetts, was one of the most successful in the United States at the time. The kennel had been started by the Gages' son, Homer, Jr., in the early 1920s. He had willed the dogs to his parents, and after his premature death in 1925 they continued the kennel with great success for several years. Four Wires were among the top winners of all breeds in 1929: in addition to Brandy Snap and Margaret, there was Ch. Talavera Gamester Lewspen and Ch. Eden Aristocrat of Wildoaks. That these dogs were all of the same breed and all imported English champions should come as no surprise, but that all four were sired by the same dog, the great Ch. Talavera Simon, is remarkable. Seldom has a single dog dominated any breed as strongly as Simon did at that time.

Ch. Weltona Frizette of Wildoaks, the top Wire Fox Terrier Best in Show winner of 1930, and like most top winners of her day, sired by the great English stud dog Ch. Talavera Simon.

The first of many Wire Fox Terriers to win big in America on a consistent basis, Ch. Talavera Margaret, Best in Show at Westminster in 1928.

Ch. Gains Great Surprise of Wildoaks, a big winner in 1927 and an important brood bitch.

Ch. Newmarket Brandy Snap of Welwire, Margaret's half brother, won ten Bests in Show in 1929.

Mr. and Mrs. Richard C. Bondy's Wildoaks Kennels, which would take on the greatest importance for the future, in both the United States and England, had already won big with the great brood bitch Ch. Gains Great Surprise of Wildoaks several years earlier. In 1930, the Bondys hit the jackpot again with Ch. Weltona Frizette of Wildoaks, yet another English-born daughter of Simon and the winner of an unprecedented thirteen Bests that year, including Morris & Essex. Four years later, another bitch from the same kennel, Ch. Leading Lady of Wildoaks, again won more than any dog of any other breed. Terrier specialist and writer John T. Marvin described Wildoaks as "probably the outstanding kennel of Wire Fox Terriers of the twentieth century," no mean compliment in view of the competition. The Bondys owned a large estate in Goldens Bridge, New York, and were also very active in the Wire Fox Terrier ring in England: a couple of dogs they bred and sent over to Bobby Barlow became champions and influential sires there. The kennel was managed in America by Mac Silver, who remained a well-known name in dogs after Wildoaks closed down in 1961.

One of the Bondys' imports, Ch. Crackley Striking of Wildoaks, achieved the distinction of winning Best in Show three times in three days in 1941—an unprecedented achievement that is still rare.

A Wire Fox Terrier won Best in Show at Westminster in 1930 and 1931 as well. However, it would be fair to say that these wins were somewhat controversial. There was no argument that Ch. Pendley Calling of Blarney was a quality Wire bitch, but she was owned and handled by John G. Bates, who held high office in the Westminster Kennel Club, which according to contemporary commentators left "wide open doorways to misunderstanding." Bates had actually been listed as the Best in Show judge at the 1930 show but apparently changed his mind and decided to participate as an exhibitor instead. According to William F. Stifel in his chronology of Westminster, *The Dog Show*, there was hissing and booing after the 1931 win, and one commentator, writing in the *AKC Gazette*, observed that "those in charge of staging this great American show" ought to "refrain from entering their dogs." Certainly in later years the powers within the club have usually gone to great lengths to

Davishill Little Man, probably the only nonchampion dog ever to win big in American all-breed competition. In 1938, Little Man won thirteen Bests in Show.

avoid such obvious appearance of conflict of interest. In any case, Pendley Calling won only a handful of Bests beyond her Westminster wins, and another Wire was winning much more during the same time period.

Far from New York, Forrest Hall had established his Hallwyre kennels in Dallas, Texas. His first big winner was Ch. Westbourne Teetotaler, who won more than any other dog in 1930. After that, the only Wire to win an important show for the next few years was Ch. Lone Eagle of Earlsmoor, who took home the Morris & Essex Best in Show in 1932. Toward the end of the 1930s, Mr. Hall came back with an even more sensational winner, a grandson of Teetotaler named Davishill Little Man—possibly the

only dog ever to win big in all-breed competition without achieving the official AKC champion title. At his peak in 1938, Little Man won thirteen all-breed Bests, impressive for any dog and unheard of for a dog that was not officially even a champion!

It would be impossible today for a dog competing consistently at top level not to become a champion, but it wasn't then. It seems that when entering Little Man in the shows, his handler, Dick Davis, took advantage of a little-known rule that allowed any dog, champion or not, to compete only in the Specials class for Best of Breed. Little Man took all his Group and Best in Show victories as a Special without competing for the points that would have given him the champion title. Reportedly, he was shown in the classes on only one occasion, and since he did not win the breed at that time, the attempt was never repeated. The AKC soon changed the rule, and as far as is known, no other dog has ever managed to win consistently in all-breed competition without also becoming a champion.

A SMOOTH FOX TERRIER TAKES OVER

Gradually, Wire Fox Terriers lost steam in the late 1930s and began to be overshadowed by other breeds. By the turn of the decade, the Fox Terrier that everyone talked about was not a Wire but a Smooth, a dog whose name is still remembered when most others have been forgotten. This was, of course, the immortal Ch. Nornay Saddler, whose brilliant career and sterling qualities have been the subject of endless articles and even a 1950 book written by Don Reynolds, titled *Champion of Champions: The True Story of Nornay Saddler, One of the Greatest Dogs in History*. Saddler was imported as a youngster from England, where he had done well as a puppy. The new owners were James Austin and his young stepdaughter Madelaine West, who were partners in the Wissaboo kennels in Westbury, New York.

Saddler's debut in America was not auspicious: at his first three shows, he placed last in small classes of three or four. The situation soon improved, and in 1937 he won his first Best in Show in America. The following year, Saddler won an almost unbelievable twenty-five all-breed Bests— over 10 percent of all the wins awarded that year. He was handled by the great professional Len Brumby, Sr., to most of his big wins. Like quite a few other famous dogs, Saddler never won Westminster, and he did

not take the top spot at Morris & Essex until 1941, having been brought out of retirement after three unsuccessful attempts at this show. It was the last Morris & Essex for several years; the show was shut down during the war years.

When Saddler retired in 1943, he was widely heralded as the top show dog ever in America. He is usually reported to have won a grand total of fifty-nine all-breed Bests in Show, which was indeed more than the tally of any other dog up to that time. However, that figure, as is clear from contemporary reports, included wins in Canada; Saddler's number of confirmed AKC Bests stands at thirty-eight, an impressive number but not, as we shall see, an all-breed record at the time. Some later critics maintained that Saddler's image was polished, and his winnings inflated, by an owner whose public relations skills exceeded those of any other. There is no question, however, that Saddler made a deep impact on the fancy both in his own time and much later.

Two judges who approved of Saddler were the early great breeders and rivals F. H. Farwell and Winthrop Rutherfurd, of Sabine and Warren fame, respectively. Saddler took his first important win under Mr. Farwell, and to Mr. Rutherfurd is attributed the ultimate compliment that an old breeder can bestow on a young winner. When discussing Saddler's virtues, or lack thereof, with a group of other Fox Terrier men, Mr. Rutherfurd, then in his late eighties, is reported to have tilted his head back, chosen his words carefully, and said, "Gentlemen, when I was a young man I knew many of those men in England who wrote the Smooth Fox Terrier standard back in 1876.

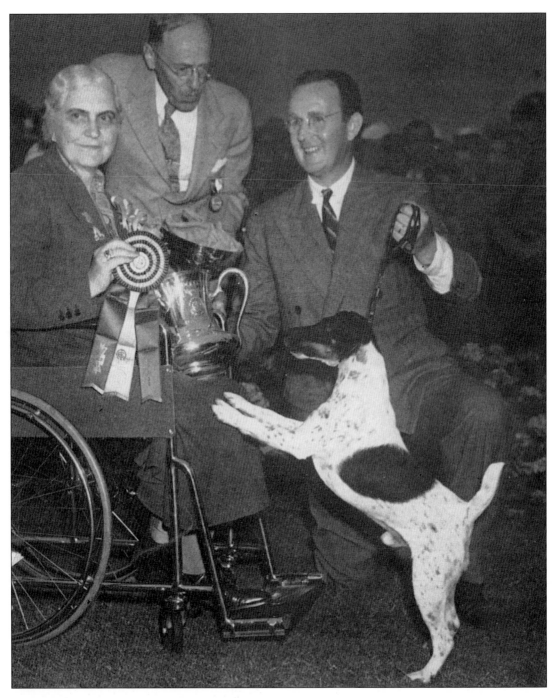

After many years of Wire dominance, the Smooth Fox Terrier came to the foreground again, through Ch. Nornay Saddler, in the late 1930s. In 1937, Saddler won Best in Show twenty-five times—a new record for any breed. He is shown after winning the famous Morris & Essex show with his owner-handler James Austin, judge Enno Meyer, and club officer Geraldine Rockefeller Dodge.

And I can tell you now that when they drew up that standard they closed their eyes and dreamed of Saddler." End of discussion.

As a sire, Saddler was said to have produced at least one champion in every single litter. However, his most important contribution after retiring from the show ring was in raising money for the war effort. His owner increased Saddler's stud fee to a then unheard of $500, with the stipulation that the fee should go to the Army Relief Fund. By lending Saddler's name to a dog-food manufacturer for advertising, Mr. Austin was able to donate $25,000 (equivalent to at least ten times that much in today's dollars) in his dog's name. Even more successful was a War Dog Fund, established by Mr. Austin as a way for average dog owners to contribute by buying a military title for their dogs. One hundred dollars made Saddler a general; other active dog people—even President Franklin D. Roosevelt and his Scottie Fala—followed suit, and the fund generated the equivalent of over a million dollars.

Other Smooth Fox Terriers have won more Bests in Show than Saddler in later decades—the Tasmanian import Ch. Ttarb The Brat in the 1980s, Ch. Broxden Rio Oso Best Dressed in the early 2000s—but none since Saddler has been Top Dog of all breeds.

The Austin family owned not one but two kennels. Mrs. Austin maintained her own high-profile Catawba Pekingese establishment and won the Toy Group at Westminster in 1938 with an English import, Ch. Tang Hao of Caversham Catawba. Her greatest star was Ch. Che Le of Matson's Catawba ("The Duck"), the first consistent Best in Show–winning Pekingese in Amer-

The top-winning modern Smooth Fox Terrier Ch. Broxden Rio Oso Best Dressed, one of the Top Ten of all breeds in 2003.

Ch. Che Le of Matson's Catawba, the first consistent Pekingese Best in Show winner in the United States, took home more than twenty all-breed Bests in the early 1940s. Che Le was owned by the Austin family of Long Island, who also owned Nornay Saddler.

English Setters dominated many of the top shows of the 1930s, 1940s, and 1950s. One of the greatest winners was Ch. Sturdy Max, Best in Show at Morris & Essex in 1937. The judge, right, was Dr. Samuel Milbank.

ica, with a total of twenty-four all-breed wins. Che Le, in spite of his name, was also an English import of the English Caversham breeding that would soon register even more and bigger wins in the American show ring.

SETTERS DOMINATE

The breeds that started to overwhelm the Fox Terriers in all-breed competition during the 1930s usually came from the Sporting Group, mostly Setters and Pointers. English Setters made their first serious inroad in all-breed competition with the appearance of the popular Ch. Blue Dan of Happy Valley, one of the top winners of the early 1930s and twice Best American-Bred at Westmin-

Max's son Ch. Maro of Maridor was the top-winning show dog in America for the first half of the twentieth century, with fifty-five recorded all-breed Bests in Show—more than any other dog up to that time. His litter brother Ch. Daro of Maridor won Westminster in 1938.

ster. He was owned by the Happy Valley Kennels, which also did well with a later star, Ch. The Country Gentleman, the top all-breed winner of 1933, as well as with several glamorous imports.

A couple of years later, another English Setter named simply Ch. Sturdy Max started an illustrious career, winning the top spot at Morris & Essex in 1937, when the entry had already shot up to more than 3,000 dogs. Max was bred and initially shown, apparently as an advertising ploy, by the Sturdy Dog Food Company and later sold to the Maridor kennels of Dwight W. Ellis, Jr., of East Longmeadow, Massachusetts. Max's son Ch. Maro of Maridor won even more than his sire did. Although largely forgotten today, Maro was the top-winning show dog in America for the first half of the twentieth century, raking in fifty-five recorded AKC all-breed Bests—considerably more than even Nornay Saddler had. Maro seems to have changed owners several times, from Mr. and Mrs. A. Biddle Duke to Charlie Parker to W. S. Kennedy. He must also have been quite a handful, unusually so for his breed. A report in *Kennel Review* in 1943 tells the story:

There's nothing like a little burst of temper to put a dog on his toes, as was demonstrated in Cincinnati Sunday night when W. S. Kennedy's English Setter, Ch. Maro of Maridor, put on one of the finest exhibitions of his career to capture his 46th Best in Show. It was a dramatic finale with the Great Dane, Ch. King von Leonehart, owned by Mr. & Mrs. William R. Field, suddenly making a lunge at the Setter

The Cocker Spaniel Ch. My Own Brucie, winner of back-to-back Bests in Show at Westminster in 1940 and 1941.

as he came into the ring and the two dogs tangling in a scrap that brought screams from the women spectators until the handlers could get them apart. Maro was anxious to finish the battle, in fact to lick anything in sight, and there was no denying his domination of the ring.

Maro should not be confused with Ch. Daro of Maridor, his litter brother. Daro won "only" five Bests, but one of them came at Westminster in 1938, a victory that eluded the otherwise much more successful Maro. Today, almost all Westminster winners are campaigned heavily before they win the big one, but that, as should be obvious from the above, did not always happen in years past. One of the most impressive records in this respect was held by another sporting dog, the Cocker Spaniel Ch. My Own Brucie, whose total of six Bests in Show included not only the 1939 Morris & Essex show (the biggest ever with 4,456 entries) but also back-to-back Bests at Westminster in 1940

The English Setter Ch. Rock Falls Colonel, top Best in Show winner of both 1952 and 1953 and the winner of a total of 100 Bests in Show. "The Colonel" is shown after winning Best in Show at Morris & Essex in 1951, owner-handled by William T. Holt, with judge Anton Rost and Geraldine Rockefeller Dodge.

and 1941. He had already won Best American-Bred at Westminster in 1939, and since his owner and breeder, Herman Mellenthin, judged the finale at Westminster in 1942, he had the unprecedented experience of being involved in the Westminster Best in Show competition for four years in a row.

As if the early achievements of English Setters weren't enough, the biggest star this breed has ever seen appeared just a few years after the rest, in the middle of the century. One reason so many great English Set-

ters from the early days have been forgotten is, in fact, that their achievements were overshadowed by those of "the great Colonel," Ch. Rock Falls Colonel. Described as having "that certain glow about him," and always owner-handled by William T. Holt, the Colonel began what would be a long career in 1950. He was a slow starter and for some time did not really show any signs that his would be an all-time great career. In 1951, the Colonel was selected as Best in Show at Morris & Essex, which made the fancy sit up and take notice. By 1952, the orange belton Colonel officially entered the realm of show dog greatness by winning 35 Bests in one year (more than any dog had ever won in so short a period), in the process relegating the famous Boxer Ch. Bang Away of Sirrah Crest to the Number Two spot. Colonel was Top Dog again in 1953, and by the end of 1954 Colonel had won 89 Bests in Show. The dog was now officially a veteran, but Mr. Holt was gunning for 100 Bests—a previously unthinkable tally. In 1955, Colonel won the 11 Bests that took him to 100; he was then—finally— retired, perhaps not without a sigh of relief from the competition.

The Gordon Setter Ch. Legend of Gael was one of the top Sporting dogs and one of the top dogs of all breeds in 1970 and 1971. He is shown with handler Jane Kamp (now Forsyth) and judge Tom Stevenson at the Mid-Hudson Kennel Club in 1970.

One of the few dogs ever to take three Group wins in a row at Westminster, the Gordon Setter Ch. Bit O Gold Titan Treasure, pictured after his first win in 1997 with handler Ken Murray and judge Dr. Bernard McGivern. The trophy presenter (right) is Robert V. Lindsay.

Irish Setters fielded many top winners, a couple of which did spectacularly well. There was the famous Ch. Higgin's Red Pat, who won the first ever Morris & Essex show in 1927 and made an impressive comeback after a few years away from the top spot, winning more Bests in Show than any other dog in 1931. Another four years passed before Pat's even more illustrious nephew Ch. Milson O'Boy repeated that achievement, defeating 4,000 dogs at Morris & Essex. O'Boy was one of the first in a long row of winners of different breeds campaigned for several decades by Mrs. Cheever Porter, whose dogs in later years were always shown by Robert and Jane Forsyth.

Despite the intrinsic beauty and glamour of the setters, none has ever won Westminster, and none has come close to the Top Dog of all breeds spot in the more than fifty years that have passed since the Colonel's glory days. Those that have placed highest in the all-breed rankings are the English Setter Ch. Goodtime's Silk Teddy (Number Four in 1989), the Irish Setter Ch.

★ CHAMPION SETTERS ★

CH. MOLLY O'DAY, *Irish Setter* ★ CH. MARO OF MARIDOR, *English Setter*
KENDARE FARMS, WILFRED S. KENNEDY, *Owner*, DETROIT, MICHIGAN

"*See and Sniff*"

says Wilfred S. Kennedy, owner of Kendare Champions—

"Make sure the dog food you buy can pass your own inspection"

"See and Sniff" is a simple test. Yet it tells the truth about your dog's food. Reveals instantly whether he's getting a wholesome, appetizing ration.

Make this easy test on Pard Dog Food. Then, like thousands of dog owners, you'll *know* how truly fresh and honestly good Pard is. This nutritionally balanced ration contains all the essential food elements, minerals, and vitamins normal dogs need—and

more. Put *your* pet on tempting, health-building Pard now!

VITAMIN RICH!

Pard, fed daily, provides all the known vitamins essential for sound dog health: Vitamin B₂ (riboflavin) for growth and healthy skin; nicotinic acid (specific in the prevention and cure of canine black tongue). Also supplies Vitamins A, B₁, D, E, K, and pantothenic acid—vital to a well-balanced diet for your dog.

GENERATION-AFTER-GENERATION PARD HEALTH
In 6 successive generations of dogs, fed Pard exclusively at Swift's Kennels, not one diet-caused ailment ever appeared. All enjoyed excellent health, full vitality always.

PARD

SWIFT & COMPANY'S NUTRITIONALLY BALANCED DOG FOOD

The Irish Setter Ch. Molly O'Day and the English Setter Ch. Maro of Maridor help promote Pard Dog Food in 1942. At that point, Maro's show career was over, and he had been transferred to the Kendare Farms of Wilfred S. Kennedy in Detroit.

Pompei's The American Way (Number Four in 1997), and the Gordon Setter Ch. Bit O Gold Titan Treasure (Number Five in 1997, Number Nine in both 1996 and 1998). The latter was also one of the very few dogs ever to win the Group at Westminster for three years running. The Irish Ch. Major O'Shannon and the Gordon Ch. Legend of Gael were among the top all-breed contenders for two years each in the late 1960s and early 1970s.

POINTER POWER

In Pointers, Robert F. Maloney from Pittsburgh had already won Westminster in 1925 with Ch. Governor Moscow. He won even more with several dogs of his own breeding, primarily Ch. Herewithem J. P., who was one of the top dogs of all breeds in the late 1920s and who won the Group at Westminster in 1929. The Herewithem dogs were successful enough to be exported back to the breed's native country, where they sired several top winners, including Best in Show at Crufts in 1958, Ch. Chiming Bells. Several decades later, they still exist far back in English Pointer pedigrees.

The Pointer Ch. Herewithem J. P., one of the top all-breed winners in the late 1920s. His owner, Robert Maloney, had won Westminster in 1925 and exported some of his homebred dogs to England.

Mrs. Dodge's Giralda kennel was successful in many breeds. One of her greatest winners was the Pointer Ch. Nancolleth Markable, Reserve Best at Crufts prior to his long and brilliant show career in America, which included Westminster Best in Show in 1932.

Early in the 1930s, Mrs. Dodge turned her attention to Pointers, and the result was a show team that traveled around the country with its handler, McClure Halley, on a victory tour that left little for the competition. Mrs. Dodge's string consisted primarily of imports, not homebreds. Ch. Benson of Crombie and Ch. Nancolleth Marquis each took home a number of Bests in Show, but the biggest wins went to Ch. Nancolleth Markable. He had won Reserve Best at Crufts, was never defeated by another Pointer during his English career, and reportedly even had a field title. In the United States, Markable took the top spot at Westminster in 1932 and embarked on a

The Giralda show string was campaigned nationwide: Ch. Nancolleth Marquis is shown during a tour of the Texas circuit in 1935, where he was shown five times and picked up five Bests in Show, handled by Giralda's kennel manager, "Mac" McClure Halley.

Vroom in 1984. Beryl also won more in all-breed competition than any other dog in 1932, making this the fourth time a Giralda dog had that distinction.

Just why Beryl had the Giralda suffix added to her name but her brother did not is unclear. Presumably, as an English champion, his name could not be altered when he arrived in the United States, whereas hers could. Many new owners at that time tended to fairly indiscriminately tack on their kennel names to their imports' already existing names in their advertisements, regardless of what the official registration certificate read. Mrs. Dodge did so as well, but in Beryl's case Giralda was actually registered as a part of her name.

Pointers have continued to be a force to be reckoned with in recent decades, although they are not nearly as prominent in Best in Show competition as they once were. The two highlights on the all-breed scene were the Westminster win in 1986 of the liver-and-white dog Ch. Marjetta's National Acclaim and the many big wins of his daughter Ch. Luftnase Albelarm Bee's Knees, who won more than fifty all-breed

career that lasted several years and included many more all-breed Bests. A litter sister to Markable from the same kennel, Ch. Nancolleth Beryl of Giralda, never won Westminster but took a total of twenty-eight all-breed Bests, a record for Pointers that stood for over a half century until broken by Ch. Cumbrian Black Pearl, shown by Corky

The Giralda dogs traveled to shows in style: a specially built Cadillac with "ample accommodations for eight dogs to ride in solid comfort."

The first Pointer to win Westminster since Markable, more than fifty years later, was Ch. Marjetta's National Acclaim, in 1986. He was handled by Michael Zollo. The judge was Anna Wanner.

Bests, a new breed record, as well as the Number Two spot of all breeds in 1989.

In the last decade of the twentieth century and the first years of the twenty-first, the Pointer's German cousin has done even better than his English relative, both in the annual ratings and at Westminster. In 1973, the German Shorthaired Pointer Ch. Gretchenhof Columbia River was Runner-up to the Top Dog position, and the following year he won Westminster as well. Fourteen years later, another of the same breed, Ch. NMK's Brittania V Sibelstein, was also second in the Top Dog competition; she did not win the top spot at Westminster but compensated for that by winning the Sporting Group there in both 1987 and 1988. There were links between the two: Colum-

National Acclaim's daughter Ch. Luftnase Albelarm Bee's Knees was handled by Mike Zollo to more than fifty all-breed Bests in Show, and was Runner-up to Top Dog of all breeds in 1989. They are shown winning at Elmira Kennel Club that year under judge Emil Klinckhardt.

The German Shorthaired Pointer Ch. NMK's Brittania V Sibelstein was Runner-up to Top Dog of all breeds in 1987. She was shown by Bruce Schultz and is pictured winning Best in Show at the Santa Barbara Kennel Club under Danish judge Ole Staunskjaer.

The Westminster Best in Show winner of 2005, the German Shorthaired Pointer Ch. Kan-Point's VJK Autumn Roses, handled by Michelle Ostermiller.

bia River was "Britt's" great-grandsire; he was handled by breeder Joyce Shellenbarger, and Britt by Shellenbarger's son-in-law at the time, Bruce Schultz. The German Shorthaired success at Westminster continued in 2005, when a distant descendant of Columbia River, Ch. Kan-Point's VJK Autumn Roses, won Best in Show.

DOBERMANS DEBUT

Although Giralda's primary breeds were German Shepherd Dogs early on, then Pointers, and finally English Cocker Spaniels, Mrs. Dodge had a soft spot for many other breeds. In addition to those already mentioned, Giralda housed Best in Show–winning Bloodhounds, Greyhounds, and (later) Golden Retrievers, and one of the kennel's greatest dogs was the odd man out, a dog with a brilliant but ultimately tragic career. In 1939, Mrs. Dodge introduced a new import to the fancy by winning Best in Show with him at Westminster at his first show in America. This was a fiery Doberman Pinscher, soon to be widely known as Ch. Ferry v. Rauhfelsen of Giralda. He was just off the boat from Europe and not even an AKC champion at the time of his momentous win.

Ferry won a dozen all-breed Bests that season and continued to win the following year, but from all accounts he was not an easy dog to handle, so it must have been

Ch. Ferry v. Rauhfelsen of Giralda, shown here on a *Kennel Review* cover, started his American show career in Mrs. Dodge's ownership with Best in Show at Westminster in 1939. He was later sold to the Randahof kennels and continued to be shown in California.

with some relief that McClure Halley saw his charge go to the Randahof kennels in California. There he caused a sensation; shown initially by Russell Zimmermann, he added a string of additional Bests to his collection, but his fate took a turn for the worse as he was passed from one handler to the next. It is impossible not to read between the lines, and from the few reliable reports that still exist, it is clear that handling Ferry in the ring could be risky business. Eventually, he ended up in the hands of a professional handler named Harold Duffy and his brother, and although they showed him with limited success for some time—he was now very far from the brilliant star who had won Westminster a couple of years earlier—the end came suddenly. Exactly what happened is not clear—perhaps Ferry attacked one of the brothers—but the end result was that Ferry was dead. His owners sued the brothers, but that didn't bring the dog back, and all the parties involved were out of dogs soon thereafter, leaving a cloud that has remained over this outstanding and unfortunate dog's memory.

Ferry's California owners, Mr. and Mrs. L. R. Randle, already owned another record-breaking Doberman import, Ch. Jockel v. Burgund. (In the late 1930s, the Randles

Doberman Pinschers started winning big in the late 1930s. The first West Coast dog to head the Best in Show league was Ch. Jockel v. Burgund, in 1936. He was owned by the Randahof kennels in California and shown by Russell Zimmermann.

advertised their establishment, perhaps with some exaggeration, as "the world's foremost kennel of Dobermans.") He had won even more than Ferry did at his best and was the top winner in all-breed competition in 1936, the first time a West Coast dog had held that position and proof positive that all the top dogs no longer lived in the East. An ad for Jockel in *Kennel Review* magazine in August 1937 gives an idea of the range that a top dog's campaign might have at that time. Over the past seventeen

months, Jockel's show record is detailed at eighty-seven Bests of Breed, thirty-seven Group Firsts, and twenty Bests in Show—and he was not through yet by a long shot.

Jockel and Ferry were not the only great Doberman stars, however. There was also Ch. Troll v. Engelsburg, who won twelve all-breed Bests in 1938. Like the other two, Troll was a German import, but he was owned by Mr. E. Bornstein of Peoria, Illinois, and was advertised as having sired "ALL of the 1938 German Siegers and Siegerins." Dobermans

The third top Dobe of the late 1930s, Ch. Troll v. Engelsburg, won a dozen Bests in Show in 1938. Like Jockel and Ferry, he was a German import and was advertised as having sired "all the German Siegers" of the day.

The step from Dobermans to Boxers isn't large. Boxers took a little longer than the Dobes to get going, but once they were established the results were spectacular. The first all-breed Best in Show winner, Ch. Check v. Hunnenstein, won that award in 1932, but it was another German import, Check's grandson Ch. Dorian v. Marienhof of Mazelaine, who really showed what the breed could do. Reportedly never defeated in the breed either in Germany or the United States, Dorian was one of the four "pillars of the breed" that are credited with creating the American Boxer. The other three, all of similar bloodlines to Dorian, were Chs. Utz, Lustig, and Sigurd (the old man of the quartet and grandsire of the other three), all carrying the vom Dom suffix. They all won well, but it was Dorian

would continue to win big after World War II and have remained one of the most consistently successful of all show breeds.

THE BRED-IN-AMERICA AWARD

Because of the overwhelming dominance of imported dogs, mostly from England and Germany, for a few years during the 1930s, the AKC held a competition for Best American-Bred Dog of the Year. The award was based not on Best in Show wins but on the greatest number of Group firsts an American-bred dog won during the year. One American-bred winner in each Group was honored in New York early the following year, establishing a custom that was revamped, opened to all dogs regardless of nationality, and continued in the 1950s with the Quaker Oats awards—now known as the *Dogs in Review* Show Dogs of the Year awards and still handed out in New York each year during the weekend preceding Westminster.

The public-relations value of the AKC awards in the 1930s was tremendous. It is easy to imagine that media interest in purebred dogs is a fairly recent phenomenon, but cameras whirred and flashbulbs popped as the AKC's top dogs were presented to the New York press in the mid- and late 1930s. *Life* magazine ran feature stories about the winners on several occasions. It was not all print stories either: as many as 50 million viewers watched the top show dogs in the newsreels that were shown before the feature films in movie theaters across America in those days.

The first Boxer to win big in America, the German import Ch. Dorian v. Marienhof of Mazelaine, won twenty-two Bests in Show in 1936 and 1937. He was also an influential sire.

who, handled by Jimmie Sullivan, won twenty-two all-breed Bests in 1936 and 1937, thereby giving a taste of what would follow for the breed and for the Mazelaine kennels in the 1940s and 1950s.

THE ROMANOFF BORZOI

The first winner of the AKC's Best American-Bred award in 1935 was the young Borzoi Ch. Vigow of Romanoff, who would go on to even greater glory in the next couple of years. His owner and breeder, Louis Murr, had come to the forefront a few years earlier with the young dog's sire and namesake, Ch. Vigow O'Valley Farm. The first Vigow was bred in a kennel whose foundation stock had been imported on a couple of adventurous trips to prerevolutionary Russia by one of the most colorful and daring dog people of the early 1900s, Joseph B. Thomas. Thomas was a master showman who generated tremendous publicity for the breed by benching a large number of his glamorous Borzoi at Westminster each year. This tradition was continued by Murr and in modern times by the Majenkir dogs of Karen Staudt-Cartabona, which descend from Romanoff stock. (Some years in the 1990s and early 2000s, as many as a dozen Majenkir champions were entered at Westminster, a few of them admittedly in different ownership.) Thomas never won the top spot at Westminster, but his Ch. Ivor O'Valley Farm won Best American-Bred in Show there in 1925.

Louis Murr continued the winning tradition from Valley Farm, taking home the AKC's Best American-Bred award once again the second year it was awarded with the now mature Vigow. He was one of the

In the 1930s, the American Kennel Club introduced a Best American-Bred award to the year's top dog. The winner in both 1935 and 1936 was the Borzoi Ch. Vigow of Romanoff. He was shown by his owner and breeder, Louis Murr.

top dogs of all breeds in both 1936 and 1937, was reportedly never defeated in breed competition, and won a total of twenty-one Bests in Show. Vigow's Best in Show record is still unsurpassed: the Canadian-born brothers Ch. Kishniga's Desert Song and Dalgarth got close in the 1970s, but no Borzoi has won more than Vigow did, either before or since. Vigow died in a tragic kennel accident, just five years old, barely a week after winning his second Hound Group at Morris & Essex,

The Borzoi Ch. Kishniga's Desert Song, Top Dog of all breeds in his native Canada in 1977. He is shown winning Best in Show at the International Kennel Club of Chicago under judge Tom Stevenson in 1978, handled by his owner and breeder, Dr. Richard Meen.

Ch. Sporting Fields Kinsman, one of the top dogs in all-breed competition in 1992, with his owner-handler, Debbie Butt, and judge Dr. Josephine Deubler.

The Greyhound Ch. Rosemont Liskeard Fortunatus won some of his seventeen Bests in Show before the beginning of official AKC reports in 1925. He is still the top-winning Greyhound male of all time.

The English-born Whippet Ch. Flornell Glamorous won twenty-one Bests in Show in the early 1940s, more than any other Whippet bitch for the next 60-plus years. She was one of the top winners of all breeds for three years.

The Greyhound Ch. Huzzah Sweet Molly Malone, a multiple Best in Show winner and one of the top Hounds in 2001.

when an ill-tempered bitch in season was accidentally let into his kennel.

There were other Vigows, as Mr. Murr tried to repeat the magic formula. He won Westminster Groups in the 1940s with two different Romanoffs and remained a popular all-breed judge for many years, but it was the second Vigow who was his greatest claim to fame. The Romanoff blood still flows in the veins of many American Borzoi today.

GREAT GREYHOUNDS, GLAMOROUS WHIPPETS

The hounds that usually won the most in top competition in the 1920s and 1930s were of another sighthound breed. The Greyhound bitch Ch. Lansdowne Sunflower was reported to have won forty-nine Bests in Show before all-breed competition became strictly regulated, but that figure is impossible to verify. Another Greyhound, Ch. Rosemont Liskeard Fortunatus, straddled the period

The Whippet Ch. Courtenay Fleetfoot of Pennyworth won Best in Show at Westminster in 1964 and was Top Dog of all breeds the same year.

before and after 1924, which means that his exact record cannot be established: of the seventeen Bests in Show he reportedly won, thirteen can be confirmed in official AKC records. Mrs. Dodge's Ch. Giralda's Cornish Man was one of the top all-breed winners of 1941 and was later part of the general exodus from the East. He found a new home in the glamorous Canyon Crest kennels in Los Angeles, which would present a large number of top Greyhounds and Whippets over the next couple of decades, as well as winners in several other breeds—Great Danes, Miniature Pinschers, and especially Standard Manchester Terriers.

Greyhounds in those years won much more than did Whippets, which had only a single top winner in the 1940s. The Mardormere Kennels on Long Island showed both breeds; the particolor Greyhound bitch Ch. Magic of Mardormere won three consecutive Groups at Westminster, and the imported Whippet bitch Ch. Flornell Glamorous won twenty-one Bests in Show, a record that stands unequaled by any other Whippet bitch through the early 2000s. How Glamorous would hold up in today's competition is uncertain; most of the photographs of her are heavily retouched. Percy Roberts, who showed both Magic and Glamorous, is long gone, but Robert Forsyth, who saw the nearly all-white Glamorous in her prime, maintains that she could still hold her own. Forsyth worked for Mardormere as a young man and later showed many top-winning Whippets before becoming one of the sport's most respected all-rounder judges.

Only a few males in this breed have won more than Glamorous in later years: Ch. Courtenay Fleetfoot of Pennyworth in the 1960s, then Ch. Sporting Fields Clansman in the late 1970s, and his great-grandson Ch. Sporting Fields Kinsman in the early 1990s. The two former were both shown by Bob Forsyth; it was while he was campaigning Clansman that Forsyth decided to retire from professional handling, and "Buoy" took his last wins owner-handled by a very young Debbie Butt, who also showed Kinsman from start to finish. Fleetfoot was brought over from a successful show career in England, was Top Dog of all breeds in the United States in 1964, and won Westminster that same year—the only one of his breed to win either of these awards. "Ricky" also turned out to be an influential stud dog and opened the gates for a flood of other English Whippet

Ch. Sporting Fields Clansman, great-grandsire of Kinsman, was among the top dogs of all breeds in both 1979 and 1980. He was initially handled by Robert Forsyth but is shown after winning his last Best in Show with owner-handler Debbie Butt.

PERCY ROBERTS

The British-born Percy Roberts was a professional handler and importer, not a breeder, but he nevertheless added his own kennel name, Flornell, to a large number of the dogs he brought from England for his American clients. Most of the imports were terriers: the two Wire Foxes Ch. Flornell Spicy Bit of Halleston and Ch. Flornell Spicy Piece of Halleston, not closely related in spite of their names, won Best in Show at Westminster for Stanley Halle's Halleston kennels in 1934 and 1937, respectively. The Welsh Terrier Ch. Flornell Rare-Bit of Twin Ponds not only won Westminster in 1944 but also was among the top-winning dogs of all breeds for at least two years. In all, Percy Roberts won the Westminster finale four times, in 1926, 1927, 1935, and 1937—more than any other handler until Peter Green equaled that record in 1968, 1977, 1994, and 1998. His influence as an all-rounder judge was equally great; he judged Best in Show at Westminster in 1967, awarding the top spot to the English-imported Scottish Terrier Ch. Bardene Bingo.

The Terrier Group at Westminster Kennel Club in 1971 was judged by Percy Roberts and won by the Kerry Blue Ch. O'Connell of Kerry Oaks, handled by Joe Waterman.

imports of similar bloodlines. By the late 1970s, the river had become a narrow trickle, but most American Whippets—including Clansman and Kinsman—still descend from a largely British background a number of generations back.

Almost all the Greyhounds and the one Whippet bitch mentioned previously were English imports, although one would not know it from their names. Flornell Glamorous, for instance, had been registered as Tiptree Honey as a puppy in England, but upon exportation to the United States her entire name was changed, as was then still permissible.

POODLE PAGEANTRY

In 1937, the AKC's Best American-Bred award was won by the black Standard Poodle Ch. Pillicoc Rumpelstiltskin. Attention was suddenly focused on a breed that was just starting to become a serious contender for the top awards. It is difficult to imagine today, with Poodles of all three varieties consistently topping the biggest shows, how exotic this breed must have appeared to both dog people and the general public in the 1930s and 1940s. However, Rumpelstiltskin was not the first great Poodle winner. A couple of years earlier, the aristocratic white Ch. Nunsoe Duc de la Terrace of Blakeen had arrived in America via a circuitous route from his native Switzerland. With English and international championship titles already under his belt, "The Duke" was an immediate sensation. His owner, Hayes Blake Hoyt, handled him to win Westminster in 1935—this historic occasion made Duc the first Poodle to take the top spot at Westminster and Mrs. Hoyt the first woman to accomplish the feat.

In the ensuing decades, the line of champions streaming from Blakeen would make this one of America's most successful kennels. Many of the dogs were handled by Mrs. Hoyt herself, impeccably dressed, always in white gloves, and if none of his children quite equaled Duc in mystique and exotic aura, they did win even more than their sire. Ch. Blakeen Jung Frau won fifteen Bests in 1938 and the Best American-Bred award; she and her brother Ch. Blakeen Eiger took turns winning scores of Bests for several years. Later on, Mrs.

INT. CH. NUNSOE DUC DE LA TERRACE OF BLAKEEN
3rd BEST IN SHOW—WESTMINSTER 1934
BEST IN SHOW—WESTMINSTER 1935
2nd BEST IN SHOW—WESTMINSTER 1936

BLAKEEN KENNELS
Poodles
MRS. SHERMAN R. HOYT, *Owner*

KATONAH, N.Y.   TELEPHONE 217

The first Poodle to win Westminster, the Swiss import Ch. Nunsoe Duc de la Terrace of Blakeen, did so in 1935. He also started a dynasty of winning white Standard Poodles.

Hoyt had equal success in Miniature and Toy Poodles. She even sent a Miniature back to England, Ch. Blakeen Oscar of the Waldorf, who became both a champion and an influential sire of white Miniatures there.

The most serious challenge to the Poodle sovereignty of the Blakeens came from the Pillicocs, owned by Mrs. Milton Erlanger and handled by German-born Henry Stoecker, later one of America's most respected all-rounder judges. Mrs. Erlanger's main weapon in this campaign was at first the widely admired Rumpelstiltskin, followed a few years later by another black, Ch. Pillicoc Aplomb, the top all-breed winner of 1939. Aplomb followed a route

Standard Poodles first came to the forefront in the 1930s, partly through Ch. Pillicoc Rumpelstiltskin, winner of the American Kennel Club's Best American-Bred award for 1937.

One of America's most successful breeders and exhibitors ever, Hayes Blake Hoyt, produced a large number of winning Poodles of the three sizes for several decades. She is shown handling Ch. Blakeen Jung Frau, winner of the Best American-Bred award in 1938.

The Standard Poodle Ch. Blakeen Eiger, one of America's top winners in Best in Show competition in the late 1930s.

The American Kennel Club's last award for Best American-Bred was made in 1939 and won by the Beagle Ch. Meadowlark Draftsman. The AKC then discontinued the award.

taken by many before him and was "exported" from the East Coast to California in 1940, where he continued to win Bests in Show. His new owner was Col. E. E. Ferguson, who maintained a friendly relationship with both of the leading East Coast Poodle ladies and also showed some of the best Blakeen Miniatures on the West Coast.

In 1939, the last time the AKC Best American-Bred award was given, the top spot was won by the Beagle Ch. Meadowlark Draftsman. It was a slightly anticlimactic win: Draftsman won seven Bests that year, which was a good record. That the Standard Poodle Aplomb won twice as many Bests did not affect the outcome of the award, which was based on the number of

Group wins only. Exactly why the AKC decided to discontinue the competition is unclear, but it appears that even then there was a strong feeling against the elitism inherent in the rankings awards, which rewarded wealthy owners who could afford to have their dogs heavily campaigned throughout the year. Similar accusations of unfair advantage are often leveled at the top competitors today; obviously, there's nothing new in this.

THE WAR YEARS AND BEYOND

By the early 1940s, the sport of showing dogs was "storming ahead full blast," as the AKC's *Blue Book of Dogs* put it. The outbreak of World War II did not stop dog show activities completely, as it did in Europe, but many shows were canceled. The total number dropped sharply, from 238 in 1941 to 130 in 1943.

When the war ended in 1945, Europe was in ruins, but America was soon ready to assert world dominance in many different areas. Arts, sports, and leisure activities were a part of this, and with a burgeoning economy, it was easy to predict that the dog fancy would soon enjoy an unprecedented boom. American Kennel Club registrations shot up from 77,400 in 1944 to more than 200,000 two years later, to about 350,000 in the mid-1950s, 500,000 in the early 1960s, and just over 1 million for the first time in 1970. Dog show activities increased as dramatically as registrations and even continued to expand when registrations eventually stalled.

More shows each year and larger entries meant keen competition for the top awards. It took a major investment of time, effort, and money to get to the top and stay there, and the dogs that succeeded had to be much more than just a pretty face. These dogs needed stamina, dependability, and a temperament that allowed them to shine in any environment. Undoubtedly as a result, the fortunes of certain breeds began to rise.

THE BOXER GLORY YEARS

Is there any breed more likely to remain upbeat and unfazed than the Boxer? The 1940s introduced a period of unparalleled show ring success for this breed. It hinged, of course, on the prewar imports, all of them bred down from Frau Stockmann's legendary vom Dom dogs in Germany. Dorian's great record had already been equaled and narrowly exceeded by a bitch named Ch. El Wendie of Rockland, who was shown by Nate Levine to Top Dog of all breeds in 1944. Unlike many other winning show bitches regardless of breed, Wendie was also a successful brood bitch and is still featured in the American Boxer Club's Register of Merit.

Mazelaine: Warlord and Brandy

The Mazelaine Kennels of John and Maizie Wagner was already producing scores of top winners, all bred from their German imports. The Wagners mated a Dorian daughter to Utz and came up with Ch. Warlord of Mazelaine, who followed in his sire's footprints to become the second Boxer to take the Group at Westminster. He did so in 1945 and repeated the win in 1946 and again in 1947, when he went all the way to Best in Show. That was impressive, but more was to follow. Warlord's litter sister, Warbaby, was bred to a Dorian grandson, thereby doubling up on Dorian, and produced Ch. Mazelaine's Zazarac Brandy, handled by Phil Marsh to a reported sixty Bests in Show, including Westminster in 1949. (It has been possible to confirm only fifty-four of these;

quite possibly the remaining six were at Boxer specialty shows.)

His large number of all-breed wins made Brandy the top-winning show dog ever in the United States, but his record did not last long.

The Phenomenal Bang Away

A new Boxer kennel, Sirrah Crest, owned by Dr. and Mrs. Raphael C. Harris of Santa Ana, California, was already providing formidable competition for Mazelaine. The Harrises had purchased their foundation stock from the Wagners, and in Ch. Bang Away of Sirrah Crest they produced what many still consider one of the greatest show dogs ever. Bang Away was a brilliant red with striking white markings—in comparison, Zazarac Brandy was brindle with much less white, and Warlord was nearly solid red. Bang Away also had a stunning physique and, most important, the charisma that didn't need any spotlights for him to stand out anywhere.

Bang Away first made his mark in 1949 as a four-month-old puppy. Friederun Stockmann, whose breeding laid the cornerstones for Boxer breeding the world over, was on an extended visit from Germany to the United States. She could not judge a regular AKC show, but the Boxer Club of Southern California arranged a match show especially for her. The entry was enormous, and her choice for Best in Match was the very young Bang Away. Frau Stockmann put the puppy up on a crate for everyone to see, pronounced him "the best Boxer in America," and predicted a brilliant future for the young dog. What the Wagners thought of all this is not clear, but that they admired their rival is a fact: Mr. Wagner was one of the first judges to put Bang Away up, and Mazelaine's last top winner several years later was a Bang Away daughter.

Even as a yearling, Bang Away was breathing down Brandy's neck. While Brandy was Top Dog of all breeds in 1950, Bang Away was second to him both as top

OBSERVING A LEGEND

John Connolly, later president of the American Boxer Club, remembers seeing Bang Away for the first time in the 1950s: "Every minute I had that day was spent watching Bang Away in his pen, in his crate, and in the ring. All the knowledgeable people were telling me he was older now, he had gone BIS the day before, he had bred a couple of bitches, so he was kind of tired. When he was in the ring you could not take your eyes off of him, you couldn't look at anything else in the ring. He easily won BIS, winning a large washing machine." According to Connolly, Bang Away completely changed the look of the Boxer breed: "Compared to the good dogs that went before him, he was streamlined and added more style and flair to the breed." Naturally, the breeders flocked to Bang Away. According to the published records, he sired a total of 228 litters, which included eighty-one champions.

The late 1940s and 1950s were golden years for American Boxers. All previous records were shattered by Ch. Bang Away of Sirrah Crest, who won Westminster in 1951 and took home a total of 121 all-breed Bests in Show—more than any other dog up to that time.

Bang Away's predecessor in the top spot, Ch. Mazelaine's Zazarac Brandy, a result of linebreeding on imported German lines, won Westminster in 1949 and was the top Best in Show winner of 1950. He won more than fifty all-breed Bests in Show.

Boxer and among all breeds in the rankings. Due to the stature of these two Boxers, it became de rigueur for serious show fanciers to follow the breed more closely than ever before. The tension between the two camps is palpable even in the reports published in the dog press of that time. The owners were certainly polite, even respectful, of each other, but this did not stop Brandy's handler, Phil Marsh, from telling the press that "I know I have a better Boxer than Bang Away and I could produce fifty judges who know it." Both dogs were heavily promoted in full-page advertisements, and the Wagners announced in bold headlines that Brandy was "THE TOP DOG OF ALL TIME!" They must have realized, however, that it was just a matter of time before Brandy's days would be over. In 1951, Bang Away was Top Dog of all breeds for the first time, with a new record of twenty-eight Bests that year alone; the now five-year-old Brandy, although still a contender, dropped down a few notches and then went into dignified retirement. The Harrises, in what must be considered the ultimate act of sportsmanship, commissioned a cartoon showing the old king, Brandy, handing the crown over to Bang Away.

Bang Away's career lasted six years, five of them as Number One or Number Two of all breeds. In the sixth year, during a temporary retirement, he dropped down to Number Three. His long reign at the top came about at least partly as a result of the intense rivalry between Bang Away and the English Setter Ch. Rock Falls Colonel. The Boxer was already heading into retirement as the top-winning show dog of all time when Colonel picked up speed and looked as if he might take over the all-time record, where-upon Bang Away was brought back into the arena and quickly established himself as Top Dog again. He won his 100th Best in Show at Bronx County Kennel Club on December 4, 1954, the first dog ever to do so—a few months before the English Setter achieved the same goal. Bang Away ended up with an all-time record of 121 Bests in Show, in the process reportedly being defeated in breed competition only five times. On one of these occasions, his loss caused such a riot, with the enraged ringside throwing chairs, that a police escort was required to get the judge safely out of the building. Bang Away was one of the first dogs to be shown consistently on both coasts, in the East by Nate Levine and in the West by Harry Sangster.

Appropriately, the last year Bang Away was Top Dog, in 1955, Number Two of all breeds was another Boxer, Bang Away's daughter Ch. Baroque of Quality Hill, owned by the Wagners. Baroque's much-admired litter brother Ch. Barrage of Quality Hill was shown by Jane Kamp, one of the handlers who would dominate the show scene in the East for the next few decades. Of course, she is now known as Mrs. Robert Forsyth and, together with her husband, makes up one of the most respected judging couples in the dog sport.

The great age of the Boxer lasted for only a couple of decades. When Bang Away won Westminster in 1951, it was the third time in five years that a Boxer had taken the top spot there. At the American Boxer Club specialty show in 1952, the three giants of the breed paraded together—Warlord now ten years of age, Brandy already a little grey around the muzzle at six, and Bang Away reaching his prime at three years old.

Other Boxer Greats

In the decades that followed, many other kennels would promote top-quality show Boxers with great success. The famous Salgray establishment in Massachusetts, for instance, turned out one top contender after another for many years and bred two dogs that scored high in the Top Dog ratings in the 1960s: Ch. Salgray's Fashion Plate and his nephew, Ch. Salgray's Ovation. Both were shown by Larry Downey, who provided a human link to the past, having grown up at the Mazelaine kennels. However, only one other Boxer would win Westminster—Ch. Arriba's Prima Donna in 1970. Depending on what statistics you look at, Prima Donna was either Number One or Number Two of all breeds in 1969 (a slight difference between the two ruling scoring systems created different winners that year). One other Boxer was Top Dog of all breeds—Ch. Treceder's Painted Lady, who

Ch. Evo-Wen's Impresario was the top Working dog for three years, won more than forty Bests in Show, and was Runner-up to Top Dog in 1960.

took that award in 1963, winning thirty all-breed Bests that year, more even than Bang Away in his prime. Both dogs were shown by professional handlers who remain active as judges in the early 2000s: Prima Donna was handled by Jane Forsyth, and Joe Gregory showed Painted Lady. A third dog, Ch. Evo-Wen's Impresario, didn't win either Westminster or Top Dog but won almost everything else. Handled alternately by Harry Sangster and Larry Downey, he was the country's top Working dog for three consecutive years in the late 1950s, among the top few of all breeds each time, and won more than forty Bests in Show.

Boxers continued to top the annual Working Group rankings consistently into the 1960s and won many all-breed Bests later in the century, but the fact that none has dominated the scene as did the earlier dogs raises questions. Are Boxers not as good as they once were? Are the judges not appreciating the good ones as they should? Are there perhaps outstanding Boxers out there that do not get the opportunities that the top dogs from the middle of the last century had? There are indications that a renaissance may be on the way. In the 1990s and early 2000s, a number of Boxers succeeded in placing high among the Top Ten of all breeds: Ch. Kiebla's Tradition of Turo, Ch. Hi-Tech's Arbitrage, Ch. Turo's Futurian of Cachet, Ch. Hi-Tech Johnny J of Boxerton, Ch. Storybook's Rip It Up, Ch. Hi-Tech's Basic Edition, and Ch. Brookwood's Mystic Warrior. The last mentioned, "Tommie," even succeeded in winning more Bests in Show than Zazarac Brandy had and retired in 2006 with sixty-three Bests, the closest to Bang Away's still unmatched record of half a century earlier.

©Custom Dog Designs

Ch. Brookwood's Mystic Warrior was one of the top dogs of all breeds in 2004 and 2005; he broke most of the old breed records and won more Bests in Show than any other Boxer male except Ch. Bang Away of Sirrah Crest in the 1950s. Handler Gary Steele shows the way.

The Boxer successes continued into the 1960s and beyond. Ch. Arriba's Prima Donna was joint Top Dog of all breeds in 1969 and won Westminster in 1970, handled by Jane Kamp (now Forsyth).

Ch. Hi-Tech's Basic Edition placed among the Top Ten of all breeds in both 2004 and 2005. He is pictured with handler Kimberly Pastella Calvacca winning Best in Show at Boardwalk Kennel Club in 2004. Judge Joseph Gregory is one of the few people approved by AKC to judge all breeds and is a past Boxer handler.

Ch. Salgray's Fashion Plate, one of a long line of the top winners carrying the Salgray prefix, was one of the top dogs of all breeds in 1965 and victor of the American Boxer Club national specialties in 1965 and 1966.

Ch. Turo's Cachet remained among the top Working Group winners for four years and among the Top Ten of all breeds for two. She was top Working dog in 1986 and is shown, handled by Kimberly Pastella, winning Best in Show at Central Ohio Kennel Club that year under judge Dr. John Shelton.

Ch. Mighty Sweet Regardless, shown with judge Mrs. Dodge (center) and handler Mrs. Claude Fitzgerald, won more Bests in Show than any other dog did in 1946.

The Boston Terrier Ch. El-Bo's Rudy Is A Dandy was the top winner of his breed for many years and placed among the top Non-Sporting dogs for three years in the early 1980s. He won Best in Show twenty-eight times during his years at the top. He is shown handled by his owner, Bob Candland, to a Group win at Sahuaro State Kennel Club in 1971 under judge Tom Stevenson.

THE BOSTON TERRIER: INSTANT ACCEPTANCE

The difference between past glories and current status has been most strongly pronounced in the Boxer's small relative, the Boston Terrier. Immediately following its official recognition by the American Kennel Club in 1893, the breed became hugely popular with both the pet-loving public and dog show fanciers. Often, 100 Boston Terriers or more would compete at the big shows, and the breed was a consistent contender for top honors from the start. The Boston Terrier, in fact, was right up there with Fox Terriers and setters as the most successful of all show breeds in the early years, winning dozens of Bests in Show in the 1920s, in the days when there were far fewer shows than there are today. The wins were usually evenly divided between a large number of different dogs, allowing no single dog to dominate the breed.

That changed after World War II with the appearance of two Boston Terriers of such charm, style, and quality that they set the dog world on its ear. It started with Ch. Mighty Sweet Regardless, owned by Claude Fitzgerald, who won twenty-five all-breed Bests and back-to-back Groups at Westminster in a three-year career starting in 1945. Mighty Sweet was, far and away, the Top Dog of all in 1946, an honor that no other Boston has achieved since. Mighty Sweet had barely stepped down when the next Boston star appeared on the scene: Charles D. Cline's owner-handled Ch. Payson's Miss Patricia CGI, who stayed close to the top among all show dogs into the 1950s and amassed almost as many big wins as Mighty Sweet did. Once the show careers of those two were done, the excitement was pretty much over for Bostons in all-breed competition. No Boston Terrier has ever headed the annual Non-Sporting Group ratings since they were inaugurated in 1956, and only one was close: Ch. El-Bo's Rudy Is A Dandy, bred, owned, and handled by Bob and Eleanor Candland, who won enough in all-breed competition to place Number Two in 1981. Why the Boston Terrier has been conspicuously absent from the winner's circle for so long is a mystery. With its distinctive markings and charming temperament, it would seem to merit more serious consideration in all-breed competition than it has received since its early glory days.

The second Boston Terrier to score big in the 1940s, Ch. Payson's Miss Patricia GCI, stayed among the top show dogs of all breeds for several years.

BULLDOG GREATS

Bulldogs have had a much more consistent run of success over the years. Among the winners of the 1950s, none was greater than the English import Ch. Kippax Fearnought. "Jock," as he was known, arrived from the breed's native country in December 1953, accompanied by glowing praise from British specialist judges. He was imported by Dr. John Saylor of Long Beach, California, a relative newcomer to the sport, and won Best in Show at his very first show in America. Handled by his owner, Jock did not do so well; Dr. Saylor recalls going "dead last" when showing his new import at the next show. Fortunately, help was at hand. The great professional Harry Sangster took one look at Jock and convinced the Saylors to let him show the dog. It would be a campaign on the owners' terms, however: Jock was shown only a couple dozen times in a career that lasted several years. That in spite of this limitation he accounted for a total of seventeen Bests in Show gives some indication of the deep impression Jock made on the fancy. For Sangster, it must have been frustrating not to be able to show this great dog extensively, but

Jock will forever be remembered for the percentage of his wins rather than the total. He went to Westminster twice, in 1954 and 1955, and won the Group both times, the first time as a youngster even before becoming a champion. On his return trip the following year, he also won the Best in Show finale under the highly esteemed judge Albert E. Van Court. He adorned the cover of *Sports Illustrated* magazine later that year—one of the very few dogs ever to do so—and he even appeared in *Playboy* magazine!

Bulldogs continued to win steadily in later years. Ch. Vardona Frosty Snowman was owner-handled by his breeder, Dr. E. M. Vardon, who had awarded Jock Best of Breed at Westminster in 1955. Snowman had a much longer career than Jock did and ruled as the top Non-Sporting dog for three years in the late 1950s and early 1960s. Although he never won the supreme award at Westminster, he was Best American-Bred in Show there in 1959 and was Group first in 1960. He won more Bests in Show than Jock did and made a significant contribution as a sire even in England through an exported son. Bulldogs have continued to win consistently ever since.

The Bulldog Ch. Banshee of Beechlyn, titled in both England and America, was one of the top Non-Sporting winners of both 1956 and 1957 in the United States.

Ch. Kippax Fearnought was exported from England to California and, in spite of a restricted show career, won back-to-back Groups at Westminster and Best in Show there in 1955. "Jock" also adorned the cover of *Sports Illustrated* and even appeared in *Playboy* magazine.

They headed the annual Non-Sporting Group competition for three years running in the 1970s (Ch. Westfield Cunomorus Stone twice and Ch. Marinebull's All The Way once), with Ch. Hetherbull Bounty's Frigate, bred by Bob and Jean Hetherington, going as far as Top Dog of all breeds in 1989. However, no Bulldog has won Westminster since Jock.

The Bulldog Ch. Vardona Frosty Snowman was one of the most successful owner-handled dogs of all time. Shown by his breeder, Dr. E. M. Vardon, Snowman was the top Non-Sporting dog in America for three consecutive years—1958, 1959, and 1960—and also placed among the Top Ten of all breeds. He was an influential sire not only in America but also in England.

Ch. Kippax Fearnought was one of the last dogs to have a spectacular career in spite of not being heavily campaigned. From the late 1950s and even more so from the 1960s onward, it was necessary to stay on the road and win consistently most weekends of the year to earn a top spot in the increasingly important annual rankings.

A LEGACY OF DOBERMAN WINS

One other dog of the early 1950s also achieved legendary status in a career that was as restricted as that of the Bulldogs. The Doberman Pinscher Ch. Rancho Dobe's Storm was bred by Mr. and Mrs. Brint Edwards in a glamorous new kennel in California, but he did his big winning on the East Coast. Owned by Len Carey, a Madison Avenue advertising executive, and handled by Peter Knoop, Storm achieved an astonishing record. According to published records, he was shown a total of only twenty-five times, was undefeated in the breed every time (except for one puppy class appearance), and won twenty-two Working Groups and seventeen Bests in Show—including back-to-back Bests at Westminster in 1952 and 1953. That's an amazing percentage, but the debate among breed fanciers swirled for many years about just how good the dog was. Some detractors felt that Mr. Carey's profession may have helped his dog's career. However, F. F. H. Fleitmann, the man who did more to establish the Doberman in the United States than anyone else, stated emphatically, "The Germans have not yet produced a dog to beat Storm."

A later dog from the same breeders, Ch. Rancho Dobe's Maestro, a descendant of Storm, provided the young Corky Vroom with one of his first great winners and was Number Two of all breeds in 1970. The Rancho Dobe name lasted longer than the kennel itself; the author recalls a big kennel sign displayed in Calabasas next to the freeway outside Los Angeles in the 1980s, but by then the Dobermans were long gone and the Rancho Pet kennel was used for boarding.

From the prewar German imports there is a direct link to Rancho Dobe (Storm's dam came from Randahof and was a granddaughter of the late great Ferry) and from there to one of the most consistently successful American kennels over the long

The Doberman Pinscher Ch. Rancho Dobe's Storm, Best in Show at Westminster in both 1952 and 1953.

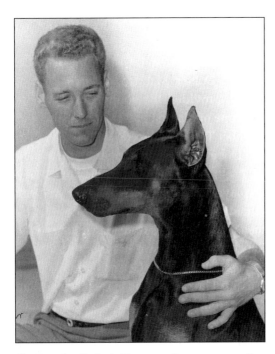

Ch. Rancho Dobe's Maestro, Runner-up to Top Dog of all breeds in 1970, with handler Corky Vroom.

Ch. Brunswig's Cryptonite, Runner-up to the Top Dog of all breeds in 1991. He was also a top sire and was handled by George Murray.

term: Marienburg. Mary Rodgers did not breed the first big winner to carry her kennel name, Ch. Sultana v. Marienburg, who had a couple of lines going back to Storm and Ferry. However, Rodgers bred innumerable other champions, including Sultana's granddaughter Ch. Marienburg's Mary Hartman. Sultana had been Number Two of all breeds in 1967, professionally handled by Rex Vandeventer and pushing her owner into the spotlight for the first time. The granddaughter went one step higher, becoming Top Dog in 1978, still owned by Rodgers but shown by Moe Miyagawa, who has remained as handler for the Marienburg dogs for several decades. Marienburg has continued with unabated success into the twenty-first century, incorporating new imported blood and, still with the assistance of Miyagawa as handler, launching its great-

est later star, Ch. Marienburg's Repo Man, as top Working dog and one of the Top Ten of all breeds in 2002. When Mary Rodgers was chosen as the AKC Breeder of the Year in 2003, it was in recognition of what she had achieved with a breeding program spanning four decades.

Dobermans have produced more Top Dog winners in the annual rankings than has any other breed in America. In 1965, Bob Hastings succeeded in winning the Top Dog all-breed competition with Ch. Ru-Mar's Tsushima with a total of only six Bests in Show—far fewer such wins than anyone for years before or after her. This was because of a drastic shift in show entries: the Working Group, especially on the West Coast, had grown so big that winning just a large number of Groups—and Tsushima won twenty-six that year—could earn a dog sufficient points to get ahead of the competition. In 1973, the new Top Dog of all breeds was Ch. Galaxy's Corry Missile Belle, shown by Corky Vroom; in 1978, it was Mary Hartman's turn to be Top Dog. A decade later, Ch. Royal Tudor's Wild As The Wind was the winner. She also won Westminster in 1989 and established her handler, Andy Linton, as one of the country's top new talents. "Indy" was the last Doberman on record to become Top Dog,

although a couple have come close since then—Ch. Brunswig's Cryptonite is remembered as an influential stud dog; he was also a successful show dog and was Number Two of all breeds in 1991. A few years after his successes, Ch. Toledobe's Serenghetti won nearly 100 Bests, stayed among the top dogs of all breeds for three years, and was Number Two in 1996.

Many other Dobes have ranked among the Top Ten dogs of all breeds, and a few

Ch. Sultana v. Marienburg, the first top winner from Mary Rodgers's famous kennel, was Runner-up to Top Dog of all breeds in 1967, handled by Rex Vandeventer.

Ch. Toledobe's Serenghetti, shown winning Best in Show at Louisville Kennel Club in 1998, handled by Andy Linton under judge Michele Billings. "Sera" stayed among the top dogs in the country for three years.

The Top Dog of all breeds in 1973, Ch. Galaxy's Corry Missile Belle, one of three Top Dog winners that Corky Vroom handled for owners Gloria and Nat Reese. Missile Belle is shown winning Best in Show in Philadelphia in 1972 under judge Alva Rosenberg.

Ch. Royal Tudor's Wild As The Wind, pictured in the Group at Westminster with her handler, Andy Linton. "Indy" won Best in Show there in 1989 and was Top Dog the previous year.

have remained there for over a year: Ch. Star Dobe's Irish Fantasy in 1981 and 1982, Ch. Eagle's Devil D in 1983 and 1984, and Ch. Aquarius Damien V Ravenswd in 1993 and 1994. Dobermans remain one of the most intensely competitive of all breeds, always with a new great star on the horizon.

THE GREAT SPRINGER DILEMMA

A breed that had done well in the prewar years began making the judges spring to attention and take notice in the 1950s: the English Springer Spaniel. The name, according to some, is a misnomer: what we call an "English" Springer Spaniel is not what Springer Spaniels look like in Great Britain. Actually, the more Springers won in the United States, the more they tended to diverge from their British ancestors. Some breed fanciers even in England maintain that the differences are mainly cosmetic, due mostly to a greater emphasis on color and markings, on trimming and showmanship, but there is no question that the English Springer Spaniel in America is a far more streamlined and glamorous animal than his British cousin. Whether it has changed to the degree that a change of name is justified is a different matter.

Ch. Chinoe's Adamant James, Top Dog of all breeds in 1971 and Best in Show at Westminster in both 1971 and 1972. He is shown with handler Clint Harris winning the Group in 1972 under judge Lee Murray.

There had been many Springer winners before the war, including such great British imports as Ch. Showman of Shotton, but it was not until 1948 that the breed really came into the limelight. Showman's grandson Ch. Frejax Royal Salute defeated such canine royalty as the Boxer Zazarac Brandy and the reigning Blakeen Poodle, Magic Fate, to become Top Dog in the country that year. Royal Salute was owned and bred by Fred Jackson, the leading Springer breeder of his

day, but it is interesting to note that his top winner was sired by a dog from a then still relatively unknown kennel named Salilyn.

It was not long, however, before Julia Gasow's Detroit-based Salilyn kennel burst forth as one of the greatest show and breeding establishments America had ever seen. Royal Salute had, in fact, barely retired before it was time for the first of a seemingly unending string of Salilyn dogs to shoot up in the charts: Ch. King Peter of Salilyn won his first Best in the early 1950s and was runner-up to the Top Dog award in 1953. In a breeding career of many peaks, the second high was reached in the late 1960s, when Ch. Salilyn's Aristocrat appeared on the scene. He was a dog of such class and prepotency that his stellar show career—which included an amazing record of forty-five all-breed Bests won in a single year, 1967—was actually eclipsed by his success as a sire. Aristocrat is credited with a total of 188 champions, more than any other dog of any breed. The greatest-winning Aristocrat son was the legendary Ch. Chinoe's Adamant James, a dog who won even more than his sire did: forty-seven Bests in 1971 and back-to-back Bests in Show at Westminster, in 1971 and 1972—only the fifth dog ever to do so. To date, no dog since Adamant James has won Westminster twice.

"D. J." was not the first English Springer to win the top spot at Westminster. Royal Salute, King Peter, and Aristocrat went only as far as to win the Sporting Group there in

The first English Springer Spaniel to win really big in America, Ch. Frejax Royal Salute, shown winning Best in Show at Harbor Cities Kennel Club in 1947 under judge Harry T. Peters. Royal Salute was shown by his breeder and owner, Fred Jackson.

1948, 1955, and 1967, respectively; but Ch. Wakefield's Black Knight, handled by Laddie Carswell, won the first Westminster Best for the breed in 1963.

The final, and probably highest, peak in Mrs. Gasow's long breeding career came in the final decade of the twentieth century. Aristocrat's descendant Ch. Salilyn's Condor won Best in Show sixty-nine times in 1992, something that would normally have guaranteed him the Top Dog spot of all breeds. However, that year will be forever remembered as one of the greatest horse races in dog show history, with the ultimate winner, the Wire Fox Terrier Ch. Registry's Lonesome Dove, scoring one of the narrowest victories ever in this type of competition. "Robert" made up for his second place, as if that were necessary, by winning Westminster in 1993 and went on to sire a daughter, Ch. Salilyn 'N Erin's Shameless ("Samantha"), who made it a unique father-daughter double victory by also winning Westminster in 2000, a few months after Mrs. Gasow's death at ninety-four years of age.

Not all the top Springer winners came from Salilyn, although most of them were related. Among the most successful were Ch. Filicia's Dividend and Ch. Telltale Royal Stuart, both of whom were among the Top Ten of all breeds for two years each in the 1980s; and Ch. Felicity's Diamond Jim (who is called "James" after his ancestor, Ch. Chinoe's Adamant James), handled by Kellie Fitzgerald to Best in Show at Westminster in 2007. Many Springer kennels contributed to the consistent success of this breed in Best in Show competition. Most of their dogs carried Salilyn blood, but there has also been cautious outreach to Springer fanciers in other countries, perhaps indicating that

The English Springer Spaniel Ch. Salilyn 'N Erin's Shameless, among the top all-breed winners in both 1998 and 1999, won Westminster in 2000. "Samantha" is shown winning at Tuxedo Park Kennel Club in 1999 under judge Chester F. Collier. Trophy presenters are club officers Glorvina and Alexander Schwartz.

there will be no need, as has been occasionally suggested, to rename the English Springer Spaniel as the American Springer Spaniel.

COCKER SPANIELS: ENGLISH AND AMERICAN

In Cocker Spaniels, unlike Springers, the split between English and American types was taken to its logical conclusion. The two had been developing in different directions and categorized at the shows as varieties of the same breed for a number of years when the American Kennel Club officially separated them into different breeds in 1946.

What are now called English Cocker Spaniels in the United States (and, logically, simply Cocker Spaniels in Great Britain) have not won nearly as much since the split as the American breed. The only English Cockers ever to place among the Top Ten of all breeds in the United States were Ch. Elblac's Bugle of Hastern in 1956 and Ch. Ancram's Simon in 1970. The red dog Ch. Chestnut's Selling The Drama came close in 2005 and achieved a record number of all-breed Bests for the breed.

By contrast, the breed named Cocker Spaniel in the United States (and termed, both logically and ultimately confusingly,

One of the few English Cocker Spaniels to rank among the Top Ten of all breeds, Ch. Ancram's Simon, shown with handler Ted Young and judge Clark Thompson in 1969.

American Cocker Spaniel in other countries) quickly developed into a show breed par excellence. The Cocker's ebullient temperament, wagging tail, flowing coat, plush face, and melting eyes have no doubt helped to seduce many a Best in Show judge.

Several of the first distinctly American-type Cockers to succeed in all-breed competition came from the Stockdale kennel in California, including the black Ch. Stockdale Town Talk, who was greatly admired in the early 1940s. The event that really took the American Cocker Spaniel to the next level, however, occurred in 1954 when Virgil

The top-winning English Cocker Spaniel Ch. Chestnut's Selling The Drama, shown winning Best in Show at Waukesha Kennel Club in 2005 under judge Dr. Steven Keating, handled by Laura King.

The 1954 Westminster Best in Show–winning Cocker Spaniel, Ch. Carmor's Rise and Shine, with handler Ted Young and judge Irene Khatoonian Schlintz.

Johnson selected Ch. Carmor's Rise and Shine as Best in Show at Westminster. It is true that the black Ch. My Own Brucie had already won Westminster twice in the early 1940s, but although he certainly was an American-type Cocker, his wins occurred before the breed had officially seceded from its British ancestors. This recognition signaled fanciers that the native Cocker was ready to be taken seriously, and in the first two years of official all-breed ratings, 1956 and 1957, the top Sporting dog in the United States was a black American Cocker Spaniel, Ch. Gail's Ebony Don D, shown alternately by Roy Nelson and Norman Austin. More was to come: in 1960, Ch. Pinetop's Fancy Parade rose to the Top Dog spot among all breeds, and in 1972 Ch. Sagamore Toccoa was also Top Dog. They were shown by two of the all-time great Cocker handlers, Norm Austin and Ted Young, respectively, both of whom were in great part responsible for the Cocker's acceptance as a top contender at all-breed shows. Since then, the Cocker's success in this type of competition has been almost repetitious. Although none has been Top Dog or won Westminster for several decades, most years have seen at least one

One of the many Cocker Spaniels to place among the top dogs of all breeds, Ch. Harrison's Peeping Tom did so in 1981, handled by Ted Young.

Cocker as a serious contender among the top Sporting dogs. The black Ch. La-Shay's Bart Simpson was Number Two of all breeds in 1994, and the following year the particolor Ch. Rendition Triple Play repeated that achievement.

RETRIEVERS: LIGHT BRIGADE, CHARLIE, AND . . . WHO?

For many years now, two retriever breeds, the Labrador and the Golden, have been more popular as both show dogs and pets than the Cocker has. In spite of this, both

Labrador Retrievers have been conspicuous mostly for their absence in the Top Dog awards. The highest achievement for the breed in America was when Ch. Shamrock Acres Light Brigade came in as top Sporting dog and Number Five of all breeds in 1968. He is shown winning at Detroit Kennel Club, handled by Dick Cooper under judge H. H. Wilson. The trophy presenter is club officer Julia Gasow.

breeds remain far less successful in all-breed competition. Labradors, in particular, seldom win the top awards and almost never score in the year-end ratings. This was not always the case: in the 1940s and 1950s, several Labradors were among the top Best in Show winners. The highest achievement the breed has ever scored in this kind of competition came in 1968, when the yellow Ch. Shamrock Acres Light Brigade was top Sporting dog and Number Five of all breeds. Goldens also had some surprisingly prolific winners at one time, but they are largely forgotten today. (Does anyone remember Ch. Golden Knolls King Alphonzo, who was among the top all-breed winners in the early 1950s?) Although many Goldens have won Best in Show in recent years, the awards have usually been divided among many different dogs. No modern winner has equaled Ch. Cumming's Gold Rush Charlie's achievement from 1974, when he was Top Sporting dog and Number Three of all breeds.

Since the days of Light Brigade and Charlie, no retriever has placed among the annual

Above: Golden Retrievers, more successful than Labradors in Best in Show competition, have had no contenders for Top Dog of all breeds since 1974, when Ch. Cumming's Gold Rush Charlie was top Sporting dog and Number Three of all breeds. He is shown winning Best in Show at Monmouth County Kennel Club, handled by William Trainor under judge J. Warwick.

Left: The Flat-Coated Retriever Ch. Flatford Zeus The Major God, JH won the Group at Westminster in 2001. He is shown winning Best in Show at Illinois Valley Kennel Club, handled by Mark Bettis under judge Gerald Schwartz.

Top Ten in the all-breed statistics in the United States. That the less popular retriever breeds have not done so either is not as surprising. One Flat-Coated Retriever, Ch. Flatford Zeus The Major God, JH, won the Group at Westminster in 2001. No Labrador and only two Goldens have done the same: Ch. Cragmount's Hi-Lo in 1968, and Ch. Chuckanut Party Favour O Novel in 2006.

THE AFGHAN HOUND EMERGES
A few years into the 1950s, a breed whose exotic appeal had already begun to attract attention sprang into full flower. In looks,

the Afghan Hound is far from what most people think of as a "regular dog," but the breed has in fact remained surprisingly unaltered since the first native imports to England in the 1920s, with a few later additions from India to the United States. It was not always easy to make reliable show exhibits of the wild mountain hounds in those days, but when the independence and haughtiness could be controlled, it was obvious that this breed had great potential in the show ring.

Two Afghan Hound kennels, one on the East Coast and one on the West, burst on the

Afghan Hounds have attracted attention at all-breed shows since the first arrivals in the 1930s. One of the most admired and influential Afghans of all time was Ch. Shirkhan of Grandeur, owner-handled to Best in Show at Westminster in 1957 and a great stud dog.

The rivalry between two great kennels in the 1950s, Grandeur in Long Island and Crown Crest in California, helped generate enthusiasm for Afghan Hounds at many levels. Ch. Taejon of Crown Crest, shown with owner-handler Kay Finch in California, also won two Groups at Westminster.

scene with spectacular success at approximately the same time. Both fanciers had done their homework and served time in the trenches. When Sunny Shay handled her exotic young Ch. Shirkhan of Grandeur to Best in Show at Westminster in 1957, she had already bred many generations of champions and won the Group there earlier with an English import, Ch. Turkuman Nissim's Laurel. Shirkhan was heavily campaigned, remained among the top dogs of

all breeds for three years, and was a fixture on the show circuit well into the 1960s. His most lasting influence, however, came as a stud dog. His champion descendants filled the ring for years and can still be found in the back of most Afghan Hound pedigrees.

Grandeur was located in Hicksville, New York, but Shirkhan was, on occasion, shown as far away as in California, and on those occasions he met stiff competition from the local Crown Crest dogs. Those dogs

Ch. Crown Crest Mr. Universe, a grandson of Taejon, was his breeder's crowning achievement and ranked among the top all-breed winners in both 1959 and 1960.

were owned, bred, and handled by Kay Finch, in her own way as flamboyant a character as Sunny Shay and every inch her match as a competitor. The dogs differed considerably in type: the Grandeurs were often blacks or blues, refined and aristocratic, while the Crown Cest dogs tended to be more substantial, heavily coated, and almost always black-masked goldens. A clash was inevitable, and most judges took sides. Mrs. Finch had already experienced great success with her exuberant black-masked silver dog Ch. Taejon of Crown Crest, who invaded Grandeur territory and won the Group at Westminster twice in the early 1950s. Shirkhan then dominated for a couple of years, but Crown Crest came back with its best winner, the "Johnny" grandson Ch. Crown Crest Mr. Universe. (So named, Mrs. Finch said, because he was born during the televised Miss Universe pageant.) "Mr. U" remained among the top all-breed winners into the early 1960s, but after that the Grandeur–Crown Crest rivalry was basically

The Saluki Ch. Sundown Alabaster Treasure, owner-handled by Karen Black to a spot among the Top Ten dogs of all breeds in 1999.

over. Typically, both breeders respected the other's achievements, and in spite of their differences the dogs meshed well in the breeding programs of many later kennels.

After Sunny Shay's death, the Grandeur name was transferred to Roger Rechler, a younger fancier who had supported Shay's breeding program in her last years. Under his ownership, Grandeur enjoyed a renaissance of the kind that would have impressed its founder. One record-breaking champion followed another, all shown by Grandeur's private handler, Michael Canalizo, and all

Ch. Tryst of Grandeur and her handler, Michael Canalizo, in the Hound Group at Westminster. Tryst was top Hound for four years in the 1990s and Top Dog of all breeds in 1995.

The Afghan Hound Ch. Kabik's The Challenger, Top Dog of all breeds in 1982, with owner-handler Chris Terrell and Afghan breeder and judge Sandra Withington Frei. "Pepsi" also won Best in Show at Westminster in 1983.

true to the type for which the kennel had always been known. The two most successful were the brindle male Ch. Triumph of Grandeur in the late 1980s and his black daughter Ch. Tryst of Grandeur. Neither would repeat Shirkhan's win at Westminster, but Tryst won the Group there and had a show career that has hardly been matched by any other dog. After ruling as America's top Hound for three years in a row, starring as Top Dog of all breeds in 1995, and winning well over 100 Bests in Show, Tryst was retired for maternal duties, in the manner of many other successful show bitches. That was not the end, however: three years later, at an age when most dogs are confined to the couch, Tryst sprang back into action, returned to the show ring, and added twenty more all-breed Bests in 1999. She was also top Hound that year (for the fourth time!) and again placed among the Top Ten

of all breeds, also for the fourth time. At the time of her retirement, Tryst was nearly nine years old but looked barely half her age.

Shortly afterward, in the early 2000s, the Grandeur kennel was closed down, but both Rechler and Canalizo remain involved in dogs. Rechler has helped sponsor the show campaigns for dogs as diverse as a Chinese Crested, a German Shepherd Dog, and most recently the Akita Ch. Redwitch Reason To Believe, a 2007 top contender. Canalizo is currently employed by the AKC.

The Afghan Hound has been represented by a large number of outstanding winners in addition to those already mentioned. Two of the most noticeable came from the Kabik Kennels of Chris and Marguerite Terrell. Most of the big names hail from either the eastern states, from California, or from somewhere in the heartland of America, where a professional handler is conveniently located for access to as many shows as possible. The Terrells did not fit into that pattern: living in the state of Washington, far off the beaten track and without resorting to a professional handler, Chris Terrell and Ch. Kabik's The Challenger became one of the dog fancy's most admired teams when they took the Top Dog of all breeds spot in 1982. The following February, they capped a brilliant career with the top award at Westminster. A few years later, the Terrells won even more with a "Pepsi" son, Ch. Kabik's The Front Runner, top Hound and among the top dogs in the country for two years running.

THE VIN-MELCA ELKHOUNDS

While Afghan Hounds remained a major force in the Hound Group, the focus in the late 1960s shifted to another, rather unlikely breed. Norwegian Elkhounds had done fairly well for many years but never quite reached the top. (In fact, Elkhounds seldom win big even in their native country, where most are hunting dogs and rarely attract large show entries.) This was about to change in America, thanks to the energy, determination, and talent of a single breeder—Patricia Craige Trotter of Carmel, California. She established her Vin-Melca breeding program based on the best Norwegian lines, and by the late 1960s judges were starting to notice. Even more remarkably,

all the top Vin-Melca dogs were owner-handled. In 1970, Ch. Vin-Melca's Vagabond forged ahead to gain the Top Dog award of all breeds, and in the following decades almost every year brought forward a new homebred winner, often as top Hound and frequently as a contender for a Top Ten spot among all breeds. The number of Vin-Melca top dogs cannot be matched by any other American kennel except Salilyn. Ch. Vin-Melca's Nimbus and Ch. Vin-Melca's Calista were both Number Two of all breeds, in 1978 and 1990, respectively. Remarkably,

A son of "Pepsi," Ch. Kabik's The Front Runner was among the top dogs of all breeds for both 1987 and 1988. He is shown with handler Chris Terrell winning a Hound Group under judge Anne Rogers Clark at the Santa Barbara Kennel Club. Trophy presenters are club officers Bo Bengtson, Dr. Richard Meen, and Marilyn and Tom Mayfield.

Ch. Vin-Melca's Nimbus, among the top all-breed winners for three years and Runner-up to Top Dog in 1978. He is shown with owner-breeder-handler Patricia Craige Trotter, winning Best in Show at Channel City Kennel Club in 1988 under Canadian judge Virginia Lyne.

Ch. Vin-Melca's Calista and Patricia Craige Trotter in the Hound Group at Westminster in 1990. Calista won the Group and was Runner-up to Top Dog for the year.

Vagabond, Nimbus, and Calista each won two Groups at Westminster. In the mid-1990s, after winning two more Groups at Westminster with Calista's daughter, Ch. Vin-Melca's Marketta, Trotter retired from campaigning her dogs to become a judge but has continued to breed top winners.

A GREYHOUND PACESETTER

In the late 1970s, in spite of the competition from the Elkhounds, another California hound rose to the top. Best in Show honors were nothing new to the Greyhound, although the breed had not enjoyed its former show-ring splendor for several decades. The blue brindle bitch Ch. Aroi Talk of the Blues, or "Punky," as she became known throughout the dog show world, was discovered in 1975 by judge Anne

Rogers Clark. Then an unruly youngster, Punky nevertheless won the Greyhound Club of America specialty in Santa Barbara under Mrs. Clark and as a mature adult went on to a brilliant career with Corky Vroom as her handler. Punky was Top Dog of all breeds in 1976, runner-up to that honor the following year, and in the process racked up well over fifty recorded Bests in

Show—more than any of her illustrious breed predecessors. To this day, no Greyhound has kept pace with Punky as a top all-breed contender.

Competing with the aristocratic sighthounds and indomitable Elkhounds has proved tough for the other breeds in the Hound Group. None beyond those already mentioned has won Westminster or Top

The only Greyhound in recent decades to feature consistently among the top winners of all breeds, Ch. Aroi Talk of the Blues. "Punky" was handled by Corky Vroom to Top Dog in 1976. They are shown winning Best in Show under judge Langdon Skarda.

Dog of all breeds, although Basset Hounds got close through Ch. Deer Hill's Great Gatsby, runner-up to the top spot in 1998 with an impressive forty-four all-breed Bests in that year alone. Most other hound breeds have only made guest spot appearances in the top rankings; the most consistent winner was probably a lone Dachshund, the Miniature Wire Ch. Spartan's Sloe Gin Fizz MW, who placed among the Top Ten in both 1976 and 1977. It would be fair to say that the hound breeds, with a few obvious exceptions, are statistically underrepresented when the top all-breed ribbons are being awarded.

CHANGES IN GROUPS

One of the most distinct trends at dog shows in the 1960s was the increasing strength of the Working Group. Both in numbers and quality, the breeds that made up that group dominated to such a degree that winning a Working Group at that time was almost as good as winning a Best in Show. That the competition was strong made sense, considering that among the competitors then participating in this group were such powerhouse breeds as Boxers and Dobermans, as well as all the herding-type breeds that did not have a group of their own at the time. The dominance of the Working breeds made it difficult for the rest of the groups to keep up: one year in the 1970s, five of the country's top six dogs came from the Working Group! Eventually it became obvious that drastic action had to be taken, and as of 1983, by American Kennel Club decree, the Working Group was divided in two, with the herding-type breeds separated from the rest to form their own independent Herding Group.

THE NEW WORKING GROUP

The balance between the seven groups has remained fairly constant since then, and because Doberman Pinschers continued to dominate as strongly as ever, only one other breed from the new Working Group has produced a Top Dog of all breeds. That was the imported Standard Schnauzer from Italy Ch. Parsifal di Casa Netzer, who carried all before him in 1996. "Pa" was co-owned by his Italian breeder, Gabrio del Torre, and Rita Holloway in the United States, with Rita's husband, Doug, as handler. Standard Schnauzers did much better than their rather low entry figures might lead anyone to expect: just a few years after Pa, another of the same breed, Ch. Charisma's Jailhouse

The Standard Schnauzer Ch. Charisma's Jailhouse Rock, winner of seventy-five Bests in Show and Runner-up to Top Dog in 2001, with handler Brenda Combs.

The most successful representative from the record-breaking Skansen kennels in California, Ch. Skansen's Tristan II, won more than fifty Bests in Show and was Runner-up to Top Dog in 1999. She is shown winning at Del Monte Kennel Club, handled by Bill McFadden under judge Dr. Robert Smith. Trophy presenters are Gerda Rayne (left) and Dr. Jacklyn Hungerland.

Rock, won even more and increased the all-time breed record to seventy-five Bests in Show. "Rocky" was Number Two of all breeds in 2001.

Giant Schnauzers had first appeared among the top winners in the 1960s but got a big boost from the activities of Skansen, a new all-conquering kennel in California. This is one of the few modern American kennels that operates on a large scale. There may be as many as 100 Schnauzers in residence at Skansen, and well over 1,000 champions have been bred since the kennel was founded in the 1960s. (Not all the champions were Giant Schnauzers; there have been quite a few Miniatures and Standards, plus a few early litters of Greyhounds—as well as the world-class llamas also bred at Skansen.) Owner Sylvia Hammarström settled in California after leaving her native Sweden in the 1950s. Working closely with breeders in Europe and utilizing stud dogs such as the early greats Ch. Lillemarks Kobuch from Denmark and Ch. Lucas de Campos de Oro from Spain, she has established a breeding program that produces a seemingly unending line of winners all over North and South America, Europe, and Asia. The chief standard bearers include Ch. Skansen's I Have A Dream, one of the top dogs of all breeds in the late 1980s and a Group winner at Westminster in 1990, and Ch. Skansen's Tristan II (a bitch, in spite of her name), who did even better a decade later, won more than fifty Bests in Show and was runner-up to the Top Dog of all breeds award in 1999.

Several other dogs demonstrated the strength of the Working Group in all-breed competition during the 1960s and 1970s. An early Giant Schnauzer, Ch. Ebenholtz D'Lux v Deberic, placed among the Top Ten of all breeds for two years even before Skansen reached its prime, and so did two Great Danes: Ch. Reggen's Madas-L of Marydane in 1966 and 1967 and Ch. Heideres Kolyer Kimbah in 1972 and 1973. Three different Working dogs were among the top dogs of all breeds for at least a couple of years each in the 1980s, and all of them were Runners-up to Top Dog: the Samoyed Ch. Quicksilver's Razz Ma Tazz in 1983, the Bullmastiff Ch. Bandog's Crawdaddy Gumbo in 1985, and the Great Pyrenees Ch. Rivergroves Run For The Roses in 1988. There is no question that the Doberman Pinscher cast a long shadow, however, and in most cases the other Working breeds have been represented by only occasional winners at the top level. In the early 2000s, when the St. Bernard Ch. Trust's Gentle Ben v Slaton was one of the country's most popular show dogs—he placed among the Top Ten in both 2000 and 2001—it was a half century since any dog of this breed had done so well. The imported Ch. Gerd v.d. Lueg v. Edelweiss had been one of the top dogs in the country in 1950, but no St. Bernard or other Working breed beyond those mentioned had produced more than an occasional top contender during the years in between.

THE HERDING GROUP

After the Groups were divided, the power gradually swung away from the Working breeds to the new Herding Group. German Shepherd Dogs had been a major force in the show rings from the start, with the Giralda imports dominating the all-breed scene for several years when the official Best in Show competition was first introduced in the 1920s. That the breed disappeared from the annual all-breed ratings for many years during and after World War II probably did not, as has been suggested, have anything to do with politics—another German breed, the Boxer, enjoyed its greatest vogue at that time. It is more likely that the German Shepherd Dog fanciers' increasing disdain for

The Bullmastiff Ch. Bandog's Crawdaddy Gumbo was among the top dogs of all breeds for three years and Runner-up to Top Dog in 1985. He is shown with handler Wayne Boyd winning Best in Show under judge Tom Mayfield.

The Great Pyrenees Ch. Rivergroves Run For The Roses, here with judge Josephine Deubler, was Runner-up to Top Dog in 1988. "T. R." was bred and owned by Jean Boyd, who also owned the Bullmastiff Crawdaddy Gumbo. The handler is Wayne Boyd.

all-breed shows and the ensuing focus on their own breed specialty competition was the reason.

German Shepherd Dog Specialties

The German Shepherd Dog Club of America's national show at its peak was one of the biggest and best-organized events of its kind, and although the entry figures have dwindled in recent years, a large number of German Shepherd Dog exhibitors still attend only specialty shows. More than 150 shows exclusively catering to the German Shepherd Dog fanciers are held each year in an atmosphere vastly different from that of most other AKC events. Almost all the han-

dlers are professionals and good runners, able to keep up with their long-striding charges. The dogs are moved, seemingly endlessly, round the ring, the focus on side gait is relentless, and double handling is generally accepted. The practice of double handling is what occurs when a dog's attention is deliberately attracted by a person outside the ring in an attempt to make the dog look naturally alert. There are those who feel that a mild form of double handling can be an excellent method for making a dog look his best without unnecessary baiting in the ring, but the AKC frowns on the practice. As performed at some German Shepherd Dog specialties, double handling

The German Shepherd Dog Ch. Ulk Wikingerblut was imported from Germany, won the Grand Victor title in Canada, and was among the Top Ten dogs of all breeds in the United States in 1961. He was also a successful stud dog.

can deteriorate into a cacophony of ringing bells, squeaking toys, and owners' calling their dogs' names, any of which would automatically disqualify everyone involved at any other show. The most extreme form of double handling involves a runner, someone whom the dog likes and wants to follow: that person circles outside the ring ahead of the dog and handler as the side gait is being assessed. The judges, in spite of AKC directives to the contrary, on occasion actually encourage double handling; it is not unknown to hear a judge catch the ringside's attention before he asks the handlers to move around the ring with their dogs as a group: "OK, runners—are you ready?" Anyone standing at ringside at that point had better make sure they don't get mowed down by a horde of fast-running German Shepherd Dog owners, each calling his or her dog's name.

At all-breed shows, such practices are taboo, and since the top specialty winners were practically never shown in competition with other breeds—and all-breed judges almost never got an opportunity to judge German Shepherd Dog specialty shows—the type of dogs winning at the different types of shows started to diverge. The specialties tended to favor dogs of extreme type and side gait, sometimes at the expense of soundness coming and going, while the usually meager all-breed entries were supported by a more "average" type of German Shepherd Dog.

It is impossible to say to what extent these circumstances affected the German Shepherd Dog's long, conspicuous lack of success in all-breed competition, but the fact is that no German Shepherd Dog made a serious dent in the all-breed ratings for many years until the early 1970s. At that time, almost simultaneously, two American-bred males, Ch. Lakeside's Gilligan's Island and Ch. Val-Koa's Roon, broke through and were among the top all-breed winners for two years each. The two were related through a common great-grandsire, Ch. Troll v. Richterbach, one of the most influential German imports of the 1950s.

The really big wins came later. In 1979, a dog that would become a household word was born in the famous Covy-Tucker Hill kennels of Cappy Pottle and Gloria Birch. They had already produced scores of top winners, and the litter that included this future great was very well bred: the sire was a son of Gilligan and the dam was Ch. Covy's Rosemary of Tucker Hill, one of the breed's greatest matrons and herself a daughter of Gilligan's litter brother. In retrospect, it may be surprising that little to-do was made of the young dog that would eventually become known by every dog show fancier in America as Ch. Covy-Tucker Hill's Manhattan, but the fact is that "Hatter" was a slow starter.

Manhattan made a first humble appearance in the breed ratings in 1981 with a couple of Group thirds and fourths. The following year, he won a few Groups and his first all-breed Best. In 1983, the first year the Herding Group was an independent entity, Hatter was already four years old, and people began to notice. He had by then found his permanent owner, Shirlee Braunstein, and also the handler who would help make him one of the greatest dog show stars ever.

The German Shepherd Dog Ch. Covy-Tucker Hill's Manhattan was one of the most successful show dogs ever and one of the most popular as well. He was already five years old when he reached the top in 1984, but he stayed there until winning Westminster as a veteran in 1987 and taking an even 200 Bests in Show. He is shown facing the press after his Westminster win.

The German Shepherd Dog Ch. Beech Hill's Benji Von Masco, one of the top winners of all breeds in 1982, shown with handler Ken Rayner and judge Robert Wills winning at Elm City Kennel Club that year.

Ch. Lynrik's Kristal, one of the top all-breed winners of 1986, is pictured with handler Leslie Dancosse and judge Ann Stevenson winning Best in Show at Bartlesville Kennel Club in 1986.

James A. Moses has an impeccable pedigree in German Shepherd Dogs: he had been brought up on breed lore, gone to the specialty shows, and learned from the great Ernest Loeb, the man who, after moving to America from Germany before the war, had become the breed's leading importer, handler, and later judge. Moses was already an established handler at the specialty shows, but he saw that although they were not where Hatter's future would lie, this dog had qualities that could turn heads in other areas.

As much as Hatter was later admired by the general dog-loving public, he was often made light of by some breed specialists. Certainly Hatter was a "real dog" of the kind that everyone could relate to, with the stable, self-possessed temperament that one dreams of; possibly he did not have all the extreme qualities that most breed specialist judges admired at the time. In the end, most German Shepherd Dog fanciers would admit that Hatter did a tremendous amount

of good for the breed's image with the general public and paved the way for the many German Shepherd Dogs that would win after him.

After winning a few Bests in 1983—still not enough to make him Number One in the breed—the stars aligned for Hatter in 1984. He had a talented handler, a supportive owner, and—not least important—the backing of Jane Firestone, a wealthy sportswoman who would be crucial in the breed's future history at AKC shows. Hatter was Top Dog of all breeds that year and took home sixty-four Bests in Show, more than any dog had ever accumulated in a twelve-month period. His biggest win came in November, when the venerated senior allrounder William L. Kendrick chose Hatter as his winner in the finale at the American Kennel Club's Centennial show in Philadelphia, the largest dog event ever held in the United States with an entry of just over 8,000 dogs.

America's top winner ever in all-breed competition, the German Shepherd bitch Ch. Altana's Mystique. Campaigned by Jimmy Moses for four years, she won Best in Show at 275 AKC shows. As far as is known, no dog anywhere has won nearly as much. At her peak, Mystique topped the Herding Group 173 times in a single year, going Best in Show 116 times—more than twice every week through the year. Born in Canada, Mystique was almost eight years old at the time of her retirement.

The following year Hatter, already a bona fide sensation, bested his own record by taking home 67 Bests and was Top Dog again. In 1986, officially a veteran, he was shown much less but added another 45 all-breed Bests, for an all-time total of 183 such wins. At this point, not much remained for Hatter to achieve, but Westminster remained elusive: after going "only" as far as Group First there in 1984 and 1986, and placing second in the Group in 1985, Hatter made a final bow in 1987. He would turn eight years old

The third German Shepherd Dog to become Top Dog of all breeds since the ratings systems were introduced in 1966 was Ch. Kismet's Sight For Sore Eyes. He won more than 100 Bests in Show and was Top Dog of all breeds in 2002. "Dallas" also became an extremely influential sire.

just a couple of months after the show but looked barely half his age. He performed flawlessly on the famous shoestring leash Moses used to show him and added the only missing jewel in his crown. After just a few more shows to make his lifetime record an even 200 Bests in Show, Hatter retired to live out his life in comfort on Jane Firestone's couch. Many years later, he is remembered as one of the most popular show dogs ever, one of those whose name is invariably brought up when dog people get together and reminisce about the great dogs of the past.

For Jimmy Moses, Manhattan's long and exhausting career was just the beginning. While not forsaking his roots and occasionally returning to win at German Shepherd Dog Club of America specialties, Moses followed Hatter with a long string of other winners at all-breed shows. Not all the German Shepherds that won big in all-breed competition since the mid-1980s were shown by Moses—there was, for instance, a much admired bitch named Ch. Lynrik's Kristal who took over Manhattan's role as a top all-breed contender in 1987 and was handled by Leslie Dancosse—but most were Moses's charges. Ch. Galewynd's Georgio Armani, Ch. Bramblewood's Custom Made, Ch. Windwalker's Leroy Brown, and Ch. Jagan's Belle Starr were all handled by Moses to a position among the Top Ten dogs of all breeds in the late twentieth century.

The Shepherd that would eventually break even Manhattan's records was a bitch that Moses, again, "inherited" as she was about to be retired. Ch. Altana's Mystique was born in Canada, descended from the Covy-Tucker Hill line on her dam's side, and—unlike Manhattan—had experienced great success on the specialty circuit although never campaigned at all-breed shows. However, she had such overall appeal and charisma that Moses, again with Firestone as a backer, embarked on a career that would leave even Hatter's record in the dust. Mystique did not start winning seriously until 1992, the year she turned five, but just like Hatter, she was a good laster: her total record when she was retired in 1995, at nearly eight years of age, includes 275 Bests in Show—more than any other dog of any breed has ever won in the United States or, as far as is known, anywhere else in the world. At her peak, in a single year, Mystique, with Moses, headed the Herding Group 173 times, of which 116 resulted in all-breed Bests. This is truly a mind-boggling achievement. For most people (and dogs), even getting to that many shows in a year would be difficult. To stay healthy and happy and go around the ring well enough to actually win at all of them indicates a stamina and determination on both the dog's and the handler's part that is almost beyond belief.

It is difficult to say if the most important German Shepherd Dog winner of all was Hatter, Mystique, or the third dog that Moses showed to Top Dog of all breeds, Ch. Kismet's Sight For Sore Eyes. Certainly Hatter got the public's vote, as any pioneer breaking new ground will do. Mystique's contribution, many felt, was a unique combination of specialist breed type with all-around appeal. However, if you take a dog's producing ability into account, the brightest star would be Sight For Sore Eyes. "Dallas," as he was called, was piloted by Moses to more than 100 all-breed Bests in the early 2000s, including Top Dog in 2002.

Mystique did not produce any puppies; Manhattan sired a number of champions but none that could begin to equal his own achievements; but Dallas proved to be a hugely influential stud dog, siring scores of champions and handing over the baton to several of his own offspring after he was retired. Two daughters, Ch. Kaleef's Genuine Risk and Ch. Kenlyn's Tenacity of Kaleef, were among the top dogs of all breeds for three years, from 2003 to 2005, and a son, Ch. Kenlyn's Calvin HiCliff Kaleef, was one of the top dogs in Canada in 2006.

Other Herding Breeds

Between all the Boxers and Dobermans that dominated the competition before the old Working Group was split and the German Shepherd Dogs afterward, not much was left for the other Herding breeds. Bouviers des Flandres were well represented, however. Ch. Galbraith's Ironeyes was Top Dog of all breeds in 1990. This was the third time that handler Corky Vroom won this award for owners Mr. and Mrs. Nathan Reese; their previous two Top Dog winners were

The Bouvier des Flandres Ch. Galbraith's Ironeyes is one of very few dogs to win Best in Show more than 100 times at AKC all-breed shows. He was Top Dog of all breeds in 1990 and is shown posing with a few winners of the dog world's equivalent of the Oscars for outstanding achievement—the Winkies, introduced by *Kennel Review* in the 1970s and resurrected by *Dogs in Review* magazine in the early 2000s.

Ch. Willets Red Jacket was not the first Pembroke Welsh Corgi to win big in America: his sire, Ch. Cote de Neige Sundew, had won Best American-Bred in Show at Westminster in 1960. Jacket won even more than his sire—he was top Working Dog for two years and runner-up to the top spot for all breeds in 1962. He was handled by Stephen Shaw, later a judge.

In 1983, the Herding breeds were split off from the Working Group and held their own competition. The first-ever top Herding Dog title went to the Pembroke Welsh Corgi Ch. Vanguard Jennelle, pictured with her handler, Ray McGinnis. Jennelle placed high among the Top Dogs of all breeds as well.

The Shetland Sheepdog Ch. Elf Dale Viking placed among the Top Dogs of all breeds for three consecutive years, 1963–1965.

The Pembroke Welsh Corgi Ch. Coventry Queue, one of the Top Dogs of all breeds in 2000, pictured with handler Michael Scott winning Best in Show at Bucks County Kennel Club that year under judge Ron Menaker. Queue won back-to-back Groups at Westminster.

the Doberman Ch. Galaxy's Corry Missile Belle in 1973 and the Greyhound Ch. Aroi Talk of the Blues in 1976. Among many other top Bouviers contenders, the Belgian import Ch. Taquin du Posty Arlequin was among the top dogs of all breeds for three years running in the 1970s, Ch. Beaucrest Ruffian was Number Two of all breeds in both 1981 and 1982, and the Canadian-born Ch. Quiche's Ivanhoe was among the Top Ten in 1988 and 1989.

Some now popular Herding breeds reached their biggest achievements in the early pre–group division days. The only Shetland Sheepdog ever to place so high among the top dogs of all breeds, Ch. Elf

Dale Viking, did this for three years running in the mid-1960s; like many of his breed, he was a great laster and took some of his top wins as a veteran. The highest-ranked Welsh Corgi ever in the United States, the Pembroke Ch. Willets Red Jacket, topped the Working Group rankings in both 1961 and 1962, going all the way to the Number Two spot among all breeds the latter year. Other Pembrokes (but no Cardigans) have soared high in the rankings since then; Ch. Vanguard Jennelle was top Herding dog in 1983, the year this group got independent status, and in 2000 Ch. Coventry Queue was top Herding dog and third in the Top Ten— just one step below Red Jacket nearly four decades earlier. Queue also won back-to-back Groups at Westminster, something that escaped Red Jacket. Few would argue that Shelties and Corgis have improved in quality over the years, yet this is hardly reflected in the all-breed annual ratings.

Old English Sheepdogs have been consistent winners over many decades, doing at least as well in the old Working Group as after the Herding breeds got their own competition. The first to make his mark in the ratings was Ch. Merriedip Duke George, handled twice to a spot among the Top Ten of all breeds in the 1950s by his owner, Mona Berkowitz in California. A few years later, it was the Fezziwig dogs back East that made news, shown professionally by Bob Forsyth: Ch. Fezziwig Raggedy Andy remained among the Top Ten dogs for three

Old English Sheepdogs from the Fezziwig kennels were consistently successful, especially in the 1960s. Ch. Fezziwig Raggedy Andy was among the Top Dogs of all breeds for three years in the mid-1960s, including Runner-up to Top Dog in 1966. He was handled by Robert Forsyth.

years and was Number Two in 1966. Ten years later, Ch. Loyalblu Hendihap reached the same position, Ch. Prince Andrew of Sherline remained among the Top Ten dogs of all breeds for two years in the late 1960s, Ch. Sir Lancelot of Barvan came from Canada to win the top spot at Westminster in 1975, and the owner-handled Lambluv dogs have done their best to challenge the all-conquering German Shepherd Dogs in the group competition in recent years.

THE TERRIER TRADITION

Terriers boast a long tradition as show dogs, with an unbroken line traceable all the way back to the earliest fancy dog exhibitions of the 1800s and to the first Crufts and Westminster shows. Fox Terriers were more popular than any other breed in those days and could attract several hundred entries at the big shows. The other terriers took second billing at first, but some—Airedales, Scotties, and Irish Terriers—did well early on and have been joined by an increasing and colorful array of breeds in later years. The terriers routinely field smaller entries than any of the other AKC groups, but the competition is often much tougher than those figures might suggest.

The Handler Connection

One reason for the high level of competition in terriers is the traditional reliance on professional handlers. The majority of the terrier breeds are wire coated and depend on a great deal of skillful trimming to look their best. Trying to show, for example, an Airedale, Scottish, Welsh, or Wire Fox Terrier without the benefit of professional quality presentation would at best be an exercise in futility. Amateurs and owner-handlers

The Airedale Terrier bitch Ch. Westhay Fiona of Harham was runner-up to Top Dog of all breeds in 1958—the highest position in all-breed competition ever for the breed in America.

who persist in competing with the professionals deserve high marks for determination, but more tangible rewards are usually scarce. The high standard set by the full-time handlers makes it difficult for most others to compete in the Terrier Group with any reasonable expectation of success.

If the history of the terriers is also the history of their handlers, this is a time-honored tradition from the days when men such as Bob Barlow and Percy Roberts brought over the cream of the British crop,

especially Wire Fox Terriers, to compete at Westminster. Barlow returned home to England after his visits, but Roberts stayed and became an all-rounder judge in America when his handling days were over. Unlike most of the terrier handlers, Roberts was also very active in many other breeds, although all four dogs he won Westminster with were terriers.

Following World War II, terriers took a long time to regain the all-breed success they had enjoyed prior to the war. The late

1940s and 1950s seemed to be dominated primarily by Boxers and English Setters. The single exception was a Scottie, Ch. Walsing Winning Trick of Edgerstoune, who after a good career in England did even better in the United States, was Top Dog of all breeds in 1949, and won Westminster in 1950. He was handled by Phil Prentice. Among the terrier kennels that straddled the war years, one of the most outstanding was Harold Florsheim's Harham establishment in Chicago. The dogs were handled by Tom Gately and included a large number of high-profile English imports of several different breeds. Among the biggest names were the Wire Fox Terrier Ch. Travella Superman of Harham and the Airedale bitch Ch. Westhay Fiona of Harham, who was Number Two of all breeds in 1958—a higher placement than any Airedale has reached in America since then. There was also Florence Alker's Twin Ponds Welsh Terriers, whose greatest star, Ch. Flornell Rare-Bit of Twin Ponds, was one of the top dogs in all-breed competition in the early 1940s. She was also the only one of her breed ever to win Westminster, which she did in 1944. Several Twin Pond winners of later vintage carried the kennel's name over into the 1950s and early 1960s. Mrs. Alker, like the Bondys, employed a private handler in the person of John Goudie.

Welsh Terriers would not win so much again for many years. Ch. Anasazi Annie Oakley was one of the top dogs of all breeds in 1985, and Ch. Anasazi Billy The Kid remained among the Top Ten for three years in the mid-1990s. Both were bred by Michael and Nancy O'Neal and shown by top terrier professionals Clay Coady and Woody Wornall, respectively.

New Dogs Prevail

It took the skills and drive of the new handlers for terriers to reclaim their earlier prominence after Word War II. In 1961, a Wire Fox Terrier bitch named Ch. Miss Skylight became the first of her kind to dominate the annual all-breed ratings since Ch. Nornay Saddler—or, discounting Smooths, since the Wildoaks dogs of the 1930s.

Miss Skylight had been imported from Ireland and was handled by the brightest young American terrier handler of the day, Ric Chashoudian, who at that time lived in California. He would go on to even greater fame as the handler of two more Top Dog winners—the Kerry Blue Ch. Melbee's Chances Are ("Tommy") in 1968 and the Lakeland Ch. Jo-Ni's Red Baron of Crofton in 1974. Chashoudian's last two great winners before he retired from handling were the Australian-born Smooth Fox Terrier Ch.

Ric Chashoudian with the Lakeland Terrier Ch. Jo-Ni's Red Baron of Crofton, the Top Dog in 1974.

The Smooth Fox Terrier Ch. Ttarb The Brat, imported from Tasmania, was one of the top all-breed winners in the 1980s and the sire of 137 champions.

Ttarb The Brat and the English-bred Wire Fox Ch. Sylair Special Edition, both among America's top show dogs in the 1980s and both later hugely influential stud dogs, with Brat siring 137 champions. Chashoudian still maintains an active interest in terriers; he is also a popular judge and a talented sculptor whose best work often reveals his expert knowledge of terriers and many other breeds.

Another terrier man who started his American handling career in California was Peter Green. Arriving from Great Britain in 1958, Green first worked as kennel manager and handler for Mrs. Joseph Urmston's Trucote kennels in Malibu, known for a long line of winning Kerry Blue, Welsh, and Wire Fox terriers. After returning to Wales for a few years, Green accepted an offer in 1963 to return to work for Mr. and Mrs. William

Lakeland Terrier Ch. Revelry's Awesome Blossom, one of the Top Dogs of all breeds in 1995 and 1996, winner of 100 Bests in Show.

Wimer of the Pool Forge Kennels, located not far from his present home in Bowmansville, Pennsylvania. Green has remained in the United States since then and began handling independently in 1967, with many breaks for return visits to look at, and sometimes judge, dogs in the United Kingdom.

A Lakeland Dynasty
In the late 1960s, Green presented the first of what would be an unequaled string of terriers to hit the high spots in all-breed competition. Mr. and Mrs. James Farrell, whose Foxden Kennels had already been established for many years in Smooth Fox Terriers and Greyhounds, asked Green to find them a top-class Lakeland Terrier. Setting his sights high, Green settled on a dog that had won the Group at Crufts in 1966. One of the conditions for purchase was that the dog should be allowed to stay and be shown at the next year's Crufts as well; he did, and went on to not only repeat the Group win but take Best in Show also, handled by Albert Langley. Ch. Stingray of Derryabah was then imported and made a successful

debit in the United States; the following February, upon going to the top at Westminster with Green as handler, he became the first dog ever to win both the world's greatest dog shows. Stingray also proved to be a great sire and was the progenitor of a long line of outstanding Lakelands, most notably his grandson Red Baron. According to Green, every Best in Show–winning Lakeland Terrier in the United States for the next fifteen years came down from Stingray. The top-winning Lakelands in more recent years have been Ch. Cozy's Mischief Maker, Ch. St. Roque's Tempermental, and Ch. Revelry's Awesome Blossom, all of whom were among the top dogs of all breeds for two

The Lakeland Terrier Ch. Stingray of Derryabah was the first dog ever to win the two top shows in England and America, Crufts and Westminster. He won Best in Show at Crufts in 1967, handled by Albert Langley, and at Westminster the following year, shown by Peter Green (pictured after the Terrier Group win with judge Terence Bresnahan). Stingray also started a dynasty of top-winning Lakelands that continues to this day.

Ch. Sunnybrook Spot On, multiple Best in Show winner in both England and the United States and winner of two Terrier Group awards at Westminster, one as a veteran. Spot On also sired the Crufts 1975 Best in Show winner.

years running—in the late 1970s, late 1980s, and mid-1990s, respectively.

Nine years after his Westminster success with Stingray, and just a year after Stingray's grandson Red Baron took the top prize there, Green won Best in Show at the Garden again, with a Sealyham Terrier. Ch. Dersade Bobby's Girl ("Binnie") was an import that Green had found during a visit to his native Wales and brought back to Pool Forge. Sealyhams had not been much in the limelight since their heyday in the 1920s and 1930s, but Binnie set new records for the breed and was the Top Dog of all breeds in 1975. To this day, Green considers Binnie the greatest of all the dogs he has shown.

The Wire Fox Terrier Ch. Galsul Excellence with his handler, Peter Green. "Paddy" was imported from Ireland and was the Top Dog of all breeds in America in both 1986 and 1987.

The Lakeland Terrier Ch. Cozy's Mischief Maker was the top-winning Terrier of both 1978 and 1979 and Runner-up to Top Dog of all breeds in 1979. She is pictured with handler Eddie Boyes and a four-legged friend.

The string of top terriers presented by Peter Green from the 1970s onward is unmatched. In Wires, there was Ch. Sunnybrook Spot On, who won two Groups at Westminster, one of them as a veteran. He was followed by the great Ch. Galsul Excellence ("Paddy"), imported from Harry O'Donoghue's famous Blackdale kennel in Ireland. With Green at the helm, Paddy was Top Dog for two years in a row, 1986 and 1987, and in his abbreviated career won more than 100 Bests in Show. Who knows what his total achievements might have been if he had not, due to a shortsighted AKC decision involving the dog's owner, been suspended from show and stud activities while still in his prime. In spite of these limitations, he managed to sire a daughter,

The Sealyham Terrier Ch. Dersade Bobby's Girl is still remembered by her handler, Peter Green, as one of the best ever. Imported from Wales, "Binnie" put Sealyhams back on the map as the Top Dog of all breeds in 1975. She is pictured after winning Westminster two years later.

Ch. Registry's Lonesome Dove, who not only matched her sire's back-to-back Top Dog achievement (1991 and 1992) but also did him one better by winning Westminster in 1992, handled by Michael Kemp.

Norwiches and Norfolks

Norwich Terriers had not previously attracted much attention at the top level and were generally considered to be impossible to win with in major competition as a less glamorous stepchild of the more high-profile, stylized terriers. Peter Green proved that assumption to be a fallacy. The breakthrough came with Ch. Thrumpton's Lord Brady, an English import who remained among the top winners of all breeds in the United States for three years and was Top Dog in 1980. Just about the only thing that Brady did not win was Westminster, but his

Norwich Terriers broke through to the top spots in America primarily through Ch. Thrumpton's Lord Brady, who was imported from the United Kingdom by Peter Green and won Top Dog in America in 1979. He is shown winning Best in Show at the Santa Barbara Kennel Club that year under judge Thomas H. Bradley, III.

THE TOP DOG OWNERS

The Wire Fox Terrier Ch. Registry's Lonesome Dove, Top Dog of all breeds in 1991 and 1992, was owned by Samuel and Marion Lawrence, two of a small but influential group of dog show exhibitors who have made a habit of sponsoring the careers of promising show dogs regardless of breed. The dogs' breeders and perhaps an original everyday owner frequently remain involved in the career, with decisions being made jointly by a sort of syndicate, mapping out the strategy and the goals for the show campaign.

No one has experienced more success in this area than the Lawrences. One account puts the number of Bests in Show won by their dogs at more than 800, a staggering figure that includes the wins of no fewer than four different dogs with at least 100 Bests each: the black Cocker Spaniel Ch. La-Shay's Bart Simpson; the Doberman Pinscher Ch. Brunswig's Cryptonite; the Maltese Ch. Ta-Jon's Tickle Me Silly; and, of course, Lonesome Dove. In what was surely a unique double victory, the Lawrences owned both the Number One and Number Two dogs of all breeds in 1991, when

Ch. Registry's Lonesome Dove took over her sire "Paddy's" spot as Top Dog in both 1991 and 1992 and also won Best in Show at Westminster in 1992. She is pictured with handler Michael Kemp, winning the Santa Barbara Kennel Club's show in 1991 under judge Virginia Lyne from Canada. Trophy presenters, left to right, are Lou and Seme Auslander, Carmen Visser, Dr. John Reeve-Newson, and Tom Bradley.

Lonesome Dove's closest competitor was their Doberman Cryptonite.

Many of the sponsoring owners are breeders and genuine dog people in their own right. The Lawrences were AKC judges and heavily involved in German Shepherd Dogs long before starting to show other breeds.

The trend of show dogs having sponsoring owners, or backers, is almost as old as the sport of dog shows in America. In other countries, where distances are shorter and the shows fewer, the top dogs are more often shown by their owners, and campaign expenses seldom reach astronomical heights, with the result that there is less need for backers of the top dogs. One of the first owners to sponsor the show careers of a large number of dogs would have been Mrs. Cheever Porter, who was largely responsible for the wins of many top dogs of different breeds (particularly Setters and Afghan Hounds), most of them shown by Robert and Jane Forsyth while they were professional handlers.

In 1997 and 1998, the top Toy Dog spot was occupied by the Maltese Ch. Ta-Jon's Tickle Me Silly, also one of the top dogs of all breeds both years. She is shown winning Best in Show at the Indianhead Kennel Club in 1998 under judge Lee Canalizo.

Other names past and present in this category include Jane Firestone (the lady behind Jimmy Moses's early German Shepherd Dog winners), Mrs. Alan Robson, Mr. and Mrs. Nathan Reese, Roger Rechler (in his post-Grandeur Afghan Hounds days), Cecelia Ruggles, and the legendary TV comedian Dr. William H. Cosby, always in partnership with Capt. Jean Heath. Without them, the high-flying careers of several dogs that either came close to or won the Top Dog of the year award could never have been realized. There are many other individuals who make sure that promising dogs of a particular breed—or even a particular bloodline—are given the opportunities they deserve to shine at the shows.

A top-level American dog show campaign can easily cost over $100,000 per year. What the sponsoring owner gets in return for this investment varies considerably. In many cases, the satisfaction of knowing that you backed a winner and helped a great young dog get noticed may be enough; and there is usually some agreement about an exchange of future puppies or stud services in return.

Top Dog of all breeds in the United States in 1997 was the Canadian-bred Norwich Terrier Ch. Fairewood Frolic. She also won Westminster in 1998.

The Wire Fox Terrier Ch. Aryee Dominator was among the top Terriers for four years and Runner-up to Top Dog of all breeds in 1975. He won more than seventy Best in Shows, handled by George Ward.

grandson Ch. Chidley Willum The Conqueror compensated for that omission by going to the top at Madison Square Garden in 1994. Just a few years later, Green showed the Canadian-born bitch Ch. Fairewood Frolic to head *both* the Top Dog and Westminster competitions. A fitting finale to an outstanding handling career was provided by the Norfolk Terrier bitch Ch. Cracknor Cause Celebre. "Coco" had been imported from England and was Top Dog of all breeds in America in 2003, handled by Green's partner, Beth Sweigart. In February 2005, the Green team went back to Coco's and Green's country of origin and created a stir: handled on this occasion by Green, Coco won Best in Show at Crufts.

"Shannon" and "Mick"

George Ward's greatest star and the top-winning terrier ever in America was a Scottish Terrier bitch named Ch. Braeburn's Close Encounter, known as "Shannon." Since the beginning of dog shows, when it comes to winning the big shows in both Great Britain and the United States, Scotties have taken second place among all breeds only to Wire Fox Terriers. None, however, had a career like Shannon's. Her stamina, quality, and endurance made her one of the most consistent winners ever in American dog show history. Born in the fall of 1978 and owned by Sonnie and Alan Novick, Shannon took her first all-breed Best in 1980 and then stayed at the top for over six years, winning her final Best in Show when she was over eight years old. Shannon amassed a career total of 214 all-breed Bests in Show, remained among the country's top show dogs for five consecutive years, was Number One in 1983, and in 1985 became the sixth Scottie to win Westminster.

The official AKC records outline Shannon's show attendance in the last couple of years of her career. (Records for the first few years are not available because the AKC first started computerizing show records in 1984.) In her last 155 recorded shows, Shannon is listed as having won the Terrier Group 154 times in a row, followed by Best in Show at 99 of those. It is entirely possible that she lost the breed competition on some occasions, as AKC records do not include any show that does not result in at least a placement. (In fact, Shannon did lose the Breed at the AKC Centennial show in 1984, an event described as "sending shock waves throughout the show and the fancy," according to one spectator!)

TERRIER HANDLERS

There were many great terrier handlers during the second half of the twentieth century. One of the most successful was Cliff Hallmark, who hit the jackpot in 1977 with a Wire Fox Terrier, Ch. Harwire Hetman of Whinlatter. Hetman had made a name for himself in his native England, winning the Grand Challenge Cup for Wires at the Fox Terrier Club's (UK) centenary show in 1976. He won Best in Show at his first outing in the United States and the following year went all the way to Top Dog. Wire Fox Terriers have done better than any other breed in this type of competition: even excluding the brilliant early years, Wires account for a half dozen Top Dog wins in the second half of the twentieth century. Hetman also went on to sire a large number of champions.

Hallmark was consistently successful with other breeds as well, for instance, the great winning West Highland White Terrier Ch. De Go Hubert, one of the top dogs of

George Ward won the Montgomery County terrier classic four times between 1940 and 1984. He is shown in 1956 with the Kerry Blue Terrier Ch. Tailteann's Marcie's Son, judge Harry Lumb, and presenter Ed Doyle.

West Highland White Terrier Ch. Elfinbrook Simon, Best in Show at Westminster in 1962.

The top Terrier of 1970, West Highland White Terrier Ch. De Go Hubert, was one of the Top Dogs of all breeds that year. He was handled by Cliff Hallmark.

1970; but there cannot be much question that the three most noteworthy terrier handlers of the postwar era were Ric Chashoudian, Peter Green, and George Ward. The third of this trio was the son and grandson of professional handlers and had begun showing dogs as a boy in Canada in the 1930s before moving to the United States. Ward had won his first Westminster in 1962 with the imported West Highland White Terrier Ch. Elfinbrook Simon, owned by Wishing Well Kennels.

One of the top show dogs of all time, the Scottish Terrier Ch. Braeburn's Close Encounter stayed among the Top Dogs of all breeds in the United States for six consecutive years, amassed more than 200 Bests in Show, and won Best in Show at Westminster in 1985. She was handled by George Ward.

However, once she won Best of Breed, Shannon was tough to beat in the Terrier Group: there is only one other show during those years where it is known for certain that Shannon did not win the Group competition. This was at the Montgomery County terrier classic in 1990, at which point she was a ripe twelve years old; at this, her last appearance in the show ring, Shannon won the Veteran Bitch class but let a new generation take over the top wins.

No other terrier ever won more than Shannon, but at least one had a career that was just as glittering, if not nearly as long.

The Kerry Blue Terrier Ch. Torum's Scarf Michael had one of the most glittering careers of any show dog. He was undefeated at his last several big shows in England, including Crufts in 2000, and was undefeated throughout most of his American career as well. He topped the Montgomery County terrier classic twice, won the resurrected Morris & Essex show in 2000, and was Best in Show at Westminster in 2003—becoming only the second dog in history to win both Crufts and Westminster. In England, "Mick" was usually handled by Geoff Corish or Michael Coad and sometimes by his breeder, Ron Ramsay; in the United States, Mick was shown by Bill McFadden.

Expectations were high in the spring of 2000 when reports started circulating that one of the greatest dogs in the United Kingdom was on his way to the United States. The Kerry Blue Terrier Ch. Torum's Scarf Michael had been undefeated at his last big shows in England, ending his career there with Best in Show at Crufts. "Mick's" handler in America would be Bill McFadden, already established as a successful terrier specialist in California. He had shown one record-breaking Kerry Blue before Mick, Ch. Kerrageen's Hotspur, in the early 1990s and also handled the Giant Schnauzer Ch. Skansen's Tristan II to Number Two of all breeds in 1999. Tristan was owned by Marilu Hansen, who would also be Mick's new American owner.

Mick's career turned into a brilliant chapter of American dog show history. Arriving shortly after Westminster, he stayed home for a couple of months before hitting two terrier group shows in California. After winning those, he waited until fall before his next venture: going East to the great Montgomery County terrier weekend, which that year also included the first Morris & Essex Kennel Club since the original show had been discontinued in 1957. Mick was the sensation of the weekend: nobody who saw him then could doubt that the American dog fancy had a new bright shining star. Not yet an American champion when he arrived, Mick won Best in Show at Morris & Essex, Devon, and Montgomery County. At Hatboro, he won the superstrong Terrier Group but was defeated in the finale by the Standard Schnauzer Ch. Charisma Jailhouse Rock, who would run close behind Mick for much of the following year's Top Dog competition.

In 2001, Mick went on the campaign trail, won 87 Bests in Show, and was Top Dog of all breeds. The following year, he was shown sparingly, was undefeated in most of his appearances, and scored another 22 Bests. In 2003, in an electrifying performance, he won the only show that had thus far eluded him—Westminster—a first for the breed. Summing up Mick's show career in America: he won Best of Breed at all but 2 of the 170 shows he went to, won the Group on all but three occasions, and won 113 Bests in Show. Some dogs won more, but few—if any—had such a high percentage of wins. That this dog had charisma and ringside appeal was obvious, but it must have felt particularly rewarding for his team that Mick also met with the breed-specific approval of old-time terrier people, including Ric Chashoudian, who had shown the previous breed record holder Ch. Melbee's Chances Are twenty-five years earlier, and Mrs. Bea Schlesinger, "Tommy's" owner, whose last Melbee champions were sired by Mick.

Dandie from Down Under

In 2006, the top dog in all-breed competition was another terrier, also imported and also shown by McFadden. Dandie Dinmont Terriers had occasionally won Bests in Show in America before Ch. Hobergays Fineus Fogg arrived in late 2005, but never as often or as consistently as "Harry" did. Born in New Zealand, with a pedigree that combined Australian, New Zealand, English, Canadian and American lines, Harry hit America fresh from having won Australia's Melbourne Royal show over more than 4,000 dogs. Handled by his Australian owner, Emma Greenway, he won his first couple of

The Dandie Dinmont Terrier Ch. Hobergays Phineus Fogg had a successful career in Australia, incorporating three Royal Bests in Show, before being campaigned to Top Dog of all breeds in the United States in 2006.

Bests in Show in America directly from the classes, and in McFadden's care he became a consistent winner in all-breed competition. Harry's American co-owners, Jean Heath and Bill Cosby, had already experienced tremendous success with their Black Watch Lakeland Terriers as well as with several other breeds. Cosby, of course, has been one of America's most popular comedians and entertainers for many years and has been a consistent supporter of top show dogs for almost as long.

POODLE POPULARITY

Few dogs create such an outrageously glamorous spectacle or generate such strong feelings as a Poodle in full show coat. Originally a sporting dog and water retriever, the Poodle can still excel at this job if given half a chance: the Poodle Club of America in recent years has organized well-attended water retrieving trials to demonstrate the breed's ability. Primarily, however, the Poodle has become the show dog par excellence, a breed whose appearance is held up

THE POODLE CLIP

The Poodle's coat pattern was originally based on the practical idea that the coat should be left longer around the chest and joints for protection in the water (with the tail pompon, carried high, functioning as an easily visible signal for the hunter on land). The manner in which Poodles are presented at dog shows today is unapologetically artificial, no doubt about it, and whether you like it or not is strictly a matter of taste; but it's important to Poodle fanciers that the show clip is not just a whim but represents a tradition that is over a century old.

There are many different variations of the clip. In some countries, almost anything goes at the shows, but in America only the Continental and English Saddle clips are accepted in the competitive classes for adult dogs. In both cases, the face, the throat, the feet, the forelegs, and base of the tail are shaved, with puffs left around the pasterns and a huge, carefully tailored jacket of hair covering the chest and neck. Both clips have shorter hair on the hindquarters, which are shaved smooth in the Continental style with only a single "bracelet" on each hock and an optional pompon on each hip. In the English Saddle clip, a short blanket of hair is left on the rear, except for a curved shaved area on each flank and two shaved bands on each hindleg. On the skull, the long topknot is held out of the dog's face with elastic bands. Poodles up to twelve months of age can also be shown in the Puppy clip, with a long coat covering the entire dog except the shaved face, throat, feet, and base of the tail. A more tailored version of the Puppy clip, the so-called Sporting clip, is accepted only for nonregular classes, such as Stud Dog and Brood Bitch.

There is, however, much more to the Poodle than its coat. Combine the striking outward appearance with a temperament that is among the happiest, most biddable, and most civilized of any dog, and you get an extroverted show dog that is impossible to miss and, at best, difficult to take one's eyes off of. The breed took some time to develop its show potential and, although exhibited ever since the late 1800s, was mostly regarded as a curiosity until the middle of the twentieth century.

as a symbol of viewers' attitudes toward dog shows, both supportive and critical.

The first kennels to successfully promote Poodles on a large scale in top-level competition in America were Blakeen and Pillicoc, whose exploits with Standard Poodles take us back to the 1930s. However, when the Poodle popularity explosion occurred, it primarily involved Miniatures. There had been a Westminster Best in 1943 for a Miniature, the black Ch. Pitter Patter of Piperscroft, imported from one of the most important foundation kennels in England, but their biggest success came in the 1950s and 1960s.

Miniatures and Toys

The first consistent Miniature Poodle winners in all-breed competition came from Blakeen. Mrs. Hoyt gradually switched to the smaller Poodle varieties in later years and quickly became as successful there as she

Maxine Beam with the English Miniature Poodle import Ch. Adastra Magic Fame and the Toy Ch. Ty-Del's Dancing Girl, both multiple Best in Show winners in the 1950s. Fame won more than forty all-breed Bests and was Runner-up to Top Dog in both 1956 and 1957.

Good rapport between handler and dog is paramount. The Miniature Poodle Ch. Surrey Spice Girl awaits her turn at the Poodle Club of America specialty with her handler, Kaz Hosaka. Spice Girl was Best in Show at Westminster in 2002.

had been with Standards. The white Ch. Blakeen Christable (the result of a sire-daughter breeding going back to Piper-scroft) shot up like a comet and won eighteen Bests in Show in 1947, more than any other dog that year. She disappeared from the show scene as quickly as she had

appeared but is behind many whites in both the United Kingdom and America through her son Ch. Blakeen Oscar of the Waldorf, who was exported to England. A black kennel mate, Ch. Magic Fate of Blakeen (the result of a half brother–sister breeding), continued to win for several years, even after being acquired by Col. Ferguson in California. Magic Fate's fifty-five all-breed Bests were advertised as a world record for Poodles in the early 1950s. Mrs. Hoyt's own white English import Ch. Snow Boy of Fircot was among the top dogs of all breeds with fourteen Bests in 1949, as was his white grandson Ch. Blakeen Van Aseltine, who won sixteen Bests in 1955.

Toy Poodles had been on the scene since the first American dog shows early in the century without ever getting themselves noticed in top competition. In the middle of

the century, they had a brief burst of glory. The black Ch. Blakeen King Doodles won a dozen Bests in 1955, making him one of the top winners of all breeds that year, and the following year the white Ch. Blakeen Ding Ding made history by winning the Top Dog spot with twenty-one Bests in Show. Not all dogs carrying the famous kennel name were owned or even necessarily bred by Mrs. Hoyt. King Doodles was both owned and handled by Robert Levy in Florida, who a few years later would win even more with Ch. Loramar's I'm A Dandee, a brown dog

The Standard Poodle Ch. Rimskittle Ruffian in the Westminster Best in Show finale in 1980, handled by Tim Brazier.

of part Blakeen breeding whose seventy Bests in Show in the 1960s remained a breed record until the mid-1990s. Ding Ding was neither owned nor bred by Mrs. Hoyt, but she was out of a Blakeen dam and owned by the renowned Washington, D.C., political society "hostess with the mostest" Perle Mesta.

Ding Ding's handler was Maxine Beam, who was having a great run of success as a Poodle handler in those years. At the same time that Ding Ding was experiencing her meteoric rise to success, Miss Beam was also winning with the white Miniature Ch. Adastra Magic Fame. He had been imported from England but was the result of several generations of transatlantic cooperation: his sire had been sent from Blakeen to England, and the sire's sire had come from England to Blakeen. When the so-called Phillips points were added up in 1956 (the first year they were collected and presented as a whole), it turned out that two Poodles shown by the same handler, Ding Ding and Magic Fame, ended up as Number One and Number Two of all breeds. Such a double victory has never again occurred for any handler, partly because the statistical chances of having two such successful dogs at the same time are so remote, but also because later handlers generally have focused on just one star dog, relegating the rest to supporting roles.

Magic Fame won even more the following year but ended up as Number Two again, defeated by a toy dog of a different breed, the Pekingese Ch. Chik T'Sun of Caversham. Miss Beam continued to show dogs of many breeds successfully for many years and later became one of America's most popular and respected judges.

Another link to the future was provided by Ding Ding's sire, Ch. Wilber White Swan. He was a top all-breed contender for several years and won Westminster in 1956. It was the first win ever at this show, not just for Toy Poodles but for any toy dog, and it was also the beginning of a long and close association that White Swan's handler, Anne Rogers Clark, would have with the Best in Show arena at America's greatest show.

Mrs. Clark had started showing dogs very early and already won well with many breeds. She soon entered the record books by winning Westminster a second time, now with the Miniature Ch. Fontclair Festoon (described by Mrs. Clark as "banker's grey" in color), in 1959, and then again with the black Toy Ch. Cappoquin Little Sister, in 1961. Three Westminster wins was a record that anyone could be proud of, but after Mrs. Clark retired from handling, she also had the ultimate satisfaction of seeing a Miniature Poodle she had co-bred, Ch. Surrey Spice Girl, win the top spot at Westminster in 2002. The Surrey prefix had been inherited by Mrs. Clark from her mother, Olga Hone Rogers, and has graced many champion Miniature Poodles (all of them descending from Mrs. Clark's old favorite, Festoon). There have also been Surrey champions in English Cockers, Norfolk Terriers, and Whippets, to mention just some of the breeds in which the Clarks have been involved. Standard Poodles were a major interest but were registered with the late James Edward Clark's prefix, Rimskittle; the most famous were the eye-catching white Ch. Rimskittle Bartered Bride and the black Westminster Group winner Ch. Rimskittle Ruffian.

By the early 1960s, the most glamorous era of the Miniature Poodle in America was

Frank Sabella with the Standard Poodle Ch. Acadia Command Performance shortly before winning Best in Show at Westminster in 1973.

in full bloom. Top imports from the best English kennels were flooding across the borders, and Miniature Poodles were attracting many of the best and the brightest of show fanciers—some as breeders, some as handlers, others just as admirers and fanciers who in some cases had the wherewithal to finance high-profile show careers for dogs they particularly admired.

A Touch of Show Business

A new handler who appeared on the scene at just the right moment in the 1950s was able to take Poodles to a new level on the West Coast. Frank T. Sabella got his first Standard Poodle in the early 1950s and

quickly realized that dog shows—and Poodles—were a hobby that could be turned into a real career. Learning the art of Poodle presentation first from Mrs. Clark, then branching out on his own and using, to great advantage, not a little of the showmanship he had acquired from his earlier professional experience in the entertainment world, Sabella's rise to the top was nothing short of meteoric. His first top winner was a brown, Ch. Cappoquin Bon Jongleur, top Poodle in 1959, but it was a pair of whites that brought Sabella the greatest notice. Ch. Estid Ballet Dancer and Ch. Tedwin's Top Billing virtually defined Poodle glamour in the early 1960s. With these two,

In the 1950s, Miniature Poodles exuded more glamour than did any other breed and gained much attention. The Miniature Ch. Tedwin's Top Billing was Top Dog of all breeds in 1962, handled by Frank Sabella.

The black English-imported Miniature Ch. Frederick of Rencroft was Top Dog of all breeds in 1966, handled by Frank Sabella. He is shown winning Best in Show at the Golden Gate Kennel Club show under judge Percy Roberts (left).

After the glory years of the 1950s and 1960s, Miniature Poodles became less prominent in all-breed competition. Ch. Bar-King's Scintilla was one of the few exceptions; she is pictured with her handler, Barbara Humphries, and judge Henry Stoecker at Westminster in 1985, the year she was among the top dogs of all breeds.

Sabella topped the Non-Sporting Group ratings for three years in a row and won or placed high among all breeds each time: Ballet Dancer, Number Three in 1961, and Top Billing, Number One in 1962 and Number Two in 1963. "Billy" was bred by the famous Cocker handler Ted Young and had started out with Mrs. Clark on the East Coast. Both dogs were sired by the great imported stud dog Ch. Summercourt Square Dancer of Fircot, and both were owned by Ernest Ferguson. Top Billing's being accorded what was, indeed, top billing in the dog show world in 1961 was the apex of Ferguson's long career in dogs, which had started with Great Danes in the 1930s.

Sabella continued to dominate the Poodle scene through the 1960s in California and often nationwide. His second victory in the all-breeds Top Dog ratings came in 1966

with the black English Miniature Ch. Frederick of Rencroft, and the third with the black Standard Ch. De Russy Lollypop. (The latter win came in 1969 and was shared with the Boxer Ch. Arriba's Prima Donna: a slight discrepancy between the two leading ratings systems resulted in two different winners that year.) Lollypop was bred by Dr. Jacklyn Hungerland, who after a successful career as a Poodle breeder went on to become a judge and the first female director of the American Kennel Club. She remains one of the most active all-rounders and judged Best in Show at Westminster in 1995.

The one show that Sabella had not yet cracked was Westminster. The opportunity came with the dramatic white Standard Ch. Acadia Command Performance ("Bart") in 1973. It was an exciting finale: according to Sabella, Bart was not an easy dog to show and had to be run around the block at Madison Square Garden several times to keep him from exploding with excitement. Although he was still quite young at the time of this win, Bart retired from show business shortly afterward when Sabella decided to turn from professional handling to judging. Bart made a major contribution to Poodles as a stud dog, and Sabella has become one of the most sought-after judges both in America and abroad.

With the retirement of several of the great Poodle handlers, there was a distinct downturn in the breed's fortunes in all-breed competition for a few years. In the 1950s and 1960s, many or most of the top Non-Sporting dogs were Poodles; during the 1970s, the numbers dropped so that by 1983, for the first time since these records were kept, not a single Poodle was included among the year's top Non-Sporting winners.

The difference was most noticeable in Miniatures. A few, all black bitches, have earned a spot among the top dogs of all breeds since the mid-1960s: Ch. Bar-King's Scintilla (1985), Ch. Surrey Capsicum (1994), Ch. Reignon Dassin Alexandra (1999), and Ch. Surrey Spice Girl (2001). The Miniatures with few exceptions have not been able to hold their own with the Standards as they once did.

The Standard Tradition

The tradition of great, mostly white Standard Poodles continued, however. The largest Poodle variety has continued to attract major breeders who are willing and

Among the most important kennels providing a foundation for future Standard Poodle breeders was Puttencove: the white Ch. Puttencove Promise won Best in Show at Westminster in 1958.

able to invest what it takes to maintain large-scale breeding programs and to promote their best dogs in the show ring. The Puttencove Kennels, owned by Mrs. George Putnam, continued the tradition from the earlier great kennels; its biggest winner, Ch. Puttencove Promise, who won Best in Show at Westminster in 1958, had one grandsire from Blakeen, the other from Pillicoc. Puttencove stock in turn helped produce the Alekai line, which has remained one of the prime purveyors of top winners of the Standard variety for several decades.

The Alekai kennel was originally owned by Mrs. Henry J. Kaiser (whose husband, founder of the Kaiser steel and aluminum companies, has been called the father of modern American shipbuilding) and located in Oahu, Hawaii. The show dogs were always sent to live with their handler, Wendell Sammet, on the mainland. He inherited the dogs from Mrs. Kaiser upon her death and has continued to breed with equal success under the same prefix, Ale Kai, with just a small typographical space change to indicate the new ownership. The most outstanding representative for the kennel's long breeding program has been Ch. Ale Kai Mikimoto On Fifth, the winner of more than eighty Bests in Show and the top Non-Sporting dog for both 2002 and 2003.

The Dassin Poodles were long among Alekai's (and Ale Kai's) main rivals in the Standard ring, with an equally long line of outstanding, but mostly black, winners. In recent years, Ale Kai and Dassin (founded by the late Bud Dickey but now owned by his partner, Joseph Vergnetti) have joined forces, resulting in several new Best in Show winners. Dassin has also produced a prolific line of black Miniature winners, of which Ch. Reignon Dassin Alexandra was the most successful exponent, with more than sixty Bests in Show and a position among the Top Ten of all breeds in the late 1900s.

The biggest Standard Poodle successes were scored by a series of whites that

The Alekai Standard Poodles were started in the 1950s and handled by Wendell Sammet from the start. He is shown winning Best in Show at the Ladies' Dog Club in 1969 with Ch. Alekai Luau. The judge was Henry Wheeler, Jr.

The Dassin kennel has produced top-winning Standard and Miniature Poodles for several decades. The black Miniature bitch Ch. Reignon Dassin Alexandra was handled by breeder Joseph Vergnetti to more than sixty Bests in Show and was among the Top Dogs of all breeds in 1999. Alexandra is shown winning at the Poodle Club of America specialty in 1997 under judge Peggy Hogg. Trophy presenters were club officials Gene Cozart and Betsey Leedy.

started in the Midwest with Ch. Lou-Gin's Kiss Me Kate in the 1970s. Those were the days when American dog shows had become so big and competition so fierce that the past all-breed records of dogs such as Bang Away, Chik T'Sun, and the Colonel seemed almost inconceivable. Those dogs had all won Best in Show 100 times, but that was twenty or twenty-five years earlier, and it seemed unlikely that such achievements would be possible again. Kiss Me Kate proved the naysayers wrong: the times were changing once again, and she was the first but not the last in a long line of members in the modern era's Century Club, the informal name given to a group of dogs that have

The Standard Poodle Ch. Whisperwind's On A Carousel won Best in Show at Westminster in 1991, remained among the country's top dogs for three years, and amassed a total of more than 100 Bests in Show.

Ch. Lake Cove's That's My Boy was Top Dog of all breeds in both 1998 and 1999. "Treson" accumulated 169 Bests in Show between 1997 and 1999. He was a grandson of On A Carousel and an influential sire.

won Best in Show 100 times or more at AKC all-breed shows. A linebred descendant of Bart (she was sired by his brother and out of his daughter) and handled by Robert Walberg, Kate embarked on a career that, when she retired in 1980, totaled 140 all-breed Bests in Show, and included such honorifics as Top Dog of all breeds in 1979 and runner-up in the same competition in 1980.

Much more was to come. A handler partnership that brought Standard Poodles to the highest peaks ever achieved in America began to attract notice in the 1980s.

Between Dennis McCoy and Randy Garren's presentation, little was left to chance, and their charges were given every earthly possibility to shine. The Randenn team worked spectacularly well with Ch. Whisperwind's On A Carousel, the 1991 Westminster winner. "Peter" descended from a long line of champions that carried the blood of Alekai, Dassin, Puttencove, and Command Performance; he stayed among the top dogs in the country for three years and won more than 100 Bests in Show. McCoy and Garren's next charge was an

The Dalmatian Ch. Green Starr's Colonel Joe, among the top Non-Sporting Dogs for three years running and one of the top winners of all breeds in 1979.

The first dog to win 100 Bests in Show since the 1950s was the white Standard Poodle Ch. Lou-Gin's Kiss Me Kate, Top Dog of all breeds in 1979. She was handled by Robert Walberg.

exotic representative of the famous Del Zarzoso kennel in Spain. Ch. Maneetas Del Zarzoso Fuego Fatuo had a very international background: he was born in England, had a Swedish sire, finished his American championship as a puppy, and went to Finland to become Top Dog there before return-

ing to the United States. With that background, it is not surprising that "Gordon" had a slightly shorter career in the United States than his predecessor did, but he was one of the top dogs of all breeds in 1993. He also proved to be a hugely popular and influential stud dog, with approximately 100 American champions to his credit, plus many more elsewhere around the world.

In the mid-1990s, McCoy and Garren took a rest from their back-breaking Poodle campaigns and focused on showing a Dalmatian instead. Ch. Spotlight's Spectacular was the top Non-Sporting dog for two years and won two Westminster Groups and more than fifty Bests in Show, staying

The liver-spotted Dalmatian Ch. Spotlight's Spectacular won the group at Westminster in 1996 and 1997. "Penny" was also the top Non-Sporting dog in 1995 and 1996.

among the Top Ten of all breeds both years. No Dalmatian had done so well since the great Ch. Four-in-Hand Mischief in the late 1930s. Ch. Roadcoach Roadster in the 1950s and Ch. Green Starr's Colonel Joe in the late 1970s were the only two other Dalmatians to place among the Top Ten in sixty years.

The zenith, both for Poodles and for the Randenn team, came in the last few years of the twentieth century, when a stunning white Standard named Ch. Lake Cove's That's My Boy made his debut. A grandson of Ch. Whisperwind's On A Carousel, "Treson" was both owned and bred by Doris Lilienthal, five generations down from Command Performance. He lived up to his pedigree: his whirlwind career included 169 Bests in Show (an all-time Poodle record) from 1997 through 1999 and Top Dog of all breeds for two years in a row. Treson was also an internationally influential sire in spite of his tragically premature death in a kennel accident.

The Changing Toy Poodles

Toy Poodles in most other countries compete in the same group as their larger cousins do. Not so in America, where the Toy Poodle—logically, in many respects—is included in the same group as the other toy-size breeds. After some great wins in the 1950s, Toy Poodles had only a few top all-breed contenders for the next few decades. The two biggest winners were bred and shown by Gary Wittmeier. Both were white, and both won the Toy Group at Westminster: Ch. Trebor of Ahs Capital Gains in 1991 and Ch. MVP of Ahs in 1994. The latter was among the Top Ten dogs in the country for two years and broke the old Toy Poodle record, adding at least a half dozen Best in

Show wins to I'm A Dandee's total of seventy from the 1950s.

The Toy Poodle type changed dramatically over the years, going from the longer-bodied, low-legged dwarf common in the early years to a well-proportioned, tiny replica of the larger Poodle varieties. The modern American Toy Poodle has become much in demand overseas, nowhere more so than in Japan, where the cult of breeding exquisite small dogs has a long tradition. Gradually, around the turn of this century, American fanciers were realizing that Toy Poodles bred from American stock in Japan were actually every bit as good as their ancestors. In fact, many of them were even better, as became apparent when the first Japanese imports started to arrive in America. In 1998, the white Ch. Dignity of Jewelry House Yoko became the first Japanese-born dog of any breed to win a Group at Westminster. He was shown by Kaz Hosaka, who himself had come over from Japan

The Toy Poodle Ch. North Well Chako JP Platina King was Top Dog of all breeds in 2004. "Coleman" was imported from Japan but descended from a long line of American and Canadian exports, including Coleman's sire. He was handled by Tim Brazier.

The Toy Poodle Ch. Hell's-A-Blazen Fagin's Pride strides out ahead of handler Richard Bauer in the Toy Group at Westminster in the late 1970s.

many years earlier to apprentice with Mrs. Clark and stayed on to become one of America's top Poodle handlers, winning Westminster in 2002 with the black Miniature Ch. Surrey Spice Girl.

Soon, the occasional Japanese Toy Poodle import turned into an avalanche. At the Poodle Club of America specialties in 2005 and 2006, practically *all* the top awards in Toys went to dogs bred in Japan. The white Japanese import Ch. North Well Chako JP Platina King was America's Top Dog of all breeds in 2004, almost a half century after Ding Ding had been in the same spot. "Coleman" was shown by Tim Brazier, a Cana-

The Toy Poodle Ch. Trebor of Ahs Capital Gains, Group winner at Westminster in 1991, handled by his owner and breeder, Gary Wittmeier. The judge was Vernelle Kendrick.

Ch. Devon Puff and Stuff was not the first Bichon Frisé to win in all-breed competition, but she captured the fancy's imagination and helped make the breed popular. She was Runner-up to Top Dog in 1986 and is pictured winning one of more than sixty Bests in Show at Bloomington Indiana Kennel Club that year, handled by Michael Kemp under judge Ann Stevenson.

dian who, like Hosaka, had earned his first big Poodle wins in the United States as the handler of the Clarks' dogs (in his case, the Rimskittle Standards Bartered Bride and Rampant). Coleman's owners were Toni and Martin Sosnoff, whose Atalanta prefix was previously best known for Standard Poodles. The Top Dog victory was a huge triumph not only for Japanese breeding but also for American Toy Poodles: Coleman's pedigree goes back to Japanese bitches that have been bred to American exported stud dogs for five generations, with more than a dozen lines to the influential Syntifny stud dogs of the 1970s and 1980s.

In 2006, another white Toy Poodle from Japan, Ch. Smash JP Win A Victory, was campaigned by Hosaka to a position among the top dogs of all breeds. She also won the Group at Westminster in 2007.

BICHONS: NEW KIDS ON THE BLOCK

Poodles often did not leave much for the other breeds in Group competitions. Bichons Frisés, however, proved extremely competitive once they were approved for AKC competition in the Non-Sporting Group in 1973 and have knocked Poodles off the top spot many times since then. The

The Top Dog of all breeds in 2000, the Bichon Frisé Ch. Special Times Just Right! with his handler, Scott Sommer, at Westminster in 2001. They won Best in Show.

The top Non-Sporting winner of both 1983 and 1984, the Chow Chow Ch. Wah-Hu Redcloud Sugar Daddy. He was among the Top Dogs of all breeds in 1983 and is shown winning the Ladies Kennel Association of America under judge Elaine Young in 1984, handled by William Trainor.

first to win consistently at all-breed level was Ch. Teaka's Erbin Einar, who stayed close to the top for three years in the early 1980s; but it was the bitch Ch. Devon Puff and Stuff whose charm and showmanship really caught the fancy's attention a few years later when she won more than sixty Bests in Show and was Number Two of all breeds in 1986.

Several other Bichons have done well since then, and the top honor goes to Ch. Special Times Just Right! ("J. R."), who walked away with the Top Dog of all breeds award in 2000. The following February, J. R. won a very popular Westminster victory; few who were present will forget his exu-berant greeting of the assembled press after his big win. His handler, Scott Sommer, is one of the most successful of his generation of professionals, and owner Cecelia Ruggles has been the power behind the throne for several of the country's most outstanding show dogs in the early 2000s.

American Bichons have helped establish breeding programs around the world and often gone to the top at big international shows. One of the most outstanding successes was scored by Ch. PaRay's I Told You So, who after three years as one of America's top Non-Sporting dogs went to the United Kingdom, where he became Top Dog of all breeds in 2004.

Heavily dominated by Poodles and Bichons, with occasional Bulldogs and Dalmatians contending for the top spots, it's obviously difficult for the other breeds in the Non-Sporting group to earn their place in the sun. The Flakkee Keeshonden and Ralanda French Bulldogs deserve their own mention in the owner-handler annals of dog show history from the 1960s and 1970s, but the only other dog that managed to top the Non-Sporting group ratings for two years in a row was a Chow Chow, Ch. Wah-Hu Redcloud Sugar Daddy, one of the country's most successful show dogs regardless of breed in 1983.

Toy Dogs at the Top

It is ironic that the English Toy Spaniels—which more than almost any other breed helped to get dog shows started in the late 1800s—met with so little appreciation from the judges in the century that followed. The breed has a devoted group of followers but has been surpassed in both numbers and prominence by newer toy breeds in their native country as well as in America. The word newer may not really be applicable, however: the leading toy dog since competition between different breeds was first organized has been the Pekingese, which of course existed in pure form in the Chinese imperial court long before the dog show fancy in the West took shape.

Prodigious Pekingese

The first Pekingese imports came to England after the looting of the Summer Palace in Beijing in 1860. The few court attendants who did not flee the invading British army committed suicide, and the little dogs that were found in the palace buildings no doubt

"bit the foreign devils," just as Empress Tzu Hsi had decreed they should do. In spite of this, a number of them were brought as war trophies back to England. One, appropriately named Looty, was given as a gift to Queen Victoria; but the monarch was not known to have shown any particular interest in the new acquisition and continued to favor her Pomeranians. Other imported

One of the top show dogs ever in America, the Pekingese Ch. Chik T'Sun of Caversham, was exported from England to Canada as a youngster. After winning Top Dog there in 1956, he embarked on a career in the United States that made him Top Dog of all breeds for the next three years. He won 126 Bests in Show at AKC all-breed shows, including Westminster in 1960, and was rarely defeated by any other dog. "Gossie" is pictured with his American owner, Mrs. Charles Venable.

Pekingese founded strains that soon produced the first show winners.

The breed's early rise to the top spots at shows in the United Kingdom has already been outlined; in America, several Pekingese won Best in Show as soon as this award was officially recognized, but the first great winner did not appear until the late 1930s. This was the previously mentioned English import Ch. Che Le of Matson's Catawba, owned by Mrs. James Austin, whose husband was at that time showing the great Smooth Fox Terrier Ch. Nornay Saddler. Che Le's record was overshadowed by another English import almost two decades later. This dog was Ch. Chik T'Sun of Caversham, whom many consider to have the greatest show record of any dog in America. He won the annual Top Dog point score for three consecutive years in the United States and is also the only dog ever to be Top Dog in both Canada and the United States.

Chik T'Sun's story is closely linked to that of one of the great international kennels of the world, St. Aubrey-Elsdon. This establishment was, and still is, located in Canada but was also active in the United Kingdom for several years and has always been extremely successful in the United States as well. One of the partners, Nigel Aubrey-Jones, started in dogs in his native Wales in the early 1940s. He studied with the masters and was a frequent visitor at the great Caversham kennel, which would prove a useful connection in future years.

Meanwhile, R. William Taylor had already started showing Pekingese in Canada. The partnership between Aubrey-Jones and Taylor began when the latter visited the United Kingdom to look at

Pekingese but was cemented with the first purchase the partners made. Ch. Caversham Ko Ko of Shanruss had been a great winner in England and won Best in Show at his very first show after being brought to America, the classic Westchester event in 1955. Among the defeated Group winners were the great Boxer Bang Away, the current Blakeen Poodle, and a host of other American stars. The dog fancy took notice. Ko Ko was soon sold to Mrs. Austin, owner of the earlier top winner Che Le, setting another precedent for the importers: of the large number of dogs purchased by the St. Aubrey-Elsdon kennels over the years, many were used in the kennel's extensive and extremely successful breeding program, but even more were sold to other fanciers, influencing the development of the Pekingese worldwide.

St. Aubrey-Elsdon branched out into many other breeds over the years, invariably with success, but it was always its Pekingese that remained the primary interest. The breeding program produced endless numbers of champions around the world, including Ch. St. Aubrey Dragonora of Elsdon, Best in Show at Westminster in 1982. Both partners became popular judges, and Taylor is one of the few to have judged a Group at both Crufts and Westminster. Since Aubrey-Jones's death in 2003, the kennel, situated in Quebec, has continued to produce champions and top winners on a smaller scale.

The partners purchased Chik T'Sun as a promising youngster in England and showed him to Top Dog of all breeds in Canada in 1956. They then took him to Westminster in 1957, where he won the Toy Group. Subsequent to that show, "Gossie,"

The Pekingese Ch. Yakee Leaving Me Breathless at Franshaw was among the Top Dogs of all breeds in both 2002 and 2003, winning the Toy Group at Westminster twice before being retired. He is pictured with handler Hiram Stewart, Toy Group judge Bettie Krause, and trophy presenter Robert E. Taylor in 2003.

as Chik T'Sun was called, was sold to Mr. and Mrs. Charles Venable from Atlanta, Georgia, who contracted the toy specialist handler Clara Alford to be his exclusive handler. In the following three years, they broke all existing records for winning. As far as is known, Gossie was defeated for Best of Breed only one time during his long career, at Westminster in 1958. On the 173 occasions that he walked into a Toy Group, he won it on all but 7 occasions. His 166 Group wins, in turn, resulted in 126 Bests in Show—a total that remains almost unbelievable and a win percentage that very few dogs have achieved before or since. During one especially memorable forty-six-day period, Gossie attended fourteen shows and won Best in Show at each. This was more than even Bang Away had won, and by the end of his career, Gossie was the top-winning dog in history in America, a title he held until the 1980s.

The Pekingese Ch. Wendessa Crown Prince won Best in Show at Westminster in 1990. He was handled by Luc Boileau under judge Frank Sabella. Trophy presenters are club officials Ronald H. Menaker and Chester F. Collier.

Ch. Coughton Sungable of Perryacre, imported from England and America's top Toy dog in 1965 and 1966, placed high among all breeds both years. He is shown with handler Elaine Rigden and judge Bea Godsol at Palm Beach County Dog Fanciers Association in 1966.

It would be nearly a half century before another Pekingese would be Top Dog of all breeds in America. In the interim period, there were several that did well in the ratings: the English import Ch. Coughton Sungable of Perryacre was shown by Elaine Rigden to top toy for two years in the 1960s, and Ch. Briarcourt's Damien Gable repeated that achievement in the early 1990s, handled by David Fitzpatrick; both ranked high in the all-breed Top Ten statistics. Just one—in addition to Gossie and Dragonora—won Westminster: Ch. Wendessa Crown Prince, handled by Luc Boileau in 1990 for owner Edward B. Jenner, who also owned the Standard Poodle Command Performance, the 1973 winner. In the early 2000s, one import from the famous Yakee kennel in Scotland

The Pug Ch. Dhandy's Favorite Woodchuck had a brilliant career in 1981, winning Best in Show at Westminster and ending the year as Top Dog of all breeds before dying in a tragic incident while traveling by airplane.

A series of glamorous Shih Tzu presented by Gilbert Kahn's long-established Charing Cross kennel in Florida won top honors in the early 2000s. Ch. Charing Cross Ragtime Cowboy was among the Top Dogs of all breeds in both 1999 and 2000.

succeeded another in the top spots: Ch. Yakee Leaving Me Breathless at Franshaw started out as Number Three of all breeds in 2002 and moved up to second place in 2003 before being retired. He won the Toy Group at Westminster for two years running, handled in the United States by Hiram Stewart but owned by John Shaw and Maria Francis from Hong Kong, already internationally known for their winning Pekingese. The following year, another Scottish import, Ch. Yakee If Only, took over. Owned by Kit Woodruff and shown by David Fitzpatrick, "Jeffrey" ended up as Runner-up to Top Dog in 2004 and then went on to win that award the following year. Each dog won more than 100 Bests in Show, adding up to an impressive total for their respective owners as well as for the Scottish kennel that had sent them over.

Pugs and Shih Tzus

The up-and-coming breeds in Toy Group competition are primarily Shih Tzu and Pugs, however. The latter had a great winner in Ch. Dhandy's Favorite Woodchuck, who had a brilliant career in 1981, winning Westminster and forty other Bests to become Top Dog of all breeds before tragically suffocating in an airplane en route to a show. A second serious Pug contender in 2005, Ch. Kendoric's Riversong Mulroney, was runner-up to the Pekingese for both top Toy Dog and Top Dog of all breeds.

Shih Tzu have been superbly represented by a series of dogs campaigned by Luke Ehricht for longtime breed specialist Gilbert Kahn in Florida. The two that reached the highest peaks of perfection were Ch. Charing Cross Ragtime Cowboy, who was Runner-up to Top Dog of all breeds in 2000, and his son Ch. Hallmark Jolei Raggedy Andy, who did the same in 2003. Kahn is thought of primarily as a toy dog fancier and specializes in these breeds as a judge, but as an exhibitor he possesses a

Maltese had a great run in the 1990s. Ch. Sand Island Small Kraft Lite was top Toy dog of 1990 and 1991 and among the Top Ten dogs of all breeds both years, winning more than seventy Bests in Show in the process. "Henry" is shown winning the Group at Westminster in 1992, handled by Vicki Abbott under judge Dawn Vick Hansen.

Sand Island Small Kraft Lite (1990 and 1991), and Ch. Ta-Jon's Tickle Me Silly (1997 and 1998). No Maltese has been Top Dog of all breeds or won Westminster so far, however. Yorkshire Terriers and Papillons have each accounted for one classic Westminster winner, Ch. Cede Higgens and Ch. Loteki Supernatural Being, respectively. The Yorkie won under Mrs. Clark in 1978, handled by his owner's daughter, Marlene Switzer; the Papillon took the top spot under Edd Bivin in 1999 and was a veteran when he did so. He had been a very popular Best in Show winner at the FCI World Show in Finland the previous year and remains the only dog to win both Westminster and the World Show, handled to both wins by British-born John Oulton. Remarkably, "Kirby" made a comeback by winning the Papillon Club of America's national specialty in 2005, at over fourteen years of age—probably the oldest dog ever to take such a win.

Although they did not win Westminster, a few other toys had such outstanding records that they must be mentioned: the Brussels Griffon Ch. Barmere's Mighty Man (sired by a St. Aubrey-Elsdon import), Top Toy in both 1962 and 1963; and three Miniature Pinschers with exceptional show records. The first of these was an amazing little dog generally known as "Little Daddy," officially registered as Ch. Rebel Roc's Casanova von Kurt, who was handled by his owner and breeder, E. W. Tipton, Jr., to a spot among the country's top toy dogs for five consecutive years in the late 1950s and early 1960s. In the process, he won a total of seventy-five Bests in Show, was the country's Number Two dog of all breeds in 1961, and sired scores of champions. In the 1970s, there were two champions from John McNamara's Jay-Mac kennels: Little Daddy's

triple record of sorts in that a Basset Hound he campaigned in 1998, Ch. Deer Hill's Great Gatsby, was also Number Two of all breeds.

Additional Toy Standouts

There have been many top contenders among Maltese, including Ch. Aennchen's Poona Dancer, who was among the Top Ten of all breeds for two years (1966 and 1967), and no fewer than four that each topped the annual toy dog ratings twice: Ch. Pendleton's Jewel (1969 and 1970), Ch. Joanne Chen's Maya Dancer (1971 and 1972), Ch.

granddaughter Ch. Jay-Mac's Impossible Dream and Ch. Jay-Mac's Dream Walking. One or the other remained among the Top Ten dogs of all breeds for five years in the 1970s. Impossible Dream also won the Miniature Pinscher Club of America's national specialty show four years in a row.

Statistically, toy breeds have won far more than their fair share compared with larger breeds in the early part of the twenty-first century. Intrinsic quality and great glamour have something to do with this record, but so, no doubt, has the basic cost of traveling. A toy breed that can be brought into the airplane cabin for a transcontinental flight is safer, less expensive, and more convenient to travel with than is a bigger dog in a crate.

Affenpinschers started winning big in the 1990s, and by 2001, Ch. Yarrow's Supernova was top Toy dog and among the top winners of all breeds. He is shown winning the Group at Westminster in 2002, handled by Beth Sweigart under judge Keke Kahn. Trophy presenter was George F. Clements, Jr.

The Maltese Ch. Pendleton's Jewel was the top Toy dog in both 1969 and 1970 and placed high among the Top Dogs of all breeds in 1970. She was owner-handled by Dorothy White.

LOOKING BACK

In the late twentieth and early twenty-first century, new records were set in most breeds, and the interest in dog shows reached a fever pitch that continues to rise exponentially. Show entries are in the millions each year, the public awareness of dog shows is greater than ever, and the adoration of the top winners at dog shows resembles what is more commonly lavished on pop stars or screen idols. It should be obvious from the above, however, that in many ways the sport of dog shows has changed less than one would expect, and as we focus on the current contenders and future stars, it helps to look back at those who broke the ground we are now treading on. What they achieved, with much fewer opportunities than we have now, was in many cases remarkable.

The Cavalier King Charles Spaniel Ch. Annatika Andreas, one of the top Toy dogs in 2001. Andreas won Best in Show eleven times during that year alone.

ALL-TIME FAVORITES

In a 2004 survey in *Dogs in Review* magazine, more than 100 active fanciers responded to the question, Which dog that was shown before your time do you most wish you could have seen in real life? Ten dogs together received over 50 percent of the answers, with the Smooth Fox Terrier Ch. Nornay Saddler from the 1930s and 1940s receiving the most votes, followed by the English Setter Ch. Rock Falls Colonel, Bulldog Ch. Kippax Fearnaught, Afghan Hound Ch. Shirkhan of Grandeur, Boxer Ch. Bang Away of Sirrah Crest, Cocker Spaniel Ch. My Own Brucie, Pekingese Ch. Chik T'Sun of Caversham, Doberman Pinscher Ch. Rancho Dobe's Storm, Kerry Blue Terrier Ch. Melbee's Chances Are, and Standard Poodle Ch. Rimskittle Ruffian.

All-time favorite, the Smooth Fox Terrier Ch. Nornay Saddler from the 1930s and 1940s.

CHAPTER 10

ON TOP AROUND THE WORLD

O ver the past century, what was originally a British pastime for the aristocracy and a rising bourgeoisie has become virtually a worldwide passion, reaching across almost every social barrier. It seems, in fact, that as soon as a country achieves a certain level of social and economic stability, one of the first activities to blossom is the keeping of what used to be called fancy dogs. A wealthy upper class is not necessary for maintaining a high level of purebred dog activities; what is required is a substantial number of people who are

Four of Scandinavia's top dogs at the turn of the century, pictured at the Helsinki show with judge Pamela Cross-Stern from Great Britain: from left, Greyhound Ch. Jet's Once Upon A Dream (Top Dog in Norway 2001); Vizsla Hookside Csaba (imported from the United Kingdom, Top Dog in Finland 2001); Scottish Terrier Ch. Raglan Rory (Top Dog in Sweden 2001); and Maltese Ch. Cinecittà Brevincontro (born in Italy, Top Dog in Denmark 2001).

able to retreat from everyday cares long enough to be susceptible to the appeal of a warm puppy. The first dog provides companionship as well as a passport into the world of active dog sports. The formation of kennel clubs and the beginning of dog shows are only a step behind.

GLOBAL OVERVIEW

Western Europe (including Scandinavia), North America, Australia, and New Zealand were the mainstays of purebred dog activities for most of the twentieth century. Latin America has a long history of dog shows and world-class dogs, although the social structure is still too divided to allow most middle-class families to become involved. Asia broke into the show dog world in the 1970s and 1980s with a splash, and after a few missteps, Japan in particular has become established as a major player. Israel and South Africa are geographically isolated outposts of dog show enthusiasm in areas with little other activity.

The traffic in judges and dogs used to be fairly one-sided from West to East but has developed into a genuine two-way street, culminating in the crowning of a Japanese-born Toy Poodle, Ch. North Well Chako JP Platina King, as America's Top Dog of all breeds for the year 2004—an achievement no one would have predicted even ten years earlier. Dogs from Australia and New Zealand have also gone to the top at an increasing number of the top British and American shows in the early twenty-first century. This is further proof that the dog show world has become increasingly global in a manner that would have been unthinkable only a few decades before.

The fall of communism in Eastern Europe in the 1990s saw that region emerge within a few short years as an almost frenzied participant on the international dog scene. Russia was going through the birth pangs involved in getting a national kennel club and international relations established at the turn of the twenty-first century and soon afterward started to make serious inroads on the top awards at European shows. The next frontier is China, long the most inhospitable place on earth for keeping dogs as pets. Now, a few years into the third millennium, an increasing number of Western dog experts are being invited to officiate at Chinese dog shows. Authorities there confidently predict that China will register 5 million dogs annually within the next decade—several times more than will any other country in the world. Whether a society that for so long has had no tradition of keeping dogs as pets will be able to become an accepted member of the international dog show community is still an open question, however.

It is doubtful whether pet dogs have a future in countries with a predominantly Muslim population, in view of the low status Islam generally accords dogs. India, which is predominantly Hindu but has a large Muslim population, joined the FCI in 2006 and is now organizing more dog shows than ever since the time of the British Raj. Other countries that would probably not have been considered likely players in the past are starting to produce dogs that can compete successfully on the world stage. Exactly where the world focus for purebred dog activities will be as the twenty-first century progresses is not certain, but it will most likely change from where it is today.

CANADA

Although the Canadian dog fancy has traditionally retained somewhat closer ties to the British roots of the sport than the United States has, the proximity and frequent exchange of dogs and judges have ensured that, in dogs at least, North America can in

The Toy Poodle Ch. Loramar's I'm A Dandee was born in California and became Canada's Top Dog of all breeds in 1963. After returning to the United States, Dandee was shown in Florida by his owner, Robert Levy, to seventy Bests in Show—a breed record that stood for several decades. Dandee was among the top winners in AKC competition for four years.

The St. Bernard Ch. Ambassadeur was the Top Dog in Canada in 1973.

The Old English Sheepdog Ch. Sir Lancelot of Barvan, Top Dog of all breeds in Canada in 1974 and Best in Show at Westminster the following February.

some ways be treated as a single entity. Many fanciers travel back and forth across the Canadian-U.S. border so often that it's difficult to separate their activities in the two countries, and Canadian breeders have made a much greater contribution to dogs in the United States than is commonly recognized. Some dogs have one Canadian and one American breeder; others may be born in Canada from American parents, or vice versa, making it difficult on occasion to determine whether a dog is, in fact, Canadian or American.

When a Canadian-born dog experiences exceptional success in the United States—which happens more often than most American fanciers are aware of—it tends to be forgotten that the dog is not, in fact, a native American product. A case in point is the German Shepherd Dog Ch. Altana's Mystique, the top show dog ever in the United States, with 275 Best in Show wins at AKC all-breed events. That Mystique was born and bred in Canada is not often recorded, nor is the fact that her handler, Jimmy Moses—who has won the Top Dog award in the United States more often than anyone else—is also an "import" from north of the border.

Canada has produced several Best in Show winners at Westminster, the first one in 1918 in the shape of a white Bull Terrier, Ch. Haymarket Faultless. The second one didn't come until 1975, when the Old English Sheepdog Ch. Sir Lancelot of Barvan won; he was also Top Dog of all breeds in his own country. There were two more Canadian Westminster winners in the next few years—the Irish Water Spaniel Ch. Oak Tree's

The Chow Chow Ch. Mi-Tu's Han Su Shang, Top Dog in Canada in 1975.

Irishtocrat in 1979 and the Pekingese Ch. St. Aubrey Dragonora of Elsdon in 1982, both owned by Anne Snelling of Ontario. The latest Canadian top winner in the United States was the Norwich Terrier Ch. Fairewood Frolic. She was born in Canada but lived in the United States, was Top Dog of all breeds there in 1997, and won Westminster in 1998.

Similarly, and unfairly, when Canadian breeding triumphs elsewhere in the world, the wins are often credited just to America, which is, of course, incorrect. The biggest success stories overseas are the two Canadian-bred Best in Show winners at Crufts: the Kerry Blue Terrier Ch. Callaghan of Leander in 1979 and the Australian Shepherd Ch. Caitland Isle Take A Chance in 2006. The Kerry Blue was living in England at the time; the Australian Shepherd was owned and handled by Americans, but it is worth noting that so far there has been no U.S.-bred Best in Show winner at Crufts.

It would be impossible to profile all the Canadian kennels that have had a major influence on their respective breeds in the United States. Standard Poodles, starting with the old Wycliffe dogs of Jean Lyle, have always had a good reputation south of the border, and the tradition continued in recent years with the Dawin standards, twice Top Dog of all breeds in Canada and consistently successful in the United States as well. The great Pekingese kennel of St. Aubrey-Elsdon is located in Canada but truly belongs to the world and is, because of its contributions to the show scene in the United States, profiled in chapter 9. Dandie Dinmont Terrier from Glahms, Borzoi from Sirhan and Kishniga, Bouviers des Flandres from Quiche, and many more have made names for themselves on the international scene; the two last mentioned also won Top Dog all breeds in their native country.

The traffic has, of course, gone both ways: some of the winners of the Top Dog award in Canada came from the United States. Among them was the Toy Poodle Ch. Loramar's I'm A Dandee, who had a great show career on both sides of the border in the 1960s: he was Top Dog in Canada before going on to become Top Dog in the United States. (Before him, the great English-born Pekingese Ch. Chik T'Sun of Caversham had won both titles.) The list of Canada's Top Dogs includes three dogs who took the award more than once: the English Miniature Poodle Ch. Tophill Orsino won in 1967 and 1968, the Boxer Ch. Scher-Khoun's Shadrack in 1969 and 1970, and the U.S.-born Great Pyrenees Ch. Rivergrove's If Looks Could Kill in 1990 and 1992. Boxers won Top Dog four times between them,

more often than any other breed: in addition to Schadrack, his son Ch. Mephisto's Soldier of Fortune won in 1976 and Ch. Haviland's Count Royal in 1979; all of them were successful sires. Three English Setters won Top Dog: Ch. Storybook's Marauder in 1981, Ch. Fantail's Sunshine Man in 1982, and Ch. Telcontar's Tahiti Sweetie in 1991. Standard Poodles did the same, more recently and in less than a decade: Ch. Dawin Hi Falutin 1995, Ch. Alias Just Give Me That Wink in 2002, and Ch. Dawin Stellar Performance in 2004. The three Bouviers des Flandres that won Top Dog were Ch. Glen Miller's Beau Geste and Ch. Glen Miller's Bandit for two consecutive years in the early 1980s, and Ch. Quiche's Zena Warrior Princess in 2003.

Canada does not produce just top dogs. Many of the most talented breeders, judges, and handlers in the United States were also born in Canada. Of the melting pot that the dog shows in the United States is made up, a very large percentage has its origins north of the border.

The Top Dog in Canada in both 1969 and 1970, the Boxer Ch. Scher-Khoun's Shadrack. Among his many victories was the American Boxer Club national specialty in 1972. He sired no fewer than 111 champions in the United States and Canada.

The Miniature Poodle Ch. Tophill Orsino, imported from the United Kingdom, was Top Dog in Canada in 1967 and 1968.

The Top Dog in Canada in 1991, English Setter Ch. Telcontar's Tahiti Sweetie, shown winning Canada's Show of Shows in 1991, handled by Doug Belter.

The Great Pyrenees Ch. Rivergrove's If Looks Could Kill was Canada's Top Dog of all breeds in both 1990 and 1992. "Looker" won more than 100 Bests in Show and is seen with handler Harold Butler and judge Anne Rogers Clark from the United States at the Arnprior Canine Association in 1990.

The Standard Poodle Ch. Dawin Stellar Performance was the Top Dog in Canada in 2004, handled by Allison Alexander-Foley.

Canada's Top Dog in 1982, the English Setter Ch. Fantail's Sunshine Man, with some of his ribbons.

The Bouvier des Flandres Ch. Quiche's Zena Warrior Princess was Top Dog in Canada in 2003.

Bouviers des Flandres repeatedly top major shows in Canada and have several times won Top Dog there. In 1983, the title holder was Ch. Glen Miller's Beau Geste.

A German Wirehaired Pointer, Ch. Ripsnorter's It's ShowTime, was Top Dog in Canada in 1996.

The English Cocker Spaniel Ch. Hobbithill Ashwood Hi Class was Top Dog in Canada in 1986.

Top Dog in Canada in 1998, the Wire Fox Terrier Ch. Britework's Bold Navigator, shown winning Best in Show at Credit Valley Kennel & Obedience Club under judge James Reynolds, handled by Doug Belter.

The Canadian Kennel Club recognizes a number of breeds not seen at AKC shows. This includes the Carelian Bear Dog, which has achieved great success in all-breed competition, primarily through Ch. Sune's Dansk Aesir, one of Canada's Top Ten dogs of all breeds in 1997 and the winner of twenty-three Bests in Show. He is shown winning Best in Show at Edmonton Kennel Club in 1997, handled by Stewart Gladstone under judge Donna Cole.

The Irish Setter Ch. Muldoon Dewitts Great One was the Top Dog in Canada in 2005, handled by William Alexander.

The number one dog in Canada for 2006 was a first for the breed: the Havanese Ch. Sonrisa's Tiny Thomas.

The Pointer Ch. Tahari's Serious Alibi, Top Dog in Canada in 1999, handled by John Griffith.

EUROPE

Dog shows have been held on the European continent for almost as long as they have existed in Great Britain. Yet it is difficult to provide an overview for the simple reason that so many dog people cross national bor-

ders as a matter of course on their way to the next show almost every weekend that it makes national boundaries largely unimportant—from a dog fancier's point of view, at least. It might be easier to consider the European continent as a single unit, but that would disregard the fact that each country has its own kennel club, its own traditions, and its own dog show culture. In the future, perhaps, there will be some annual award for the top show dogs in Europe, but for the time being, the overview picture is splintered and not easily summarized.

IRELAND

Some top Irish dog people—and dogs—have become fixtures on the international dog scene, and kennels of the native Irish breeds have provided foundation stock for other fanciers around the world. Ballykelly and Nutstown are names known to Irish Wolfhound fanciers everywhere; the latter is still active and has produced champions in England, America, and many other countries. One of the early names in Kerry Blue Terriers, Shillelagh, was started by Joe Delmar, whose son Séan has carried on the kennel and is currently president of the Irish Kennel Club.

Probably Ireland's best-known name on the world stage is Blackdale, the Wire Fox Terrier kennel owned by Harry O'Donoghue,

Ireland's Top Dog of 2005 and 2006, the Pomeranian Ch. Belliver Latest Creation, is shown winning Best in Show at the St. Patrick's show in Dublin. Runner-up to Best in Show was the Norfolk Terrier Ch. Nordach Magic Moment. The judge, Michael Drennan, stands between the two winners; at left is Irish Kennel Club president Sean Delmar and Olga Greer.

who has been producing champions world-wide for over forty years. O'Donoghue is also a popular international judge. The Tirkane family prefix in Boxers and Poodles is carried on in the second generation by Ann Ingram, who is also a much-respected international judge. The Barnesmore Whippet kennel in County Down is also a family operation and has produced champions in many parts of the world. One of the Irish kennels that has had the most success in England in recent years has been Belliver Pomeranians, owned by Séan Carroll and his nephew James: their Ch. Belliver Latest Creation won Best of Breed at Crufts as a puppy and was the Irish Kennel Club's Dog of the Year in both 2005 and 2006.

Exhibitors have always traveled freely across the border between the Republic of Ireland and Northern Ireland. Almost half the entries at many IKC shows come from the north, where many of the most ambitious breeders are located (including Tirkane and Barnesmore). Even during what is euphemistically termed "the troubles" in the late 1960s, dog people from the north supported the IKC shows, although traveling to the shows then was sometimes very dangerous. There is not, and never has been, a quarantine situation between Ireland and Great Britain, so exhibitors could travel freely between all parts of the British Isles.

GERMANY AND FRANCE

The two largest European dog-showing countries, Germany and France, usually play a smaller part on the international stage than do many countries with lower registration figures. As far as world-class exports go, Germany has a near monopoly on providing the rest of the world with top-quality German Shepherd Dogs, but in some of the other native breeds, the lead has been taken by other countries. In fact, besides German Shepherds, the most internationally respected breeder in Germany today is deeply involved in a British breed. Alex Möhrke's Bismarckquelle Fox Terriers were initially started by his father in the early 1950s, and he has been known for top-quality Wires around the world for decades. His international success is equaled by one other German-born breeder, Christina Bailey, who began showing her Zottel's Old English Sheepdogs in her native country but brought them to even greater renown after moving to England in the 1980s.

Of the German breeds, the Boxer was primarily created from pre–World War II stock descending from Friederun Stockmann's vom Dom Kennels, but in the second half of the twentieth century, the influence of direct German exports dwindled, with primarily American and British descendants of the original German imports dominating in most countries. Doberman Pinschers and Schnauzers everywhere go back to German foundation stock but often via circuitous routes across many countries. Giant Schnauzers, for example, have become a truly international melting pot, with influential breeding programs established in countries as far apart as Spain, Finland, Russia, and the United States. The smaller-size Schnauzers have been supported by two world-class kennels in Belgium, the late Countess Claudine de Pret's van de Stedeke and Cyriel de Meulenaer's van de Havenstad. The latter has even had success with American-bred Miniatures in the FCI countries, something that would not normally be easy.

The most spectacular Schnauzer success story in Europe, however, came from Italy, in the form of the sensational Standard Schnauzer Ch. Parsifal di Casa Netzer. In the mid-1990s, "Pa" won everything a dog could win in America, including Top Dog of all breeds in 1996; he capped his brilliant career by winning Westminster in 1997, a breed first.

Italy has, in fact, an impressive record for winning at the world's top shows. As early as 1975, an Italian-owned Wire Fox Terrier named Ch. Brookewire Brandy of Layven won Crufts. Brandy was owned by Beppe Benelli and Paolo Dondina, one of Italy's top international judges, but she was bred in England and shown by British handler Albert Langley. A decade later, two terriers that were born in Italy had great success in England: the Kerry Blue Ch. Balboa King Regal was Top Dog of all breeds in 1986 and the Airedale Ch. Ginger Xmas Carol won Crufts the same year after having been Top Dog in 1985. These were impres-

The Italian-born Standard Schnauzer Ch. Parsifal di Casa Netzer not only took home Top Dog all breeds in the United States in 1996 and the top spot at Westminster in 1997 but also won Best in Show during the FCI World Show circuit in Puerto Rico the same year. He was handled by Doug Holloway under judge Carla Molinari from Portugal. At right is club official Roberto Vélez Pico.

It's raining confetti over the Best in Show–winning Newfoundland from 10,000 dogs entered at the Europe Winner show in Helsinki in 2006, Ch. Skipper's King of Helluland, a bitch in spite of her name. She was handled by Gabor Maroti from Hungary and is pictured with Hans Lehtinen (left) and Kari Järvinen (right), two of Finland's top international judges.

sive victories for Italian breeders, although both dogs were of entirely British ancestry.

Almost no breed is more international than the Newfoundland. A large number of talented breeders in various countries seemingly work toward the same goal, and many of the best dogs have remarkably cosmopolitan pedigrees. Central Europe has several Newfoundland strongholds, which breeders around the world recognize and which were shown to shining example when Ch. Darbydale's All Rise PouchCove won Westminster in 2004. It was not widely noted at the time, but "Josh's" sire, Ch. Midnight Lady's Especially For You, was bred in Hungary and sired Josh during a visit to the PouchCove Kennels in America, which made him a top sire there. When it comes to homebred stock competing at the international level, no Newfoundland kennel can compete with Manlio Massa's Cayuga establishment in

Basset Hounds from Portugal have done well at the major shows in Europe. Ch. Come and Get Me Dos Sete Moinhos was Portugal's Top Dog of all breeds in both 2000 and 2001.

Italy, however. Starting with Danish stock in the late 1970s, Massa quickly established a breeding program that has produced scores of top winners in continental Europe, in the United States, and in England, including a Best of Breed winner at Crufts.

The Alaskan Malamute Ch. Giving-A-New-Royal-Star de Jungla Negra, pictured winning BIS at Luxemburg in 2006, was born in Spain but owned by and descended from the famous del Biago kennel in Italy. The dog also won the Working Group at Crufts 2007. The handler is Monika Kubiak.

SPAIN AND PORTUGAL

As mentioned earlier, the Giant Schnauzer has long been one of Spain's proudest international products. Sylvia Hammarström's celebrated Skansen kennel in California is only one of many around the world that credit the famous Spanish breeders, primarily de Pichera and Campos de Oro, with much of their success. However, by far the highest-profile and internationally most successful Spanish kennel since the 1970s has been the Del Zarzoso Standard Poodles. Originally started by Carlos Renau and Juan Cabrera and later carried on by Renau alone, the kennel was founded on the best Anglo-American lines and was soon able to produce dogs capable of harvesting laurels all across continental

International all-rounder judge Luis Pinto Teixeira from Portugal awards Group First at the FCI World Show in Poland 2006 to the top-winning Grand Basset Griffon Vendéen Ch. Bassbar Hermitage, bred by British breeder Bill O'Loughlin in Italy but owned in the Netherlands.

Europe, in England, and in both North and South America. One of the most famous dogs associated with this kennel, Ch. Maneetas Del Zarzoso Fuego Fatuo, was actually born in England and was Top Dog of all breeds in Finland as a youngster before going on to make his indelible mark in the United States both as a show dog and as a sire.

Portugal has produced a couple of the world's top all-rounder judges in Carla Molinari and Luis Pinto Teixeira. The only Portuguese show dogs that have really penetrated the world stage, however, are the Basset Hounds from the Dos Sete Moinhos kennel, which have made their presence felt not only at the World Shows but in England as well.

THE NETHERLANDS

The Netherlands, although one of the smallest countries in Europe, has a long tradition of breeding quality dogs. Among the oldest and best known abroad is the Doberman Pinscher kennel van Neerlands Stam, founded by Mrs. V. Knijff-Dermout in the 1940s. Dogs of her breeding have been exported virtually around the whole world, but the international win that meant the most must have been the Sieger title at the German Doberman Pinscher Club's centennial show in 1999, won by Ch. Graaf Zeppelin v. Neerlands Stam. Another Dutch kennel that became world famous early was Eta Pauptit's van de Oranje Manege Afghan Hound establishment. Its most famous export, Ch. Ophaal, came to California in 1956, promptly won Best in Show at Santa Barbara even before becoming an American champion, and went on to sire an array of top winners as the exclusive stud in Kay

The Saluki Ch. Abrisa vom Felsenkeller, one of the few dogs ever to win the FCI World Show twice: in the Netherlands in 1985 and in Austria in 1986. Abrisa was owned and shown by the Dutch Samoem kennels.

Finch's Crown Crest Kennels. (His twenty-seven AKC champion sons and daughters, many of them Best in Show winners, from a total of only seven litters must be a record of its kind.) Dutch Afghan Hounds had a strong following in the United States, England, Australia, and Scandinavia for many years. The Oranje Manege suffix can also be found far back in many of the world's Saluki and Shih Tzu pedigrees.

Another Dutch sighthound breeder of international importance is Tim Teillers, of the Samoem Salukis and Whippets. The former were founded on a combination of desert breeding and British lines, the latter mostly English with a dash of North American influence. The Samoem Salukis succeeded in winning Best in Show at the World Show three times, and a homebred Whippet, Ch. Samoems Silent Knight, was exported to Barbara Wilton-Clark's Shalfleet Kennels in England in 1979 and became the first imported Whippet ever to become a champion there.

SCANDINAVIA

Scandinavia forms a clearly defined geographic entity, with huge shows and a very well-organized, sophisticated dog fancy. The interest in dogs is, on a percentage basis, perhaps the strongest in the world—certainly comparable to that of the United Kingdom, probably greater than America's. The Swedish Kennel Club, for instance, in a country populated by barely 9 million people, has some 300,000 members, and is one of that country's largest nonprofit organizations. The figures in the other Scandinavian countries are comparable, if not greater: at present the largest Scandinavian dog shows are often held in Finland. Even Iceland, where for many years it was illegal to keep dogs as pets, now has a small but very active group of dog show fanciers.

Denmark, the smallest of the Scandinavian countries, has fewer shows and lower registration totals than the others but has provided world-class stock in many breeds. When the Shih Tzu became established as a breed in the United States in 1969, it was largely through descendants of Astrid Jeppesen's closely linebred Bjørneholm dogs. A similar development occurred in the 1980s, when the Petit Basset Griffon Vendéen began attracting notice as a serious dog show contender in many countries. Best in Show at the 1989 FCI World Show in Denmark was Ch. Chouan Gimlet, whose extroverted charm persuaded many new fanciers of the appeal this happy breed could have.

Following that achievement, dogs bred by the Chouan kennels of Gunnar Nymann and Holger Busk helped establish the breed in many other countries, especially the United States, where for a few years most of the top PBGVs seemed to have a Chouan

background. The kennel has also had success in other breeds, notably Siberian Huskies, where the American import Ch. Kontoki's Gibson Girl was Denmark's top dog for two years in the 1990s, and her son Ch. Chouan Breaking The Waves repeated that achievement in Sweden in 2000.

Another breed that made Denmark known in international circles in the 1980s was the Afghan Hound, with especially the Boxadan kennel of Lotte Jørgensen providing the background for many top winners across the Continent, in England, and in America. Their eyecatching Ch. Boxadan Hey Ma Look At Me was one of the top dogs in Europe for several years and even

The Petit Basset Griffon Vendéen Ch. Chouan Gimlet attracted great attention to his breed by winning Best in Show at the FCI World Show in Denmark in 1989. He is shown with his owner and breeder, Gunnar Nymann, whose breeding is behind many top winners, especially in America.

The Danish-born Afghan Hound Ch. Boxadan Hey Ma Look At Me was Top Dog of all breeds in her native country before having a short but successful career in the United States. She is shown in Denmark in 1987 with American breeder-judge Sandy Withington Frei of the Stormhill Afghans.

gained her American championship in short order (nine days from start to finish!) under the sponsorship of the Grandeur Kennels. One of Great Britain's top Afghan Hounds in recent years, Ch. Exxos Gameboy of Zharook, was born in Denmark and goes back to the same Swedish El Khyria lines as the Boxadan dogs.

Denmark has also produced world-class Beagles, Basset Hounds, and Newfoundlands, among other breeds. Appropriately, its best-known judge, Ole Staunskjaer, breeds Great Danes and is in demand at top shows around the world.

SWEDISH HEADLINERS

Long the dominant force in the Scandinavian dog fancy, Sweden has a larger population of both people and dogs than its neighboring countries do. Beginning early in the 1900s, many top Swedish kennels imported heavily from England, sometimes from Central Europe, but for the better part of the century, it was almost unheard of for aspiring fanciers to cast their eyes further.

One of the most glamorous and successful of all Swedish kennels for several decades was the Toyhome establishment, situated on its own small islet not far from

The Swedish Kennel Club's centennial show in 1989 was won by the Welsh Springer Spaniel Ch. Metzgard's Moonlight Valley, handled by Karin Brostam under judge Ulla Segerström. Also pictured are FCI President Hans Müller (in white jacket) and Swedish Kennel Club official Karl-Gustav Fredricson. Note the French Bulldog pattern on the judge's dress, indicating her own breed affiliation.

the city of Stockholm. Owner Aina Rossander was an imperious presence at the shows, usually making a grand entrance with a team of well-trained kennel girls in her wake, each carrying one of the Toyhome private wooden kennel boxes painted light yellow with the kennel name printed on top in purple script, each box inhabited by an exquisite jewel of a toy dog. In its early years, the kennel did not restrict itself to any particular toy breed; in the 1950s, however, it began focusing exclusively on Pekingese

and Pomeranians. Mrs. Rossander made a shopping trip to England each year to purchase the next year's show string and usually swept the shows with her glamorous imports. She was also a talented breeder and won Best in Show twice at the big annual Stockholm show with her homebred Pekingese Ch. Toyhomes Bi-No-Tu and Ch. Toyhomes Yat-Sen.

There were also Vivian Ahlberg's Miniature Poodles, who won the Stockholm show three times. Ch. Tarrywood Black Countess

(1954), Ch. Royalblue of Burdiesel (1961), and Ch. Furor of Montfleuri (1970) were all English imports, impossibly glamorous for their time, and superbly presented. Mrs. Ahlberg and her husband, Stig Ahlberg of the Ragtime Airedales, were greatly respected in the best British and American circles and served as an inspiration for many younger fanciers, including the author.

A major change occurred in the 1950s, when Curt and Ulla Magnusson returned to Sweden after living in South America for some years. Stopping over in the United States, they had fallen in love with Great Danes and brought back with them the brindle bitch Ch. Duyster's Joan of Arc and her sensational fawn daughter Ch. Duyster's Euclid of Ralwin. The Airways Great Dane kennels were soon established and did much to promote a more stylish, elegant type in the breed than had been seen before in Scandinavia.

The homebred champions were legion, not just in Sweden but also from farther away: Ch. Airways Wrangler of Impton won Group second at Crufts, and Mona Maytag in America, later mainly active in Whippets, started her career in dogs with an Airways champion. Ulla Magnusson on one memorable occasion in the 1970s handled a black Great Dane sired by one of her dogs, Ch. Duralex Bernando of Impton, to Best in Show at Three Counties championship show—probably the greatest Scandinavian success in England up to that time. The most successful of the later Airways imports from America were the fawn bitch Ch. Harmony Hill Linda of Airways, Top Dog of all breeds in 1969, and the brindle male Ch. Gerjo's Shilo of Airways, Best in Show at the 1980 Stockholm show under Anne Rogers Clark.

Two very different breeds that caught the eye of many international judges visiting Sweden were the Cairn Terrier and the Greyhound. In the former, which seldom wins much in all-breed competition in other countries, three different kennels—Sarimont, Hjohoo's, and Rottrivers—each produced a Best in Show winner at the big Stockholm show in the 1980s and 1990s. American breed specialist Lydia Coleman Hutchinson told the author that the best group of dogs she ever saw in her long international career as a judge was a class of Cairn Terriers at the Stockholm show in

The leading dog show exhibitor in Sweden from the 1950s and for many years later was Vivian Ahlberg, three times Best in Show at the Stockholm show with her imported Miniature Poodles. She is shown with her homebred Ch. Vivihills Soldier Boom in 1984.

One of the top Swedish kennels of the early to mid-1900s was Toyhome, twice Best in Show at the Stockholm show with homebred Pekingese. The owner, Aina Rossander, is shown left with a group of her dogs in the late 1940s; her son, Lennart Rossander (center) continued the kennel in later years.

2006! Swedish Greyhounds have a long international reputation. The Sobers kennel had bred a few successful Greyhound litters in the 1950s and 1960s but eventually focused almost exclusively on Italian Greyhounds. The old Sobers blood, based on a solid Treetops foundation, produced champions for world-class Greyhound establishments such as Rudel in America and Solstrand in England; it also helped jump-start kennels such as Gulds in Sweden and Jet's in Norway. When the original owner's granddaughter, Bitte Ahrens, took over Sobers in the 1980s, she picked up the old

family line by importing two bitches from Solstrand and breeding them to Gulds and Jet's dogs, with extremely successful results. Currently residing in Italy, Sobers has continued an old tradition by producing new champions in America but also won Best of Breed at Crufts for two years in a row in the early 2000s.

By the early 1980s, the very existence of a Top Dog award in Sweden—always an extremely egalitarian country—drew enough criticism that the award was discontinued for some time. Since being reintroduced, it has been won not only by glam-

THE GOLDEN DOG

In the mid-1960s, an official Top Dog of the Year award was initiated in Sweden: the Golden Dog trophy. The first winner, in 1965, was a white Toy Poodle import from England, Ch. Sudbrook Sunday Hymn. His owner, Kerstin Grauers, had established her Stortuvan kennels on a grand scale, purchasing a large number of top-quality Toy and Miniature Poodles from England and soon producing generations of homebred champions that were at least as good as their ancestors. Stortuvan, in fact, was one of the first Scandinavian kennels to export a number of their own breeding that became champions in both the United States and the United Kingdom.

Among the other early Top Dog winners was a German Shepherd bitch from the Triumph kennels of Bo Nyman, a legendary breeder who would produce two winners of this competition, and a third dog that won the big Stockholm show in 2005, a few months after Nyman's death. There were two Top Dog winners also from the world-class Racketeer Standard Poodles of Margareth Vear and a sensational Tibetan Terrier, Ch. Tintavon Desdemona, who moved from England to Sweden in the late 1970s with her owner and breeder, Paul Stanton. He has continued to breed top-quality Tibetan Terriers and Lhasa Apsos in his adopted country.

The Swedish-born Norwich Terrier Ch. Cobby's Timothy Gyp won Best of Breed at Crufts in 1992. He was shown in the Terrier Group by breeder Renée Sporre-Willes. Cobby's was earlier best known for Pugs, later for the Italian Lagotto Romagnolo; and Sporre-Willes became an international judge.

The Racketeer Standard Poodles, originally located in Norway and later in Sweden, have had great influence on breed development in both England and America. The breeder, Margareth Vear, is shown in the 1980s with Ch. Racketeer's White Angel, presented in acceptable Scandinavian show trim.

The Top Dog in both Sweden and Finland in 1979 was the Tibetan Terrier Ch. Tintavon Desdemona. She and her owner, Paul Stanton had moved from England to Sweden. Tintavon Lhasa Apsos were also successful, and Stanton is a much-traveled judge.

INTERNATIONAL JUDGES

Even in the 1960s, before international air travel had become commonplace, three female Swedish judges were officiating at top shows in England, America, and most other major dog countries. As a female counterpoint to the later "fabulous Finns," they opened doors in every direction, both showing the rest of the world that top judges could be found in what was then considered unlikely places and informing local dog fanciers about the world beyond the national borders. Ulla Segerström was the stern, eagle-eyed arbiter with a soft spot especially for toy dogs and French Bulldogs; Carin Lindhé was everyone's favorite grandmother, whose background lay primarily in terriers and sighthounds; while Marianne Fürst-Danielson's wide influence in many breeds is only equaled by the fact that she started what became "the world's most successful breeder ever" on the road to success: Sylvia Hammarström, of a thousand-and-one later Skansen Schnauzer champions in California, began as a teenage kennel girl working with Fürst-Danielson's Jidjis Greyhounds in Sweden.

Carin Lindhé was one of the first Scandinavian judges to officiate at top shows worldwide, including in England, Australia, and America. She is pictured with her homebred Irish Wolfhound Ch. Mountebanks Barrabas, a Best in Show winner in the 1970s.

orous imports but also, on at least a couple of occasions, by native breeds that are not usually associated with major success in all-breed competition. Ch. Härkilas Mach I, Sweden's Top Dog of all breeds for two years in the 1980s, is without much question the top-winning Drever in the history of the breed anywhere. The Drever is a Swedish scenthound, popular primarily with the hunting fraternity and rarely seen at dog shows outside Scandinavia. It most closely resembles a Beagle with some Foxhound

© Per Undén

A breed seldom seen outside Sweden, and even more rarely at the top in all-breed competition, is the Drever. An exception was the great Ch. Härkilas Mach I, Top Dog of all breeds in Sweden in both 1986 and 1988. His admirers included international judges: Mach is pictured winning Best in Show in Sätila under top British judge Robert M. James.

The Airescot kennel is one of the few to have won Top Dog of all breeds with two different breeds: Norwich Terrier and Scottish Deerhound. The Deerhound Ch. Airescot Lazuli was Sweden's Top Dog in 1977 and won Best in Show at Stockholm the same year. He is pictured relaxing at home with a young Norwich friend.

© Per Undén

The Swedish Lapphund is a native breed that, unlike the Drever, has a strong following among exhibitors in its own country. In 1994, Ch. Anthrazith's Droy was Top Dog of all breeds. He is shown winning under judge Marlo Hjernquist.

The Wire Fox Terrier Ch. Ash Grove Highwaystar, born in Italy, Top Dog in Sweden 2005 and in Denmark 2006, handled by owner Agneta Åström.

and Dachshund added to the mix. In 1994, the Top Dog winner was a Swedish Lapphund, Ch. Anthrazith's Droy, a Spitz-type breed that is quite popular in Sweden but has yet to catch on outside its native country. (The Finnish Lapphund, a separate but markedly similar breed, has gained a foothold in England.)

One of the most international kennels in Sweden for many years has been Cobby's,

Renée Sporre-Willes's prefix first for Pugs and then for Norwich Terriers. Sporre-Willes was one of the first Scandinavians to win Best of Breed at Crufts with a homebred champion, a Norwich, in the days when such achievements were still highly unusual. She later helped promote the Lagotto Romagnolo—a Poodle-like truffle-hunting dog from Italy—in Scandinavia with great success.

Equally international in scope is the Airescot kennel, owned by Nenne Runsten, who won Top Dog of all breeds in Norway with a Norwich Terrier and in Sweden with a Scottish Deerhound. Airescot's most lasting contribution, however, has been to import several top-class Whippets, mostly of American breeding, which in turn have produced high-class champions in many countries, including England. Both Sporre-Willes and Runsten are widely traveled international judges.

There are no professional handlers in Scandinavia, but there are many talented amateur handlers. One of the most successful, Agneta Åström, first made a name for herself as a relative newcomer in the late 1980s by winning Top Dog of all breeds in Sweden with her Wire Fox Terrier Ch. Louline Promotion. This breed is not commonly exhibited with any degree of success by novices, but Åström repeated the win a few years later with a dog she had bred herself, Ch. Crispy High 'N Low, and once again in 2005 with the Italian-born Ch. Ash Grove Highwaystar.

The Scottie is probably the terrier breed that has made the most prominent headlines internationally. Ch. Raglan Rose Maiden at Brio was born in Sweden but exported to England and owner-handled by Jane Miller throughout a brilliant career, which came to a climax with Reserve Best in Show at Crufts in 2004. By any standard, this must be classified as one of Scandinavian dogdom's greatest international triumphs. Rose Maiden's breeder, Dan Ericsson, showed her to the top spot at Windsor and has turned out generations of top-winning Scotties since the 1970s. In 2001, Sweden's Top Dog award for all breeds went to Rose Maiden's sire Ch. Raglan Rory. Ericsson is also an internationally recognized judge.

One other exhibitor who has won the Top Dog award three times is Ingela Wallström Dahlander with her Old English Sheepdogs: first with the American import Ch. Bahlamb's Barnyard Baron in 1996, then with his daughter Ch. Drover's Roll Those Dice in 1999, and then again with Ch. Bahlamb's Benevolent Brethren in

Old English Sheepdogs won Sweden's Top Dog award of all breeds three times in the late 1990s and early 2000s. All three were shown by Ingela Wallström Dahlander. She is seen with the 1999 winner, Ch. Drover's Roll Those Dice, and judge Kenneth Edh.

2002. This represented a full circle of sorts for the Bahlamb Old English Sheepdog kennels, which had been started by Caj Haakansson in Sweden in the 1960s, later became extremely successful in the United States, and remain influential since his death in 1996.

One breed of Swedish dogs to hit early headlines was the Papillon, with exports from different kennels doing well as far apart as England, America, and Asia. On the home front, however, the Flat-Coated Retriever engendered the most favorable comments from international judges. About a thousand are registered each year, and entries can be in the hundreds at the big shows. The most influential kennel is Almanza, started by Ragnhild Ulin in the late 1970s. A study of the catalog from the 2005 Stockholm show indicates that in an entry of more than 200 Flat-Coats, almost half were bred by Almanza or sired by an Almanza dog. The first great winner in the 1980s and early 1990s was Ch. Almanza Larry O'Grady, five times Best in Show at the large annual Swedish show for spaniels and retrievers, the last time at ten years of age. Since then, the breeding program has expanded, the winners have proliferated, and the rest of the world has taken notice.

Few breeds in Sweden have attracted more international attention than the Flat-Coated Retriever. Most of the top winners carry the Almanza prefix; the kennel's first big star was Ch. Almanza Larry O'Grady, shown with breeder and owner Ragnhild Ulin in 1990. He won Best in Show at the Stockholm show the following year.

With numerous champions in many countries, including the United States, Australia, and England, Almanza has become a kennel of truly global importance. It is worth noting that a number of the top show dogs have also gained titles in the field, as tracking dogs, or in obedience. Among the best-known homebred show winners are Ch. Almanza Emergency Brake, Top Dog of all breeds in Sweden in 1995, and Ch. Almanza I Hate Mondays, a good winner in England and handled by his breeder to Runner-up in the Gundog Group at Crufts 2006. Swedish-born Flat-Coats, in fact, have an amazing record at this show: I Hate Mondays' sire, Ch. Almanza Far & Flyg, won the Group at Crufts in 2007, and his sire, Ch. Inkwells Named Shadow, did the same in 2003!

The Almanza-bred teams have had spectacular success in the breeders' competitions that are such an important feature at Swedish shows. They are based not on an individual dog's wins but on the overall quality and impression of a team: four dogs from the same breeder compete against teams from other kennels and of other breeds. At the major shows, with the best team of each breed entering the ring in file for the final competition, the Best Breeder competitions are often quite spectacular. A couple of hundred dogs may be in the ring at one time, and the top teams, moving in unison, exhibit a degree of style that is further enhanced by well-practiced presentation, with handlers often dressed in matching outfits.

The main threat to Almanza's position as the top Swedish kennel in recent years has come from the Diplomatic's Great Danes, presenting a long line of uncropped and mostly fawn champions, and from

Scandinavian Salukis have been much admired internationally. Ch. Qirmizi Cartago was one of the all-breed top winners and won Best in Show at the Stockholm show in 2003. He is shown with his breeder, Nicklas Eriksson.

another breed whose quality is internationally recognized, the Saluki. The Badavie teams of homebred Saluki champions, usually all black and tans, have successfully challenged the Almanza retrievers in the Best Breeder competitions on many occasions. However, they are not the only ones making international Saluki headlines. Individual dogs from the Qirmizi establishment have won even more in Group and Best in Show competitions, and an export from a third breeder, Baklava, gained high American honors: Ch. Baklava's Rafi Rasi of Khiva was a multiple Best in Show winner in the early 2000s.

One of the top Scandinavian breeders, Geir Pedersen, started his Louline Wire Fox Terriers in Norway but later moved to England and America, where his dogs have experienced great success. He is shown with his homebred Ch. Louline High 'n Mighty in Sweden in 1982.

The Music Kerry Blue Terriers originated in Norway but moved to Canada in the 1970s. Ch. Music's Right On moved back to Norway and was Top Dog both there and in Finland in 1978. He was owner-handled by Jul Hamlot.

NOTABLE NORWEGIANS

Norway, in spite of having a smaller population than Sweden does, has made big news on the world's dog scene for many years. The first to do so was, appropriately, a Norwegian Elkhound, Ch. Tortåsens Bjønn II, who won the Hound Group at Westminster in 1959 and was important in establishing one of America's top breeding establishments, the Vin-Melca's kennels of Patricia Trotter. In later years, only a few Norwegian Elkhound exports have made major contributions to their breed overseas, but Norwegian specialist judges continue to officiate at major specialties abroad. The Norwegian Elkhound Association of America, which holds a national specialty only every other

year, has employed almost all the top specialist judges from Norway for this event.

In the 1960s and 1970s, a Kerry Blue Terrier breeder from Norway, Knut Egeberg, won top honors at Scandinavian shows before immigrating with his Music's dogs to Canada, where he continued doing well. The terrier tradition was sustained by another Norwegian, Geir Pedersen, who first came to prominence in the mid-1970s with the Welsh Terrier Ch. Deveraux Janore. Pedersen's main breed was destined to be the Wire Fox Terrier, however, and after spectacular success with the Irish import Ch. Blackdale Starbright, a long line of immaculately presented homebreds carrying the Louline prefix took over. They garnered a stream of top

This Standard Poodle from Norway, Ch. Topscore Contradiction, is the first—and so far only—dog to win Best in Show at both the FCI World Show and Crufts. The former win came in Amsterdam in 2002; the latter came earlier that year and also made "King" the first foreign dog to travel to Crufts and win Best in Show. King is shown with his handler, Mikael Nilsson, and breeder Astrid Giercksky.

wins, first in Scandinavia, then later in the breed's native country and in America. In the United States alone, the Louline dogs won more than 200 Terrier Groups and more than fifty all-breed Bests in Show in the 1990s. Following their marriage, Geir and his wife, Gerd Flyckt of Sweden, along with their dogs, moved first to England and then, in 2006, to the United States. Between them, their Louline and Hubbestad kennels have shown champions in more breeds than most, from Norfolk and Lakeland Terriers to English Cocker Spaniels, Whippets, and Greyhounds.

The biggest international success from Norway was yet to come, however. Scandinavian Poodles have done well in many parts of the world, often as a result of breeding programs that incorporate dogs from many different countries. Norway's top Poodle breeder for many years was Astrid Giercksky, best known for her Topscore black Miniatures. She bred an occasional Standard Poodle litter as well, and in late 1998, she had a promising homebred white puppy that was sold to novice owners. Ch. Topscore Contradiction matured into an exuberant, charismatic show dog and became one of the most admired international winners ever from this part of the world. As a youngster in 2001, "King" started out as one of Norway's Top Dogs of all breeds, but it was in 2002 that the rest of the dog world took notice. Accompanied by his handler, Mikael Nilsson, and his owners, Kari and Stein Glenna, King went on to win Sweden's big Stockholm show and Italy's glamorous and very international Golden Collar competition.

King and his entourage, the Glennas, now dedicated dog show fans, then traveled to Crufts in 2002 and created a sensation by going all the way to Best in Show over 22,000 dogs. It was the first time that a genuinely foreign dog and handler had won the top spot at this show. The impact on the British and the rest of the world's dog fanciers was resounding. It was not exactly that the fortress had crumbled, but King made it clear that a good dog, regardless of background, *could* win even such a prestigious show as Crufts. It did not hurt that the judges who helped launch King on this singular success were among Britain's most respected arbiters: Norman Butcher of the old-established Tuttlebees Poodles awarded King the breed win, Terry Thorn judged the Group, and Pamela Cross-Stern was the Best in Show judge.

Later the same year, King traveled to the FCI World Show in Amsterdam and won Best in Show there, in an entry of nearly 15,000 dogs. After all the wins in Europe, only one conquest remained for King: Westminster. Because America's top show is open only to AKC champions of record, King flew across the Atlantic in June and qualified for participation in great style. At his first American show, the huge Poodle Club of America event in Maryland, King won Best of Winners; then he proceeded to win Best in Show on each of the three following days, adding an American champion title to his others in record time. This spectacular debut indicated that King might have what it took to do as well in the United States as he had already done in Europe. The Westminster entry form was duly submitted but turned out to be one of the many that were not accepted. Westminster is one of the few dog shows in the world that must limit the number of dogs shown: only the

The FCI sets the rules for international shows in most countries outside the English-speaking world. Among the most important FCI events is the European Winner Show, held each year in a different country. In 2005, it was hosted by Austria and won by the young Pharaoh Hound Ch. Enigma Surprise Me from Sweden.

first 2,500 opened entries are accepted. Whether King would, in fact, have done well at Madison Square Garden will be a question that remains unanswered, but a number of his champion children in America and Europe have continued his stellar legacy.

INTER-SCANDINAVIAN COOPERATION

King has always been shown by Mikael Nilsson, who is not only an experienced and talented groomer but also a skillful handler and able to deal with his charge's exuberant antics in the ring. Nilsson started breeding

The FCI classifies four size varieties of Poodles: the Dwarf is bigger than a Toy but smaller than a Miniature. Ch. Kudos The Knockout, one of the all-time top winners of this variety, was Top Dog of all breeds in Sweden in 2003, the next year in Norway. He is pictured with his breeder and owner-handler, Mikael Nilsson.

Poodles in partnership with his mother in Sweden in the 1980s and showed the home-bred black Dwarf Poodle Ch. Kudos The Knockout to Top Dog of all breeds twice, first in Sweden in 2003 and then in Norway the following year. ("Tyson" would be considered a small Miniature in the United States. The dog fancy in English-speaking countries recognize only Standard, Miniature, and Toy Poodles, but the FCI has four different Poodle sizes—Standard, Miniature, Dwarf, and Toy. This leads to the odd situation in which a dog may be classified as being of one variety in one country and another in the next country.)

When King was defeated as Norway's Top Dog in 2001, the winner was a brindle Greyhound bitch, Ch. Jet's Once Upon A Dream. The Jet's involvement in Greyhounds had been established by Kari Engh in the 1950s and has continued successfully, with an increasing emphasis on international connections, in the hands of her son Espen. The first Top Dog award was followed by another in 2003: the red Ch. Jet's Something In The Way U Smile. Both these top show Greyhounds are lure-coursing champions, among the few of their breed anywhere with both field and conformation titles. Jet's champions have won in most countries where Greyhounds are known, and Engh regularly judges top sighthound shows around the world, including several national specialties in the United States.

Equally international in scope are the Hotpoint Pekingese and Great Danes, owned by Borghild Moen and twice winner of the Top Dog spot with imported Pekingese, and the Bernegården St. Bernards. The latter kennel was started by Britt Marit Halvorsen in Norway in the 1970s, based on a combination of European and American dogs. In 1993, Ch. Bernegården's Valentin was Top Dog in Norway, and other Bernegården dogs have done well in many other countries, including England, where Ch. Bernegården's Hold Your Horses at Snowfordhill is a top sire. Halvorsen has experienced great success in Scandinavia, Belgium, and the rest of the European continent, most recently with her Swedish-born Ch. Courmayeur's Nobody Like Me (sired by Ch. Bernegården's Ragtime), Top Dog of all breeds in Norway in 2005.

As in Sweden, the Top Dog title has on occasion been won by breeds not normally associated with Best in Show competition. One of the first Top Dog awards in Norway, in 1972, went to a Norwegian Buhund, simply named Ch. Caro, and in 1987, the country's top-winning show dog was a Greenland Dog, Ch. Togo av Angiaq. Both breeds belong to the Spitz Group, and although the Buhund has become established on the British show scene, neither of these two breeds is commonly seen at dog shows in most countries.

THE FINNISH MIRACLE

Finland lagged behind the other Scandinavian countries in dog show enthusiasm for many years, but in the 1970s and 1980s, a revolution of sorts took place that catapulted this country to the forefront of the world's dog shows. That this relatively small nation, with a population of just more than 5 million inhabitants and situated far off the dog world's jet-setting tracks, can organize dog shows that are among the biggest in the world is something of a miracle. The reason for this development is difficult to establish. Certainly the emergence of several internationally recognized judges has had significant influence. First Hans Lehtinen and then Rainer Vuorinen became

The Greyhound Ch. Jet's Once Upon A Dream, one of the top-winning dogs ever in Scandinavia, with nine Bests in Show at FCI international shows. In 2001, "Vera" topped the big year-end shows in Stockholm, Helsinki, and Oslo and was Top Dog of all breeds in Norway.

The Silky Terrier Ch. Curiosity Luxury of Silk demonstrates that undocked breeds can win big: in 2002, he was Top Dog of all breeds in Finland. He was shown successfully outside of Scandinavia as well, winning a Group placement at Crufts in 2004.

Poodles from the Spanish kennel Del Zarzoso have been winning in many countries around the world. Ch. Maneetas Del Zarzoso Fuego Fatuo was actually born in England and was Top Dog in Finland in 1991 before becoming a top winner and sire in America. "Gordon" is shown winning Best in Show in Finland, handled by Juha Palosaari under judge Ritva Raita.

Top Dog of all breeds in Finland in 1983 was the American-born Standard Schnauzer Skansen's Faenrik.

The Standard Poodle Ch. Canmoy's Rubiazo, a double grandson of Fuego Fatuo, took the Top Dog award himself five years later. He also followed his famous ancestor to America and became a big winner there as well. Rubiazo is shown winning Best in Show in Finland under Italian judge Marisa Brivio Cellini, handled by breeder Tiina Taulos. At right is Argentinian judge Enrique Filippini.

established, beginning in the 1970s, in the front rank of the world's all-rounder judges, equally popular in the United States, Great Britain, Australia, Asia, and Europe. With the emergence of a third name, Kari Järvinen, the trio of internationally recognized fabulous Finns was complete.

When the FCI World Show was held in Finland for the first time ever in 1998, the rest of the dog world realized what Scandinavians already knew: Finland had become a world-class dog country. That year's event was one of the biggest World Shows ever. More than 15,000 dogs were entered and the finale was spectacular, with judge Kari Järvinen awarding the top spot to a Papillon

from America, Ch. Loteki Supernatural Being, who would also go on to win Westminster a few months later.

Although Finland's greatest claim to international fame remains its judges, it is also the birthplace of many high-class show dogs. The two kennels that have had the most international success are the Canmoy Poodles and the Finnsky Skye Terriers. Tiina Taulos' successful Canmoy Poodles first stepped into the limelight in 1991, when the imported white Standard Ch. Maneetas Del Zarzoso Fuego Fatuo rocketed to Top Dog of all breeds in Finland; five years later, his homebred double grandson Ch. Canmoy's Rubiazo did the same. Both dogs went on to

Finnish Salukis have a high reputation worldwide. In 1987, Ch. El Hamrah Giah was Top Dog of all breeds, owner-handled by Chrisse Schrey-Grandell.

The Giant Schnauzer Ch. Stablemaster's Northern Hope, Top Dog of all breeds in Finland for three consecutive year, 2003–2005, handled by breeder Frances Fabergé.

become top winners in the United States, and both were shown in Finland by Tiina's talented ex-husband handler, Juha Palosaari, who is also a successful breeder with two Top Dog wins credited to Wire Fox Terriers carrying his Starring prefix.

Skye Terriers have been a Finnish specialty for many years, and breeders continue to succeed in maintaining the highest international quality in spite of low numbers. Only a handful of litters are registered annually. The Skyeline kennel of Hjördis Westerholm was founded in the 1960s, producing a number of dogs that won well in many foreign countries, including a Best of Breed win at Crufts during the 1980s. The Finnsky kennel of Thea and Rolf Dahlbom, started a decade later partly on Skyeline blood, has done even better on the interna-

Top Dog of all breeds in Singapore in 2002, the Australian-born Whippet Ch. Taejaan Ms Martini, pictured with owner-handler Dr. Arnold Tan winning Best in Show under judge William Stevenson from Australia.

Australia's leading Best in Show winner in 2005 and 2006, the Siberian Husky Ch. PVT STK's Fire In The Sky, imported from the United States. He is pictured handled by Simon Briggs, winning Best in Show at Sydney Royal show in 2006 under Japanese judge K. Wada.

tional stage. This is particularly true in the United States, where several homebred Finnskys have won Best of Breed at Westminster, including a Group first there for Ch. Finnsky Oliver in 1996.

The most successful breed at the shows in Finland in the late 1900s and early 2000s, however, is the Giant Schnauzer. Between them, four different Giants have won the Top Dog award six times in Finland in less than two decades. Two of the dogs were bred by the Pectus kennel, two by Stablemaster's—both names that crop up in international Schnauzer pedigrees with some frequency. Ch. Stablemaster's Northern Hope must be considered the top-winning dog in Finland ever, since he took home the Top Dog award for three years in a row, 2003–2005.

ON TOP DOWN UNDER

Australia and New Zealand have an unbroken history of dog shows since the 1800s. The long distances to most other dog-breeding countries and strict quarantine regulations kept these countries relatively isolated from the rest of the world even late in the twentieth century. The business of importing dogs and putting them through the required quarantine was very expensive, complicated, and drawn out. A six-month stay in quarantine was compulsory; furthermore, because all imported dogs had to have been born in England or have spent a minimum of six months in residence there, for many decades it was almost impossible to bring in dogs from any other country.

THE ROYAL SHOWS

The British influence is reflected in the honor rolls of early winners at the prominent Royal

Australia's leading exhibitor for many years, David Roche of the Fermoy kennels in Adelaide, was the first foreign judge to officiate for Best in Show at Crufts. He also judged at Morris & Essex in the United States and at shows in many other countries. One of his first great winners was the Afghan Hound Ch. Mazari of Carloway, imported from England but of half-American parentage. Mazari won Best in Show at three of the big Royal shows in Australia—Adelaide, Sydney, and Melbourne—in 1965, and then won again at the Melbourne Royal show in 1968.

The white Standard Poodle Grand Ch. Picardy Step Aside Boys was bred from an American bitch imported in whelp to the all-time top Poodle, Ch. Lake Cove That's My Boy. "Marco" won numerous Best in Shows, including the first Poodle National show in Australia. He is pictured with judge Liz Cartledge from England and his owner-handler, Lorraine Boyd.

The Kerry Blue Terrier Ch. Blue Fire's Double Trouble of Fermoy was titled in England, America, and Canada before coming to Australia, where he was a Royal Show Best in Show winner. He was also an influential sire.

The Old English Sheepdog Ch. Hartwyn Royal Pageant, CDX, Best in Show at Melbourne Royal Show in 1990.

shows in Australia, so-called not because of direct royal patronage but simply because the dog shows were a part of the Royal Agricultural Society's big annual events in each state. The Royal shows, particularly those in New South Wales and Victoria, are huge week-long events that feature every aspect of the traditional Australian country lifestyle: the dog sections alone usually incorporate several thousand entries.

In spite of the difficulty in importing dogs, many of the early Australian winners came from the best-known English kennels. The of Ware Cocker Spaniels were particularly successful, with no fewer than four different Royal Best in Show winners in the first few decades of the twentieth century. An English-born Afghan Hound, Ch. Mazari of Carloway, set a record by winning both the Melbourne and Sydney Royals in the 1960s—and he won Melbourne twice, something no other dog has done. Mazari's owner, David Roche of the Fermoy kennels in Adelaide, is one of the dog world's most cosmopolitan figures, successful with a long line of Kerry Blue Terriers, Afghan Hounds,

English Foxhounds have experienced more success in Australia than in most other countries. Ch. Peelhunt Ruler won Best in Show at Sydney Royal show in 2002; he is pictured with Swedish judge Moa Persson.

Best in Show at Melbourne Royal show in 2001 was judged by Hiroshi Kamisato from Japan. He is pictured with his four finalists. The winner was the Irish Setter Ch. Tullane Fiery Thyme; the runner-up was the Australian Terrier Ch. Rebelglen Catmandoo; third, the Whippet Ch. Bonnymead Red Pepper; and fourth, the Chinese Crested Ch. Pearlylane Little Flirt.

and other breeds in Australia for several decades and also a judge of international repute. He had the unique distinction of judging one of the last Morris & Essex shows in America as a young man, and in 1969 was the first foreigner to be invited to judge Best in Show at Crufts. The only other non-British judge to receive this singular honor was another Australian, Dr. Harry L. Spira, in 1985.

International Afghans

Mazari's wins were a foretaste of things to come. In the 1960s and 1970s, as air travel made it easier to bring international judges to the top shows, word began to get out about impressive entries—sometimes several hundred strong—of top-quality Afghan Hounds at shows in Australia. Other kennels gave Fermoy a run for its money: names such as Furbari, Alaqadar, Quom, and Calahorra became known around the world, and all of them produced Best in Show winners at the Royal shows in Melbourne or Sydney. Calahorra alone, a large establishment that incorporated bloodlines from many different kennels around the world, succeeded in producing three different dogs that won Sydney Royal show Best. Registrations and entry figures declined in the 1980s, but Australian Afghan Hounds have retained a solid international reputation and

Australian Afghan Hounds became world famous in the late 1970s. One of the most glamorous was Ch. Calahorra Turban, Best in Show at Sydney Royal show in 1975. Turban was the first of three Afghans from the same kennel to take the top spot at this show.

The Australian-born Afghan Hound Ch. Gengala Been There was Sweden's Top Dog in 1997. He is pictured with his owner and handler, Elisabet Levén.

One of the most legendary dogs ever to come from Australia, the Smooth Fox Terrier Ch. Ttarb The Brat, was among the top show dogs in America for two years in the early 1980s and sired more than 100 champions. He is pictured winning Best in Show at Santa Barbara Kennel Club in 1983, on this occasion handled by Peter Green under judge Derek Rayne. The trophy presenters (left to right) are Frank Sabella, Abbe Shaw, Tanis Hammond, and Tom Bradley.

have infiltrated the pedigrees of top winners all over the world. Names such as Khandhu, Karakush, and Gengala are well known wherever Afghan Hounds are shown.

Spectacular Smooths

Another breed from down under that caused big headlines, especially in the United States, was the Smooth Fox Terrier. Several different Smooths won Best in Show at the Royal shows. One of the most admired was Ch. Farleton Don Pedro, carrying a kennel name that was known in England in the same breed but under different ownership. He was much admired by both Australian specialists and foreign judges

and won the top spot at Melbourne Royal in 1975 under Winifred Heckman, one of America's top judges. Don Pedro stayed in Australia, but another Farleton offspring, Ch. Ttarb The Brat (sired by Ch. Farleton Captain Sandy), arrived in the United States in the late 1970s. He was an immediate sensation and, under the care of the talented terrier specialist handler Ric Chashoudian, succeeded in winning more than any other Australian-born dog in the United States before or since. The Brat ended his career with sixty Bests in Show to his credit—including two years in a row at the Santa Barbara Kennel Club. That was more than even the great Ch. Nornay Saddler had done several decades before him. As a stud dog, The Brat did even better: few American-bred Smooth Fox Terriers in the early 2000s do not include his name in the backgrounds of their pedigrees.

Basenjis of Note

Basenjis have long been one of the breeds for which Australia is most noted. In the 1970s, after British judges of such stature as Catherine Sutton and Robert James had remarked on the high quality of the Basenjis down under, the legendary breeder Veronica Tudor-Williams made a visit and pronounced them "unquestionably the best in the world." In the early 1980s, she imported a dog that went back, many times over but through several generations of Australian breeding, to the hugely influential bitch puppy Miss Tudor-Williams had imported from Africa in 1959, Fula of the Congo. The Australian dog Ch. Afrika Royal Challenge

In the early 1980s, the Australia-born Basenji Ch. Afrika Royal Challenge of the Congo was exported to England, where he quickly became a champion and had great influence as a sire.

of the Congo ("Aussie") quickly became an English champion after his arrival in Britain and, more important, proved to be extremely successful as a stud dog. His descendants in more recent years have done well, too: the only Basenji to win Best in Show at Crufts, Ch. Jethard Cidevant in 2001, has six lines in his pedigree going back to Aussie.

AMERICAN ONSLAUGHT

By the 1980s, dogs brought in from other countries had gradually begun making inroads among all the British exports. As the quarantine regulations eased at the end of the century, a flood of American imports of different breeds were brought in, and the competition between sometimes widely divergent British and American types in some breeds came into stark contrast. The first American-born dog to win one of the biggest Royal shows was a Wire Fox Terrier at Melbourne in 1986, Ch. Santeric Res Ipsa Loquitur, brought over from the United States by Lee Pieterse after she had spent time in America and worked as an apprentice for Ric Chashoudian. Frank and Lee Pieterse's Statuesque kennel has won more Royal shows than most with several different breeds. Their most successful show dog may have been the Australian Terrier Ch. Tahee Dirty Harry, who won multiple Royal Bests in Show. The Tahee-bred dogs have proven to be among the most influential Australian imports of any breed in the United Kingdom in recent years. The Pieterses' most important contribution to dogs overseas has been the Whippet Ch. Statuesque Extortion, who has sired champions in more countries than most stud dogs—from England to the United States,

The Australian-born Airedale Terrier Ch. Oldiron Margaret River was one of the Top Dogs of all breeds in the United States in 2005, winning twenty-five Bests in Show that year alone. She was one of the last dogs shown by Peter Green before his retirement from professional handling; they are pictured winning the Great Lakes Terrier Association under judge Dr. Samuel Draper.

from Scandinavia to Asia, and from Eastern Europe to New Zealand.

Statuesque imported dogs from both England and America: Extortion, although born in Australia, was of all American breeding. A harmonious blend of British and American breeding has become the hallmark of many of Australia's top kennels. None is more typical of that development than the Troymere Poodle kennels of Troy Tanner and Lex Henery, whose Miniatures and Toys are based on imports from both

countries and whose homebreds have had great influence on breeding in other countries. Their most spectacular wins, however, have come with black Standards. Ch. Troymere Believe Inme, a combination of British, American, Canadian, and Australian breeding, won Melbourne Royal in 1993. Some years later came Ch. Troymere Diva D'Amour, the result of breeding an American sire to a bitch of mostly Australian ancestry, who became one of the few dogs ever to win both the Sydney and Melbourne

The Wire Fox Terrier Ch. Santeric Res Ipsa Loquitur was bred by Ric Chashoudian in the United States and brought to Australia by Lee Pieterse. Lee handled "Ricky" to Best in Show at the Melbourne and Brisbane Royal shows in 1986 and 1988, respectively. Left is owner Frank Pieterse.

Royals, and the only one since Mazari of Carloway to do so in the same year, 2000. That the Sydney Royal win came under the great American judge and Poodle specialist Anne Rogers Clark no doubt made the win even more memorable.

LABRADOR RETRIEVER RECOGNITION

Nowhere else are Labrador Retrievers as successful in competition with other breeds as in Australia. This is almost entirely the result of a single kennel, Driftways, owned by Guy Spagnolo, whose dogs descend from the best British blood, often through several generations of homebred stock. Although Labradors seldom win in all-breed competition elsewhere, international judges of almost every background have

The Australian Terrier Ch. Tahee Dirty Harry won Best in Show at Brisbane Royal show in both 1987 and 1989. He also won the Sydney Royal show in 1990, owner-handled by Lee Pieterse.

Nowhere do Labrador Retrievers win more than they do in Australia. Grand Ch. Driftway Serenade is pictured with breeder and handler Guy Spagnolo and judge Richard G. Beauchamp from the United States.

The biggest winning export from Australia to England, the Vizsla Sh. Ch. Hungargunn Bear Itn Mind, was Top Dog of all breeds in the United Kingdom in 2006. He is pictured, with handler John Thirlwell and judge Geoff Corish, winning Best in Show at the Scottish Kennel Club. Also pictured are show officials Myra Orr, Anne Macdonald, and Aitken Johnston.

been sufficiently impressed to put Labradors up at major all-breed events in Australia. One of the greatest names is Gr. Ch. Driftway Regal Oak, sired through artificial insemination by Sh. Ch. Rocheby Royal Oak from England but homebred for several generations on his dam's side. His daughter Gr. Ch. Driftway Serenade, grandson Gr. Ch. Driftway Flash Dancer, and many others have followed in his footsteps.

Australia's most successful export to Great Britain is of yet another gundog breed. The Vizsla Sh. Ch. Hungargunn Bear Itn Mind, bred by Andrew and Naomi Cragg in New South Wales, came from a successful career in his native country and took Great Britain by storm soon after his debut there in 2005; he was far and away Top Dog of all breeds in the United Kingdom in 2006. He is Australian-bred for several generations but also has some lines going back to central European and North American imports.

LEADING HERDING DOGS

Australia's leading kennel for exports, regardless of destination or category, is the Cordmaker Puli establishment. Bred by Sue

A long line of winning Pulik from the Cordmaker kennels in Australia is illustrated by the multititled Ch. Cordmaker Mississippi Mud, one of the top Herding dogs in America in both 2000 and 2001. He is pictured winning Best in Show at the Hoosier Kennel Club in 2001, handled by Linda Pitts under judge Dorothy Hutchinson.

Huebner, the Cordmaker dogs travel the world and take home more international titles than any others. With a strong influence from American dogs, particularly from Bokar, the top Cordmaker champions have titles in a dizzying array of countries. One of the best-known dogs, Ch. Cordmaker One Spy Too Many, started out by getting a Grand Champion title and a fistful of all-breed wins in his native Australia, then left for the United Kingdom, where he won another title as well as a Best in Show in Ireland. He then went to the United States, won several all-breed Bests there, and for good measure added a World Winner and

champion title in Argentina. Along the way, he also managed to get a New Zealand championship. Only slightly less titled is Ch. Cordmaker Mississippi Mud (with championships in Australia, the United States, and Canada), who can lay claim to the position of world's top-winning Puli with more than fifty Bests in Show to his credit, most in the United States.

For obvious reasons, with a long tradition of livestock production, Australia has a large number of quality dogs in the herding breeds. Many of these have been appreciated by breed fanciers worldwide. Pembroke Welsh Corgis from both Australia

One of the top Herding dogs in America for three years in a row—2003, 2004, and 2005—the Australian-born Border Collie Ch. Borderfame Spellbound. He won the Group at Westminster in 2005.

and New Zealand have been very influential in the United States and Europe. Border Collies have done even better, with dozens of champions from top Australian kennels—Borderfame, Nahrof, Korella—in most of the major countries. Borderfame, a particularly successful breeding establishment, was started in the early 1980s by Helen Fitzgerald in Perth in Western Australia, an area that is isolated from main dog activities even by Australian standards. Among the many AKC champions bred at this kennel, the best known is Ch. Borderfame Spellbound, a Group winner at Westminster in 2005. In England, Ch. Borderfame Heart N'Soul won Best of Breed at Crufts in 2002 and is titled in the United States and Europe.

The Pride of New Zealand

Border Collies are as much a New Zealand specialty as an Australian one. In fact, New Zealand's best-known kennel on the world stage may be the Clan-Abby Border Collie establishment, started by Judy Vos and based on early Australian imports in the 1970s. The breeding program has been so successful that fanciers in other countries, from Africa to Scandinavia, soon took notice. Clan-Abby dogs are behind many of the current Australian kennels, and the first AKC Border Collie champion came from Clan-Abby; but it is Great Britain that particularly benefited from the New Zealand exports. Several homebred dogs have been sent back to the breed's home country and become champions there, with Ch. Clan-Abby Blue Aberdoone winning Best of Breed at Crufts in 1991. He also became an influential sire, with one of his offspring, Sh. Ch. Dykebar Future Glory, taking the breed's only Best in Show in Great Britain, as well as Reserve Best at Crufts in 1994.

New Zealand has quality dogs of many breeds. Because of the country's relative isolation from the rest of the world, the significance of imports within the gene pool has been, and still is, vital for the continued success and existence of many breeds. Just how good the New Zealand dogs can be was not clear to the rest of the world until the early 2000s, when a few dogs born on these small and distant isles started to figure in the all-breed ratings in England and America. The Rottweiler Ch. Rolex Rumour Has It by Fantasa, bred by Shelley Reeves, was already a mature three-year-old when he won New Zealand's top dog show, the Pedigree National, in 2002. "Ronan" was titled in both Australia and his native country before

Ch. Crookrise Firebrand, New Zealand's top Best in Show winner in both 1980 and 1981, was imported from the classic Crookrise kennels in England.

arriving in England, where he was among Britain's Top Dogs of all breeds for two years in a row, winning a record number of CCs for his breed. Ronan has won no fewer than seven Bests in Show at British all-breed championship shows, ensuring him a place among the all-time top winners in the United Kingdom.

Other contemporary New Zealand–bred winners in England include the exotic top-winning Afghan Hound Ch. Rainbow Aladin of Jhanzi; the English Toy Terrier (Toy Manchester Terrier in America) Ch. Juleko Henry James at Amalek, who has proved an influential stud dog; and most recently the Pointer Ch. Chesterhope Lets Be Serious of Kanix, sired by artificial insemination by an American dog, Ch. Be Serious Lord Jim, and winner of the 2005 NZKC National Show.

In the United States, the Top Dog of all breeds in 2006 was a Dandie Dinmont Terrier, Ch. Hobergays Fineus Fogg, who was imported into the United States after a great run of success in Australia but was actually born in New Zealand. His pedigree reads like an international Who's Who of the breed and incorporates dogs not only from down under but from England, Canada, and the United States as well.

SOUTH AFRICA

South Africa's first foray into major international competition was in 1980, when Gary and Anna Kartsounis traveled from Johannesburg to the FCI World Show in Italy with their Whippet, Ch. Beseeka Knight Errant Of Silkstone. "Whiskey" had been imported from England after winning the Hound Group at Crufts a couple of years earlier and must have been one of the most trav-

eled show dogs in the world in his day. At the World Show, he won the Group under the author and Best in Show under Italy's senior all-rounder judge, Paolo Ciceri—making Whiskey one of the most long-distance World Show winners ever. The Kartsounises' Tula kennel included a large number of top-class English imports in the 1960s and 1970s. Some of their exports to the United States did well and produced an American Whippet Club specialty winner in the 1980s.

In later years, the Shih Tzu Ch. Midnightdream Simply The Best has been a top dog in South Africa. He won both the annual point scores twice between 2001 and 2004, in addition to twenty-eight all-breed Bests in Show. "Leo" also found time to go to North America and went back home with both American and

The first time South Africa registered a major international win was at the FCI World Show held in Milan, Italy, in 1980. The Whippet Ch. Beseeka Knight Errant of Silkstone was born in England and had won the Group at Crufts before going to South Africa, where he became a top winner. His owner and handler, Gary Kartsounis, took his dog to the World Show, won the Group under judge Bo Bengtson (pictured), and later also won Best in Show.

The Shih Tzu Ch. Midnightdream Simply The Best has taken home most of the Top Dog awards in his native South Africa. "Leo" was also shown in the United States and Canada and came back with two more champion titles. He is pictured being shown by his owner, Riekie Erwee.

Canadian champion titles. Bred by Riekie and Maartin Erwee, he was born in South Africa from imported parents, Ch. Keepsakes Midnight Dream and Ch. Moonglow's Private Dancer, and his pedigree is full of American and Canadian winners.

EMERGING DOG FANCY COUNTRIES

Although there are many world-class kennels in the rest of the world—in Latin America, Asia, Russia, and Eastern Europe—few have as yet had significant impact on the top awards in the major dog-showing countries. Individual breeders have occasionally sent dogs to America or (less frequently) England, and although most have done well, with a couple of notable exceptions they have not been campaigned to the top spots. This is likely to change as the twenty-first century progresses and an increasing

number of dog people from these countries want to try their luck in the big leagues.

LATIN AMERICA

Latin America has world-class dogs, as attested to by the international experts who travel there to judge, and many of those dogs deserve to be better known in the rest of the world. Some of them have been campaigned successfully in North America, and it is most likely only a matter of time before one of them breaks through to the Top Dog spot. In most breeds, there is a preponderance of imports from the United States and Canada, and some breeders cooperate on a regular basis with fanciers in the North. Nowhere is this more evident than in Doberman Pinschers. Probably the best-known South American dog in the United States is a Doberman, Ch. Nello's Lex Luthor, who was bred in Argentina by Ana Maria Sinatra and

The Pekingese Ch. Baron of Chyld Dog is titled in Brazil, Argentina, and Uruguay. He is Brazil's top winner in all-breed competition ever, having won ninety Bests in Show there.

The Boxer Ch. Elharlen's Iago Gaigas, born and bred in Brazil, is one of the all-time top winners in that country, with eighty-one all-breed Bests in Show.

The 2004 FCI World Show, held in Rio de Janeiro, Brazil, was won by the Pug Ch. Double D Cinoblu's Masterpiece. "Paco" had been the Top Dog of all breeds in Brazil the previous year. The judge was Sérgio Meira Lopes de Castro. To the handler's right is FCI president Hans Müller (in yellow tie).

In 1999, Mexico hosted the FCI World Show. Best in Show went to the Belgian Tervuren from the United States Ch. Tacara's Santer Savar.

Eliberto Lugueros. He won the national specialty in his home country for the first time under breed specialist William Shelton from the United States in 1997, repeated the win the following year, and later became a top sire in both North and South America. Among his best-known sons in the United States were the Westminster Group winner in 2000 Ch. Ravenswood Southern Cross and the top Working dog in 2002 Ch. Marienburg's Repo Man.

One of the most successful South American fanciers who exhibits her dogs regularly in the United States, Zuleika Borges Torrealba, owns the da Maya Poodles in Brazil. Many of her top winners are American born, but a glamorous white Standard bitch of her own breeding, Ch. Teodora da Maya, was among

The FCI World Show was held in San Juan, Puerto Rico in 1997. Best in Show was won by the American Cocker Spaniel Ch. Afton's Absolut, handled by Flavio Werneck. The judge was Rafael de Santiago; left is Roberto Vélez Pico, right FCI's Hans Müller and Paolo Dondina.

the top Non-Sporting dogs in the United States in 2005. The Torquay kennel of Alessandra and Marco Flávio Botelho in Brazil has also experienced great success in America: both the Smooth Fox Terrier Ch. Torquay S Demetrio and the fifteen-inch Beagle Ch. Torquay Central Station were top contenders in Best in Show competition in 2006 and 2007.

The biggest individual success scored by a South American dog fancier on the international stage, however, belongs to Flavio Werneck. Already a top handler, with a World Show Best in Show to his credit in 1997, he was one of the owners of America's Top Dog in 2000, the Bichon Frisé Ch. Special Times Just Right. Some credit for "J. R.'s" stunning success should go to his sire, Ch. Dreams Came True's Oliver, bred in Cristina Martins da Veiga's successful ken-

nel in São Paulo. Werneck was killed in a car accident in his native Brazil the same year J. R. won Best in Show at Westminster. He did not get the opportunity to fulfill his promise in the dog show world, but he had already achieved more than most fanciers do in a much longer lifetime.

RUSSIA JOINS THE DOG WORLD

The Russian dog world is still in its infancy in the early years of the twenty-first century, but some breeds, particularly Schnauzers and Kerry Blue Terriers, have already impressed visiting judges in both numbers and quality, and a new native breed, the Russian Black Terrier, has attracted attention both in Europe and in the United States. There is no national ranking of the top dogs in Russia; when an award was given to

The Miniature Poodle Ch. Milamarten Bonaparte, imported from Finland, is the top-winning dog in Russia since the introduction there of dog shows patterned after those in Western countries after the fall of the Soviet Union in the 1990s.

The Miniature Smooth Dachshund from Russia Ch. Pigalitsa Moi iz Mishkinogo Doma has been successful in her native country as well as at top shows in Europe. She is pictured with owner Yulia Chalova.

Russia's Top Winning Dog at the international show in Moscow in 2005, it was simply given to the dog that it was believed had won more than any other dog since the introduction of modern shows in the early 1990s. The award went to the Finnish-born black Miniature Poodle Ch. Milamarten Bonaparte. At the same show, an announcement of Russia's Top Breeder was also made, with this award going to the Gloris kennels of Miniature Schnauzers, bred by Olga Seliverstova. Gloris breeding is now behind winning dogs in both Europe and America.

In 2006, in what is surely a sign of the future, Russian dogs made a first, successful crusade to Crufts, with an undocked Airedale Terrier, Ch. Rus Kornels Zvedznaya Koroleva, winning Best of Breed and making the cut in the Terrier Group.

THE IMPACT OF ASIA

Asia is leading the way in toy breeds: Papillons from Japan (usually with a mixed Scandinavian and English background) have done well at the top American shows for many years, and at Westminster in 2006, both the Best of Breed and Best of Opposite Sex in a large entry of Pomeranian champions went to dogs bred by the Tokie kennels of Chaivat Tangkaravaku and Prakit Chularojmontri in Thailand. By far the strongest influence has come from Japanese Toy Poodles, however. After importing a large number of American champions over many years, Japanese breeders have started to reverse the flow, and in the early 2000s, the American Toy Poodle rings were filled with top-winning Japanese dogs. Two of the biggest names have been the Top Dog of all breeds in the United States in 2004, Ch. North Well Chako JP Platina King; and one of the 2006 top contenders among all breeds in 2006 and 2007, Ch. Smash JP Win A Victory. Japanese Toy Poodles have won well in many other parts of the world as well, including England and Scandinavia.

The most popular breed in India is the Labrador Retriever, followed by German Shepherd Dogs, Boxers, Great Danes, and Doberman Pinschers. There are high-quality Smooth Dachshunds and Pugs as well. The top winners in all-breed competition in the early 2000s have been imported from Australia and South America and include the Siberian Husky Ch. Suthanlites Law Breaker, the Wire Fox Terrier Ch. Holy Ground's Special Edition, and the Doberman Ch. Lex Luthor Dupont. There are also several native breeds that are as yet not recognized by the FCI, although they are exhibited at their own country's kennel

Best in Show at the 1999 FCI Asian show, the Pembroke Welsh Corgi Ch. Lorien It's A Guy Thing, imported from the United States. The judge was Rainer Vuorinen from Finland.

Best in Show at the 1997 FCI Asian show, the Japanese-born Golden Retriever Ch. Puddleby Palace JP Lake Hunter, with judge Dr. Robert Berndt from the United States.

Japan Kennel Club officials with the Best in Show winner at the FCI Asian show in 2000, the Siberian Husky Ch. Generous JP Prime Stage. The judge was Uwe Fischer from Germany.

Toy Poodles from Japan started to win worldwide in the early 2000s. On the home grounds, the white Ch. Smash JP Samba de Amigo won Best in Show at the FCI Asian show in 2002. The handler was Martin Gregory from the United States, the judge Graham Head from Australia.

The Maltese Ch. Funny Ladies Segarl was born in Japan and a champion there as well as in Thailand and the United States before becoming a multiple Best in Show winner in Europe in 2005. He is shown winning Best in Show at Tulln, Austria, handled by Laurent Heinesche under judge Dr. Andreas Schemel.

club shows. The most notable is, perhaps, the ancient Caravan Hound, a sighthound breed that used to follow the traders and mercenaries traveling in caravans from various parts of Asia. India has produced two well-traveled international judges: Philip John and, more recently, C. V. Sudarsan, the secretary of the Kennel Club of India.

For countries such as New Zealand, Australia, Norway, and Japan to have pro-duced the top show dogs in the United Kingdom and America would have been unthinkable just a decade or two earlier. Dogs from Russia, Greece, and Slovenia have taken major wins at Crufts; others from Latin America and Asia have made serious inroads at Westminster. This illustrates how thinking outside the box in combination with relaxed quarantine regulations has changed the international dog scene in the twenty-first century.

CHAPTER 11

How to Be Number One

S o you want a dog that has whatever it takes to become a top winner, Number One, world famous—or at least so well known that everyone in the fancy will know your name (or your dog's). How do you go about accomplishing that?

There are two versions of the usual scenario. Either you have a dog you're convinced can be a great winner, or you're looking for one. In either case, there are certain basic qualities that a dog must possess for it to have any chance of winning at the biggest dog shows, and they aren't necessarily those you might expect. If you own the dog, of course you think it's wonderful—who doesn't think his or her own dog is wonderful?—but that doesn't mean it's going to impress the cognoscenti or the judge on the day of the show.

The first "officially" top-rated dog, the Toy Poodle Ch. Blakeen Ding Ding, Top Dog 1956.

NUMBER ONE U.S. SHOW DOGS: 1957–1961

Pekingese Ch. Chik T'Sun of Caversham, Top Dog 1957, 1958, and 1959, with handler Clara Alford and judge Forest N. Hall at Nebraska Kennel Club.

Cocker Spaniel Ch. Pinetop's Fancy Parade, Top Dog 1960, handled by Norman Austin.

Wire Fox Terrier Ch. Miss Skylight, Top Dog 1961, shown here handled by Ric Chashoudian.

FIND THE DOG FIRST

If you are still looking, how do you find a dog that's capable of becoming a top contender? It isn't going to be easy: you will need to rely on, in varying degrees, a combination of luck, homework, money, and expert guidance. You will have to attend shows, visit kennels, talk to breeders and judges, and make it clear that you would be able to do a great dog justice. Future great show dogs aren't easy to find, but to have any chance of success, your search will be a little easier if you know what to look for.

THE RIGHT BREED

Consider which breed you plan to show. If you are already devoted to a particular kind of dog, you are not going to change your mind, but it helps to know that some breeds

consistently win much more than others. Why that is so is a different subject, but it's a fact you must be aware of. Some popular breeds, no doubt, benefit from the fact that most judges are familiar with them and feel comfortable pointing in their direction. However, with these breeds you will have a much more difficult time breaking through at the breed level, as the competition there is so strong. Not all the popular breeds do equally well: Labrador Retrievers, for instance, often attract huge entries but are notorious for their lack of success in Group and Best in Show competition.

It may be wise to start with a breed for which the competition in the early stages is less strong, so at least your dog has more of a chance to compete at the Group level. However, in Group competition, it will really

NUMBER ONE U.S. SHOW DOGS: 1962–1964

The Miniature Poodle Ch. Tedwin's Top Billing, Top Dog 1962.

The Boxer Ch. Treceder's Painted Lady, Top Dog 1963, handled by Joe Gregory.

The Whippet Ch. Courtenay Fleetfoot of Pennyworth, Top Dog 1964, with handler Robert Forsyth.

need something a little extra to catch the judge's eye, probably more so than in one of the more established breeds. Rare breeds seldom do well in all-breed competition, but there are exceptions. Take, for instance, the Sussex Spaniel Ch. Clussexx Three D Grinchy Glee, one of a very small number of this breed to be shown, yet an unprecedented top contender among all breeds in 2004; or the Ibizan Hound Ch. Luxor's Playmate of the Year, a representative from another numerically small breed who did equally well in 2003. Both of them, in fact, won Group firsts at Westminster, proving that rare breeds—on rare occasions—*can* win big.

THE GROOMING FACTOR

You must consider the amount of show preparation your dog will need as well.

Some breeds, such as Doberman Pinschers, Whippets, and Pointers, are practically wash and wear—ready to go into the ring at almost a moment's notice with very little preparation beyond regular everyday grooming. However, those breeds can't hide a flabby waistline or lack of muscle tone, so long-term conditioning probably matters even more than it does in breeds in which a mass of hair can hide a multitude of sins. Poodles and most of the harsh-coated terriers win a lot in all-breed competition, but these breeds require a huge amount of expert coat preparation to be considered for any of the top awards.

A WINNING ATTITUDE

Once you have settled on a breed and are sure that your dog will be perfectly

NUMBER ONE U.S. SHOW DOGS: 1965–1967

The Doberman Pinscher Ch. Ru-Mar's Tsushima, Top Dog 1965.

The Miniature Poodle Ch. Frederick of Rencroft, Top Dog 1966, with handler Frank Sabella and judge Tom Stevenson.

The English Springer Spaniel Ch. Salilyn's Aristocrat, Top Dog 1967, with handler Dick Cooper and judge Maurice Baker at Lafayette Kennel Club.

groomed, the first question you should ask yourself is whether the dog has the right disposition for a grueling life in show business. Most dogs are lovable at home, and if they know how to behave well in public, it certainly helps. But does your dog have enough stamina, stability, and relentless cheerfulness to come out of the crate with tail wagging even after the 100th show of the season?

Let's consider the male advantage for a moment. There are more top male dogs than top bitches, partly because a little macho swagger helps in the ring and partly because males don't come in season twice a year with the attendant problems of coat loss, mood swings, and other headaches. It's the handler's job to keep his charge happy and well throughout the show career, but if the dog

doesn't have a show attitude, no amount of coaxing by the handler can create it.

The advantage of a positive attitude cannot be emphasized strongly enough. No dog looks good if he or she feels miserable, and most breeds require a happy tail and proud head carriage to do well in the ring. The few that do not, when in fact the tail *should* be carried low, present a special problem. The dog needs to look happy but still carry its tail in the fashion prescribed by the breed standard. Many Salukis, Borzoi, and Whippets may actually have to be taught to carry their tails low however happy they may be. Above all, the dog needs to love people and always be on its best behavior when there are people around. It must be a little like a movie star or politician who knows not to yawn or pick his or her teeth

NUMBER ONE U.S. SHOW DOGS: 1968–1969

The Kerry Blue Terrier Ch. Melbee's Chances Are, Top Dog 1968, with handler Ric Chashoudian and judge Heywood Hartley at the Santa Cruz Kennel Club.

The Boxer Ch. Arriba's Prima Donna, joint Top Dog 1969, with handler Jane Kamp (now Forsyth) and judge Langdon Skarda.

in public since there's always some critic with a camera around. It's not enough for the dog to look pretty in the ring during the official moments of judging, because a top dog is judged by ringside spectators, competitors, and passing judges every moment it is in the public eye.

NO AGGRESSION

Most important, absolutely no sign of temper can ever be allowed. Being off and looking tired in the ring is bad enough and will not help any dog win what is essentially a beauty contest; refusing to be handled for examination or, worse, snapping at the judge is the deadliest of sins. Who can blame a dog for getting a little irritable when the judge gets intimate—checking teeth, feeling testicles—for the 150th time?

But showing aggression toward any human (judge, handler, or spectator) will immediately get a dog excused from the ring or even disqualified if, in the judge's opinion, the dog attacks any person in the ring. That means it cannot be shown again until extenuating circumstances have been proven, whereupon the dog may be reinstated—but by that time, many shows have gone by and a reputation has possibly already been ruined.

The fact that shows of aggression toward people happen so seldom is testimony to the basically solid, patient, and people-loving temperament that show dogs universally seem to possess. I remember one show where the Terrier Group winner went for the judge's nose in the Best in Show finale, and another occasion when one of

NUMBER ONE U.S. SHOW DOGS: 1969–1971

The Standard Poodle Ch. De Russy Lollypop, joint Top Dog 1969, with handler Frank Sabella.

The Norwegian Elkhound Ch. Vin-Melca's Vagabond, Top Dog 1970.

The English Springer Spaniel Ch. Chinoe's Adamant James, Top Dog 1971, with handler Clint Harris at Forsyth Kennel Club.

America's top dogs—generally known as an amiable, level-headed character—for no apparent reason tried to bite a judge during a routine examination. Temporary disqualification was the result.

Professional handler Bill McFadden has told of his experiences when showing the great Kerry Blue Terrier Ch. Torum's Scarf Michael ("Mick"), a dog both feisty and friendly, whose best buddies were the young sons of his British breeder. Yet Bill was worried on a few occasions toward the end of Mick's career about his reluctance to let the judges check his private parts, mandatory during the initial examination routine. (Any dog not having two fully developed testicles normally descended into the scrotum must be disqualified, per American Kennel Club rules.) It turned out that Mick had a medical problem that made any probing in that area painful for him. Quite possibly, something similar was the reason for the other incident mentioned earlier, which ruined a glittering show career.

Being fond of other dogs, as opposed to people, is not necessarily a requirement for a top winner, provided the handler is experienced and knows how to control the dog. A certain amount of swagger, even a little bristling, may help the dog get up on his feet, arch his neck, and present a striking picture for the judge. In some breeds—terriers, working dogs—the males would not be expected to be friendly toward each other (and bitches can be the same way toward other bitches), whereas in others, any sign of hostility toward another dog in the ring would be very much frowned on. In any

NUMBER ONE U.S. SHOW DOGS: 1972–1974

The Cocker Spaniel Ch. Sagamore Toccoa, Top Dog 1972, with handler Ted Young and judge Frank Landgraf at Lakes Region Kennel Club.

The Doberman Pinscher Ch. Galaxy's Corry Missile Belle, Top Dog 1973, with handler Corky Vroom and judge Irene Khatoonian Schlintz at the Del Monte Kennel Club.

The Lakeland Terrier Ch. Jo-Ni's Red Baron of Crofton, Top Dog 1974, with handler Ric Chashoudian and judge Mrs. C. Bede Maxwell at the San Luis Obispo Kennel Club.

case, it is the handler's job to make sure there are no fights. This is one reason children and inexperienced exhibitors must never be allowed into a show (or anywhere else, for that matter) with a dog that is less than 100 percent tolerant of other dogs.

One of the potentially most damaging acts of dog aggression was on view at a recent Westminster Kennel Club show, where two Irish Wolfhound males very nearly got into a fight in the ring. Once started, such a fight would have been extremely difficult to break up, and the damage to dogs and handlers—not to mention possibly bystanders and, in view of all the media present, to the breed's and the sport's reputation—could have been nearly irreparable. It looked frightening enough from ringside with two such giants going at

each other, and it was only the quick thinking of one of the handlers, who simply dragged her dog out of the ring without even asking to be excused, that saved the day. It was learned subsequently that earlier in the day one of the dogs had tried to scale the partition separating them on the bench to attack his rival; nothing happened then, but both dogs obviously remembered the incident when they faced each other in the ring.

The fact that so many thousands of dogs and people are squeezed into tight quarters at shows every weekend of the year with almost no problems speaks volumes both for the essentially good nature of the dogs and for the vigilance and good sense of their handlers.

Good condition is a basic requirement for show circuit success, so as a part of the

NUMBER ONE U.S. SHOW DOGS: 1975-1976

The Sealyham Terrier Ch. Dersade Bobby's Girl, Top Dog 1975, with handler Peter Green and judge Henry Stoecker at the Detroit Kennel Club.

The Greyhound Ch. Aroi Talk of the Blues, Top Dog 1976, with handler Corky Vroom.

generally level-headed and easygoing approach to life expected in a top show dog, it helps to have one that's able to accept new and sometimes peculiar conditions, that wolfs down his dinner, that doesn't mind traveling by car or plane, that will exercise and answer nature's call on a strip of dead grass just about anywhere if necessary, and that will then settle in happily for a snooze in his crate. This dog will have a huge advantage over the competition, which may not be quite so relaxed about these matters.

THE CASE FOR CRATES

A word about the use of crates is necessary. To the uninitiated, these "cages" may look like prisons, with bars across the closed gates, and it is not uncommon to hear spectators express pity for the poor dogs that are shut up and locked away like prisoners. If you could ask the dogs, you would hear a different story. Most dogs regard their crates as a safe retreat, a sort of combined private condo and king-size bed where nobody bothers them, so they get some privacy and peace. Show dogs, who are often fed in their crates, usually can't wait to get back in them after showing or exercise. There are only so many times you can smile for the cameras, flirt with the judges, and let the public paw at you. After that, even a show dog just wants to be alone!

There are exceptions: dogs that either were not crate-trained as puppies or that suffer from separation anxiety whenever they are shut in a crate or a room on their own. All puppies, regardless of whether they are to be show dogs or not, should be

NUMBER ONE U.S. SHOW DOGS: 1977–1979

The Wire Fox Terrier Ch. Harwire Hetman of Whinlatter, Top Dog 1977, with handler Cliff Hallmark and judge Langdon Skarda at the Harford County Kennel Club.

The Doberman Pinscher Ch. Marienburg's Mary Hartman, Top Dog 1978, handled by Moe Miyagawa under judge Mrs. Augustus Riggs IV at the Santa Barbara Kennel Club.

The Standard Poodle Ch. Lou Gin's Kiss Me Kate, Top Dog 1979, with handler Robert Walberg.

taught to be alone in a crate for at least an hour or two when they can't be watched, perhaps overnight as well. It is natural for a puppy to protest the solitary confinement at first, but if you do this right and the dog remains miserable, howling and scratching in the crate, chances are it has a temperament problem. A dog with separation anxiety should not be shown, would most likely not be successful anyway, and would make both itself and others miserable in the process.

Yet crates are so convenient that there is a risk of abuse. No dog should spend most of its show life cooped up in a crate, but as long as the dog is allowed an active life, companionship, and exercise with its peers, the crate is the dog's safe haven away from home, on the road and at the shows.

READY TO TAKE THE PLUNGE: THE TRIAL RUN

So, provided your dog has a perfect show dog temperament, what about conformation? What about that cute face, those liquid eyes, the shiny coat, and all the other handsome features your dog exhibits? Of course, you need a dog that conforms to the basic requirements of the breed standard, but unless you have a lot of experience, you may not be able to tell whether the dog in front of you can be a top winner.

What you need to do is take that dog to a few shows—not necessarily to win, but first to see how the dog reacts to a show environment, and second to get an idea of how it looks in the ring. Preferably, you should watch from ringside, not show the dog yourself; therefore, you need to find a sympa-

The Norwich Terrier Ch. Thrumpton's Lord Brady, Top Dog 1980, with handler Peter Green and judge Robert Graham at the Charlottesville-Albemarle Kennel Club.

The Pug Ch. Dhandy's Favorite Woodchuck, Top Dog 1981, with handler Bob Barlow and judge Ann Stevenson at Westminster Kennel Club.

thetic handler who is willing to take on a raw dog and is likely to make it a pleasant experience. You also need a few trusted mentors at your side, people who are willing to cast a critical eye over the dog while it's being judged and who will tell you honestly what they think—not so much what they see as what they can predict for the future. You shouldn't expect to win at these shows; it's great if you do, but that isn't the point of the exercise. The dog will not be completely ring-trained, and the performance with a new handler won't be very smooth, so the idea is to get a feel for the dog's potential and attitude more than anything else.

When should the dog be started on a trial run? Provided that the temperament and positive attitude are there, you can start early, at six to ten months, depending on the breed. (Bigger breeds usually mature later than small ones do.) Certainly, the dog will not reach its peak until it's two or three years old, older in some breeds, but it does no harm to make the errors early, before the dog is famous. Starting early also allows you and the dog time to pick up a few pointers before the pressure is on. Just don't overdo it. Above all, make sure that the shows are fun for the dog: unless it looks forward to every outing and enjoys being in the ring, it's never going to become a good show dog.

WHERE TO SHOW: ALL-BREED VERSUS SPECIALTY

You must also be aware that a dog may succeed in one type of competition but not do equally well in another. In most breeds, there

NUMBER ONE U.S. SHOW DOGS: 1982–1983

The Afghan Hound Ch. Kabik's The Challenger, Top Dog 1982.

The Scottish Terrier Ch. Braeburn's Close Encounter, Top Dog 1983, with handler George Ward and judge E. W. Tipton, Jr., at the Detroit Kennel Club.

is at least some slight differentiation between the kind of dog that wins well at a breed specialty show and the kind that wins at an all-breed show. In some breeds, the two winners almost appear to be two different breeds. This, of course, shouldn't be so: the breed standard is the same. It is natural, however, for judges who officiate at big specialty shows—most likely people with a long, deep background in that particular breed but often with limited experience of other breeds—to emphasize different characteristics than an all-rounder would. The all-breed judge may know something about most breeds but cannot possibly have the same depth of understanding of every breed he or she judges. Generally speaking, the specialist judges tend to focus on either a certain look or fine details of breed type, whereas the all-

rounder tends to reward general balance, soundness, and glamour, perhaps without being aware that the dog may lack some subtle, but important, breed points.

In an extreme case, you may have an all-rounder's type of dog, in which case you may not win at specialties but can focus on events at which the breed competition is less intense and at which your dog—if he wins the breed—will shine at the all-breed level. If you have a specialist's type of dog, you may win any number of important breed events but will still be overlooked in the Group or even be defeated in mediocre breed competition if you find yourself at the mercy of an all-rounder judge. There are dogs that amass huge Best in Show records yet hardly ever win a specialty, and there are others that win national specialties over

NUMBER ONE U.S. SHOW DOGS: 1984–1988

The German Shepherd Dog Ch. Covy-Tucker Hill's Manhattan, Top Dog 1984 and 1985, with handler Jimmy Moses and judge Anne Rogers Clark at the Santa Barbara Kennel Club.

The Wire Fox Terrier Ch. Galsul Excellence, Top Dog 1986 and 1987, with handler Peter Green and judge Frank Sabella at Bucks County Kennel Club.

The Doberman Pinscher Ch. Royal Tudor's Wild As The Wind, Top Dog 1988, with handler Andy Linton and judge Charlotte Clem McGowan at Westminster Kennel Club.

hundreds of their peers yet hardly ever top even a single Group. The greatest dogs, needless to say, are those rare individuals that excel under all types of judges—and that is, of course, what you want.

STAR QUALITY

Much has been said about the somewhat nebulous characteristic often termed star quality. When speaking of show dogs, it is impossible to quantify it or explain exactly what it consists of. Sometimes, it may exist only in the eye of the beholder, as a sort of kennel blindness that hits even the most experienced dog fancier when he or she falls for a dog (or "believing is seeing," to twist a cliché). However, just as certain people— actors, public speakers, even the occasional politician—may possess an ineffable quality

that keeps an audience riveted, so some dogs seem to have a natural charisma that makes it difficult for anyone, judge or ringside spectator, to miss them. Perhaps it involves a certain natural carriage, a way of moving, an attitude, but if it is paired with even the basics of correct conformation it is worth gold in a show dog.

Charisma may even compensate for some glaring structural faults. There was a lovely Miniature Poodle in the 1960s that possessed star quality in spades but had an obviously incorrect front construction, moving like the proverbial eggbeater when viewed head on. She had a wonderful show career nevertheless, and when a defeated competitor sourly asked the English judge how she could fail to notice the front action as the dog moved up and back in the ring,

The Bulldog Ch. Hetherbull Bounty's Frigate, Top Dog 1989, with owner-handler Jean Hetherington and judge Tom Stevenson at Vacationland Dog Club.

The Bouvier des Flandres Ch. Galbraith's Ironeyes, Top Dog 1990, with handler Corky Vroom and judge Lou Harris at Westminster Kennel Club.

the judge blithely answered, "Oh, my dear, that's when I powder my nose."

OWNER-HANDLER OR PROFESSIONAL?

One of the most important questions to ask yourself is whether you should show the dog yourself or turn it over to a professional handler. This applies primarily in the United States, of course, where handlers dominate the show scene; in most other countries, there are few or no professionals, so you would either have to show the dog yourself or find a talented friend who is willing to do so. It can be thrilling to win with your own dog, no question about it: you will become a team, travel a lot together, and most likely experience much joy—and probably some disappointments—

together. In the end, you will have the satisfaction of knowing that what you achieved, you and your dog did on your own.

Even if your dog is good enough to defeat the big guns, you must ask yourself if you are able to do it justice and compete on equal terms with skilled professionals. It can be done, and having the luxury of focusing entirely on one dog, not a whole string as the professionals must, gives you a built-in advantage: you and your dog will know each other better than most of the professional teams do. In theory, this means that your dog will show better for you than it would for a handler it doesn't know as well—but that advantage is balanced, and sometimes outweighed, by the fact that a professional handler will probably have much more experience than you do. He or

NUMBER ONE U.S. SHOW DOGS: 1991–1995

The Wire Fox Terrier Ch. Registry's Lonesome Dove, Top Dog 1991 and 1992, with handler Michael Kemp and judge Melbourne T. L. Downing at Westminster Kennel Club.

The German Shepherd Dog Ch. Altana's Mystique, Top Dog 1993 and 1994, with handler Jimmy Moses and judge Michele Billings at Santa Barbara Kennel Club.

The Afghan Hound Ch. Tryst of Grandeur, Top Dog 1995, with handler Michael Canalizo and judge Lydia Coleman Hutchinson at the Burlington Wisconsin Kennel Club.

she will have gone to hundreds, possibly thousands, of shows for years and will know all the ins and outs of traveling, conditioning, picking suitable shows with good (for his dogs!) judges, and all the other imponderables. Perhaps because the handler is less emotionally involved in the dogs, he or she is also often better able to assess their real quality and less likely to be kennel blind than a doting owner is. When you make your livelihood from showing dogs, you just cannot afford to fool yourself the same way many loving owners do when they look at their prodigies in soft focus.

OUTSTANDING OWNER-HANDLERS

In spite of the overwhelming odds against them, owner-handlers can break through the professional ranks. The most famous case was when Patricia Craige Trotter campaigned her Vin-Melca's Norwegian Elkhounds to top honors year after year from the 1960s to the early 1990s, at which point she settled down to a career as a judge. In 1970, Trotter became the first owner-handler to win the Top Dog award since the ratings systems began with her Ch. Vin-Melca's Nimbus. Trotter still shows her dogs successfully but no longer campaigns them. In the early 1980s, the Afghan Hound Ch. Kabik's The Challenger won both Westminster and the award for Top Dog of all breeds, owner-handled by his breeder Chris Terrell, and in 1989 the Bulldog Ch. Hetherbull Bounty's Frigate, handled by his owner, Jean Hetherington, became the third and so far last amateur owner-handled winner of the Top Dog of all breeds award.

NUMBER ONE U.S. SHOW DOGS: 1996–1999

The Standard Schnauzer Ch. Parsifal di Casa Netzer, Top Dog 1996, with handler Doug Holloway and judge Charles E. Trotter at Westminster Kennel Club.

The Norwich Terrier Ch. Fairewood Frolic, Top Dog 1997, with handler Peter Green and judge Kari Järvinen from Finland at the Montgomery County Kennel Club.

The Standard Poodle Ch. Lake Cove That's My Boy, Top Dog 1998 and 1999, with handler Dennis McCoy and judge Robert Fisher at Old Dominion Kennel Club.

In the United States, at least, showing a dog competitively is almost a full-time job. You will need to be away from home most weekends and many weekdays if you aspire to reach a spot among the top dogs, and you will need the financial means to either pay for considerable travel and many hotel nights or invest in a motor home. Often it is less expensive, all told, to send the dog with a handler.

FINDING A SPONSOR

When you add up all the costs for a top campaign, you may be ready to quit before you start. Good show campaigns have been built on less than $50,000 per year, but you must expect to keep the dog going for at least one warm-up year before the big wins come, and if you are really ambitious and want to promote your dog in the glossy trade publications (not required but certainly helpful), the annual cost can easily creep up into the six figures. Showing dogs does not have to be expensive in itself, but getting your dog into the top rankings almost invariably is, in the United States, at least. If you have a potentially great dog, or a reputation as a good breeder, you may easily find someone willing to sponsor the dog—which will involve a whole new set of problems and new opportunities, with written agreements, co-owner contracts, and other elements. There are many different variations of co-owner agreements: usually the sponsor agrees to pay a certain sum for entries, handling, traveling, advertising, and other components for a specified period of time in return for official title of co-owner

NUMBER ONE U.S. SHOW DOGS: 2000–2001

The Bichon Frisé Ch. Special Times Just Right! Top Dog 2000, with handler Scott Sommer and judge Jane Forsyth at the Detroit Kennel Club.

The Kerry Blue Terrier Ch. Torum's Scarf Michael, Top Dog 2001, with handler Bill McFadden and judge Peter Luyten from Australia at the Montgomery County Kennel Club.

and, often, first choice of the dog's future puppies.

PICKING YOUR SPOTS

Another way to deal with the constraints of time and money is to set your sights on different goals. Obviously, most people are neither able nor willing to make the huge investment of both time and money that is required for an all-breed Top Dog campaign in the United States. For the all-breed Top Dog rankings, it is almost always necessary to compete in more than 100 shows in a year. But if you aim instead for Number One at the breed level, it's often possible—if you have an outstanding dog and plan carefully—to go to far fewer shows, win a few of the most competitive weekends, and still walk away with the top spot. The public

renown may not be quite as glorious, but the satisfaction should be almost as great.

Let us assume that you have a wonderful young dog that has taken some nice early wins and shows every promise of developing into a top-class show dog. What's the next step?

This is where experience and planning play a big part. Ideally, you find the right shows with the right judges, people who are especially likely to appreciate your particular dog. If the dog does well, chances are that other people will notice, word of mouth will spread, and soon the dog world—or at least a sizeable part of it—may be buzzing about your promising newcomer. There is no better show to take an aspiring star to than Westminster, provided the dog's temperament is such that he can take the bustle

NUMBER ONE U.S. SHOW DOGS: 2002–2003

The German Shepherd Dog Ch. Kismet's Sight For Sore Eyes, Top Dog 2002, with handler Jimmy Moses and judge Eileen Pimlott at Westminster Kennel Club.

The Norfolk Terrier Ch. Cracknor Cause Cele-bre, Top Dog 2003, with handler Beth Sweigart and judge Robert Stein at the Evans-ville Kennel Club.

of Manhattan and the crowds at Madison Square Garden. Putting in a good performance at Westminster has spawned many a young dog's show career. Most of the country's top dog people are watching, and a promising newcomer will be noticed, whether he wins or not.

GETTING THE WORD OUT

You may want to ensure that word of mouth really goes out by advertising your young dog in some of the trade periodicals. In the United States alone, there are several different publications whose primary source of income is the promotion and advertising of show dogs, and dog magazines in other countries have started to follow the lead of the Americans. These advertisements are driven in about equal degrees by a proud sense of achievement ("Look what we won!") and a sometimes naive expectation that judges will be impressed and therefore more likely to look favorably on the advertised dog when they next see it in their rings. This is a controversial subject: on one hand, no judges worth their salt will reward a dog just because they know it has won at other shows; on the other hand, not all judges *are* worth their salt. Judging is, in any case, a complicated psychological process; it is conceivable that judges, however honest, could subconsciously, when the competition is very close, favor a dog they have recently admired in an ad over an unknown dog.

It is also easy for the advertising to backfire: if the sales pitch is too blatant, it won't work. Often, the advertising goes

NUMBER ONE U.S. SHOW DOGS: 2004–2006

The Toy Poodle Ch. North Well Chako JP Platina King, Top Dog 2004, with handler Tim Brazier and judge Patricia Laurans at Somerset Hills Kennel Club.

The Pekingese Ch. Yakee If Only, Top Dog 2005, with handler David Fitzpatrick and judge Dr. Harry Smith at Catonsville Kennel Club.

The Dandie Dinmont Terrier Ch. Hobergays Fineus Fogg, Top Dog 2006, with handler Bill McFadden and judge Paula Hartinger.

unnoticed by everyone but the dog's owner and friends anyway; very few dog fanciers, let alone busy judges, have the time or patience to leaf through the many hundreds of glossy advertising pages that the kennel presses produce every month. The intelligent fancier will make an effort to counteract this by presenting the dog in a publication that consists of more than ads. Obviously, if a magazine has solid editorial content, the judges are more likely to read—and save—that publication and therefore notice the photo of your dog in it. Yet, as evidenced by the tons of glossy advertising pages wasted each year, perhaps it really is more a way of showing off for friends than a serious attempt to influence the decision makers.

There is no question that good advertising helps educate the judges, at the same time making your dog a household name within the fancy. Most top dogs are regularly advertised, but there are always exceptions to the rule.

CHAPTER 12

BREEDS THAT WIN AND BREEDS THAT DON'T

All breeds are equal in the judge's eye—or should be. Yet it does not require more than a cursory look to realize that some breeds win much more than others do. A glance through any of the illustrated dog show trade magazines (as well as this book) will prove that the biggest rosettes and silver cups usually go to dogs from a rather small number of breeds. Theoretically speaking, any dog regardless of breed has as good a shot at Best in Show as any other dog—provided it is good enough to win. If that is true, however, why do certain breeds win so frequently, and why is it so hard for others to make it past the Group ring? Are some breeds just that much better than the rest? In reality, many different factors play a part in the final decision.

The Sporting Group competition in America is often dominated by Setters and Cockers. The Clussexx heavy Spaniels, bred by Jeane Haverick and Douglas Johnson, have included many top-winning Clumbers as well as the Sussex Spaniel Ch. Clussexx Three D Grinchy Glee, the top Sporting Dog and one of the Top Dogs of all breeds in 2004. He won thirty-seven Bests in Show that year, handled by Scott Sommer.

Some rare breeds win more than their fair proportional share of the top awards. Often a ground-breaking top winner opens the door for others of the same breed. Ibizan Hounds had won Best in Show before "Bunny," but none had placed among the top Hounds until Ch. Luxor's Playmate of the Year soared right through to top Hound in 2003. She won thirty-nine all-breed Bests in Show that year and was Number Three of all breeds, one of the most momentous achievements ever for a rare breed. She also won the Hound Group at Westminster twice. Bunny received her name because of an almost perfect Playboy bunny mark on her back. She was handled by Clint Livingston during the most active part of her campaign.

SURPRISING UNDERDOGS

Certainly a dog must be both physically and mentally sound to win consistently in top competition. Since there is a natural relationship between quality and numbers, this may explain why so many established popular breeds win so much. A breed with high registration figures is likely to be supported by many talented breeders, so it is reasonable that a large number of quality puppies will be born, with a good chance that many will get the opportunities they deserve in the show ring. Therefore, it comes as no surprise that the populations of a number of the most popular breeds include many high-quality competitors capable of winning at the biggest shows. It also helps that more judges are likely to recognize a top-quality dog of a well-known established breed than one of a less common breed. There are exceptions to this rule, however.

The Labrador Retriever is the most popular breed of all at dog shows in most countries, yet it seldom reaches the top spot in all-breed competition. In fifty years of AKC ratings, only three Labradors have placed among the year's top five Sporting Dogs, and only one succeeded in doing so for two consecutive years. This was Ch. Aquarius Centercourt Delight, who won twenty-three all-breed Bests in Show and was among the top Sporting Dogs in both 2003 and 2004. "Buzz" also won several big specialty shows, including the National. American-bred for the first two generations, Buzz is linebred to the top-producing English import Ch. Receiver of Cranspire. He is shown with handler Joy Quallenberg, winning Best in Show under judge Dr. Ronald Spritzer at the Framington Valley Kennel Club in 2003.

In spite of low registration figures, the Otterhound has produced a remarkable number of top winners in all-breed competition. Ch. Scentasia's Hostile Takeover won more than 20 Bests in Show and ranked among the country's top Hounds in 2003. She is shown winning at the Tuxedo Park Kennel Club, handled by Kitty Burke under judge Carol Reisman. The trophy presenter is Glorvina Schwartz.

THE LABRADOR EXCEPTION

In most countries, Labrador Retrievers are usually absent when top honors in all-breed competition are awarded. This has been true for so many years that it is almost taken for granted in dog show circles. In spite of the fact that it is by far the number-one breed in popularity in both America and the United Kingdom, no Labrador has ever been a serious contender for the Top Dog spot since these competitions were first instituted; none has ever won Westminster, and none has won Crufts since the 1930s. The Labrador Retriever is not a glamorous breed, certainly, but in spite of many indications to the contrary, it is not necessary for a

breed to be glamorous to win well in all-breed competition. A recent example comes in the Otterhound, a breed that even in top show form may appear scruffy and actually less glamorous than the Labrador does. It is also one of the rarest breeds in AKC registrations, yet in recent years it has managed to win just about as much in all-breed competition as the incomparably much more numerous Labrador Retrievers did.

In a 2003 breed survey in *Dogs in Review* magazine, a number of breed-specialist judges were asked why Labradors so consistently fail to match the Group and Best in Show records of other breeds. Most of the respondents explained this fact primarily by

One of the few American Water Spaniels to win Best in Show, Ch. Waterway-Game Crk Mare-Z Dotes, is pictured after winning at Indianhead Kennel Club in Wisconsin in 2004 with judge Jon Cole.

referring to the Labrador's lack of flash and glamour, but two highly respected authorities were more specific. Dr. Bernard W. Ziessow, who has been involved in the breed since the 1950s and whose Franklin kennel has produced more than seventy-five champions, wrote:

> Those of us who have been in the breed for many years are deeply concerned with the condition—dogs that have had Bests in Show or multiple Group wins in the past couldn't win a ribbon today. Unfortunately, they would look like another breed compared to the Labradors shown today. Who's at fault? Authors of recent books on the breed and contributors to dog magazines have compared the [current] breed to

Mack trucks, Sherman tanks and draft horses. This is contrary to the breed standard and the description of the breed by the eminent English sportswoman and breeder of Labradors, Lorna, Countess Howe, who compared the breed to a thoroughbred Irish hunter.

Australian breeder-judge Guy Spagnolo added that "having judged the breed in a few places, my impressions are [that] whilst there have been some wonderful and typey dogs present, a great many are not conditioned correctly enough to do battle at Group level with the glamorous breeds. A show Labrador needs to be fit and appear capable of work. Fat does not replace substance." Spagnolo pointed out that in Australia, Labrador Retrievers enjoy huge success at the all-breed level (it is, in fact, the only major dog-showing country where the breed does so); his own greatest star, Gr. Ch. Driftway Regal Oak, won fifty-three Bests in Show, including the Brisbane Royal Show twice.

The Curly-Coated Retriever Ch. Fairway It's My Party, handled by Mary Dukes to Best in Show at San Luis Obispo Kennel Club in 2001 under judge Dana Cline.

WHAT ABOUT GOLDENS?

If adding attractive furnishings were the answer to all-breed success, why is the Golden Retriever—which in many ways looks like a Labrador decked out in a glamorous coat—not doing much better than it is? Almost as popular as the Labrador, the Golden has failed to produce a single dog that has won either Westminster or Crufts, and none has been a close contender for Top Dog of all breeds since Ch. Cumming's Gold Rush Charlie, Number Three in the all-breed ratings in 1974. Individual Goldens win a fair number of Bests in Show, however, certainly more than Labradors do, but few win consistently enough to make a mark in the annual ratings. In any case, if coat were the deciding factor, how could one explain the huge success of Doberman Pinschers and Boxers, breeds that don't have a stitch of extra hair to hide faults or flatter the outline? Yet they have been consistent Top Dog contenders for decades. It is probably only a matter of time before the tide turns for both Labradors and Goldens—certainly the opportunities are there for the right dog and the right handler.

Golden Retrievers are often competitive in all-breed competition, but none has gone as far as Top Dog all breeds. In 2000, Ch. Touchstone's Ooh Whad Ya Dooh was among the top Sporting dogs. She is shown with handler Beth Johnson and judge William Hixson winning one of her fifteen Best in Shows that year at Lake Shore Kennel Club.

The Field Spaniel Ch. Marshfield's Boys' Night Out is pictured taking Group Second at Westminster in 2002, a rare achievement for the breed. "Henry" was also a multiple Best in Show winner. He is shown with judge Erik Bergishagen and handler Christy Marley.

THE RISE AND FALL OF TOP BREEDS

It is easy to understand why some breeds so often go to the top. However, the fact that a breed does well at a particular period of time does not in any way guarantee that this will always be the case. The dog show history books are full of examples to the contrary: breeds that once ruled the roost but hardly ever take a top win today; others that used to be minor players—or simply didn't exist in the past—yet rose to great prominence in competition with other breeds at the world's top dog shows.

THE STAR BREEDS

The Wire Fox Terrier was king of the shows for several decades, and anyone who has watched a professionally trimmed and prepared Wire in the ring will agree that it is a very dynamic work of art. The combination of highly stylized conformation with a tough, go-get-'em temperament was what helped make the Wire Fox Terrier so difficult for other breeds to conquer for so long. The other established terrier breeds, many almost equally stylish, usually got their fair share of the spoils—Airedales, Scotties, Welshes, and Lakelands—but it was long felt that the little scruffy terriers, primarily the Norfolks and Norwiches, could not be taken seriously as contenders even for best terrier, let alone Best in Show. That changed in the late 1970s, when the first of a series of top winners appeared, notching a row of successes that included three wins as Top Dog of all breeds in the United States alone (two Norwiches, one Norfolk), and Best in Show wins at both Westminster and Crufts in just a couple of decades.

The Poodle's appeal as a show dog has more in common with that of the Wire Fox Terrier than might at first seem likely. The highly stylized look relies greatly on talented grooming for its impact, but it was the combination of visual appeal with self-confidence and obvious charm that made all the difference in the show ring. Nobody would imagine either a Wire Fox Terrier or a Poodle going to the top unless it is also a happy, exuberant show-off—undeniable proof that a rock-solid temperament is the first requirement for a top-winning show dog. The biggest difference between Fox Terrier and Poodle show histories is that it took Poodle fanciers much longer to polish their product sufficiently to attract the judges' eyes. Although quite popular by the late nineteenth century, Poodles did not start reaching dog show stardom consistently until the late 1930s, and Standard

The Glen of Imaal Terrier Ch. Royalty's Star Over Coleraine won Best in Show at the Gloucester County Kennel Club in October 2004, just two weeks after the breed was fully recognized by AKC. The judge was Anitra Cuneo.

Poodles have now remained a major show breed for several decades without any sign of slackening. Toys are winning more nowadays than they ever did before, but Miniatures, after a tremendous burst of success in the middle of the twentieth century, have not done quite as well in recent years.

FALLING STARS

Whatever happened to the Sealyham Terrier, one of the glories of the show rings in the past, with three Westminster wins in the 1920s and 1930s? Sealyham victories in later decades, in spite of a few exceptions, hardly add up to more than a year's worth in the breed's heyday. The Sealyham Terrier offers a fairly extreme example of how a breed's dominance may rise or fall in comparison with that of other breeds. There are others as well. English Setters are still a serious all-breed contender almost everywhere in the world, but the breed has never regained the strong influence it had in the American show ring from about 1930 through the early

1950s. The Boston Terrier's development has been downright distressing for lovers of this charming breed: it was one of the most popular choices for top awards in America during the early twentieth century but, although still quite popular, is very seldom considered for Best in Show honors today.

THE NEW COMPETITORS

The new breeds added to the roster almost every year don't make it any easier for some of the old favorites to maintain their standings. Usually it takes a few decades for a newly approved breed to become established before individual dogs start winning really big. A notable exception is the Bichon Frisé, which existed in Europe for centuries without ever being widely noticed. When the Bichon was approved for AKC competition in 1973, it very soon started to win big, supported by a group of talented, highly motivated fanciers: within a few years, the Bichon was a frequent Best in Show contender, climaxing with Top Dog and Best in Show at Westminster in 2001. In the United Kingdom, in an even shorter time, Bichons have done even better, winning Top Dog three times—in 1990, 1999, and 2004.

CONFLICTING CONCLUSIONS

After studying the question of what helps a breed win in all-breed competition, it is impossible not to come to a number of sometimes conflicting conclusions:

- Sound conformation and solid temperament are necessary. You can fool some of the judges most of the time and most of the judges some of the time, but you can't fool all of the judges all of the time,

The top-winning Terrier of 1998, Ch. Sweetsound's King 'O' Rockn Roll, is pictured winning Best in Show at Harrisburg Kennel Club in 1999 under judge Edd E. Bivin, handled by Kathleen Ferris.

so there has to be more than flash, glamour, and showmanship to help any dog reach the top.

- Certainly, a breed that lends itself to being shaped into a striking outline often has an advantage. Coated breeds that can be sculpted into an attractive silhouette take far more than their share of the top wins than is statistically justified. However, there are many exceptions to this rule.

- Popularity helps. A good dog of an established breed familiar to every judge will usually enjoy an edge over an equally good dog of a lesser-known breed. This can also work both ways, since a minor fault that will be noted by most judges in a popular breed may easily pass unnoticed on a dog of a less familiar breed.

- A single big star can benefit a whole breed. Once one dog of a breed has

become established in all-breed competition, it is easier for other dogs of similar quality to go even further. This can also backfire, however: if the first headliner compiles a huge record and looks very different from others of his kind, it may actually be more difficult for the dogs that follow to get a second look.

- Good public relations always help. A progressive breed club, a good writer, a well-orchestrated advertising campaign may help the dog fancy—including the judges—look with new interest and fresh eyes on a previously unnoticed breed.

- A talented, competitive, dedicated group of breeders and handlers who compete with the same goal in mind is probably the single most conducive factor to major all-breed success. Would the Standard Poodle have become established so suddenly without the Blakeen versus Pillicoc rivalry in the 1930s? Would the Miniature Poodle have become the big winner of the 1950s without handlers such as Anne Rogers Clark and Frank Sabella? Would the Bichon Frisé have gone to the top so quickly without Richard Beauchamp and a group of like-minded, devoted breeders? Would Norwich and Norfolk Terriers ever have been taken seriously in top competition without Peter Green and his charges?

Trends Then and Now

A study of the Best in Show awards in the United States and the United Kingdom for two different time periods, one just after World War II and one in the early 2000s, shows some clear trends. The figures may not be statistically reliable because of the varying number of shows between past and present and from the United Kingdom to the United States. The three-year period from 1943 to 1945 included 558 shows in the United States; a similar time period, 2003 to 2005, included 4,151 shows, indicating how the number of shows had grown during the intervening six decades. Because there are far fewer shows in the United Kingdom, a five-year period was analyzed: during the period from 1947 to 1951, there were 77 shows; in the period from 2001 to 2005, there were 121 shows. The number of shows in the United Kingdom had increased far less significantly than the size of these shows, many of which now number more than 10,000 dogs.

In the United Kingdom

Considering the situation in the United Kingdom first, the wins were widely spread out, with most breeds taking only a single Best in

One of the few Boston Terriers to hit the top spots since the 1950s, Ch. Star Q's Brass Buttons won multiple Bests in Show in 1970 as well as the Non-Sporting Group at Westminster; shown here handled by Harry Clasen under judge William Kendrick.

Very few Löwchens have won Best in Show in AKC competition, but Ch. Touche Pearlbrook Heartbeat is shown taking one of several such wins at the Midland Michigan Kennel Club in 2004 under judge Lydia Coleman Hutchinson, owner-handled by Richard Lawless.

In 2005, the Mastiff Ch. Southforks Sherman was the first of his breed to rank among the top five Working dogs in the United States. He is shown winning Best in Show at Silver State Kennel Club under judge Judy Doniere, handled by Pamela Reid.

Show each in the first few years after World War II. A few won twice, but only seven different breeds had more than two Best in Show winners during this period. Easily the two leading breeds after World War II were Cocker Spaniels (English, of course), with six different individuals accounting for a total of seventeen Bests in Show—more than twice as many as any other breed—and Wire Fox Terriers, seven of which won Best in Show, none more than once. Three Airedale Terriers won eight Bests, and four Pekingese, three Chow Chows, three Miniature Poodles, and three Scottish Terriers all won a single Best in Show each. The breeds with two Best in Show winners were Smooth Fox Terriers,

An old breed that was fully recognized by the AKC only in 1999, the Havanese has quickly become a popular contender for top honors. Ch. Blanch-O's Tease The Boys is pictured winning at the Shawnee Kennel Club in 2006 under judge Carol Esterkin.

Lakeland Terriers, Pointers, and Whippets. With so few shows, naturally many breeds did not win a single Best in Show during this time period.

Which representatives of the six Groups won Best in Show most often? The stage in those early years was heavily dominated by Terriers and Gundogs; between them, they won 62 percent of the shows—Terriers 33 percent, Gundogs 29 percent. This left little for the rest: 12 percent for the Utility breeds, 10 percent for Hounds, and 8 percent each for the Toy and Working breeds (or 4 percent for Working and 4 percent for Herding breeds, if they are counted separately, although the Herding Group was not introduced until 1984).

Despite the fact that more shows were held during the 2001–2005 period, only three different breeds had more than two Best in Show winners in that time. Wire Fox Terriers were on top with four winners taking a total of six Bests in Show, three Bulldogs won four Bests between them, and three American Cocker Spaniels also won four Bests in Show. Interestingly, not a single English Cocker Spaniel won Best in Show in its native country during the first few years of the new century.

Nine different breeds were represented by two Best in Show winners each. This included the Giant Schnauzer, which through a long line of big wins for one single dog added up to a total of thirteen Bests for the breed—more wins than any other breed. Kerry Blue and Scottish Terriers each had two winners with four Bests in Show between them; two Maltese took three wins, and two Boxers, two Vizsla, two Irish Wolfhounds, two Norfolk Terriers, and two Whippets won once each.

The Belgian Malinois is not among the most common winners at all-breed level, but in 2005, Ch. Broadcreek's Mirabella took nine Best in Show wins and was among the top Herding Dogs in the United States. She is shown taking one of two back-to-back wins during the Hilton Head Island Kennel Club's weekend in South Carolina under judge James J. Ham.

The wins had leveled off considerably among the different Groups compared with those in earlier years, with both Terriers and Gundogs having dropped off a great deal. Most of the winners now came from the Working Group (22 percent), followed by the Toy and Utility Groups (17 percent each), Terriers (16 percent), Hounds (11 percent), Gundogs (9 percent), and the newly formed Pastoral Group (8 percent).

IN THE UNITED STATES

In the United States during the three-year period at the end of World War II in which shows were analyzed, the dominant breeds were Boxers, Cocker Spaniels, and Wire Fox Terriers, in roughly that order. Thirteen Boxers won seventy-seven Bests in Show, and even more Cocker Spaniels (all of the American breed, recently separated from its English cousin), nineteen in all, took home fifty-eight

The Chesapeake Bay Retriever Ch. Chestnut Hills Copper Solid achieved a rare Best in Show victory for his breed at Shawnee Kennel Club in 2002 under judge Sari Brewster Tietjen; the following year, he repeated the win at, appropriately, the Chesapeake Kennel Club in Maryland.

The American Eskimo Dog Ch. Silveroaks Juneau Arnold, the only one of his breed to experience major all-breed winning for several years, took a dozen Bests in Show from 2003 to 2006. He is shown with handler Randy Benns, winning at the Bonneville Basin Kennel Association in Utah under judge Loraine Boutwell.

Bests. The Wire Fox Terrier was going strong, with fourteen winners taking forty-three Bests. English Setters had only six winners but forty wins; Kerry Blue Terriers, by contrast, produced eleven winners with twenty-eight wins. Other breeds with at least five Best in Show winners during this time period were Pointers, Scottish Terriers, Irish Setters, Afghan Hounds, Standard Poodles, Doberman Pinschers, Whippets, and Miniature Poodles.

The distribution of the Best in Show wins between the different Groups was extremely uneven in those days. The Sporting breeds won 39 percent of the time. Terriers won 28 percent of the shows, Working breeds 18 percent (or 19 percent if we include the Herding breeds that were then a part of the Working Group), Hounds just 6 percent, and Non-Sporting and Toy breeds each took only 4 percent of the wins.

During 2003–2005, the number of shows had multiplied more than sevenfold. The Doberman Pinscher produced the most Best in Show winners, twenty-nine in all, followed by twenty-four wins for Standard Poodles and twenty-three winners each for both Boxers and Cocker Spaniels (with the three color varieties combined). However, none of these breeds won as many Bests in Show as the Pekingese, with 245 wins for eight dogs—again due to an exceptionally high number won by a couple of unique campaigners. The other top breeds took between 100 and 180 wins. At least twenty-seven breeds were represented by no fewer than ten Best in Show winners, including German Shepherd Dogs, Pugs, Smooth Fox Terriers, Pomeranians, English Springer Spaniels, Whippets, Newfoundlands, Rottweilers, Siberian Huskies, Australian Shep-

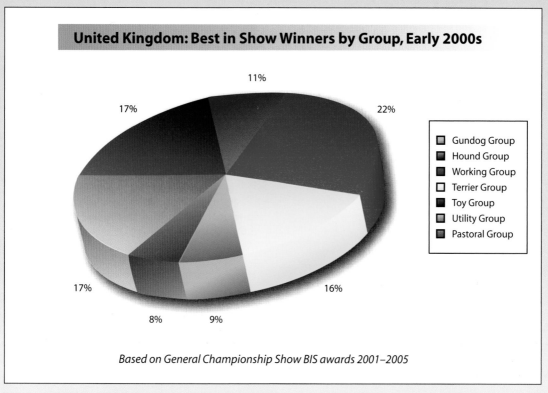

United Kingdom: Best in Show Winners by Group, Early 2000s

11%

17%   22%

Gundog Group
Hound Group
Working Group
Terrier Group
Toy Group
Utility Group
Pastoral Group

17%   16%

8%   9%

Based on General Championship Show BIS awards 2001–2005

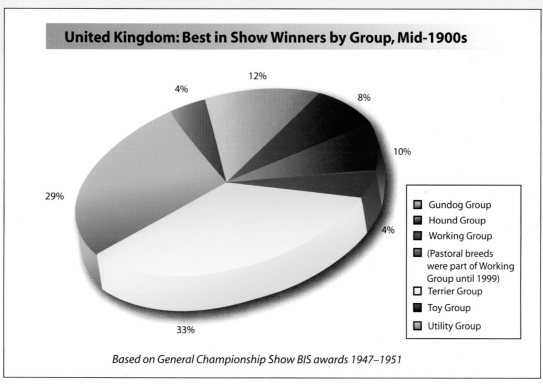

United Kingdom: Best in Show Winners by Group, Mid-1900s

12%

4%   8%

10%

29%

Gundog Group
Hound Group
Working Group
(Pastoral breeds were part of Working Group until 1999)
Terrier Group
Toy Group
Utility Group

4%

33%

Based on General Championship Show BIS awards 1947–1951

herds, Irish Setters, Old English Sheepdogs, Bichon Frisés, Wire Fox Terriers, Golden Retrievers, Basset Hounds, Great Danes, Scottish Terriers, Shetland Sheepdogs, Norwich Terriers, Afghan Hounds, Alaskan Malamutes, Bulldogs, Samoyeds, Lhasa Apsos, and West Highland White Terriers.

If the American Kennel Club was striving for equality between the seven variety Groups, it could hardly have achieved greater success, especially compared with the figures sixty years earlier. The difference between the two Groups that won most (Toys and Working, 18 percent of the total each) and the one that won the least (Non-Sporting, 11 percent) is fairly insignificant. The Hound

The Kuvasz Ch. Glacier Creek's Artic Spirit, one of the few of his breed to win Best in Show in AKC competition, is shown winning at Oakland Kennel Club in Michigan in 2003 with judge Suzanne Dillin.

Group won at 12 percent of the shows, the Herding Group at 13 percent, and the Terrier and Sporting Group each at 14 percent.

The Papillon Ch. Caprice N Flashpt Ghost Buster, a multiple Best in Show winner in 2004 and 2005.

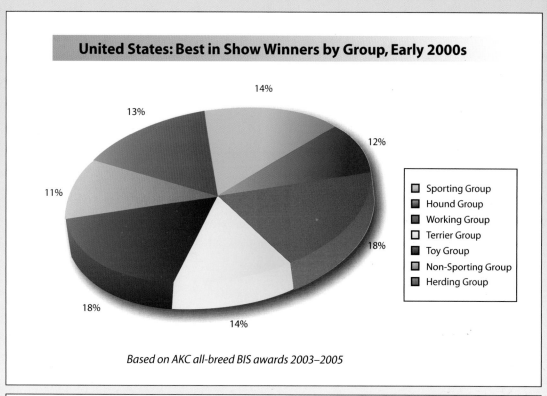

United States: Best in Show Winners by Group, Early 2000s

14%
13%
12%
11%
18%
18%
14%

Legend:
- Sporting Group
- Hound Group
- Working Group
- Terrier Group
- Toy Group
- Non-Sporting Group
- Herding Group

Based on AKC all-breed BIS awards 2003–2005

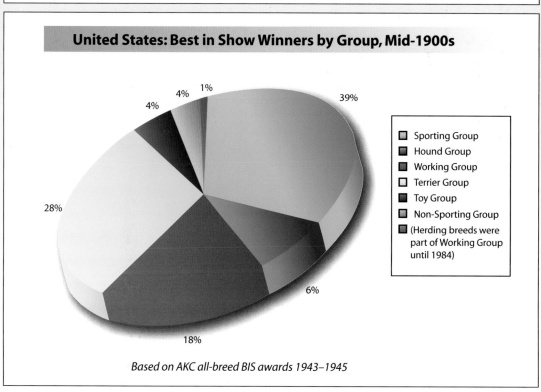

United States: Best in Show Winners by Group, Mid-1900s

1%
4%
4%
39%
28%
6%
18%

Legend:
- Sporting Group
- Hound Group
- Working Group
- Terrier Group
- Toy Group
- Non-Sporting Group
- (Herding breeds were part of Working Group until 1984)

Based on AKC all-breed BIS awards 1943–1945

AKC Sporting Group Highlights

Top Sporting dog of 1985, the Irish Setter Ch. Windwood's Night Hawk, handled by Ken Murphy under judge Arlene Thompson Brown.

The Brittany Ch. Magic Sir-ly You Jest, JH was one of the top Sporting dogs in the country in 1999 and 2000. In 2003, at nearly eight years of age, he made a comeback by winning the Group at Westminster. He was handled by Clint Livingston under Canadian judge Virginia Lyne.

The only Vizsla to win the Sporting Group at Westminster, Ch. Harann's Tulipann, did so under breed specialist judge Dr. Bernard McGivern, Jr., in 1983. The handler was Bobby Barlow.

The Weimaraner Ch. Valmar's Pollyanna, Best in Show at San Gabriel Valley Kennel Club in 1984 under judge Charlotte Clem McGowan. The trophy presenters are Mrs. Thomas F. Powers and Mrs. Ralph Roberts. Pollyanna was among the top Sporting dogs in the annual ratings that year.

The top Sporting dog of 2000, the German Shorthaired Pointer Ch. Khrispat's Megan A Point, with handler Valerie Nunes Atkinson and judge Ralph Del Deo at Somerset Hills Kennel Club in 2000.

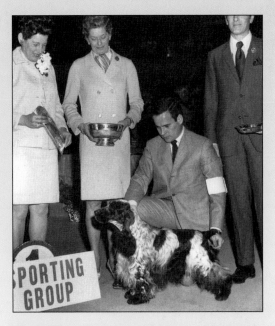

The English Cocker Spaniel Ch. Dunelm Galaxy with handler Richard Bauer and judge Connie Bosold at the International Kennel Club of Chicago 1964. Trophy presenters are Mr. and Mrs. Gordon Pirie.

The only German Wirehaired Pointer ever to place among the Top Ten dogs of all breeds, Ch. Wildefire's Bentley, pictured with handler Jane Myers and judge Dr. Robert Smith in 2000.

The Welsh Springer Spaniel Ch. Rolyart's Still The One, a Best in Show winner in all-breed and specialty competition, shown with judge James Covey at Westminster in 2002.

AKC HOUND GROUP HIGHLIGHTS

The Petit Basset Griffon Vendéen Ch. Celestial CJ's Jolly Fairchild, top Hound in 2006, with judge Patricia Mowbray-Morgan and handler Greg Strong at Asheville Kennel Club in 2006.

The 13-inch Beagle Ch. Kahootz Chase Manhattan, a top Hound for three years, was handled by Mike Kurtzner to Best in Show in 1998 under judge Sandra Goose Allen.

The Basenji Ch. Reveille Re-Up, a top Hound for three years, was handled by Damara Bolté to Best in Show at the Virginia Kennel Club in 1971 under judge Nelson Groh.

The Saluki Ch. Karim Zahab al Bokay, a top Hound for four years, won Best in Show as a veteran at Louisville Kennel Club's 100th anniversary show in 1986. The handler was Eugene Blake, and the judge was Robert Waters, Canada.

The Wire Dachshund Ch. Starbarrack Malachite, Westminster Group winner in 1997. The handler was Robert Fowler, and the judge was Gloria Reese.

The Petit Basset Griffon Vendéen Ch. Afterglow Woody Woodpecker, top Hound in 2005 and also a top winner in England. The handler was Clint Livingston, and the judge was Patricia Gellerman.

AKC Hound Group Highlights

The Miniature Wire Dachshund Ch. Spartan's Sloe Gin Fizz, one of the Top Ten dogs of all breeds in 1976 and 1977. Handler Jerry Rigden is shown with Fizz and judge Tom Stevenson at Savannah Kennel Club in 1978.

The top Hound of 2000, Bloodhound Ch. Ridgerunner Unforgettable, shown with handler Bruce Schultz winning Best in Show at the Kennel Club of Palm Springs in 2001 under judge Wayne Burton from Australia.

The Black and Tan Coonhound Ch. Southchase's Warrior Princess was among the top Hounds in America for three consecutive years in the late 1990s. She is shown winning Best in Show at Huntingdon Valley Kennel Club in 1999, handled by Victor Capone under judge Carol Esterkin.

The only Irish Wolfhound to be top Hound in the United States and place among the Top Ten of all breeds, Ch. Aodh Harp of Eagle, did so in 1984. He is shown winning the Group at Westminster in 1985, handled by his breeder and owner, Sam Ewing, under judge Anna Wanner.

The Basset Hound Ch. Deer Hill's Great Gatsby was handled by Bryan Martin to top Hound and runner-up among all breeds in 1998. They are shown taking one of forty-four Bests in Show won that year alone at Bryn Mawr Kennel Club under judge Richard Bauer.

The Rhodesian Ridgeback Ch. Filmmaker's Never Surrender of FM, rated among the top Hounds for three years in the late 1990s, with handler Frank Murphy and judge Ralph Lemcke at Jupiter-Tequesta Dog Club in April, 1998.

The American Foxhound Ch. Polk's Impressive Sundance, among the top winners in the Hound Group in 1999, is shown winning Best in Show at Steel City Kennel Club that year, handled by Stanley Flowers under judge Roxanne Peterson Berton.

AKC WORKING GROUP HIGHLIGHTS

In 1999, the Working Group at Westminster was judged by Lynette Saltzman. Her winner was the Bernese Mountain Dog Ch. Mentmore's Windy Meadow, handled by Diane Kiester. The trophy presenter was Dr. Charles M. Curry, Jr.

The Samoyed Ch. Tarahill's Everybody Duck, a top Working dog in 1993, with handler Chris Jones.

The Great Dane Club of America's national specialty in 2000 had 478 dogs present and competing. Best of Breed was the veteran dog Ch. Our Danes Fabulous Fabio.

The only St. Bernard ever to place among the Top Ten Dogs of all breeds in America, Ch. Trust's Gentle Ben V Slaton, did so in both 2000 and 2001. He is pictured with handler Joe Wolff winning Best in Show at Harrisburg Kennel Club in 2000 under judge Thomas H. Bradley, III.

Competitions for Best Veteran are seldom held at AKC shows. At Monitowoc County Kennel Club's show in 1999, the Alaskan Malamute Ch. Storm Kloud's Corner The Market won Best Veteran in Show under judge Dr. Robert Indeglia.

The Samoyed Ch. Quicksilver Razz-Ma-Tazz, one of the Top Dogs of all breeds in both 1983 and 1984, is shown winning the Samoyed Club of America national specialty in 1983 under judge Anne Rogers Clark. The handler was Roy Murray.

The Bernese Mountain Dog Ch. Shersan Chang O'Pace V Halidom, one of the top dogs of all breeds in 1986, handled by Bobbi Kinley-Blewitt.

Dorothy Collier awarding Best of Breed at the American Rottweiler Club's national specialty in 1997 to the German import Ch. Champ vom Vilstalerland.

AKC Terrier Group Highlights

The Irish Terrier Ch. Rockledge Mick Michael, one of the top Terriers of the early 1980s, won Best of Breed as a veteran at the Great Western Terrier specialties in 1997. The handler was Woody Wornall, and the judge was Ann Stevenson.

The Best in Show–winning Parson Russell Terrier Ch. Fox Valley Frolic with handler Michael Scott in the Group ring at Westminster in 2001.

The only Soft Coated Wheaten Terrier to win a Group at Westminster, Ch. Andover Song 'N Dance Man, did so in 1989, handled by Sally George under judge William Bergum.

Best in Show at Louisville Kennel Club in 1997 was the Miniature Schnauzer Ch. Sole Bay's Johnar, handled by Maripi Wooldridge. The judge was Betty-Anne Stenmark.

The American Staffordshire Terrier Ch. Fraja EC Gold Standard is shown winning the Breed under judge Elliott Weiss at Westminster in 2001. He also had a successful career in Europe and was one of the Top Dogs in Finland.

Top Terrier of both 1971 and 1972, the Welsh Terrier Ch. Golden Oak Jim Royal is shown with handler Dora Lee Wilson winning a Group at Council Bluffs Kennel Club in 1970 under judge Haskell Schuffman.

AKC Terrier Group Highlights

The Monty-Ayr Bull Terriers produced several Best in Show winners in the 1950s. Ch. Masterpiece of Monty-Ayr is shown winning at Butler County Kennel Club, owner-handled by his breeder, Dr. E. S. Montgomery, under judge William L. Kendrick, all-rounder and Bull Terrier expert.

One of the few Border Terriers to win Best in Show on a consistent basis, Ch. Skyline Spice Girl, ranked among the top Terriers in 1999 and won the top spot of all breeds fourteen times that year. She is shown winning at Oshkosh Kennel Club on May 22 that year under Terrier specialist judge Ric Chashoudian, handled by Ken Murray.

The Welsh Terrier Ch. Copperboot's Wee Blastie is pictured at her first show, winning Best of Breed "from the classes" under judge Derek Rayne at the Great Western Terrier specialties in 1977, handled by Clay Coady. Wee Blastie went on to be one of the top Terrier winners for the following three years.

The Miniature Schnauzer Ch. Blythewood National Acclaim, a top winner at all-breed and specialty shows in the 1980s, handled by owner and breeder Joan Huber. He was also a top sire.

The Irish Terrier Ch. Tralee's Rowdy Red, handled by Robert Fisher to Best in Show at Wall-kill Kennel Club in 1984 under judge Dr. W. Edward McGough. Rowdy was a Top Dog of all breeds that year.

The first Staffordshire Bull Terrier to win Best in Show in America, Ch. Guardstock's Red Atom, is pictured with handler Judith Daniels and judge Ann Stevenson, taking the top award at Tucson Kennel Club in 1983.

The Bedlington Terrier Ch. Willow Wind Tenure, the top Terrier and one of the Top Dogs of all breeds in 2000. "Ten" was handled by Taffe McFadden and is shown winning Best in Show under judge W. Everett Dean, Jr., at the Del Monte Kennel Club in 1999.

AKC Toy Group Highlights

One of the few Brussels Griffons ever to score in the annual Top Ten ratings for all breeds, Ch. Wallin's Charlie Brown was the top Toy of 1983. He is shown with handler Leslie Boyes and judge Tom Stevenson at the Chico Dog Fanciers Association in 1982.

Judge Dorothy Macdonald awards Best in Show at the Del Valle Dog Club of Livermore in 1998 to the Pug Ch. Glorys Fantasy Tugboat Willy, one of the top Toy dog winners for four years. He was handled by Corky Vroom. The trophy presenter was Betty-Anne Stenmark.

The Smooth Chihuahua Ch. ELH's Mighty Lunar of Dartan, a top-winning Toy Dog of 1983, was handled by Michael Diaz to Best in Show at Coos Kennel Club that year. The judge was Glenn Fancy.

The Silky Terrier Ch. Shalee Tawny Mist Royal Silk, one of the top Toy dogs of the late 1990s, winning at Owensboro River City Kennel Club in 1999 under judge Michael Sosne. Royal Silk won Best in Show fifteen times that year and was runner-up to the top Toy spot.

The Italian Greyhound Ch. Westwind's Sweet and Sassy was one of the top Toy dogs of both 1986 and 1987. She is pictured with her handler, Don Rogers, after winning the Italian Greyhound Club of America's national specialty in 1985.

One of the most successful owner-handlers in the early 2000s, Janet York, has handled a series of Cavalier King Charles Spaniels to top spots. She is shown with her Dutch import, Ch. Fredrik van het Lamslag, who was among the top Toy dogs of 2006, winning Best in Show at Southern Maryland Kennel Club in 2006 under judge Glenda Dawkins.

The Japanese Chin Ch. Briarhill Rock and Roll, the first of his breed to win the Group at Westminster in more than a half century, is pictured with handler Scott Sommer and judge Gilbert Kahn after the 1997 win.

AKC Toy Group Highlights

Ch. Moonvale Infatuation, Best of Breed at the American Cavalier King Charles Spaniel Club's specialty 2004 under British specialist judge Molly Coaker.

The English Toy Spaniel Ch. Dreamridge Dear Charles, winner of the Toy Group at Santa Barbara Kennel Club 1980, is shown with handler Tom O'Neal, judge Anne Rogers Clark, and trophy presenter Wendy Streatfield.

The Miniature Pinscher Ch. Jay-Mac's Impossible Dream, the top Toy dog of 1975 and also one of the Top Dogs of all breeds that year. She is pictured with handler Joe Waterman and judge Ann Stevenson, winning at the Colorado Kennel Club in 1974.

Jay-Mac Miniature Pinschers were among the top Toy dogs in America for five years running in the 1970s. Ch. Jay-Mac's Dream Walking was top Toy in 1976 and among the Top Ten of all breeds for both 1976 and 1977. She is shown winning at Laporte Kennel Club in 1976, handled by Bob Condon under judge Kenneth Peterson.

Best in Show at Metro Mile-Hi Kennel Club's Toy Dog show 2004, the Cavalier King Charles Spaniel Ch. Hurleaze Bristol Blue, with handler Clint Livingston and judge Doris Cozart.

The Chinese Crested Ch. Bayshore Cruis'n The Casbar, one of the top Toy dogs for 2002 and 2003, winning at Owenboro's River City Kennel Club in 2003 under judge Ron Menaker, owner-handled by Barbara Cassidy.

The Shih Tzu Ch. Dragonwyck The Great Gatsby was one of the top winners in the Toy Group for three years in the mid-1970s. Gatsby won Best in Show forty times during his years at the top.

The Silky Terrier Ch. Weeblu's Trailblazer of Don El, a top Toy dog 1981 and 1982, at Del Monte Kennel Club with handler Florence Males and judge Michele Billings.

AKC Non-Sporting Group Highlights

Chinese Shar-Pei Ch. Asia's Toon Towne Northern Lights, rated among the top Non-Sporting winners in both 2001 and 2002, is shown with handler Susan Capone winning Best in Show at Penn Ridge KC in 2000 under judge Desmond Murphy.

Tibetan Terrier Ch. Sim-Pa Lea's Razmatazz, a top Non-Sporting dog for three years, at Del Monte Kennel Club 2001, with owner-handler David Murray and judge Virginia Lyne, Canada. The trophy presenter is Dorothy Macdonald.

No Schipperke has yet won Group at Westminster, but Ch. DeLamer's Fire Island Fox placed in the Non-Sporting finale in 2001. The judge was Dr. Robert Indeglia.

The top-winning Non-Sporting dog in 1977 was the Lhasa Apso Ch. Yojimbo Orion, shown with handler John Thyssen and judge Tom Stevenson at the Kennel Club of Beverly Hills that year.

For the first time in forty years, a French Bull-dog was top Non-Sporting dog in 2004. Ch. Bandog's Jump For Joy is shown winning one of her sixteen Bests in Show that year at Central Indiana Kennel Club, handled by Larry Cornelius under judge Kent Delaney.

Chow Chow Ch. Lov-Chows Risen Star was one of the top Non-Sporting winners of the early 1990s and the Westminster Group winner of 1992.

Dalmatian Ch. Tuckaway Winged Foot was among the top Non-Sporting dogs for four years in the 1990s. He is shown winning Best in Show at Santa Clara Valley Kennel Club in 2000, handled by Mike Stone under judge Anne Rogers Clark. "Jack" won the Dalmatian Club of America's national specialty in 1999.

The Bulldog Ch. Cherokee Yancy is pictured winning Best in Show at the Marion Ohio Kennel Club in 1985, handled by owner Cody Sickle under judge Dona Hausman.

AKC HERDING GROUP HIGHLIGHTS

The Bearded Collie Ch. Ha'Penny Moon Shadow, one of the top Herding dogs in 1988, with handler Cliff Steele.

The Belgian Tervuren Ch. Corsair's Beaujangles, one of the top Herding dogs of 1983 and 1984. He is shown winning Best in Show at Monroe Kennel Club in 1983, handled by owner and breeder Steve Sorensen under judge Maxine Beam.

Ch. Raby du Posty Arlequin, one of several Bouviers des Flandres that were imported by Chester F. Collier and successful in the 1960s and 1970s. Raby is shown with handler Roy Holloway winning Best in Show under judge Doris Wear.

The Shetland Sheepdog Ch. Zion's Man About Town won the Herding Group at Westminster in 1997, handled by Linda Guihen under judge Betty Moore.

The first Cardigan Welsh Corgi to score high among the top Herding dogs, Ch. Kingsbury Carbon Copy, did so in both 1994 and 1995. He is shown as a veteran winning Best of Breed at Westminster in 2000 under judge Dorothy Welsh.

The only Rough Collie ever to place among the Top Ten of all breeds, Ch. Fancy Hi Honeybrook However, shown with handler Frank Ashbey and judge Louis Murr. This occurred in 1958.

Most of the numerically small breeds only rarely achieve all-breed success; an exception is the Polish Lowland Sheepdog Ch. Ponwoods Fancy Girl, who won Best in Show at Packerland Kennel Club in 2001, handled by Nancy Martin. The judge was Bernard Schwartz.

Welsh Corgis dominated the Herding Group at Westminster in recent years, with four wins in five years. In 2004, the winner—and one of the Top Ten dogs of all breeds—was Ch. Hum'nbird Kepn Up'pearances, handled by Frank Murphy under judge Lester Mapes.

The Pembroke Welsh Corgi Ch. Fox Meadows Obsession, one of the top Herding dogs for three years in the early 1990s, is shown with handler and co-owner John Wilcox.

The Australian Shepherd Ch. Bayshore's Russian Rhoulette was successful in Canada, the United States, and England, where she won the Group at Crufts in 2003. She is pictured after winning the United States Australian Shepherd Association's Specialty in May 2002, handled by co-owner Leon Goetz. The judge was Houston Clark.

CHAPTER 13

DOG SHOWS AND THE MEDIA

The media play a vitally important role in the dog sport, perhaps more so than in most other activities, and dog periodicals have been an inextricable part of the sport almost as long as there have been dog shows. The forerunners of today's publications began to appear in the late 1800s, and specialized newspapers about dogs have proliferated with increasing frequency in every corner of the world since. The stream of new publications shows no sign of abating, but with the arrival of the Internet, the role of the printed press is gradually changing, focusing less on breaking news and more on information that can be saved and referred to as needed in the future. Film and television showed an interest in purebred dogs as a source of entertainment or social comment early on, and this, too, increased in the late twentieth century.

In 2004, the Westminster Best in Show winner, Newfoundland Ch. Darbydale's All Rise Pouch-Cove, and his handler, Michelle Ostermiller, were guests on the *Late Show with David Letterman.*

THE PERIODICALS

The world's dog press can be divided into fairly distinct categories. In almost every country, the national kennel club will publish an official mouthpiece—the *Kennel Gazette* in the United Kingdom and the *AKC Gazette* in the United States are two outstanding examples. Many of these publications are beautifully produced, informative, and well edited. Some also achieve wide circulation: the Swedish Kennel Club's magazine, *Hundsport*, for example, has a monthly circulation of more than 100,000 copies.

In most cases, however, the official kennel club publication is not able to satisfy the need for debate and critical appraisal of the sport that the dog fancy demands, and this has led to the creation of a large number of independent dog publications. Most of these cover all dog show activities; some focus on only one breed (*Poodle Variety*, the *Rottweiler Quarterly*) or group of breeds (*Just Terriers*, *Sighthound Review*). The publications for general dog owners form a separate category, although some of them may also cover dog shows: in the United States, *Dog Fancy* and *Dog World* are the two with the widest distribution, both with a monthly circulation of, respectively, 250,000 and 50,000 copies.

THE BRITISH WEEKLIES

In England, early canine events were first covered mostly by sporting journals or the general press, but by the 1890s, the dog world was sufficiently established to support specialist publications. Possibly the first one was the *British Fancier*, a weekly newspaper that, in addition to its canine coverage, catered to poultry and pigeon fanciers. In the mid-1890s, the *British*

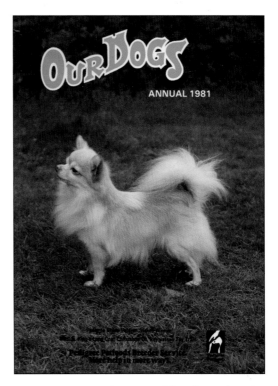

***Our Dogs Annual* cover, 1981, featuring the Long Coat Chihuahua Ch. Raygistaan Toy Train.**

Fancier's editor, Theo Marples, persuaded several fellow canine enthusiasts to form a publishing company capable of producing a weekly newspaper dedicated to the canine world. *Our Dogs*, originally edited by Marples, has continued to serve the canine world since its first appearance on newsstands on January 5, 1896. Marples was an experienced dog fancier and judge. He had officiated at dog shows since 1873 and—in spite of an apparently rocky relationship with Charles Cruft—judged at England's top show several times as well as in the United States, Canada, Russia, South Africa, and reportedly nearly every city in Europe. Marples also wrote several books, notably *Show Dogs: Their Points and Characteristics* and *How to Breed for Prizes and Profit*, the latter of which was published in 1907 and had several later editions.

The interest in purebred dogs soon grew strong enough to support more than one publication, and a second weekly newspaper, *Dog World*, quickly developed into a worthy rival of *Our Dogs*. It was started in 1902 as the *Illustrated Kennel News* and was given its present name by its popular and influential editor, Phyllis Robson, following a change in ownership after World War I. Robson was one of the emerging dog world's first international celebrities, almost as well known in America from her frequent visits as in her own country, and she was instrumental in forging many of the transcontinental friendships that led to such a large number of dogs traveling across the Atlantic. Although Robson was at one point an active Bulldog breeder, her best-known show dog was the black and tan Afghan Hound Ch. Asri-Havid of Ghazni.

Robson was a great admirer of American dog shows, as is obvious from the following quotes attributed to her in Arthur Fredrick Jones's report from the 1935 Morris & Essex Kennel Club show: "Oh, a grand show . . . nothing like it anywhere! That super catalogue . . . so well indexed . . . [is] particularly appealing to the journalist. . . . I wish we had something like it in England. And what good sports you have in America . . . no grousing over the awards during the whole day. Your system of choosing Best in Show is so much more spectacular than England's. . . . people are breathless waiting for the judge's decisions."

Dog World has had a long line of extremely well-respected people at the helm as editors. The brilliant international all-rounder judge Leo Wilson was in charge of editorial policy for many years and bred top-winning Smooth Fox Terriers carrying his own initials (Ch. Lethal Weapon et al.). However, since Robson (who retired from judging when she became editor of *Dog World*), no one has been better known worldwide than Ferelith Somerfield, whose family is steeped in dog show history. The family's kennel name, Oudenarde, was first used by Somerfield's aunts in the 1920s; continued by her mother, Diana Hamilton; and remains a force to be reckoned with in Cairn Terriers. Ferelith Hamilton started at

The legendary Phyllis Robson, editor of *Dog World* in England and frequent visitor to America, with her Afghan Hound Ch. Asri-Havid of Ghazni.

Dog World as a subtrainee editor in 1955 and gradually worked her way up to become editor, a position she held for many years. In 1977, she married Stafford Somerfield, former editor of London's biggest Sunday paper, *News of the World*, and the author of a popular column in *Dog World* as well. Mrs. Somerfield retired as editor but remained chairman of the company. She is one of the most respected judges in the United Kingdom and abroad and has judged Best in Show at Crufts and at most other top shows in the United Kingdom as well as in America, Australia, Scandinavia, and the rest of Europe. Following in Somerfield's shoes cannot have been easy, especially for a young fancier, but Simon Parsons—editor for several years and a second-generation Pembroke Welsh Corgi breeder—has been aided in his editorial duties by an encyclopedic knowledge of practically every facet of the sport in the United Kingdom.

The British dog press is a necessity for anyone who requires weekly information—not just about the British Isles but about world dog affairs in general. Like the British dog shows that they cover, *Our Dogs* and *Dog World* have become considerably more cosmopolitan than they once were. Both big British weekly dog newspapers are filled with news, show reports, special features, and editorials by the dog world's most respected experts to such a degree that these publications do not have an equal anywhere else in the world.

In light of the dominance and success of *Dog World* and *Our Dogs* in the British dog world, glossy all-breed magazines for show fanciers have generally fared less well in the United Kingdom. *Dog World* especially provides many color supplements and special

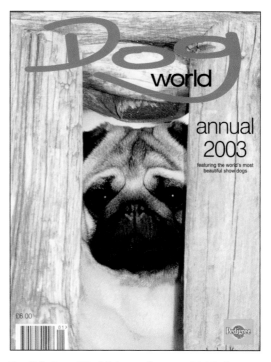

English *Dog World Annual* cover, 2003, featuring the Pug Ch. Broughcastl Bugatti, one of the top-winning Toy dogs in America.

feature editions. Both major weeklies also publish thick, colorful Christmas annuals—with year-end summaries, world reports, and a large number of glossy kennel advertisements—that serve as excellent reference libraries from past years.

THE GROWTH OF THE AMERICAN DOG PRESS

That the American dog press would eventually develop along very different lines from that in the United Kingdom was not apparent from the start. The longest-lasting American publication devoted exclusively to show dogs, *Kennel Review*, was founded in 1898, only two years after *Our Dogs* in England, but would not hit its stride for another few decades. Long published in Kansas City, Missouri, by its founder, Dorothy

Buttles (later to become Mrs. Bert Heath), *Kennel Review* had already absorbed some other early publications by the 1920s, such as *The Collie* and *Dogology,* but remained primarily a regional publication. In the early years, *Kennel Review* had to compete for the fancy's attention with other periodicals, such as *Dogdom* and *Field and Fancy.*

In 1935, *Dogdom* and *Field and Fancy* were incorporated with what had previously been an illustrated weekly named *Popular Dogs,* which emerged as the leading monthly national kennel journal of the 1940s and 1950s. Under the dynamic leadership of a series of female editors—Josephine Z. Rine, Mary Scott, Alice Wagner, and Joan McDonald Brearley—*Popular Dogs* became the first publication anywhere to start rating the year's top dogs in order of merit. This was initially done in the late 1930s on a fairly casual basis, based simply on who had won the most Bests in Show during the year. The intricate annual ratings system that included detailed exact numbers of defeated competitors did not appear until 1966. *Popular Dogs* statistician Irene Phillips Khatoonian Schlintz worked out the retroactive point scores to 1956, published in 1967 as *Great Show Dogs of America.*

Kennel Review

By the 1960s, as the sport started to grow exponentially, the focus shifted increasingly to the West Coast, where *Kennel Review* had already been relocated in the 1930s by Bert Heath, following the death of his wife. The

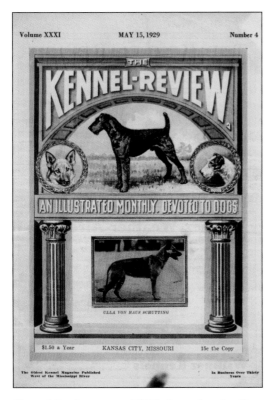

Kennel Review **cover, 1929, featuring the German Shepherd Dog Ulla von Haus Schütting.**

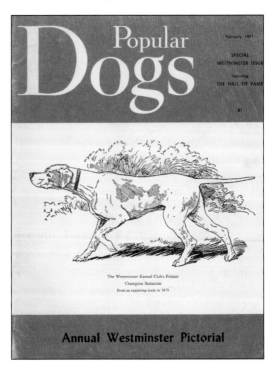

Popular Dogs **cover, 1971, showing an illustration of the Pointer Ch. Sensation, a dog that was owned by Westminster Kennel Club in the late 1800s.**

small, rather drab magazine from early in the century had received a face-lift and was now difficult to recognize, having gotten the full "California treatment" of larger size, glossier paper, and many more illustrations. In 1961, Bert Heath died, and Francis X. Holdenreid assumed ownership until 1964, when Richard G. Beauchamp, who would remain closely identified with the magazine for more than a quarter century, purchased it. Under Beauchamp's expert guidance, *Kennel Review* broke new ground and essentially invented the modern American dog magazine, going from regional to national and becoming a force to be reckoned with as an increasingly stylish monthly bible of the show dog fancy. Beauchamp, who then lived in Hollywood, California, had a history in real show business, as was evident by his approach to the magazine. With the now obligatory monthly ratings already appearing in *Popular Dogs*, Beauchamp provided his own twist on the concept, with the result that the same dog's score might differ somewhat from one publication to another. On at least one famous occasion, in 1969, there were not one but two winners of the Top Dog award, the identity of the Top Dog dependent on which publication you consulted. The *Popular Dogs* winner was the Standard Poodle Ch. De Russy Lollypop, shown by Frank Sabella; *Kennel Review*'s winner was the Boxer Ch. Arriba's Prima Donna, handled by Jane Forsyth. Their year-end scores were so close that the winner depended on whether one counted points won at shows actually held during the calendar year or at shows whose results were published during the calendar year.

With the death of its publisher, George F. Foley (of the Foley Dog Show Organiza-

Richard G. Beauchamp, publisher of the hugely influential and innovative *Kennel Review* magazine from 1964 to 1992. Beauchamp was also one of the creators of the modern Bichon Frisé and is an AKC multigroup judge.

tion), in June 1970, *Popular Dogs* gradually lost ground to *Kennel Review*, changed ownership, and eventually ceased publication.

Kennel Review's prestige was such that it single-handedly succeeded in organizing the annual *Kennel Review* Awards, based on Beauchamp's experiences of the motion picture industry's Academy Awards. Instead of Oscars, the awards were named Winkies, and each year, during a gala ceremony held either in Los Angeles or some other suitable location, the best of the sport in several different categories—best judge, best show,

Kennel Review cover, May 1960. The Smooth Dachshund Ch. White Gables Ristocrat was one of the top Hounds in 1961 and 1962, owned by Albert and Ramona Van Court, later among the most respected judges in America.

The Great Dane Ch. Hansi of Garricrest, one of the first West Coast dogs to win enough Bests in Show to make him one of America's top winners in the early 1940s. He is shown on the cover of *Kennel Review* magazine's January 1941 issue.

best professional handler, best owner-handler—were honored by their peers. The nominees were announced in advance, the dog fancy voted by ballot, and the name of the winner was kept a secret until its announcement during the evening of the event, Oscar style. The awards were initiated in the 1960s and remained a highlight of the dog show years, with some interruptions, into the late 1980s. In the early twenty-first century, with Beauchamp's assistance, the Winkies have been successfully reintroduced by the monthly *Dogs in Review* magazine in an awards ceremony prior to the Westminster dog show in New York each February. This event also incorporates the

old Quaker Oats awards to the top winners in each group during the previous year—now known as the Show Dogs of the Year awards.

In addition to the awards, *Kennel Review* hosted a glamorous Tournament of Champions contest, a gala event to which the top dogs in the country were invited and at which they competed under a select committee of experienced but not necessarily AKC-approved judges. The tournament was among the first of its kind, and although it is no longer held, it spawned latter-day descendants in many other countries. It was the first major all-breed dog event in the United States that was not sanctioned by the AKC, although many of the club's officers attended as guests and some participated as judges.

One of the most far-reaching efforts that *Kennel Review* pioneered was the use of imaginative advertising for show dogs. The urge to brag about one's dog (and, by extension, oneself) is a fundamental one, and dog publications have been used for this purpose since the very beginning: some of the claims from the early 1900s are, in fact, far more outrageous than what is seen today. (Modern ads seem positively tame compared with such old-time claims as "The Most Perfect Fox Terrier Ever Exhibited," "The Greatest Bulldog Ever Brought to America," and "Championship Guaranteed!") Prior to Beauchamp's time, however, the promotion almost inevitably consisted of just a plain photo and some text. With imaginative ideas, striking layouts, and catchy headlines, *Kennel Review* changed the look of the sport forever. The dog fancy responded with enthusiasm, and the number of pages skyrocketed: the monthly issues often numbered more than 300 pages, and the year-end annual issues on occasion encompassed some 800 pages in the 1970s and 1980s.

Success of this kind takes a toll on its creator, and the *Kennel Review* era ended in 1992: the last issue was published in July of that year. Much missed, *Kennel Review* inspired countless young dog lovers both in America and abroad with enthusiasm for the sport. It occupies a unique niche in American dog show history.

One of the reasons for *Kennel Review*'s success was that Beauchamp, more than most American dog-magazine publishers, has a solid background in dogs. His initial

Cover of *Kennel Review*'s 800-page seventy-fifth anniversary issue in December, 1973. The Bichon Frisé had been approved for full AKC recognition that year, and the cover dog, Ch. Chaminade Syncopation, was its first Best in Show winner. "Snidely Whiplash," as he was called, was among the top Non-Sporting dogs in both 1973 and 1974.

interest lay primarily in Cocker Spaniels, but he was also instrumental in spearheading the dog world's acceptance of the Bichon Frisé as a new breed in the 1970s. With nearly 100 champions to his Beau Monde kennel's credit, Beauchamp is now a multigroup judge both at AKC shows and abroad. In other countries, a dog magazine publisher can also be an approved judge. In the United States, the AKC for many years has considered these two occupations to be mutually exclusive, as the publisher would presumably derive much of his or her income from advertising paid for by the exhibitors.

Modern American Publications

The success and eventual demise of *Kennel Review* inspired the birth of a number of other dog show publications, many of which had only short life spans. The newspaper format, which had been so successful in the United Kingdom, was tried first by *Canine Chronicle* in the 1970s, initially published by Ric Routledge as a weekly but later reformatted as a glossy monthly and now published by Tom Grabe in Ocala, Florida. Its main competitor, *Showsight*, was started by Duane Doll and Joel McGinnis in the early 1990s, also in Florida. Both publications feature hundreds of beautiful pages of color advertising for current dog show winners, articles by well-known regular contributors, and—

most important—many pages of current statistics: the top dogs of all breeds, of each of the seven groups, and the top ten winners in each breed, based on both all-breed and individual breed competition.

The newspaper format is represented by the widely read and extremely influential *Dog News*, a large-format New York weekly that has been published since the mid-1980s. The driving force behind this publication since its inception has been the partnership of Matt Stander and Eugene Zaphiris, with the latter as editor. Both have a long background in publishing and in dogs, with experience primarily in Bloodhounds and Skye Terriers—including a 1996 Westminster Group win in Skyes through the Finnish import Ch. Finnsky Oliver.

A 2007 cover of *Canine Chronicle*, showing handler Pam Lambie with the Hawaii-born Rhodesian Ridgeback Ch. Pupukearidge Ikaika O Spring Valley, an all-breed and specialty Best in Show winner.

***Showsight* cover from 2005, featuring handler Tammie Wilcox with the Japan-born Papillon Ch. Queen Bless JP Royal Silk and the Cavalier King Charles Spaniel Ch. Courtlore Slammin Sammy.**

Advertising: A Way of Life

One feature all American dog show publications share is a high reliance on advertising. Compared with the British weeklies, for instance, the editorial content in the American publications is slight, and the percentage of display advertising exponentially greater. The British weeklies depend on a large number of paid subscriptions for their income (according to reliable estimates, around 30,000 dog fanciers pay to have *Dog World* or *Our Dogs* delivered to their homes every week), whereas most of the American publications are given away free. At almost every dog show in America, boxes of magazines are strategically placed so that visitors and (especially) exhibitors can take a free copy—

Cover of the weekly *Dog News* in 2005, showing the Dalmatian Ch. Merry Go Round Mach Ten, the top Non-Sporting dog of 2006.

obviously designed to promote further advertising. One magazine proudly claims to distribute 15,000 free copies every month. Paid subscriptions are not a priority, and the mailing lists consist mainly of AKC judges, all of whom are given complimentary subscriptions.

Because the exhibitors' desire to spend money on seeing their dogs in print appears almost inexhaustible, the equation still works to the publishers' economic advantage. According to a 2006 estimate, a total of more than a thousand pages of paid dog show advertising are published in the all-breed periodicals combined in an average month. In a sense, most American dog show publications are more advertising catalogs than traditional news magazines.

In 1996, the author—after contributing articles to many of the aforementioned periodicals—started a slightly different type of show dog publication in partnership with Paul Lepiane, who had already published successful breed magazines for many years. When the first issue of *Dogs in Review* appeared in January 1997, its nonglamorous newspaper format, serious editorial content, and relatively low percentage of advertising pages made it distinctly different from other American dog show publications. However, in spite of enthusiastic support from a rather small but influential group of readers (primarily judges, senior club officials, and longtime breeders and exhibitors), it became clear that to reach as many fanciers as possible, a show dog publication in America needs both heft and color. The magazine was adjusted accordingly, and since 2000, *Dogs in Review* has been presented in approximately the same format as the other monthly magazines. The content, however, remains different

Dogs in Review, cover, July 2006, featuring the top Whippet Ch. Brushwood's Moxi of Endeavor.

insofar as the many pages of show statistics, which are a staple of the other magazines, are replaced by editorial features. In 2003, *Dogs in Review* was sold to BowTie, Inc., but the author has remained, first as editor and later as editor at large, with Allan Reznik (earlier of *Dogs in Canada*, currently also editor of the American *Dog World* and *Dog Fancy*) as editor in chief and Christi McDonald as editor. Over the years, many of the best-known names in the dog world have contributed to the publication's content, including Ferelith Somerfield, Anne Rogers Clark, Richard G. Beauchamp, and hundreds of other judges and specialists.

Australian Dog Press

One of the best dog publications anywhere in recent decades, *National Dog*, was produced in Australia for many years by British immigrant Frances Sefton, an experienced journalist, international judge, and breeder of the famous Cheska Lhasa Apsos. Started as a newspaper in the 1970s, it followed the same route as many other publications and eventually evolved into a glossy monthly. Following Sefton's death in the 1990s, *National Dog* merged with another Australian dog periodical, *The Ring Leader*. It is now published as a large-format, monthly color tabloid by Wendye and Stuart Slatyer, owners of the world-famous Calahorra Afghan Hound kennels outside Sydney. Most countries outside England and the United States, however, do not have a sufficiently large (or sufficiently well-funded) group of dog fanciers to support independent dog show periodicals beyond those published by their respective kennel clubs.

Breed Periodicals

The vast array of dog publications is further enlarged by a high number of specialized breed periodicals. Currently, they are primarily an American specialty, but it was not always so. Certainly *The Fox Terrier Chronicle*, whose office address was at 77 Fleet Street in London, was already doing well in 1897 and must have been one of the first publications ever to focus on just one breed. There are few British single-breed magazines today; in recent decades, the tradition centers primarily on yearbooks, produced by various breed clubs, that sum up the season's show wins and other activities. The best of these books are professionally produced and provide an invaluable, lasting source of reference for serious fanciers. In America, by contrast, there is at least one periodical for almost every breed; some are published by breed clubs, others independently. There is a great deal of variation in format, size, and

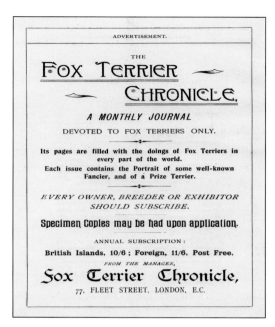

Ad for the *Fox Terrier Chronicle* in 1897—most likely the world's first breed magazine.

frequency as well as in the degree of professionalism displayed: these range from glossy color magazines to newsletters consisting of photocopied pages stapled together. With so many fanciers spread out so thinly over such a vast area as the United States, these various publications serve an important function of connecting the various breed fanciers and affording them the opportunity to communicate on a regular basis. Many clubs in other countries publish similar breed-specific newsletters or magazines.

THE MAINSTREAM PRESS

Mainstream publications seldom cover dog shows other than Westminster and Crufts. A notable exception was provided for many years by the *New York Times*, which published serious and informed regular dog show reports by "the dean of canine journalism," Walter Fletcher, whose working career lasted from 1927 to his retirement in 1976 and

beyond. Fletcher continued to report from Westminster for both *Dog World* and the *New York Times* through 1995. Another name equally revered by dog writers is that of Maxwell Riddle, a founding member of the Dog Writers Association of America (DWAA) in 1935 and later president of that organization. Riddle was an international judge and kennel club officer, wrote about dogs for the *Cleveland Plain Dealer* for thirty years, and penned a monthly column for American *Dog World* for over fifty years. The DWAA's most coveted annual award for journalists, the Maxwell, was named after Riddle. A rival organization to DWAA, the Alliance of Purebred Dog Writers, was started in the early 2000s, "dedicated to excellence in writing about purebred dogs and issues of interest to owners, breeders, and others in the fancy."

MEMORABLE COVER DOGS

In spite of the generally cavalier treatment of dog shows, it was not unknown for major national publications to feature famous show dogs, although more as cover eye candy than anything else. The Doberman Pinscher that won Westminster in 1939, Ch. Ferry v. Rauhfelsen of Giralda, was on the cover of *Newsweek* two weeks after the show. The Afghan Hound's exotic look long made it a favorite of cover photographers. In the 1940s, both *Life* and the *Saturday Evening Post* featured Marion Florsheim's glamorous top winner Ch. Rudiki of Prides Hill on their covers, and in March 1956, the dual Westminster Group–winning Ch. Taejon of Crown Crest adorned the cover of *Sports Illustrated*. Only a few months later, the 1955 Westminster winner, the Bulldog Ch. Kippax Fearnought, was also given that honor by the same publication.

LOST DOG PUBLIC FASCINATION

Whippet Ch. Bohem C'est la Vie (known to the public as Vivi), beloved show dog turned urban legend, is shown at Westminster 2006 with handler Paul Lepiane less than twenty-four hours prior to her disappearance at Kennedy Airport.

A vivid illustration of the general public's fascination, even obsession, with show dogs was provided as an aftermath to Westminster in 2006. The day after the show, one of the contestants, a Whippet that had flown in from California to compete at Madison Square Garden, was lost at JFK Airport in New York. Exactly what happened was never made clear: the dog's owner—Olympic equestrienne Jil Walton of Los Angeles—checked in her dog "Vivi" (alias Ch. Bohem C'est la Vie) as usual, but somewhere between check-in and loading, Vivi got out of her crate and was pursued down the runway by airport security vehicles before escaping through a barbed wire fence.

The media coverage that followed was unprecedented and without much question intensified by the Westminster connection, perhaps also by the fact that Vivi was a well-known Best in Show winner of a fragile-looking breed, seemingly not likely to fend successfully for itself in New York winter and traffic. Newspapers worldwide, including the *New York Times* and *Los Angeles Times*, printed front-page, illustrated stories; *People* magazine ran not one but two full-page articles several months apart; and practically all the major TV stations covered the story with interviews of the humans involved and clips of Vivi in the ring at Westminster.

The fact that Vivi was sighted many times for several months, allowing herself to be fed and even petted but never caught, kept the public's interest alive. The search efforts included hordes of volunteers, psychics, teams of search dogs, Port Authority officials in wetsuits searching the surrounding marshlands, helicopters, night-vision cameras, a hotline phone number, a $5,000 reward, and more than 50,000 Lost Dog posters pasted on practically every post in Queens and surrounding boroughs. In spite of intense, more than year-long efforts from a team of dedicated volunteers, Vivi was never found.

Many months after her disappearance, the runaway Whippet entered what amounts to New York near-mythology: on November. 24, 2006, CBS News headlined an article about Vivi, "Wayward Whippet Becomes Urban Legend."

Part of the problem was that Vivi, contrary to general perception and surface appearance, was a hardy dog, used to running miles and supporting herself hunting rabbits on a farm. As Vivi's co-owner and handler Paul Lepiane said in an ESPN interview, "If she had been a couch potato, maybe she would have gone up to the first person and begged to be taken home and given some food." As Vivi's breeder, this book's author experienced the entire rescue effort at close quarters.

Although the amount of time and money spent on the search of a single dog was considered excessive by many, one positive aftermath of the Vivi hunt was the fact that the volunteers in the process of looking for her found and rehomed more than sixty dogs and cats. As Lepiane said, "We could do a lot worse than have that be Vivi's legacy."

SHIPPING SHOW DOGS

There are no figures to show how many dogs travel by air in pursuit of show ring success. The number attending dog shows overseas is probably still limited to fewer than a thousand flights per year—consisting mostly of adventurous American fanciers seeking victory on foreign shores, plus a few European or South American exhibitors bringing their dogs to America. Quarantine restrictions make it difficult for dog show fanciers in Great Britain and the Southern Hemisphere to bring their dogs to other countries, and almost regardless of where you live in Europe, dog show destinations are usually accessible by driving.

However, in the United States, it became increasingly common in the 1990s and early 2000s for handlers to fly their top dogs to shows. The long distance effectively prohibits most West Coast fanciers from driving to New York for Westminster, and the ever-increasing number of shows around the country tempts a handler in pursuit of ratings success to pick the most suitable events for the dog almost regardless of location, adding thousands of miles on his or her Frequent Flyer account.

Generally, flying dogs is no less safe than any other form of transportation, but it can be a nerve-wracking experience for the owner, if not the dog. A dog that has developed a fear of flying should obviously not be subjected to such an ordeal, but most show dogs are experienced travelers and settle into their crates without any problems. It is left to the human in charge to deal with the airline, paperwork, crate securing, flight restrictions (primarily maximum or minimum airport temperatures), and, of course, the Transportation Security Administration, which can remove a dog from its crate for a checkup at any time, without the owner being present, a scenario that frightens any concerned dog owner.

The fact that so few serious incidents occur—Vivi getting out of her crate in 2006, the famous Pug Ch. Dhandy's Favorite Woodchuck asphyxiated in his crate in 1982—is proof that flying a dog is not generally an unsafe procedure. The fact that incidents occur at all will always have dog owners worried until their dogs arrive at their destinations, tails wagging and wondering what the fuss was about.

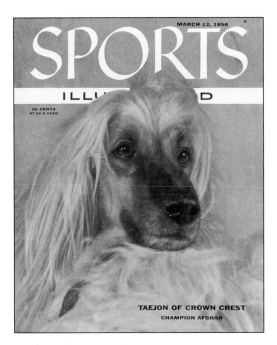

The top-winning Afghan Hound Ch. Taejon of Crown Crest on the cover of *Sports Illustrated* in March 1956.

Cover of *The New Yorker* magazine, before Westminster in 1998.

WESTMINSTER IN *LIFE*

One of the most extensive show dog features published in a major mainstream magazine appeared in *Life* on February 7, 1964. The magazine was then at the peak of its fame as America's leading weekly illustrated news publication, and the eight-page spread, with eye-catching color photographs of ten top contenders at the Westminster Kennel Club show, which would start three days later, titillated the public's interest to an unprecedented degree. The photographer, Patricia Hunt, wrote that the hardest part was to "choose from all the show dogs of America the ones that . . . were not only great enough but also had the personality to make wonderful pictures." The featured dogs became America's canine sweethearts for the time: the Chow Chow Ch. Ah Sid's The Dilettante, the Skye Terrier Ch. Jacinthe de Ricelaine, the Great Dane Ch. Daneridge Caliban, the Brussels Griffon Ch. Barmere's Mighty Man, the German Shorthaired Pointer Ch. Gretchenhof Moonshine, the Boxer Ch. Treceder's Painted Lady (Top Dog of all breeds in 1963), the French Bulldog Ch. Ralanda Ami Francine, the Old English Sheepdog Ch. Fezziwig Ceiling Zero, the Miniature Poodle Ch. Tedwin's Top Billing (Top Dog of 1962), and the Whippet Ch. Courtenay Fleetfoot of Pennyworth. Four days later, the last mentioned won Best in Show at the Garden, went on to become Top Dog of 1964, and was also featured in a two-page follow-up story in *Life* on February 21, showing him on the way to his big win and resting with his trophies afterward.

Later in the twentieth century, show dogs did not make front page news very often. *Life* magazine disappeared from the

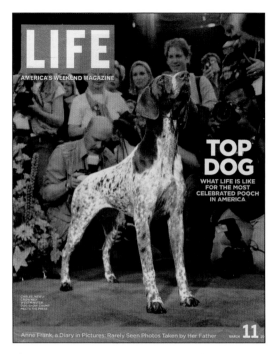

The 2005 Westminster winner, the German Shorthaired Pointer Ch. Kan-Point's VJK Autumn Roses, graced the cover of *Life* the month after her win and was also the subject of a four-page story in the magazine.

newsstands for a few years but reappeared as a weekend supplement to local newspapers nationwide in the early 2000s. Complete with its famous logo, *Life* turned its attention to a Westminster winner again in 2005. The March 11 issue that year featured the German Shorthaired Pointer Ch. Kan-Point's VJK Autumn Roses ("Carlee") on the cover, with a four-page feature inside, outlining the twenty-four frenzied hours after the Best in Show win. Cameramen and reporters followed Carlee and handler Michelle Ostermiller to numerous TV interviews at CNN (where a staffer remarked that Carlee's entourage "is bigger than Jennifer Aniston's"), on *Good Morning America, Fox & Friends,* CBS's *The Early Show,* the *Today* show with Katie Couric, *The Tony*

Danza Show, and two hours of TV interviews via satellite at the Hotel Pennsylvania, unofficial headquarters of the dog show crowd during Westminster. Carlee was scheduled for a guest spot on *Live with Regis and Kelly* as well but just couldn't make it.

THE PHOTOGRAPHERS

The art and business of taking dog photographs goes back almost as far as the history of dog shows. The oldest, and most famous, name in dog photography worldwide, Thomas Fall, started his professional career in London in 1875, initially concentrating on family portraits, especially children. Toward the end of the century, he increasingly turned to animals, dogs in particular. Among his clients were the royal family: Fall's portraits of royalty and their pets gave both his career and the hobby of purebred dogs a boost.

Fall died in 1900, but his name has lived on into modern days first through Edward Hitchings Parker and later through Barbara Bourn Burrows, who started as Parker's assistant in 1927 and continued to operate under the Thomas Fall business name until her retirement in 1990. Almost all the top dogs from the legendary kennels in Great Britain for the better part of the twentieth century had their portraits taken by Mrs. Burrows. Most were shot in black and white, some later ones were in color, and some were painstakingly hand-colored portraits. All were adorned with the famous Thomas Fall signature. Simon Parson wrote in English *Dog World* that "If necessary and so desired, imperfections in the photo would be removed; Barbara was known to have quite a collection of Bull Terrier tails, for example, the most suitable of which she would add on subtly if the dog wasn't too keen to cooperate. Sometimes one would be allowed to look through the incomparable Fall archive, and it was fascinating to see the other, possibly less flattering, pictures taken of great dogs in the same session as that most frequently reproduced."

In America, the first great photographer of show dogs was Rudolf Tauskey, a German immigrant whose incomparably glamorous portraits of the top-winning East Coast dogs from primarily the 1940s up to the 1960s also often owed something to art. On occasion, it was said, Mr. Tauskey would make considerable improvements to the original subject: his knowledge of anatomy and the different breed specific traits was vast. The effect was undeniably striking, but sometimes a latter-day fancier is hard-pressed to know just what the top winners of the past really looked like. Tauskey's counterpart on the West Coast was the legendary Joan Ludwig, who first started going to dog shows in the 1930s but really got her start as a photographer after the war and continued to take incomparably beautiful—

The great dog show photographer Joan Ludwig was honored with an exhibition of her work at the Santa Barbara Kennel Club in 1988. Here she is awarded All-time Best in Show by Tom Stevenson, himself a Hall of Fame inductee.

and usually unretouched—portraits of the top show dogs almost up to her death in 2004. The controversy about retouched show dog photographs is certainly nothing new: as early as in 1952, a kennel advertisement in *Kennel Review* announces, probably facetiously, that the owner is a member of the "Breeders Association for Unretouched Dog Photography"!

Dog show photography, especially in the United States, has become big business. All AKC shows have official photographers on the grounds whose job it is to record each win at the exhibitor's request. The traditional subject matter includes not only the dog but also the handler, the judge (with ribbon in hand), and possibly—for an important win—one or more trophy presenters and club officials. From a pictorial point of view, dog shows must be among the best-documented events of any kind, with several hundred official win photos taken at even a moderate-size event. The fact that almost none of the official dog show photographs is retouched means that the visual record for posterity, for better or worse, is usually an honest rendition of what the judge saw that day. For this reason, as much as for anything else, the best American dog show photographers—the Ashbey and Booth signatures are among the longest established and most respected—have made invaluable contributions to the sport.

In addition to the bread-and-butter win photography, dog shows are also a natural environment for more or less candid ringside snapshots and posed portraits. These pictures are taken by what is usually a separate group of photographers, none more famous than Gay Glazbrook, whose groundbreaking work regularly adorns advertisements for the top winners in the

Before (below) and after (left): the art of retouching in the age before computers is graphically illustrated by this Poodle photograph, prepared for publication in the 1950s. The dog is the same, but few aspects of the conformation were left untouched; the handler was eliminated and a new background added.

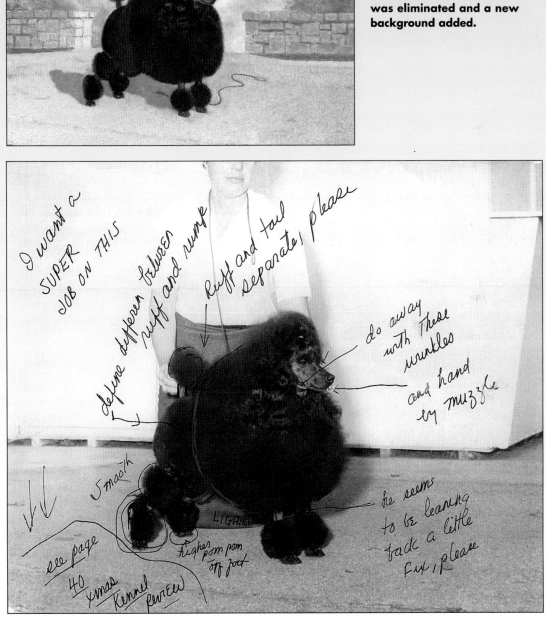

Joan Ludwig seldom retouched her photographs. But here, the original portrait (left) of this Italian Greyhound in California, Ch. Queen's Alfa vom Bayerischen Meer, has been given a more suitable background (below), and the dog's neck, tail, and topline have been lightly airbrushed. Alfa was the top Italian Greyhound in the United States in 1960.

The weather can be the photographer's best friend (left) and worst enemy (below). Most of Joan Ludwig's classic photographs were taken outside in the California sun, as in this shot of Virginia Withington and her top Afghan Hound in the 1960s, Ch. Pandora of Stormhill.

This is quite a different scene. Even on a rainy day, the show must go on: the judge is Bert Shoendorf.

American dog press. There is no pretense that these images are unretouched: the object is not so much realism as art.

THE IMPACT OF FILM AND TELEVISION

In the 1930s, show dogs received a burst of media attention from a different source. According to William Stifel's *The Dog Show: 125 Years of Westminster*, motion-picture cameras made a first appearance at Westminster in 1921, and newsreel coverage began in the 1930s. That coverage appeared in the short film reels that were for many years shown before the main features in movie theaters. They usually included fairly light news of the sort that would today be shown on television, and both Westminster and the AKC's annual awards to the top American-bred dogs were popular subjects.

In the late 1940s, the emerging television industry began taking over the news coverage, and it is through TV that dog shows have received their widest coverage. Even at that time, it was the Westminster Kennel Club dog show that was the focus of attention. "Television promises to do more for the pure-bred dog in one year than all of the words written in a lifetime!" wrote Alice Wagner, prophetically and with only slight exaggeration, in *Popular Dogs* in 1949, while around the same time, Arthur Frederick Jones of the *American Kennel Gazette* was impressed that the event could be "enjoyed by television set owners as far away as the Middle West," predicting correctly that the "cable" would reach all the way to the Pacific Coast in the future. Hayes Blake Hoyt of Blakeen Poodle fame was the expert commentator in those early years, a role later taken over by James Edward Clark and his

Mass media took an immediate interest in dog show winners: Merv Griffin interviewed Peter Green on his TV show after Green's Westminster win in 1968 with the Lakeland Terrier Ch. Stingray of Derryabah.

wife, Anne Rogers Clark, for twenty years in the 1970s and 1980s.

DOG SHOW COVERAGE IN THE MODERN MEDIA

It was in the early 1990s that the annual TV coverage of Westminster started to grow. Much of the credit for this development goes to Westminster Kennel Club's then show chairman and later president Chester F. Collier, a longtime network television producer and executive with seven Emmy Awards to his credit. With his mass-media background and expertise, Collier was able to oversee the entire production and help create a unique, successful live television event. Collier's solid background in dogs, as both a multigroup judge and successful earlier exhibitor of Bouviers des Flandres, must have helped also. Since then, coverage has proliferated as local TV stations discovered that dog shows can provide entertaining footage at a comparatively low cost. Several regularly featured shows provide elaborate and professional reports, including the Crufts programs, which are shown in both the United Kingdom and the United States, hosted by dog experts Wayne Cavanaugh from America and Frank Kane and Jessica Holm from the United Kingdom, and co-hosted by Peter Purves of the BBC TV show *Blue Peter* fame and Leanza Cornett of *Entertainment Weekly* from the United States. The TV coverage of the AKC National Championship appears on the Animal Planet cable network, with commentator Ron Reagan, Jr. (son of the late president), as one of the well-informed hosts.

No other dog show programs, however, are as in-depth or as well produced as the live annual Westminster broadcast, which attracts between 3 million and 4 million viewers on the USA cable network each year. Most of the TV coverage is focused on the Group and Best in Show judging, but with the introduction of a camera in every breed ring in 2005, it was possible for Internet viewers anywhere in the world to access the judging of every breed on their computer screen within a couple of hours of the completion of breed judging. Predictably, this innovation proved hugely popular, with 1.5 million streams from 140 countries requested the first year, even more the next. The live TV coverage is spiced up by added human-interest (and canine-interest)

The face of Westminster Kennel Club: television announcer David Frei. Frei has a solid background in dogs and is an AKC licensed judge.

stories about some of the major stars, which are produced in advance. It all adds up to three hours of viewing each day for two days in a row, covering virtually the entire judging of the finals.

In a masterstroke of casting, in 1990 the producers assigned one of the host spots to David Frei, an AKC judge with a solid background in sports, media, and dogs who has since become the TV face of Westminster. In contrast to Frei and his insider dog knowledge, a commentator without special dog knowledge was given the role of asking the questions the general public would want answered; the most successful of these was Joe Garagiola, a former Major League catcher and veteran sports announcer for NBC. With Frei acting as the straight man, Garagiola was free to act the part of a lovable ignoramus with whom the audience could identify without risk of alienating hard-core dog fanciers in the TV audience. Watching a sporting event on television is never as exciting as experiencing it live, but the Westminster TV coverage comes close.

Dog shows figure in regular TV entertainment only on rare occasions, but at least one of them was memorable. Anyone who watched Academy Award–winning actress Glenn Close's parody of a pompous dog show judge on *Saturday Night Live* will never feel quite the same way when watching certain judges in action again. Close often attends Westminster as a spectator and has a great-aunt, Mrs. Augustus Riggs IV, who judged Best in Show at Westminster in 1973. Widely publicized but less entertaining, according to both reviews and most dog fanciers, was the infamous *Showdog Moms & Dads* series, shown on the Bravo cable network in 2005, an eight-part "reality" show that, in fact, was highly edited and contrived to make its participants—most of them regular dog show exhibitors—look as freakishly outlandish as possible.

A BEST IN SHOW MOVIE

Westminster—although it was never really spelled out—also served as the inspiration for the film *Best in Show*, which caused a stir among both dog show fanciers and independent movie fans when it opened to excellent reviews in 2000. Directed and cowritten by Christopher Guest, a Hollywood veteran with such independent classics as *This Is Spinal Tap* (1984) and *Waiting for Guffman* (1996) to his credit, the mock documentary takes a satirical yet affectionate look at a number of hard-core dog show fans

The dog show world was brilliantly—and good-humoredly—parodied in the "mockumentary" film *Best in Show*, an independent Castle Rock Entertainment hit in 2000.

and their charges, leading up to the finale at an all-important, fictitious Westminster look-alike, the Mayflower Kennel Club Dog Show in Philadelphia. The producers went to great lengths to ensure that Guest's ensemble of character actors look like authentic dog fanciers, even hiring a well-known AKC judge, Dany Canino, as technical adviser and to act as one of the judges in the film. The actors got the hang of it and look as if they would make pretty good handlers at a real dog show; Parker Posey and Jane Lynch are especially convincing as, respectively, a *very* competitive Weimaraner

exhibitor and a Poodle handler who discovers her true self. Bob Balaban as Mayflower Club official Dr. Theodore W. Millbank III even shares his name with a real past Westminster member and Best in Show judge, Dr. Samuel Milbank. Fred Willard does a brilliant riff on Garagiola's inane patter as the show commentator. Most of the dogs used in the film were Canadian champions, but any veteran of real dog shows will notice that neither the dogs nor the characters are nearly as far over the top in mannerisms as many originals. If the film has a weakness, in fact, it is that the dog show scenes fall a little flat and don't really give much feeling for the wonderful weirdness that is Westminster: the film's budget would probably have to be increased considerably to succeed at that level.

Many dog show people were upset by the film's light-hearted satire and refusal to treat the subject matter with sufficient respect. However, as one reviewer wrote, "Though the film pokes fun at the dog show circuit, it also reveals a fondness for the people involved. It may not inspire you to become a dog show person, but it just may have you looking in the classifieds to see when the next real-life show is coming to your town." Guest himself summed it up, not necessarily talking about *Best in Show*: "I am interested in the notion that people can become so obsessed by their world that they lose sense of awareness of how they appear to other people. They are so earnest about it. But that's true of so many things."

Appendix A:
How It Works: Rules and Regulations

Most dog shows everywhere follow a recognizable pattern. The dogs initially compete with others of the same breed, and each breed is divided into a number of classes whose criteria are usually based on the participants' sex, age, and previous awards. After being examined by a judge, the participants advance through an elimination process, with one chosen as Best of Breed (BOB). This dog may continue to compete against the winners of other breeds in the Group judging (for all purposes, a semifinal), and the Group winners finally compete for the title of Best in Show, awarded to the one undefeated dog at that particular show.

Many rules, however, differ from one country to another. Even to an experienced dog person on a first visit to a foreign show, it may not always be clear what is going on in the ring, as each country has developed its own increasingly complex system over time. If you are new to dog shows, or one of the thousands who enjoys traveling and showing your dogs abroad, or one of the increasing number of jet-setting judges who fly from one international dog show to another, you need to know at least the basics about how the shows you visit are run.

Two Camps: Anglo and FCI

The dog world can be roughly divided into two camps: the English-speaking countries versus all the rest. In spite of all their differences, British and American dog shows have much more in common with each other than they do with those in FCI member countries, and so do those in Canada, Australia, and New Zealand. The FCI is based in Belgium but sets the rules for international dog shows in more than eighty member countries across the European continent, in Scandinavia, Russia, most of Asia, and all of Latin America.

Occasionally, some national clubs from the English-speaking world have flirted with the idea of FCI membership—most disastrously Australia, where after the initial honeymoon in the 1990s, something akin to civil war erupted among active dog fanciers. Many were not happy with the new regulations imposed by the FCI, and the association was soon unceremoniously dropped. South Africa is officially a member of the FCI, but only one annual show there is run according to the FCI model; the rest follow the old British rules. In 2005, the Irish Kennel Club, founded in 1922, took the drastic step of becoming a full FCI member. How this will play out in the long run remains uncertain. Will Irish breeders be left between a rock and a hard place, with their old British-style shows and breed standards set aside in favor of the sometimes very different FCI requirements?

The basic approach to dog shows on each side of the divide is so different that a merger between the FCI and the kennel clubs of the English-speaking world isn't likely to occur anytime soon. The biggest difference between the two major systems is how the judges approach their tasks. Dog shows in the English-speaking world are based on the premise that the judge's principal duty is to place the dogs in each class in order of merit compared with each other—usually from First through Fourth place. In the FCI countries, the emphasis is traditionally more on grading the exhibits: each dog receives one of several awards, or grades, corresponding to its quality, from Excellent all the way down to Insufficient. Any number of dogs in a class, or none at all, may be of superior quality, which would be reflected in the grades awarded at FCI shows. In some cases, all of the dogs in a class, even in an entire breed, may receive an Excellent rating—or, at the other extreme, they may all receive an Insufficient quality grade. In other words, the FCI judge at this stage is comparing the dogs not with each other but against the imaginary ideal of the breed that should be indelibly imprinted in each judge's mind. Only after the grading are the best dogs in the class placed in order of merit at FCI shows as well.

The Anglo system is easy to understand for both participants and spectators and no doubt helped make dog shows popular with the public in the early days. The FCI version is more cumbersome and does not present a particularly exciting spectacle from ringside: watching judging at FCI shows can be about as enthralling as watching paint dry. At an FCI show, exhibitors always receive an award, which at least theoretically tells how good a dog is; a participant in a big class at an Anglo-type show may easily leave the ring without anything to show that he or she even competed.

Even in the English-speaking countries, a judge may withhold awards if he or she feels the quality is lacking. There is always controversy when this happens: How bad is bad enough for a dog not to get a ribbon? Is it possible to go second in a class of one? Is it better to refuse a class placement or to make a strong statement by withholding the top award that would allow a class-winning (but possibly inferior) dog to become a champion? Whatever a judge does, exhibitors will probably be unhappy. So far, at least, no judge in any country has been known to withhold an award in Group or Best in Show competition: this would be perceived as the ultimate insult.

CRITIQUES

The FCI shows often require judges to furnish a written critique of every dog shown, specifying both faults and virtues. A copy of this critique is given to the dog's handler, in the ring. (The original is kept by the club; a triplicate is often published in the breed magazines.) When used correctly, a critique helps exhibitors understand their dogs' virtues and faults; it also obliges judges to give reasons for their decisions. Sometimes the critique is delivered orally in the ring for other exhibitors and the ringside to hear. On the judge's part, this obviously requires considerable knowledge and self-confidence (and a voice that carries!) as well as a certain degree of tact. A judge must be frank without hurting exhibitors' feelings—a delicate balance to achieve, as so many owners consider their beloved pets faultless and do not take kindly to criticism.

Because FCI judges have to produce critiques on a regular basis, they are usually better prepared to justify their actions than are judges from English-speaking countries. In the United States, judges are actually advised not to tell the exhibitors too much about what they think for fear of getting into an argument, and American dog people—both judges and exhibitors—usually are not accustomed to the frank give-and-take routine found in most FCI countries. In Scandinavia, for instance, exhibitors tend to get upset if they don't learn just what the judge thinks is wrong with their dogs. Being equally up front in the United States would almost certainly get a judge in trouble with the official AKC representative.

Yet critiques, verbal or written, are among the best tools for giving breeders, exhibitors, and spectators at a dog show a glimpse into the judge's mind as well as a way to hold the judge accountable. It is much easier for a judge to point to a random winner if he does not have to explain why that dog is better than the others.

ADVANTAGES OF ORAL CRITIQUES

Although widely used in other forms of animal judging in many countries, oral critiques are seldom heard at dog shows. At cattle or sheep exhibitions, and even cat shows, the judge is likely to pick up a microphone after each class and explain just why he placed the competitors as he did. It's invariably interesting, and often educational: I have learned more about cows and sheep on such occasions than I would ever have expected. Exactly why oral critiques are not more popular at dog shows is unclear. A lack of confidence on the part of many judges may have something to do with it, but more likely it is the close emotional bond between dog and owner that makes anything even remotely resembling public criticism so sensitive. It is usually much more difficult for a dog owner to hear in public that his beloved Cocker does not have a perfect bite or proper rear angulation than it is for a cattle farmer to hear that his Dexter bull has thin horns or excessively short legs.

There is, however, a little-known provision that allows judges to give oral critiques on the spot in the ring, even in the United States. Provided that the club requests it in advance, the AKC may give permission for this procedure on a show-by-show basis. In several decades of attending American dog shows, I can think of only three or four occasions—all major specialty shows—when this has been done. It is easy to understand how, in the fast-paced atmosphere at most American all-breed shows, thoughtful critiques from all the judges are not a realistic expectation. Still, it is surprising that more specialty clubs, with fewer time restraints and more focus on a specific breed, do not ask their judges to tell the ringside exactly why they did what they did.

POLITE CRITIQUES

The dog press in Great Britain will print the judges' comments about their top placements in a summary report that can be as entertaining, educational, or bland as the judge in question is capable of making it. Since these comments are written after the event, they usually make up in tact what they may lack in spontaneity. Sometimes even the polite British veneer gives way to sarcasm: no doubt the reason the dog press there started limiting judges' comments from the top three to the first two in each class was to conserve space, but it also eliminated the opportunity for a breed judge to place a serious competitor's dog in third place just so he could criticize the animal in print. The subtle but deadly comment "Never looked better and therefore deserved third place," about a very famous dog, is a classic example, although possibly apocryphal.

In America, critiques are seldom printed in the general dog press, but some breed publications may ask judges to write postshow comments after a major specialty show. These are usually pretty general in content and seldom identify specific faults in particular dogs.

DOG SHOWS IN GREAT BRITAIN

No other country has as many big dog shows as Great Britain has. Almost every week during the summer, there is at least one mammoth event that would be a record-breaker anywhere else in the world; in the United Kingdom, it's just par for the course that about 10,000 dogs get together at most of the big championship shows. During the winter months, the shows are less frequent, but some of the world's biggest dog shows—Crufts, Manchester, the Ladies Kennel Association—are held indoors between December and March.

The twenty-five big all-breed shows are just the top of the pyramid, however, closely followed by one or two championship shows for each of the various groups and a varying number of single-breed championship events. There are more types of shows in Great Britain than anywhere else: a descending scale with Championship shows at the top and Open shows one step below, via Limited shows to Companion shows at the bottom. Some of the Open shows are bigger than most major shows in other countries, yet by definition do not have championship status. The others are of decreasing importance for serious competitors—the Companion shows, for instance, are basically informal pet events on the village green, perhaps with a local celebrity awarding prizes to the dog with the sweetest expression or the one that looks the most like its owner. All of these shows, regardless of status, provide an excellent training ground for those, both people and dogs, who aspire to greater things, but there is no question that championship shows are where the real action takes place.

CHALLENGE CERTIFICATES

What makes championship shows so important is that they are where the Challenge Certificates (CC) can be awarded: one to the best dog, one to the best bitch in a breed, provided the judge feels that the winner is of such outstanding quality

that it is worthy of the champion title. Although it consists only of a piece of cardboard, the CC—also called simply a ticket—is the building block upon which the dog sport in the United Kingdom is built. It is so important that even getting the runner-up award, the Reserve CC, is quite an important achievement in its own right. Three CCs won under three separate judges make a dog a champion under Kennel Club rules. It sounds simple, but it isn't easy: a champion title won in the United Kingdom carries more prestige than does any other in the world, not necessarily because British dogs are better but simply because the title is so much more difficult to attain there than in most other countries.

The Challenges of the Challenge Certificates

It is not easy to earn a CC. The number awarded in a breed is determined by The Kennel Club each year and based on past show entries. If the entry figures go up, a breed may gain a new set of CCs; if they drop, the breed may lose some CCs. The most popular breeds, those with high entry figures and heavy competition, are allocated CCs at more shows than are the numerically smaller breeds. Labrador and Golden Retrievers, for instance, may compete for more than forty sets of CCs per year—one at each of all the regular all-breed shows, a couple at Gundog Group shows, and a dozen or so more at various breed club shows. Less popular breeds may be allocated as few as a half dozen shows with CCs per year, which almost guarantees that there will be reasonable competition at these. (In addition, years of participation with no chance of any champion titles at all are required for new breeds before they can compete for CCs. The road to championship status is long and rocky, marked by participation in Imported Register and Any Variety classes. The Kennel Club will not grant the first crucial sets of CCs to a new breed until it has become an established part of the dog show scene, with sufficient numbers and recorded history to justify a dog of this breed's carrying the champion title.)

Only a few big shows—Crufts, Birmingham National, and the Welsh and Scottish Kennel Clubs—can consistently offer CCs for all the eligible breeds. At most of the other all-breed championship shows, CCs will be awarded only in a limited number of breeds—probably to most of the popular breeds, but not to all. Some breeds will have classes with CCs, others may have classes but no CCs, and others have no classes at all. The only way a dog of an unclassified breed can compete at such a show would be to qualify for one of the Variety classes that are usually offered, such as Any Variety Not Separately Classified.

Because the number of Challenge Certificates is so limited, competition at the shows where they are offered is almost invariably strong. Even relatively rare breeds often have large entries, and some breeds regularly attract a couple of hundred dogs at almost every championship show. Because Great Britain is not particularly large, it is possible for most of the top dogs to be at nearly all the big shows.

In addition, there is never more than one set of CCs on offer for a breed anywhere on any given day. This, in turn, means that one cannot run away from the competition to smaller shows for cheap wins, as exhibitors in many other countries may do if the going gets too tough at the big events.

As if the above did not make it difficult enough to gain a champion title, the coup de grâce for many hopeful exhibitors is the fact that there is no Champion class at shows in the United Kingdom. The CCs go to the best dog and the best bitch of the breed even if they are champions already and technically don't need any more CCs. On occasion, when a couple of heavily campaigned superstars dominate a breed, hardly any other dogs get a foot in the door, and it can be a long dry spell without a single new champion in that breed until the top dog is finally retired or knocked off its pedestal by an upstart nonchampion. Some top dogs may win fifty or sixty CCs in their prime (and possibly beyond), which means that they may have prevented fifteen or twenty other dogs from becoming champions in the process.

Changing the System?
Suggestions to change the British system—which has been in place ever since Challenge Certificates were first awarded in 1901—have often

been made, especially, of course, by those who keep collecting a large number of Reserve CCs to the ruling champions. (It is interesting to note, incidentally, that late in the 1800s, prior to the current rules, it was a specified number of class wins that made a dog a champion. Some of the class wins could be worth more points than others, and at least one had to be in a Champion class. Obviously, some of these ideas were picked up in the American dog sport and are still in use on the other side of the Atlantic, over 100 years later.) Some exhibitors feel that a dog should retire as soon as it has won three CCs and a title; some feel that a maximum number of CCs ought to be allowed per dog; a few even favor the introduction of a Champion class. The bottom line, however, is that nobody has come up with a viable suggestion for a change that would not also mean lowering the value of the UK champion title.

ADDITIONAL CHAMPIONSHIP REQUIREMENTS

Other than three Challenge Certificates awarded by three different judges, the only requirement for the champion title in Great Britain is that the dog must be at least twelve months old at the time of its qualifying win. In other words, a successful puppy may win any number of CCs but still does not become a champion until it has won a qualifying CC after it has turned a year old. Gundog breeds are called Show Champion (Sh. Ch.) when they have won the required three CCs until they are qualified in the field, at which point they become full champions. This is distinct from Dual Champion, awarded to the few dogs that so excel in both conformation and field activities that they achieve the championship title in both. The same regulations apply to only one breed outside the Gundog Group: Border Collies can only become Show Champions when they prove their worth working with livestock. Only one has become a full champion so far.

With these facts in view, it is no wonder that each new champion in Great Britain is greeted with quite a bit more fanfare than is customary elsewhere. As a rough guide, it's about ten times more difficult to make up a champion in the United Kingdom as it is to finish one in the United States, to use the expressions commonly employed. (It is unclear why getting a dog to its champion title is described by different terms in Great Britain and the United States. This is especially peculiar because for an American dog, the champion title is often only the beginning, not the finish, of its serious show career, whereas for a dog in the United Kingdom, that third CC might not come until the very end of that career.) The comparison is borne out pretty well by statistics: few breeds in the United Kingdom have more than 10 or 15 new champions per year, as opposed to 100 or 200 for the same breeds in the United States. A stud dog with as many as 10 or 15 UK champion offspring to his credit would almost certainly be considered as great as an American sire with 100 champions. Once a fancier has bred 2 or 3 champions in England, he or she may be considered a serious and accomplished breeder by most people; in the United States, it would probably take 20 or 30 champions to reach a similar plateau.

OTHER BRITISH TITLES

Obviously, only a small percentage of the show dogs in England can ever become champions. In 2003, The Kennel Club introduced a new title that is considerably easier to get: the Show Certificate of Merit. Only wins at Open all-breed or Group shows count, and as in the United States, there is a point system. A dog gets one point for Best of Breed, five for Best in Show, and two to four points for a Group win or placement. After a total of twenty-five points won in both Breed and Group competition at both Championship and Open shows, an owner can apply for the certificate and add the abbreviation ShCM after the dog's name. Many dogs that started out with a ShCM have gone on to earn the "real" champion title, but because the

ShCM is not based on wins at the championship level, it is obviously not taken as seriously.

Another title that has been part of the British scene for many years is a de facto youth championship. Known as the Junior Warrant, it may be awarded to any dog between the ages of six and eighteen months that collects a total of twenty-five points at Championship or Open shows. Each class win at a show with CCs for the breed earns three points, each class win at a show without CCs earns one point, and there must be at least two other dogs present in each class. Just like the ShCM, the Junior Warrant is awarded upon application to The Kennel Club. The abbreviation JW will be added to the dog's name in all official documents. Many Junior Warrant winners go on to become adult champions; some do not, and conversely, some dogs that failed to earn a Junior Warrant may blossom later, winning many CCs.

SHOW FORMATS

The number of breed classes offered at shows in the United Kingdom varies from show to show and from breed to breed. At big shows, breeds with large entries will have more classes than will less popular breeds at the same event; at small shows, some breeds may only have two or three classes, other breeds perhaps a single class or none at all, in which case they go into one of the Any Variety classes that lump different breeds together.

A full array of classes would include: Minor Puppy (six to nine months), Puppy (six to twelve months), Junior (six to eighteen months), Yearling, Novice, Undergraduate, Graduate, Post Graduate, Minor Limit, Mid Limit, Limit, and Open classes, all separated by sex. On special occasions, such as breed club shows, there may be a bewildering array of additional classes restricted to dogs of certain color, weight, or

SPECIAL COMPETITIONS

In addition to the regular shows, there is a large variety of annual special events in the British dog world's calendar: the Pup of the Year competition and the Contest of Champions are two of the best known. Best described as a mixture of dog show and social event, they are usually held in a conveniently located hotel ballroom, accompanied by dinner and even dancing, with both judges and exhibitors in evening wear. Various dog food companies and insurance companies host these events, offering the invited public an opportunity to see a large number of the top dogs in a particular category compete in a congenial setting under one roof. Although they have no official status and are not governed by the usual dog show rules, these competitions require permission from The Kennel Club before they can be held. The contests are often glamorous, prestigious, and even lucrative for the winning exhibitors. There has been nothing like this in the United States since *Kennel Review* magazine held its lamented Tournament of Champions in the 1980s, but many other countries stage similar events with varying degrees of glamour and panache.

other criteria. (There was even a special class for dogs Handled by a Lady, but that was a long time ago.) Instead of ribbons, class placements are rewarded with prize cards, which are traditionally displayed on the dog's bench.

Eligibility requirements are such that unshown dogs, those that have never won anything, or very young dogs can be entered in any or all classes, whereas those that have established a winning record are restricted to the upper classes. Challenge Certificate winners and champions can compete in any age class for which they are eligible, but beyond that, CC winners can be shown only in the Limit and Open classes, and champions only in the Open class. At shows in the United Kingdom, most dogs can be, and often are, entered in more than one class. This practice is less popular now than it once was, but in the old days, with lower entry fees and substantial prize money, a successful, daring exhibitor could on occasion make a killing. I remember

one show at which the late Bobby James, before he became a famous judge, showed a young Whippet in every single dog class, from Puppy to Open, winning them all, including the CC and BOB. Such cases were unusual then and probably don't occur at all today.

In each class, the dogs are placed First, Second, Third, and Reserve (never called Fourth). Most shows offer Very Highly Commended for fifth place; a Highly Commended and Commended to the sixth and seventh placements, respectively, may even be offered at a very big show as a sort of honorary consolation prize. Once all the classes have been judged, the unbeaten winners are called back to compete first for Best Dog (and, if it's offered, the Challenge Certificate), then for Reserve Best Dog (and Reserve CC). After the same procedure has been followed in bitches, the two CC winners compete for Best of Breed.

Breed winners, of course, are eligible for Group competition, which offers placements for

First through Fourth. The Group winners advance to Best in Show competition, in which a winner and a Reserve are chosen. The seven Groups—Gundogs, Hounds, Working, Terriers, Toys, Utility, and Pastoral—are fairly similar to AKC divisions, but there are differences. The Bichon Frisé is in the UK Toy Group but in the AKC Non-Sporting Group, for instance; and the Utility Group, which otherwise closely corresponds to the Non-Sporting Group in America, includes the Akita, the Canaan Dog, the Miniature and Standard Schnauzers, the Shih Tzu, and the Toy Poodle—which are, respectively, in the Working, Herding, Terrier, Working, and Toy Groups in the United States. Neutered dogs and spayed bitches can be shown in regular competition in the United Kingdom. All that is required is for the owner to notify The Kennel Club that the animal has been neutered. This is different from the United States, where spayed or neutered dogs cannot participate at all-breed shows, only in veteran classes and nonregular competition at independently held specialty shows.

A DISTINCTIVE ATMOSPHERE

The major difference between dog shows in the United Kingdom and shows in America is not included in the rule book but concerns the overall atmosphere at the events. A first-time overseas visitor to a British dog show is almost invariably taken aback by how low-key it all seems. There may be several thousand dogs present, but there's not much noise, very little visible stress, hardly any applause except a few polite claps for some popular new champion. The exhibitors generally dress and behave far more casually than most American fanciers would. Even the biggest shows often resemble a large county fair, with exhibitors appearing far less regimented than do their counterparts in America. Much less emphasis is placed on Group and Best in Show judging, with almost none of the high-strung, bait-throwing, overdressed, and carefully choreographed atmosphere that is evident at many dog shows in some other countries. The Crufts finale has become a very sophisticated event, but the show itself still seems quite informal compared with its American counterpart in New York.

There are good reasons for the low-key atmosphere. For one, all the general championship shows are benched, which means that each dog is provided with its own space on a raised bench—for easy viewing by the public—with high side dividers providing privacy from neighboring dogs. Only Westminster and a very few other shows in the United States are benched. These shows give each dog and exhibitor their own place to spend the day and relax, avoiding much of the chaos of unbenched shows, at which exhibitors have to bring their own crates and exercise pens and set up a space for their dogs in a designated area, as is the custom at most American shows. At benched shows, the dogs are usually required to remain the entire day, whereas at the unbenched events, they usually have to stay only for the duration of the breed judging, not all day.

In addition, the British tradition of understatement and a stiff upper lip applies to dog shows as to everything else: regardless of the occasion, one doesn't expect to hear ringside screaming for the favorite or to witness an exhibitor breaking down in tears after an emotional win. However, this is changing, at least in some breeds: a new generation of British exhibitors in the twenty-first century is much more inclined to displays of emotion both in and outside of the ring than their ancestors ever would have been.

Another reason for the fairly low-key atmosphere is that showing dogs is a much bigger national pastime in Great Britain than anywhere else, so you will see thousands of people—and dogs—who participate just to have a good day out and don't really expect to win much. Obviously, as there are so many more dogs competing, the odds of winning are much smaller, which means that the exhibitors in general tend to take things more easily. Many participate for years without going higher than class placements, barely dreaming of Challenge Certificates, not to mention Group or Best in Show awards. In addition, almost everyone is an owner-handler, which means that winning or losing won't affect an exhibitor's livelihood, so they can afford to be a little more cavalier about the results.

Do not misread the atmosphere, however. The exhibitors may look casual, and handling and presentation are traditionally not emphasized as much as they are in America, but the seriousness of purpose and depth of dog knowledge at a big championship show in the United Kingdom can hardly be matched anywhere else. When you know who the players are, it can be awesome to watch some of the most influential breeders in the world, owner-handlers all, pitting their best homebreds against each other. In many ways, the top British all-breed shows can more easily be compared with specialty shows in the United States; such is the emphasis on specialized breed judging.

DOG SHOWS IN THE UNITED STATES

Dog shows in the United States have a common background with those in Great Britain, but the sport has developed over the years so that they are now very different. The reasons for this are

many, most of them based on geography and demographics.

The figures tell a clear story: the United Kingdom, whose Kennel Club registers about 300,000 dogs per year, has more than 60 million inhabitants crowded into an area of less than 100,000 square miles. The United States, where the American Kennel Club registers almost a million dogs per year, has about 300 million inhabitants spread out across a continent of nearly 3.7 million square miles.

This means that although there may be three times as many purebred dogs in the United States as in Great Britain and five times as many people, these dogs and people are spread very thinly over an area that's about thirty-seven times larger than that of the British Isles. With a mostly widespread, scattered population, the dog shows are much smaller, much more numerous, and often located so far apart that dog people have to travel long distances to get to them. Over the years this, in turn, has resulted in many of the features that make dog shows in North America such a different experience from those in Great Britain.

An American dog fancier may look with envy at the paradise of easily accessible large shows in Great Britain, but it must have been obvious early on that the sport would have to develop along different lines in the United States. Although dog shows, like most other activities early in the twentieth century, were mainly clustered along the eastern seaboard, people—and their dogs—continued to move westward across the continent. At a corresponding rate, a large number of new clubs and dog shows were created in the midwestern and western areas of the country (new ones are still being founded today). By the 1920s, more than 100 annual all-breed shows were held across the United States. That figure doubled before the outbreak of World War II, and after a slight wartime drop in the mid-1940s, doubled again a decade later. The numbers kept increasing year by year: there were more than 500 shows by 1965, more than 700 by 1975, 1,000 by the mid-1980s. By 2000, there were already more than 1,400 AKC all-breed shows, and the figure keeps increasing.

The number of dogs competing at these shows is also impressive. Even by the mid-1950s, there were more than 200,000 *dogs in competition*, to use the AKC's convenient but slightly misleading term, which indicates the cumulative number of times all dogs were shown in a year. By the late 1950s, the annual total was more than 500,000, by 1980 just over a million, and by 2000 there were 1.32 million dogs in competition. (How many individual dogs participate in a given year is rarely mentioned; the figure is a little over 150,000, which means that each dog was shown an average of about nine times. Some of these dogs may participate at as many as 100 shows a year; others, perhaps only at 1 or 2.)

As must be obvious from the above, the number of shows has increased even faster than the number of dogs. In the 1950s, at an average AKC all-breed show, some 500 dogs were usually entered; there was a sharp upturn in the 1960s, and by 1970 the average entry figure was already higher than it is today. In the mid- to late 1970s, the size of the average AKC all-breed show reached an all-time peak, with almost 1,300 dogs entered; today that figure is barely 950 dogs per show. These figures reflect not a decreased interest among dog people but simply the much greater number of shows that exhibitors can choose from. Almost everyone who cares about the sport—including professional handlers who make their livelihood from these shows—agrees that there are too many shows in the United States. The American Kennel Club itself has professed inability to rein in the increasingly bloated show calendar—and if the AKC can't, who can?

The figures above are taken from published AKC records and pertain only to what is listed as all-breed shows. It appears, however, that the AKC is including the Group shows, those limited to one variety Group of breeds—such as Terriers, Toys, Hounds—in their so-called all-breed annual statistics. This would at least partly explain the downturn in average entry figures, because many more Group shows are held now than in the past, and most of them obviously have fewer entries than all-breed events do.

The AKC is not the only dog registry in the United States. Its main competitor is the United Kennel Club, which has coexisted with the AKC for over 100 years. The United Kennel Club focuses more on performance dogs than on shows, does not allow professional handlers to exhibit dogs for others at their conformation events, and registers 300,000 dogs per year, making it bigger than most, if not all, of the world's other kennel clubs, except the AKC. The United Kennel Club operates out of Kalamazoo, Michigan, and incorporates many individuals who have been active in AKC events. Its president, Wayne Cavanaugh, was an AKC judge for several Sporting breeds until the AKC introduced restrictions in 2006 that prohibit their judges from being active within other American all-breed organizations. There is also the American Rare Breed Association, which caters to about 130 breeds not yet fully recognized by the AKC, and a large number of for-profit registries that do not offer much beyond a piece of official-looking paper in exchange for the registration fee.

The fact that American dog shows are both smaller and more numerous than those in Great Britain has had an effect on many other aspects of the sport in the United States. At a British show with 10,000 dogs, entries in most reasonably popular breeds will probably give each judge a full day's work. In the United States, with fewer than 1,000 dogs at the average all-breed show, a single-breed specialist judge is ordinarily not of much use, and each judge must be prepared to earn his or her keep by being capable of going over many breeds each day. A breed entry at AKC all-breed shows consists of only six or seven dogs on average (more for the most popular breeds, fewer for the rest), and because a full day's work would consist of judging 150–175 dogs, simple economics decrees that all-rounders and multibreed judges are the order of the day. The effect is strengthened by the fact that in an effort to minimize the expense and difficulties of long-distance traveling, several shows may be held in the same place over a long weekend, so many judges are expected to pass over a large number of breeds for three or even four days in a row.

As a result of these conditions, few of the more than 3,000 judges approved by the American Kennel Club are content to judge just one or two breeds. If they do, they won't be in much demand by most clubs. Whether it is good for the sport that most judges try to graduate to multibreed, Group, and Best in Show status as quickly as possible is debatable, but it has certainly had an effect on the judging, as breed specialists and all-rounder judges often develop slightly different preferences. To generalize, single-breed judges usually tend to prioritize finer points of breed type over general impression and showmanship, whereas all-rounders do the opposite.

Another side effect of the long distances has been the prevalence of professional handlers in America. If you must drive several hundred miles to a show and take several days off work to do so, it might be a good idea to pay a handler to take the dog on the road while you stay at home. In addition, if you want your dog to place in the top dog ratings in America, you would need to go to so many shows and be gone so many weekends—and weekdays—that for most people it would be impossible to participate without hiring a professional handler.

How the Judging Works

All AKC shows use basically the same classifications for all breeds: a Puppy class (usually split into six-to-nine-months and nine-to-twelve-months divisions); a twelve-to-eighteen-months class, a Novice class, a Bred-by-Exhibitor class, and an American-Bred class, which are self-explanatory; and finally Open, which is just that—open to any dog of any age. (Champions are also eligible to compete in the Open class as well as for Best of Breed only, but it is considered extremely unsportsmanlike to enter a champion in the Open class.) All these classes are subdivided by sex, and the competitors are awarded satin ribbons for First, Second, Third, and Fourth place in each class. The undefeated class-winning males compete for the Winners Dog award (and Reserve) before the bitch classes, which culminate in the equivalent: Winners Bitch and Reserve. Foreign judges should note that Winners and Reserve are not awarded at the same time, as frequently happens in other countries. In the United States, once Winners has been awarded, the dog placed second in the class to Winners returns to compete for Reserve. This applies only if Winners does not come from a class of one, as often happens in small entries.

CHAMPIONSHIP POINTS

Going Winners (yes, it's an ungrammatical plural: "My dog went Winners!" with no apostrophe either) isn't like winning a Challenge Certificate in England. The Winners award (unlike the CC) can be worth anything from a maximum of five points, if the competition is really strong, to nothing at all if there is no or only negligible competition. Fifteen points are needed for a dog to become an AKC champion. With a lot of luck and a really great dog, it is possible to gain a champion title in just three shows, but usually it takes much longer, with single-point wins punctuating the majors (as three- to five-point wins are called). The majors are crucial. If all your dog gets are one- and two-point wins, it doesn't matter how many points your dog has: at least two of the wins making up the fifteen-point total must consist of majors. The majors must be awarded by at least two different judges, and at least one additional judge must award one or more of the minor points.

The point score for each breed—just how many dogs have to be present and competing for the various points to be awarded—varies among breeds, from one region to another, and from dogs to bitches. The particulars are reevaluated by the AKC annually according to a complex system and (in a manner reminiscent of the allocation of CCs in Great Britain) based on previous years' entries in each sex, each breed, and each region. For these purposes, the AKC has divided the United States into thirteen geographic areas, usually consisting of a group of neighboring states. Alaska,

HOW MANY CHAMPIONS?

In most breeds and point regions, a dog must defeat at least twenty-some competitors to win a major, which means that even in some popular breeds, it is possible to attain an AKC champion title by defeating as few as fifty or sixty entries. Most new titlists don't have it that easy, but with well over 20,000 new champions finished each year in the United States, obviously this title does not have quite the cachet here that it has in Great Britain. In most breeds, you can count from 1 to 200 new conformation champions each year. In 2005, according to AKC records, Havanese, Cavalier King Charles Spaniels, and Papillons had the most, with 348, 345, and 310 new champions, respectively. (Cocker Spaniels and Dachshunds had more than 600 new champions each, and Poodles 512, but that's due to the fact that the different varieties—three colors in Cockers, three coat types in Dachshunds, three sizes in Poodles—each compete for their own points.) Other breeds with close to 300 new champions that year were Golden Retrievers, Great Danes, and Pomeranians. Beagles had 303 new champions but are judged in two different size varieties; Chihuahuas had 391 and Collies 388, but both compete in two separate coat varieties. The breeds with the fewest new champions that year, each with fewer than twenty titlists, were American Water Spaniels, Black and Tan Coonhounds, American and English Foxhounds, Komondorok, Neapolitan Mastiffs, and Canaan Dogs.

California, Hawaii, and Puerto Rico each have their own point scores.

A new point score is presented by the AKC each April, effective at shows held on or after a specified date in May. Dogs in some less numerous breeds don't have to defeat more than three competitors to win major points. However, because finding any competition at all is difficult in these breeds, and because dogs still need to defeat at least one other competitor to get even a single point, it takes not just a good dog but also a great deal of determination on the part of the handler to win both the majors and the fifteen-point total. The minimum number of entries it is necessary to defeat to become an AKC champion, even in the rarest of breeds and in the most isolated areas, would be fifteen—and that's an extreme case. (It does not necessarily have to be fifteen dogs—it could, at least theoretically, be the same three dogs being defeated over and over again.)

At the other end of the scale, if you were showing a dog of a popular breed such as a Labrador Retriever in Delaware, New Jersey, and Pennsylvania (Division 2), one of the most densely populated regions in terms of dog show competition in 2005, you would have had to find an entry of at least 138 Labrador bitches, and they would all have had to be present and competing to result in a five-point major. In California in 2005, a five-point major for Labrador bitches required "only" 86 competitors, and in other parts of the country much fewer: in Puerto Rico, you would have needed to defeat just 7 Labrador bitches to take that five-point win.

You could, of course, simply get on a plane if you're really desperate to win those points. Some people do search out areas where the point rating is low, but there is no guarantee that enough dogs will be entered to make the trip worthwhile—and even if the show looks good on paper, just one absentee may be enough for the point value to drop. A different way around the problem, more frequently employed in the bygone days of big kennels and plentiful staff, is to bring your own competition and "invade" a show in a low-point area with, say, a dog that just needs a major to finish, plus a handful of rather immature youngsters. You then have to hope that the judge chooses the right one—and that no inconvenient outside competition turns up.

Many have suggested that the AKC should create an additional superior championship title, one less easily attainable than the current one. Thus far, the AKC has resisted all requests to do so, somewhat surprisingly, as almost all the AKC performance titles are incremental, with a consistently successful dog adding to the initial, basic title. Most other countries have different conformation titles for different levels of achievement, and an AKC Grand Champion title (awarded to a dog that has won at least ten Best of Breeds in major entries, for example) would no doubt be welcomed by most exhibitors.

CAMPAIGNING CHAMPIONS

The awarding of Winners points is not the highlight of AKC breed judging, as is the competition for the CC at shows in the United Kingdom. The most important competition starts after that, in the Best of Breed competition, which is open only to dogs that are already AKC champions and to the Winners Dog and Winners Bitch on the day. (At certain events, the winners of special classes for veterans, field trial dogs, and so on may also compete; these classes are mostly offered only at big specialty shows.) The dogs entered in Best of Breed competition constitute, in effect, a champion class, with dogs and bitches competing together. The number of champions participating varies greatly, from only one (or none) at the smaller shows to dozens or, in exceptional instances, more than a hundred champions—sometimes so many that the ring, literally, isn't large enough to fit them all at once.

Should a dog from the classes (Winners Dog or Winners Bitch) succeed in defeating the champions for Best of Breed, then the points won earlier in the day may be increased: the champions are added to the total number that the Best of Breed winner defeated for Winners. Should a class dog go Best of Opposite Sex, the defeated champions in the winner's own sex will, again, be added to the total—and either way, a Best of Winners (BOW) is always selected from the two Winners, with the BOW credited with whichever point score is highest. (When there are only one or two points available in the dog classes but a major in bitches, the Winners Dog award tends to be Best of Winners more often than statistically would be expected. Ring stewards have been known to "helpfully" remind the judge that the major is in bitches. This is not what judging dogs is supposed to be about, of course, but it's probably human nature. However, a good judge could not care less about what points are available and whether the awards affect the point score.)

At an AKC show, Best of Breed, Best of Winners, and Best of Opposite Sex are awarded simultaneously; the judge should never designate Best of Breed and then start looking around for the remaining awards. It is customary for the judge to move his or her choices up to the front of the line—first Best of Breed, followed by Best of Winners, then Best of Opposite Sex—and ask the whole class to move around the ring in that order before pointing to the three final winners. It could be just two dogs that share the ribbons, of course: Best of Breed may be awarded to the Winners Dog, which then automatically is Best of Winners, with either a champion bitch or the Winners Bitch as Best of Opposite Sex; or Best of Breed could go to a champion bitch, with the Winners Dog as Best of Winners, and either that same Winners Dog or a champion male as Best of Opposite Sex. It's logical but requires the judge to do a bit of thinking before pointing his or her finger. It does not inspire much confidence if the judge tries to award, for instance, both Best of Breed and Best of Opposite Sex to dogs of the same sex, as has on occasion happened.

At many leading all-breed shows and at an increasing number of national specialty shows, special awards are given to the strongest contenders for Best of Breed. These may be called Awards of Merit, Selects, or something similar but are always used as a tool for the judge to indicate which dogs—beyond the ultimate winners—were of particularly high quality in a large entry of champions. The number of Selects will usually vary depending on the size of the entry, and judges are sometimes even requested to place the dogs in descending order of merit—which basically amounts to the same as champion class placements at FCI shows. Most exhibitors will treasure a Select award at a National Specialty far higher than any win at smaller shows. (See chapter 4 for a discussion of specialty shows.)

The Best of Breed winner is eligible to continue and compete in one of the seven Groups (Sporting, Hound, Working, Terrier, Toy, Non-Sporting, and Herding), and the winners of each Group then compete for Best in Show. There is never a Reserve Best in Show award or any other placement of the Group winners at AKC shows today, but as late as in the 1960s, there was often a separate Best American-Bred Dog in Show award, a remnant of the days when imports ruled the American show ring more than they do today. Westminster offered a Reserve Best in Show award for a few years early in the twentieth century, but it didn't catch on, and the general attitude now seems to be that it's best to let all those who don't win think they were the judge's second choice.

Some AKC shows also feature Brace and Team classes, with one exhibitor handling two (or more) dogs at the same time. The best brace and team in each breed compete for a Best in Group award, and the Group winners then compete for the Best Brace in Show or Best Team in Show awards. These competitions were very popular in the past, and Best Brace in Show was a high-profile event at Westminster for many years, but it is no longer offered there or at most other shows.

OTHER COMPETITIONS

In addition to the regular AKC dog shows, at which championship points are awarded, there are a couple of other types of conformation competitions in the United States, although nothing like the variety offered in Great Britain. Match shows were a popular, vital part of the dog show scene, especially in the 1960s and 1970s. These informal events, resembling British Open or Limited shows, were good training grounds for serious competitors and future judges. At their peak, match shows could attract hundreds of exhibitors, but as wins there do not qualify for any titles, support for matches has gradually eroded. The AKC still requires new clubs to hold several match shows to prove they

will be able to organize a "real" dog show, but matches are now far less important in the dog scene than they once were.

Two other forms of competition are popular at breed club specialty shows: sweepstakes and futurity classes. Sweepstakes judging is a kind of show within the show, limited to young dogs or veterans and judged by someone who is not necessarily an AKC judge but usually has a solid background in the breed. Futurity classes are similar to sweepstakes, the main difference being that entry is limited to dogs nominated by their breeder as puppies or even before birth. The nomination and entry fees can add up to several thousand dollars, of which a large part is paid back to those who bred the winning puppies. This is one of the rare occasions when it can actually be financially profitable to have bred a winning show dog!

A relatively new feature is provided at an increasing number of all-breed shows that organize unofficial competitions for Best Puppy, Best Bred-by-Exhibitor, and Best Veteran in Show. A regularly approved AKC judge selects the winners in each breed, but final selections in these categories may be made by judges who are not necessarily approved for all the participating breeds.

KEEPING UP APPEARANCES

A first-time visitor to AKC shows, especially one from abroad, is usually surprised by the formality and careful orchestration of these events, with their multitude of written and unwritten rules of behavior from which one strays at one's own peril. The basic organization is almost invariably first class, thanks to the presence of professional event superintendents, who are in charge of the nuts and bolts of the show, making sure that the judging rings fit the minimum requirements, that ring matériel is in place, that everyone knows what time the judging for each breed will start, and so on. The dogs are almost invariably well trained and on their best behavior. The judges and handlers conduct themselves professionally and are well dressed in either business or appropriate sporting attire. At least at first glance, everyone involved appears supremely polite. You always congratulate the winner, no matter how tough it may be. You never argue with the judge, however tempting. Of course, there are exceptions to these largely unwritten rules, but American dog show exhibitors are exceptionally good at keeping up a civilized public front; if they need to vent, they usually wait until they get back to their setups, or at least some distance away from the ring.

Part of the reason for the emphasis on good form is that many handlers are business-people and as such cannot afford either to appear less than presentable or to act unprofessionally. They set the example, and ambitious amateurs who want to win naturally take their leads from the pros in both dress and attitude. Another strong motivation for good behavior is the presence of the official AKC representative, a sometimes feared individual who functions as a sort of combined Miss Manners and security guard, making sure that everyone behaves appropriately and that every rule is meticulously followed. The AKC rep can, if necessary, call a bench hearing, which may result in an offending participant's suspension from all organized club activities for a specified period of time. Obviously, that is not something a professional handler can afford to risk. Occasionally, as reported in the monthly *AKC Gazette*, tempers flare to the degree that some punishment must be meted out, but considering the thousands of people involved at several thousand events every year, the American dog

show fancy must be one of the best regulated anywhere.

Dog Shows in Canada

Canada occupies a geographic area that is larger than the United States but has only one-tenth of the population and even fewer dogs per square mile than does its neighbor to the south. In a country so vast and sparsely populated, many of the conditions governing the sport in the United States are similar or even more pronounced. The Canadian Kennel Club (CKC) registers around 70,000 dogs per year and approves just over 600 all-breed shows annually, with a total of about 160,000 entries. This means that the average Canadian show will have an entry of just over 260 dogs. The Golden Retriever has the highest entries, with an average of 13 dogs entered per show. Canadian shows offer classes for several breeds that are not currently recognized in the United States—the Greenland Dog, the Berger Picard, the Drever, and the Carelian Bear Dog, for instance. The inclusion of these breeds makes the average breed entry smaller but the Groups more competitive. There are also around 300 specialty shows annually with about 15,000 entries total.

To become a champion in Canada, only ten points are needed and no majors are required, with the result that the CKC title is usually considerably easier to achieve than is the AKC equivalent. The Canadian Kennel Club is reportedly planning to introduce a superior title, Grand Champion, which would be more difficult to earn and therefore more highly regarded.

The classes offered at Canadian shows are similar but not identical to those at AKC events: Junior Puppy (six to nine months); Senior Puppy (nine to twelve months); twelve to eighteen months (formerly offered only at specialty events, but as of January 2006, an official class at all-breed shows as well); Canadian-Bred; Bred-by-Exhibitor; Open; and Specials Only, which "shall be for any dog that has a recorded CKC Registration or Event Registration Number and has attained the required points for Championship status." As in the United States, there can be additional nonregular classes at specialties.

Taking the lead from their British forebears, the Canadian shows are beginning to more often offer Reserve Best in Show competition. This used to be the case in the United States in the distant past but has not been seen since the 1930s south of the border. The Reserve Best award is offered at the discretion of the club, offers no points, and holds no official title or position. Reserve Best in Show can be awarded either to one of the remaining six dogs after the winner has been chosen or to the dog that placed Group Second behind the Best in Show winner. Prizes often consist of cash awards.

One distinct difference between Canada and the United States is that Canadian shows always have a Best Puppy award, given to the best dog in each breed that is still under twelve months old, even if it is already a champion or entered in an adult class. There is also Best Puppy in Group and Best Puppy in Show judging. Only one puppy is selected in each Group; puppies are not placed First through Fourth as the adults are.

The main difference between shows in Canada and the United States is something as subtle as atmosphere. For a tightly controlled American exhibitor, it often feels a bit of a relief to attend Canadian shows: similar enough not to feel quite foreign, but distinctly lower key, more informal, and retaining a real feeling of hobby about them.

DOG SHOWS IN AFRICA AND DOWN UNDER

The English-speaking dog world beyond Great Britain and North America consists of South Africa, New Zealand, and Australia. All have large groups of active dog show fanciers, mainly steeped in the British tradition, although subjected to other influences in recent years, from both America and central Europe.

SOUTH AFRICA

South Africa is now a fully affiliated member of the FCI and holds one show per year at which the CACIB can be awarded. (See "FCI Judging Procedure" below for a discussion of the CACIB.) The breeds at this show are divided into ten different Groups according to the FCI requirements. The other shows—about forty-five per year, with the show season lasting from March until October—are run according to the Kennel Union of Southern Africa (KUSA) rules, with the breeds divided into seven Groups similar to those in the United Kingdom. Entries range from about 3,000 at the premier events in Johannesburg to just 100 or 200 dogs at shows in the more remote areas, which include Namibia, an independent republic that still falls under the jurisdiction of the KUSA. To become a champion in South Africa, a dog must win five Challenge Certificate points, all of which must be won when the dog is more than nine months of age, and at least one when it is more than eighteen months old. The five CCs must be awarded by five different judges and in at least four different geographic areas. If there are more than ten dogs competing for the CC, two points are awarded instead of one.

Among the most important special events in South Africa are the Goldfields Dog of the Year competition, the TKC Kennel Club's Supreme

Champion competition, and the KUSA's own national show, at which a National Dog is chosen from the entered breed champions. (In the past, *TKC* stood for Transvaal Kennel Club, but when Transvaal province was renamed Gauteng, the club was forced to change its name. It settled on simply using initials as its official moniker.) There are also two different point scores for top dog each year, one run by *Animaltalk* magazine and one by the KUSA.

NEW ZEALAND

The New Zealand Kennel Club (NZKC) was founded in 1886, registers approximately 10,000 dogs per year, and has 4,600 active kennel owners. About 130 all-breed championship shows are scheduled annually on the northern and southern islands, not counting breed and group specialty shows. A Challenge Certificate can be awarded to the best dog of each sex, and just as in the United Kingdom, champions continue to compete for the CCs—which means that a new dog must defeat the established winners to gain the title. A dog cannot become a champion until it has won a qualifying CC at more than twelve months of age. For a Grand Champion title, a dog must have won fifty CCs and three times Best in Show under three different judges at all-breed shows.

The seven NZKC Groups are Toys, Terriers, Gundogs, Hounds, Working, Utility, and Non-Sporting, similar but not identical to those in America and Great Britain. After the best in each Group has been selected, the dog that was runner-up to Best of Breed in the Group winner's breed is brought back to compete for Reserve Best in Group. The same procedure is followed for Reserve Best in Show, so it's possible for two dogs of the same breed to take the top spots in both Group and Best in Show competition. In addition, there is judging

for best Baby Puppy (four to six months), Puppy (six to twelve months), Junior (twelve to twenty-four months), Intermediate (twenty-four to thirty-six months), New Zealand–Bred, and Open (any exhibit over six months, champion or not) in each Group. An entry from the Baby Puppy class is eligible to compete for Best of Breed and may even win the Group and Best in Show; but even if it should defeat all the older dogs on the day, a puppy cannot be awarded the CC until it is six months old.

The top event for purebred dogs is the NZKC National Dog Show, held annually in Wellington in the past half century, starting in 1955. Since 2004, the show has been moved to different locations each year—Auckland, Christchurch, and Palmerston North—and been supported by a series of different sponsors.

After many years in the shadow, New Zealand has come into its own as a producer of world-class show dogs in the twenty-first century, with several of the top all-breed winners in Great Britain, Australia, and the United States born and bred in what a local dog person has described as a "very isolated" part of the world.

AUSTRALIA

Australia first emerged as a world-class dog country in the last few decades of the twentieth century. The first dog show down under was held in Hobart on the island of Tasmania in 1862. It had ninety-one dogs entered, was open to the general public ("including ladies," it was noted), and was judged by three gentlemen, two of whom exhibited their own dogs and carried home some of the top prizes—shades of that English show in Newcastle just three years earlier. An impressive variety of breeds was on view: the usual setters, pointers, and spaniels as well as Greyhounds,

Harriers, Beagles and retrievers, Bulldogs, Bull Terriers, Fox Terriers, Newfoundlands, something described as Rough Esquimaux Poodles (the mind boggles!), and a Smithfield Colley. The second documented dog show, and the first on mainland Australia, was held in Melbourne in 1864, attracting 381 dogs and hosted by the Acclimatisation Society, which was responsible for the introduction of many of the British species of birds, mammals, and plants into the Australian colonies.

A unique feature of the Australian dog world in the past was that the rules could differ considerably from one part of the country to another. This was a result of long distances and a sparse population, which encouraged the development of independent regional rules. The widely scattered kennel clubs wrote their own breed standards and awarded their own champion titles, so that a dog might be a champion in Victoria but not in New South Wales. The six states and two territories each still have their own kennel control (the ruling body for the dog world in that state or territory), but the days of regional autonomy are long past. The kennel controls are now united by the Australian National Kennel Council (ANKC), with each kennel control having representation at regular ANKC meetings, ensuring unity in important issues such as breed standards and championship rules. A uniform allocation of Challenge points was introduced in the early 1960s.

Although Australia has a relatively small population on a vast landmass (20 million people on a continent not much smaller than the United States), the activity is so strongly concentrated along the eastern and southeastern coasts that the major Australian shows are at least as big as—sometimes bigger than—the top shows in America.

The Quarantine Factor

The great distances and unusually strict import regulations long kept Australia almost completely isolated from the rest of the world. Until the mid-1970s, dogs could be imported into Australia only via Great Britain or New Zealand, and even then only by boat, followed by six long months in quarantine. This means that in practice it was almost impossible to export dogs from America to Australia: they would first have to go through quarantine to get into England before even contemplating the trip down under.

The reason for the long quarantine was a strong fear of rabies in a country whose economy was, and is, very dependent on livestock. The concern about damage to the native sheep industry resulted in what practically amounted to a demonization of the German Shepherd Dog for several decades. Australia was, in fact, one of the first countries in the world to introduce breed-specific legislation. By 1929, it had banned all importation of German Shepherd Dogs because of the alleged risk that the dogs would cross with dingoes and produce "a race of super sheep-killers." A German Shepherd Dog breed council was eventually formed in 1960, with the stated aim of convincing the authorities to lift the ban. They finally succeeded in 1972, and the German Shepherd Dog has become the most popular breed in Australia, with a large number of dogs imported from Europe, especially Germany.

The gradual easing of import restrictions saw a huge influx of dogs from many countries and a decided shift toward American bloodlines in some breeds. The increase in air travel also helped break the long isolation from the rest of the world, and Australia emerged as a major international influence in dogs, combining much of what was best from its

British past with newer influences from the United States.

Dog Shows Aussie Style

The Australian dog show system is a hybrid of English and American formats. As in England, Challenge Certificates are the stepping-stones to a champion title. To win a CC (or Challenge, as it is called here), you have to knock off the reigning champions; there is no separate class for champions. Titled dogs, in fact, can crop up in any class, even in Puppy and Junior classes if they should be titled very young. The differences from shows in the United Kingdom are obvious, too: Challenges are available for every breed at all shows, regardless of the size of the entry, but each Challenge comes with a varying number of American-style points based on how many dogs are entered. Each Challenge is worth five points, with one additional point added for every dog exhibited (including the challenge winner itself), up to a maximum of twenty-five points. The Best of Breed winner gets an extra point for each exhibit defeated of the opposite sex. This practice continues in Group competition, with the winner getting one additional point for every dog defeated in the Group, up to the maximum of twenty-five points. A total of 100 points are required for the Australian Champion title, so the minimum number of shows needed to win it is four. As in Canada, majors are not required, and it is at least theoretically possible to compete frequently at small shows and eventually achieve a championship title without ever having defeated a single competitor.

At one time, an Australian Grand Champion title was offered to dogs that had won twice as much as what was needed for a regular title. This designation eventually fell out of favor but was reintroduced in 1997, with considerably heightened requirements. Only the best dogs and the most energetic exhibitors can hope to accumulate the 1,000 breed points required for a modern Grand Champion title—ten times what is needed for a basic Australian championship.

The judging leading up to Best in Show (or General Specials, as it is usually called) is a long, drawn-out affair with what's called "in Show" awards for every possible class: Best Baby Puppy in Show, Best Puppy in Show, Best Junior in Show, Best Intermediate in Show, Best Australian-Bred in Show, and Best Open in Show. There is a Runner-up award to Best in Show as well. At least in the past, the competition for second best was taken to its logical conclusion, with a runner-up selected in each breed. If an Afghan Hound won the Hound Group—as happened frequently in the 1970s and 1980s when Australian Afghans became world famous—the Runner-up Best Afghan would also compete for Runner-up Best Hound. Thus, the same breed could win both top spots in the Group. It could, and on occasion did, happen that even the Best in Show and the Runner-up to Best in Show winners were of the same breed. Strong forces in some states are lobbying for a simplification of the complicated and time-consuming in Show competitions as this book went to press. There was even to be a Champion class at the Sydney Royal show.

THE FCI COUNTRIES

Theoretically, the international shows governed by the FCI (or the International Canine Federation) ought to be identical regardless of where in the world they are held. That is not necessarily the case: geography and tradition exert strongholds, sometimes stronger than do the official regulations. Some FCI member countries, especially in Asia and Latin America, are so far from FCI headquarters in Brussels, and so strongly influenced by American customs, that it is difficult to take their FCI memberships at face value. Query a kennel club official in one of those countries on basic policies and procedures on which the FCI and the AKC differ, such as breed standards and judges, and you might find that the FCI hardliners from Europe would not be completely satisfied with the answers.

The FCI was founded on May 22, 1911, its stated aim to "promote and protect cynology and purebred dogs" by uniting kennel clubs from different countries. Austria, Belgium, France, Germany, and the Netherlands were the five foundation members. The FCI was disbanded during World War I but reconstituted in 1921, gradually adding more members to its roster over the years and organizing World Congresses on a regular basis since 1932. The total now exceeds eighty member countries, including all the national kennel clubs in continental Europe, all those in Scandinavia, most in South America and Asia, and most recently and perhaps most important, Russia, with the possibility of China being added to the fold. (China is, in fact, listed by the FCI as a member country, in spite of the fact that China does not yet have a nationally recognized kennel club.) Although neither The Kennel Club in England nor the American Kennel Club (nor the clubs in any of the other English-speaking countries except Ireland and South Africa, as mentioned earlier) is a member of the FCI, each recognizes the organization's authority and cooperates when necessary as far as the different regulations allow.

The FCI sees as its responsibility to ensure that registrations, pedigrees, kennel names, breed standards, and judges in its member countries are mutually recognized. By incorpo-rating just a single national kennel club from each country and making sure that this club's activities are accepted in all the other member countries, the FCI has made possible a great level of international exchange in a sport that would most likely have descended into chaos without generally accepted rules.

Currently, the FCI recognizes 353 different breeds—more than twice as many as either The Kennel Club or the AKC. (The total figure depends a little on exactly how you define *breed*: there are different size, coat, and color varieties within many of the FCI breeds that may be labeled as separate breeds. In that case, the total is closer to 500.) Each of these breeds is considered the property of its native country, and the breed standard drawn up in each breed's country of origin is automatically accepted, in translation if necessary, in all the FCI member countries. The fact that in many cases, Great Britain and even more so the United States have breed standards that sometimes differ drastically from those approved by the FCI is one of the dog world's most enduring bones of contention.

FCI SHOWS

The calendar for international shows in the member countries as approved by the FCI provides some interesting data. At last count, there were about 400 international FCI shows per year, the number per country varying widely. Most of the shows are held in Europe; about 100 combined in the Caribbean, South American, and Central American member countries; and a few dozen in Asia. The FCI member country with by far the highest registration figures in the last available year—more than 500,000—was Japan, followed by Brazil, France, Germany, Italy, and Russia, all with between approximately 100,000 and

150,000 registrations. Yet Japan hosted only fourteen FCI international shows in the same year, while Brazil and France had forty-two and thirty-six, respectively, followed by Italy, Russia, Spain, and Sweden, each of which hosted at least twenty international shows. Russia had by far the highest number of FCI-approved judges (1,350), followed by Germany (856) and France (676).

The number of active purebred dog fanciers listed for each FCI country also varied strongly, to some extent due to different national kennel club membership requirements. With more than 600,000 individual members, Germany has more organized purebred dog fanciers than has any other FCI country, followed by more than 500,000 in France, nearly 300,000 in Sweden, fewer than 200,000 in Japan, and more than 100,000 in Ukraine. Figures for some countries are not available, but it is clear that there is little activity in some of the member countries. The kennel club in Bulgaria, for instance, had a total of 734 registered dogs in the year recorded, and Cuba had about the same, yet both countries were able to organize several dog shows. According to the FCI statistics, Uzbekistan had only a few hundred registrations yet held

eighty-eight national (but no international) dog shows. A few countries, such as Bahrain, appear to have no dog show activity at all, yet are listed among FCI member countries.

In addition to the FCI international events, the member countries organize national shows, ranging from just a handful to a couple of hundred each, for a total of 4,000 to 5,000 per year. Naturally, each country has more autonomy at these events, but it is almost invariably the international shows that attract the biggest entries.

OUTSTANDING EVENTS

The most important of all the FCI shows is the World Dog Show, hosted by a different member country each year. The FCI also has annual so-called Section shows—one show in each region is selected as that area's top show for the year: the European Winner show, the FCI Asian International show, and the Las Americas y El Caribe show in Latin America. The last-mentioned show has in recent years become as important as the other big dog event in this part of the world, the SICALAM (Sociedad de Intercambio de la Canofilia Latinoamericana). The European Winner Show invariably gets huge entries—almost 10,000 in

EVEN THEN, THEY BASHED THE JUDGES
Some of the reports from the early shows are more entertaining than historically informative, as demonstrated by the 1892 report of a Victorian country show: "The dogs were a sorry lot, but it is most remarkable that the judge threw out nearly all the best dogs. This was most noticeable in the Bull Terrier and Fox Terrier classes. There was a fair brindle dog but the judge gave the decision to a pug-nosed half-bred brute of no value whatever. The Fox Terriers were never worse judged. We understand the judge was a local production. Well, we pity him, for his want of knowledge."

Helsinki in 2006, which was considerably bigger than even some World Show totals.

Other events may also be called Europe shows although they are not quite the same, and the Scandinavian countries select one show each year as the Nordic Winner show. The multitude of title shows explains, at least to some extent, the long, complex titles carried by many crowned heads of European dog aristocracy. In abbreviation, they look like nothing so much as alphabet soup, but written out they can sound impressive, if cumbersome. Here's one not unusual example—take a deep breath: DKUCH INTUCH NORDUCH NORDV-02 NORDV-03 NORDV-04 NV-01 NV-03 SV-02 WW-03 — all of which appears before the dog's registered name and is printed in show catalogs. Written out and translated, it would read something like "Danish, International, and Nordic Show Champion; Nordic Winner 2002, 2003, and 2004; Norwegian Winner 2001 and 2003; Swedish Winner 2002; World Winner 2003." With titles such as these, or only somewhat

shorter, included many thousand times over in an average show catalog (titles for each dog's sire and dam are often also printed in full), it is easy to be grateful to the AKC for accepting only the simple *Ch.* abbreviation. (The AKC does not, in fact, accept any foreign titles, does not include them in their pedigrees, and does not print them in the show catalogs. The reasons for this have probably more to do with practicality than with chauvinism, but there is a deep-rooted suspicion of foreign championships within the AKC.)

FCI JUDGING PROCEDURE

The basic judging procedure at the international shows is similar regardless of where they are held. The dogs are graded before being placed in their respective classes, some kind of critique is often (but not always) provided, and—most important—the international certificate, the CACIB (Certificat d'Aptitude au Championnat Internationale de Beauté) can be awarded to the best dog and bitch over fifteen months of age. Younger dogs may compete for

GRADINGS

The different gradings deserve an explanation. During the individual examination of each dog, the judge is expected to determine the dog's overall quality and award it the grade it merits. The top grade is Excellent, which as far as such a subjective term can be defined has been officially described as "a dog which could be set up as a goal for breeders to aim at." In some countries, the Excellent is termed Certificate Quality, meaning that the dog is worthy of becoming a champion (even if it should not win on that day). The second-highest grade is Very Good or First class, followed by plain Good or Second grade, Acceptable or Third grade, and finally Unacceptable, which means that the dog is not typical of its breed or has a temperament problem—for instance, a dog that tries to bite cannot be awarded anything else, regardless of conformation. Exactly how freely a judge awards the higher grades varies considerably, but at least limiting the Excellent to dogs of champion quality is a fairly consistent requirement—in theory.

a national certificate (CAC, or Certificat d'Aptitude au Championnat), depending on local regulations, but even if this dog should go on to take Best of Breed over adult champions, it cannot be awarded a CACIB until it is at least fifteen months of age.

The chief attraction of the CACIB is that it marks a first step up the ladder to the official title of International Champion. Normally, a minimum of four CACIB wins under three judges in three different countries, with at least one year's time between the first and the qualifying win, are required for FCI's International Champion title. In some countries, where geography and a lack of neighboring FCI member countries make showing abroad difficult, the International Champion title can be awarded to a dog that has simply won the CACIB four times provided the judges come from different FCI member countries. In a number of breeds, show ring success isn't enough for a champion title; field or working achievements are also required.

In certain breeds, additional CACIBs can be awarded for separate color varieties. In Great Danes, for instance, there is one CACIB for brindles and fawns, another for blacks and harlequins, and a third for blues. Poodles have separate CACIB awards for several of the different color varieties—except Toy Poodles, which have only one CACIB per sex, regardless of color. Even some of the breeds themselves are categorized differently by the FCI than in countries with English-based show systems: Poodles, again, are divided into four, not three, size varieties (Standards, Miniatures, Dwarfs, and Toys); Dachshunds are divided into nine different varieties—combinations of three different coats (Smooth, Wire, and Long) and three different sizes (Standard, Miniature, and Kaninchen, or Dwarf).

Sometimes international titles that are not sanctioned by the FCI are advertised in the American press. Anyone whose dog wins a title in more than one country can presumably call it an international champion, and becoming a triple champion in England, the United States, and Canada is certainly as impressive an achievement as gaining any number of FCI titles. However, normally when the term *International Champion* is used in the dog world, it is the FCI title that is indicated. The AKC does not issue international titles, nor does the United Kennel Club. A few little-known American dog organizations do, but these are not affiliated with any major kennel club and their titles are barely worth the ink spilled in writing them out.

The classification at FCI shows is similar, if not identical, from one member country to another. Puppy classes may or may not be offered but are never part of the official competition. There is a Junior class, an Intermediate or Young Adult class, an Open class, a separate Working class in the breeds for which field or utility trials are organized, a Champion class, and a Veteran class—all split by sex.

The Best Dog and Best Bitch compete for Best of Breed at FCI shows in the same way as they do in England, but how they get to that point may differ from one country to another. In Denmark, Norway, and Sweden, for instance, the four best dogs and the four best bitches have to be placed in order prior to Best of Breed judging. This can be a somewhat unnerving experience for a first-time visiting judge, as not only the class winners but all dogs the judge rewarded with the highest grade that day (Excellent, or Certificate Quality) come into the ring at the same time, regardless of class placement, and have to be assessed once again. In a large entry among which top grades have been freely awarded, this can amount to many dogs—but it is logical that, for example, the second in the Champion class might well place ahead of the Open class winner for Best Dog, and those final Best Dog and Best Bitch placements are taken very seriously by the exhibitors.

Japan, by contrast, does not have any Best of Breed judging at all. The Best Dog and the Best Bitch compete in separate Groups for Kings and Queens, and not until a Best King and a Best Queen have been designated do the two meet to compete for Best in Show.

In every other way, the Group judging is identical at all FCI shows. There are ten different Groups, the majority of which look very different from those in most of the English-speaking world, and because of the large number of breeds classified at FCI shows, they can also be very large. Four placements are made in each Group, sometimes with a fifth as reserve. In the Best in Show judging, usually there are not only a winner and a reserve but also a third and a fourth placement. On occasion, judges are requested to place all the ten Group winners in descending order!

IRELAND

Some countries are in the peculiar position of being FCI members in spite of having close links to other kennel clubs. South Africa has already been mentioned. The Republic of Ireland became a member of the FCI in 2005, after developing its own dog show history for many decades and cooperating mainly with The Kennel Club in London, which governs canine affairs in Northern Ireland, officially still part of the United Kingdom. The Irish Kennel Club was founded in January 1922, only a few weeks after the British offered dominion status to Ulster and southern Ireland. Around

30,000–35,000 dogs are registered per year and about 20 all-breed championship shows are held each year, most of them during the summer. The most important event has always been the Irish Kennel Club's own St. Patrick's show, in the past held at the Royal Dublin Society's horse show arena. For many years, the general public flocked to the dog show after watching the St. Patrick's Day parade—although there may have been more than dog interest at stake, since the dog show was the only place in town where a pint of Guinness was available, as the pubs were closed on St. Patrick's Day. Since 1995, the show has moved to a March weekend following Crufts and usually attracts upward of 3,000 dogs. Starting in 2007, the Irish Kennel Club show is moving to a summer date, which is more practical considering the weather and the number of entries the show gets.

To become an Irish champion, a dog needs to win seven Green Stars under seven different judges. At least one of the wins must come after the dog has turned fifteen months old. The Green Stars are Ireland's answer to the British CCs, and just as champions continue to compete for CCs in the United Kingdom, so the Green Stars in Ireland are on offer for champions and nonchampions alike. The seven Green Stars requirement is new, as of 2007; prior to that year, a point system, somewhat similar to that in the United States, was employed. The division of breeds into different Groups will parallel that of the FCI, with ten different Groups instead of the usual seven in most other English-speaking countries.

Since Ireland became an FCI member, the coveted CACIB awards, which serve as stepping-stones toward an official International Champion title, are available at a few of the shows: the St. Patrick's show, the Combined Canine show on

BREAKING THE RULES

As an example of how FCI rules may not always be observed at some FCI shows, the following is an experience from the author's own past. While I was judging at one of the shows during the FCI World Show in Puerto Rico in 1997, there appeared in my ring a couple of dogs with clearly disqualifying color, according to the FCI breed standard (although not AKC's). The dogs were otherwise quite handsome, but because this was an FCI show, I had no choice but to disqualify the dogs. The handler politely informed me that the dogs won "all the time" under American judges. As it turned out, he was proven right at the show the very next day, also an FCI event, when a fellow American judge gave the same dogs the highest honors. In other words, judges at FCI shows do not always judge by the FCI standards.

The same situation was even more clearly illustrated by another judge, one with a high standing in Europe, who judged the FCI Asian International show in Tokyo. This is the premier dog event in that part of the world and one of the most important FCI shows anywhere. Encountering a large champion class where almost all the dogs were of a color that was, again, clearly disqualifying according to the FCI standard, the judge was at a loss what to do. He called in the club officials, who told him to "judge by the American standards, like we usually do."

Equally clearly in violation of both regulations and common sense, an Australian judge officiating for the first time at an FCI show in Europe reports having been assigned a breed for which she was not approved in her home country, in fact had never in her life previously judged. The club told her to just go ahead and judge it anyway.

It is certainly not only the FCI that does not stick to the rules. In many countries, I have been asked, even scheduled, to judge breeds for which I am not officially approved. Being invited to award Challenge Certificates for the "wrong" breed in England probably does not happen often, and if I had been unwise enough to accept, The Kennel Club most likely would not have approved the assignment. However, being invited to judge at one of Australia's huge Royal shows is, well, almost a royal command, and refusing to fulfill an assignment of several breeds that were not on the list I had agreed to judge created a great stir at the time. Being assigned the Group finals for breeds in which I had no previous experience at an international FCI show in Europe was easier to get out of, as was refusing to judge an entry of Dogos Argentino at a show in South America. Even the normally careful American Kennel Club slipped up once and scheduled me to judge Rhodesian Ridgebacks on one of my first assignments in the United States. It was a small entry, and after some persuasion from a fellow judge, I actually judged them, which means that I am now in the perhaps unique position of having judged a breed at an AKC show for which I am as yet not approved by the American Kennel Club.

Easter Saturday, Swords, Monkstown, and Clonmel. These events attract bigger entries than the rest and usually include a good number of visitors from Great Britain as well.

In the early 2000s, a few kennel clubs in Northern Ireland seceded from The Kennel Club in London, affiliating themselves with the Irish Kennel Club and running their shows according to IKC rules.

INDIA

On the other side of the globe, India in some respects mirrors the Irish developments both in its early ties and later its independence from The Kennel Club in London. The Kennel Club of India was founded in 1896, before most others except the AKC and a few in Europe. During the years of British sovereignty, it was natural for the ruling class to introduce the social and sporting clubs that were a part of their life back home. Carefully selected, aristocratic, wealthy Indians were invited to participate in the sport. As a result, India saw the importation of some extremely fine dogs from England, but because the sport was in the hands of a select few, it was difficult to build up a significant depth of quality.

Because the national club was closely affiliated with The Kennel Club in London, it generally followed the same rules and accepted British breed standards. Currently, however, the Kennel Club of India is a full member of both the FCI and the Asian Kennel Union, and the British influence on India's dog game is waning.

The Kennel Club of India has about fifty affiliated all-breed clubs and a handful of specialty clubs, each of which hold a minimum of two shows per year. Most shows have only a few hundred dogs, with the national show held by the Kennel Club of India once a year attracting around 600–700 dogs.

Increasing affluence and a rising middle class have resulted in renewed interest in pedigree dogs in recent years. One obstacle to dog ownership has been a reluctance to cook and feed meat products, as a large percentage of India's population is vegetarian and follows traditional religious restrictions on handling meat. With the advent of commercially processed dog food, this problem has been largely overcome.

With more and more distant countries becoming members of the FCI, the central government in Belgium faces increasing pressure to adjust to different dog show cultures. Most likely, the organization will eventually split up into regional sections—FCI Europe, FCI Asia, FCI Latin America, and so on—but will no doubt continue to serve as a unifier for international dog shows.

Appendix B: Registerable Breeds

American Kennel Club Registerable Breeds

The AKC official list of breeds does not indicate varieties within a breed, such as the coat varieties of Dachshund or the size varieties of Poodle.

Sporting Group

American Water Spaniel
Brittany
Chesapeake Bay Retriever
Clumber Spaniel
Cocker Spaniel
Curly-Coated Retriever
English Cocker Spaniel
English Setter
English Springer Spaniel
Field Spaniel
Flat-Coated Retriever
German Shorthaired Pointer
German Wirehaired Pointer
Golden Retriever
Gordon Setter
Irish Setter
Irish Water Spaniel
Labrador Retriever
Nova Scotia Duck Tolling Retriever
Pointer
Spinone Italiano
Sussex Spaniel
Vizsla
Weimaraner
Welsh Springer Spaniel
Wirehaired Pointing Griffon

Hound Group

Afghan Hound
American Foxhound
Basenji
Basset Hound
Beagle
    (Not exceeding 13 inches;
    over 13 inches but not
    exceeding 15 inches)
Black and Tan Coonhound
Bloodhound

Borzoi
Dachshund
    (Longhaired; Smooth; Wirehaired)
English Foxhound
Greyhound
Harrier
Ibizan Hound
Irish Wolfhound
Norwegian Elkhound
Otterhound
Petit Basset Griffon Vendéen
Pharaoh Hound
Plott
Rhodesian Ridgeback
Saluki
Scottish Deerhound
Whippet

Working Group

Akita
Alaskan Malamute
Anatolian Shepherd Dog
Bernese Mountain Dog
Black Russian Terrier
Boxer
Bullmastiff
Doberman Pinscher
German Pinscher
Giant Schnauzer
Great Dane
Great Pyrenees
Greater Swiss Mountain Dog
Komondor
Kuvasz
Mastiff
Neapolitan Mastiff
Newfoundland
Portuguese Water Dog
Rottweiler

Saint Bernard
Samoyed
Siberian Husky
Standard Schnauzer
Tibetan Mastiff

Terrier Group

Airedale Terrier
American Staffordshire Terrier
Australian Terrier
Bedlington Terrier
Border Terrier
Bull Terrier
Cairn Terrier
Dandie Dinmont Terrier
Glen of Imaal Terrier
Irish Terrier
Kerry Blue Terrier
Lakeland Terrier
Manchester Terrier
Miniature Bull Terrier
Miniature Schnauzer
Norfolk Terrier
Norwich Terrier
Parson Russell Terrier
Scottish Terrier
Sealyham Terrier
Skye Terrier
Smooth Fox Terrier
Soft Coated Wheaten Terrier
Staffordshire Bull Terrier
Welsh Terrier
West Highland White Terrier
Wire Fox Terrier

Toy Group

Affenpinscher
Brussels Griffon
Cavalier King Charles Spaniel

Chihuahua
Chinese Crested
English Toy Spaniel
Havanese
Italian Greyhound
Japanese Chin
Maltese
Manchester Terrier
   (Toy)
Miniature Pinscher
Papillon
Pekingese
Pomeranian
Poodle (Toy)
Pug
Shih Tzu
Silky Terrier
Toy Fox Terrier
Yorkshire Terrier

NON-SPORTING GROUP

American Eskimo Dog
Bichon Frisé
Boston Terrier
Bulldog
Chinese Shar-Pei
Chow Chow
Dalmatian
Finnish Spitz
French Bulldog
Keeshond
Lhasa Apso
Löwchen
Poodle
   (Miniature; Standard)
Schipperke
Shiba Inu
Tibetan Spaniel
Tibetan Terrier

HERDING GROUP

Australian Cattle Dog
Australian Shepherd
Bearded Collie
Belgian Malinois
Belgian Sheepdog
Belgian Tervuren
Border Collie
Bouvier des Flandres
Briard
Canaan Dog
Cardigan Welsh Corgi
Collie
German Shepherd Dog
Old English Sheepdog
Pembroke Welsh Corgi
Polish Lowland Sheepdog
Puli
Shetland Sheepdog

MISCELLANEOUS BREEDS

In addition to maintaining the registry of its officially recognized breeds, which appear in the Stud Book of the American Kennel Club, the AKC provides for a regular path of development for miscellaneous breeds, which may result in these breeds' full recognition. The requirement for admission to the Stud Book is clear and categorical proof that a substantial, sustained nationwide interest and activity in the breed exists. This includes an active parent club, with serious and expanding breeding activity over a wide geographic area. When in the judgment of the AKC Board of Directors such interest and activity exists, a breed is admitted to the Miscellaneous Class. Breeds in the Miscellaneous Class may compete and earn titles in AKC Obedience, Tracking, and Agility events. Miscellaneous breeds are also eligible to compete in Junior Showmanship. They may also compete at conformation shows, but are limited to competition in the Miscellaneous Class and are not eligible for championship points.

Beauceron (regularly registerable as of March 1, 2007, but still listed on AKC Web site as Miscellaneous on January 28, 2007)
Dogue de Bordeaux
Norwegian Buhund
Pyrenean Shepherd
Redbone Coonhound
Swedish Vallhund (regularly registerable as of March 1, 2007, but still listed on AKC Web site as Miscellaneous on January 28, 2007)

FOUNDATION STOCK SERVICE BREEDS

The following breeds are accepted for recording in the AKC's Foundation Stock Service. This service is provided by the AKC to allow these breeds to continue to develop while providing them with the security of a reliable and reputable avenue to maintain their records. These breeds are not eligible for AKC registration. Several of the FSS breeds are approved to compete in AKC Companion Events (Obedience, Agility, Tracking, and Rally).

American English Coonhound
Appenzeller Sennenhund
Argentine Dogo
Azawakh
Belgian Laekenois
Bergamasco
Black and Tan Coonhound
Bluetick Coonhound

Bolognese
Boykin Spaniel
Bracco Italiano
Cane Corso
Catahoula Leopard Dog
Caucasian Mountain Dog
Central Asian Shepherd Dog
Cesky Terrier
Chinook
Coton de Tulear
Czechoslovakian Wolfdog
Entlebucher Mountain Dog
Estrela Mountain Dog
Finnish Lapphund
German Spitz
Grand Basset Griffon Vendéen

Icelandic Sheepdog
Irish Red and White Setter
Kai Ken
Karelian Bear Dog
Kooikerhondje
Lagotto Romagnolo
Lancashire Heeler
Leonberger
Mudi
Norwegian Lundehund
Perro de Presa Canario
Peruvian Inca Orchid
Portuguese Podengo
Portuguese Pointer
Pumi
Rafeiro do Alentejo

Rat Terrier
Russell Terrier
Schapendoes (new on FSS list as of 2007)
Sloughi
Small Munsterlander Pointer (new on FSS list as of 2007)
South African Boerboel (new on FSS list as of 2007)
Spanish Water Dog
Stabyhoun
Thai Ridgeback
Tosa
Treeing Tennessee Brindle
Treeing Walker Coonhound
Xoloitzcuintli

THE KENNEL CLUB (UNITED KINGDOM) REGISTERABLE BREEDS

GUNDOG GROUP
Bracco Italiano
Brittany
English Setter
German Longhaired Pointer
German Shorthaired Pointer
German Wirehaired Pointer
Gordon Setter
Hungarian Vizsla
Hungarian Wirehaired Vizsla
Irish Red and White Setter
Irish Setter
Italian Spinone
Kooikerhondje
Korthals Griffon
Lagotto Romagnolo
Large Munsterlander
Pointer
Retriever (Chesapeake Bay)
Retriever (Curly Coated)
Retriever (Flat Coated)
Retriever (Golden)
Retriever (Labrador)
Retriever (Nova Scotia Duck Tolling)
Small Munsterlander
Spaniel (American Cocker)
Spaniel (Clumber)

Spaniel (Cocker)
Spaniel (English Springer)
Spaniel (Field)
Spaniel (Irish Water)
Spaniel (Sussex)
Spaniel (Welsh Springer)
Spanish Water Dog
Weimaraner

HOUND GROUP
Afghan Hound
Azawakh
Basenji
Basset Bleu de Gascogne
Basset Fauve de Bretagne
Basset Griffon Vendéen (Grand)
Basset Griffon Vendéen (Petit)
Basset Hound
Bavarian Mountain Hound
Beagle
Bloodhound
Borzoi
Dachshund (Long Haired)
Dachshund (Miniature Long Haired)
Dachshund (Smooth Haired)
Dachshund (Miniature Smooth Haired)
Dachshund (Wire Haired)

Dachshund (Miniature Wire Haired)
Deerhound
Norwegian Elkhound
Finnish Spitz
Foxhound
Grand Bleu De Gascogne
Greyhound
Hamiltonstövare
Ibizan Hound
Irish Wolfhound
Otterhound
Pharaoh Hound
Portuguese Podengo (Warren Hound)
Rhodesian Ridgeback
Saluki
Segugio Italiano
Sloughi
Whippet

WORKING GROUP
Alaskan Malamute
Beauceron
Bernese Mountain Dog
Bouvier des Flandres
Boxer
Bullmastiff
Canadian Eskimo Dog

Dobermann
Dogue de Bordeaux
Entlebucher Mountain Dog
German Pinscher
Giant Schnauzer
Great Dane
Greenland Dog
Hovawart
Leonberger
Mastiff
Neapolitan Mastiff
Newfoundland
Portuguese Water Dog
Pyrenean Mastiff
Rottweiler
Russian Black Terrier
St. Bernard
Siberian Husky
Tibetan Mastiff

TERRIER GROUP
Airedale Terrier
Australian Terrier
Bedlington Terrier
Border Terrier
Bull Terrier
Bull Terrier (Miniature)
Cairn Terrier
Cesky Terrier
Dandie Dinmont Terrier
Fox Terrier (Smooth)
Fox Terrier (Wire)
Glen of Imaal Terrier
Irish Terrier
Kerry Blue Terrier
Lakeland Terrier
Manchester Terrier
Norfolk Terrier
Norwich Terrier
Parson Russell Terrier
Scottish Terrier
Sealyham Terrier
Skye Terrier
Soft Coated Wheaten Terrier
Staffordshire Bull Terrier

Welsh Terrier
West Highland White Terrier

TOY GROUP
Affenpinscher
Australian Silky Terrier
Bichon Frisé
Bolognese
Cavalier King Charles Spaniel
Chihuahua (Long Coat)
Chihuahua (Smooth Coat)
Chinese Crested
Coton de Tulear
English Toy Terrier (Black and Tan)
Griffon Bruxellios
Havanese
Italian Greyhound
Japanese Chin
King Charles Spaniel
Lowchen (Little Lion Dog)
Maltese
Miniature Pinscher
Papillon
Pekingese
Pomeranian
Pug
Yorkshire Terrier

UTILITY GROUP
Akita
Boston Terrier
Bulldog
Canaan Dog
Chow Chow
Dalmatian
Eurasier
French Bulldog
German Spitz (Klein)
German Spitz (Mittel)
Japanese Shiba Inu
Japanese Spitz
Keeshond
Lhasa Apso
Mexican Hairless
Miniature Schnauzer

Poodle (Miniature)
Poodle (Standard)
Poodle (Toy)
Schipperke
Schnauzer
Shar Pei
Shih Tzu
Tibetan Spaniel
Tibetan Terrier

PASTORAL GROUP
Anatolian Shepherd Dog
Australian Cattle Dog
Australian Shepherd
Bearded Collie
Belgian Shepherd Dog (Groenendael)
Belgian Shepherd Dog (Laekenois)
Belgian Shepherd Dog (Malinois)
Belgian Shepherd Dog (Tervueren)
Bergamasco
Border Collie
Briard
Collie (Rough)
Collie (Smooth)
Estrela Mountain Dog
Finnish Lapphund
German Shepherd Dog (Alsatian)
Hungarian Kuvasz
Hungarian Puli
Komondor
Lancashire Heeler
Maremma Sheepdog
Norwegian Buhund
Old English Sheepdog
Polish Lowland Sheepdog
Pyrenean Mountain Dog
Pyrenean Sheepdog
Samoyed
Shetland Sheepdog
Swedish Lapphund
Swedish Vallhund
Welsh Corgi (Cardigan)
Welsh Corgi (Pembroke)

FÉDÉRATION CYNOLOGIQUE INTERNATIONALE REGISTERABLE BREEDS

The FCI incorporates national kennel clubs in more than eighty member countries, including all those in Europe except the United Kingdom, as well as most in Asia and South America. Breed names listed below are those officially used by the FCI, with English translations in parentheses, when available.

GROUP 1: SHEEPDOGS AND CATTLE DOGS (EXCEPT SWISS CATTLE DOGS)

Australian Cattle Dog
Australian Kelpie
Bearded Collie
Berger de Beauce (Beauceron)
Berger de Brie (Briard)
Berger de Picardie (Berger Picard)
Berger des Pyrénées à face rase
   (Pyrenean Sheepdog, smooth faced)
Berger des Pyrénées à poil long
   (Long-haired Pyrenean Sheepdog)
Border Collie
Bouvier des Ardennes (Ardennes Cattle Dog)
Bouvier des Flandres/Vlaamse Koehond (Flanders Cattle Dog)
Ca de Bestiar-Perro de pastor mallorquín
   (Majorca Shepherd Dog)
       a. Short-haired
       b. Long-haired
Cane da pastore Bergamasco (Bergamasco Shepherd Dog)
Cane da pastore Maremmano-Abruzzese (Maremma and
   Abruzzes Sheepdog)
Cão da Serra de Aires (Portuguese Sheepdog)
Chien de Berger Belge (Belgian Shepherd Dog)
       a. Groenendael
       b. Laekenois
       c. Malinois
       d. Tervueren
Collie, Rough
Collie, Smooth
Deutscher Schäferhund (German Shepherd Dog)
Gos d'Atura Catalá-Perro de pastor catalán (Catalan Sheepdog)
       a. Long-haired
       b. Smooth-haired
Hollandse Herdershond (Dutch Shepherd Dog)
       a. Short-haired
       b. Long-haired
       c. Rough-haired
Hrvatski Ovcar (Croatian Sheepdog)
Ioujnorousskaïa Ovtcharka (South Russian Shepherd Dog)
Komondor
Kuvasz
Mudi
Nederlandse Schapendoes (Dutch Schapendoes)
Old English Sheepdog (Bobtail)
Polski Owczarek Nizinny (Polish Lowland Sheepdog)
Polski Owczarek Podhalanski (Tatra Shepherd Dog)
Puli
Pumi
Saarlooswolfhond (Saarloos Wolfdog)
Schipperke Ceskoslovenský Vlcak (Czeslovakian Wolfdog)
Shetland Sheepdog
Slovenský Cuvac (Slovakian Chuvach)
Welsh Corgi, Cardigan
Welsh Corgi, Pembroke

GROUP 2: PINSCHERS AND SCHNAUZERS, MOLOSSOID BREEDS, SWISS MOUNTAIN AND CATTLE DOGS, AND OTHER BREEDS

Affenpinscher
Appenzeller Sennenhund (Appenzell Cattle Dog)
Berner Sennenhund (Bernese Mountain Dog)
Broholmer
Bulldog
Bullmastiff
Cão da Serra da Estrela (Serra da Estrela Mountain Dog)
       a. Smooth-haired
       b. Long-haired
Cão de Castro Laboreiro (Castro Laboreiro Dog)
Chien de l'Atlas (Aïdi) (Atlas Shepherd Dog)
Chien de Montagne des Pyrénées (Pyrenean Mountain Dog)
Coban Köpegi (Anatolian Shepherd Dog)
Deutsche Dogge (Great Dane)
Deutscher Boxer (German Boxer)
Deutscher Pinscher (German Pinscher)
Dobermann
Dogo Argentino
Dogue de Bordeaux
Do-Khyi (Tibetan Mastiff)
Entlebucher Sennenhund (Entlebuch Cattle Dog)
Fila Brasileiro
Grosser Schweizer Sennenhund (Great Swiss Mountain Dog)

Hollandse Smoushond (Dutch Smoushond)
Hovawart
Jugoslovenski Ovcarski Pas-Sarplaninac
   (Yugoslavian Shepherd Dog-Sharplanina)
Kavkazskaïa Ovtcharka (Caucasian Shepherd Dog)
Kraski Ovcar (Karst Shepherd Dog)
Landseer (europäisch-kontinentaler Typ)
   (Continental-European type)
Leonberger
Mastiff
Mastín del Pirineo (Pyrenean Mastiff)
Mastín español (Spanish Mastiff)
Mastino Napoletano (Neapolitan Mastiff)
Newfoundland
Österreichischer Pinscher (Austrian Pinscher)
Perro dogo mallorquín (Ca de Bou) (Majorca Mastiff)
Rafeiro do Alentejo (Alentejo Mastiff)
Riesenschnauzer (Giant Schnauzer)
Rottweiler
Schnauzer
Shar Pei
Sredneasiatskaïa Ovtcharka (Central Asia Shepherd Dog)
St.Bernhardshund (Bernhardiner) (Saint Bernard Dog)
        a. Short-haired
        b. Long-haired
Tchiorny Terrier (Black Terrier)
Tosa
Zwergpinscher (Miniature Pinscher)
Zwergschnauzer (Miniature Schnauzer)

GROUP 3: TERRIERS
Airedale Terrier
American Staffordshire Terrier
Australian Silky Terrier
Australian Terrier
Bedlington Terrier
Border Terrier
Bull Terrier
            a. Bull Terrier (Standard)
            b. Miniature Bull Terrier
Cairn Terrier
Ceský Teriér (Cesky Terrier)
Dandie Dinmont Terrier
Deutscher Jagdterrier (German Hunting Terrier)
English Toy Terrier (Black and Tan)
Fox Terrier (Smooth)
Fox Terrier (Wire)
Irish Glen of Imaal Terrier

Irish Soft Coated Wheaten Terrier
Irish Terrier
Jack Russell Terrier
Kerry Blue Terrier
Lakeland Terrier
Manchester Terrier
Nihon Teria (Japanese Terrier)
Norfolk Terrier
Norwich Terrier
Parson Russell Terrier
Scottish Terrier
Sealyham Terrier
Skye Terrier
Staffordshire Bull Terrier
Welsh Terrier
West Highland White Terrier
Yorkshire Terrier

GROUP 4: DACHSHUNDS
a. Standard
            Smooth-haired
            Long-haired
            Wire-haired
b. Miniature
            Smooth-haired
            Long-haired
            Wire-haired
c. Rabbit Dachshund
            Smooth-haired
            Long-haired
            Wire-haired

GROUP 5: SPITZ AND PRIMITIVE TYPES
Akita
Alaskan Malamute
American Akita
Basenji
Canaan Dog
Chow Chow
Cirneco dell'Etna
Deutscher Spitz (German Spitz)
            a. Wolfspitz (Keeshond)
            b. Grossspitz (Giant Spitz)
            c. Mittelspitz (Medium-size Spitz)
Eurasier (Eurasian)
Grønlandshund (Greenland Dog)
Hokkaïdo

Islenskur Fjárhundur (Icelandic Sheepdog)
Jämthund (Swedish Elkhound)
Kai
Karjalankarhukoira (Karelian Bear Dog)
Kishu
Kleinspitz (Miniature Spitz)
Korea Jindo Dog
Lapinporokoira (Finnish Reindeer Herder)
Nihon Supittsu (Japanese Spitz)
Norrbottenspets (Norrbottenspitz)
Norsk Buhund (Norwegian Buhund)
Norsk Elghund Grå (Norwegian Elkhound grey)
Norsk Elghund Sort (Norwegian Elkhound black)
Norsk Lundehund (Norwegian Lundehund)
Perro sin pelo del Perú (Peruvian Hairless Dog)
      a. Large
      b. Medium-size
      c. Miniature
Pharaoh Hound
Podenco Canario (Canarian Warren Hound)
Podenco Ibicenco (Ibizan Warren Hound, Ibizan Podenco)
      a. Rough-haired
      b. Smooth-haired
Podengo Português (Portuguese Warren Hound, Portuguese
Podengo)
      a. Wire-haired
            Large
            Medium-size
            Miniature
      b. Smooth-haired
            Large
            Medium-size
            Miniature
Russko-Evropeïskaïa Laïka (Russian-European Laïka)
Samoiedskaïa Sabaka (Samoyed)
Shiba
Shikoku
Siberian Husky
Suomenlapinkoira (Finnish Lapphund)
Suomenpystykorva (Finnish Spitz)
Svensk Lapphund (Swedish Lapphund)
Thai Ridgeback Dog
Västgötaspets (Swedish Vallhund)
Volpino Italiano
Vostotchno-Sibirskaïa Laïka (East Siberian Laïka)
Xoloitzquintle (Mexican Hairless Dog)
      a. Standard
      b. Intermediate

      c. Miniature
Zapadno-Sibirskaïa Laïka (West Siberian Laïka)
Zwerspitz (Pomeranian)

GROUP 6: SCENTHOUNDS AND RELATED BREEDS

Alpenländische Dachsbracke (Alpine Dachsbracke)
American Foxhound
Anglo-français de petite vénerie
Ariégeois
Basset artésien normand (Artesian-Norman Basset)
Basset bleu de Gascogne (Blue Gascony Basset)
Basset fauve de Bretagne (Fawn Brittany Basset)
Basset Hound
Bayrischer Gebirgsschweisshund
   (Bavarian Mountain Scenthound)
Beagle
Beagle-Harrier
Billy
Black and Tan Coonhound
Bosanski Ostrodlaki Gonic Barak (Bosnian Coarse-haired
   Hound, called Barak)
Brandlbracke (Vieräugl) (Austrian Black and Tan Hound)
Briquet griffon vendéen (Medium Griffon Vendéen)
Chien d'Artois (Artois Hound)
Chien de Saint-Hubert (Bloodhound)
Crnogorski Planinski Gonic (Montenegrin Mountain Hound)
Dalmatinac (Dalmatian)
Deutsche Bracke (German Hound)
Drever (Swedish Dachsbracke)
Dunker (Norwegian Hound)
English Foxhound
Erdélyi Kopó (Transylvanian Hound)
Français blanc et noir (French White and Black Hound)
Français blanc et orange (French White and Orange Hound)
Français tricolore (French Tricolour Hound)
Grand anglo-français blanc et noir (Great Anglo-French White
   and Black Hound)
Grand anglo-français blanc et orange (Great Anglo-French
   White and Orange Hound)
Grand anglo-français tricolore (Great Anglo-French Tricolour
   Hound)
Grand Basset griffon vendéen (Grand Basset Griffon Vendéen)
Grand bleu de Gascogne (Great Gascony Hound)
Grand gascon saintongeois (Great Gascon Saintongeois)
Grand griffon vendéen (Grand Griffon Vendéen)
Griffon bleu de Gascogne (Blue Gascony Griffon)
Griffon fauve de Bretagne (Fawn Brittany Griffon)

Griffon nivernais
Haldenstøvare (Halden Hound)
Hamiltonstövare (Hamilton Hound)
Hannover'scher Schweisshund (Hanoverian Scenthound)
Harrier
Hellinikos Ichnilatis (Hellenic Hound)
Hygenhund (Hygen Hound)
Istarski Kratkodlaki Gonic (Istrian Short-haired Hound)
Istarski Ostrodlaki Gonic (Istrian Coarse-haired Hound)
Ogar Polski (Polish Hound)
Otterhound
Petit Basset griffon vendéen (Petit Basset Griffon Vendéen)
Petit bleu de Gascogne (Small Blue Gascony Hound)
Petit gascon saintongeois (Small Gascon Saintongeois)
Poitevin
Porcelaine
Posavski Gonic (Posavaz Hound)
Rhodesian Ridgeback
Sabueso Español (Spanish Hound)
Schillerstövare (Schiller Hound)
Schweizer Laufhund-Chien Courant Suisse (Swiss Hound)
    a. Bernese Hound
    b. Jura Hound
    c. Lucerne Hound
    d. Schwyz Hound
Schweizerischer Niederlaufhund-Petit chien courant suisse
  (Small Swiss Hound)
    a. Small Bernese Hound
        Smooth-haired
        Coarse-haired
    b. Small Jura Hound
    c. Small Lucerne Hound
    d. Small Schwyz Hound
Segugio Italiano (Italian Hound)
    a. Short-haired
    b. Coarse-haired
Slovenský Kopov (Slovakian Hound)
Smålandsstövare (Småland Hound)
Srpski Gonic (Serbian Hound)
Srpski Trobojni Gonic (Serbian Tricolour Hound)
Steirische Rauhhaarbracke (Styrian Coarse-haired Hound)
Suomenajokoira (Finnish Hound)
Tiroler Bracke (Tyrolean Hound)
Westfälische Dachsbracke (Westphalian Dachsbracke)

GROUP 7: POINTING DOGS
Bracco Italiano (Italian Pointing Dog)
Braque d'Auvergne (Auvergne Pointing Dog)

Braque de l'Ariège (Ariege Pointing Dog)
Braque du Bourbonnais (Bourbonnais Pointing Dog)
Braque français, type Gascogne (grande taille) (French Pointing Dog, Gascogne type)
Braque français, type Pyrénées (petite taille) (French Pointing Dog, Pyrenean type)
Braque Saint-Germain (St.Germain Pointing Dog)
Ceský Fousek (Bohemian Wire-haired Pointing Griffon)
Deutsch Drahthaar (German Wire-haired Pointing Dog)
Deutsch Kurzhaar (German Short-haired Pointing Dog)
Deutsch Langhaar (German Long-haired Pointing Dog)
Deutsch Stichelhaar (German Rough-haired Pointing Dog)
Drentse Patrijshond (Drentse Partridge Dog)
Drotzörü Magyar Vizsla (Hungarian Wire-haired Pointing Dog)
English Pointer
English Setter
Epagneul bleu de Picardie (Blue Picardy Spaniel)
Epagneul Breton (Brittany)
Epagneul de Pont-Audemer (Spaniel de Pont-Audemer)
Epagneul français (French Spaniel)
Epagneul picard (Picardy Spaniel)
Gammel Dansk Hønsehund (Old Danish Pointing Dog)
Gordon Setter
Griffon d'arrêt à poil dur Korthals (French Wire-haired Korthals
  Pointing Griffon)
Grosser Münsterländer (Large Munsterlander)
Irish Red and White Setter
Irish Red Setter
Kleiner Münsterländer (Small Munsterlander)
Perdigueiro Português (Portuguese Pointing Dog)
Perdiguero de Burgos (Burgos Pointing Dog)
Pudelpointer
Rövidszörü Magyar Vizsla (Hungarian Short-haired Pointing
  Dog)
Slovenský Hrubosrsty Stavac (Ohar) (Slovakian Wire-haired
  Pointing Dog)
Spinone Italiano (Italian Wire-haired Pointing Dog)
Stabyhoun (Frisian Pointing Dog)
Weimaraner
    a. Short-haired
    b. Long-haired

GROUP 8: RETRIEVERS, FLUSHING DOGS, AND WATER DOGS
American Cocker Spaniel
American Water Spaniel
Barbet (French Water Dog)
Cão de agua Português (Portuguese Water Dog)

a. Curly
b. Long and wavy
Chesapeake Bay Retriever
Clumber Spaniel
Curly Coated Retriever
Deutscher Wachtelhund (German Spaniel)
English Cocker Spaniel
English Springer Spaniel
Field Spaniel
Flat Coated Retriever
Golden Retriever
Irish Water Spaniel
Kooikerhondje (Small Dutch Waterfowl Dog)
Labrador Retriever
Lagotto Romagnolo (Romagna Water Dog)
Nova Scotia Duck Tolling Retriever
Perro de agua español (Spanish Water Dog)
Sussex Spaniel
Welsh Springer Spaniel
Wetterhoun (Frisian Water Dog)

GROUP 9: COMPANION AND TOY DOGS
Bichon à poil frisé (Bichon Frisé)
Bichon Havanais (Havanese)
Bolognese (Bolognese)
Boston Terrier
Bouledogue français (French Bulldog)
Caniche (Poodle)
a. Standard
b. Medium-size
c. Miniature
d. Toy
Cavalier King Charles Spaniel
Chihuahua
a. Smooth-haired
b. Long-haired
Chin (Japanese Chin)
Chinese Crested Dog
a. Hairless
b. Powder Puff with veil coat
Coton de Tuléar
Epagneul nain Continental (Continental Toy Spaniel)
a. Papillon (with erect ears: 1.5–2.5 kilos/
2.5–4.5 kilos)
b. Phalène (with drooping ears: 1.5–2.5 kilos/
2.5–4.5 kilos)
Griffon belge (Belgian Griffon)

Griffon bruxellois (Brussels Griffon)
King Charles Spaniel
Kromfohrländer
Lhasa Apso
Maltese
Pekingese
Petit Brabançon (Small Brabant Griffon)
Petit chien lion (Little Lion Dog)
Pug
Shih Tzu
Tibetan Spaniel
Tibetan Terrier

GROUP 10: SIGHTHOUNDS
Afghan Hound
Azawakh
Chart Polski (Polish Greyhound)
Deerhound
Galgo Español (Spanish Greyhound)
Greyhound
Irish Wolfhound
Magyar Agar (Hungarian Greyhound)
Piccolo Levriero Italiano (Italian Greyhound)
Russkaya Psovaya Borzaya—Barzoï (Borzoi)
Saluki
a. Fringed
b. Short-haired
Sloughi (Arabian Greyhound)
Whippet

PROVISIONALLY ACCEPTED BREEDS
Dogs of provisionally accepted breeds are not eligible for the CACIB.

Australian Shepherd, Group 1
Australian Stumpy Tail Cattle Dog, Group 1
Berger Blanc Suisse (White Swiss Shepherd Dog), Group 1
Cane Corso Italiano (Italian Corso Dog), Group 2
Cào Fila de Sào Miguel, Group 1
Ciimarron Uruguayo (Uruguayan Cimarron), Group 2
Ciobanesc Romanesc Carpatin (Romanian Carpathian Shepherd
   Dog), Group 1
Ciobanesc Romanesc Mioritic (Romanian Mioritic Shepherd
   Dog), Group 1
Dogo Canario, Group 2
Russkiy Toy (Russian Toy), Group 9
Tatiwan Dog, Group 5
Terier Brasileiro (Brazilian Terrier), Group 3

Appendix C:
Top Dogs in the United States 1925–2006

An annual Top Dog award for the most successful show dog of all breeds was first designated by *Popular Dogs* magazine in the late 1930s. This was based simply on number of Bests in Show won during the year. Using that system, a Top Dog has been designated retroactively to 1925, the first year that Best in Show awards were consistently published by the AKC. Starting in 1956, the top dogs each year were rated based on number of defeated competitors in both Group and Best in Show competition. Following the dog's name and breed are the number of Best in Shows won during the year and, from 1956 forward, the point score rounded to the nearest thousand. The list is compiled from records published in *Great Show Dogs of America* (1956–1965), *Popular Dogs, Kennel Review,* and by the American Kennel Club and other authoritative sources.

2006

1. Ch. Hobergays Fineus Fogg (imp. NZ)	Dandie Dinmont Terrier	57	87,000
2. Ch. Felicity's Diamond Jim	English Springer Spaniel	34	81,000
3. Ch. Bayview Some Like It Hot	Boxer	35	66,000
4. Ch. Stonebroke Right On The Money	Sealyham Terrier	35	65,000
5. Ch. Smash JP Win A Victory (imp. Japan)	Toy Poodle	38	62,000

2005

1. Ch. Yakee If Only (imp. UK)	Pekingese	64	100,000
2. Ch. Kendoric's Riversong Mulroney	Pug	42	61,000
3. Ch. Brookwood's Mystic Warrior	Boxer	24	58,000
4. Ch. Stonebroke Right On The Money	Sealyham Terrier	28	56,000
5. Ch. Telltale Salute	English Springer Spaniel	32	52,000

2004

1. Ch. North Well Chako JP Platina King (imp. Japan)	Toy Poodle	56	95,000
2. Ch. Yakee If Only (imp. UK)	Pekingese	58	90,000
3. Ch. Kaleef's Genuine Risk	German Shepherd Dog	51	73,000
4. Ch. Clussexx Three D Grinchy Glee	Sussex Spaniel	37	65,000
5. Ch. San Jo's Born To Win	Cocker Spaniel (Parti)	34	59,000

2003

1. Ch. Cracknor Cause Celebre (imp. UK)	Norfolk Terrier	47	86,000
2. Ch. Yakee Leaving Me Breathless at Franshaw (imp. UK)	Pekingese	54	71,000
3. Ch. Luxor's Playmate of the Year	Ibizan Hound	39	67,000
4. Ch. Kaleef's Genuine Risk	German Shepherd Dog	43	65,000
5. Ch. Blue Chip Purple Reign	Doberman Pinscher	35	63,000

2002

1. Ch. Kismet's Sight For Sore Eyes	German Shepherd Dog	59	86,000
2. Ch. Hallmark Jolei Raggedy Andy	Shih Tzu	51	76,000
3. Ch. Yakee Leaving Me Breathless at Franshaw (imp. UK)	Pekingese	58	67,000
4. Ch. Torum's Scarf Michael (imp. UK)	Kerry Blue Terrier	22	52,000
5. Ch. Marienburg's Repo Man	Doberman Pinscher	29	51,000

2001

1. Ch. Torum's Scarf Michael (imp. UK)	Kerry Blue Terrier	87	138,000
2. Ch. Charisma Jailhouse Rock	Standard Schnauzer	41	58,000
3. Ch. Deco's Hot Fudge V Legend	Doberman Pinscher	27	57,000
4. Ch. Kismet's Sight For Sore Eyes	German Shepherd Dog	33	56,000
5. Ch. Yarrow's Super Nova	Affenpinscher	30	56,000

2000

1. Ch. Special Times Just Right!	Bichon Frisé	76	123,000
2. Ch. Charing Cross Ragtime Cowboy	Shih Tzu	52	78,000
3. Ch. Coventry Queue	Pembroke Welsh Corgi	49	72,000
4. Ch. Willow Wind Tenure	Bedlington Terrier	27	53,000
5. Ch. Storybook's Rip It Up	Boxer	25	51,000

1999

1. Ch. Lake Cove That's My Boy	Standard Poodle	65	90,000
2. Ch. Skansen's Tristan II	Giant Schnauzer	29	72,000
3. Ch. Hi-Tech Johnny J of Boxerton	Boxer	27	70,000
4. Ch. Salilyn 'N Erin's Shameless	English Springer Spaniel	30	70,000
5. Ch. Sweethearts Space Jam	Cocker Spaniel (Black)	39	65,000

1998

1. Ch. Lake Cove That's My Boy	Standard Poodle	64	96,000
2. Ch. Deer Hill's Great Gatsby	Basset Hound	44	66,000
3. Ch. Toledobs Serenghetti	Doberman Pinscher	25	64,000
4. Ch. Ta-Jon's Tickle Me Silly	Maltese	52	60,000
5. Ch. Salilyn 'N Erin's Shameless	English Springer Spaniel	17	52,000

1997

1. Ch. Fairewood Frolic (imp. Canada)	Norwich Terrier	67	104,114
2. Ch. Nanuke's Take No Prisoners	Alaskan Malamute	50	82,000
3. Ch. Toledobes Serenghetti	Doberman Pinscher	25	71,000
4. Ch. Pompei's The American Way	Irish Setter	42	70,000
5. Ch. Bit O Gold Titan Treasure	Gordon Setter	37	67,000

1996

1. Ch. Parsifal di Casa Netzer (imp. Italy)	Standard Schnauzer	51	93,000
2. Ch. Toledobes Serenghetti	Doberman Pinscher	44	86,000
3. Ch. Revelry's Awesome Blossom	Lakeland Terrier	44	72,000
4. Ch. Anasazi Billy The Kid	Welsh Terrier	32	55,000
5. Ch. Tryst of Grandeur	Afghan Hound	38	52,000

1995

1. Ch. Tryst of Grandeur	Afghan Hound	52	84,000
2. Ch. Rendition Triple Play	Cocker Spaniel (Parti)	36	62,000
3. Ch. Kontoki's E-I-E-I-O	Siberian Husky	35	58,000
4. Ch. Revelry's Awesome Blossom	Lakeland Terrier	37	54,000
5. Ch. MVP of Ahs	Toy Poodle	32	73,000

1994

1. Ch. Altana's Mystique (imp. Canada)	German Shepherd Dog	89	112,439
2. Ch. La-Shay's Bart Simpson	Cocker Spaniel (Black)	51	84,000
3. Ch. Tryst of Grandeur	Afghan Hound	41	66,000
4. Ch. Hi-Tech's Arbitrage	Boxer	33	65,000
5. Ch. Gaelforce Post Script	Scottish Terrier	26	50,000

1993

1. Ch. Altana's Mystique (imp. Canada)	German Shepherd Dog	116	169,980
2. Ch. Chidley Willum The Conqueror	Norwich Terrier	50	87,000
3. Ch. Maneetas Del Zarzoso Fuego Fatuo (imp. UK)	Standard Poodle	31	55,000
4. Ch. Holyrood's Hotspur O'Shellybay	West Highland White Terrier	27	53,000
5. Ch. Registry's Lonesome Dove	Wire Fox Terrier	38	48,000

1992

1. Ch. Registry's Lonesome Dove	Wire Fox Terrier	85	115,815
2. Ch. Salilyn's Condor	English Springer Spaniel	69	114,319
3. Ch. Altana's Mystique (imp. Canada)	German Shepherd Dog	67	94,000
4. Ch. Kiebla's Tradition of Turo	Boxer	11	45,000
5. Ch. Heldenbrand's Jet Breaker	Boxer	17	43,000

1991

1. Ch. Registry's Lonesome Dove	Wire Fox Terrier	72	104,000
2. Ch. Brunswig's Cryptonite	Doberman Pinscher	58	96,000
3. Ch. Bramblewood's Custom Made	German Shepherd Dog	32	68,000
4. Ch. Galbraith's Ironeyes	Bouvier des Flandres	34	60,000
5. Ch. Sand Island Small Kraft Lite	Maltese	42	60,000

1990

1. Ch. Galbraith's Ironeyes	Bouvier des Flandres	47	82,000
2. Ch. Vin-Melca's Calista	Norwegian Elkhound	45	80,000
3. Ch. Whisperwind's On A Carousel	Standard Poodle	49	66,000
4. Ch. Brunswig's Cryptonite	Doberman Pinscher	27	56,000
5. Ch. Sand Island Small Kraft Lite	Maltese	31	50,000

1989

1. Ch. Hetherbull Bounty's Frigate	Bulldog	29	51,706
2. Ch. Luftnase Albelarm Bee's Knees	Pointer	19	51,399
3. Ch. Galewynd's Georgio Armani	German Shepherd Dog	34	51,091
4. Ch. Goodtime's Silk Teddy	English Setter	18	45,000
5. Ch. Rivergrove's Run For The Roses	Great Pyrenees	17	43,000

1988

1. Ch. Royal Tudor's Wild As The Wind	Doberman Pinscher	28	60,000
2. Ch. Rivergrove's Run For The Roses	Great Pyrenees	23	51,000
3. Ch. Kabik's The Front Runner	Afghan Hound	21	39,000
4. Ch. Skansen's I Have A Dream	Giant Schnauzer	14	37,000
5. Ch. Brawbridge TNT of Kris	Gordon Setter	15	35,000

1987

1. Ch. Galsul Excellence (imp. Ireland)	Wire Fox Terrier	50	84,000
2. Ch. NMK's Brittania V Sibelstein	German Shorthaired Pointer	30	63,000
3. Ch. Kabik's The Front Runner	Afghan Hound	25	45,000
4. Ch. Lynrik's Kristal	German Shepherd Dog	26	42,000
5. Ch. Telltale Royal Stuart	English Springer Spaniel	16	39,000

1986

1. Ch. Galsul Excellence (imp. Ireland)	Wire Fox Terrier	54	78,000
2. Ch. Devon Puff And Stuff	Bichon Frisé	33	54,000
3. Ch. Covy-Tucker Hill's Manhattan	German Shepherd Dog	45	49,000
4. Ch. Telltale Royal Stuart	English Springer Spaniel	28	47,000
5. Ch. Kirsch's Rodeo of Halo	Standard Poodle	34	39,000

1985

1. Ch. Covy-Tucker Hill's Manhattan	German Shepherd Dog	67	82,000
2. Ch. Bandog's Crawdaddy Gumbo	Bullmastiff	14	43,000
3. Ch. Anasazi Annie Oakley	Welsh Terrier	24	42,000
4. Ch. Braeburn's Close Encounter	Scottish Terrier	31	34,000
5. Ch. Devon Puff and Stuff	Bichon Frisé	20	33,000

1984

1. Ch. Covy-Tucker Hill's Manhattan	German Shepherd Dog	64	83,000
2. Ch. Braeburn's Close Encounter	Scottish Terrier	70	76,000
3. Ch. Quicksilver's Razz Ma Tazz	Samoyed	26	42,000
4. Ch. Tralee's Rowdy Red	Irish Terrier	18	33,000
5. Ch. Cumbrian Black Pearl	Pointer	14	30,000

1983

1. Ch. Braeburn's Close Encounter	Scottish Terrier	54	59,000
2. Ch. Quicksilver's Razz Ma Tazz	Samoyed	24	35,000
3. Ch. Wah-Hu Redcloud Sugar Daddy	Chow Chow	23	31,000
4. Ch. Wallin's Charlie Brown	Brussels Griffon	13	30,000
5. Ch. Vanguard Jenelle	Pembroke Welsh Corgi	14	29,000

1982

1. Ch. Kabik's The Challenger	Afghan Hound	31	55,000
2. Ch. Beaucrest Ruffian	Bouvier des Flandres	13	41,000
3. Ch. Beech Hill's Benji V Masco	German Shepherd Dog	13	33,000
4. Ch. Salilyn's Private Stock	English Springer Spaniel	23	33,000
5. Ch. Mike Mars China Dragon	Pekingese	18	27,000

1981

1. Ch. Dhandy's Favorite Woodchuck	Pug	40	60,000
2. Ch. Beaucrest Ruffian	Bouvier des Flandres	46	46,000
3. Ch. Ttarb The Brat (imp. Australia)	Smooth Fox Terrier	23	37,000
4. Ch. Thrumpton's Lord Brady (imp. UK)	Norwich Terrier	22	35,000
5. Ch. Star Dobe's Irish Fantasy	Doberman Pinscher	17	34,000

1980

1. Ch. Thrumpton's Lord Brady (imp. UK)	Norwich Terrier	43	61,000
2. Ch. Lou-Gin's Kiss Me Kate	Standard Poodle	52	59,000
3. Ch. Bahlamb's Beach Boy	Old English Sheepdog	14	31,000
4. Ch. Sporting Fields Clansman	Whippet	17	30,000
5. Ch. Siegal's Top Contender	Boxer	14	29,000

1979

1. Ch. Lou-Gin's Kiss Me Kate	Standard Poodle	56	63,896
2. Ch. Cozy's Mischief Maker	Lakeland Terrier	42	63,369
3. Ch. Marienburg's Mary Hartman	Doberman Pinscher	22	54,000
4. Ch. Vin-Melca's Nimbus	Norwegian Elkhound	20	48,000
5. Ch. Sporting Fields Clansman	Whippet	25	43,000

1978

1. Ch. Marienburg's Mary Hartman	Doberman Pinscher	18	43,000
2. Ch. Vin-Melca's Nimbus	Norwegian Elkhound	22	40,000
3. Ch. Salilyn's Hallmark	English Springer Spaniel	23	38,000
4. Ch. Cozy's Mischief Maker	Lakeland Terrier	21	32,000
5. Ch. Lou-Gin's Kiss Me Kate	Standard Poodle	23	29,000

1977

1. Ch. Harwire Hetman of Whinlatter (imp. UK)	Wire Fox Terrier	34	57,000
2. Ch. Aroi Talk of the Blues	Greyhound	33	55,000
3. Ch. Vin-Melca's Nimbus	Norwegian Elkhound	18	38,000
4. Ch. Cede Higgens	Yorkshire Terrier	23	33,000
5. Ch. Spartan's Sloe Gin Fizz MW	Wire Dachshund	23	33,000

1976

1. Ch. Aroi Talk of the Blues	Greyhound	18	43,000
2. Ch. Loyalblu Hendihap	Old English Sheepdog	6	42,000
3. Ch. Taquin du Posty Arlequin (imp. Belgium)	Bouvier des Flandres	18	41,000
4. Ch. Spartan's Sloe Gin Fizz MW	Wire Dachshund	28	40,000
5. Ch. Oak Tree's Irishtocrat	Irish Water Spaniel	14	36,000

1975

1. Ch. Dersade Bobby's Girl (imp. UK)	Sealyham Terrier	35	60,000
2. Ch. Aryee Dominator	Wire Fox Terrier	38	53,000
3. Ch. Jo-Ni's Red Baron of Crofton	Lakeland Terrier	24	49,000
4. Ch. Jay-Mac's Impossible Dream	Miniature Pinscher	24	47,000
5. Ch. Salilyn's Classic	English Springer Spaniel	18	36,000

1974

1. Ch. Jo-Ni's Red Baron of Crofton	Lakeland Terrier	27	50,000
2. Ch. Sunnybrook Spot On (imp. UK)	Wire Fox Terrier	27	46,000
3. Ch. Cumming's Gold Rush Charlie	Golden Retriever	17	34,000
4. Ch. Talak of Kotzebue	Alaskan Malamute	6	34,000
5. Ch. Galaxy's Corry Carina	Doberman Pinscher	13	34,000

1973

1. Ch. Galaxy's Corry Missile Belle | Doberman Pinscher | 20 | 56,000
2. Ch. Gretchenhof Columbia River | German Shorthaired Pointer | 20 | 42,000
3. Ch. Heideres Kolyer Kimbayh | Great Dane | 16 | 39,000
4. Ch. Val-Koa's Roon | German Shepherd Dog | 11 | 32,000
5. Ch. Vin-Melca's Valley Forge | Norwegian Elkhound | 11 | 29,000

1972

1. Ch. Sagamore Toccoa | Cocker Spaniel (ASCOB) | 29 | 45,000
2. Ch. Joanne-Chen's Maya Dancer | Maltese | 29 | 41,000
3. Ch. Lakeside's Gilligan's Island | German Shepherd Dog | 14 | 33,000
4. Ch. Val-Koa's Roon | German Shepherd Dog | 9 | 28,000
5. Ch. Heideres Kolyer Kimbayh | Great Dane | 7 | 25,000

1971

1. Ch. Chinoe's Adamant James | English Springer Spaniel | 47 | 63,000
2. Ch. Lakeside's Gilligan's Island | German Shepherd Dog | 21 | 43,000
3. Ch. Dolph v Tannenwald | Doberman Pinscher | 16 | 36,000
4. Ch. Weichardt's A Go Go | Doberman Pinscher | 7 | 32,000
5. Ch. Abner Lowell Davis | Great Dane | 5 | 28,000

1970

1. Ch. Vin-Melca's Vagabond | Norwegian Elkhound | 15 | 31,000
2. Ch. Rancho Dobe's Maestro | Doberman Pinscher | 10 | 25,000
3. Ch. Pendleton's Jewel | Maltese | 18 | 25,000
4. Ch. Prince Andrew of Sherline | Old English Sheepdog | 3 | 22,000
5. Ch. De Go Hubert | West Highland White Terrier | 17 | 21,000

1969

1. Ch. Arriba's Prima Donna* | Boxer | 20 | 35,000
2. Ch. De Russy Lollypop* | Standard Poodle | 28 | 34,000
3. Ch. Salgray's Ovation | Boxer | 21 | 26,000
4. Ch. Vaught's John Paul | American Foxhound | 12 | 22,000
5. Ch. Honeygold v. Overcup | Great Dane | 5 | 22,000

1968

1. Ch. Melbee's Chances Are | Kerry Blue Terrier | 29 | 40,000
2. Ch. Flakkee Sweepstakes | Keeshond | 25 | 23,000
3. Ch. Prince Andrew of Sherline | Old English Sheepdog | 8 | 21,000
4. Ch. Big Kim of Belladane | Great Dane | 12 | 21,000
5. Ch. Shamrock Acres Light Brigade | Labrador Retriever | 12 | 18,000

1967

1. Ch. Salilyn's Aristocrat | English Springer Spaniel | 45 | 42,000
2. Ch. Sultana von Marienburg | Doberman Pinscher | 26 | 31,000
3. Ch. Aennchen's Poona Dancer | Maltese | 19 | 20,000
4. Ch. Reggen's Madas L of Marydane | Great Dane | 12 | 19,000
5. Ch. Rivermist Dan Patch | Old English Sheepdog | 6 | 18,000

* These statistics are from *Kennel Review*. In the same year, *Popular Dogs* had Ch. De Russy Lollypop as Number 1 and Ch. Arriba's Prima Donna as Number 2. This is the only time the award is known to have gone to different dogs.

1966

1. Ch. Frederick of Rencroft (imp. UK)	Miniature Poodle	26	25,000
2. Ch. Fezziwig Raggedy Andy	Old English Sheepdog	11	24,000
3. Ch. Reggen's Madas L of Marydane	Great Dane	8	17,000
4. Ch. Coughton Sungable of Perryacre (imp. UK)	Pekingese	16	15,000
5. Ch. Salilyn's Aristocrat	English Springer Spaniel	18	15,000

1965

1. Ch. Ru-Mar's Tsushima	Doberman Pinscher	6	18,000
2. Ch. Coughton Sungable of Perryacre (imp. UK)	Pekingese	25	17,000
3. Ch. Sahadi Shikari	Afghan Hound	17	16,000
4. Ch. Salgray's Fashion Plate	Boxer	13	15,000
5. Ch. Fezziwig Raggedy Andy	Old English Sheepdog	4	12,000

1964

1. Ch. Courtenay Fleetfoot of Pennyworth (imp. UK)	Whippet	21	25,000
2. Ch. Carmichael's Fanfare	Scottish Terrier	21	20,000
3. Ch. Elf Dale Viking	Shetland Sheepdog	5	14,000
4. Ch. Ralanda Ami Francine	French Bulldog	16	10,000
5. Ch. Fezziwig Raggedy Andy	Old English Sheepdog	3	10,000

1963

1. Ch. Treceder's Painted Lady	Boxer	30	23,000
2. Ch. Tedwin's Top Billing	Miniature Poodle	25	18,000
3. Ch. Gretchenhof Moonshine	German Shorthaired Pointer	9	11,000
4. Ch. Jacinthe de Ricelaine (imp. France)	Skye Terrier	11	11,000
5. Ch. Fezziwig Ceiling Zero	Old English Sheepdog	7	11,000

1962

1. Ch. Tedwin's Top Billing	Miniature Poodle	21	15,000
2. Ch. Willets Red Jacket	Pembroke Welsh Corgi	10	12,000
3. Ch. Ralanda Ami Francine	French Bulldog	20	11,000
4. Ch. Ah Sid's The Dilettante	Chow Chow	15	11,000
5. Ch. Jacinthe de Ricelaine (imp. France)	Skye Terrier	11	11,000

1961

1. Ch. Miss Skylight (imp. Ireland)	Wire Fox Terrier	14	12,000
2. Ch. Rebel Roc's Casanova v. Kurt	Miniature Pinscher	28	12,000
3. Ch. Estid Ballet Dancer	Miniature Poodle	18	11,000
4. Ch. Bettina's Kow-Kow	Pekingese	15	9,000
5. Ch. Willets Red Jacket	Pembroke Welsh Corgi	5	9,000

1960

1. Ch. Pinetop's Fancy Parade	Cocker Spaniel (ASCOB)	28	16,000
2. Ch. Evo-Wen's Impresario	Boxer	14	11,000
3. Ch. The Ring's Banshee	Basset Hound	12	11,000
4. Ch. Rebel Roc's Casanova v. Kurt	Miniature Pinscher	24	10,000
5. Ch. Cappoquin Little Sister	Toy Poodle	10	10,000

1959

1. Ch. Chik T'Sun of Caversham (imp. UK)	Pekingese	36	17,000
2. Ch. Salilyn's MacDuff	English Springer Spaniel	27	16,000
3. Ch. Crown Crest Mr. Universe	Afghan Hound	12	12,000
4. Ch. Rider's Sparklin' Gold Nugget	Pomeranian	12	9,000
5. Ch. Evo-Wen's Impresario	Boxer	13	9,000

1958

1. Ch. Chik T'Sun of Caversham (imp. UK)	Pekingese	44	19,000
2. Ch. Westhay Fiona of Harham (imp. UK)	Airedale Terrier	17	12,000
3. Ch. Evo-Wen's Impresario	Boxer	10	8,000
4. Ch. Artru Hot Rod	Cocker Spaniel (ASCOB)	10	8,000
5. Ch. Shirkhan of Grandeur	Afghan Hound	9	8,000

1957

1. Ch. Chik T'Sun of Caversham (imp. UK)	Pekingese	44	19,000
2. Ch. Adastra Magic Fame (imp. UK)	Miniature Poodle	30	14,000
3. Ch. Merriedip Duke George	Old English Sheepdog	8	10,000
4. Ch. Gail's Ebony Don D	Cocker Spaniel (Black)	10	8,000
5. Ch. Westhay Fiona of Harham (imp. UK)	Airedale Terrier	7	7,000

1956

1. Ch. Blakeen Ding Ding	Toy Poodle	21	11,000
2. Ch. Adastra Magic Fame (imp. UK)	Miniature Poodle	9	10,000
3. Ch. Barrage of Quality Hill	Boxer	15	9,000
4. Ch. Gail's Ebony Don D	Cocker Spaniel (Black)	13	8,000
5. Ch. Elblac's Bugle of Hastern	English Cocker Spaniel	5	7,000

1955

1. Ch. Bang Away of Sirrah Crest	Boxer	21

1954

1. Ch. Bang Away of Sirrah Crest	Boxer	24

1953

1. Ch. Rock Falls Colonel	English Setter	24

1952

1. Ch. Rock Falls Colonel	English Setter	35

1951

1. Ch. Bang Away of Sirrah Crest	Boxer	28

1950

1. Ch. Mazelaine's Zazarac Brandy	Boxer	17

1949
1. Ch. Walsing Winning Trick of Edgerstoune (imp. UK)   Scottish Terrier   19

1948
1. Ch. Frejax Royal Salute   English Springer Spaniel   13

1947
1. Ch. Blakeen Christable   Poodle (Miniature)   18

1946
1. Ch. Mighty Sweet Regardless   Boston Terrier   15

1945 (TIE)
1. Ch. Erin's Beau Brummell   Irish Setter   5
1. Ch. Magic of Mardormere   Greyhound   5
1. Ch. Quo Schmerk of Marienland   Doberman Pinscher   5

1944
1. Ch. El Wendie of Rockland   Boxer   18

1943
1. Ch. Maro of Maridor   English Setter   11

1942
1. Ch. Maro of Maridor   English Setter   10

1941
1. Ch. Maro of Maridor   English Setter   14

1940
1. Ch. Maro of Maridor   English Setter   12

1939
1. Ch. Pillicoc Aplomb   Poodle (Standard)   14

1938
1. Ch. Nornay Saddler (imp. UK)   Fox Terrier (Smooth)   25

1937
1. Ch. Dorian v. Marienhof of Mazelaine (imp. Germany)   Boxer   11

1936
1. Ch. Jockel v. Burgund (imp. Germany)   Doberman Pinscher   14

1935
1. Ch. Milson O'Boy   Irish Setter   10

1934
1. Ch. Leading Lady of Wildoaks   Fox Terrier (Wire)   8

1933
1. Ch. The Country Gentleman   English Setter   9

1932
Ch. Nancolleth Beryl of Giralda (imp. UK)   Pointer   19

1931
1. Ch. Higgin's Red Pat   Irish Setter   12

1930
1. Ch. Weltona Frizette of Wildoaks (imp. UK)   Fox Terrier (Wire)   13

1929
1. Ch. Newmarket Brandy Snap of Welwire (imp. UK)   Fox Terrier (Wire)   10

1928 (TIE)
1. Ch. Delf Discriminate of Pinegrade   Sealyham Terrier   6
1. Ch. Cito v. d. Marktfeste (imp. Germany)   German Shepherd Dog   6

1927
1. Ch. Cito v. d. Marktfeste (imp. Germany)   German Shepherd Dog   7

1926
1. Ch. Teuthilde vom Hagenschiess (imp. Germany)   German Shepherd Dog   6

1925
1. Ch. Teuthilde vom Hagenschiess (imp. Germany)   German Shepherd Dog   8

Appendix D:
Top Dogs in the United States by Group 1956–2006

The top-rated dog in each of the seven AKC Groups, based on number of dogs defeated.

TOP SPORTING DOGS

2006: Ch. Felicity's Diamond Jim, English Springer Spaniel
2005: Ch. Telltale Salute, English Springer Spaniel
2004: Ch. Clussexx Three D Grinchy Glee, Sussex Spaniel
2003: Ch. Drakkar's She's All That, German Wirehaired Pointer
2002: Ch. Set'r Ridge Wyndswept In Gold, English Setter
2001: Ch Magic Sir-ly You Jest, Brittany
2000: Ch. Khrispat's Megan A Point, German Shorthaired Pointer
1999: Ch. Salilyn 'N Erin's Shameless, English Springer Spaniel
1998: Ch. Salilyn 'N Erin's Shameless, English Springer Spaniel
1997: Ch. Pompei's The American Way, Irish Setter
1996: Ch. Bit O Gold Titan Treasure, Gordon Setter
1995: Ch. Rendition Triple Play, Cocker Spaniel (Parti-Color)
1994: Ch. La-Shay's Bart Simpson, Cocker Spaniel (Black)
1993: Ch. Jordean All Kiddin' Aside, Brittany
1992: Ch. Salilyn's Condor, English Springer Spaniel
1991: Ch. Salilyn's Condor, English Springer Spaniel
1990: Ch. Goodtime's Silk Teddy, English Setter
1989: Ch. Luftnase Albelarm Bee's Knees, Pointer
1988: Ch. Brawbridge TNT of Kris, Gordon Setter
1987: Ch. NMK's Brittania V Sibelstein, German Shorthaired Pointer
1986: Ch. Telltale Royal Stuart, English Springer Spaniel
1985: Ch. Windwood's Night Hawk, Irish Setter
1984: Ch. Cumbrian Black Pearl, Pointer
1983: Ch. Filicia's Dividend, English Springer Spaniel
1982: Ch. Salilyn's Private Stock, English Springer Spaniel
1981: Ch. Harrison's Peeping Tom, Cocker Spaniel (Black)
1980: Ch. Kamp's Kaptain Kool, Cocker Spaniel (Parti-Color)
1979: Ch. Prelude's Echo, English Springer Spaniel
1978: Ch. Salilyn's Hallmark, English Springer Spaniel
1977: Ch. Salilyn's Hallmark, English Springer Spaniel
1976: Ch. Oak Tree's Irishtocrat, Irish Water Spaniel
1975: Ch. Salilyn's Classic, English Springer Spaniel
1974: Ch. Cumming's Gold Rush Charlie, Golden Retriever
1973: Ch. Gretchenhof Columbia River, German Shorthaired Pointer

1972: Ch. Sagamore Toccoa, Cocker Spaniel (ASCOB)
1971: Ch. Chinoe's Adamant James, English Springer Spaniel
1970: Ch. Major O'Shannon, Irish Setter
1969: Ch. Counterpoints Lord Ashley, Pointer
1968: Ch. Shamrock Acres Light Brigade, Labrador Retriever
1967: Ch. Salilyn's Aristocrat, English Springer Spaniel
1966: Ch. Salilyn's Aristocrat, English Springer Spaniel
1965: Ch. Forjay's Sundown, Cocker Spaniel (ASCOB)
1964: Ch. Bigg's Snow Prince, Cocker Spaniel (ASCOB)
1963: Ch. Gretchenhof Moonshine, German Shorthaired Pointer
1962: Ch. Headliner The Flaming Beauty, Irish Setter
1961: Ch. Wakefield's Black Knight, English Springer Spaniel
1960: Ch. Pinetop's Fancy Parade, Cocker Spaniel (ASCOB)
1959: Ch. Salilyn's MacDuff, English Springer Spaniel
1958: Ch. Artru Hot Rod, Cocker Spaniel (ASCOB)
1957: Ch. Gail's Ebony Don D, Cocker Spaniel (Black)
1956: Ch. Gail's Ebony Don D, Cocker Spaniel (Black)

TOP HOUNDS

2006: Ch. Celestial CJ's Jolly Fairchild, Petit Basset Griffon Vendéen
2005: Ch. Afterglow Woody Woodpecker (imp. UK), Petit Basset Giffon Vendéen
2004: Ch. Heathers Knock On Wood, Bloodhound
2003: Ch. Luxor's Playmate of the Year, Ibizan Hound
2002: Ch. Vin-Melca's Silver Shadow, Norwegian Elkhound
2001: Ch. Topsfield Bumper Cars, Basset Hound
2000: Ch. Ridgerunner Unforgettable, Bloodhound
1999: Ch. Tryst of Grandeur, Afghan Hound
1998: Ch. Deer Hill's Great Gatsby, Basset Hound
1997: Ch. Zindika's Johnny Come Greatly, Basenji
1996: Ch. Tryst of Grandeur, Afghan Hound
1995: Ch. Tryst of Grandeur, Afghan Hound
1994: Ch. Tryst of Grandeur, Afghan Hound
1993: Ch. Lanbur Miss Fleetwood, Beagle (13-inch)
1992: Ch. Sporting Fields Kinsman, Whippet
1991: Ch. Triumph of Grandeur, Afghan Hound
1990: Ch. Vin-Melca's Calista, Norwegian Elkhound
1989: Ch. Vin-Melca's Calista, Norwegian Elkhound

1988: Ch. Kabik's The Front Runner, Afghan Hound
1987: Ch. Kabik's The Front Runner, Afghan Hound
1986: Ch. Brundox Daiquiris Kid MW, Wirehaired Dachshund
1985: Ch. Baskerville's Sole Heir, Bloodhound
1984: Ch. Aodh Harp of Eagle, Irish Wolfhound
1983: Ch. Mr. Stewart's Cheshire Winslow, English Foxhound
1982: Ch. Kabik's The Challenger, Afghan Hound
1981: Ch. Bigdrum Close Call v. Westphal, Smooth Dachshund
1980: Ch. Sporting Fields Clansman, Whippet
1979: Ch. Vin-Melca's Nimbus, Norwegian Elkhound
1978: Ch. Vin-Melca's Nimbus, Norwegian Elkhound
1977: Ch. Aroi Talk of the Blues, Greyhound
1976: Ch. Aroi Talk of the Blues, Greyhound
1975: Ch. Slippery Hill Hudson, Basset Hound
1974: Ch. Vin-Melca's Homesteader, Norwegian Elkhound
1973: Ch. Vin-Melca's Valley Forge, Norwegian Elkhound
1972: Ch. The Whims Buckeye, Beagle (13-inch)
1971: Ch. Glenhaven's Lord Jack, Basset Hound
1970: Ch. Vin-Melca's Vagabond, Norwegian Elkhound
1969: Ch. Vaught's John Paul, American Foxhound
1968: Ch. Jay Bees Toreador, Smooth Dachshund
1967: Ch. Holly Hill Desert Wind, Afghan Hound
1966: Ch. Holly Hill Desert Wind, Afghan Hound
1965: Ch. Sahadi Shikari, Afghan Hound
1964: Ch. Courtenay Fleetfoot of Pennyworth (imp. UK), Whippet
1963: Ch. Courtenay Fleetfoot of Pennyworth (imp. UK), Whippet
1962: Ch. Gay Boy of Geddesburg, Beagle (15-inch)
1961: Ch. The Ring's Ali Baba, Basset Hound
1960: Ch. The Ring's Banshee, Basset Hound
1959: Ch. Crown Crest Mr. Universe, Afghan Hound
1958: Ch. Shirkhan of Grandeur, Afghan Hound
1957: Ch. Shirkhan of Grandeur, Afghan Hound
1956: Ch. Crown Crest Zardonx, Afghan Hound

TOP WORKING DOGS

The Herding Group was separated from the Working Group in 1983. Prior to that year, the Working Group included breeds that now compete in the Herding Group.

2006: Ch. Bayview Some Like It Hot, Boxer
2005: Ch. Brookwood's Mystic Warrior, Boxer
2004: Ch. Brookwood's Mystic Warrior, Boxer
2003: Ch. Blue Chip Purple Reign, Doberman Pinscher
2002: Ch. Marienburg's Repo Man, Doberman Pinscher

2001: Ch. Charisma Jailhouse Rock, Standard Schnauzer
2000: Ch. Storybook's Rip It Up, Boxer
1999: Ch. Skansen's Tristan, Giant Schnauzer
1998: Ch. Toledobe's Serenghetti, Doberman Pinscher
1997: Ch. Nanuke's Take No Prisoners, Alaskan Malamute
1996: Ch. Parsifal Casa di Netzer (imp. Italy), Standard Schnauzer
1995: Ch. Kontoki's E-I-E-I-O, Siberian Husky
1994: Ch. Hi-Tech's Arbitrage, Boxer
1993: Ch. Aquarius Damien V Ravenswod, Doberman Pinscher
1992: Ch. Kiebla's Tradition of Turo, Boxer
1991: Ch. Brunswig's Cryptonite, Doberman Pinscher
1990: Ch. Brunswig's Cryptonite, Doberman Pinscher
1989: Ch. Rivergroves Run For The Roses, Great Pyrenees
1988: Ch. Royal Tudor's Wild As The Wind, Doberman Pinscher
1987: Ch. Sheenwater Gamble On Me, Great Dane
1986: Ch. Turo's Cachet, Boxer
1985: Ch. Bandog's Crawdaddy Gumbo, Bullmastiff
1984: Ch. Quicksilver's Razz Ma Tazz, Samoyed
1983: Ch. Quicksilver's Razz Ma Tazz, Samoyed
1982: Ch. Beaucrest Ruffian, Bouvier des Flandres
1981: Ch. Beaucrest Ruffian, Bouvier des Flandres
1980: Ch. Bahlamb's Beach Boy, Old English Sheepdog
1979: Ch. Marienburg's Mary Hartman, Doberman Pinscher
1978: Ch. Marienburg's Mary Hartman, Doberman Pinscher
1977: Ch. Covy-Tucker Hill's Finnegan, German Shepherd Dog
1976: Ch. Loyalblu Hendihap, Old English Sheepdog
1975: Ch. Taquin du Posty Arlequin (imp. Belgium), Bouvier des Flandres
1974: Ch. Talak of Kotzebue, Alaskan Malamute
1973: Ch. Galaxy's Corry Missile Belle, Doberman Pinscher
1972: Ch. Lakeside's Gilligan's Island, German Shepherd Dog
1971: Ch. Lakeside's Gilligan's Island, German Shepherd Dog
1970: Ch. Rancho Dobe's Maestro, Doberman Pinscher
1969: Ch. Arriba's Prima Donna, Boxer
1968: Ch. Prince Andrew of Sherline, Old English Sheepdog
1967: Ch. Sultana von Marienburg, Doberman Pinscher
1966: Ch. Fezziwig Raggedy Andy, Old English Sheepdog
1965: Ch. Ru-Mar's Tsushima, Doberman Pinscher
1964: Ch. Elf Dale Viking, Shetland Sheepdog
1963: Ch. Treceder's Painted Lady, Boxer
1962: Ch. Willets Red Jacket, Pembroke Welsh Corgi
1961: Ch. Willets Red Jacket, Pembroke Welsh Corgi
1960: Ch. Evo-Wen's Impresario, Boxer
1959: Ch. Evo-Wen's Impresario, Boxer
1958: Ch. Evo-Wen's Impresario, Boxer
1957: Ch. Merriedip Duke George, Old English Sheepdog
1956: Ch. Barrage of Quality Hill, Boxer

TOP TERRIERS

2006: Ch. Hobergays Fineus Fogg (imp. New Zealand), Dandie Dinmont Terrier

2005: Ch. Stonebroke Right On The Money, Sealyham Terrier

2004: Ch. Cracknor Cause Celebre (imp. UK), Norfolk Terrier

2003: Ch. Cracknor Cause Celebre (imp. UK), Norfolk Terrier

2002: Ch. Torum's Scarf Michael (imp. UK), Kerry Blue Terrier

2001: Ch. Torum's Scarf Michael (imp. UK), Kerry Blue Terrier

2000: Ch. Willow Wind Tenure, Bedlington Terrier

1999: Ch. The Duke of Copperplate, Norfolk Terrier

1998: Ch. Sweetsound's King 'O' Rockn Roll, West Highland White Terrier

1997: Ch. Fairewood Frolic (imp. Canada), Norwich Terrier

1996: Ch. Revelry's Awesome Blossom, Lakeland Terrier

1995: Ch. Revelry's Awesome Blossom, Lakeland Terrier

1994: Ch. Gaelforce Post Script, Scottish Terrier

1993: Ch. Chidley Willum The Conqueror, Norwich Terrier

1992: Ch. Registry's Lonesome Dove, Wire Fox Terrier

1991: Ch. Registry's Lonesome Dove, Wire Fox Terrier

1990: Ch. Kerrageen's Hotspur, Kerry Blue Terrier

1989: Ch. Killick of the Mess (imp. UK), Wire Fox Terrier

1988: Ch. Talludo Minstrel of Purston (imp. UK), Wire Fox Terrier

1987: Ch. Galsul Excellence (imp. Ireland), Wire Fox Terrier

1986: Ch. Galsul Excellence (imp. Ireland), Wire Fox Terrier

1985: Ch. Anasazi Annie Oakley, Welsh Terrier

1984: Ch. Braeburn's Close Encounter, Scottish Terrier

1983: Ch. Braeburn's Close Encounter, Scottish Terrier

1982: Ch. Braeburn's Close Encounter, Scottish Terrier

1981: Ch. Ttarb The Brat (imp. Australia), Smooth Fox Terrier

1980: Ch. Thrumpton's Lord Brady (imp. UK), Norwich Terrier

1979: Ch. Cozy's Mischief Maker, Lakeland Terrier

1978: Ch. Cozy's Mischief Maker, Lakeland Terrier

1977: Ch. Harwire Hetman of Whinlatter (imp. UK), Wire Fox Terrier

1976: Ch. Roderick of Jenmist (imp. UK), Sealyham Terrier

1975: Ch. Dersade Bobby's Girl (imp. UK), Sealyham Terrier

1974: Ch. Jo-Ni's Red Baron of Crofton, Lakeland Terrier

1973: Ch. Purston Pinmoney Pedlar, West Highland White Terrier

1972: Ch. Golden Oak Jim Royal, Welsh Terrier

1971: Ch. Golden Oak Jim Royal, Welsh Terrier

1970: Ch. De Go Hubert, West Highland White Terrier

1969: Ch. Special Edition, Lakeland Terrier

1968: Ch. Melbee's Chances Are, Kerry Blue Terrier

1967: Ch. Stingray of Derryabah (imp. UK), Lakeland Terrier

1966: Ch. Bardene Bingo (imp. UK), Scottish Terrier

1965: Ch. Zeloy Mooremaide's Magic (imp. UK), Wire Fox Terrier

1964: Ch. Carmichael's Fanfare, Scottish Terrier

1963: Ch. Jacinthe de Ricelaine (imp. France), Skye Terrier

1962: Ch. Jacinthe de Ricelaine (imp. France), Skye Terrier

1961: Ch. Miss Skylight (imp. Ireland), Wire Fox Terrier

1960: Ch. Miss Skylight (imp. Ireland), Wire Fox Terrier

1959: Ch. Cudhill Kalypso of Harham (imp. UK), Wire Fox Terrier

1958: Ch. Westhay Fiona of Harham (imp. UK), Airedale Terrier

1957: Ch. Westhay Fiona of Harham (imp. UK), Airedale Terrier

1956: Ch. Ivory Jock of Iradell, Skye Terrier

TOP TOY DOGS

2006: Ch. Smash JP Win A Victory (imp. Japan), Toy Poodle

2005: Ch. Yakee If Only (imp. UK), Pekingese

2004: Ch. North Well Chako JP Platina King (imp. Japan), Toy Poodle

2003: Ch. Yakee Leaving Me Breathless at Franshaw (imp. UK), Pekingese

2002: Ch. Hallmark Jolei Raggedy Andy, Shih Tzu

2001: Ch. Yarrow's Supernova, Affenpinscher

2000: Ch. Charing Cross Ragtime Cowboy, Shih Tzu

1999: Ch. Charing Cross Ragtime Cowboy, Shih Tzu

1998: Ch. Ta-Jon's Tickle Me Silly, Maltese

1997: Ch. Ta-Jon's Tickle Me Silly, Maltese

1996: Ch. Loteki Supernatural Being, Papillon

1995: Ch. MVP of Ahs, Toy Poodle

1994: Ch. Shanlyn Rais'n Raucous, Maltese

1993: Ch. Briarcourt's Damien Gable, Pekingese

1992: Ch. Briarcourt's Damien Gable, Pekingese

1991: Ch. Sand Island Small Kraft Lite, Maltese

1990: Ch. Sand Island Small Kraft Lite, Maltese

1989: Ch. Wendessa Crown Prince, Pekingese

1988: Ch. Starbeck Silken Starshine (imp. UK), Brussels Griffon

1987: Ch. Holiday Gold Jubilee, Smooth Coat Chihuahua

1986: Ch. Salutaire Surely You Jest, Toy Manchester Terrier

1985: Ch. St. Aubrey Bees Wing of Elsdon (imp. Canada), Pekingese

1984: Ch. Fairview No Nonsense, Toy Poodle

1983: Ch. Wallin's Charlie Brown, Brussels Griffon

1982: Ch. Mike Mars China Dragon, Pekingese

1981: Ch. Dhandy's Favorite Woodchuck, Pug

1980: Ch. Joanne-Chen's Mino Maya Dancer, Maltese

1979: Ch. Lennis's Tar Lacy Foxfire, Pomeranian

1978: Ch. Funfair's Pinto O'Joe Dandy, Pomeranian
1977: Ch. Cede Higgens, Yorkshire Terrier
1976: Ch. Jay-Mac's Dream Walking, Miniature Pinscher
1975: Ch. Jay-Mac's Impossible Dream, Miniature Pinscher
1974: Ch. Randy's Jolly Wee Peppi, Pomeranian
1973: Ch. Witches Wood Yum Yum, Shih Tzu
1972: Ch. Joanne-Chen's Maya Dancer, Maltese
1971: Ch. Joanne-Chen's Maya Dancer, Maltese
1970: Ch. Pendleton's Jewel, Maltese
1969: Ch. Pendleton's Jewel, Maltese
1968: Ch. Dan Lee Dragonseed, Pekingese
1967: Ch. Aennchen's Poona Dancer, Maltese
1966: Ch. Coughton Sungable of Perryacre (imp. UK),
       Pekingese
1965: Ch. Coughton Sungable of Perryacre (imp. UK),
       Pekingese
1964: Ch. Loramar's I'm A Dandee, Toy Poodle
1963: Ch. Barmere's Mighty Man, Brussels Griffon
1962: Ch. Barmere's Mighty Man, Brussels Griffon
1961: Ch. Rebel Roc's Casanova v. Kurt, Miniature Pinscher
1960: Ch. Rebel Roc's Casanova v. Kurt, Miniature Pinscher
1959: Ch. Chik T'Sun of Caversham (imp. UK), Pekingese
1958: Ch. Chik T'Sun of Caversham (imp. UK), Pekingese
1957: Ch. Chik T'Sun of Caversham (imp. UK), Pekingese
1956: Ch. Blakeen Ding Ding, Toy Poodle

TOP NON-SPORTING DOGS

2006: Ch. Merry Go Round Mach Ten, Dalmatian
2005: Ch. Greg-Mar Glory Bound, Standard Poodle
2004: Ch. Bandog's Jump For Joy, French Bulldog
2003: Ch. Ale Kai Mikimoto On Fifth, Standard Poodle
2002: Ch. Ale Kai Mikimoto On Fifth, Standard Poodle
2001: Ch. Surrey Spice Girl, Miniature Poodle
2000: Ch. Special Times Just Right!, Bichon Frisé
1999: Ch. Lake Cove That's My Boy, Standard Poodle
1998: Ch. Lake Cove That's My Boy, Standard Poodle
1997: Ch. Sterling Rumor Has It, Bichon Frisé
1996: Ch. Spotlight's Spectacular, Dalmatian
1995: Ch. Spotlight's Spectacular, Dalmatian
1994: Ch. Surrey Capsicum, Miniature Poodle
1993: Ch. Maneetas Del Zarzoso Fuego Fatuo
       (imp. UK), Standard Poodle
1992: Ch. El's Image of Belle, Standard Poodle
1991: Ch. Whisperwind's On A Carousel, Standard Poodle
1990: Ch. Whisperwind's On A Carousel, Standard Poodle
1989: Ch. Hetherbull Bounty's Frigate, Bulldog
1988: Ch. Alpenglow Ashley du Chamour, Bichon Frisé
1987: Ch. Alekai Airy, Standard Poodle

1986: Ch. Devon Puff And Stuff, Bichon Frisé
1985: Ch. Devon Puff And Stuff, Bichon Frisé
1984: Ch. Wah-Hu Redcloud Sugar Daddy, Chow Chow
1983: Ch. Wah-Hu Redcloud Sugar Daddy, Chow Chow
1982: Ch. Teaka's Erbin Einar, Bichon Frisé
1981: Ch. Teaka's Erbin Einar, Bichon Frisé
1980: Ch. Lou-Gin's Kiss Me Kate, Standard Poodle
1979: Ch. Lou-Gin's Kiss Me Kate, Standard Poodle
1978: Ch. Lou-Gin's Kiss Me Kate, Standard Poodle
1977: Ch. Yojimbo Orion, Lhasa Apso
1976: Ch. Marinebull's All The Way, Bulldog
1975: Ch. Westfield Cunomorus Stone, Bulldog
1974: Ch. Westfield Cunomorus Stone, Bulldog
1973: Ch. Acadia Command Performance, Standard Poodle
1972: Ch. Chen Korum Ti, Lhasa Apso
1971: Ch. Tally Ho Tiffany, Miniature Poodle
1970: Ch. Flakkee Jackpot, Keeshond
1969: Ch. De Russy Lollypop, Standard Poodle
1968: Ch. Flakkee Sweepstakes, Keeshond
1967: Ch. Flakkee Sweepstakes, Keeshond
1966: Ch. Frederick of Rencroft (imp. UK), Miniature Poodle
1965: Ch. Alekai Pokoi, Standard Poodle
1964: Ch. Ralanda Ami Francine, French Bulldog
1963: Ch. Tedwin's Top Billing, Miniature Poodle
1962: Ch. Tedwin's Top Billing, Miniature Poodle
1961: Ch. Estid Ballet Dancer, Miniature Poodle
1960: Ch. Vardona Frosty Snowman, Bulldog
1959: Ch. Vardona Frosty Snowman, Bulldog
1958: Ch. Vardona Frosty Snowman, Bulldog
1957: Ch. Adastra Magic Fame (imp. UK), Miniature Poodle
1956: Ch. Adastra Magic Fame (imp. UK), Miniature Poodle

TOP HERDING DOGS

Prior to 1983, the Herding breeds were part of the
Working Group and did not have a separate Herding
Group competition.

2006: Ch. Bugaboo's Big Resolution, Old English Sheepdog
2005: Ch. Kenlyn's Tenacity of Kaleef, German Shepherd Dog
2004: Ch. Kaleef's Genuine Risk, German Shepherd Dog
2003: Ch. Kaleef's Genuine Risk, German Shepherd Dog
2002: Ch. Kismet's Sight For Sore Eyes, German Shepherd
       Dog
2001: Ch. Kismet's Sight For Sore Eyes, German Shepherd
       Dog
2000: Ch. Coventry Queue, Pembroke Welsh Corgi
1999: Ch. Fox Meadows Forest Gump, Pembroke Welsh Corgi
1998: Ch. Windwalker's Leroy Brown, German Shepherd Dog

1997: Ch. Lambluv's Desert Dancer, Old English Sheepdog

1996: Ch. Diotima Bear Necessity (imp. UK), Bearded Collie

1995: Ch. Aristes Hematite Dragon, Bouvier des Flandres

1994: Ch. Altana's Mystique (imp. Canada), German Shepherd Dog

1993: Ch. Altana's Mystique (imp. Canada), German Shepherd Dog

1992: Ch. Altana's Mystique (imp. Canada), German Shepherd Dog

1991: Ch. Bramblewood's Custom Made, German Shepherd Dog

1990: Ch. Galbraith's Ironeyes, Bouvier des Flandres

1989: Ch. Galewynd's Georgio Armani, German Shepherd Dog

1988: Ch. Quiche's Ivanhoe (imp. Canada), Bouvier des Flandres

1987: Ch. Lynrik's Kristal, German Shepherd Dog

1986: Ch. Covy-Tucker Hill's Manhattan, German Shepherd Dog

1985: Ch. Covy-Tucker Hill's Manhattan, German Shepherd Dog

1984: Ch. Covy-Tucker Hill's Manhattan, German Shepherd Dog

1983: Ch. Vanguard Jennelle, Pembroke Welsh Corgi

An award to the top dog of the year exists in most countries, based on the cumulative records of Best in Show competitions held during the year. Only countries with established, generally acknowledged rating systems are included in the following; several countries, such as Australia and New Zealand, have more than one Top Dog award based on different criteria.

USA

See Appendix C.

UNITED KINGDOM

Rating systems for Top Dog of all breeds were introduced in the 1950s but were not consistently published until the early 1970s. Records prior to 1958 are based on highest number of Best in Show wins earned each year.

2006: Ch. Hungargunn Bear Itn Mind (imp. Australia), Hungarian Vizsla

2005: Sh. Ch. Afterglow Douglas Fashion, American Cocker Spaniel

2004: Ch. PaRay's I Told You So (imp. US), Bichon Frisé

2003: Ch. Jafrak Philippe Olivier, Giant Schnauzer

2002: Ch. Zottel's You Don't Fool Me, Old English Sheepdog

2001: Ch. Yakee A Dangerous Liaison, Pekingese

2000: Ch. Potterdale Prophet, Bearded Collie

1999: Ch. Roxara He Drives You Wild, Bichon Frisé

1998: Ch. Saxonsprings Tradition, Lhasa Apso

1997: Sh. Ch. Boduf Pistols at Dawn with Afterglow, American Cocker Spaniel

1996: Ch. Ozmilion Mystification, Yorkshire Terrier

1995: Ch. Myriehewe Rosa Bleu, Shetland Sheepdog

1994: Ch. Pamplona Something Special, Standard Poodle

1993: Ch. Bassbar O'Sullivan, Basset Hound

1992: Ch. LamedaZottel Flamboyant, Old English Sheepdog

1991: Ch. LamedaZottel Flamboyant, Old English Sheepdog

1990: Ch. Si'Bon Fatal Attraction at Pamplona, Bichon Frisé

1989: Ch. Nutshell of Nevedith, Whippet

1988: Ch. Olac Moon Pilot, West Highland White Terrier

1987: Ch. Ozmilion Dedication, Yorkshire Terrier

1986: Ch. Balboa King Regal (imp. Italy), Kerry Blue Terrier

1985: Ch. Ginger Xmas Carol (imp. Italy), Airedale Terrier

1984: Ch. Montravia Tommy-Gun, Standard Poodle

1983: Ch. Jokyl Gallipants, Airedale Terrier

1982: Ch. Saxonsprings Fresno, Lhasa Apso

1981: Ch. Sternroc Dikki, Japanese Chin

1980: Ch. Grayco Hazelnut, Toy Poodle

1979: Ch. Perrancourt Playful, Airedale Terrier

1978: Ch. Groveview Jubilee, Welsh Terrier

1977: Ch. Blairsville Royal Seal, Yorkshire Terrier

1976: Ch. Blairsville Royal Seal, Yorkshire Terrier

1975: Ch. Briarghyll Falstaff, Pyrenean Mountain Dog (Great Pyrenees)

1974: Ch. Beechlyn Golden Nugget of Denbrough, Bulldog

1973: Sh. Ch. Hawkhill Connaught, English Springer Spaniel

1972: Ch. Cripsey Townville T'Other Un, Wire Fox Terrier

1971: Ch. Ukwong King Solomon, Chow Chow

1970: Ch. Ukwong King Solomon, Chow Chow,

1969: Ch. Gosmore Kirkmoor Craftsman, Wire Fox Terrier

1968: Ch. Gosmore Eilburn Miss Hopeful, Scottish Terrier

1967: Ch. Gosmore Eilburn Admaration, Scottish Terrier

1966: Ch. Bibelot's Tall Dark and Handsome (imp. Canada), Standard Poodle

1965: Ch. Iceberg of Tavey, Dobermann Pinscher

1964: Ch. Gisbourne Inca, Wire Dachshund

1963: No clear winner

1962: Ch. Horningsea Khanabad Suvaraj, Afghan Hound

1961: Ch. Riverina Tweedsbairn, Airedale Terrier

1960: Ch. Riverina Tweedsbairn, Airedale Terrier

1959: Ch. St. Margaret Steve, Sealyham Terrier

1958: Ch. Frenches Honeysuckle, Standard Poodle

1957: No clear winner

1956: Ch. Colinwood Silver Lariot, Cocker Spaniel

1955: No clear winner

1954: Ch. Caversham Ku Ku of Yam, Pekingese

1953: No clear winner

1952: Ch. Caversham Ko Ko of Shanruss, Pekingese

1951: Sh. Ch. Tracey Witch of Ware, Cocker Spaniel

1950: Ch. Weycroft Wyldboy, Airedale Terrier

1949: Ch. Murose Replica, Airedale Terrier

1948: Sh. Ch. Tracey Witch of Ware, Cocker Spaniel

1947: No clear winner

IRELAND

2006: Ch. Belliver Latest Creation, Pomeranian

2005: Ch. Belliver Latest Creation, Pomeranian
2004: Ch. Merrybear Enrique, Newfoundland
2003: Ch. Pamplona Private Dancer, Standard Poodle
2002: Ch. Watervalley Marvin Gaye of Merrybear,
    Newfoundland
2001: Ch. Allmark Goes Ballistic with Scallywag,
    Old English Sheepdog
2000: Ch. Kensbridge Karbon Kopy, Kerry Blue Terrier
1999: Ch. Pamplona Norma Jean, Standard Poodle
1998: Ch. Risepark Favorite Fella, Miniature Schnauzer
1997: Ch. Lowerpark Limited Edition, Rough Collie
1996: Ch. Hallsblu Seventh Wonder, Kerry Blue Terrier
1995: Ch. Barnesmore Circus Paint, Whippet
1994: Ch. Babiton Bedazzled by Scallywag,
    Old English Sheepdog
1993: Ch. Pahlavi Pandemonium (imp. US), Afghan Hound
1992: Ch. Manton High Society, Pembroke Welsh Corgi
1991: Ch. Trendicote Cappucino, Toy Poodle
1990: Ch. Bellablue Nikita, Old English Sheepdog
1989: Ch. Oriana of Saxonsprings, Lhasa Apso
1988: Ch Penmyn Coolamber at Meloth, Pekingese
1987: Ch. Tiopepi Mad Louie, Bichon Frisé
1986: Ch. Tirkane Secret Weapon, Toy Poodle
1985: Ch. Burtonswood Black Domino, St. Bernard

CANADA
As published in the Canadian Kennel Club's *Dogs in Canada*

2006: Ch. Sonrisas' Tiny Thomas, Havanese
2005: Ch. Muldoon Dewitts Great One, Irish Setter
2004: Ch. Dawin Stellar Performance, Standard Poodle
2003: Ch. Quiche's Zena Warrior Princess, Bouvier
    des Flandres
2002: Ch. Alias Just Give Me That Wink, Standard Poodle
2001: Ch. Freespirit's Far And Away, Doberman Pinscher
2000: Ch. Taeplace Monet, Pekingese
1999: Ch. Tahari's Serious Alibi, Pointer
1998: Ch. Britework's Bold Navigator, Wire Fox Terrier
1997: Ch. Classic Image Of A Legend, Bearded Collie
1996: Ch. Ripsnorter's It's Show Time, German Wirehaired
    Pointer
1995: Ch. Dawin Hi Falutin, Standard Poodle
1994: Ch. Serenade's Family Tradition, English Springer
    Spaniel
1993: Ch. Quailfield's Mak'N Business, Irish Setter
1992: Ch. Rivergrove's If Looks Could Kill, Great Pyrenees
1991: Ch. Telcontar's Tahiti Sweetie, English Setter
1990: Ch. Rivergrove's If Looks Could Kill, Great Pyrenees
1989: Ch. Jamelyn Second Edition, Lakeland Terrier

1988: Ch. Shente's Christian Dior, Shih Tzu
1987: Ch. McCamon Impressario, Irish Setter
1986: Ch. Hobbithill Ashwood Hi Class, Cocker Spaniel
    (English)
1985: Ch. Shisaido's Frostkist Footman, Siberian Husky
1984: Ch. Glen Miller's Bandit, Bouvier des Flandres
1983: Ch. Glen Miller's Beau Geste, Bouvier des Flandres,
1982: Ch. Fantail's Sunshine Man, English Setter
1981: Ch. Storybook's Marauder, English Setter,
1980: Ch. Le Dauphin of Limberlost, Great Pyrenees
1979: Ch. Haviland's Count Royal, Boxer
1978: Ch. Hornblower's Long John Silver, Newfoundland
1977: Ch. Kishniga's Desert Song, Borzoi
1976: Ch. Mephisto's Soldier of Fortune, Boxer
1975: Ch. Mi-Tu's Han Su Shang, Chow Chow
1974: Ch. Sir Lancelot of Barvan, Old English Sheepdog
1973: Ch. Ambassadeur, St. Bernard
1972: Ch. Davos Baroness Zareba, Great Dane
1971: Ch. Lulhaven's Snowmist Eternal Design, Samoyed
1970: Ch. Scher-Khoun's Shadrack, Boxer
1969: Ch. Scher-Khoun's Shadrack, Boxer
1968: Ch. Tophill Orsino (imp. UK), Miniature Poodle
1967: Ch. Tophill Orsino (imp. UK), Miniature Poodle
1966: Ch. Ja-Mar's Avenger of Arbor, German Shepherd Dog
1965: Ch. Outdoors Bonanza (imp. UK), Bulldog
1964: Ch. Stoney Gap Sugar Daddy of Mahnraf, West
    Highland White Terrier
1963: Ch. Loramar's I'm A Dandee, Toy Poodle

MEXICO
2006: Ch. Dazzles Bad Tad for Bear Paw, Smooth Chihuahua
2005: Ch. Mukwa's Four-on-the-Floor Seabrook,
    Newfoundland
2004: Ch. Great Hart, Rottweiler
2003: Ch. Sir Roccos Sing It To Me, Boxer
2002: Ch. As Time Goes By, Cocker Spaniel (American)
2001: Ch. Di Dolce Chance, Bichon Frisé
2000: Ch. Peace Breaker, Lakeland Terrier
1999: Ch. Del Zarzoso Mission Impossible, Standard Poodle
1998: Ch. Endo von Herman, Rottweiler
1997: Ch. Roderich, Mastiff
1996: Ch. DJ Carbon Copy, Pekingese
1995: Ch. Hubert's Desert Star Atila, Bull Terrier
1994: Ch. Jontus Henry Jones Junior, Cocker Spaniel
    (American)
1993: Ch. HHH Texas Two Step, Pomeranian
1992: Ch. Al Hara's Urey, Azawakh
1991: Ch. Hycourt's Tijuana Brass, Scottish Terrier
1990: Ch. Skansen's Lonesome Stranger, Giant Schnauzer

1989: Ch. OBJ's Shochmo Ku San, Akita
1988: Ch. Icobod de l'Esprit, Bouvier des Flandres
1987: Ch. Camshron's Falon, Kerry Blue Terrier
1986: Ch. Lee Vee Sonic Boom, English Springer Spaniel
1985: Ch. Rustic's Cry'n Out Loud, Afghan Hound
1984: Ch. Karaseva's Cinnamon Candy, Siberian Husky
1983: Ch. Nombre Alca's All The Way Popeye, Bulldog
1982: Ch. Pat Way Gummo's Son, Basset Hound
1981: Ch. Emir Yamel, Afghan Hound
1980: Ch. Lancelot Petersen von Bauer, Miniature Poodle
1979: Ch. Empire Ginger Golden Passion, Afghan Hound
1978: Ch. Cinko Duba Csebi, Puli
1977: Ch. Jim Pat's Assai, Boxer
1976: Ch. Vannan's Devastating Lady, Boxer
1975: Ch. Highlights Windermere, Lakeland Terrier
1974: Ch. Rebel, German Shepherd Dog
1973: Ch. Rebel, German Shepherd Dog
1972: Ch. Chinoe's Prodigy, English Springer Spaniel

SCANDINAVIA

Champion titles cannot be assumed even for the biggest winners at Scandinavian dog shows. Most of the dogs listed are
champions, but many breeds require field or working credits
before even a show champion title is awarded. Country of birth
is listed only when outside Scandinavia.

SWEDEN

2006: Caci's Cute Carmen at Ld's, American Cocker Spaniel
2005: Ash Grove Highwaystar (imp. Italy), Wire Fox Terrier
2004: Redwitch The Heat Is On (imp. UK), Akita
2003: Kudos The Knockout, Dwarf Poodle
2002: Bahlamb's Benevolent Brethren (imp. US), Old English
    Sheepdog
2001: Raglan Rory, Scottish Terrier
2000: Chouan Breaking The Waves, Siberian Husky
1999: Drover's Roll Those Dice, Old English Sheepdog
1998: Ulf van de Havenstad (imp. Belgium), Miniature
    Schnauzer
1997: Gengala Been There (imp. Australia), Afghan Hound
1996: Bahlamb's Barnyard Baron (imp. US), Old English
    Sheepdog
1995: Almanza Emergency Brake, Flat-Coated Retriever
1994: Anthrazith's Droy, Swedish Lapphund
1993: Syringa Set Me Free, Afghan Hound
1992: Extrem's Ovation of Osyth (imp. UK), Bulldog
1991: Racketeer's Exquisite Sinner, Standard Poodle
1990: Crispy High N'Low, Wire Fox Terrier
1989: Louline Promotion (imp. UK), Wire Fox Terrier

1988: Härkilas Mach I, Drever
1987: Triumphs Blaze, German Shepherd Dog
1986: Härkilas Mach I, Drever
1985: Sperringgårdens Cylvester, Cavalier King Charles Spaniel
1984: Tyegarth Lucifer (imp. UK), Bulldog
1983: No award
1982: Bushey's Magic Storm, West Highland White Terrier
1981: Parcvern Smuggler (imp. UK), Yorkshire Terrier
1980: Blackdale Starbright (imp. Ireland), Wire Fox Terrier
1979: Tintavon Desdemona (imp. UK), Tibetan Terrier
1978: Artru Sundance Pacemaker (imp. US), American Cocker
    Spaniel
1977: Airescot Lazuli, Scottish Deerhound
1976: Gaywyn Dandin (imp. UK), West Highland White Terrier
1975: Racketeer's Play It Again Sam, Standard Poodle
1974: Deveraux Janore (imp. UK), Welsh Terrier
1973: Paling Corinthian (imp. UK), French Bulldog
1972: Wedge Hollow's Sam's Son (imp. US), Boxer
1971: Powhatan Sentry (imp. UK), Labrador Retriever
1970: Annasline Diadem (imp. UK), Beagle
1969: Harmony Hill Linda of Airway (imp. US), Great Dane
1968: Brackenford Ballinderry Patricia (imp. UK), Irish
    Wolfhound
1967: Triumphs Heidi, German Shepherd Dog
1966: Chicos Pierre Boy, Standard Poodle
1965: Sudbrook Sunday Hymn (imp. UK), Toy Poodle

NORWAY

2006: Raptures Prelude to Ovations (imp. Canada), Shih Tzu
2005: Courmayeur's Nobody Like Me, St. Bernhard
2004: Kudos The Knockout, Dwarf Poodle
2003: Jet's Something in the Way U Smile, Greyhound
2002: Topscore Contradiction, Standard Poodle
2001: Jet's Once Upon A Dream, Greyhound
2000: Paper Moon's Parisian Maiden, Whippet
1999: Desloupiots Wesson O'Innisfree (imp. US),
    Siberian Husky
1998: Tiny Jewel's Toystar, Pomeranian
1997: Stjernelia's O'la, German Shepherd Dog
1996: Stablemaster's Super Play (imp. Finland),
    Giant Schnauzer
1995: Thatledom Perfect Partner (imp. UK), Boxer
1994: Jaraluv's Indelible (imp. US), Scottish Deerhound
1993: Bernegården's Valentin, St. Bernard
1992 (Tie): Bradir Chuck Norris, Briard; Eik von Haus Schlüter
    (imp. Germany), Leonberger
1991: Penda Passion at Louline (imp. UK), Wire Fox Terrier
1990: Surprising's Thelma, Labrador Retriever
1989: Royceland Lapaloma for Toydom (imp. UK), Pekingese

1988: Triglyph the Sorcerer (imp. UK), Boxer

1987: Togo av Angiaq, Greenland Dog

1986: Saxonspring Fol-de-Rol (imp. UK), Lhasa Apso

1985: Talk About Topscore, Miniature Poodle

1984: Lillvretens Quintus, Norwich Terrier

1983: Siggens Hi-Fi, Pembroke Welsh Corgi

1982: Sunsalve Come Play with Me at Toydom (imp. UK), Pekingese

1981: Casa de Oro 10000 Volt, Kerry Blue Terrier

1980: Blackdale Starbright (imp. Ireland), Wire Fox Terrier

1979: Silverlings Sun Dancer, Wire Fox Terrier

1978: Music's Right On (imp. Canada), Kerry Blue Terrier

1977: Flannon Connel, Irish Wolfhound

1976: Kanix Vagant, Bouvier des Flandres

1975: Starline Midnight Sascha, Standard Poodle

1974: Deveraux Janore (imp. UK), Welsh Terrier

1973: Min Susi Wong, Pug

1972: Caro, Norwegian Buhund

1971: Leander Midnight Cowboy (imp. UK), Standard Poodle

1970: Mountebanks Nicola, Scottish Deerhound

1969: Stanolly Star Gem (imp. UK), Bedlington Terrier

1968: Yorken Gallant Knight (imp. UK), Pembroke Welsh Corgi

1967: Thorholms Goodwill, Boston Terrier

1966: Driv av Kotofjell, Norwegian Elkhound

FINLAND

2006: Leonhard's Supertramp (imp. Germany), West Highland White Terrier

2005: Stablemaster's Northern Hope, Giant Schnauzer

2004: Stablemaster's Northern Hope, Giant Schnauzer

2003: Stablemaster's Northern Hope, Giant Schnauzer

2002: Curiosity Luxury of Silk, Silky Terrier

2001: Hookside Csaba (imp. UK), Hungarian Viszla

2000: Starring Flir, Wire Fox Terrier

1999: El Hamrah Farraar, Saluki

1998: Freckle-Face Cobra, Miniature Wire Dachshund

1997: Pectus Zaicca, Giant Schnauzer

1996: Canmoy's Rubiazo, Standard Poodle

1995: Stablemaster's Super Play, Giant Schnauzer

1994: Starring Name Game, Wire Fox Terrier

1993: Pectus Bistro, Giant Schnauzer

1992: Stårups Ruud Gullit, Wire Fox Terrier

1991: Maneetas Del Zarzoso Fuego Fatuo (imp. UK), Standard Poodle

1990: Straight Fire Dynamite of Reistos, Maltese

1989: Hejano Grandee Curare (imp. UK), Bull Terrier

1988: Zep Hild v. Axmagal (imp. Netherlands), Bouvier des Flandres

1987: El Hamrah Giah, Saluki

1986: Tjällmoras Dandy, Irish Terrier

1985: Tjällmoras Dandy, Irish Terrier

1984: Choice Wild West, Afghan Hound

1983: Skansen's Faenrik (imp. US), Standard Schnauzer

1982: Wintell's Dark Debora, Miniature Poodle

1981: Mistyway Saucy Red Tiger, American Cocker Spaniel

1980: Lochlannaigh Embassy Man, Kerry Blue Terrier

1979: Tintavon Desdemona, Tibetan Terrier

1978: Music's Right On (imp. Canada), Kerry Blue Terrier

1977: Miradel Magnus (imp. UK), Miniature Poodle

1976: Brimstone's Dacapo, Clumber Spaniel

1975: Astrawin Apollo (imp. UK), English Cocker Spaniel

Appendix F:
Bests in Show

WESTMINSTER KENNEL CLUB
New York City, US

Note: There was no Best in Show award in 1923. The American Kennel Club barred interbreed competition for 1923 except in the Miscellaneous Class. Comprehensive new rules for Group and Best in Show judging were adopted effective 1924. Best in Show winners prior to 1924 were not necessarily undefeated at the show.

2007: Ch. Felicity's Diamond Jim, English Springer Spaniel
2006: Ch. Rocky Top's Sundance Kid, Bull Terrier (Colored)
2005: Ch. Kan-Point's VJK Autumn Roses, German Shorthaired Pointer
2004: Ch. Darbydale's All Rise PouchCove, Newfoundland
2003: Ch. Torum's Scarf Michael (imp. UK), Kerry Blue Terrier
2002: Ch. Surrey Spice Girl, Poodle (Miniature)
2001: Ch. Special Times Just Right, Bichon Frisé
2000: Ch. Salilyn 'N Erin's Shameless, English Springer Spaniel
1999: Ch. Loteki Supernatural Being, Papillon
1998: Ch. Fairewood Frolic (imp. Canada), Norwich Terrier
1997: Ch. Parsifal di Casa Netzer (imp. Italy), Standard Schnauzer
1996: Ch. Clussexx Country Sunrise, Clumber Spaniel
1995: Ch. Gaelforce Post Script, Scottish Terrier
1994: Ch. Chidley Willum The Conqueror, Norwich Terrier
1993: Ch. Salilyn's Condor, English Springer Spaniel
1992: Ch. Registry's Lonesome Dove, Fox Terrier (Wire)
1991: Ch. Whisperwind's On A Carousel, Poodle (Standard)
1990: Ch. Wendessa Crown Prince, Pekingese
1989: Ch. Royal Tudor's Wild As The Wind, Doberman Pinscher
1988: Ch. Great Elms Prince Charming, II, Pomeranian
1987: Ch. Covy-Tucker Hill's Manhattan, German Shepherd Dog
1986: Ch. Marjetta's National Acclaim, Pointer
1985: Ch. Braeburn's Close Encounter, Scottish Terrier
1984: Ch. Seaward's Blackbeard, Newfoundland
1983: Ch. Kabik's The Challenger, Afghan Hound
1982: Ch. St. Aubrey Dragonora of Elsdon (Canada), Pekingese
1981: Ch. Dhandy's Favorite Woodchuck, Pug
1980: Ch. Innisfree's Sierra Cinnar, Siberian Husky

1979: Ch. Oak Tree's Irishtocrat (Canada), Irish Water Spaniel
1978: Ch. Cede Higgens, Yorkshire Terrier
1977: Ch. Dersade Bobby's Girl (imp. UK), Sealyham Terrier
1976: Ch. Jo-Ni's Red Baron of Crofton, Lakeland Terrier
1975: Ch. Sir Lancelot of Barvan (Canada), Old English Sheepdog
1974: Ch. Gretchenhof Columbia River, German Shorthaired Pointer
1973: Ch. Acadia Command Performance, Poodle (Standard)
1972: Ch. Chinoe's Adamant James, English Springer Spaniel
1971: Ch. Chinoe's Adamant James, English Springer Spaniel
1970: Ch. Arriba's Prima Donna, Boxer
1969: Ch. Glamoor Good News, Skye Terrier
1968: Ch. Stingray of Derryabah (imp. UK), Lakeland Terrier
1967: Ch. Bardene Bingo (imp. UK), Scottish Terrier
1966: Ch. Zeloy Mooremaide's Magic (imp. UK), Fox Terrier (Wire)
1965: Ch. Carmichael's Fanfare, Scottish Terrier
1964: Ch. Courtenay Fleetfoot of Pennyworth (imp. UK), Whippet
1963: Ch. Wakefield's Black Knight, English Springer Spaniel
1962: Ch. Elfinbrook Simon (imp. UK), West Highland White Terrier
1961: Ch. Cappoquin Little Sister, Poodle (Toy)
1960: Ch. Chik T'Sun of Caversham (imp. UK), Pekingese
1959: Ch. Fontclair Festoon (imp. UK), Poodle (Miniature)
1958: Ch. Puttencove Promise, Poodle (Standard)
1957: Ch. Shirkhan of Grandeur, Afghan Hound
1956: Ch. Wilber White Swan, Poodle (Toy)
1955: Ch. Kippax Fearnought (imp. UK), Bulldog
1954: Ch. Carmor's Rise and Shine, Cocker Spaniel (ASCOB)
1953: Ch. Rancho Dobe's Storm, Doberman Pinscher
1952: Ch. Rancho Dobe's Storm, Doberman Pinscher
1951: Ch. Bang Away of Sirrah Crest, Boxer
1950: Ch. Walsing Winning Trick of Edgerstoune (imp. UK), Scottish Terrier
1949: Ch. Mazelaine's Zazarac Brandy, Boxer
1948: Ch. Rock Ridge Night Rocket, Bedlington Terrier
1947: Ch. Warlord of Mazelaine, Boxer
1946: Ch. Hetherington Model Rhythm, Fox Terrier (Wire)
1945: Ch. Shieling's Signature, Scottish Terrier
1944: Ch. Flornell Rare-Bit of Twin Ponds (imp. UK), Welsh Terrier

1943: Ch. Pitter Patter of Piperscroft (imp. UK), Poodle
(Miniature)

1942: Ch. Wolvey Pattern of Edgerstoune (imp. UK), West
Highland White Terrier

1941: Ch. My Own Brucie, Cocker Spaniel (Black)

1940: Ch. My Own Brucie, Cocker Spaniel (Black)

1939: Ch. Ferry v. Rauhfelsen of Giralda (imp. Germany),
Doberman Pinscher

1938: Ch. Daro of Maridor, English Setter

1937: Ch. Flornell Spicy Piece of Halleston (imp. UK), Fox
Terrier (Wire)

1936: Ch. St. Margaret Magnificent of Clairedale (imp. UK),
Sealyham Terrier

1935: Ch. Nunsoe Duc de la Terrace of Blakeen
(imp. Switzerland), Poodle (Standard)

1934: Ch. Flornell Spicy Bit of Halleston (imp. UK),
Fox Terrier (Wire)

1933: Ch. Warland Protector of Shelterock (imp. UK),
Airedale Terrier

1932: Ch. Nancolleth Markable (imp. UK), Pointer

1931: Ch. Pendley Calling of Blarney (imp. UK),
Fox Terrier (Wire)

1930: Ch. Pendley Calling of Blarney (imp. UK),
Fox Terrier (Wire)

1929: Laund Loyalty of Bellhaven (imp. UK), Collie (Rough)

1928: Ch. Talavera Margaret (imp. UK), Fox Terrier (Wire)

1927: Ch. Pinegrade Perfection (imp. UK), Sealyham Terrier

1926: Ch. Signal Circuit of Halleston (imp. UK),
Fox Terrier (Wire)

1925: Ch. Governor Moscow (imp. UK), Pointer

1924: Ch. Barberryhill Bootlegger, Sealyham Terrier

1922: Ch. Boxwood Barkentine, Airedale Terrier

1921: Ch. Midkiff Seductive, Cocker Spaniel (Parti-Color)

1920: Ch. Conejo Wycollar Boy (imp. UK), Fox Terrier (Wire)

1919: Ch. Briergate Bright Beauty (imp. UK), Airedale
Terrier

1918: Ch. Haymarket Faultless (Canada), Bull Terrier (White)

1917: Ch. Conejo Wycollar Boy (imp. UK), Fox Terrier (Wire)

1916: Ch. Matford Vic (imp. UK), Fox Terrier (Wire)

1915: Ch. Matford Vic (imp. UK), Fox Terrier (Wire)

1914: Ch. Slumber (imp. UK), Old English Sheepdog

1913: Ch. Strathay Prince Albert (imp. UK), Bulldog

1912: Ch. Kenmare Sorceress (imp. UK), Airedale Terrier

1911: Ch. Tickle 'Em Jock (imp. UK), Scottish Terrier

1910: Ch. Sabine Rarebit, Fox Terrier (Smooth)

1909: Ch. Warren Remedy, Fox Terrier (Smooth)

1908: Ch. Warren Remedy, Fox Terrier (Smooth)

1907: Ch. Warren Remedy, Fox Terrier (Smooth)

MORRIS & ESSEX KENNEL CLUB

2005: Ch. Rocky Top's Sundance Kid, Bull Terrier (Colored)

2000: Ch. Torum's Scarf Michael (imp. UK), Kerry Blue Terrier

1958–1999: No shows held; beginning in 2000, show held
every five years

1957: Ch. Fircot L'Ballerine of Maryland (imp. UK), Poodle
(Miniature)

1956: Ch. Roadcoach Roadster, Dalmatian

1955: Ch. Baroque of Quality Hill, Boxer

1953: Ch. Toplight Template of Twin Ponds, Welsh Terrier

1952: Ch. Wyretex Wyns Traveller of Trucote (imp. UK),
Fox Terrier (Wire)

1951: Ch. Rock Falls Colonel, English Setter

1950: Ch. Tyronne Farm Clancy, Irish Terrier

1949: Ch. Walsing Winning Trick of Edgerstoune (imp. UK),
Scottish Terrier

1948: Ch. Rock Ridge Night Rocket, Bedlington Terrier

1947: (Ch.) Rock Ridge Night Rocket, Bedlington Terrier

1946: Ch. Benbow's Beau, Cocker Spaniel

1942–1945: No shows held

1941: Ch. Nornay Saddler (imp. UK), Fox Terrier (Smooth)

1940: Ch. Blakeen Jung Frau, Poodle (Standard)

1939: Ch. My Own Brucie, Cocker Spaniel

1938: Ch. Ideal Weather, Old English Sheepdog

1937: Ch. Sturdy Max, English Setter

1936: Ch. Mr. Reynal's Monarch, Harrier

1935: Ch. Milson O'Boy, Irish Setter

1934: Ch. Gunside Babs of Hollybourne, Sealyham Terrier

1933: Epping Eveille of Blarney, Fox Terrier (Wire)

1932: Ch. Lone Eagle of Earlsmoor, Fox Terrier (Wire)

1931: Ch. Fionne von Loheland of Walnut Hall
(imp. Germany), Great Dane

1930: Ch. Weltona Frizette of Wildoaks (imp. UK),
Fox Terrier (Wire)

1929: Ch. Little Emir, Pomeranian

1928: Ch. Delf Discriminate of Pinegrade, Sealyham Terrier

1927: Ch. Higgin's Red Pat, Irish Setter

CRUFTS

London/Birmingham, UK

(Ch.) indicates that the winner was not a champion at the time
of the Crufts win but gained the title subsequently.

Sh. Ch. stands for Show Champion (for Gundogs only).

2007: Ch. Araki Fabulous Willy, Tibetan Terrier

2006: Am. Ch. Caitland Isle Take A Chance (imp. Canada
to US), Australian Shepherd

2005: Ch. Cracknor Cause Celebre (exp. UK to US), Norfolk Terrier
2004: Ch. Cobyco Call The Tune, Whippet
2003: Ch. Yakee A Dangerous Liaison, Pekingese
2002: Ch. Topscore Contradiction (Norway), Poodle (Standard)
2001: Ch. Jethard Cidevant, Basenji
2000: Ch. Torum's Scarf Michael, Kerry Blue Terrier
1999: Sh. Ch. Caspians Intrepid, Irish Setter
1998: Ch. Saredon Forever Young, Welsh Terrier
1997: Ch. Ozmilion Mystification, Yorkshire Terrier
1996: Sh. Ch. Canigou Cambrai, Cocker Spaniel
1995: Sh. Ch. Starchelle Chicago Bear, Irish Setter
1994: Ch. Purston Hit and Miss from Brocolitia, Welsh Terrier
1993: Sh. Ch. Danaway Debonair, Irish Setter
1992: Ch. Pencloe Dutch Gold, Whippet
1991: Sh. Ch. Raycroft Socialite, Clumber Spaniel
1990: Ch. Olac Moon Pilot, West Highland White Terrier
1989: Ch. Potterdale Classic of Moonhill, Bearded Collie
1988: Sh. Ch. Starlite Express of Valsett, English Setter
1987: Ch. Viscount Grant, Afghan Hound
1986: Ch. Ginger Xmas Carol (imp. Italy), Airedale Terrier
1985: Ch. Montravia Tommy-Gun, Poodle (Standard)
1984: Ch. Saxonsprings Hackensack, Lhasa Apso
1983: Ch. Montravia Kaskarak Hitari, Afghan Hound
1982: Ch. Grayco Hazelnut, Poodle (Toy)
1981: Ch. Astley's Portia of Rua, Irish Setter
1980: Ch. Shargleam Blackcap, Flat-Coated Retriever
1979: Ch. Callaghan of Leander (imp. Canada), Kerry Blue Terrier
1978: Ch. Harrowhill Huntsman, Fox Terrier (Wire)
1977: (Sh. Ch.) Bournehouse Dancing Master, English Setter
1976: Ch. Dianthus Buttons, West Highland White Terrier
1975: Ch. Brookewire Brandy of Layven (Italian-owned), Fox Terrier (Wire)
1974: Ch. Burtonswood Bossy Boots, St. Bernard
1973: (Ch.) Alansmere Aquarius, Cavalier King Charles Spaniel
1972: Ch. Abraxas Audacity, Bull Terrier
1971: Ch. Ramacon Swashbuckler, German Shepherd Dog (Alsatian)
1970: Bergerie Knur, Pyrenean Mountain Dog (Great Pyrenees)
1969: Ch. Hendrawen's Nibelung of Charavigne, German Shepherd Dog (Alsatian)
1968: Ch. Fanhill Faune, Dalmatian
1967: Ch. Stingray of Derryabah, Lakeland Terrier
1966: (Ch.) Oakington Puckshill Amber Sunblush, Poodle (Toy)

1965: Ch. Fenton of Kentwood, German Shepherd Dog (Alsatian)
1964: Sh. Ch. Silbury Soames of Madavale, English Setter
1963: Ch. Rogerholm Recruit, Lakeland Terrier
1962: Ch. Crackwyn Cockspur, Fox Terrier (Wire)
1961: Ch. Riverina Tweedsbairn, Airedale Terrier
1960: (Ch.) Sulhamstead Merman, Irish Wolfhound
1959: Ch. Sandstorm Saracen, Welsh Terrier
1958: Ch. Chiming Bells, Pointer
1957: Ch. Volkrijk of Vorden, Keeshond
1956: (Ch.) Treetops Golden Falcon, Greyhound
1955: Ch. Tzigane Aggri of Nashend, Standard Poodle
1954: Show canceled
1953: Ch. Elch Edler of Ouborough, Great Dane
1952: Ch. Noways Chuckles, Bulldog
1951: (Ch.) Twynstar Dyma-Fi, Welsh Terrier
1950: (Sh. Ch.) Tracey Witch of Ware, Cocker Spaniel
1949: No show, to adjust to date change from October to February
1948: (Sh. Ch.) Tracey Witch of Ware, Cocker Spaniel
1940–1947: No shows held
1939: (Sh. Ch.) Exquisite Model of Ware, Cocker Spaniel
1938: (Sh. Ch.) Exquisite Model of Ware, Cocker Spaniel
1937: Ch. Cheverells Ben of Banchory, Labrador Retriever
1936: Ch. Choonam Hung Kwong, Chow Chow
1935: (Sh. Ch.) Pennine Prima Donna, Pointer
1934: Ch. Southball Moonstone, Greyhound
1933: Ch. Bramshaw Bob, Labrador Retriever
1932: (Ch.) Bramshaw Bob, Labrador Retriever
1931: (Sh. Ch.) Lucky Star of Ware, Cocker Spaniel
1930: (Sh. Ch.) Lucky Star of Ware, Cocker Spaniel
1929: (Ch.) Heather Necessity, Scottish Terrier
1928: Primley Sceptre, Greyhound

Prior to 1928, there was no official Best in Show award at Crufts, but a challenge bowl for Best Champion in the Show was introduced in 1906 and served a similar purpose.

1924–1927: No award recorded
1923: Ballochmyle Lightening, Skye Terrier
1921–1922: No award recorded
1918–1920: No shows held
1917: No award recorded
1916: Ch. Chequebook of Notts, Fox Terrier (Wire)
1915: Sonneburgh Squire, Rough Collie
1914: Ch. St. Blaise, Greyhound
1913: No award recorded
1912: Ch. The Pride of Sussex, St. Bernard

1911: Ch. Collarbone of Notts, Fox Terrier (Wire)
1910: Ch. Broadwater Banker, Greyhound
1909: Ch. Clareholm Dora, Field Spaniel
1908: Ch. Shelton Viking, Newfoundland
1907: Ch. The Sable Mite, Pomeranian
1906: Ch. Wishaw Leader, Rough Collie

RESERVE BEST IN SHOW CRUFTS

2007: Ch. Travella Show Stopper, Wire Fox Terrier
2006: Ch. El Rays Snowtaire Iceni Payback (imp. US),
      Wire Fox Terrier
2005: Sh. Ch. Bournehouse Royal Colours, English Setter
2004: Ch. Raglan Rose Maiden at Brio (imp. Sweden),
      Scottish Terrier
2003: Ch. Torum's Tunde Bayou, Kerry Blue Terrier
2002: Ch. Yakee A Dangerous Liaison, Pekingese
2001: Ch. Penliath Shooting Star, Pembroke Welsh Corgi
2000: Sh. Ch. Wiljana Waterfall, Cocker Spaniel
1999: Ch. Redwitch Dancin' In The Dark, Akita
1998: Ch. Towsushet's The Mistress, Chow Chow
1997: Sh. Ch. Boduf Pistols at Dawn with Afterglow,
      American Cocker Spaniel
1996: Ch. Jokyl This Is My Song, Airedale Terrier
1995: Ch. Purston Leading Lady at Wigmore, Welsh Terrier
1994: Sh. Ch. Dykebar Future Glory, Border Collie
1993: Ch. Drakesleat Odyt, Irish Wolfhound
1992 : Sh. Ch. Homestead's Tiffany with Boduf (imp. US),
      American Cocker Spaniel
1991: Ch. Caswell Copper Tiger, Papillon
1990: Ch. Nutshell of Nevedith, Whippet
1989: Ch. Yakee For Your Eyes Only, Pekingese
1988: Ch. Brannigan of Brumberhill, Border Terrier
1987: Ch. Killick of the Mess, Fox Terrier (Wire)
1986: Ch. Tyegarth Jacob of Kelloe, Bulldog
1985: Ch. Micklee Roc's Ru-Ago, Pekingese
1984: Ch. Lirevas Shooting Star, Pomeranian
1983: (Sh. Ch.) Corriecas Fagan, Irish Setter
1982: Kenmil's Bellisima of Danala, German Shepherd Dog
1981: Sablecomb White Polar at Leander, Poodle (Standard)
1980: Ch. Castilla Linajudo, Miniature Schnauzer
1979: Ch. Belmuriz Brevier, Chihuahua (Smooth Coat)
1978: Ch. Blairsville Royal Seal, Yorkshire Terrier
1977: Ch. Binate Plantagenet, Kerry Blue Terrier
1976: Ch. Maytheas Delila, Maltese
1975: Ch. Beechlyn Golden Nugget of Denbrough, Bulldog
1974: Ch. Blairsville Most Royale, Yorkshire Terrier
1973: Sh. Ch. Daviam Titus Lartius, Pointer
1972: Ch. Dondelayo Duette, Whippet

1971: Ch. Rozavel Tarina Song, Chihuahua (Long Coat)
1970: Ch. Ouaine Chieftain, Cocker Spaniel
1969: Sh. Ch. Lochranza Strollaway, Cocker Spaniel
1968: Ch. Bergerie Diable, Pyrenean Mountain Dog
      (Great Pyrenees)
1967: Ch. Bibelot's Tall Dark and Handsome (imp. Canada),
      Poodle (Standard)
1966: Sh. Ch. Blakeshay Avant Tout, Pointer
1965: Ch. Forrardon Appeline Beeswing, Beagle
1964: Ch. Burydown Freyha, Saluki
1963: Sh. Ch. Silbury Soames of Madavale, English Setter
1962: (Sh. Ch.) Colinwood Black Eagle, Cocker Spaniel
1961: (Sh. Ch.) Silbury Soames of Madavale, English Setter
1960: Ch. Pixietown Serenade of Hadleigh, Pomeranian
1959: Ch. Ruler of Blaircourt, Labrador Retriever
1958: Ch. Ambassadorson of Buttonoak, Bullmastiff
1957: Ch. Shiplake Dean of Crombie, English Setter
1956: Ch. Caradochouse Spruce, Fox Terrier (Wire)
1955: (Ch.) Melba of Quernmore, Borzoi
1954: Show canceled
1953: Ch. Netheroyd Alibaba, Afghan Hound
1952: Ripleygate Topnote, English Setter
1951: Edana of Combehill, German Shepherd Dog (Alsatian)
1950: Ch. Adastra Magic Beau, Poodle (Miniature)
1949: No show, to adjust to date change from October to
      February
1948: (Ch.) Drakehall Dairymaid, Fox Terrier (Wire)
1940–1947: No shows held
1939: Ch. Choonam Hung Kwong, Chow Chow
1938: Ch. Ruler of Ouborough, Great Dane
1937: Kren of the Hollow, Elkhound
1936: Silver Templa of Ware, Cocker Spaniel
1935: Ch. Choonam Hung Kwong, Chow Chow
1934: (Sh. Ch.) Whoopee of Ware, Cocker Spaniel
1933: Ch. Rose Marie of the Rookes, Scottish Terrier
1932: (Ch.) Another Prince of the Chevin, Kerry Blue Terrrier
1931: Ch. Nancolleth Markable, Pointer
1930: Ch. Heather Necessity, Scottish Terrier
1929: (Sh. Ch.) Stainton Spruce, Pointer
1928: (Sh. Ch.) Stainton Spruce, Pointer

FCI WORLD SHOW

The Fédération Cynologique Internationale's World Show is
hosted by a different country each year. Entry figures fluctuate
greatly, from more than 15,000 dogs when the World Show is
held in Europe to 2,000–3,000 dogs in South or Central
America. In parentheses after the Best in Show winner's name

is the country of birth. FCI does not maintain a list of past winners; the following has been compiled by the author. Records from the first years' shows are not available.

2007: Mexico City, Mexico: Ch. Smash JP Talk About (Japan), Toy Poodle

2006: Poznan, Poland: Ch. Alex del Monte Alago (Italy), Bracco Italiano

2005: Buenos Aires, Argentina: Ch. Homero del Alcazar (Brazil), Lhasa Apso

2004: Rio de Janeiro, Brazil: Ch. Double D Cinoblu's Masterpiece (Brazil), Pug

2003: Dortmund, Germany: Ch. Propwash Syzygy (US), Australian Shepherd

2002: Amsterdam, Netherlands: Ch. Topscore Contradiction (Norway), Poodle (Standard)

2001: Oporto, Portugal: Ch. Atwater Crazy-Diamond Borgoleonardo (Italy), Newfoundland

2000: Milan, Italy: Ch. Giacherbee dell'Angelo del Summane (Italy), Bracco Italiano

1999: Mexico City, Mexico: Ch. Tacara's Santer Savar (US), Belgian Tervuren

1998: Helsinki, Finland: Ch. Loteki Supernatural Being (US), Papillon

1997: San Juan, Puerto Rico: Ch. Afton's Absolut (US), Cocker Spaniel (American)

1996: Vienna, Austria/Budapest, Hungary: Ch. Sanallah's Jerome (US), Afghan Hound

1995: Brussels, Belgium: Ch. Humphrey dos Sete Moinhos (Portugal), Basset Hound

1994: Bern, Switzerland: Ch. Artic's Blue Senator (US/Spain*), Siberian Husky

1993: Buenos Aires, Argentina: Ch. Eddie Tato von Norwalfer (Argentina), Great Dane

1992: Valencia, Spain: Ch. Caligola di Ponzani (Italy), Neapolitan Mastiff

1991: Dortmund, Germany: Ch. Fanto vom Hirschel (Germany), German Shepherd Dog

1990: Brno, Czech Republic: Ch. Chakpori's Mao (Holland), Lhasa Apso

1989: Copenhagen, Denmark: Ch. Chouan Gimlet (Denmark), Petit Basset Griffon Vendéen

1988: Lima, Peru: Ch. Northwind's Rising Star (US), Samoyed

1987: Tel Aviv, Israel: Ch. Northwind's Rising Star (US), Samoyed

1986: Tulln, Austria: Ch. Abrisa vom Felsenkeller (Germany), Saluki

1985: Amsterdam, Netherlands: Ch. Abrisa vom Felsenkeller (Germany), Saluki

1984: Acapulco, Mexico: Ch. Kishniga's Diaghilev (Canada), Borzoi

1983: Madrid, Spain: Ch. Tigre (Spain), Spanish Mastiff

1982: Tokyo, Japan: Ch. Fujimiland Julia (Japan), Yorkshire Terrier

1981: Dortmund, Germany: Ch. Saliha's Deianeira (Holland), Saluki

1980: Verona, Italy: Ch. Beseeka Knight Errant of Silkstone (UK), Whippet

FCI ASIAN SHOW

The FCI Asian show has been held each year since 1984 in Tokyo except in 1990, when it was held in Chiba, and in 1996 and 1997, when it was in Yokohama. The Japan Kennel Club has provided the following information.

2007: Ch. Border Lane JP Moonshining, Border Collie

2006: Ch. North Well Chako JP Marble Queen, Poodle (Toy)

2005: Ch. Riverside King's Sweet Emblem, Maltese

2004: Ch. Masada's Trumpet Player (imp. North America), Keeshond

2003: Hadleigh Sweet Serenade, Pomeranian

2002: Ch. Smash JP Samba de Amigo, Poodle (Toy)

2001: Ch. Larchmont's Michael (imp. North America), Pembroke Welsh Corgi

2000: Ch. Generous JP Prime Stage, Siberian Husky

1999: Ch. Lorien It's A Guy Thing (imp. North America), Pembroke Welsh Corgi

1998: Ch. Nautilus Sugar Smacks (imp. North America), Golden Retriever

1997: Ch. Puddleby Palace JP Lake Hunter, Golden Retriever

1996: Ch. Innisfree's Ice T (imp. North America), Siberian Husky

1995: Ch. Dragon Fall Miwa JP Oh My God, Shih Tzu

1994: Ch. Misty Wood JP Wishing Star, American Cocker Spaniel

1993: Ch. Sweet Evening of Fortune, Shetland Sheepdog

1992: Ch. Oreia Instnt Replay Sumrwnd (imp. North America), Afghan Hound

1991: Ch. Wisdom's James Bros Franky (imp. North America), Saluki

1990: Ch. Satari's Pride N Joy (imp. North America), Siberian Husky

* Bred by Rhonda Hayward, of an American military family that was temporarily stationed in Spain and has since returned to the United States.

1989: Ch. Teru Noble's Sun Miracle, Miniature Schnauzer
1988: Ch. Zaimar's Scarlet Ribbons (imp. North America), Siberian Husky
1987: Ch. Birnam Wood's Vilanova Punch (imp. North America), Golden Retriever
1986: Ch. Innisfree's Gilpak's Macho (imp. North America), Siberian Husky
1985: Ch. Telly of Iris New Hakodate Sato, Pomeranian
1984: Ch. Beckwith Goldwing Drambuie (imp. North America), Golden Retriever

STOCKHOLM INTERNATIONAL SHOW SWEDEN

Country of origin is indicated only when outside Scandinavia.

2006: Ch. Caci's Cute Carmen at Ld's, American Cocker Spaniel
2005: Triumphs Izaro, German Shepherd Dog
2004: Ch. Topscore Contradiction, Poodle (Standard)
2003: Ch. Qirmizi Cartago, Saluki
2002: Ch. Topscore Contradiction, Poodle (Standard)
2001: Ch. Jet's Once Upon A Dream, Greyhound
2000: Ch. Sentling Zenzero (imp. UK), Italian Spinone
1999: Ch. Drover's Roll Those Dice, Old English Sheepdog
1998: Ch. Tiny Jewel's Toystar, Pomeranian
1997: Ch. Porrigito Claypot, Norfolk Terrier
1996: Ch. Bahlamb's Barnyard Baron (imp. US), Old English Sheepdog
1994: Ch. Kontoki's Gibson Girl (imp. US), Siberian Husky
1994: Ch. Almanza Emergency Brake, Flat-Coated Retriever
1993: Ch. Rottrivers Black Pearl, Cairn Terrier
1992: Ch. Extrem's Ovation of Osyth (imp. UK), Bulldog
1991: Ch. Almanza Larry O'Grady, Flat-Coated Retriever
1990: Ch. Hjohoo's I Love Hjo Yeh! Yeh! Yeh! Cairn Terrier
1989: Ch. Metzgard's Moonlight Valley, Welsh Springer Spaniel
1988: Ch. Carillo Art of Noice, American Cocker Spaniel
1987: Ch. Triumphs Blaze, German Shepherd Dog
1986: Ch. Triumphs Blaze, German Shepherd Dog
1985: Ch. Gilroy Mr. Margeaux, Lakeland Terrier
1984: Ch. Vanitonia Holy Moses (imp. UK), Poodle (Toy)
1983: Ch. Sarimont Skallagrim, Cairn Terrier
1982: Ch. Bushey's Magic Storm, West Highland White Terrier
1981: Ch. Gulds Heroine Honey, Greyhound
1980: Ch. Gerjo's Shilo of Airways (imp. US), Great Dane
1979: Ch. Tintavon Desdemona (imp. UK), Tibetan Terrier
1978: Ch. Music's Right On, Kerry Blue Terrier

1977: Ch. Airescot Lazuli, Scottish Deerhound
1976: Ch. Groveview Red Rum (imp. UK), Welsh Terrier
1975: Ch. Martlesham Bronson (imp. UK), Pug
1974: Ch. Piruett, Greyhound
1973: Ch. Kennelgarth Samson (imp. UK), Scottish Terrier
1972: Ch. Stanolly Sandpiper (imp. UK), Bedlington Terrier
1971: Ch. Leander Midnight Cowboy (imp. UK), Poodle (Standard)
1970: Ch. Furor of Montfleuri (imp. UK), Poodle (Miniature)
1969: Ch. Cedewain Comedy (imp. UK), Welsh Terrier
1968: Ch. Glenessa Helmsman (imp. UK), Golden Retriever
1967: Ch. Triumphs Heidi, German Shepherd Dog
1966: Ch. Chicos Pierre Boy, Poodle (Standard)
1965: Ch. Akka, Västgötaspets (Swedish Vallhund)
1964: Ch. Bombax Ericus Rex, Border Terrier
1963: Ch. Laguna Locomite (imp. UK), Whippet
1962: Ch. Crackwyn Cockspur (imp. UK), Fox Terrier (Wire)
1961: Ch. Royalblue of Burdiesel (imp. UK), Poodle (Miniature)
1960: Ch. Chiquita of Mathena (imp. UK), Pekingese
1959: Ch. Lucklena Musician (imp. UK), Cocker Spaniel
1958: Ch. Toyhomes Yat-Sen, Pekingese
1957: Ch. Örlidens Cossack II, Cocker Spaniel
1956: Ch. Tomahawk-Uncas von der Aue (imp. Germany), Boxer
1955: Ch. Örlidens Starlight, Cocker Spaniel
1954: Ch. Tarrywood Black Countess, Poodle (Miniature)
1953: Ch. Fasansparets Fairy, Fox Terrier (Wire)
1952: Strandborg Minx, Boxer
1951: Ch. Arabella av Boyan, Great Dane
1950: Ch. Flickery Flies, Bulldog
1949: Ch. Toyhomes Bi-No-Tu, Pekingese

MELBOURNE ROYAL SHOW AUSTRALIA

2006: Gr. Ch. Ryangaye Rhythm N Time, Cocker Spaniel
2005: Gr. Ch. Hobergays Fineus Fogg (imp. NZ), Dandie Dinmont Terrier
2004: Ch. Chebaco's Bridgewood Guard (imp. US), English Setter
2003: Ch. Saynthaven I Gotcha, St. Bernard
2002: Gr. Ch. Kjavu Air Jordan, Afghan Hound
2001: Ch. Tullane Fiery Thyme, Irish Setter
2000: Ch. Troymere Diva D'Amour, Poodle (Standard)
1999: Ch. Liebendane Baby Grand (imp. A.I.), Great Dane
1998: Gr. Ch. Eirannmada at Tulane, Irish Setter
1997: Ch. Graphic American Dream (imp. US), Poodle (Standard)

1996: Ch. Vlandyn Countryman, Pembroke Welsh Corgi
1995: Ch. Fernsglen Irish-Mike (imp. NZ), Kerry Blue Terrier
1994: Ch. Transwind Divine Madness, Afghan Hound
1993: Ch. Troymere Believe Inme, Poodle (Standard)
1992: Ch. Swelegant Once Again, Cocker Spaniel (American)
1991: Ch. Taratan Show Bonnet, Boxer
1990: Ch. Hartwyn Royal Pageant, CDX, Old English Sheepdog
1989: Ch. Bon Jovi Bacchante (imp. Ireland), Poodle (Miniature)
1988: Ch. Wongan Chiffon, English Springer Spaniel
1987: Ch. Dygae Superspark, Pembroke Welsh Corgi
1986: Ch. Santeric Res Ipsa Loquitur (imp. US), Fox Terrier (Wire)
1985: Ch. Rossfort Nijinski (imp. UK), Siberian Husky
1984: Ch. Planhaven Big Mac, Newfoundland
1983: Ch. Maykel Wei Lin, Pekingese
1982: Ch. Cherrymount Lucette, Dalmatian
1981: Sampenny Vendetta, German Shepherd Dog
1980: Ch. Wybong Just Hooper, Bulldog
1979: Ch. Alaqadar De Fauves, Afghan Hound
1978: Ch. Pangtoy Mardi Gable, Pekingese
1977: Doggestadt Jadd, Great Dane
1976: Ch. Letomi Hi There, Boxer
1975: Ch. Farleton Don Pedro, Fox Terrier (Smooth)
1974: Ch. Bowmore Mark Time, Pembroke Welsh Corgi
1973: Ch. Bowmore Sonnatag, Pembroke Welsh Corgi
1972: Ch. Dulcannina Kansas, Australian Silky Terrier
1971: Ch. Horand Prince Huzzar, German Shepherd Dog
1970: Ch. Zarel Rusty, English Setter
1969: Ch. Garrleigh Golden Sands, Fox Terrier (Smooth)
1968: Ch. Mazari of Carloway (imp. UK), Afghan Hound
1967: Ch. Zaukera Shah, Afghan Hound
1966: Ch. Womack Wright Royalshow (imp. UK), Dachshund (Smooth)
1965: Ch. Mazari of Carloway (imp. UK), Afghan Hound
1964: Ch. Konig Brave Lustre, Doberman Pinscher
1963: Ch. Lambrigg The Squatter, Cocker Spaniel
1962 : Ch. Bernlore Kaisers Gold, German Shepherd Dog
1961: Tynycoed Cherie, Pembroke Welsh Corgi
1960: Ch. Suyian Aladdin, Pekingese
1959: Ch. Wulfreda Rhapsody (imp. UK), Kerry Blue Terrier
1958: Ch. Panorama Huzzar, German Shepherd Dog
1957: Ch. Ahfoo Chinkee, Pekingese
1956: Ch. Hawlock Daffodil, Pomeranian
1955: Ch. Reptonite, Greyhound

1954: Ch. Sedora Syntax of Ware (imp. UK), Cocker Spaniel

SYDNEY ROYAL SHOW AUSTRALIA

2007: Ch. Karakush In Champagne, Afghan Hound
2006: Ch. PVT STK's Fire In The Sky (imp. US), Siberian Husky
2005: Ch. Tarquin Once Is Not Enough, English Setter
2004: Buldawg Our Man Godfrey, Bulldog
2003: Ch. Illahee Summer Fun, Siberian Husky
2002: Ch. Peelhunt Ruler, English Foxhound
2001: Ch. Patrician Phantom (imp. NZ), Maltese
2000: Ch. Troymere Diva D'Amour, Poodle (Standard)
1999: Gr. Ch. Kiabe Qariban, Saluki
1998: Ch. Hillacre Wee Macgregor, Shetland Sheepdog
1997: Ch. Taejaan Ms Margarita, Whippet
1996: Ch. Tobalsk Royal Secret, Samoyed
1995: Ch. Silkstone Jewel in the Crown (imp. UK), Whippet
1994: Ch. Aldonza Kiss And Tell, Samoyed
1993: Ch. Grauhund Nite Moves, Weimaraner
1992: Ch. Azucroft Jumpin Jack, English Springer Spaniel
1991: Ch. Keeshee Cute Ncuddley, Keeshond
1990: Ch. Tahee Dirty Harry, Australian Terrier
1989: Ch. Peelhunt Genevieve, English Foxhound
1988: Ch. Leander White Blaze (imp. So. Africa), Poodle (Standard)
1987: Ch. Walista Wan Chai, Pekingese
1986: Ch. Mirolinda Superstar, Fox Terrier (Smooth)
1985: Ch. Aberdeen Fordyce, Scottish Terrier
1984: Ch. Sagaces Merryman, Basset Hound
1983: Ch. Calahorra Boccaccio, Afghan Hound
1982: Ch. Lehearn Lovemn Leavem, Cocker Spaniel
1981: Ch. Balandra Delta Darius, Golden Retriever
1980: Ch. Wybong Just Hooper, Bulldog
1979: Ch. Quom Starspangled Banner, Afghan Hound
1978: Ch. Deleve MacGregor, Scottish Terrier
1977: Ch. Calahorra Benedictus, Afghan Hound
1976: Ch. Regalen Saladin, Pekingese
1975: Ch. Calahorra Turban, Afghan Hound
1974: Ch. Kingsmens Witchcraft (imp. UK), German Shepherd Dog
1973: Ch. Tinee Town Talktime, Australian Terrier
1972: Ch. Fermoy Mahnfred, Afghan Hound
1971: Ch. Lourdale Tzamark, Samoyed
1970: Ch. Furbari Shalakhan, Afghan Hound
1969: Ch. Vondobe The Maharajah, Doberman Pinscher
1968: Ch. Baymark Famous, English Foxhound
1967: Ch. Almark Black Prince, German Shepherd Dog

1966: Ch. De Montfort Much Ado, Fox Terrier (Wire)
1965: Ch. Mazari of Carloway (imp. UK), Afghan Hound
1964: Ch. Rakcal Jiky, Poodle (Miniature)
1963: Ch. Mighty Rare of Ware (imp. UK), Cocker Spaniel
1962: Ch. Foxwyre Flash Gem, Fox Terrier (Wire)
1961: Ch. Chetwyn Merthytydill, Pembroke Welsh Corgi
1960: Ch. Starya of Kobe (imp. UK), Samoyed

1959: Ch. Fairtrough Jonta (imp. UK), Bulldog
1958: Ch. Ahfoo Chinkee, Pekingese
1957: Ch. Ceba of Kon Tik (imp. NZ), Poodle (Miniature)
1956: Ch. Moonta Mazilla (imp. UK), Scottish Terrier
1955: Ch. Su Huo of Alderbourne (imp. UK), Pekingese
1954: Ch. Tablow Tallulah, Irish Setter

GLOSSARY

affix: the part of a dog's registered name that identifies its family heritage, usually the owner or breeder; *see also* prefix and suffix

agent: term used by the AKC to indicate a dog's handler

AKC: *See* American Kennel Club

all-breed show: conformation show open for all breeds

all-rounder judge: judge approved for all (or, used loosely, most) breeds

American-Bred class: class for dogs bred in the United States

American Kennel Club: the largest and most influential organization governing pure-bred dog activities in the United States

angulation: angles between the joints in a dog, such as between shoulder blade and upper arm, stifle and hock

Any Variety class: UK class open for multiple breeds; sometimes limited as Any Variety Hound, Any Variety Gundog, and so on

AOM: Award of Merit

armband: number worn on a handler's arm that corresponds to the dog's catalog number

Award of Merit: unofficial award available at selected, usually large, AKC shows

bait: object or food (usually dried liver or dog cookie) used by a handler to attract the dog's attention during judging

bench show: show where each dog entered is kept in a designated, predetermined stall (bench) while not being judged

Best in Show: the dog judged as best in a show; the only dog undefeated in Breed, Group, and Best in Show competition at that event

Best in Specialty Show: the dog judged as best in a show limited to only one breed

Best King: term in Japan for the best male dog in a show

Best of Breed: the dog judged as best of its breed in a show

Best of Opposite Sex: the dog judged as best of its sex in a show but defeated by the Best of Breed winner

Best of Variety: the dog judged as best of its variety in a show; *see* variety

Best of Winners: the dog judged as best of Winners Dog and Winners Bitch in a show

Best Queen: term in Japan for best female in show

BIS: Best in Show

BISS (or SBIS): Best in Specialty Show; also Specialty Best in Show (both terms are used interchangeably)

BOB: Best of Breed

BOS: Best of Opposite Sex

BOW: Best of Winners

Brace class: class for two dogs that are shown by the same owner

Bred-by-Exhibitor class: class for dogs owned and shown by their breeder or co-breeder

breed: a race of dog, usually selected and maintained by man, with a common gene pool, function, and appearance

breeder: the owner or lessee (at the time of mating) of a bitch that produced a litter

breed standard: written description of characteristics possessed by each breed

brindle: coat pattern including stripes of black hair against a lighter (usually brown, gray, or fawn) background

Brood Bitch class: class including a dam with at least two of her offspring, judged on the merits of the quality of the offspring, not the dam

buff: off-white or light gold color

CAC: often called just certificate; Certificat d'Aptitude au Championnat

CACIB: Certificat d'Aptitude au Championnat Internationale de Beauté

Canine Good Citizen: program that tests a dog's behavior

CC: *See* Challenge Certificate

Certificat d'Aptitude au Championnat: national award in FCI countries; a varying number of CACs qualify for the national champion title

Certificat d'Aptitude au Championnat Internationale de Beauté: international award at FCI shows; usually four awards are required for the international champion title

Certificate quality: highest individual grading, equalling Excellent grade (Scandinavia)

CGC: Canine Good Citizen

Ch.: Champion, commonly abbreviated and always listed in front of a dog's registered name

Challenge: top award to best dog and bitch in breed judging at Australian shows

Challenge Certificate: top award to best dog and bitch in breed judging at UK championship shows

champion: title conferred by most national kennel clubs to dogs that have fulfilled certain specified requirements at conformation shows, sometimes including performance achievements

Championship show: conformation show where awards that may qualify a dog for the title of champion are available

circuit: group of events held in the same region on consecutive or close dates; *see also* cluster

class: subdivision within the breed judging, usually based on each dog's sex, age, and previous wins

class dog: nonchampion (US)

cluster: a number of shows (usually four) held on consecutive days in the same location

conformation: form and structure; arrangement of body parts

co-owners: two or more individuals recorded as the official owners of a dog

crate: container for transporting or housing dogs; also referred to as cage or kennel

critique: written or verbal comment by the judge of the dogs exhibited; can take the form of individual critiques of each dog or general remarks about the entry as a whole

crop: to surgically cut or trim ear leather to encourage the ear to stand erect

cryptorchid: male whose testicles are not developed or descended into the scrotum; *see also* monorchid

cynology: the study of dogs (canines)

dam: a dog's mother

disqualification: characteristic described in the breed standard that makes a dog ineligible for any award at a show, usually as determined by the officiating judge

dock: to surgically shorten the tail

double handling: the act of attracting a dog's attention during judging by a person outside the ring to make the dog look alert or show better

Dual Champion: a dog who has won titles both in conformation and performance

entire: male dog whose reproductive organs are complete; not a cryptorchid or monorchid

excercise pen: portable enclosure for dogs used at dog shows; also called ex pen

fault: undesirable characteristic as specified in the breed standard

FCI: *See* Fédération Cynologique Internationale

Fédération Cynologique Internationale: international organization that governs competition at dog shows in most of the world, with the major exceptions of the United States, Canada, United Kingdom, and Australia

finish: US term: to make a dog into a champion

front: forepart of the dog's body: front legs, chest, brisket, and shoulder

Futurity: nonregular competition for puppies and young dogs at specialty shows for which nominations, usually prior to birth, are required and at which a portion of entry and nomination fees are awarded to the winners

gait: a dog's movement, action

get: offspring

gradings: judging method at FCI shows in which each dog exhibited is graded on a scale of excellence based on its adherence to the breed standard

Grand Champion: superior champion title, indicating that the titlist has won considerably more than the requirements for the regular champion title (Australia and New Zealand)

group: designated division of breeds, primarily in order to facilitate judging: the number of groups at shows in North America and the United Kingdom is seven; at FCI shows, it is ten

Group show: conformation event limited to one of the designated groups of breeds

gundog: UK term for Sporting Dog

handler: person who presents a dog in the ring during judging; *see also* agent

homebred: a dog that's bred by its owner

inbreeding: the mating of two closely related dogs, usually half-sibling to half-sibling, sire to daughter, son to dam

interbreeding: the mating of dogs of different breeds; also called crossbreeding

International Champion: official title awarded to a dog who has won the CACIB four times, usually at shows in at least three different countries and over a minimum time of one year

junior handler: young handler between the ages of at least 9 and under 18 years

Junior Showmanship: classes for young handlers in which the abilities of the handlers, not the quality of the dogs, are taken into account

Junior Warrant: title awarded to young dogs at UK shows that have won a specified number of classes prior to 18 months of age

Junior World Winner: title awarded at the FCI World Show to the best Junior dog and bitch of each breed

KC: The Kennel Club (UK)

kennel: building for housing dogs; figuratively, family of dogs all owned by the same individual(s)

Kennel Club: the national organization for purebred dogs in the United Kingdom

kennel manager: employee in charge of running a kennel, usually a large establishment

kennel name: family name used by one person (or partners) when registering dogs bred (sometimes owned) by that kennel

licensed show: official AKC championship event

Limited show: UK show at which awards for champion title cannot be won and that is not open to all dogs

linebreeding: the deliberate mating of dogs with one or more common ancestors, usually not closer than in the third generation; *see also* inbreeding

litter: sibling puppies born of the same whelping

major: a US Winners Dog or Winners Bitch award that consists of 3, 4, or 5 points; at least two majors must be part of the

15 points required for the AKC champion title

match: informal dog show at which championship points are not awarded

Miscellaneous class: US class for breeds not yet fully recognized by the AKC

monorchid: male with one testicle normally developed and one that is hidden and not descended into the scrotum; *see also* cryptorchid

move-up: a dog that completed its championship after closing of entries for a show and has been transferred to the Specials class at this show; *see* Specials class

national specialty: event held by a breed's parent club, usually indicating the most important event in that breed's annual calendar

Open show: UK conformation event open to all dogs, or all dogs of a breed, but without CCs on offer

outcross: breeding of unrelated dogs of the same breed

owner-handler: handler who shows a dog of which he or she is also listed in the catalog as the dog's owner or co-owner

parent club: national organization representing a specific breed

particolor: dog with two or more distinct broken body colors, one of which is white

pedigree: written record of a dog's ancestry, usually incorporating at least three generations (parents, grandparents, and great-grandparents)

PHA: Professional Handlers' Association

Phillips System: the first attempt at rating show dogs, named after its innovator, Irene Phillips Khatoonian Schlintz, and based on annual records of number of dogs defeated in breed, group, and Best in Show competitions

points: (1) credits toward a champion title at shows in, for example, the United States, Canada, and Australia; the number of points awarded on each occasion is usually dependent on the number of competitors defeated: (2) credits in the annual ratings, where usually one point is awarded per defeated competitor in Breed, Group, and Best in Show competitions; (3) specific features of a breed

prefix: part of a dog's registered name, preceding the dog's individual name, usually indicating breeder or owner (such as Salilyn in Salilyn's Aristocrat); *see also* suffix

premium list: official announcement of an upcoming event containing details of classes, judges, trophies, and so on

professional handler: person who makes a livelihood from showing dogs for a fee

provisional judge: a judge who has been approved by the AKC to officiate for specified breeds on a temporary basis and whose performance is evaluated prior to becoming a regularly approved judge

puppy: a dog under 12 months of age

Puppy class: class open only for puppies, usually divided into one class for puppies ages 6–9 months and one for puppies ages 9–12 months

purebred: dog whose sire and dam belong to the same recognized breed

registration certificate: document issued by the national kennel club to the owner of a dog that includes the dog's individual registration number, date of birth, parentage, breeder, owner, and so on

Reserve (UK): fourth placement in a class

Reserve Best in Show: award to the dog that has defeated all dogs at a show except the Best in Show winner

Reserve Challenge Certificate: award to a dog that has been defeated only by the CC winner

Reserve Winners: award to a dog that has been defeated only by the Winners Dog or the Winners Bitch

ringside: spectators watching judging from outside the ring

ring steward: person in charge of the running of a ring during judging, distributing armbands, getting the right dogs into the ring for each class, preparing ribbons, and so on

SBIS (also BISS): *see* Specialty Best in Show

scenthound: any breed of the Hound group that hunts by smell, not vision

Schutzhund: literally "guard dog"; a sport that involves training Working Group breeds to protect their owners

Sh. Ch.: Show Champion

Show Certificate of Merit: UK title indicating that a dog has achieved a certain measure of success at open and championship shows

Show Champion: UK title awarded to gundog breeds and Border Collies that have fulfilled the conformation requirements for the champion title

show circuit: a number of shows located closely enough in time and place to each other to attract roughly the same exhibitors

show schedule: list of judging times with details of each judge's assignment, entry, and ring number

side gait: a dog's action when viewed from the side

Sieger (fem. Siegerin): German: literally "winner"

sighthound: breeds that hunt by the aid of vision, not scent

sire: a dog's father

sound: mental and physical health, when all the dog's organs and faculties are functioning normally

special: U. S. champion, especially a top quality champion worth campaigning

specialist judge: a judge whose interest is focused on one or a small number of breeds

Specials class: U. S. champion class for both dogs and bitches

Specialty Best in Show: the dog judged as best in a show limited to only one breed

sponsor: (1) person who finances a dog's show career, usually listed as official

co-owner; (2) organization supporting a show or event

stack: to position a dog for the judge's inspection

standard: *see* breed standard

steward: *see* ring steward

stud book: register of dogs and bitches with details of their breeding activities, litters produced, and so on that allows a student to trace a dog's ancestry

Stud Dog class: class including a sire with at least two of his offspring, judged on the quality of the offspring, not the sire

suffix: part of a dog's registered name that follows after the dog's individual name and usually indicates breeder or owner (such as Ware in Tracey Witch of Ware); *see also* prefix

superintendent: US individual or organization licensed by the AKC to be responsible for the practical organization of a dog show or other event

sweepstakes: nonregular competition offered at specialty shows or supported entries at all-breed shows, usually limited to puppies, young dogs, or veterans

tail male/female line: unbroken line from father to son or from mother to daughter for several generations

ticket: casual reference to the Challenge Certificate in the United Kingdom

type: the combined characteristics that distinguish one breed from another or dogs of one family within a breed from another family

UKC: *see* United Kennel Club

United Kennel Club: second-largest purebred dog registry in the United States

variety: subdivision of certain breeds; AKC divides nine breeds (Cocker Spaniels, Beagles, Collies, Dachshunds, Bull Terriers, Manchester Terriers, Chihuahuas, English Toy Spaniels, and Poodles) into separate varieities based on size, coat, or color

Veterans class: class for older dogs, usually seven years or older

WB: Winners Bitch

WD: Winners Dog

Winkie: the Oscars of dogdom, awarded to outstanding individuals in different categories during a ceremony preceding Westminster Kennel Club Dog Show in New York each year

Winners (Dog or Bitch): AKC award given to the best non-champion dog and bitch in each breed at a show

World Winner: title awarded to the best dog and the best bitch of each breed at the FCI World Show

RESOURCES

The American Kennel Club Blue Book of Dogs. New York: Garden City Publishing, 1938.

Barnes, Duncan, ed. *The AKC's World of the Pure-Bred Dog.* New York: Howell Book House, 1983.

Hier, Anne. *Dog Shows Then and Now.* West Redding, CT: Images in Print, 1999.

Jackson, Frank. *Crufts: The Official History.* London: Pelham Books, 1990.

Miller, Harry, ed. *Who's Who in American Dogdom.* Chicago: The National Research Bureau, 1958.

Nesbit, Kerry, ed. *Who's Who in Handling.* Winston-Salem, NC: Kerry Nesbit & Co., 1993.

O'Neill, Charles A.T., ed. *The American Kennel Club 1884–1984: A Source Book.* New York: Howell Book House, 1985.

Schlintz, Irene Castle Khatoonian. *Great Show Dogs of America.* New York: Howell Book House, 1968.

The Westminster Kennel Club 1877–1976. New York: The Westminster Kennel Club, 1976.

William F. Stifel, *The Dog Show: 125 Years of Westminster.* New York: Westminster Kennel Club, 2001.

PHOTO CREDITS

Title page
Carol Beuchat

Preface
8: Unknown. **11:** Paul Lepiane.

Acknowledgments
12: Unknown. **14:** Kerrin Winter-Churchill. **15:** Miguel/Infocus-bymiguel.com.

Introduction
16: Carol Ann Johnson. **18:** Jim and Kathy Corbett. **19:** Unknown.

Chapter 1
20: From the collection of Walter Goodman. Photo by Robert Lorenzson. **22, 43:** Unknown. **23, 24:** From *La Livre de la Chasse*. **25:** From *The New Book of the Dog*. **26:** Clipart.com. **27, 29, 35:** Courtesy of the Kennel Club Picture Library. **30:** From *London Labour and the London Poor*. **31:** From *Illustrated London News*. **33, 36:** Mary Evans/Thomas Fall. **34, 42:** Ken Spooner. **37:** From *The Illustrated Book of the Dog*. **39, 40:** From *The Book of the Dog*. **41:** Photo Axel Lindahls Fotografiaffär.

Chapter 2
44–49, 51, 55 (top) , 57 (bottom left): Unknown. **52:** Gay Glazbrook. **54 (left):** Mary Evans/Thomas Fall. **54 (right):** Gunderson Photography. **55 (bottom):** Evelyn M. Shafer. **56 (top and bottom right), 57 (top right):** Ashbey Photography. **56 (top and bottom left), 57 (top left):** Carol Ann Johnson. **57 (bottom right):** Kitten Rodwell/Flashkat. **58:** Paula Heikkinen-Lehkonen.

Chapter 3
60, 70 (bottom), 72, 75, 76 (top and bottom right), 77 (bottom), 79 (second from right): Westminster Kennel Club. **61, 62, 63 (top), 64, 66 , 67, 68 (top and bottom), 69:** Courtesy of the Kennel Club Picture Library. **63 (bottom), 98 (bottom), 99:** Unknown. **68 (bottom right):** Mary Evans/Thomas Fall. **70 (top):** Evelyn M. Shafer. **73:** Peter Green. **74, 78 (bottom), 79 (left):** William P. Gilbert. **76 (top left):** Miguel/Infocusbymiguel.com. **77 (top):** Kerrin Winter-Churchill/Dog-Photo.com. **78 (top):** Kennel Review Archives. **79 (second from left):** Ashbey Photography. **79 (right):** Lisa Croft-Elliott courtesy of the Westminster Kennel Club. **80:** Carol Beuchat. **81:** Nancy Spelke/Custom Dog Design. **83, 84, 86:** Wayne Ferguson, Morris & Essex Kennel Club. **87 (top):** Lisa Croft-Elliott. **87 (bottom):** Morris & Essex Kennel Club. **88:** Williamson Aircraft Company. **89 (top):** Fox & Cook/mydogphoto.com. **89 (bottom):** Author's Collection. **90, 91:** Meg and Jim Callea/Callea Photo. **92:** Kitten Rodwell/Flashkat. **94:** Photo by Trafford. **95, 96 (bottom), 97, 100:** Karl Donvil. **96 (top):** RBT/Harold Gay. **98 (bottom):** Per Undén. **98 (top):** Zoophoto. **101:** Caes de Fato.

Chapter 4
102, 108, 122 (top): Bill Kohler. **103, 105 (bottom) 125:** Fox & Cook/mydogphoto.com. **104:** Missy Yuhl. **105 (top), 112 (bottom), 122 (bottom):** Evelyn M. Shafer. **106:** Joan Ludwig. **107:** Tom and Linda Nutting/Photo by Tom Nutting. **110:** Tatham Photography.

111, 112 (top), 113 (top), 114, 118, 121: Ashbey Photography. 113 (bottom): William P. Gilbert. 115: Unknown. 116 (top): Meg and Jim Callea/Callea Photo. 116 (bottom): Les Alberti courtesy of Collie Expressions. 117: Bill Meyer. 119: Roberto Photography. 120: Bo Bengtson. 123: Lorie Crain. 124 (top): Magnus Hagstedt. 124 (bottom): Showdog Publications.

Chapter 5
126: Nancy Spelke/Custom Dog Design. 129, 151, 152 (top): Mary Evans/Thomas Fall. 131, 146 (bottom): Meg and Jim Callea/Callea Photo. 133, 142, 144: Evelyn M. Shafer. 134: Frasie Studio. 138, 139 (left), 149, 150: Ashbey Photography. 139 (right), 143 (top): Joan Ludwig. 140: Tauskey Photography. 141, 143: Westminster Kennel Club. 142 (bottom): Ross Photography. 146 (top): Pegini Photography. 147: Fox & Cook/mydogphoto.com. 148: Unknown. 153: Barkleigh Shute.

Chapter 6
154, 173 (bottom): Brown Photography. 155, 174 (right): Meg and Jim Callea/Callea Photo. 156 (left), 158 (bottom), 173 (top), 175 (bottom): Unknown. 156 (right), 157 (left), 161, 172 (top), 174 (left), 178 (left), 183: Ashbey Photography. 157 (right), 164, 165, 170, 181: Kim Booth/Booth Photography. 158 (top), 160, 166: Nancy Spelke/Custom Dog Design. 159: Stillman Photography. 162, 175 (top), 177 (top): Joan Ludwig. 163: January Photography. 167: Fox & Cook/mydogphoto.com. 168, 169: David Dalton. 171: Ladin Photography. 172 (bottom): William P. Gilbert. 176: Evelyn M. Shafer. 177 (bottom): Robert Photography. 178 (right): Harkins Photog-

raphy. 179, 180: Miguel/Infocusbymiguel.com. 182, 185: Carol Beuchat. 184: Paula Heikkinen-Lehkonen.

Chapter 7
186, 188–191, 196, 197, 201, 205, 207 (top left): Unknown. 187: Joan Brearley. 188 (middle): Jovan. 193: Joan Ludwig. 194, 203, 204: Mary Evans/Thomas Fall. 195: Ron Willbie. 198: Karl Donvil. 199, 207 (bottom): William P. Gilbert. 200, 206, 209 (left): Booth Photo. 202 (bottom): Jayne Langdon. 202 (top): Bill Williams Studio. 207 (top right), 208, 209 (right): Ashbey Photography. 211: Rich Bergman.

Chapter 8
212, 229 (bottom left), 230, 242 (bottom): Courtesy of the Kennel Club Picture Library. 215, 276, 277, 283, 284 (top), 285 (bottom): Carol Ann Johnson. 215 (bottom), 217: From *The Twentieth Century Dog*, by Herbert Compton. 216 (top), 219: From *The Dog Book*, by James Watson. 218, 221, 222 (bottom), 223 (right), 229 (bottom right), 233 (bottom), 236 (top), 237, 238, 244–247, 254, 280, 282 (bottom): Unknown. 220, 231, 232, 233 (top), 234, 239, 241 (bottom), 248, 251, 265, 267: Mary Evans/Thomas Fall. 222 (top), 223 (left), 225: From *The Complete Book of the Dog*, by Robert Leighton. 224: From *Hutchinson's Dog Encyclopedia*. 226, 236 (bottom): From *The Book of Dogs*, by Stanley West. 227, 243: Courtesy of *Dog World*. 229 (top): From *The New Complete Scottish Terrier*, by John T. Marvin. 235, 274: Karl Donvil. 241, 253 (left), 263 (bottom), 278: Paula Heikkinen-Lehkonen. 241 (right), 242 (top), 249, 256, 259, 260, 264 (top), 268, 271–273: Sally Anne Thompson. 250,

263 (top), 266, 275: David Dalton. 252: Garwood Photography. 255: F. W. Simms Photography. 258: Cooke Photography. 264 (bottom), 270: Diane Pearce. 269: From *The Afghan Hound,* by Charles Harrisson. 279: Photo Hartley. 281: Diane Johnson. 282 (top): Photo by Trafford. 284 (bottom): Photo Corsair. 285 (top): Bo Bengtson.

Chapter 9
286–289, 291, 292, 296, 300–302, 306–308, 310–312, 314 (top), 315–319, 321 (top), 326, 327, 336–339, 341, 343, 344 (bottom), 347, 350, 357, 372, 373 (top), 375, 377, 381 (top), 402, 405 (left), 407, 412, 417 (right), 420, 421 (bottom): Unknown. 293: Photo Shannon. 295: Wayne Ferguson, Morris & Essex Kennel Club. 298: *AKC Gazette.* 299, 325, 332, 335 (top right): Tauskey Photography. 304: Percy T. Jones. 305 (top), 333: Nancy Spelke/Custom Dog Design. 305 (bottom): Mary Evans/Thomas Fall. 309, 324, 379, 416 (bottom): Evelyn M. Shafer. 309 (bottom), 313, 323, 335 (top left), 348, 351, 364, 368 (left), 374, 401 (right), 404, 409 (bottom), 415, 416 (top), 418, 419: Ashbey Photography. 314 (bottom), 408: Carol Beuchat. 320, 321 (bottom right), 335 (bottom), 344 (top), 349 (bottom), 353 (bottom), 378 (right), 385, 387, 390, 406 (right), 410, 417 (left): Kim Booth/Booth Photography. 321: Rich Bergman. 322, 400, 413: *Time Life* Pictures/Getty Images. 330 (top), 376, 388: Brown Photography. 330 (bottom), 340, 389 (bottom): Frasie Studio . 334, 346, 349 (top), 353 (top), 382, 389 (top), 403: William P. Gilbert. 342 (left), 354–356, 358, 361, 366, 373 (bottom left), 378 (left), 380, 383, 395, 401 (left): Joan Ludwig. 342 (right): McNealy Photography. 345, 360 (bottom): Michele Perlmutter. 352: Frank

Photography. 359, 384: Fox & Cook/mydogphoto.com. 360 (top), 381 (bottom), 405 (right): Missy Yuhl. 362, 370, 386, 391, 411, 421 (top): Gay Glazbrook. 363, 397, 406 (left), 409 (top): Meg and Jim Callea/Callea Photo. 365: Janet Photography. 367: Westminster Kennel Club. 368 (right): Don Petrulis Photography. 369, 396: Vicky Holloway/Holloway Photo. 373 (bottom right): B. A. Photography. 393: Sally Stasytis. 399: Dagmar Kenis.

Chapter 10
422, 446, 450 (right), 456–458: Paula Heikkinen-Lehkonen. 424 (left), 427 (top), 430: Mikron Photography. 424 (right)–426, 427 (bottom right), 428 (bottom right), 429 (top and bottom left), 431 (top and bottom left): *Dogs in Canada.* 427 (botom left): Lisa Croft-Elliott. 428 (top): J. Rick Photography. 428 (bottom left): Alex Smith, courtesy of *Dogs in Canada.* 429, 431 (bottom right): Alex Smith Photography, Ltd. 432: Crawford-Manton Photography. 434, 474: Ashbey Photography. 435 (top), 436, 451, 453, 473 (top), 479: Karl Donvil. 435 (bottom): Marcelino Pozo Ruiz. 437: Dierenfotografie Ruud Vinck. 438: Photo OBC. 439: Tell Photography. 440, 443 (middle), 450 (left), 471 (bottom left): Gunnar Lindgren. 441, 443 (right), 445 (top and bottom right), 447-449, 454: Per Undén. 443 (left): David Dalton. 444, 445 (bottom left): Andréas Photography. 455: Elisabeth Espedal. 459 (left), 460 (top), 461 (top), 464, 466 (top), 470, 473 (bottom), 475, 477 (bottom), 478: Unknown. 459 (right), 466 (bottom): Barbara Killworth. 460 (bottom left), 462 (top): Photo by Trafford. 460 (bottom right), 461 (bottom): Sally Stasytis. 462 (bottom): Sven Westerblad. 463: Fox &

Cook/mydogphoto.com. **465, 468:** Kim Booth/Booth Photography. **467:** Carol Ann Johnson. **469:** Miguel/Infocus-bymiguel.com. **471 (bottom right):** Joan Whittingham. **472:** Caes de Fato. **476:** Aleksey Kalashnikov. **477 (top):** Mari Nakashima.

Chapter 11
480, 483 (left), 485 (left and right), 489 (left): Unknown. **481(left):** Frasie Studio. **481 (middle):** Brown Photography. **481 (right), 483 (middle), 486 (middle and right):** Joan Ludwig. **482 (left):** Tauskey Photography. **482 (middle):** Neetzel Photography. **482 (right):** Evelyn M. Shafer. **483 (right):** Ritter Photography. **484 (left):** Stillman Photography. **484 (right), 486 (left), 488 (left):** William P. Gilbert. **485 (middle):** Smolley Photography. **487, 490 (right), 493 (right), 495 (left), 496 (right):** Kim Booth/Booth Photography. **488 (middle):** Missy Yuhl. **488 (right):** Meg and Jim Callea/Callea Photo. **489 (right), 491 (middle and right), 492 (right), 493 (left), 494, 495 (right), 496 (left), 497:** Ashbey Photography. **490 (left), 491 (left), 493 (middle):** Fox & Cook/mydogphoto.com. **492 (left):** Tatham Photography.

Chapter 12
498: Vicky Holloway/Holloway Photo. **499:** Carol Beuchat. **500, 501, 504, 506, 514 (top right and bottom left), 515 (top left), 516 (top), 517 (top right), 518 (bottom left), 519 (top), 520 (top left and bottom right), 523 (bottom left), 527 (bottom), 530 (left), 532 (top left and bottom right), 533 (bottom left):** Ashbey Photography. **502 (top right):** Susan and Lennah. **502 (bottom), 516 (bottom left), 520 (bottom left), 522 (left), 526 (top right):** Kit Rodwell. **503,** **507 (bottom), 512, 514 (top left), 515 (bottom right), 517 (top left), 519 (bottom), 521 (left), 522 (bottom right), 523 (top), 524 (top right), 527 (top left), 529 (top right), 531 (top left and bottom right), 532 (top right), 533 (top right):** Kim Booth/Booth Photography. **505, 508 (bottom), 510 (left):** Tom DiGiacomo. **507 (top), 533 (top middle):** Evelyn M. Shafer. **508 (top). 510 (right), 529 (top left):** Bill Kohler. **509:** Susan and Lennah. **511, 513:** Heather Powers. **514 (bottom right), 529 (bottom right):** Rich **Bergman. 515 (top right), 533 (top midle):** Evelyn M. Shafer. **515 (bottom right):** Tatham Photography. **516 (bottom right), 525 (top left), 532 (bottom left), 533 (top left):** William P. Gilbert. **517 (bottom):** Luke Allen Photography. **518 (top left):** Earl Graham. **518 (top right) 525 (top right and bottom), 530 (top right):** Fox & Cook/mydogphoto.com. **518 (bottom right), 520 (top right), 521 (bottom left), 527 (top right), 531 (top right):** Unknown. **521 (top right):** Alex Smith Photography, Ltd. **522 (top right):** Joan Ludwig. **523 (bottom right:** Lloyd W. Olson Studio. **254 (top left):** Bo Bengtson. **524 (bottom), 528 (top right), 530 (bottom right), 533 (bottom middle):** Missy Yuhl. **526 (top left):** Mikron Photography. **526 (bottom), 528 (top left), 531 (bottom left), 533 (bottom right):** Meg and Jim Callea/Callea Photo. **528 (bottom left):** Bennet Associates. **528 (bottom right):** Booth Photography. **529 (bottom left):** Bennet Associates.

Chpater 13:
534: Westminster Kennel Club. **535:** *Our Dogs.* **536, 539, 445, 550, 551, 554:** Unknown. **537:** *Dog World.* **538 (left):** *Kennel Review.* **538 (right):** *Popular Dogs.* **540, 541:** *Kennel Review,* Romaine

Photography. **542 (left):** *Canine Chronicle.* **542 (right):** *Showsight,* Family Tree Photography. **543:** *Dog News,* Lisa Croft-Elliot. **544:** *Dogs in Review.* **546:** S. Surfman. **548 (top):** *Sports Illustrated.* **548 (bottom):** *The New Yorker.* **549:** *Life magazine.* **552, 553:** Joan Ludwig. **555:** Sharon Sakson. **556:** Castle Rock Entertaiment.

DOG NAME INDEX:

The titles of the dogs have been omitted for easy reference. Page references for photos are in bold type.

Huzzah Sweet Molly Malone, Greyhound, **321**
Hycourt's Tijuana Brass, Scottish Terrier, 610

I

Iccabod Olympic Gold, Miniature Schnauzer, 277
Iceberg of Tavey, Doberman Pinscher, 214, **268**, 269, 609
Icobod de l'Esprit, Bouvier des Flandres, 611
Ideal Weather, Old English Sheepdog, 614
Ightfield Dick, Pointer, 31
Illahee Summer Fun, Siberian Husky, 619
Inkwells Named Shdow, Flat-Coated Retriever, 449
Innisfree's Gilpak's Macho, Siberian Husky, 618
Innisfree's Ice T, Siberian Husky, 617
Innisfree's Sierra Cinnar, Siberian Husky, **79**, 613
Inverdruie Scorchin, Scottish Terrier, 257
Ivor O'Valley Farm, Borzoi, 318
Ivory Jock of Iradell, Skye Terrier, 606

J

Jacinthe de Ricelaine, Skye Terrier, **176**, 548, 600, 606
Jacquet's Urko, Boxer, **99**
Jafrak Philippe Olivier, Giant Schnauzer, 214, 269, **283**, 609
Jagan's Bell Starr, German Shepherd Dog, 371
Ja-Mar's Avenger of Arbor, German Shepherd Dog, 610
Jamelyn Second Edition, Lakeland Terrier, 610
Jaraluv's Sindar Star Image, Scottish Deerhound, **106**
Jaraluv's Indelible, Scottish Deerhound, 611
Jaszkoseri Kocos Csupor, Komondor, **96**
Jay Bees Toreador, Smooth Dachshund, 605
Jay-Mac's Dream Walking, Miniature Pinscher, 419, **528**, 607
Jay-Mac's Impossible Dream, Miniature Pinscher, 419, 528, 598, 607
Jethard Cidevant, Basenji, 464, 615
Jet's Once Upon A Dream, Greyhound, **422**, 454, **455**, 611, 618
Jet's Something in the Way U Smile, Greyhound, 454, 611
Jim Pat's Assai, Boxer, 611
Joanne Chen's Maya Dancer, Maltese, **142**, 418, 599, 607
Joanne Chen's Mino Maya Dancer, Maltese, 606
Jockel v. Burgund, Doberman Pinscher, 315–**16**, 602
Jokyl Gallipants, Airedale Terrier, 203, 214, 259, 609
Jokyl This Is My Song, Airedale Terrier, 260, 616
Jo-Ni's Red Baron of Crofton, Lakeland Terrier, **377**, **486**, 598, 606, 613
Jontus Henry Jones Junior, American Cocker Spaniel, 610
Jordean All Kiddin' Aside, Brittany, 604
Juleko Henry James at Amalek, English Toy Terrier, 470

K

Kabik's The Challenger, Afghan Hound, 176, **358**, **490**, 493, 597, 605, 613

Kabik's The Front Runner, Afghan Hound, 358, **359**, 596, 597, 605
Kahootz Chase Manhattan, Beagle, **516**
Kaleef's Genuine Risk, German Shepherd Dog, **52**, 297, 372, 594, 607
Kamp's Kaptain Kool, American Cocker Spaniel, 604
Kanix Vagant, Bouvier des Flandres, 612
Kanix Zulu, Bouvier des Flandres, 214, 282
Kan-Point's VJK Autumn Roses, German Shorthaired Pointer, 181, **314**, 315, **549**, 613
Karakush In Champagne, Afghan Hound, 619
Karamoor Llacue's Edelweiss, Afghan Hound, **185**
Karaseva's Cinnamon Candy, Siberian Husky, 611
Karim Zahab al Bokay, Saluki, **517**
Karolaska Bristol Bay, Great Pyrenees, **178**
Katawampus, Schipperke, 217
Kazor's Johnny Come Greatly, Basenji, **122**
Keepsakes Midnight Dream, Shih Tzu, 472
Keeshee Cute Ncuddley, Keeshond, 619
Kemphurst Superb, Wire Fox Terrier, 225–26
Kendoric's Riversong Mulroney, Pug, **150**, 417, 594
Kenlyn's Calvin HiCliff Kaleef, German Shepherd Dog, 372
Kenlyn's Tenacity of Kaleef, German Shepherd Dog, **180**, 372, 607
Kenmare Sorceress, Airedale Terrier, 614
Kenmil's Bellisima of Danala, German Shepherd Dog, 619
Kennelgarth Samson, Scottish Terrier, 618
Kennelgarth Viking, Scottish Terrier, 203, 257
Kensbridge Karbon Kopy, Kerry Blue Terrier, 610
Kerrageen's Hotspur, Kerry Blue Terrier, 392, 606
Kerryfair Night Fever, Irish Setter, 203
Khafka's Exotic Spice, Afghan Hound, **124**
Khayam Apollo, Afghan Hound, **55**
Khinjan American Express, Standard Schnauzer, 215, 277
Khrispat's Megan A Point, German Shorthaired Pointer, **515**, 604
Kiabe Qariban, Saluki, 619
Kiebla's Tradition of Turo, Boxer, 332, 596, 605
Killick of the Mess, Wire Fox Terrier, 606, 616
Killucan Dreadnought, Rough Collie, 219
King Peter of Salilyn, English Springer Spaniel, 200, 346–47
Kingsbury Carbon Copy, Cardigan Welsh Corgi, **533**
King's Champagne Taste, Standard Poodle, 202
Kingsmens Witchcraft, German Shepherd Dog, 619
Kippax Fearnought, Bulldog, 338, **339**–40, 421, 545, 613
Kirsch's Rodeo of Halo, Standard Poodle, 597
Kishniga's Desert Song, Borzoi, 319, **320**, 610
Kishniga's Diaghilev, Borzoi, 617
Kismet's Sight For Sore Eyes, German Shepherd Dog, 297, **370**, 371–72, **496**, 594, 595, 607

Kjavu Air Jordan, Afghan Hound, 618
Konig Brave Lustre, Doberman Pinscher, 619
Kontoki's E-I-E-I-O, Siberian Husky, 178, 595, 605
Kontoki's Gibson Girl, Siberian Husky, 438, 618
Kontoki's One Mo' Time, Siberian Husky, **57**, 178
Kren of the Hollow, Elkhound, 616
Ku-Chi of Caversham, Pekingese, 248
Kudos The Knockout, Dwarf Poodle, **454**, 611
Ku-Jin of Caversham, Pekingese, 248
Kwetu Oakhurst Bronco, Rhodesian Ridgeback, 124, **139**

L

Laguna Locomite, Whippet, 618
Lajosmegyi Dahu Diga, Komondor, **174**
Lake Cove's That's My Boy, Standard Poodle, 180, 297, **405**, 408, 460, **494**, 595, 607
Lakeside's Gilligan's Island, German Shepherd Dog, 366, 599, 605
Lambluv Desert Dancer, Old English Sheepdog, **178**, 608
Lambluv Moptop Show Stopper, Old English Sheepdog, **178**
Lambrigg The Squatter, English Cocker Spaniel, 619
LamedaZottel Flamboyant, Old English Sheepdog, 215, 282, 283, 609
Lanbur Miss Fleetwood, Beagle, 604
Lancelot Petersen von Bauer, Miniature Poodle, 611
Lansdowne Sunflower, Greyhound, 290, 320
Larchmont's Michael, Pembroke Welsh Corgi, 617
La-Shay's Bart Simpson, American Cocker Spaniel, 297, 351, 384, 596, 604
Latest Dance of Bournehouse, English Setter, 203
Laund Loyalty of Bellhaven, Rough Collie, 225, 614
Laund Luetta, Smooth Collie, 224–25
Laund Lynne, Smooth Collie, 224–**25**
Leading Lady of Wildoaks, Wire Fox Terrier, **295**, 301, 603
Leander Midnight Cowboy, Standard Poodle, 612, 618
Leander Stockbroker of Montravia, Standard Poodle, 261
Leander Tia Maria, Toy Poodle, 264
Leander White Blaze, Standard Poodle, 619
Le Dauphin of Limberlost, Great Pyrenees, 610
Lee Vee Sonic Boom, English Springer Spaniel, 611
Legend of Gael, Gordon Setter, **309**, 310
Lehearn Lovemn Leavem, English Cocker Spaniel, 619
Lennis's Tar Lacy Foxfire, Pomeranian, 606
Leonhard's Supertramp, West Highland White Terrier, 612
Letomi Hi There, Boxer, 619
Levenside Luke, Smooth Fox Terrier, **221**
Lex Luthor Dupont, Doberman Pinscher, 476
Liebendane Baby Grand, Great Dane, 618
Lillemarks Kobuch, Giant Schnauzer, 363
Lillvretens Quintus, Norwich Terrier, 612
Lin-Yu-Tang of Alderbourne, Pekingese, **36**

Page references for photos are in bold type. For technical reasons, the letters å, ä, ö, and ü are alphabetized as if they were English letters.

Poole, William and Rebecca, 208
Popular Dogs (magazine), 228, **538**, 539
Porter, Mrs. Cheever, 310, 385
Portugal, 437
Portugal FCI World Show, 95–97
Posey, Parker, 556
Potterdale Bearded Collies, 267–68
Pottle, Cappy, **186**
PouchCove Newfoundlands, 206, 209
Powers, Mrs. Thomas F., **514**
Prentice, Phil, 377
the press, 545–49
Pret, Countess Claudine de, 433
Price, Nadia, 245
Price, Philippe Howard, 245, **246**
Price-Jones, Rita, 245–46
prize money, 82
professional handlers, 163–70, 170–73,
    180–81, 492–93
Professional Handlers Association, 162,
    184
Provisionally Accepted Breeds Group
    (FCI), 593
Puerto Rico FCI World Show, 434, 474, 583
Pugs, 26, 198, 208, 209, 417
Pulik, 467–68
puppies: crate training, 487–88; finding
    homes for non-show quality pups,
    192; Pup of the Year competition, 564;
    puppy clip for Poodles, 394; training,
    156–59
Purston Terriers, 260–61
Purves, Peter, 555
Putnam, Mrs. George, 402
Puttencove Standard Poodles, 402
Pyrenean Mountain Dog. *See* Great
    Pyrenees

Q
Qirmizi Salukis, 449
Quaker Oats award, 179, 317
Quallenberg, Joy, **500**
quarantine, 69–70, 459, 547, 576–77
Queen's Head Tavern (London), **27**, 28
Quiet Creek Bloodhounds, 209
Quigley, Anna, 208
Quirk, Joseph, **87**
Quom Afghan Hounds, 462

R
Racketeer Standard Poodles, 443
Radford, Pam, 277
Ragtime Airedales, 441
Ragus Norwich Terriers, 261
Rainey, Mrs. Roy A., 290
Raita, Ritva, **456**
Ralanda French Bulldogs, 413
Ramsay, Carol, 280–81
Ramsay, Ron, 280–81, 391
Randahof Doberman Pinchers, 315–16
Randall, Mr. and Mrs. L. R., 315–16
Rangel, Gabriel, **126**
Rank, James V., 234, 236
Rank, Patsy, **236**
rating systems, 293–94, 538
rat-killing matches, 27, 28–30
Raycroft Clumber Spaniels, 243
Rayne, Derek, 137, **147**, **175**, **463**, **524**
Rayne, Gerda, **147**, **363**
Rayner, Ken, **368**
Reagan, Ron, Jr., 555
Reasin, Lee Anthony, 137

Rechler, Roger, 196, 197, 356–57, 358, 385
Redwitch Akitas, 277
Reese, Gloria, **517**
Reese, Mr. and Mrs. Nathan, 180, 344, 372,
    374, 385, 517
Reeve-Newson, John, **147**, **384**
Reeves, Shelley, 470
Regency Miniature Schnauzers, 209
registerable breeds lists: AKC, 585–87; FCI,
    589–93; The Kennel Club, 587–88
regulations. *See* rules and regulations
Reid, Pamela, **508**
Reisman, Carol, 106, **501**
Renau, Carlos, 436
Rendu, Stephen, **184**
Reserve Best in Show awards, 290, 574,
    615–16
Reserve CC, 560, 562
Reserve Winners Dog and Reserve Win-
    ners Bitch awards, 568
retouched show dog photographs, **550–54**
Retrievers: Chesapeake Bay, 510; Curly-
    Coated, 216–17; Flat-Coated, 198, 208,
    448–49; Golden, 240, 243, 352, 353, 503.
    See also Labrador Retrievers
Retrievers, Flushing Dogs, and Water
    Dogs Group (FCI), 592–93
Reveille Basenjis, 209
Reynolds, Don, 85, 303
Reynolds, James, 56, 78, **102**, **107**, 138, **143**,
    145, **429**
Reznik, Allan, 544
Riddle, Maxwell, 112, 137, 145, 545
Rigden, Elaine, **416**
Rigden, Jerry, **518**
Riggs, Mrs. Augustus, IV, 137, 152, **488**,
    555–56
Rine, Josephine Z., 538
The Ring Leader (magazine), 544
ringside pickups, 170
Risepark Miniature Schnauzers, 277–78
Ritter, Michele, 208
Rizzi, Augusto, 114
Roberts, Erin, **122**
Roberts, Mrs. Ralph, **514**
Roberts, Percy, **73**, 142, **295**, 323, **324**, 376, **401**
Robson, Phyllis, 228, 385, **536**
Roche, David, 86, 150, **153**, 280, **460**, 461–62
Rocheause Bouviers des Flandres, 209
Rocky Top Bull Terriers, 208
Rodgers, Marita Gibbs, 262, **263**
Rodgers, Mary, 206, 342, 343
Rogers, Anne Hone, 154. *See also* Clark,
    Anne Rogers
Rogers, Don, **527**
Rogers, Olga Hone, 398
Romanoff Borzoi, 318–20
Roosevelt, Franklin D., 305
Rosenberg, Alva, 142, **344**
Rossander, Aina, 440, **442**
Rossander, Lennart, **442**
Rossut Beagles, 147–48, 272–73
Rost, Anton, **308**
Rotherwood Deerhounds, **204**
Rottrivers Cairn Terriers, 441
Rottweilers, 48–49, 58, 269, 470
Rough Collies, 115, 149, 218–19, 225, 533
Routledge, Ric, 542
Royal Agricultural Society, 95, 461
Royal shows in Australia, 94–95, 459–62,
    618–20
Rozavel Kennel, 265

RP breeding program, 281
Rudel Greyhounds, 442
Rufkins Lhasa Apsos, 208
Ruggles, Cecelia, 385, 412
rules and regulations: about, 557; Aus-
    tralian, 575–77; collusion of judges vs.,
    20–21, 38, 130, 575. *See also* FCI rules
    and regulations; Great Britain rules
    and regulations; United States rules
    and regulations
Rumney English Setters, 218
Runsten, Nenne, 447
Russell, J. D., **108**
Rusell, Judith M., 209
Russia, 100, 423, 474–75
Russian Black Terrier, 474
Rutherford, Winthrop, **288**, 289, 303, 305

S
Sabella, Frank: with Acadia Command
    Performance, **399**, 402; at Afghan
    Hound World Congress, **103**; at Bucks
    County Kennel Club, **491**; with De
    Russy Lollypop, **485**; Dog World's
    Hall of Fame award, 145; with Freder-
    ick of Rencroft, **401**, **483**; as Poodle
    handler, 180, 399–402; as trophy pre-
    senter, **113**, **463**; at Westminster, 139,
    140, **146**, **183**, **416**
Sabine Smooth Fox Terriers, 289
Salgray Boxers, 332
Salilyn English Springer Spaniels, 346–47
Saltzman, Lynette, **521**
Saluki Club of America, 114
Salukis, 198, 275, 437, 449
Sameja, Osman, 252–53
Sammet, Wendell, 181, 206, **403**
Samoem Salukis and Whippets, 437
Samoyeds, 204, 268
Sandringham Kennels, 65
Sandylands Labrador Retrievers, 240, 242
Sangster, Harry, **171**, 180, 228, 331, 332, 338
San-Jo Cocker Spaniels, 208
Santa Barbara Kennel Club, 88–91, 147
Santiago, Rafael de, **98**, **474**
Sarimont Cairn Terriers, 441
Saturday Evening Post, 545
Saturday Night Live, 555
Saxonsprings Lhasa Apsos, 278–79
Saylor, John, 338
Scandinavia: Denmark, 438–39; Finland,
    97, 418, 438, 455–59, 612; Norway,
    450–55, 611–12; shows in, 99–100,
    438–39, 453–55, 558; Top Dogs lists,
    611–12. *See also* Sweden
Scawthorne, David, 261
Scenthounds and Related Breeds Group
    (FCI), 591–92
Schemel, Dr. Andreas, **479**
Schlesinger, Bea, 392
Schlintz, Irene Phillips Khatoonian, **293**,
    294, **350**, **486**, 538
Schnauzers: British winners, 269, 277–78;
    German foundation stock, 433; Giant,
    197, 269, 363–64, 433, 436, 459; Minia-
    tures, 115, 120, 209, 277–78, 433, 476;
    Standard, 362–63, 434; U.S. winners,
    362–64
Schnauzers and Pinschers Group (FCI),
    589–90
Schoenberg, Isidore, 137
Schoenfeld, Bobby, **105**